This book provides a clear and accessible intro
linguistic framework. It presupposes no previ
students step-by-step from simple predicat
interpretation through to Montague's intensional l ... where
they can tackle the primary technical literature. It a ... sic knowledge of
linguistics, but aims to be as non-technical as pos ... within a technical subject.
Formal semantics will be welcomed by students and researchers in linguistics, artificial intelligence and cognitive science alike.

CAMBRIDGE TEXTBOOKS IN LINGUISTICS

FORMAL SEMANTICS

In this series:

P. H. MATTHEWS *Morphology* Second edition
B. COMRIE *Aspect*
R. M. KEMPSON *Semantic Theory*
T. BYNON *Historical Linguistics*
J. ALLWOOD, L.-G. ANDERSON, Ö. DAHL *Logic in Linguistics*
D. B. FRY *The Psysics of Speech*
R. A. HUDSON *Sociolinguistics*
J. K. CHAMBERS and P. TRUDGILL *Dialectology*
A. J. ELLIOT *Child Language*
P. H. MATTHEWS *Syntax*
A. RADFORD *Transformational Syntax*
L. BAUER *English Word-formation*
S. C. LEVINSON *Pragmatics*
G. BROWN and G. YULE *Discourse Analysis*
R. HUDDLESTON *Introduction to the Grammar of English*
R. LASS *Phonology*
B. COMRIE *Tense*
W. KLEIN *Second Language Acquisition*
A. CRUTTENDEN *Intonation*
A. J. WOODS, P. FLETCHER and A. HUGHES *Statistics in Language Studies*
D. A. CRUSE *Lexical Semantics*
F. R. PALMER *Mood and Modality*
A. RADFORD *Transformational Grammar*
M. GARMAN *Psycholinguistics*
G. CORBETT *Gender*
H. GIEGERICH *English Phonology*
R. CANN Formal Semantics

FORMAL SEMANTICS

An introduction

RONNIE CANN

Department of Linguistics, University of Edinburgh

CAMBRIDGE
UNIVERSITY PRESS

Published by the Press Syndicate of the University of Cambridge
The Pitt Building, Trumptington Street, Cambridge CB2 1RP
40 West 20th Street, New York, NY 10011-4211, USA
10 Stamford Road, Oakleigh, Victoria 3166, Australia

First published 1993
Reprinted 1994

Printed in Great Britain at the University Press, Cambridge

A catalogue record for this book is available from the British Library

Library of Congress cataloguing in publication data applied for

ISBN 0 521 37463 4 hardback
ISBN 0 521 37610 6 paperback

AU

For Bertie

CONTENTS

FIGURES

PREFACE

Although billed as an introduction to formal semantics in general, this textbook is concerned primarily with what has come to be called Montague Semantics and is therefore based primarily on Montague (1970a; 1970b; 1973). A good deal of research within Montague's general framework has been carried out since the 1970s and this has led to many changes in, and many variations of, the original theory. Other research has also led to reactions to Montague's programme and the development of rival theories. Only a few of these revisions and extensions to Montague's theory have, however, found their way into the text of the book. This may seem retrogressive, but it is my conviction that many of the questions being asked in formal semantics and the directions of research are best understood by learning about the more radical elements of Montague's original approach, particularly the semantic analysis of noun phrases and the theory of intensionality. Once these have been grasped, later developments can be understood more easily. For this reason, the exposition develops an account of the now classical version of Montague's theory, but references are given for the major revisions and extensions at the end of each chapter for readers to pursue as their interests dictate. Furthermore, there is no attempt in this book to give more of the logical and mathematical background than is necessary to understand how such things can help in the analysis of the semantics of natural languages. This is not an introduction to formal semantics for logicians, but for linguists. No discussion of completeness, consistency, formal proofs, or axiomatisation will therefore be found in these pages. This book thus provides an introduction to certain techniques in formal semantics as applied to natural languages (exemplified by English). Although readers may find that the domain of meaning that appears to be amenable to the sort of semantic analysis discussed in this book is somewhat small, the fundamental ideas of truth-conditional semantics and the possibility of applying the techniques of formal semantics to natural languages remain important for the development of linguistic semantics.

As an introduction, no logical or mathematical background is assumed for the reader, but some knowledge of Linguistics is taken for granted, particularly with regard to syntax, but acquaintance with an introductory book in general linguistic semantics would be helpful. An explanation of all the relevant concepts from logic and set theory is, however, provided within the text, and references to other textbooks that deal with these concepts are given in the further reading sections of each chapter. Readers who have a knowledge of basic predicate logic may skip Chapters 2 and 3, but those who do not are advised to take each chapter in turn. It is, moreover, advisable to attempt the exercises as they come along, provided that the reader does not get stuck on them. It is better to move on to the rest of the text than to spend many fruitless hours struggling over a single problem (in the exercises or in the reading). The answers to some of these exercises appear at the end of the book, but none are given for those that have an asterisk in front of them. These latter are in the nature of research exercises designed to make readers consider some of the sorts of problems and difficulties that are encountered in providing formal semantic analyses of the sentences of a natural language. References to particular solutions to some of these exercises may, however, be found in the further reading.

This project began as a joint venture between myself and Lesley Stirling. Unfortunately, circumstances conspired against our co-authorship and the final text was written entirely by myself. Lesley wrote an early draft of Chapter 1 and some notes for Chapter 8 and, while none of her original text appears in this final version, her ideas in our early discussions have obviously influenced its final shape. Co-teaching with her in 1986/7 also influenced the way that my later courses in formal semantics developed and thus ultimately how certain of the topics in this book are presented. For these, alas now unidentifiable, benefits, she has my heartfelt thanks. My thanks also go to John Lyons who acted as a very careful editor. This book has benefited greatly from his meticulous notes on the manuscript and his numerous criticisms of substance and style and his positive suggestions have helped to improve the text considerably. I also wish to thank my colleagues Jim Hurford and Jim Miller, for their many comments on earlier versions of the text. Chapter 8 benefited greatly from the latter's careful comments. Thanks also to Ruth Kempson for her comments on the earliest text written by myself and Lesley Stirling and to Marguerite Nesling for her insightful comments on the philosophical aspects of the text. The book has grown out of a series of courses in formal semantics for undergraduate and first year postgraduate students and I have to thank all the students at Edinburgh University, too numerous to mention by name, who took the Advanced Semantics class between the academic years 1986/7 and 1991/2. Their vociferous suffering over the numerous typos of the various versions of the text and their confusion at wrong diagrams and impossibly difficult exercises inspired me to change things well after the time that I thought I had a finished version. The text is the better for their complaints. None of those mentioned here are, of course, responsible for any remaining mistakes or infelicities for which the computer is entirely to blame.

Judith Ayling and her staff at Cambridge University Press have my gratitude for their careful editing of the final text and their considerable help with the preparation of the camara ready copy from which this book is printed. Robert Bradford helped a good deal with the latter stages of the production of the text, the final version of which was prepared on a NeXTstation.

Many thanks too to Fiona Chapman who heroically produced the illustrations while simultaneously building a house and looking after three children. Thanks also to Tom and Betty Watson for endless gin and sympathy and to those people in the village who were continually surprised that I had still not finished the book. Finally, my thanks to Robert Bradford for all his help and support, emotional, financial and computational. His help in solving the repetitive tasks in word-processing and his patience in listening to endless rantings about logic, time and the meaning of meaning went far beyond the realms of duty. I dedicate this book to him with my love.

Pool o' Muckhart

SYMBOLS

Logical symbols

&	conjunction (*and*)
$\vee$	inclusive disjunction (*or*)
$\vee_e$	exclusive disjunction
$\rightarrow$	material implication (*if...then*)
$\leftrightarrow$	equivalence (*if, and only if,*)
=	identity operator
~	negation (*not*)
λ	lambda operator
»	λ-converts into
$\forall$	universal quantifier (*all/every*)
$\exists$	existential quantifier (*a/some*)
Pres	present tense operator
Past	past tense operator
Fut	future tense operator
Perf	perfective operator
Impf	imperfective operator
$\diamond$	possibility operator
$\Box$	necessity operator
f(a)	functor f applied to argument a
Pred_n	n-place predicate
t	type of a formula
e	type of an individual
<a,b>	complex type
<s,a>	intensional type
$\vdash$	entailment
$\dashv\vdash$	paraphrase
$\models$	contradiction

Variables

x,y,z	individual (type e)
r	individual concept (type <s,e>)
P,Q	set (type <e,t>)
A	property (type <s,<e,t>>)
R	binary relation (type <e,<e,t>>)
$\Re$	relation in intension (type <s,<e,<e,t>>>)
p,q,r	propositional (type t or (ch. 10) <s,t>)
P	generalised quantifier (type <<e,t>,t>)
$\wp$	intensional generalised quantifier (type <s,<<e,t>,t>>)

Set theory

{a,..,b}	set consisting of elements a,...,b
{x | f(x)}	set of elements x satisfying property f
<a,b>	ordered pair of elements
<a,b,c>	ordered triple of elements
$\varnothing$	the null (or empty) set
$\in$	set membership (*is a member of*)
$\notin$	set non-membership (*is not a member of*)
$\cap$	set intersection
$\cup$	set union
$\subset$	proper subset relation
$\supset$	proper superset relation
$\subseteq$	subset relation
$\supseteq$	superset relation
$\leq$	is less than or equal to
$\geq$	is greater than or equal to
$>$	is greater than
$\|A\|$	cardinality of set A
$A \times B$	cartesian product of sets A and B ({<a,b> | a $\in$ A & b $\in$ B})
A^B	set of functions from domain B to range A

Model theory

$[\alpha]^{M,g,w,i}$	interpretation of α with respect to M, g, w and i
1	truth
0	falsity
M	Model
A	set of entities
F	denotation assignment function
T	set of times
I	set of temporal intervals defined on **T**
$<$	precedence relation
W	set of possible worlds
R	accessibility relation on **W**
g	assignment of values to variables
$\mathbf{g}^{a/u}$	assignment of values to variables where element g(u) = a.
D_α	denotation type of expressions of type α
$[t_i,t_j]$	temporal interval between times t_i and t_j
$[t_i]$	moment of time
$\circ$	overlap relation (of temporal intervals)
$\subseteq$	subinterval relation
$\Im[\phi]^{M,g}$	intension of ϕ with respect to M and g
$\Sigma[\phi]^{M,g}$	sense of ϕ with respect to M and g

Grammatical symbols

S	sentence
NP	noun phrase
N_{pr}	proper noun
Pro	pronoun
N	common noun
CNP	common noun phrase
Det	determiner
A	adjective
A[-PRD]	attributive adjective
VP	verb phrase
VP[PAS]	passive verb phrase
V_i	intransitive verb
V_t	transitive verb
V_{dt}	ditransitive verb
V_0	impersonal verb
[±FIN]	finite/non-finite (verb)
Adv	adverb
CONJ	conjunction
NEG	negative
PP_{by}	*by* prepositional phrase
PP_{to}	*to* prepositional phrase
[±PAST]	past/non-past
$\rightarrow$	rewrite arrow
$\Rightarrow$	translates as

1 Introduction

1.1 Semantics and semantic theory

In its broadest sense, semantics is the study of meaning and linguistic semantics is the study of meaning as expressed by the words, phrases and sentences of human languages. It is, however, more usual within linguistics to interpret the term more narrowly, as concerning the study of those aspects of meaning encoded in linguistic expressions that are independent of their use on particular occasions by particular individuals within a particular speech community. In other words, semantics is the study of meaning abstracted away from those aspects that are derived from the intentions of speakers, their psychological states and the socio-cultural aspects of the context in which their utterances are made. A further narrowing of the term is also commonly made in separating the study of semantics from that of pragmatics. Unfortunately, the nature of the object of inquiry of the discipline (what constitutes semantic meaning, as opposed to pragmatic meaning) and the domain of the inquiry (what aspects of meaning should be addressed by the discipline) remain difficult and controversial questions. There are, however, three central aspects of the meaning of linguistic expressions that are currently accepted by most semanticists as forming the core concern of linguistic semantics. These central concerns of semantic theory, adapted from Kempson (1977:4), are stated in (1) and may be adopted as criteria for ascertaining the adequacy of semantic theories which apply in addition to the general conditions on scientific theories of falsifiability and rigour.

(1) **A semantic theory must**:
- a. capture for any language the nature of the meaning of words, phrases and sentences and explain the nature of the relation between them;
- b. be able to predict the ambiguities in the expressions of a language;
- c. characterise and explain the systematic meaning relations between the words, the phrases and the sentences of a language.

One may add to these the condition that a semantic theory should provide an account of the relation between linguistic expressions and what may be called 'things in the world'. In other words, it is a primary concern of a semantic theory to explain how human beings can use their language to convey information about the external world. We may thus require a semantic theory to conform also to the criterion of adequacy in (2).

(2) A semantic theory must provide an account of the relation between linguistic expressions and the things that they can be used to talk about.

There are many other aspects of meaning that can be included in the domain of linguistic semantics, but a theory conforming to the four criteria in (1) and (2) will cover the main ground of the discipline and provide a firm basis for further research. In this book, we will be looking at a particular theory of semantics that goes a long way towards satisfying these criteria and that has been very influential in linguistic semantics over the last two decades. This theory is a formal theory of semantics and is distinguished from **general linguistic semantics** by its greater use of mathematical techniques and reliance on logical precision. This is not to say that **formal semantics** and general linguistic semantics are completely separate disciplines. It sometimes appears that these two approaches to the semantics of natural languages are mutually incompatible, but this is not obviously true. The former draws heavily on the long tradition of research in the latter which in turn benefits from the greater precision of the former. Both approaches enable us to understand more about meaning and greater integration between them would doubtless bring greater benefits to the discipline.

Formal semantics itself was devised as a means of providing a precise interpretation for **formal languages**, i.e. the logical and mathematical languages that are opposed to **natural languages** that are spoken or written as the native languages of human beings. Many logicians considered it to be impossible to apply the same rigour to the semantics of human languages, because of their supposedly inexact syntax, their vagueness and their ambiguity. In the late nineteen-sixties, however, the philosopher Richard Montague asserted that it was possible to use the same techniques in analysing the meanings of sentences in English. In three articles, *English as a formal language*, *Universal grammar* and *The proper treatment of quantification in English*, all published or presented in 1970, Montague gave arguments for his hypothesis that:

> There is in my opinion no important theoretical difference between natural languages and the artificial languages of logicians; indeed, I consider it possible to comprehend the syntax and semantics of both kinds of language within a single, natural and mathematically precise theory.
>
> Montague (1974: 222)

Throughout the nineteen-seventies, after his tragic death in 1971, Montague's work had a radical effect on the study of semantics in linguistics. Indeed, his ideas on the semantics of human languages have become central to the understanding of many of the questions and theories being discussed in linguistic semantics today. Owing to the relatively recent application of the tools of formal semantics to the analysis of natural languages, however, there are many topics in linguistic semantics that have not yet been formally analysed, but it is hoped that ultimately a good deal of linguistic meaning will be amenable to the sort of rigorous treatment envisaged by Montague. It is the exposition of Montague's theory in its now classical form that constitutes the subject matter of this book, but, before the main points of his semantic theory are introduced, the four criteria of adequacy in (1) and (2) above will be discussed in more detail in order to provide a clearer idea of the fundamental issues that underlie the development of the theory in later chapters.

1.1.1 Compositionality

A fundamental property that any semantic theory must have is the ability to pair the syntactic expressions of a language with their meanings. In the first condition of adequacy in (1.a), above, this property is characterised as a requirement that a semantic theory account for the nature of the meaning of linguistic expressions and be able to pair every expression in a language (words, phrases and sentences) with an appropriate meaning. As already mentioned, the characterisation of meaning is a controversial matter, but whatever meanings are taken to be within a theory, it is obvious that there must be some way of associating them with appropriate linguistic expressions. This is not a trivial matter, however, and there are a number of important points that need to be discussed with respect to this property.

In the first place, let us consider more closely what it is that is to be assigned meanings by a semantic theory. Condition (1.a) refers to words and sentences as the carriers of meaning. The term **sentence** here is being used in its abstract sense, common in linguistics, as the largest unit of syntactic description, independently of its realisation in spoken or written texts. Like the term sentence, **word** is also ambiguous in everyday English. Within semantics, the notion of word that is most useful is that of the **lexeme** which is an abstract grammatical construct that underlies a set of **word forms** which are recognised as representatives of 'the same word' in different syntactic environments. For example, the word forms *sing, sings, singing, sang* and *sung* are particular inflectional variants of a lexeme which we may represent for the time being as *SING*. It is to lexemes and not to word forms that meanings should be assigned, because while the inflectional properties of the verb *SING* may vary in different syntactic environments, the sort of action described by the verb remains the same. For this reason, the meaning of words is referred to in this book as **lexical meaning**, rather than word meaning.

Although it is possible for the meanings assigned to lexemes and sentences to be very different from each other, it is reasonable to expect the meanings of sentences to be related to the meanings of the lexemes underlying the word-forms they contain. It is intuitively implausible for there to be a language where the relation between the meaning of a sentence and the meanings of its component lexemes is entirely random. While languages do contain idiomatic phrases and sentences where lexical and sentential meaning are not transparently related (e.g. *kick the bucket* meaning the same as *DIE* in English), this is never the general situation. If there were no direct relation between lexical and sentential meaning, of course, the meaning of each sentence in a language would have to be listed. Since the number of sentences that make up a language is infinite, this would mean that no human being would be able to determine the meanings of all the sentences of any language owing to the finite resources of the brain. This is absurd, of course, and just as sentences are defined recursively by syntactic rules, taking words (or morphemes) as their basis, so their meanings should also be defined recursively from the meanings ascribed to the lexemes they contain.

Thus, in addition to associating each expression in a language with a meaning, an adequate semantic theory must also be able to explain how the meanings of smaller expressions contribute to the meanings of larger ones that contain them. A theory that derives the meaning of larger expressions from those of smaller ones is said to be **compositional**. The **Principle of Compositionality**, given an initial definition in (3), is generally attributed to the German philosopher Gottlob Frege, and is thus sometimes referred to as the **Fregean Principle of Compositionality** or just the **Fregean Principle**, although it is unlikely that he ever stated the principle in precisely this way.

(3) The meaning of an expression is a function of the meaning of its parts.

The notion of a **function** will be discussed in more detail in Chapter 4, but essentially it is an operation that derives a single result given a specified input. Thus, the principle (3) minimally requires that the meaning of a larger expression be uniquely determined from the meanings of its component parts. This cannot be all there is to compositionality, however, since, otherwise, we would expect that sentences containing the same words mean the same thing. This is, of course, not true. The sentence *Jo kicked Chester* does not mean the same as *Chester kicked Jo*. It must also be the case, therefore, that the syntactic structure of an expression is relevant to the derivation of its meaning. Indeed, we may strengthen the principle of compositionality so that, in deriving the meaning of a composite expression, the meaning of its component expressions are combined in some way that refers to the way they are combined by the syntax. This implies that wherever meanings are combined in a particular way to derive the meaning of a composite expression, all other composite expressions of the same sort have their meanings determined in the same way. In other words, the construction of meanings is **rule-governed**, in the same way that the construction of the well-formed syntactic expressions of a language is rule-governed. For example, whatever rule derives the meaning of the sentence *Jo sang* from the subject *Jo* and intransitive verb *sang* applies to all declarative sentences derived by combining a subject noun phrase with the appropriate form of an intransitive verb.

Furthermore, it is a general property of human languages that all the sub-expressions of a grammatically well-formed phrase have a role to play in the interpretation of a sentence, even if, on occasions, this role is predictably redundant (as, for example, in double negative constructions in certain dialects of English like *I never did nothing* where the second negative expression merely reinforces the idea of negation introduced by the first). Semantic rules should, therefore, not be allowed to delete meanings during the derivation of the meaning of a composite expression. The effect of this restriction is to make the creation of the meanings of larger expressions **monotonic** with respect to their component parts where a derivation is said to be monotonic if all properties of previous parts of a derivation are maintained throughout. In other words, once information is introduced into a monotonic derivation, it is not lost thereafter. The initial definition of compositionality in (3) may thus be strengthened to give the statement in (4).

(4) **The principle of compositionality**: The meaning of an expression is a monotonic function of the meaning of its parts and the way they are put together.

The implications of this interpretation of the principle of compositionality is that meanings should be ascribed not only to lexemes and sentences but also to other syntactic constituents. It is thus generally assumed that meanings should be assigned to all the well-formed constituents of a language, not just to its words (lexemes) and sentences. Indeed, the concept of syntax as a bridge between phonology and semantics, current in many grammatical theories, would seem to require that all constituents be assigned a meaning by the semantics and, furthermore, that (surface) syntactic structure should directly determine how the meanings of sentences are derived. It is common to assume that semantic constituency parallels syntactic constituency and hence that an adequate semantic theory must be able to ascribe appropriate meanings to noun phrases like *the old cat, Jo's mother*, *Chester* and verb phrases like *sang*, *kicked the cat*, *ran slowly*, etc, according to their syntactic structure.

One way in which this may be achieved is to adopt the hypothesis that for each syntactic rule of the grammar (or syntactic structure admitted by the grammar) there is a corresponding semantic rule that derives the meaning of the resultant expression (or structure). For example, assuming that there is a rule that defines a sentence in English as consisting of a noun phrase plus a verb phrase, then the adoption of the **rule-to-rule hypothesis** in (5), together with the principle of compositionality in (4), requires that there be a corresponding semantic rule deriving the meaning of the sentence from the meanings of its immediate constituents, NP and VP.

(5) **Rule-to-rule hypothesis**: For each syntactic rule there is a corresponding semantic rule.

The principle of compositionality in (4) is assumed to be a constraint on semantic theories and, indeed, will be seen to be the primary motivator behind much of the discussion in later chapters. The rule-to-rule hypothesis, on the other hand, is not a necessary requirement of a semantic theory, but a means of achieving compositionality. We will have cause to question the validity of this hypothesis in the later chapters of this book, but it is used in the earlier chapters to maintain a transparent relation between syntactic structures and semantic representations.

1.1.2 Meaning relations

Another aspect of meaning that must be accounted for by any semantic theory is the systematic relations that hold between different expressions in a language. According to the condition of adequacy in (1.b), a theory must satisfactorily analyse the intuitions speakers of English have about the semantic relations between lexemes and between sentences. This assumes that expressions in a language which may not be syntactically related may be related semantically and, indeed, such is the case. Consider the sentences in (6). Assuming that the reference of the name *Jo* and the discourse context are held constant for all the sentences in (6), then the sentences in (6.b) to (6.i) are semantically related to that in (6.a), even though it is not always the case that there is a direct syntactic relation between them.

(6) a. Jo stroked a cat.
b. A cat was stroked.
c. There was a cat.
d. No-one stroked a cat.
e. There are no such things as cats.
f. A cat was stroked by Jo.
g. It was Jo who stroked the cat.
h. Jo touched a cat.
i. Jo stroked an animal.

The relation between the sentences in (6.a) and those in (6.b) and (6.c) is one of **entailment**, as it is intuitively impossible for it to be true that Jo stroked a cat on some occasion without it also being true that a cat was stroked or that there existed a cat to be stroked on that occasion. We may thus define a sentence S_1 as **entailing** a sentence S_2 if the latter truly describes a situation whenever the former also does. The negation of an entailment always derives a **contradiction** and a sentence S_1 may be said to **contradict** a sentence S_2 if the former must be false when the latter is true (or vice versa). For example, the assertion that Jo stroked a cat is contradicted by the non-existence of cats, making (6.e) a contradiction of (6.a). The relation between (6.a) and the sentences in (6.f) and (6.g) is also primarily semantic, although most syntactic theories recognise a syntactic relation between the sentences as well. Using a common term in a technical way, we may say these sentences are **paraphrases** of each other, since they all have the same core meaning. Another way of putting this is to say that they mutually entail each other. Hence, we may say that a sentence S_1 is a paraphrase of a sentence S_2 if S_1 entails S_2 and S_2 entails S_1. An adequate theory of semantics must, therefore, provide an account of entailment, contradiction and paraphrase that allows one to identify which sentences are entailed by, or contradict or paraphrase, another in a language. Indeed, this concern, along with compositionality, is a major motivation for the theoretical programme developed in this book.

Other sorts of **implication** between sentences are also recognised in general linguistic semantics. Some of these derive from lexical meaning as in (6.h) and (6.i) which are related to (6.a) by virtue of the meanings of the lexemes *STROKE* and *CAT*, respectively. It is part of the meaning of the lexeme *STROKE* that an action of stroking also involves an action of touching, so that (6.a) implies (6.h). Furthermore, it is part of the meaning of *CAT* that anything that is a cat is also an animal and thus (6.a) implies (6.i). The meaning relations that hold between the lexemes of a language (or between lexemes and larger expressions) are called **sense relations** and include **hyponymy**, which holds if the sense of one lexeme includes that of another (e.g. between *CAT* and *ANIMAL*); **synonymy**, where two lexemes have the same sense (e.g. between *MERCURY* and *QUICKSILVER*); and **oppositeness**, where two lexemes have opposing senses (e.g. *BIG* and *SMALL* and *DEAD* and *ALIVE*). Hence, an adequate theory of semantics must give some account of lexical meaning and, in particular, of the sense relations that hold between lexemes in a particular language.

Other implicational meaning relations hold between sentences in addition to those that have been noted above. One of these is so-called **conversational implicature**, which is derived not from the conventional meanings of words or sentences, but from principles of discourse and context. For example, in the exchange in (7), the apparent irrelevance of Ethel's reply in (7.b) to Bertie's question in (7.a) leads the latter to infer (7.c). The reason behind inference has to do with Bertie's expectations about Ethel's co-operativeness in providing him with the information he needs. The fact that she has not given a straight answer leads Bertie, not to assume that she is being deliberately unhelpful, but to look for some piece of information that is relevant to his question that is indirectly implied by Ethel's response. This example is discussed in more detail in Section 1.3.1 below.

(7) a. Bertie: Is Fiona a good lecturer?
  b. Ethel: She has a good line in sweaters.
  c. Bertie (thinks): Fiona is not a good lecturer.

Another sort of implication between sentences is called **presupposition**. A sentence is said to presuppose another if its truth and that of its negation both imply that the presupposed sentence is also true. In other words, presupposition deals with aspects of meaning that are assumed to hold of a situation when a sentence is uttered to describe that situation. For example, the use of the definite article in a noun phrase is said to presuppose the existence of something that has the property described by the common noun in the same NP. This is illustrated in (8) where the truth of the sentences in (8.c) and (8.d) is presupposed by that of (8.a) and its negation in (8.b), because of the use of *the* in the subject noun phrase. (8.c) is not implied by (8.e) which replaces *the* in the subject NP by *every* (as shown by the bracketed causal clause which denies the truth of (8.c), apparently without contradiction) and, while (8.f) implies (indeed, according to the discussion above, entails) (8.c), its negation in (8.g) does not.

(8) a. The Duchess of Muckhart terrorised the village.
    b. The Duchess of Muckhart didn't terrorise the village.
    c. There is a Duchess of Muckhart.
    d. There is a village.
    e. Every Duchess of Muckhart terrorised the village (because there is no Duchess of Muckhart).
    f. A Duchess of Muckhart terrorised the village.
    g. A Duchess of Muckhart didn't terrorise the village.

It is usually assumed that implicatures such as that in (7) result from principles of conversation and thus form part of the domain of pragmatics rather than semantics (see Chapter 7 for some further discussion). More controversial, however, is the status of presupposition. Whether it should be included in semantic or pragmatic theory is an extremely vexed question, as indeed is the definition and status of the phenomenon itself. As the inclusion of this topic would require considerable discussion, it is omitted from consideration in this book. This is for convenience only and should not be taken to reflect on the importance of the topic, only on the controversiality of its analysis. The reader is referred for further information on this vexed topic to the books and articles mentioned at the end of this chapter.

In addition to accounting for these semantic relations, a semantic theory may also be required to provide some account of **anomaly** in the meaning of expressions in some language. It should, therefore, be able to explain why certain expressions which are syntactically well-formed are unacceptable or deviant from the semantic point of view. For example, the sentence in (9.a) is syntactically well-formed and semantically coherent in English. Those in (9.b) and (9.c), however, are semantically anomalous despite the fact that they have the same syntactic structure as (9.a). Such sentences can, however, be given some sort of non-literal interpretation (although (9.c) is harder to find an interpretation for than (9.b)), unlike the completely ill-formed expression in (9.d) which is simply not English. This decline in acceptability from (9.a) to (9.c) and the incoherence of (9.d) should thus be explained by an adequate theory of semantics.

(9) a. Green Wellington boots are very popular now.
    b. Green ideas are very popular now.
    c. Green corollaries are very popular now.
    d. *very Wellington are boots popular now green.

1.1.3 Ambiguity

The third area of meaning that Kempson (1977) suggests must be explained by a semantic theory is **ambiguity**. A sentence is said to be ambiguous whenever it can be associated with two or more different meanings. Ambiguity can arise in a sentence for a number of reasons: through the ascription of multiple meanings to single words (e.g. (10.a)); through the assignment of different syntactic structures to a sentence (e.g. (10.b)); or through the use of certain expressions that may have different semantic **scope** (e.g. (10.c)).

(10) a. Ethel's punch was impressive.
b. The strike was called by radical lecturers and students.
c. Every good politician loves a cause.

The first sort of ambiguity occurs where an expression is associated with two or more unrelated meanings, as in (10.a) where the word *punch* may be interpreted as a drink or as an action. Lexemes whose word forms have this property are called **homonyms** and can be subdivided into **homophones**, where the forms of the lexeme sound the same but may be written differently, e.g. *draft* and *draught* which can both be represented phonemically as /draft/, and **homographs**, e.g. *lead*, which are written the same, but which are pronounced differently. Some lexemes are both homophones and homographs, like *PUNCH*. Homonyms can be divided into full homonyms (like *BANK*, *PUNCH*), where all of the lexeme's associated word forms are phonetically or orthographically identical, and partial homonyms (like *FIND*, *FOUND*), where just some of its word forms are identical.

Homonymy is often contrasted with **polysemy**. A polysemous lexeme is one that is interpreted as having multiple senses that are not entirely distinct, as is the case in the standard examples of homonyms. The classic example of a polyseme in English is the lexeme *MOUTH* which has different interpretations depending on what sort of entity is described as having a mouth. There are, for example, human mouths, mouths of caves, mouths of bottles, mouths of rivers, and so on. In each of these cases, the properties of the entity described by *MOUTH* are different, but not absolutely different, as each one refers to an opening of some sort. The difference between homonymy and polysemy is one of degree, and precise definitions of these terms are difficult and controversial. As this book is not primarily concerned with lexical meaning, no attempt will be made to differentiate the two notions or to incorporate polysemy within the theory at all. As will be seen in Chapter 2, the approach to homonymy taken here is very simplistic: the senses of homonymous lexemes are simply differentiated formally by the use of superscripts, where necessary. Although an account of polysemy and a better approach to homonymy may be possible within the theory of formal semantics presented in later chapters, these matters are not central to the concerns of this book and an adequate discussion of the issues involved would only serve to increase the size of the book without serving any great purpose. The decision to exclude polysemy from consideration and to take a simplistic view of homonymy is taken on the grounds of expository convenience and readers are again referred to the further reading noted at the end of the chapter.

A more interesting source of ambiguity from the point of view of the formal semanticist is illustrated in (10.b). Here the ambiguity results from the possibility of assigning two or more syntactic structures to a single grammatical string of words. To ascertain the meaning of (10.b), for example, it is necessary to know whether the adjective *radical* modifies the nominal phrase, *lecturers and students*, in which case both the lecturers and the students who called the strike are all radical, or whether it modifies just the noun *lecturers*, in which case the lecturers who called the strike are said to be radical but the political attitude of the students who did so is not specified. These two readings are illustrated in (11) where the labelled bracketings of the agentive noun phrase in (11.b) and (11.d) correspond to the readings indicated in (11.a) and (11.c), respectively.

(11) a. The strike was called by lecturers who are radical and by students.
b. $[_{NP}\ [_{N1}\ [_{N1}$ radical lecturers] and students]].
c. The strike was called by lecturers who are radical and by students who are radical.
d. $[_{NP}\ [_{N1}$ radical $[_{N1}$ lecturers and students]]].

In the above example, what is at issue is the scope of the adjective, *radical*. In (11.a), it modifies, and thus has scope over, the noun *lecturers*, while in (11.b) its scope is the nominal phrase *lecturers and students*. Scope is an important concept in semantics and a primary source of ambiguity which involves not only adjectives, but also conjunctions, like *and*, *or*, etc and quantifiers, like *every*, *all*, and *some* in English. **Structural ambiguity** of this sort thus has its source in the syntax of a language, but there are other scope ambiguities that do not directly depend on the syntactic structure of a sentence. Such ambiguity usually involves negation (*not*), quantification (*every, some*) and other elements like tense, which do not vary their syntactic position according to the reading of the sentence. For example, the two readings of the sentence in (10.c) can be made clear by those in (12). In (12.a), there is only one cause that every good politician loves, while in (12.b) each politician may love a different cause. The sentence in (10.c), however, is usually only assigned a single surface constituent structure, so that this ambiguity cannot be directly attributed to a syntactic source and is referred to as a **semantic scope ambiguity**.

(12) a. Every politician loves a cause and that is their own career.
b. Every good politician loves a cause and each one loves a cause that everyone else loathes.

An adequate semantic theory must thus be able to predict where structural ambiguity is likely to arise in a language and provide a means of differentiating the interpretations of the different structures to an ambiguous sentence by the grammar, where this is relevant. It should also ensure that sentences that have two (or more) syntactic derivations, but only one semantic interpretation, are not assigned more than one meaning (see Chapter 3 for examples involving the conjunctions *and* and *or*). The theory should also provide an account of scope ambiguities where these are not directly reflected in syntactic derivations, and be able to differentiate the scopes of particular expressions independently of the syntax.

1.1.4 Denotation

The final criterion of adequacy that is considered here is stated in (2), above, and is the most important for our purposes, since it forms the basis of the semantic theory to be proposed in the rest of this book. This criterion requires a semantic theory to give an account of the relation between linguistic expressions and what they can be used to talk about. Since language can be used to talk about what is outside the linguistic system, it is essential that a semantic theory should be able to associate linguistic expressions with extra-linguistic objects. Language is not used solely to talk about itself, but rather it is most commonly used to convey information about the situations in which human beings find themselves. Since a listener can in general understand the meaning of what is being said by a speaker, meanings must be publicly accessible in some sense. One way that this public accessibility must be realised is in the association of linguistic expressions with publicly identifiable entities and situations. For example, the utterance of a sentence like *The book is on the table* conveys information about two entities, one of which is conventionally called a book in English and one of which is conventionally called a table, and the relation between them. Someone who hears an utterance of this sentence associates it with the situation pictorially represented in (13). Although (13) is itself a representation of an actual (or possible) situation, it is nonetheless a non-linguistic representation and a theory of semantics should be capable of relating the meaning of the sentence to the picture and, indeed, to concrete, non-representational situations where there is a (single) book on the table.

The association between the sentence *The book is on the table* and the situation represented in (13) depends in part on there being, in the situation described, an instance of a thing that is conventionally called a book and one that is conventionally called a table in English. In other words, part of the meaning of the sentence depends on the sorts of extra-linguistic **entities** that can be referred to by the lexemes *BOOK* and *TABLE*. The aspect of the meaning of an expression that concerns its relation to such objects is called its **denotation** and an expression is said to **denote** particular sorts of extra-linguistic objects. Although this relation has often been called the **reference** of an expression, this book follows the usage of Lyons (1977) and reserves this latter term for the act of picking out a particular entity denoted by the expression through the utterance of that expression on some occasion. For example, in uttering the sentence *The book is on the table*, a speaker is said to be referring to two particular, contextually unique, entities. The entities being referred to by the use of the definite noun phrases, *the book* and *the table*, are single elements in the class of entities denoted by the lexemes *BOOK* and *TABLE*.

Thus, a speaker may use linguistic expressions to refer, but linguistic expressions themselves denote. No more will be said here about the act of reference, and the differences between denotation and reference, but for more details the reader is urged to consult the further reading at the end of this chapter.

Informally, we may think of the denotation as the relation between an expression and a class of various sorts of individuals, events, properties and relations that may be referred to by the use of the expression on some particular occasion. The lexeme *BOOK* may, therefore, be thought of as denoting the set of all books, *TABLE* as denoting the set of all tables, while the preposition *ON* may be thought of as denoting

(13) **The book is on the table**

the set of all the pairs of entities of which one is on the other. It is easy to grasp the notion of denotation with respect to lexemes that denote concrete entities like books and tables, but the question arises about whether abstract lexemes like *LOVE*, *KNOWLEDGE* or *THEOREM* or ones denoting fictitious entities like *UNICORN* or *HOBBIT* have denotations in the same way. The answer is, as might be expected, controversial, but here the position is taken that there is no essential difference between such expressions and those that denote concrete entities. Thus, the noun *LOVE* is taken to denote a set of entities just like *BOOK*. The difference between them is that the entities denoted by the former are abstract while those denoted by the latter are concrete. Although the postulation of abstract entities of this sort may cause problems from a philosophical point of view, it does have the advantage of reflecting the fact that the same sorts of linguistic expressions (e.g. nouns) are used in many, if not all, languages to refer to both abstract and concrete things.

In a similar fashion, lexemes describing fictitious entities like hobbits, or entities that are no longer extant like dodos, are also assumed to have a denotation. It is, however, useful to distinguish between the denotations of lexemes that may be used to refer to entities that exist in the real world (including abstract ones) and those that do not. We can do this by making a distinction between two aspects of denotation. Nouns like *BOOK* may be used to refer to entities in the world, but the entities of which one can truthfully say *That is a book* all share a certain common property, their 'bookness', so to speak. In the same way, the set of entities that are red all have the property of redness and the set of entities that run all have the property of running. In other words, we distinguish between the property denoted by a common noun like *BOOK*, adjective like *RED* or intransitive verb like *RUN* and the entities it can be used to refer to. The former part of the meaning of the lexeme is often referred to as its **sense** and is opposed to the idea of its reference. However, just as the latter term is used here for a different notion, so too is that of sense which is used solely with respect to the sense relations that hold between the lexemes of a language (see Section 1.2 and Chapter 7). The distinction between the different aspects of the meaning of *BOOK* noted above are treated as a distinction between the **intension** of an expression and its **extension**. The former corresponds to the property aspect of common nouns, whereas the latter corresponds to the entities that they may be used to refer to in the world. Thus, the extension of the lexeme *BOOK* is the set of all books whilst its intension is the property of being a book. Both properties and sets of entities are external to the linguistic system and thus constitute aspects of denotation. This distinction allows a differentiation between entities like books which have existence in the real world and those like unicorns that, presumably, do not. In the latter case, the lexeme *UNICORN* has no extension in the real world, but it does have an intension, the property of being a unicorn. Thus, we may speak about unicorns and other entities without them needing to exist in the real world. This distinction is discussed in more detail in Chapters 9 and 10, where a specific theory of intensionality is put forward. Until then, we will be concerned primarily with the notion of extension and thus be concentrating on the relation between linguistic expressions and existing entities.

It is not necessary to restrict the notion of denotation to lexemes, but it may be extended to all well-formed linguistic expressions. For example, the verb phrase *kicked a cat* may be taken to denote the class of actions involving the kicking of a cat, which is distinct from the class of all actions involving kicking a dog which would be denoted by the expression *kicked a dog*, and so on. The denotations of other expressions, like quantified noun phrases, are less easy to specify informally, but we will see in Chapter 6 how they can be defined. Those expressions that are not used to pick out external entities in any way may also have denotations. Such expressions are typically described as **functional** or **grammatical** expressions, like determiners and conjunctions, as opposed to the **content** expressions, like nouns, verbs and adjectives. This distinction amongst the syntactic categories of a language is a traditional (and very useful) one and can be reflected in semantics by assigning rather different sorts of denotation to the two sorts of expression. Grammatical expressions are taken to denote logical relations between groups of entities that are denoted by content expressions. This subject is dealt with in proper detail in later chapters of the book, where the differences between the denotations of content and functional elements will become clear.

A theory of denotation is thus not a trivial one and any semantic theory that provides an account of this important relation has already achieved a great deal. Throughout this book the terms denotation, denotes, intension and extension are used a great deal. Although denotation most properly refers to the relation between an expression and some entity, event, property or relation, it will also be used below to refer to what an expression denotes (what Lyons (1977) calls the **denotatum** of an expression). The term is used in this way in discussions of general importance that include both extensional and intensional denotation. Where reference is being made to what a specific expression denotes, the terms extension or intension are used, depending on which aspect of denotation is relevant. Thus, the extension of an expression is taken below to refer to what the expression extensionally denotes, and similarly for the term intension. This terminology should cause no confusion, but the reader is asked to pay special attention to their use in the earlier chapters of this book.

1.2 Interpretation and representation

In the last section, we looked at those aspects of meaning that constitute the minimum domain of an adequate theory of linguistic semantics. For the rest of this book, we will be exploring a theory that attempts to provide an account of such phenomena and, in so doing, to define what semantic meaning is. There are a number of competing theories of meaning and the one that is adopted in this book starts from the premiss that one of the most important aspects of language is to talk about entities in the world. The **central core** of meaning in this theory is thus determined by the relation between linguistic expressions and the entities that they can be used to refer to. In other words, denotation, and specifically extensional denotation, forms the basis of the theory of meaning developed here. Although this theory has many critics and gives rise to a number of difficult problems, it nevertheless continues to have a large amount of support and has proved extremely fruitful in the study of linguistic semantics. In this section, a general overview is presented of the major aspects of the theory that are presented in more detail in the following chapters.

The main question that arises at this point is where the analysis should start. Many semantic theories have taken the meaning of words (lexemes) as basic and derived sentential (and phrasal) meanings from it. Whatever the successes or failures of such theories, for a theory whose basis resides in the informational content of language, what languages may be used to talk about, it is more appropriate to begin with sentence meaning and derive the meanings of its constituent parts from this. Declarative sentences are typically used to make statements which convey information directly about some state of affairs. Expressions smaller than a sentence, however, require more information from context for their interpretation than sentences do. For example, in a situation in which there are two people, one of whom is searching for a particular book, the second person knows that the book that the first is looking for is on the table and may utter any of the four expressions in (14) to convey this information to his or her partner. Only the first, a full declarative sentence, is complete and unambiguous, requiring the minimum amount of extra information to be provided by the context. Thus, while (14.a) may be used to describe a situation like that depicted in (13), it cannot be used to describe truthfully the one depicted in (15) in which the book is not on the table, but under it. The utterance of the expressions in (14.a) to (14.d) could, however, be used to describe this situation (i.e. where the speaker is referring to the vase being on the table, not the book) and a good many more, depending on the context.

(14) a. The book is on the table.
b. On the table.
c. The table.
d. Table.

Declarative sentences, when uttered to make statements, thus form the basis of our investigation into semantic meaning. Such expressions, uttered to such a purpose (and not, for example, indirectly as a polite command or a question), are said by philosophers to express **propositions** and this usage has become commonplace in linguistics. Like most useful and interesting ideas, however, propositions have had a controversial and contentious life and been variously defined. Lyons (1977)

(15) **The book is not on the table**

provides the definition in (16.a), while Hurford and Heasley (1983) give that in (16.b). Other definitions ascribe them the further properties in (16.c) and (16.d).

(16) **A proposition**:
a. is what is expressed by a declarative sentence when that sentence is uttered to make a statement. Lyons (1977:141)
b. is that part of the meaning of a sentence that describes a state of affairs. Hurford and Heasley (1983:19)
c. may be true or false.
d. may be known, believed or doubted.

We will sidestep the controversy surrounding definitions like those in (16) and adopt all four statements as descriptions of the properties that propositions have and make the assumption that declarative sentences (which we will henceforth assume to be uttered only as statements, thus ignoring other uses of such sentence forms) express propositions on particular occasions of utterance. According to (16.c), the proposition expressed by a sentence may be true or false and this truth or falsity may vary with respect to different occasions on which the sentence is uttered. For example, the proposition expressed by the sentence *The book is on the table* uttered with respect to the situation depicted in (13) is true, but it is false, if uttered with respect to the situation pictorially illustrated in (15). Propositions may thus vary in their **truth value** from utterance occasion to utterance occasion. In terms of denotation, we may, therefore, think of sentences as extensionally denoting truth values on particular occasions of utterance (and, in Chapter 10, it will be suggested that sentences intensionally denote propositions). This rather abstract idea of a sentence extensionally denoting truth or falsity forms the starting point of the semantic theory to be pursued through the rest of this book and it is to a consideration of what it means for something to be true that we now turn.

1.2.1 Truth-conditions

The definition of what it means for a statement to be true that is adopted in this book is the **correspondence theory of truth** given in (17) which is so called because a statement is defined as being true if, and only if, the state of affairs described by the statement holds.

(17) **The correspondence theory of truth**: A statement in some language is true if, and only if, it corresponds to some state-of-affairs.

The definition in (17) applies to statements in any language, whether a natural language learnt and spoken by human beings or an artificial language devised for specific purposes. Since declarative sentences are used to make statements in English (and other languages) and since, according to (16.a) above, declarative sentences are taken to express propositions when uttered as statements, we can revise (17) to apply to the particular case of human languages as in (18).

(18) The proposition expressed by a declarative sentence uttered as a statement is true on some particular occasion if, and only if, that proposition corresponds to some state-of-affairs that obtains on that occasion.

This definition makes specific reference to a state-of-affairs that holds on the occasion of the utterance of the sentence, and this is an important point. As we have seen, the proposition expressed by an utterance of *The book is on the table* is true with respect to the situation depicted in (13), but not to that depicted in (15), because in the latter case there is no correspondence between the state-of-affairs described by the sentence and that portrayed in the picture. The situation in which, or with respect to which, a sentence is uttered constitutes an important part of the interpretation of sentences, and other expressions, to be discussed in later chapters of the book.

Just knowing whether a statement is true or false does not, of course, itself tell us what the statement means. Speakers of a language know the meaning of a sentence in their language even if they do not know the truth or falsity of the proposition expressed by that sentence. For example, *Ronnie has just dropped a cup of tea on the floor* is a perfectly comprehensible sentence in English whose meaning is clear, irrespective of whether readers know whether it describes a true state-of-affairs. Although readers may not know whether the proposition expressed by the sentence is true or false, they do know the conditions that must obtain for it to be true, i.e. they know what the world must be like for the statement to correspond to some actual state-of-affairs. This idea forms the basis of **truth-conditional** semantics, whose central hypothesis is that the **core meaning** of a sentence is its truth-conditions.

(19) To know the core meaning of a sentence uttered as a statement is to understand the conditions under which it could be true.

The theory thus equates core meaning with knowledge of how the truth of a declarative sentence can be ascertained without requiring the truth or falsity of a sentence to be known or knowable in any particular situation. Every sentence in the language whose semantics is being defined must, therefore, be associated by the theory with at least one set of **truth-conditions** (more if the sentence is ambiguous). Hence, for our semantic theory to be adequate, it must be able to derive an infinite set of statements of the form of (20.a) where *S* is a sentence in the object language and **p** is a set of truth-conditions. By hypothesis, the statement in (20.a) is equivalent to that in (20.b). (Here, and elsewhere, the abbreviation *iff* stands for the phrase *if, and only if.*)

(20) a. *S* is true iff **p**.
b. *S* centrally means that **p**.

Under this interpretation of meaning, the statement in (21) gives the core meaning of the sentence *The book is on the table.*

(21) *The book is on the table* is true iff the book is on the table.

Of course, (21) is not very informative and it appears that the meaning of the sentence is being defined in terms of itself, making the theory hopelessly circular. However, this apparent circularity is caused by the fact that the language that is being used to explicate the truth-conditions of the sentence is the same as the language of the sentence itself. A language that is being analysed is called an **object language** and that used to talk about an object language is called a **metalanguage**. The apparent circularity on (21) is lessened if the object language and the metalanguage differ. For example, if we change the object language to Modern German, as in (22.a), or adopt Modern French as the metalanguage, as in (22.b), the statements become more informative and less apparently circular.

(22) a. *Das Buch ist auf dem Tisch* is true iff the book is on the table.
b. *The book is on the table* est vrai si, et seulement si, le livre est sur la table.

Even using English as both the object language and the metalanguage, we can state the truth-conditions for our example sentence in a way that makes the import of (20.a) clearer. The statements in (23) specify the truth-conditions of the object sentence *The book is on the table* and must all hold if the proposition it expresses is true on some particular occasion of utterance. According to the equivalence hypothesised between (20.a) and (20.b), the specification of the truth-conditions shown in (23) thus provides a theory of the core meaning of the sentence *The book is on the table.*

(23) a. There is a contextually unique entity which is in the (extensional) denotation of the lexeme *BOOK*.
b. There is a contextually unique entity which is in the (extensional) denotation of the lexeme *TABLE*.
c. The entity in (a) stands in the relation of being on the entity in (b).

Much of what is done in later chapters concerns the development of a metalanguage, still based on English but with a rigorous interpretation, that may be used to specify the truth-conditions of a range of English sentence types (and by hypothesis equivalent types in other human languages). This metalanguage is used to connect the proposition(s) expressed by a sentence to states-of-affairs by detailing the relationship between the syntactic structure of the sentence and the denotations of the lexemes and other expressions that make this up. In this way, the core meaning of the constituent expressions of a sentence is defined as the contribution they (or more strictly their denotations) make to the truth-conditions associated with that sentence.

1.2.2 *Formalisation, models and sets*

The notion of truth introduced in the previous subsection is based on the work of the logician Alfred Tarski who intended that the correspondence theory of truth would be used to provide a semantics for **formal** or **logical** languages quite unlike the languages that are spoken by human beings. Hence, the application of the truth-conditional method has often been referred to as **formal semantics**. Its formal nature also resides in the fact that it utilises very precise notations and concepts to define as accurately and as rigorously as possible how expressions in the object language are to be interpreted. All aspects of the metalanguage in which the semantics is defined are precisely determined. There is no room for ambiguity, vagueness or inaccuracy and hence much of the specification of the metalanguage is mathematical or logical in form. One of the advantages of constructing a formal metalanguage with a precise interpretation is that it is thereby possible to check the consequences of one's theory and prove, or disprove, that such-and-such a consequence results from the way the semantics is set up. Within logic, the construction of formal semantic systems is bound up with the idea of proving that certain forms of argument within some formal language are **valid** whilst others are not. For example, within **propositional logic** the pattern of inference in (24) is valid, whilst that in (25) is not and these patterns are reflected in the English sentences that accompany the logical expressions below. There is nothing in the syntax of the logical statements in (24) that determines that the inference in (24.c) is valid and it is the purpose of the semantic theory to show that whatever p and q stand for, the truth of the expression $p \rightarrow q$ and of p always guarantees the truth of q while the truth of $p \rightarrow q$ and q does not always guarantee the truth of p.

(24)	a.	$\mathrm{p} \rightarrow \mathrm{q}$	If Ethel is singing, the cat is unhappy.
	b.	p	Ethel is singing.
	c.	q	Therefore, the cat is unhappy.
(25)	a.	$\mathrm{p} \rightarrow \mathrm{q}$	If Ethel is singing, the cat is unhappy.
	b.	q	The cat is unhappy.
	c.	p	Therefore, Ethel is singing.

It is interesting to note here that while formalisation within syntactic theory has been accepted as a useful, if not a necessary, part of syntactic analysis, its adoption within semantics remains a subject of considerable debate. However, the adoption of a formal interpretation procedure for a particular object language makes it possible to ascertain accurately whether or not one's theory is correct as an account of the meaning of particular object languages, just as a formalisation of syntax into formal rules or principles enables the syntactician to test whether they generate ungrammatical expressions or fail to generate grammatical ones. It is furthermore possible with such systems to prove that a semantics is **consistent** (i.e. contains no internal contradictions) and **complete** (i.e. it derives the set of all valid arguments of the language as **theorems**). Although these last two aspects of formal semantics will not be discussed in this book, the fact that these things can be more easily be proved with respect to semantic theories that are formalised than to those that are not will be taken as positive, if implicit, arguments in favour of formalisation as a tool of the semantic analysis of human languages.

In the discussion above, much has been made of the fact that the propositions expressed by declarative sentences may differ in truth value with respect to different situations. In other words, their truth is not absolute but depends on when the sentence expressing the proposition is uttered, on the location and other aspects of the context of utterance (including the modality of the sentence itself). This idea may be formalised by constructing **mathematical models** of a state-of-affairs and defining truth with respect to particular models. For example, a mathematical model can be constructed of the situation depicted in (13) with respect to which the propositions expressed by the sentences in (26) are all true. A model of the situation depicted in (15) does not, however, support the truth of (26.a), (26.b) or (26.d) but does support that of the other two sentences. We thus speak of truth with respect to a particular model which represents the general context with respect to which a sentence is uttered.

(26) a. The book is on the table.
b. There is a book on the table.
c. The book is open.
d. A table is supporting a book.
e. There is no cup of coffee.

As will be seen in more detail from Chapter 3 onwards, **model-theoretic interpretation** has two parts. In the first place, there is a model that represents precisely what events, properties and relations make up the situation being modelled. The model provides a description of the denotations of all the basic expressions (content lexemes) in the object language. This reflects the fact that human beings make statements in order to convey information about some state-of-affairs. Although one can know the meaning of a sentence without knowing what specific situation is being talked about (by knowing its truth-conditions), the sentence conveys no information unless it is associated with particular individuals and the relations that hold between them.

The second part of the theory provides the rules for interpreting expressions in the object language with respect to any arbitrary model. It does this by providing a **recursive definition** that specifies how the denotations of composite expressions are constructed from those of their component parts. In other words, the **model theory** provides a specification of the truth-conditions of the sentences in the object language. The truth-conditions as specified by the model theory hold independently of particular models, but the interpretation of particular sentences may be carried out only with respect to some model or other. One may also think of model theory as constraining the sorts of model that are admissible for the interpretation of some language. Not all possible models are interpretable according to a particular model theory and there is thus a two-way relation between the theory and the model. On the one hand, models are constructed to represent a given set of phenomena and, on the other, the way that phenomena can be represented is constrained by the theory of interpretation. From the linguistic perspective, the theory of meaning thus influences the way states-of-affairs can be represented and talked about.

It has been said that the models used to represent situations with respect to which sentences are to be interpreted are mathematical. In fact, the models in this book are based on **set theory**. The denotations of lexemes are thus modelled as sets containing various sorts of entity or as mathematical **functions** over these. The model theory uses fundamental notions from set theory, like set membership, union and intersection, etc., to specify how the denotations of more composite expressions can be constructed from these. Ultimately the notion of truth is characterised according to the axioms of set theory, thus providing the rigorous and formal metalanguage for interpretation that was discussed above. No previous knowledge of set theory is, however, assumed in the discussion of later chapters and all relevant concepts are introduced as and when they are needed.

1.3 Beyond truth-conditions

In the discussion of the last section, it was suggested that the central meaning of a sentence is the set of conditions that guarantee its truth with respect to any occasion of utterance. This does not mean that truth-conditions exhaust the whole of sentence meaning, let alone all aspects of linguistic meaning. A complete explication of the latter requires considerably more than just truth-conditions. However, the hypothesis that truth-conditional meaning is central predicts that other aspects of meaning interact with this to derive the meaning of an utterance. In other words, we may think of linguistic meaning being determined by the interaction of a number of theories dealing with particular domains of meaning. This section takes a brief look at some of the other theories of meaning that are needed to interact with truth-conditional interpretation to provide a more adequate account of meaning than is possible using truth-conditions on their own.

1.3.1 Knowledge, behaviour and use

In the discussion of truth-conditions, we have referred only to the interpretation of declarative sentences uttered as statements. But, of course, declarative sentences may be used to ask questions and issue commands, as well as make statements, and there are other sentence types that are typically used in the latter ways. For example, the sentence in (27.a) is a declarative that is typically used to make a statement. The addition of a question mark in the orthography as in (27.b), or rising intonation at the end of the sentence in spoken English, turns the statement into a question that has the same meaning as the interrogative in (27.c). Finally, the imperative sentence in (27.d) is typically used in issuing a command.

(27) a. Jo kicked the cat again.
b. Jo kicked the cat again?
c. Did Jo kick the cat again?
d. Kick the cat again, Jo!

Although the sentences in (27) sentences are all typically used to do different things (make statements, ask questions and issue commands), they contain a shared component of meaning: they all make reference to a situation in which someone called Jo engages in the activity of kicking a (contextually unique) cat and that this is not the first time he or she has done so. These are, of course, the truth-conditions associated with the declarative sentence in (27.a), and the truth-conditions of a declarative sentence may be equated with its **propositional content**, which is distinct from the proposition expressed by a sentence and from the truth or falsity of that proposition on some occasion of utterance. It is propositional content that may be considered to be the common core of meaning that syntactically related sentences share, whatever their surface form. Thus, each of the sentences in (27) share the same propositional content but in their different uses bear a different relation to that content. (27.a) states that the situation described by the propositional content actually occurred. On the other hand, (27.b) and (27.c) ask whether the situation described by the propositional content has occurred or not, i.e. whether the proposition expressed by (27.a) is true or false with respect to some context of utterance, and (27.d) is typically uttered to bring about a situation in which the proposition expressed by (27.a) is true.

The sentences in (27) thus possess the same propositional content but differ in their **illocutionary force**. The way content relates to use forms the study of **speech act theory** which concentrates, not so much on the abstract meaning of a sentence, but on what people are doing when they utter it. It, therefore, takes into account extralinguistic information like speaker intentions (what **perlocutionary effect** a speaker intends to have by the utterance of an expression), socio-cultural knowledge (whether the utterance of some expression is **felicitous** or not) and so on. Such things do not form part of truth-conditional meaning, but can form the basis of the relation between abstract sentence meaning and the meaning that an utterance of that sentence has in particular situations.

Another aspect of meaning that does not come within the realm of truth-conditional semantics has its basis in discourse behaviour. This concerns the sorts of **inferences** that are drawn by participants in a discourse. In Section 1.2, we looked at the sorts of meaning relations between sentences that are within the possible domain of truth-conditional semantics. These relations allow inferences to be drawn from utterances because the truth of a paraphrase or an entailment, or the falsity of a contradiction, are guaranteed by the truth of the proposition expressed by the original sentence. The assumption that participants in a discourse are being co-operative and, in general, telling the truth is one of the **conversational maxims** put forward by the philosopher Paul Grice in the nineteen-sixties. This assumption allows inferences to be made from entailments even if the participants have no way of checking the truth or falsity of any assertion.

As mentioned in Section 1.1.2, inferences can be drawn from discourse that do not follow directly from the truth-conditions of a sentence. We have already seen an example in (7) above which is repeated below.

(7) a. Bertie: Is Fiona a good lecturer?
b. Ethel: She has a good line in sweaters.
c. Bertie (thinks): Fiona is not a good lecturer.

The inference in (7.c) from the sentences in (7.a) and (7.b) is not guaranteed by the truth-conditional meaning of the latter, but by the apparent flouting of a conversational maxim. Ethel, the speaker of (7.b), replies to Bertie's question in (7.a) in an apparently irrelevant manner. In order for Bertie to maintain the assumption that the former is sticking to the **co-operative principle** in (28), he must look for some relevant piece of information that Ethel has not given that answers the original question. Since Ethel has been obviously irrelevant and not answered the question in (7.a) directly, thus flouting the **maxim of relation** in (29.c), the most consistent inference to make is that she is intending to convey that Fiona is not a good lecturer, but does not wish to say so directly.

(28) **The co-operative principle**: make your contribution such as is required, at the stage at which it is required, by the accepted purpose or direction of the talk exchange in which you are engaged.

Grice suggested a number of conversational maxims, which are given in (29). The interaction of these maxims with the truth-conditional import of the full sentences that underlie the expressions uttered in any discourse gives rise to **conversational implicatures** that allow a speaker to convey information over and above what is actually said (i.e. in terms of truth-conditions) in any exchange. Implicatures of the sort illustrated by (7) are highly context-specific and often rely on assumptions being made by the hearer that are cmpletely dependent on the context. For example, a similar exchange to that in (7.a) and (7.b) where the context contains information to the effect that there is a good lecturer who has a good line in sweaters will lead Bertie to infer the opposite of (7.c), i.e. that Fiona is a good lecturer. Since entailments result from truth-conditional meaning, which is constant from context to context, implicatures must form part of a theory of meaning that is non-truth-conditional. Grice's theory of conversation has been very successful in accounting for some of the non-truth-conditional meaning of certain expressions, giving further support to the idea that truth-conditions form a central core of meaning that interacts with other modular theories to account for a greater range of phenomena.

(29) a. **Maxim of quantity**:
- i. make your contribution as informative as is required (for the current purposes of the exchange).
- ii. do not make your contribution more informative than is required.

b. **Maxim of quality**:
- i. do not say what you believe to be false.
- ii. do not say that for which you lack adequate evidence.

c. **Maxim of relation**:
make your contribution relevant.

d. **Maxim of manner**:
- i. avoid obscurity of expression.
- ii. avoid ambiguity.
- iii. be brief.

Grice's work has not gone unchallenged or unrevised in the literature and, in recent years, an attempt has been made to reduce the maxims in (29) to a single explanatory principle that guides all inference making. **Relevance theory** reduces all the maxims to one, essentially the maxim of relation, and defines relevance in terms of **cognitive effect** (the amount and importance of information contained in an inferred proposition for a particular participant in a particular situation) balanced against **processing effort** (the number of steps that need to be taken to get to the inferred proposition). A definition of these ideas is given in (30).

(30) **Theory of relevance**:

a. Other things being equal, the greater the cognitive effect achieved by the processing of a given piece of information, the greater its relevance for the individual who processes it.

b. Other things being equal, the greater the effort involved in the processing of a given piece of information, the smaller its relevance for the individual who processes it.

Wilson and Sperber (1988:140)

Relevance theory has currently developed into a theory of cognition, rather than a theory of linguistic meaning specifically, and, although it has some advantages over the Gricean approach, it is less well known and there is, as yet, no basic introduction to the subject. For these reasons, it will not be used in Chapter 7 where inference is discussed in more detail.

1.3.2 Context

One of the most important influences on meaning is that of the **context of utterance**. The context plays a vital role in determining how a particular utterance is to be interpreted on any occasion. In particular, it is needed to restore **ellipses**, resolve ambiguity, provide referents for **deictic** elements and resolve anaphoric dependencies.

The dialogue in (31) illustrates how important context is in enabling interpretation to be carried out.

(31) a. Fiona: Hello?

b. Jo: In here!

c. Fiona: Any chance of a coffee?

d. Jo: There's no milk in the fridge.

e. Fiona: Oh hell! I bought some yesterday. You must have used it all in that disgusting punch you made.

As (31) shows, sentences in discourse (or written texts) may not be complete realisations of full sentences and so not sufficient for the purposes of truth-conditional interpretation. To interpret (31.b) and (31.c), it is necessary to recover the system sentences that underlie them: to *I'm in here* and *Is there any chance of a coffee?*, respectively. The resolution of such ellipsis is dependent on the context, since an utterance of the expression in (31.b) could be interpreted as asserting that any number of entities are *in here*, depending on the circumstances.

Just restoring ellipses is not sufficient to enable the interpretation of (31) to take place, however. The context must also provide referents for all the **deictic expressions**. The term **deixis** is derived from the Classical Greek verb *deiknumi* meaning 'to point out' or 'show' (the Latin translation being *demonstrativus*, hence the term *demonstrative pronoun*). The purpose of deictic elements is to link aspects of the meaning of the sentence containing them to the context in which it is uttered, either spatially, temporally or in terms of the participants in the discourse. Deixis may be realised as words, particles or morphological processes. For example, in (31) the **indexical pronoun** *I* in (31.b) (restored from context) refers to Jo, but in (31.e) it refers to Fiona, i.e. the respective speakers of the expressions. Similarly, the pronoun *you* in (31.e) refers to the hearer in the discourse who happens to be Jo in this instance, but could be someone else in another context. Furthermore, context is required to indicate the location indicated by the term *here* in (31.b) (i.e. near the speaker) and the time when Fiona bought the milk in (31.e) (the day before the day on which the utterance of the sentence is made). Grammatical tense is also deictic and serves to refer to times relative to the context of utterance at which the situations described by any declarative sentences are deemed to take place. Thus, in (31.b), (31.c) and (31.d), the relevant time is the present (the time of utterance) whilst in both sentences in (31.e) (ignoring the interjection) the relevant time is prior to the time of utterance.

Other aspects of the dialogue in (31) also require the assistance of the context to enable interpretation to take place. For example, the pronoun *some* in (31.e) is to be interpreted as *some milk*, picking up on the mention of milk in the previous utterance. The anaphoric pronoun *it* in the final sentence refers to the milk that Fiona bought yesterday, information that is not explicitly stated in the utterance. In addition to anaphoric resolution of this sort, the context resolves the ambiguity of the homonym *PUNCH* which is interpreted as the drink and not the action because of the fact that the subject of this latter part of the conversation is milk, something that is drunk.

This short example indicates the extent to which interpretation relies on the context of utterance. The relation between context and interpretation is, however, extremely complex. Although there are certain aspects that have been incorporated into truth-conditional semantics (as, for example, tense, cf. Chapter 8, and certain sorts of anaphora), exactly how the context resolves ambiguities, anaphoric dependencies and ellipsis and the way participants in a discourse tie up referential expressions to particular individuals remains obscure. In what follows, it is recognised that the context is almost always required to fix the reference of expressions (and disambiguate ambiguous utterances), but we will proceed on the assumption that a theory of truth-conditional interpretation accounts for the meaning of sentences considered as abstract units of the language system. The definition of the meaning of a sentence is given in the discussion above in terms of truth-conditions and truth-conditions are associated with propositional content. Since the latter is independent of context, then truth-conditional meaning may also be treated independently of context, even though, as we have seen, the actual interpretation of a specific utterance requires information provided by the context. Whether or not a theory of context can be constructed that can interact with truth-conditional meaning to provide a fuller account of utterance interpretation than is yet available is a topic for future research.

1.4 A note on method

The scene has now been set for the development of the theory that is to be the subject of the rest of this book. A sketch has been given of those aspects of meaning that form the central domain of inquiry, of some of those that do not, and of the main tenets of the theory to be adopted below. Before starting on the long road to Chapter 10, however, something must be said about the methodology adopted in the following chapters.

In order to avoid problems with context, like those discussed in the last section, all interpretation is carried out, not directly on the sentences of a language or even on their structural descriptions, but on a **logical language** into which the object language is **translated**. The logical translation of a declarative sentence is intended to represent the proposition expressed by the utterance of that sentence on some particular occasion. As it fully represents all the information supplied by the context of utterance, it represents only one reading of an ambiguous sentence at a time, the one intended on a particular occasion. For this reason, the **translation language** must be a **disambiguated language**, i.e. permit no ambiguity. Furthermore, translation resolves all anaphoric, deictic and referential uncertainties of the utterance of the sentence, thus making sure that each expression has a determinate denotation. Essentially, the translation of a sentence can be thought of as the representation of the proposition derived from the sentence plus its context of utterance. It acts, therefore, as an intermediate step between the syntactic analysis of an expression and its truth-conditional semantic interpretation. Whether this level of representation is necessary, or not, is a controversial issue. Richard Montague assumed that it was merely convenient rather than necessary, but later linguistic research has indicated that, at least as far as anaphoric and deictic reference is concerned, a representation intermediate between syntax and interpretation is required. It is assumed henceforth that translation is an intrinsic part of any semantic analysis. Interpretation is carried out on the logical translation of a sentence, and so provides an indirect interpretation of the latter.

It is usual within formal semantics to provide not only an explicit semantic theory for an object language, but also an explicit syntax. Only by doing this can it be guaranteed that the principle of compositionality is being maintained. In studying the formal semantics of human languages, it would be a difficult task to specify a complete (and formally rigorous) definition of the syntax of a particular language before tackling the semantics. Hence, it is customary to define **grammar fragments** that determine only a subset of the set of grammatical sentences of the object language with the semantic interpretation specified for these sentences (via their translation into a logical language). Once this interpretation has been successfully defined, the coverage of the fragment is extended to take in more constructions. In this way, it is hoped that ultimately a complete formal grammar of a language, containing both an explicit syntax and semantics, can be obtained (this hope is, however, still a very long way from realisation). This method will be pursued in Chapters 2 to 6 of this book, beginning with a formal analysis of a fragment of English including proper names and simple intransitive, transitive and ditransitive sentences. This is expanded into an explicit account of co-ordination, passives and noun phrases. In the final chapters, the syntactic aspect of the analysis is not so explicit, because of the debates about the proper syntactic treatment of such things as tense, modality and finite and non-finite complementation. Some discussion will, however, be given of some of the difficulties presented by these constructions for the syntax.

It is commonplace nowadays to assume that interpretation depends on the surface constituent structure of a sentence, although different theories adopt a more or less abstract interpretation of this level of syntactic representation. It is not the intention of this book to support or criticise any particular theory of syntax, however. The semantic method outlined below can be adapted to many different syntactic theories and each one has its own merits and leads to its own problems from the semantic point of view. To maintain relative neutrality between theories, the syntactic framework that is adopted in this book is that of simple **context-free phrase structure grammar**. This type of grammar has advantages and disadvantages, but has the merit of being well known and easily describable. Each grammar fragment in the following pages, therefore, takes the form of a set of context-free phrase structure rules together with an appropriate lexicon. The translation of each sentence generated by the grammar into a disambiguated logical language is carried out in parallel with its **derivation** according to the specified phrase structure rules, in accordance with the rule-to-rule hypothesis in (5) above.

Finally, before we move on to the real work of the book, it should be noted that until time is introduced into the model in Chapter 8, every example sentence is given in its simple past tense form. It is usual within most introductions to logic in linguistics to put sentences into the present tense. Unfortunately, the present tense in English is rarely used to report events neutrally, but has aspectual and futurate interpretations that can sometimes obscure the intended sense of an example. No such problems are associated with the simple past, however, and this is used throughout Chapters 2 to 6. The proper interpretation of this tense is not, however, discussed until Chapter 8.

1.5 Further reading

Each of the chapters in this book ends with a section of further reading. These give references to other introductory texts that cover all or some of the topics discussed in each chapter and also to one or two more advanced books or articles on specific topics that have been mentioned in the text. Not all the topics that are discussed in the text are given further reading and the references that are given are very selective, only those works that the current author thinks are accessible and/or of reasonable importance being given. Although these references, and the accompanying bibliography, are in no way comprehensive, it is hoped that readers will use them to get more details of specific issues and to treat them as suitable starting points for more protracted research.

There are a number of basic introductions to general linguistic semantics that make good background reading for this book: see especially Lyons (1981) and Hurford and Heasley (1983), but Palmer (1981) and Leech (1974) may also be consulted, although the latter two books are somewhat idiosyncratic. Other introductory textbooks to general linguistic semantics and logic for linguists are Chierchia and McConnell-Ginet (1990), Kempson (1977), Allwood, Andersen and Dahl (1977) and McCawley (1981) which will be referenced below for specific topics.

The criteria of adequacy for semantic theory in (1) above are introduced and discussed in Kempson (1977: ch. 1), Chierchia and McConnell-Ginet (1990: ch. 1) discusses the domain of semantics, and the distinction between semantics and pragmatics is discussed in Levinson (1983: 1-35). Compositionality is discussed in Partee (1984) and Partee, ter Meulen and Wall (1990: 317-338) (although both presuppose some familiarity with formal semantic concepts). The logical meaning relations of entailment, paraphrase and contradiction are discussed mainly in textbooks on logic: see Guttenplan (1986: 1-41) for a good and simple introduction to the notion of logical inference (other references are given in Chapter 7). Levinson

(1983: ch. 3) provides an introduction to implicature and Ch. 4 of that book discusses presupposition, as does McCawley (1981: ch. 9). A more recent discussion of the phenomenon with extensive references is Burton-Roberts (1989) and, for a somewhat different view, see also Chierchia and McConnell-Ginet (1990: 286-317). The distinction between homonymy and polysemy is discussed at length in Lyons (1977: 550-573) and ambiguity (and vagueness, a topic not touched on here) is discussed in Kempson (1977: ch. 8), McCawley (1981: 5-11) and Lyons (1977: 396-409). On denotation, reference and sense, see Chierchia and McConnell-Ginet (1990: 46-60; 77-88) and Lyons (1977: 174-215). For a technical discussion of the difference between extension and intension, see Carnap (1956: 16-32) and McCawley (1981: 401-406). On propositions, see Lyons (1981: 106-109, passim), Hurford and Heasley (1983: 15-24) and Allwood, Andersen and Dahl (1977: ch. 3). For an outline of the sort of truth-conditional semantics pursued in this book, see Dowty, Wall and Peters (1981: ch. 1) (which gives an introduction to Montague semantics, but at a much more difficult level than that given in this book), Partee, ter Meulen and Wall (1990: ch. 5; 200-203) and for a general discussion of mathematical versus psychological approaches to meaning, see Partee (1979). On truth and truth-conditions, consult Lyons (1977: 167-173), Kempson (1977: ch. 3), Chierchia and McConnell-Ginet (1990: 61-65), Lycan (1984: 13-43), and, for a philosophical view, essays 1 to 5 in Davidson (1984). Speech act theory is discussed in Levinson (1983: ch. 5) and for context, see Lyons (1981: ch. 9) and Levinson (1983: passim). Kempson (1977: chs. 4 & 5) also discusses language use and pragmatics, and relevance theory is discussed in Sperber and Wilson (1986), Wilson and Sperber (1988) and Blakemore (1987).

2 Predicates and arguments

2.1 Translating English into a logical language

In this chapter and the next, we will lay the foundations on which a good deal of logical semantics is built. In accordance with the discussion in Chapter 1, we first define a **logical language** into which sentences of English are **translated** in order to circumvent the problems of ambiguity and underdeterminacy found in the object language. Having defined the translation language, and specified the procedure for translating simple English sentences into it, our attention will turn to the interpretation of these logical expressions in terms of their truth-conditions, thus providing an indirect interpretation of the corresponding English sentences.

2.1.1 The syntax of L_P

Like all languages, natural or artificial, logical languages have a **syntax**, i.e. a set of rules for constructing composite expressions from simpler ones. The logical language described in this chapter, called $\mathbf{L_P}$, contains expressions that fall into one of four logical categories: **individuals**, **predicates**, **formulae** and **operators** (or **connectives**). Expressions in each of the first three categories can be further subdivided into two sorts: **constants**, which have a fixed interpretation, and **variables**, which do not. These two sorts of expression correspond, roughly, to **content words** (e.g. *table*, *run*, *Ethel*) and **pronominal** expressions (e.g. *she*, *they*) in natural languages, respectively. This chapter deals only with constants, but variables will become increasingly important in later chapters.

Sentences in natural languages translate into formulae in L_P which have the logical category **t** (as sentences have the syntactic category S). Such expressions are constructed by combining individual and predicate expressions in much the same way that sentences are composed of combinations of noun phrases and verbs. Just as certain noun phrases in a sentence can be described as the **complements** of the main verb, so individual expressions, of logical category **e**, perform the role of **arguments** of the predicates in a formula. Predicates in L_P may take zero or more individuals as arguments and the number of arguments that a predicate takes is referred to as the **valency** of the predicate. Predicate constants and variables are **subcategorised** according to their valency, just as verbs are subcategorised according to whether they are **intransitive**, **transitive** or **ditransitive**, etc. All predicates are classed as members of the logical category **Pred** and their subcategorisation according to the number of individual arguments they take is shown by the use of a subscripted number to the right of the category symbol. Thus, for example, the category $\mathbf{Pred_1}$ contains all those predicates that take just one individual as an argument, the category $\mathbf{Pred_2}$ contains all those predicates that take two individual arguments, and so on. Unlike verbs in natural languages, however, there is no upper limit on the number of arguments a predicate in L_P can take; thus the language may contain an infinite number of subcategories of predicates, $\mathbf{Pred_n}$, where n is any number between zero and infinity. For the purposes of translating from English into L_P, however, we can safely ignore all predicates that have a valency higher than 3. Thus, only four of the possible subcategories of Pred are used below: $Pred_0$, $Pred_1$, $Pred_2$ and $Pred_3$.

The basic syntactic rule for constructing formulae in L_P is one that combines a predicate expression with the number of individual arguments it requires. Thus, an expression in $Pred_1$ combines with one individual expression to make a formula, an expression in $Pred_2$ combines with two individual expressions to make a formula and, in general, an expression in $Pred_n$ combines with n individual expressions to make a formula, where n is some positive whole number. The predicate is written to the left of the arguments which are enclosed within round brackets and separated from each other by commas. The appropriate rule appears in (1) where the superscripted number appearing with the individual category symbol, e, does not represent a subcategory of individual, but simply the number of the individual in the **argument structure** of the predicate. This ensures that predicates appear with the right number of arguments for their valency. The symbol $\leq$ in (1) is read as *is less than, or equal to*, so that in the rule n may be zero or any number greater than zero. $Pred_0$ is, therefore, a valid subcategory of L_P, but one that takes no arguments to make a formula. Hence, $Pred_0$ is equivalent to a formula, i.e. $Pred_0 = t$. We shall meet some English verbs that may be associated with this category in the next section.

(1) $t \rightarrow Pred_n(e^1,e^2,\ldots,e^n),\ 0 \leq n.$

Given the syntactic rule in (1) and some (abstract) expressions in L_P (*a, b, c, d* being individual constants, *P* a one-place predicate, *Q* a two-place predicate and *R* a three-place predicate), then all the expressions in (2) are **well-formed formulae** (often abbreviated as **wff**) in L_P, but those in (3) are not.

(2) a. P(a). b. Q(c,d). c. R(b,a,d).
d. R(c,b,c). e. P(b). f. Q(b,b).

(3) a. Q(c). b. R(b,a,b,b). c. P(a,a).
d. a(P). e. Rabc. f. P(e).

2.1.2 A grammar fragment for English

Having defined the (very simple) syntax of L_P, we are in a position to translate sentences of English into it. To show how translation works, we shall provide a grammar for a small fragment of English and then develop a translation procedure that associates every sentence generated by the grammar with at least one logical expression. As discussed at the end of Chapter 1, grammars for parts of a language are called **grammar fragments** and are often used in formal semantics to develop specific and precise theories about the meanings of the expressions they analyse. The grammar developed in this chapter and in Chapter 3 covers only a very small part of English and a syntactically very unexciting part at that. Although we begin by analysing a rather small and uninteresting set of sentences, by the time we get to the end of the book, we will have covered a quite considerable number of English constructions and have armed ourselves with the machinery to tackle many more. From the apparent triviality of the initial examples, a powerful semantic theory of a range of constructions in English will be developed.

The type of syntactic grammar adopted in this book is a simple **context-free phrase structure grammar**. There are many other forms of grammar, of course, that may well be syntactically more adequate than this, but context-free phrase structure grammars have the advantage of being easy to understand and simple to use. For example, it is always possible using a context-free phrase structure grammar to decide in a finite number of steps whether some string of words is generated by the grammar and it is therefore quite easy to check whether it generates ill-formed sentences of the object language. On the other hand, the well-known disadvantages of context-free phrase structure grammars are not particularly relevant for our purposes, since we are interested in semantics rather than syntax and the points made should be relevant to almost any syntactic theory. The adoption of phrase structure grammar in this book is for expository purposes only and the syntactic analyses presented are not intended to be definitive. Readers are invited to try to apply the semantic methods used in later chapters to the analyses of the same constructions determined by their favourite syntactic theory.

The sentences that are generated by the grammar in this chapter are of the simplest sort. They contain between one and three noun phrases, consisting of either a single **proper noun** or a **common noun** plus the **definite article**, *the*, together with a single **verb**, subcategorised according to the number of noun phrases it can appear with. (4) gives examples of five sentence types which contain intransitive (4.a), transitive (4.b) and ditransitive (4.c & d) verbs. The final sentence, (4.e), contains an impersonal verb which appears with the meaningless subject pronoun, *it*.

(4) a. Chester ran.
b. Chester ate the cake.
c. Ethel gave the cake to Jo.
d. Ethel gave Chester the cake.
e. It rained.

The sentences in (4) (and many, but finitely many, more besides) can all be generated by the grammar in (5), which is called $\mathbf{G_1}$, in conjunction with the simple lexicon in (6). Common abbreviations for categories are adopted. Thus, S stands for sentence, NP for noun phrase, N_{pr} for proper noun, N for common noun, V_i for intransitive verb, V_t for transitive verb and V_{dt} for ditransitive verb. Impersonal verbs are assigned to the category V_0. A **syntactic feature**, symbolised as [+FIN], indicates that a verb (of any subcategory) is **finite** (and, until tense is introduced in Chapter 8, in the **past tense**, as mentioned in Chapter 1). In Chapter 3, non-finite verbs, i.e. verbs in their **bare stem** or **citation** forms, are introduced using the feature [-FIN]. In rules $3G_1$, $5G_1$ and $7G_1$, below, the items *to*, *it* and *the* are introduced directly in the syntactic rule and do not appear in the lexicon. These, and some other expressions, are treated in this way, either because they do not contribute significantly to the semantics of a phrase and so have no translation in L_P, as with *to* and *it*, or because their contribution to the semantics of an expression is stated directly in the translation of the rule itself (as with *didn't* below). The definite article *the* is treated in the same way for expository reasons only. It is introduced here in order to increase the interest of the grammar fragment which would otherwise only contain proper names as exemplars of NPs. The semantics of *the* will be dealt with more fully in Chapter 6, while the means to rectify the other departures from the principle of compositionality will also be provided in later chapters when other theoretical machinery has been introduced.

Another non-standard feature of the rules in (5) is the fact that the noun phrases are given subscripted numbers. These numbers are strictly unnecessary from the syntactic point of view, but essential for translation and interpretation purposes. They may be thought of as marking the **grammatical function** of the noun phrase within the sentence: so that NP_1 functions as the **syntactic subject**, NP_2 as the **syntactic direct object** and NP_3 as the **syntactic indirect object**. For the sake of variation, three, not very sophisticated, rules giving the passive counterparts of the transitive and ditransitive rules $2G_1$, $3G_1$ and $4G_1$ are given in (7).

(5) a. $1G_1$: S → NP_1 V_i[+FIN].
b. $2G_1$: S → NP_1 V_t[+FIN] NP_2.
c. $3G_1$: S → NP_1 V_{dt}[+FIN] NP_2 to NP_3.
d. $4G_1$: S → NP_1 V_{dt}[+FIN] NP_2 NP_3.
e. $5G_1$: S → it V_0[+FIN].
f. $6G_1$: NP → N_{pr}.
g. $7G_1$: NP → the N.

(6) a. N_{pr} → {*Prudence, Ethel, Chester, Jo, Bertie, Fiona*}.
b. N → {*book, cake, cat, golfer, dog, lecturer, student, singer*}.
c. V_i[+FIN] → {*ran, laughed, sang, howled, screamed*}.
d. V_t[+FIN] → {*read, poisoned, ate, liked, loathed, kicked*}.
e. V_{dt}[+FIN] → {*gave*}.
f. V_0[+FIN] → {*rained, snowed*}.

(7) a. 8G1: S → NP1 was Vt[PAS] by NP2.
b. $9G_1$: S → NP_1 was V_{dt}[PAS] to NP_2 by NP_3.
c. $10G_1$: S → NP_1 was V_{dt}[PAS] NP_2 by NP_3.
d. V_t[PAS] → {*read, poisoned, eaten, liked, loathed, kicked*}.
e. V_{dt}[PAS] → {*given*}.

A grammar like G_1 is said to **generate** a sentence, Σ, if (and only if) there is a **derivation** of Σ from the symbol S using the syntactic rules and the lexicon. The derivation of a sentence is the procedure whereby, starting with S, one category in a string is expanded at a time using a rule of the grammar until the string contains only words in the lexicon. The derivation of the sentence *Ethel poisoned the cat* using the grammar, G_1, is shown in (8) where each line in the derivation has a number on the right hand side showing the rule used to derive the new string of symbols from the line before. The symbol *Lex* indicates that lexical substitution has taken place and this is represented in (8.e) as having taken place all at once. Equivalently, the generation of a sentence can be shown by a **phrase structure tree** as in (9).

(8) a. S.
b. NP_1 V_t[+FIN] NP_2. $2G_1$
c. N_{pr} V_t[+FIN] NP_2. $6G_1$
d. N_{pr} V_t[+FIN] the N. $7G_1$
e. Ethel poisoned the cat. Lex

(9)

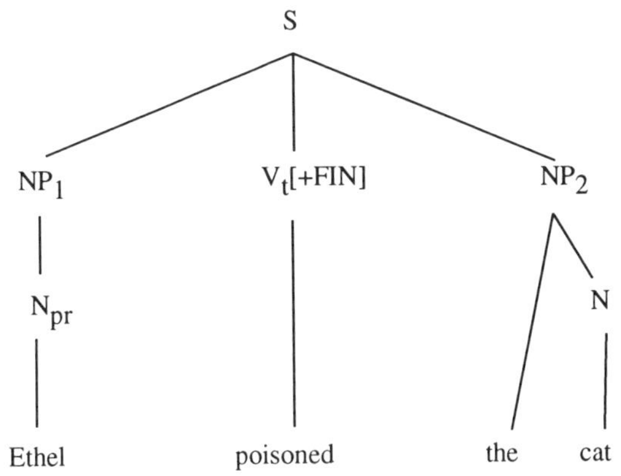

The notion of derivation and the use of phrase structure trees are important, because, as we will see in the next section, translation from English into L_P is not done on the strings of words that make up sentences, but on the syntactic structures of those sentences. Before going on to translation, however, let us first add another two rules to the grammar, both of which introduce the third person singular past tense form of the **copular verb** *be*. This verb has a number of semantic functions, one of which is to equate two entities, to indicate that they are identical. The rule in (10) allows the generation by G_1 of sentences containing this use of the copula (often called **equative** sentences) like those in (11).

(10) $11G_1$: S → NP_1 was NP_2.

(11) a. Fiona was the singer.
b. Chester was the dog.
c. Jo was Jo.

Another copular construction in English involves **predicative adjectives**. Here, the copula does not seem to have any real semantic function (except to carry information about tense which we are ignoring for the moment), but serves instead to provide a means of associating an adjective with the subject NP, as in (12).

(12) a. Chester was crazy.
b. The singer was messy.

Syntactically we can analyse the sentences in (12) as consisting of a noun phrase followed by the verb *was* followed by an adjective. This is provided by the rule in (13.a) with the additions to the lexicon in (13.b).

(13) a. $12G_1$: S → NP was A.
b. A → {*happy, crazy, messy, disgusting, wealthy*}.

2.1.3 The translation procedure

Having defined this small grammar, we can proceed to translate the sentences it generates into logical expressions in L_P. First of all, it is necessary to associate the syntactic categories in G_1 with their corresponding logical categories in L_P. As already mentioned, all proper nouns and definite noun phrases are associated with **individual constants**, i.e. they translate into L_P as expressions of category e. For the moment, common nouns are assigned to no logical category as they have no direct interpretation in this fragment. This situation will be rectified in Chapter 6 when the interpretation of noun phrases is tackled in more detail.

Verbs, which combine with noun phrases to form sentences, are naturally associated with the general semantic category of predicate. As verbs may take different numbers of noun phrases to make grammatical sentences, so they translate into different subcategories of predicate according to the number of noun phrases, including subjects, that appear with them in sentences of English. Hence, intransitive verbs, which take no objects but do have a subject, translate into one-place predicates. Transitive verbs, on the other hand, which subcategorise for a direct object and appear with a subject, thus translate into two-place predicates. Ditransitive verbs have three dependent noun phrases including their subjects and so translate into three-place predicates in L_P. Although impersonal verbs do appear with a syntactic subject in English, the **dummy subject pronoun**, *it*, has no semantic significance and has no denotation. Hence, *it* may be ignored in the logical translation and impersonal verbs translate into zero place predicates.

Predicative adjectives semantically behave in a similar fashion to verbs. For example, they may be used to ascribe properties to entities, as in the sentence *Chester was disgusting* where the adjective ascribes the property of being disgusting to the entity denoted by the word *Chester*. Such adjectives translate them into 1-place predicates. (We ignore two-place predicative adjectives like, *afraid of Jo*, here.) Finally, the logical category assigned to S is t, the category of formulae. The correspondences between categories of G_1 and those of L_P are summarised in (14), where the symbol $\Rightarrow$ means *translates into*.

(14) a. $NP \Rightarrow e$.
b. $N_{pr} \Rightarrow e$.
c. $V_0 \Rightarrow Pred_0$.
d. $V_i \Rightarrow Pred_1$.
e. $V_t \Rightarrow Pred_2$.
f. $V_{dt} \Rightarrow Pred_3$.
g. $A \Rightarrow Pred_1$.
h. $S \Rightarrow t$.

The category assignments given in (14) determine the way the translation of expressions containing members of the different syntactic categories are carried out. According to the L_P construction rule in (1), above (repeated below), an n-place predicate combines with n individual expressions to make a formula.

(1) $t \rightarrow Pred_n(e^1,e^2,...,e^n)$.

Hence, a predicate that translates an intransitive verb combines with the individual expression that translates its subject, while a predicate translating a transitive verb combines with the translations of the subject and object noun phrases to make a formula, and so on. This is not sufficient, however, to get the right translations for any English expression generated by grammar G_1, because the order in which arguments appear when combined with a predicate has yet to be specified. For example, the transitive verb construction analysed in G_1 by rule $2G_1$ (repeated in (15.a)) translates into an expression containing a two place predicate translating the verb and the two individuals which translate the subject and object noun phrases. There are two possible well-formed formulae that meet this description depending on the relative orders of the two individual expressions. These alternatives are shown in (15.b) and (15.c) where the superscript prime, ', following the syntactic category symbol stands for the L_P expression that translates an English expression analysed by that symbol in some actual derivation. A symbol like V_t', therefore, stands in place of the translation of the actual transitive verb that is introduced under the node V_t in some particular sentence. In translation rules, V_t' thus operates as a variable over the translations of all transitive verbs in the grammar. Just as the usual category symbols allow the statement of regular rules of combination without the need to specify their internal structure, so this notation allows the generalisation of translation rules regardless of the particular expressions that actually appear in any given sentence.

(15) a. $2G_1$: S → NP_1 V_t[+FIN] NP_2.
b. V_t'(NP_1',NP_2').
c. V_t'(NP_2',NP_1').

In L_P, as in English, the order in which arguments appear is semantically significant, so that, as we will see in Section 2.2.3, (15.b) is interpreted differently from (15.c). Since ordinary transitive sentences like *Ethel poisoned Chester* are not ambiguous in English, only one of the translations in (15) must be chosen as the translation of rule $2G_1$. Thus, in addition to the logical category assignment in (14), we also need rules to tell us how to combine predicates and their arguments to obtain the translations of particular English constructions.

In Chapter 1, one of the criteria for adequacy for a semantic theory is that it should adhere to the principle of compositionality. This requires the interpretation of an expression to be a function of the meanings of its component parts and the way they are put together. In other words, to interpret an expression we need to have access to the syntactic rules by which it is constructed. Because we are interpreting natural languages indirectly, via translation into L_P, we must show compositionality in the translation procedure and thus take syntactic information into account as we build up L_P representations. This can be done by providing a translation rule for each syntactic rule in the grammar, so that $2G_1$, for example, is paired with only one of the possible translations in (15). As discussed in Chapter 1, this approach to compositionality adheres to the rule-to-rule hypothesis because each rule in the syntax is paired with a corresponding translation rule and, thus, indirectly with a rule of semantic interpretation, as we will see below. In accordance with this hypothesis, therefore, every rule in G_1 is matched with a corresponding translation rule. These appear in (16) with numbers that parallel those of the syntactic rules of Section 2.1.2. Thus, $T1G_1$ translates rule $1G_1$, $T2G_1$ translates rule 2, and so on.

(16) a. $T1G_1$: $S \Rightarrow V_i'(NP')$.
b. $T2G_1$: $S \Rightarrow V_t'(NP_1',NP_2')$.
c. $T3G_1$: $S \Rightarrow V_{dt}'(NP_1',NP_2',NP_3')$.
d. $T4G_1$: $S \Rightarrow V_{dt}'(NP_1',NP_3',NP_2')$.
e. $T5G_1$: $S \Rightarrow V_0'$.
f. $T6G_1$: $NP \Rightarrow N_{pr}'$.
g. $T7G_1$: $NP \Rightarrow$ the-N'.
h. $T8G_1$: $S \Rightarrow V_t'(NP_2',NP_1')$.
i. $T9G_1$: $S \Rightarrow V_{dt}'(NP_3',NP_1',NP_2')$.
j. $T10G_1$: $S \Rightarrow V_{dt}'(NP_3',NP_2',NP_1')$.

This leaves the two copular rules, $11G_1$ and $12G_1$, to be translated. In the latter rule, which introduces predicate adjectives, the copula has no significant semantic effect (other than to signal tense) and so is ignored in the translation, leaving the one-place predicate translating the adjective to apply directly to the translation of the subject, as shown in (17).

(17) $T12G_1$: $A'(NP')$.

In the equative construction, rule $11G_1$, however, the copula does have semantic effect, as it identifies the two entities named by the subject and complement noun phrases and so must have a representation in L_P. Since the word *was* is introduced directly by the rule, it does not appear in the lexicon and so its semantic effect must be captured directly in the translation of the rule. One of the reasons for treating the equative copula in this way is that it has an interpretation defined in the logic itself, as we will see later in this chapter, which differentiates it from normal lexical items, which translate as arbitrary constants. The logical nature of the meaning of *was* in this rule is directly shown in its translation. Instead of following the usual method for translating words discussed below, it is represented by a new sort of expression in L_P, a **logical operator** which appears between the L_P expressions that are its arguments. The logical operator associated with the equative copula is =, the equals sign, requiring the new syntactic rule for L_P shown in (18.a). This yields the translation of $11G_1$ shown in (18.b), completing the set of translation rules for G_1.

(18) a. $t \rightarrow (e = e)$.
b. $T11G_1$: $(NP_1' = NP_2')$.

Before these rules can be used to translate sentences of English generated by G_1, however, some way must be specified of translating English words into expressions of L_P. Firstly, in order to bring out the fact that different inflectional forms of the same 'word' do not differ in their fundamental meaning (ignoring tense and number information), each word is stripped of any inflectional markers. In translating into L_P, therefore, we are interested only in **lexemes** and not **word forms** as such. Thus, the English word forms *give, gives, given* and *gave* are translated into L_P as a single form because they are all forms of the same lexeme, the same meaning unit. Because L_P is an artificial language, it is possible to translate lexemes into arbitrary symbols which then function as basic words or constants in the language. This is usually done, for example, in exercises in predicate logic where the relation between the symbols of the logic and the lexemes of English (or any other language) is not significant. Hence, the symbol P might translate a verb like *run, runs, ran*, Q could stand for *eat, eats, ate*, and so on. Associating English words with completely arbitrary symbols in this way, however, would mean that someone using L_P would have to learn vocabulary lists that give the translations of all English words, just like learning a foreign natural language. This is possible, of course, but unnecessarily tedious and serves no real purpose as there are no native speakers of L_P to tell us what the words of their language translate as. Thus, instead of translating lexemes of English into arbitrary symbols that need to be learned for each lexeme, we can state a simple rule that provides the L_P symbol that translates any lexeme in the object language. This rule translates any word in English as its **citation form** (which is taken to be the base form of the expression without any inflectional affixes; cf. Huddleston (1984:102)), with capital letters replaced by their lower-case counterparts and followed by a prime, '. The latter indicates that the symbol is not a word in the object language, e.g. English, but an expression in the translation language, i.e. L_P. For example, the English word forms *gives, give, gave, given* are all associated with the citation form *give* and the translation of any of these word forms into L_P is thus *give'*. More examples appear in (19). This way of translating content words into L_P is, of course, just one of many possible ways of representing the logical constants associated with such expressions in a logical language. Other writers use other means of representing translations: for example, Lyons (1977) uses the base form of a word in double quotes, e.g. "give", while Hurford and Heasley (1983) puts the form into capitals, e.g. GIVE, and other representation are possible. The one adopted here is the one adopted by Montague and is the one very commonly used by formal semanticists.

It is very important in translating into L_P to bear in mind that an expression followed by a prime is not an expression of English but an expression of L_P. They are **translation equivalents**, but not the same word. It is essential for the reader to keep in mind the fact that L_P expressions are not English, even if they appear to be similar.

(19) a. Ethel ⇒ ethel'.
b. cake ⇒ cake'.
c. gave ⇒ give'.
d. sang ⇒ sing'.
e. ate ⇒ eat'.
f. eaten ⇒ eat'.
g. messy ⇒ messy'.

Because L_P is an unambiguous language, it is necessary to be able to distinguish the different meanings of **homonyms**. Homonyms are different lexemes which are associated with the same word forms but which have different meanings. For example, the English noun *punch* may describe a kind of drink or a physical action. In L_P, these meanings must be kept separate, so that simple translation into a citation form plus prime is not quite sufficient to provide the procedure for translating words in English into constants of L_P. To resolve this, we can resort to the simple expedient of associating each constant in L_P with a superscripted number, so that *gives* translates into *give*^{1}*'* and not just *give'*. Where a word form is homonymous, it translates into a number of different constants in L_P which have the same basic form but differ in their superscript. For example, the two senses of the noun *punch* are represented as $punch^{1}$' (the drink) and $punch^{2}$' (the action). In this way, the translation of a homonymous word in any sentence results in a unique representation in L_P, ensuring, as required, that the translation is unambiguous. The same approach can be taken for proper names that may have more than one referent. If, for example, there were two people called Jo, one man and one woman, they would be distinguished in L_P as jo^{1}' and jo^{2}' and so on. The selection of which Jo is meant or which meaning of a homonym is intended is determined by context and no attempt is therefore made here to provide a way of getting to the intended referent or meaning. All that is necessary for the purpose of interpretation is that this disambiguation is done by the context and that L_P representations invoke only one of a range of alternatives. In general, of course, most word forms are not homonymous and so there is no need to distinguish their different senses. In these cases, the superscript associated with the translation is omitted in the exposition that follows for ease of representation, since there is no possible ambiguity. (As discussed in Chapter 1, polysemy is not incorporated into the current system and is thus ignored here and elsewhere.)

The full rule for translating words of English into L_P is given in (20). This provides the means for translating any word in the object language into an appropriate constant in the logical language together with a means of showing all possible alternative readings of the word.

(20) **Lexical translation rule (TLex)**: If *W* is a set of inflectionally related word forms $\{w_1, w_2, ..., w_m\}$ of which w_i is the citation form, then the translation of any word, w_i, in *W*, is w_i^{n}' where n is greater than or equal to 1.

We are now in a position to translate any sentence generated by the grammar, G_1, into L_P. The **translation procedure** is entirely mechanical and is based on the syntactic derivation of the object language sentence. The procedure provides each line in the derivation of an English sentence with a translation of that line as determined by the translation counterpart of the syntactic rule used to derive that line. For example, if there is a line in a derivation NP V_i, with translation V_i'(NP') then the NP can be expanded as N_{pr} using Rule $6G_1$. This rule is associated with the translation rule in (16.f) which equates the translation of the noun phrase with that of the proper noun it contains. The next line in the derivation is therefore N_{pr} V_i with translation V_i'(N_{pr}'). Hence, just as one line in a syntactic derivation is derived from the previous one by substituting the string on the right of a syntactic rule for an instance of the symbol on its left, so the translation of the sentence is derived by substituting the translation of the expanded symbol with the translation of the syntactic rule that was used.

To illustrate this further, (21) shows the derivation and parallel translation of the sentence *Jo laughed* according to G_1. The first line shows the start symbol S which tells us that we are deriving a sentence. This symbol is then rewritten as the string in (21.c) using rule $1G_1$ which has the translation in (21.d) according to $T1G_1$ in (16.a). The NP node in (21.c) is then expanded using rule $6G_1$, giving the string in (21.e) and translation in (21.f), as discussed above. Now we can substitute lexical items for all the symbols in (21.e) to give (21.g). At the same time we apply the lexical translation rule in (20) to each word in the English sentence and substitute the result in the appropriate place in the translation in (21.f), yielding (21.h) as the translation of the

English sentence. The numbers on the right of the examples in (21) (and below) indicate the rules that license each step in the derivation. The translation procedure is formally defined in (22), and, as mentioned above, it is entirely mechanical. If the rules are applied correctly, any sentence generated by G_1 can be paired with its translation in L_P. A more complex translation than that in (21) is shown in (23) to give a better idea of the method.

(21) a. S.
b. S'.
c. NP V_i. — $1G_1$
d. V_i'(NP'). — $T1G_1$
e. N_{pr} V_i. — $6G_1$
f. V_i'(N_{pr}'). — $T6G_1$
g. Jo laughed. — Lex
h. laugh'(jo'). — TLex

(22) **Translation procedure**: If i is a line in a syntactic derivation with a translation i' and A is a category in i with translation A' in i', then if the next line in the derivation i+1 is obtained from i by expanding A as a string X by Rule n or Lex, then the translation of i+1 is obtained by replacing A' in i' by X' the translation of X obtained by applying Translation Rule n or TLex.

(23) a. S
⇒ S'.
b. NP_1 was V_t[PAS] by NP_2 — $8G_1$
⇒ V_t'(NP_2',NP_1').
c. The N was V_t[PAS] by NP_2 — $7G_1$
⇒ V_t'(NP_2',the-N').
d. The N was V_t[PAS] by N_{pr} — $6G_1$
⇒ V_t'(N_{pr}',the-N').
e. The cat was poisoned by Ethel — Lex
⇒ poison'(ethel',the-cat').

Exercise 2.1:
Show the derivations and translations of the following English sentences using the format of (23):
i. Ethel poisoned the cat.
ii. The student gave the cake to the lecturer.
iii. The dog was crazy.

The procedure described in (22) and illustrated in (23) is called a **top down** derivation and translation, but a sentence can also be translated **bottom up**. With this method a sentence is translated by building a phrase structure tree, starting with the translations of the lexical items and then combining them in the way specified by different syntactic rules. This results in a translation tree that parallels the syntactic one and the translation of the whole sentence appears at the top. This can be shown

(24)

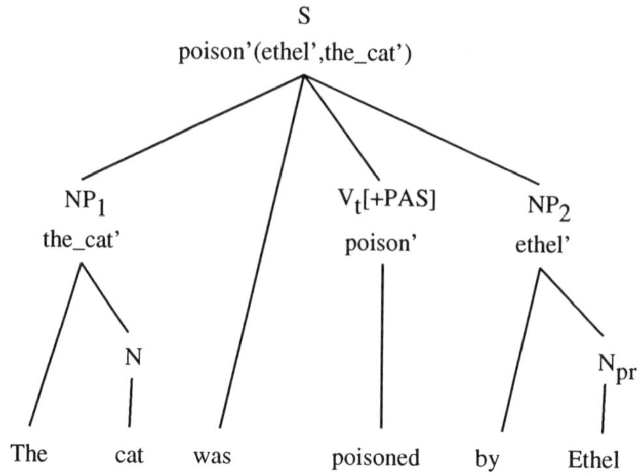

by annotating each node in a phrase structure tree with its associated translation as done in (24) which gives the bottom-up version of the sentence *The cat was poisoned by Ethel* that was derived by the top-down method in (23). Trees like this are referred to as **analysis trees** in this book. Although the phrase structure tree representation is often more perspicuous and reveals the parallelism of the translation to the syntax very clearly, the derivation procedure illustrated in (23) is the safer method and readers are recommended to stick to that way of translating until they are confident of their translating skills. Once the technique has been mastered, however, the rigorous derivational method may be dispensed with, provided that it is clear that the translation given for each phrase in the sentence is licensed by some rule. If there is any doubt, the appropriate translation rule should be referred to.

Exercise 2.2:
Draw analysis trees like that in (24) for the sentences in Exercise 2.1.

2.2 Interpreting L_P

We have now devised a procedure for translating (a restricted set of) sentences in English into a formal language, L_P. As we have seen, formulae in L_P are unambiguous and have all contextual uncertainties resolved in order to provide a representation of the semantic content of the sentences in the object language which they translate. Translation into a logical language in this way is a useful method of representing the intended meaning of an English sentence on some occasion of utterance, but does not in itself constitute a theory of semantics. What needs to be done to complete the project is to **interpret** the formulae of L_P in terms of their **truth-conditions**, as discussed in Chapter 1. In this way, the English sentences generated by G_1 are provided with an indirect interpretation.

There are two parts to the interpretation procedure. In the first place, interpretation takes place, not in a vacuum, but with respect to a representation of some state-of-affairs. Such a representation is called a **model** and models have two parts: an **ontology** and a **denotation assignment function** or **naming function**. The word *ontology* comes from the Greek word meaning to be or exist and refers to that branch of philosophy (a subpart of metaphysics) that has to do with the study of what exists in the world or some part of the world. The ontology of the model provides the basis for interpretation in that it defines what exists and so what can be talked about. If something is not recognised as existing in the model then it cannot be referred to or discussed by any language that the model is being used to interpret. This means, of course, that a model must contain abstract, as well as material, entities, otherwise we could never talk about things like love or virtue, etc. The assumption that abstract things exist just as concrete ones do may seem strange, but the differences between them may be captured by structuring the ontology in different ways. For example, it is possible to put different **entities** (the things that exist) into different **sorts** according to their basic properties. A basic distinction can be made between all entities depending on whether they are of an abstract or concrete sort. The semantic properties of the words that are associated with these two sorts of entity may differ from each other in predictable ways. Exactly what sorts of entity should be recognised as making up adequate ontologies for natural language interpretation is a vexed and controversial issue. Indeed, much current debate in formal semantics centres around just this question. The problem will, however, not be addressed in this book. The models that are defined in this and later chapters all contain only concrete, physically manifested, entities. For present purposes, therefore, it is not necessary to worry about any fundamental differences between the entities in a model.

The important thing that we are concerned with is the relation between the entities in the model and expressions of the language being interpreted. Once the things that exist in the state-of-affairs being modelled have been determined, it is necessary to associate the basic expressions of the language being interpreted with the entities that constitute the ontology. The basic expressions of the object language are here taken to mean the expressions of the language belonging to the major parts of speech (e.g. nouns, verbs, adjectives) in contrast to the **grammatical** (or **functional** expressions (e.g. determiners, conjunctions, auxiliary verbs)). In L_P, the basic expressions are the individual and predicate **constants** associated with the nouns, verbs and adjectives of the language being translated in contrast with the purely **logical** expressions like operators and quantifiers (see later chapters). Logical expressions take their interpretation, not from the model, but from the theory of interpretation, the model theory itself, thus reflecting the fact that such expressions have an invariant interpretation independent of the particular situation being modelled. The denotations of constant expressions, however, may change from model to model. For example, the name *Prudence* could be associated with a cat in one model, but a human being in another, or two entities could be singing in one model, but not in another, and so on. On the other hand, the equative copula *was* does not change its function of identifying two entities from situation to situation. Thus, the interpretation of a constant expression must be defined for each model, but those of grammatical expressions are fixed by the theory of interpretation.

The association of constants with entities in the model is done by the denotation assignment function. As discussed in Chapter 1, the **denotation** of an expression is the relation between the expression and things that exist in the world. Since the world for our purposes is given by the model of the world or situation, what is denoted by an expression in L_P is something in the model. The denotation of an expression has two aspects: an **extension**, the sorts of things in the world that an expression can be used to refer to, and an **intension**, the concept that determines the extension of the expression. A discussion of the latter aspect of denotation is left until the final four chapters of the book and the semantics defined in Chapters 2 to 6 is purely **extensional**. Hence, the denotation assignment functions of the models in these chapters associate each constant in the logic with its extension. In the discussion that follows, therefore, the denotation of any expression is given by its extension, and what particular expressions denote are referred to as their extensions. The general term denotation is used when talking about the relation between classes of expressions in the object language and the sorts of thing (entities, sets or relations) in the model that those expressions are associated with. This latter term is neutral between intension and extension, and, while Chapters 2 to 6 deal only with extensional denotations, what is said about denotation in these chapters is relevant to intensional denotation as it is defined in Chapters 8 to 10.

Since the relation between a constant (or **content word** in English) and the entities it denotes is **conventional** and **arbitrary**, the denotation assignment function provides the necessary foundation for talking about the entities in the model by specifying precisely what is happening in the situation being modelled. For example, consider a simple situation in which there are three entities, a book, a chair and a child, where the latter is sitting on the chair reading the book. A model of this situation has an ontology consisting of the three entities involved in it: the book, the chair and the child. The denotation assignment function of the model specifies that the English words *book*, *chair* and *child* (extensionally) denote the book, the chair and the child, respectively. It also specifies that the transitive verbs *read* and *sit on* (extensionally) denote a relation between the child and the book in the first case and the child and the chair in the second and that the verbs *sit* and *read* both denote things that the child is doing, and so on.

Together, the specification of an ontology and an assignment of denotations to basic expressions in a language thus gives a complete description of some state of affairs. From this complete description we can ascertain the truth or falsity of any formula in the language to be interpreted. How this is done is determined by the **model theory** which constitutes the second part of the interpretation procedure. This provides a definition of how the denotations of non-basic (i.e. composite) expressions in L_P are to be determined from the denotations of their constituent parts in accordance with the principle of compositionality. Ultimately, it defines what it is for a formula to be true with respect to some model by specifying the truth-conditions for formulae in L_P. It thus constitutes the central part of the theory of semantics pursued in this book.

The rest of this chapter is given over to defining a model of a fairly simple (but non-trivial) situation, and providing an informal account of the model theory. The interpretation procedure thus defined may be used to interpret any formula in L_P. Where these formulae translate sentences generated by G_1, the procedure provides an indirect interpretation of this fragment of the grammar of English.

2.2.1 *Individuals and identity*

As discussed above, model-theoretic interpretation provides the definition of the truth-conditions of formulae with respect to a model of some state-of-affairs. In order to interpret L_P, therefore, we must first specify a model and then detail a set of rules for ascertaining the truth or falsity of formulae with respect to this model. The model defined in this chapter is a very simple one, containing eight entities: two men, two women, a cake, a cat, a dog and a book. The ontology of this model, called M_1, could thus be represented pictorially as in (25). Using pictures to represent the entities that exist in particular models helps to bring out the way that the theory of semantics presented in this book associates linguistic expressions with non-linguistic objects. However, they are somewhat inconvenient (and expensive) to have in a textbook and the entities in models will thus be represented using symbols, rather than pictures. Any symbols may be used to represent these entities, provided only that there is no ambiguity in the symbols used. A unique symbol should thus represent each separate entity in the model. For example, one might represent the eight entities in M_1 by using the first eight Arabic positive whole numbers, as in (26.a), or the last eight letters of the Roman alphabet in their uppercase form, as in (26.b).

(25) **The entities in M_1**

(26) a. 1 2 3 4 5 6 7 8.
b. S T U V W X Y Z.

The fact that there are eight different symbols in (26.a) and (26.b) indicates that there are eight different entities in the model whose properties are determined by the denotation assignment function. However, since the entities in the model M_1 are two men, two women, a cat, a dog, a book and a cake, it is more convenient for mnemonic purposes to represent these entities by using English words in boldface uppercase letters with subscripts differentiating entities where necessary, as in (27). The English words in upper case letters in (27) are intended to represent actual entities and are not expressions of English. This is an important point and it should be borne in mind throughout the book that symbols like **MAN**$_1$ only ever stand for entities and never for expressions in English, L_P or any other language.

(27) The entities in M_1:

MAN$_1$ **MAN**$_2$ **WOMAN**$_1$ **WOMAN**$_2$ **CAT** **DOG** **BOOK** **CAKE**.

Entities in the world are typically referred to by using proper names or definite descriptions, i.e. types of noun phrase. In the translation procedure developed earlier, such noun phrases are translated into individual constants in L_P, which are therefore analysed as denoting entities in the model. The denotation assignment function in model **M**$_1$ thus associates each individual constant in L_P with a single entity in the model, the entity that the constant denotes. Only one entity is associated with each individual constant because L_P is an unambiguous language and so each constant must have an unambiguous denotation in a particular model. In M_1, all the entities except for the book and the cake have proper names. One of the women is called Fiona, the other woman is called Ethel, the men are called Jo and Bertie, the dog is called Chester and the cat is called Prudence. So, part of the denotation assignment function associates the L_P constants translating these names with the appropriate entities, as shown in (28).

(28) a. jo' DENOTES **MAN**$_1$.
b. bertie' DENOTES **MAN**$_2$.
c. ethel' DENOTES **WOMAN**$_1$.
d. fiona' DENOTES **WOMAN**$_2$.
e. chester' DENOTES **DOG**.
f. prudence' DENOTES **CAT**.

The grammar G_1 also contains simple definite NPs so that we can refer to the other entities in M_1 despite the fact that they do not have proper names. Although definite NPs in English are composite phrases (consisting at least of the definite article *the* and a common noun), the translation procedure treats them as basic expressions very much like proper names and translates them as individual constants in L_P. Since individual constants denote entities in the model, the denotation assignment function directly associates particular definite noun phrases with particular entities, ensuring that each definite description picks out only one entity. For example, the expression *the-book'* is associated with **BOOK** and *the-cake'* with **CAKE** by the denotation assignment function.

Although an individual constant may be associated with only one entity in the model, entities may themselves be identified by more than one expression in a language. In M_1, the entity **$\mathbf{WOMAN_2}$** is denoted not only by the expression *fiona'* but also by the expressions *the-lecturer'* and *the-singer'*, while the L_P expression *the-student'* denotes the entity, **$\mathbf{MAN_1}$** and **DOG** is denoted by *the-dog'* as well as *chester'*. (29) gives the extensions in M_1 for all the referring expressions in L_P, thus indirectly associating all noun phrases generated by G_1 with some entity in the model.

(29) a.	jo'	DENOTES	**$\mathbf{MAN_1}$**.
b.	the-student'	DENOTES	**$\mathbf{MAN_1}$**.
c.	bertie'	DENOTES	**$\mathbf{MAN_2}$**.
d.	ethel'	DENOTES	**$\mathbf{WOMAN_1}$**.
e.	the-golfer'	DENOTES	**$\mathbf{WOMAN_1}$**.
f.	fiona'	DENOTES	**$\mathbf{WOMAN_2}$**.
g.	the-singer'	DENOTES	**$\mathbf{WOMAN_2}$**.
h.	the-lecturer'	DENOTES	**$\mathbf{WOMAN_2}$**.
i.	the-cat'	DENOTES	**CAT**.
j.	prudence'	DENOTES	**CAT**.
k.	chester'	DENOTES	**DOG**.
l.	the-dog'	DENOTES	**DOG**.
m.	the-cake'	DENOTES	**CAKE**.
n.	the-book'	DENOTES	**BOOK**.

We are already in a position to assess the truth or falsity of some formulae that translate some of the sentences generated by the grammar fragment G_1: those that contain the equative copula, *be*. Sentences like *Bertie is the golfer* are used to assert that two descriptions refer to the same entity. Hence, we interpret formulae that translate such sentences, e.g. *bertie' = the-golfer'*, as being true only where the entity denoted by *bertie'* and that denoted by *the-golfer* are one and the same. This statement describes the truth-conditions for formulae containing the identity operator = which can be stated more formally as (30) which forms part of the model theory. (The subscripts on the NPs are given by the translation rule for equative sentences in (18.b), above.)

(30) **Truth-conditions for identity**: A formula of the form (NP_1' = NP_2') is true if, and only if, the entity denoted by NP_1' is the same entity as that denoted by NP_2'.

The expression *if, and only if* used in (30) is not a common one in everyday English but is used a lot in semantics which borrows the use from logic. The conjunction of two sentences using this expression is interpreted to mean that the two sentences are semantically equivalent. The first *if* in the conjunction expresses the idea that the truth of the proposition expressed by the second sentence is **sufficient** to guarantee the truth of the proposition expressed by the first, while the *only if* expresses the idea that the truth of the proposition expressed by the second sentence is **necessary** for the proposition expressed by the first to be true. The second sentence in the conjunction thus provides the necessary and sufficient conditions that guarantee the truth of the proposition expressed by the first sentence. In logical terms, as we shall see in Chapter 3, the semantic equivalence of two formulae that translate two sentences is guaranteed if both formulae have the same truth value. Hence, given a true equivalence, if one of the formulae is true then so is the other and if one is false, then so is the other. Consequently, if *chester'* = *the-dog'* is true then the entity denoted by *chester'* is exactly the same as that denoted by *the-dog'* and conversely, if the entities denoted by *chester'* and *the-dog'* are identical then the formula *chester'* = *the-dog'* is true. The phrase *if, and only if* thus imposes a strong relation between the two sentences it connects. The expression *if, and only if* is often abbreviated to *iff* and this will be the practice in giving numbered definitions from now on.

Exercise 2.3:
Translate the following sentences into L_P and then ascertain their truth or falsity with respect to M_1:

i. Ethel was the golfer.
ii. The student was the singer.

2.2.2 *A little light set theory*

In addition to expressions that denote entities, languages contain expressions that describe properties that entities have and the relations that they enter into. In English, properties and relations are generally expressed by verbs and adjectives whose equivalents in L_P are, as we have seen, n-place predicates. In order to complete the interpretation procedure for L_P, therefore, it is necessary to determine the sorts of extensional denotations that predicates have and to give a definition of the truth-conditions for formulae containing them in such a way as to capture our intuitions about the properties and relations English verbs and adjectives describe. In order to do this, we need to look at **set theory**, on which the semantic theory in this book is based. This section provides a short introduction to the necessary concepts, and further information can be obtained from the references at the end of this chapter.

A **set** is a collection, or group, of items which are called the **elements** or **members** of that set. This collection may consist of concrete objects like the computer I am typing this book on, the mug of coffee I have just finished, the Wallace Monument, and so on, or of abstract items like the meridian, the number 99, the fourth of April 1991, or a set of symbols or indeed any combination of abstract, concrete and symbolic elements. Finite sets (i.e. those containing a finite number of elements) may be symbolised by putting the names of their members, separated by commas, within curly brackets, { and }. This is called the **list notation** for sets and there can be either **closed sets** where all its members are listed or **open sets** where only part of.the set is listed. Examples of sets in the list notation are given in (31). (31.a) gives the closed set consisting of all and only the first five letters of the Roman alphabet. (31.b) defines an open set which contains these symbols and more besides and (31.c) lists the set of entities in the model M_1.

(31) a. {a,b,c,d,e}.
b. {a,b,c,d,e,...}.
c. {$\mathbf{MAN_1}$, $\mathbf{MAN_2}$, $\mathbf{WOMAN_1}$, $\mathbf{WOMAN_2}$, **CAT**, **DOG**, **BOOK**, **CAKE**}.

In order to show that some element, *a*, is a **member** of a particular set, the symbol $\in$, which is read as *is a member of,* is written between the element, *a*, on its left and the set on its right. Thus, the expression a $\in$ {a,b,c,d,e} asserts that a is a member of the set consisting of all and only the first five letters of the Roman alphabet. The complementary relation *is not a member of* is symbolised by $\notin$ and so the expression $\mathbf{MAN_1} \notin$ {**CAT**, **DOG**, **BOOK**} asserts that the entity, $\mathbf{MAN_1}$ is not a member of the set consisting of the entities, **CAT**, **DOG** and **BOOK**. An element must either be a member of a specific set or not be a member of that set. It cannot be both a member and a non-member of a set nor can it be neither a member nor a non-member of a set.

Sets may have any number of members. Those with just one member are often called **singleton sets** (or just singletons). For example, the set {$\mathbf{MAN_1}$} is the set consisting only of the entity called Jo in the model, M_1. It is important to remember that a singleton set is not the same as the entity that is its sole member. Thus, the set consisting only of the letter a, i.e. {a}, is not the same as the letter a. A singleton set is not, however, the smallest possible set, as a set may contain no members at all. There is, in fact, only one set with no elements and it is called the **empty** or **null set,** written as $\varnothing$. It may be thought that having a set with nothing in it is somewhat pointless and that it can hardly be described as a set at all. But, like the number zero, it is a very useful notion to have when stating general rules that apply to all sets irrespective of the number of members they have, including, of course, none. Because the empty set contains no members, statements of the form $x \in \varnothing$ (where x is some element) are never true while those of the form $x \notin \varnothing$ are always true.

Sets may share some or all of their members with other sets. In certain cases, all the members of one set, A, are members of another, B. Sets like A are called **subsets** of sets like B and sets like B are called **supersets** of sets like A. To symbolise the subset relation we use the symbols $\subseteq$ or $\supseteq$. The different symbols have the same interpretation but differ in the direction in which they are read. Both $A \subseteq B$ and $B \supseteq A$ mean that A is a subset of B, but we can read the first as *A is a subset of B* and the second as *B is a superset of A.* A formal definition of the notion of subset and superset is given in (32):

(32) Given two sets A and B, A is a subset of B ($A \subseteq B$) if, and only if, every member of A is a member of B, in which case B is a superset of A ($B \supseteq A$).

According to (32), the sets {a,b,c} and {c,d,e} are both subsets of {a,b,c,d,e} but {a,b,f} is not a subset of this, because it contains one element, f, that is not in {a,b,c,d,e}. This definition has two important consequences. In the first place, it entails that every set is a subset of itself, because (32) just requires all the members of the subset to be in the superset. Where two sets have exactly the same members, and are thus identical, the definition is trivially satisfied. In order to specify that the subset is actually smaller than the superset, the symbols $\supset$ and $\subset$ are used. $A \subset B$ is read *A is a **proper subset*** of B while $B \supset A$ is read as *B is a **proper superset*** of A. For example, {a,b,c} is a proper subset of {a,b,c,d} because the latter set contains one element, d, not in the former and so the statement, $\{a,b,c\} \subset \{a,b,c,d\}$ is true. However, while $\{a,b,c\} \subseteq \{a,b,c\}$ is true, $\{a,b,c\} \subset \{a,b,c\}$ is not, because the two sets contain exactly the same elements.

The other result of the definition of subset and superset in (32) is that the empty set is a subset of every set. One can see that this must be so by considering what would have to be the case for it not to be a subset of some set. From (32), we deduce that A cannot be a subset of B, if (and only if) there is some element in A that is not in B. Since the empty set contains no members, then it is not possible for it to have a member not in any other set. Hence, $\varnothing \subseteq A$ is a true statement, whatever set A happens to be.

Some sets share members with others without being subsets or supersets of each other. For example, the set {a,b,c,d} shares the elements c and d with the set {c,d,e,f} and thus we say that the **intersection** of these two sets, written $\{a,b,c,d\} \cap \{c,d,e,f\}$, is the set {c,d}. The definition of this relation given in (33) has three important consequences: firstly, where two sets have no common elements, their intersection is the null set, $\varnothing$; secondly, where two sets are identical, their intersection is equal to both sets; and, finally, the intersection of two sets is a subset of them both.

(33) The intersection of two sets A and B, $A \cap B$, is the set containing exactly those members of A that are members of B.

We may also join sets together to form larger sets. This is known as **set union** and the union of two sets, A and B, written $A \cup B$, is the smallest set containing all the members of both A and B. Thus, the union of the sets {a,b,c,d} and {c,d,e,f} is that set that contains the six elements that appear in both these sets, i.e. {a,b,c,d,e,f}. The definition of set union in (34) has two consequences: the union of a set with the empty set is the same as the original set; and both sets joined by the union operation are subsets of the resultant set.

(34) The union of two sets A and B, $A \cup B$, is the set which contains all and only those elements which are in A or which are in B, or both.

There is one further property of sets that it is necessary to know at the moment. This is a basic assumption of set theory that two sets with the same members are identical. For example, the listed set {z,y,x,w,v,u} is identical to the set described as the last six letters of the English alphabet while the set consisting of the first 10 prime numbers {1,2,3,5,7,11,13,17,19,23} is identical to the set {23,19,17,13,11,7,5,3,2,1} which is identical to the set {1,11,3,23,7,13,5,17,2,19}. This property is called the **Axiom of Extension** and is defined in (35).

(35) **Axiom of extension**: Two sets A and B are identical iff they have the same members.

(35) is called an **axiom** because it is a primitive of set theory and its truth cannot be derived from the truth of other statements in the theory. The term **extension** has the same meaning as the term discussed above and in Chapter 1 with respect to denotation, i.e. it refers to the elements in a set and not to the property or properties that are common to those elements. The axiom of extension thus says that whatever name is given to a set and however a set is represented, it is fully defined by the elements it contains. Therefore, if some set of elements has two names or two different representations, this does not mean that it is two different sets. If two sets have precisely the same members then they are extensionally identical. This is similar to the notion of identity between two entities discussed in Section 2.2.1 above. No

matter how an entity is named (or indeed represented), if two names or definite descriptions denote the same entity then they are extensionally identical. The interpretation of the logical language L_P thus does not depend on the expressions used to describe entities in a model, but on what those expressions denote. This important property is the basis of extensional systems like the semantic theory that is developed in Chapters 2 to 6, but fails in the intensional ones developed in Chapters 8 to 9 (see the discussion in Sections 9.1 and 10.3, in particular). Until then, however, the Axiom of Extension is assumed to hold and this has two important consequences. In the first place, (35) entails that sets are **unordered**. This means that no matter what order the elements appear in a listed set, provided that the different orderings involve all the same elements, then the differently ordered lists define the same set. Thus, {z,y,x,w,v,u} is the same set as {u,v,w,x,y,z} which is the same as {z,u,y,v,x,w}. Secondly, the Axiom of Extension guarantees that a set with repeated specifications of the same element is identical to the same set with only one listing of the element. For example, the set {u,v,w,w,x,x,x} is identical to {u,v,w,w,x} which is identical to {u,v,w,x}.

Exercise 2.4:
Given the sets defined below, which of the following statements are true?

A = {1,3,5,7}	B = {a,c,e,g,i}	C = {1,a,3,5,e,7}
D = {7,3,1,5}	E = {e,a,i,c,i,g}	F = {{1},{1,3},{1,3,5},{1,3,5,7}}

1. A = B.	2. E = B.	3. D = the first four positive odd numbers.
4. e $\in$ C.	5. a $\in$ D.	6. {1} $\in$ A.
7. D $\in$ F.	8. A $\in$ C	9. {1,3} $\supseteq$ A.
10. D $\subset$ C.	11. D $\subset$ F.	12. E $\subseteq$ B.
13. B $\subset$ E.	14. A $\cap$ D = A.	15. A $\cup$ D = D.
16. C $\cap$ B = $\varnothing$.		

2.2.3 *Interpreting predicates*

After that brief interlude, we can now go back to the interpretation procedure and assign extensions to predicates and specify the truth-conditions of formulae containing them. We begin by looking at one-place predicates.

Let us assume that the situation being modelled by M_1 is one of which the statements in (36) are all true and other statements containing the intransitive verbs and adjectives in G_1 are all false. This situation can be represented by dividing the set of entities in the model into subsets according to whether they ran, or laughed, or were crazy, and so on. These sets provide the extensions of the one-place predicates that translate the intransitive verbs and predicative adjectives of G_1. Thus, while individual constants denote entities in the model, one-place predicates denote sets of entities, just those entities of which it is true to say that they ran, laughed, were crazy, etc. Hence, the denotation assignment function of a model associates each one-place predicate in L_P with some set of entities. The assignment for M_1 according to the situation described in (36) is given in (37).

(36) a. Jo was happy and laughed.
b. Ethel was happy and laughed.
c. Fiona sang and was happy.
d. Bertie was wealthy.
e. The dog ran and howled.
f. The cat ran.
g. The cake was disgusting.
h. No-one screamed or was crazy or messy.

(37) a.	run'	DENOTES	{**DOG,CAT**}.
b.	laugh'	DENOTES	{$\mathbf{MAN_1}$, $\mathbf{WOMAN_1}$}.
c.	howl'	DENOTES	{**DOG**}.
d.	sing'	DENOTES	{$\mathbf{WOMAN_2}$}.
e.	scream'	DENOTES	∅.
f.	crazy'	DENOTES	∅.
h.	disgusting'	DENOTES	{**CAKE**}.
i.	wealthy'	DENOTES	{$\mathbf{MAN_2}$}.
k.	happy'	DENOTES	{$\mathbf{MAN_1}$,$\mathbf{WOMAN_2}$,$\mathbf{WOMAN_1}$}.
l.	messy'	DENOTES	Ø.

The generalisation that all one-place predicates extensionally denote sets can only be maintained if we accept the existence of the empty set. According to (37), in M_1 ∅ functions as the extensions of *crazy'*, *messy'* and *scream'*. It might be thought that one could interpret predicates that are true of no entities in the model by leaving them out of the denotation assignment function. This is not possible, however. To interpret a sentence, it is necessary to know what each of the content words in the sentence means. This is what the denotation assignment function does. It makes sure that each basic expression in the language is matched with something in the model and thus represents what the particular constants denote. If no extension is assigned to some basic expression, then that expression and every expression that contains it is strictly speaking meaningless. It has no denotation and therefore no sentence or formula containing the item can be assigned a truth value. For example, a (pseudo-)English sentence like *Fiona glipped the egg* could be a well-formed expression in English (since it conforms to the phonological and syntactic rules of the language). It has no interpretation, however, because the item *glipped* is an invented word and thus has no denotation. It is very important, then, that when defining a model, every constant (predicate or individual) in L_P (and thus indirectly every content word in the grammar under consideration) receives a denotation, even if nothing in the model has the property represented by the predicate. Hence, the empty set is used to indicate that nothing in the model is in the extension of particular expressions, thus enabling the interpretation procedure to function in the most general manner.

Once the extension of a one-place predicate is determined, it is an easy matter to determine whether a formula containing that predicate is true or false. All that is necessary is to see whether the entity denoted by the argument of the one-place predicate is in the set of entities it denotes. If it is, then the formula is true, if not, then it is false. Thus, the formula *run'(the-dog')* is true in M_1 because the entity denoted by *the-dog'*, i.e. **DOG**, is, according to (37), a member of the set of entities denoted by the predicate, *run'*, i.e. {**CAT,DOG**}. By the same reasoning, *run'(bertie')* is false with respect to M_1, because **MAN_2** is not a member of {**CAT,DOG**}, i.e. Bertie is not one of the entities that are running. This provides the definition of the truth-conditions for formulae containing one-place predicates which is restated more formally in (38).

(38) **Truth-conditions for one-place predicates**: A formula V_i'(NP') or A'(NP') is true with respect to a model iff the entity denoted by NP' in the model is a member of the set of entities denoted by V_i' or A' in the model. The formula is false otherwise.

From (38) it follows that a formula like *messy'(the-cat')* is true if and only if the entity **CAT**, the extension of the argument expression, *the-cat'*, is a member of the extension of the predicate *messy'*. Since the extension of the predicate is, according to (37), $\varnothing$, the empty set, nothing in the model is messy and, because **CAT** $\in \varnothing$ is false, then so is the formula *messy'(the-cat')*. Again this illustrates the usefulness of treating $\varnothing$ as a set in the same way as other sets. If we did not do this, we would have to have separate truth-conditions for formulae containing predicates that are true of no entities in a model, clearly missing a generalisation.

Exercise 2.5:
Translate the following sentences into L_P and ascertain whether they are true or false with respect to the model M_1.

i. The cat laughed.
ii. Jo was happy.
iii. Fiona ran.

Loosely speaking, intransitive verbs and adjectives (i.e. one-place predicates in L_P) ascribe properties to entities, but not only do entities have properties, they also enter into **relations** with each other. So, for example, two entities, say Jo and Ethel, might like each other, but not like a third, say Chester. In other words, there is a *relation of liking* between Ethel and Jo and vice versa but not one between Jo and Chester or Ethel and Chester. Let us further specify the situation described by the model M_1 by relating the entities in the model to each other using the transitive verbs in the grammar, G_1, as in (39).

(39) a. Jo liked Ethel, Fiona, Bertie and himself.
b. Ethel liked Jo and Fiona.
c. Fiona liked the cat and Ethel.
d. The women, the men and the cat all loathed the dog and Fiona loathed Jo.
e. Chester ate the cake.
f. The cake poisoned the dog.
g. Bertie and Ethel both read the book.
h. Nothing kicked anything else.

We can represent these relations, and others like them, as sets of **pairs of entities**, according to whether the first entity bears a particular relation to the second.

So, for example, we can represent the liking relation in M_1 by grouping together into pairs Jo and Ethel, Jo and Fiona, Jo and Bertie, Jo and himself, Ethel and Jo, Ethel and Fiona, and so on. In other words, two-place predicates translating transitive verbs denote sets of pairs of entities. Thus, like one-place predicates, two-place predicates denote sets, but sets with members that are not single entities but pairs of entities. Relations denoted by the verbs in G_1 specify a direction in which the relation goes. Hence, in the definition of the relation denoted by *like'* in M_1 the pair Jo and Ethel must be distinguished from the pair Ethel and Jo, because in the former Jo is the one doing the liking while in the latter it is Ethel who does it. Thus, in the same way that *Jo liked Ethel* means something different from *Ethel liked Jo*, we must make sure that the pairs that make up the extensions of two-place predicates are properly ordered. The extensions of two-place predicates are, therefore, defined as sets of **ordered pairs** of entities. Ordered pairs of elements are conventionally written between angle brackets, **<, >,** and separated by a comma. Hence, the two ordered pairs corresponding to Jo and Ethel and Ethel and Jo are written as **<MAN$_1$,WOMAN$_1$>** and **<WOMAN$_1$,MAN$_1$>**. Because order is significant, these pairs represent different things: the first pair shows a relation between **MAN$_1$** and **WOMAN$_1$** and the latter a relation between **WOMAN$_1$** and **MAN$_1$**. As a rough and ready principle that will suffice for the moment: the first member of an ordered pair corresponds to the entity denoted by the first argument of a predicate (the translation of the syntactic subject of an active sentence), and the second member corresponds to the entity denoted by the second argument of the predicate (the translation of the syntactic direct object of an active sentence). Letting two-place predicates denote sets of ordered pairs of entities, we may further specify the denotation assignment function for M_1 as in (40).

(40) a. like' DENOTES {**<MAN$_1$,WOMAN$_1$>**,
<MAN$_1$,MAN$_2$>,
<MAN$_1$,WOMAN$_2$>,
<MAN$_1$,MAN$_1$>,
<WOMAN$_1$,WOMAN$_2$>,
<WOMAN$_1$,MAN$_1$>,
<WOMAN$_2$,CAT>,
<WOMAN$_2$,WOMAN$_1$>}.

b. loathe' DENOTES {**<MAN$_1$,DOG>**,
<MAN$_2$,DOG>,
<WOMAN$_1$,DOG>,
<WOMAN$_2$,DOG>,
<WOMAN$_2$,MAN$_1$>,
<CAT,DOG>}.

c. poison' DENOTES {**<CAKE,DOG>**}.

d. eat' DENOTES {**<DOG,CAKE>**}.

e. read' DENOTES {**<WOMAN$_1$,BOOK>**,
<MAN$_2$,BOOK>}.

f. kick' DENOTES $\varnothing$.

The truth-conditions of a formula containing a two-place predicate are similar to those involving one-place predicates, in that set-membership is the important criterion. Such a formula is true with respect to some model, if the ordered pair formed by taking the entity denoted by the first argument of the predicate as the first element and that denoted by the second argument of the predicate as the second element is in the set of ordered pairs denoted by the two-place predicate. For example, to compute the truth value of the formula *like'(the-student',fiona')* with respect to M_1 the entities denoted by the two arguments, *the-student'* and *fiona'*, are identified. According to the denotation assignment in (29), the first expression denotes **MAN$_1$** and the second denotes **WOMAN$_2$**. The relevant ordered pair that is formed from these two entities is **<MAN$_1$,WOMAN$_2$>** because this reflects the order of the arguments in the formula. The extension of the predicate *like'* is then identified to see if the ordered pair is a member of this set. (40) shows that this is the case and that **<MAN$_1$,WOMAN$_2$>** is indeed in the extension of *like'*. Hence, the formula *like'(the-student',fiona')* is true with respect to M_1. On the other hand, the formula that translates the sentence *The student is liked by Fiona* is false in M_1, because the ordered pair **<WOMAN$_2$,MAN$_1$>** is not in the extension of *like'*. The translation rules ensure that it is not the pair **<MAN$_1$,WOMAN$_2$>** which is checked for being in the extension of the predicate. This is because the translation of the sentence is *like'(fiona',the-student')* and not *like'(the-student',fiona')*. The interpretation rule for two-place predicates given in (41) ensures that the order of arguments in a predicate-argument representation is significant and so the differences in the translation rules of active and passive sentences are semantically significant.

(41) **Truth-conditions for two-place predicates**: A formula V_t'(NP_1',NP_2') is true with respect to a model iff the ordered pair <E_1,E_2> is in the set of ordered pairs denoted by V_t' in the model, where E_1 is the entity denoted by NP_1' and E_2 is the entity denoted by NP_2' in the model. The formula is false otherwise.

Exercise 2.6:
Translate the following sentences into L_P and ascertain whether the formulae they are associated with are true or false with respect to the model, M_1.

i. The cat was liked by the lecturer.
ii. Ethel kicked the student.
iii. The cake poisoned the cat.

If transitive verbs describe relations between two entities, ditransitive verbs describe relations between three entities. For example, in the relation of giving there has to be an entity who does the giving, an entity that is given, and an entity to whom the latter is given. Thus, the extensions of three-place predicates that translate such verbs are represented as sets of **ordered triples** of entities. An ordered triple is like an ordered pair except that it contains three members, not two, but again the order is significant and fixed. The order of the entities in each of the triples that make up the extension of a three-place predicate follows the order of the arguments of the predicate. Thus, the entity denoted by the first argument forms the first element in the triple, that denoted by the second argument forms the second element and that denoted by the third argument forms the third element.

The only ditransitive verb in fragment G_1 is *gave, given* and it receives the extension in (42) which represents a situation in which Jo gave the cake to the dog, Fiona gave the cake to Jo, Jo gave the book to Bertie, Bertie gave it to Ethel and Jo gave Fiona the cat.

(42) give' DENOTES {**<WOMAN$_2$,CAKE,MAN$_1$>,
<MAN$_1$,CAKE,DOG>,
<MAN$_1$,BOOK,MAN$_2$>,
<MAN$_2$,BOOK,WOMAN$_1$>,
<MAN$_1$,CAT,WOMAN$_2$>**}.

The definition of the truth-conditions for formulae containing three-place predicates follows the same pattern as for the other predicates. The formula *give'(the-student',prudence',the-lecturer')* is true if (and only if) the ordered triple **<MAN$_1$,CAT,WOMAN$_2$>**, representing the entities denoted by the three arguments of the predicate in order, is in the set of ordered triples denoted by *give'*.

(43) **Truth-conditions for three-place predicates**: A formula V_{dt}'(NP_1',NP_2',NP_3') is true if and only if the ordered triple <E_1,E_2,E_3> is in the set of ordered triples denoted by V_{dt}', where E_1 is the entity denoted by NP_1', E_2 is the entity denoted by NP_2' and E_3 is the entity denoted by NP_3'. The formula is false otherwise.

Exercise 2.7:
Translate the following sentences into L_P and say whether they are true or false with respect to the model M_1.

i. The golfer gave the book to the golfer.
ii. The student gave the lecturer the book.
iii. Ethel was given the book by Bertie.

Exercise 2.8:
Write a general rule giving the truth-conditions for formulae containing any **n-place predicate** along the lines of (41) and (43).

2.2.4 Finishing up

We have now given the extensions for almost all the basic expressions in L_P and provided the truth-conditions for almost all the simple formulae derived by translating the English sentences generated by the grammar G_1. The only thing that remains is to interpret the zero-place predicates, *rain'* and *snow'*. Unlike the other predicates, these do not denote sets, because they have no arguments. Instead they are directly assigned truth values, because they are, in effect, basic formulae. The denotation assignment function of the model must, therefore, assign them either the value true or the value false, thus directly specifying their truth as part of the model. No separate statement of their truth-conditions in the theory is thus required to interpret them. For the sake of completeness, then, let us assume that in the situation modelled by M_1 it was raining but not snowing. The denotation assignment function of M_1 is thus completed by the statements in (44).

(44) a. rain' DENOTES **true**.
b. snow' DENOTES **false**.

All basic expressions of the grammar fragment, the constants in L_P that translate the lexemes in English, have now been assigned a denotation. Furthermore, the rules defining the truth-conditions of the simple formulae resulting from the translation of sentences in G_1 together constitute a complete theory of interpretation for those formulae in L_P. Hence, the truth or falsity of the formulae that translate any of the simple sentences generated by G_1 can be ascertained with respect to M_1 or indeed any other model that assigns denotations to the constants of L_P. The interpretation procedure outlined above remains the same for all possible models of situations that can be described by sentences generated by G_1. Hence, it forms a theory of interpretation independent of particular situations represented by models. In the next chapter, the interpretation discussed in this section is put on a more formal footing, but before this is done the grammar fragment G_1 will be extended to generate simple conjoined sentences.

2.3 Further reading

The language L_P is based on part of **predicate logic** and there are many introductions to this logical system, although they all begin with an introduction to **propositional logic** which is discussed in Chapter 3. The basic syntax of this language is introduced in Allwood, Andersen and Dahl (1977: 58-61) and the semantics is given in Allwood, Andersen and Dahl (1977: 72-75). The most accessible logic textbook is Guttenplan (1986), of which pp. 166-175 are the most relevant here. Most introductions to classical phrase structure grammar are to be found in older introductory textbooks to linguistics (see, particularly, Bach (1974)), but Borsley (1990) discusses more modern approaches to such grammars with respect also to transformational and unification grammars. Formal grammar theory and a formal account of phrase structure grammar can be found in Partee, ter Meulen and Wall (1990: 433-454; 492-505). Introductions to set theory are again legion: see, inter alia, Allwood, Andersen and Dahl (1977: chs. 1 & 2), Lyons (1977: 154-161), Partee, ter Meulen and Wall (1990: 3-30), and Martin (1987: ch. 2).

3 Negation and Co-ordination

3.1 Compound sentences

The grammar presented in Chapter 2 generates some very basic sentences of English and the translation procedure enables each one to be associated with at least one representation in L_P (more than one, if it contains a homonym). While the number of sentences generated by the grammar, G_1, is relatively large (and can be made larger if more words are added to the lexicon), the language it generates is still **finite**. One of the properties that all natural languages are assumed to have is that they contain an infinite number of sentences. Since one of the goals of a theory of semantics, as we saw in Chapter 1, is to pair each sentence in a natural language with an interpretation, the theory must contain the means to provide an infinite number of interpretations. Furthermore, because natural languages are here being interpreted indirectly via a logical representation, the logical translation language must itself be infinite.

The reason that natural languages are infinite is that they are **recursive**. This means that expressions in certain categories may contain other expressions of the same category. For example, sentences may contain other sentences conjoined by the expressions *and* or *or*, or they may be connected by *if...then*, or a sentence may contain one or more repetitions of the expression *it is not the case that*. Some examples based on the grammar G_1 are given in (1).

(1) a. Ethel poisoned the cat and the dog howled.
   b. The lecturer gave the cake to the dog or the student gave the cake to the lecturer and the lecturer laughed or the dog howled.
   c. If the dog ate the cake, then the student poisoned the dog or the lecturer poisoned the dog.
   d. If it was not the case that it rained or it snowed, then it was not the case that it was not the case that it rained and it was not the case that it snowed.

The somewhat formal sentences in (1) (and an infinite number of others) can be generated by adding three recursive rules to the grammar, G_1, and a set of conjunctions to the lexicon. These are given in (2). The first rule, $13G_1$, introduces the conjunctions *and* and *or*, the second, $14G_1$, analyses *if...then* sentences and the third, $15G_1$, provides a type of recursive negative sentence.

(2) a. $13G_1$: S $\rightarrow$ S CONJ S.
   b. $14G_1$: S $\rightarrow$ if S_1, then S_2.
   c. $15G_1$: S $\rightarrow$ it is not the case that S.
   d. CONJ $\rightarrow$ {and, or}.

The negative sentences generated by Rule $15G_1$ are not elegant and in order to obtain more natural negative sentences, we can incorporate a set of non-recursive negation rules that provide the negative counterparts of the basic sentence rules of Chapter 2. Essentially, all the rules in G_1 that introduce a finite verb (V_i[+FIN], V_t[+FIN], V_{dt}[+FIN] and V_0[+FIN]) have a negative counterpart containing the word *didn't* which appears after the subject and before the non-finite, [-FIN], form of the verb, as in (3). The non-finite form of a verb in English is its base (or citation) form, without any tense or participial suffixes or other morphological modification.

(3) a. $1G_1$ (neg): S → NP didn't V_i[-FIN].
b. $2G_1$ (neg): S → NP_1 didn't V_t[-FIN] NP_2.
c. $3G_1$ (neg): S → NP_1 didn't V_{dt}[-FIN] NP_2 to NP_3.
d. $4G_1$ (neg): S → NP_1 didn't V_{dt}[-FIN] NP_3 NP_2.
e. $5G_1$ (neg): S → it didn't V_0[-FIN].

All the rules introducing the copula, on the other hand, have negative counterparts with *was* replaced by *wasn't*, as in (4).

(4) a. $8G_1$ (neg): S → NP_1 wasn't V_t[PAS] by NP_2.
b. $9G_1$ (neg): S → NP_1 wasn't V_{dt}[PAS] to NP_2 by NP_3.
c. $10G_1$ (neg): S → NP_1 wasn't V_{dt}[PAS] NP_2 by NP_3.
d. $11G_1$ (neg): S → NP_1 wasn't NP_2.
e. $12G_1$ (neg): S → NP wasn't A.

It would be better from the syntactic point of view, of course, if these negative rules could be directly related to their positive counterparts. The machinery for doing this will be introduced in Chapter 5, but for the moment we adopt the rules in (3) and (4) without any attempt at providing syntactic adequacy. However, the grammar now generates more natural sounding negative sentences like those in (5).

(5) a. If the dog didn't eat the cake, then Ethel wasn't happy.
b. It didn't rain and it didn't snow.
c. It was not the case that Bertie didn't sing.

3.2 Complex formulae

Having defined a set of negation and co-ordination rules, it is necessary to specify the way the sentences that are generated by those rules are translated into L_P and ultimately interpreted. Because the new syntactic rules are recursive, they allow the generation of an infinite number of sentences, as already mentioned. It is in situations like these that the reasons for the rule-to-rule translation procedure set up in Chapter 2 become apparent. The translation of a finite language may be achieved by listing the sentences generated by the grammar with their appropriate translations, but that of an infinite language cannot be achieved in the same way. The pairing up of syntactic and translation rules in the procedure discussed in the last chapter has the advantage that, provided that both the object language and the logical translation language can be defined by recursive rules, any sentence in the language can be paired with its translation, no matter how long it is. Indeed, it is theoretically possible to provide the translation of an infinitely long sentence in this way, even though no human being could produce such a sentence. Hence, the rule-to-rule hypothesis not only helps maintain compositionality, but also ensures that the translation of any sentence in the object language generated by a particular grammar has a well-formed and determinate translation (and hence interpretation).

In order to translate the syntactic rules in Section 3.1, the syntax of L_P itself has to be extended to make it recursive. Two new L_P syntactic rules are given in (6.a) and (6.c) introducing two new logical categories, Op_2 for two-place **propositional operators**, connecting two formulae and Op_1 for **one-place propositional operators** which modify only one formula. These categories contain only a few, logical, expressions which are given in (6.b) and (6.d). The operators in (6.b) and (6.d) have particular logical functions, shown by their common names: & is the **conjunction operator**, ∨ is the **disjunction operator**, → is the symbol for **material implication**, ↔ is the **equivalence operator** and ~ is the **negation operator**.

(6) a. $t \rightarrow t\ Op_2\ t$.
b. $Op_2 \rightarrow \{\rightarrow, \vee, \&, \leftrightarrow\}$.
c. $t \rightarrow Op_1(t)$.
d. $Op_1 \rightarrow \{\sim\}$.

The expressions in (6.b) and (6.d) are used to translate the English conjunctions introduced by the rules in (2.a) and (2.b) and in translating negative sentences. Like the copula in equative sentences, conjunctions and negative expressions are not translated using the general rule for translating lexical items given in (21) of Chapter 2. Instead, the relationship between the logical expressions and their English counterparts is specified directly by the rules in (7).

(7) a. and ⇒ &.
b. or ⇒ ∨ .
c. if...then ⇒ → .
d. it is not the case that ⇒ ~.

Given these correspondences and the L_P construction rules in (6), rules $13G_1$, $14G_1$ and $15G_1$ have the obvious translations given in (8). In these rules, the brackets that are introduced are important to the translation because they ensure that the logical expressions are unambiguous, as we will see below.

(8) a. $T13G_1$: S ⇒ (S' CONJ' S').
b. $T14G_1$: S ⇒ (S_1' → S_2').
c. $T15G_1$: S ⇒ ~(S').

The translation rules for all the negative rules in (4) and (5) are formed by putting the negation operator, ~, in front of the translation of the positive version of the rule. For example, $1G_1$ (neg) has the translation ~(V_i'(NP')), $8G_1$ (neg) has the translation ~(V_t'(NP_2,NP_1)), and $11G_1$ (neg) has the translation ~(NP_1 = NP_2) and so on.

Translation proceeds as described in Chapter 2: for each line in the derivation of a sentence, there is a corresponding translation of that line into L_P. An example derivation is given in (9) of the compound sentence *The cake was eaten by the dog and if Ethel laughed, then Ethel poisoned the dog.*

(9) a. S
$\Rightarrow$ S'.

b. S CONJ S — $13G_1$
$\Rightarrow$ (S' CONJ' S').

c. S CONJ if S_1 then S_2 — $14G_1$
$\Rightarrow (S' \text{ CONJ}' (S_1' \rightarrow S_2'))$.

d. NP_1 was V_t[PAS] by NP_2 CONJ if S_1 then S_2 — $8G_1$
$\Rightarrow (V_t'(NP_2',NP_1') \text{ CONJ}' (S_1' \rightarrow S_2'))$.

e. NP_1 was V_t[PAS] by NP_2 CONJ if NP V_i then S_2 — $1G_1$
$\Rightarrow (V_t'(NP_2',NP_1') \text{ CONJ}' (V_i'(NP') \rightarrow S_2))$.

f. NP_1 was V_t[PAS] by NP_2 CONJ if NP V_i then NP_3 V_t NP_4 — $2G_1$
$\Rightarrow (V_t'(NP_2',NP_1') \text{ CONJ}' (V_i'(NP') \rightarrow V_t(NP_3',NP_4')))$.

g. the N was V_t[PAS] by NP_2 CONJ if NP V_i then NP_3 V_t NP_4 — $7G_1$
$\Rightarrow (V_t'(NP_2',\text{the-N}') \text{ CONJ}' (V_i'(NP') \rightarrow V_t(NP_3',NP_4')))$.

h. the N was V_t[PAS] by N_{pr} CONJ if NP V_i then NP_3 V_t NP_4 — $6G_1$
$\Rightarrow (V_t'(N_{pr}',\text{the-N}') \text{ CONJ}' (V_i'(NP') \rightarrow V_t(NP_3',NP_4')))$.

i. the N was V_t[PAS] by N_{pr} CONJ if N_{pr} V_i then NP_3 V_t NP_4 — $6G_1$
$\Rightarrow (V_t'(N_{pr}',\text{the-N}') \text{ CONJ}' (V_i'(N_{pr}') \rightarrow V_t(NP_3',NP_4')))$.

j. the N was V_t[PAS] by N_{pr} CONJ if N_{pr} V_i then N_{pr} V_t NP_4 — $7G_1$
$\Rightarrow (V_t'(N_{pr}',\text{the-N}') \text{ CONJ}' (V_i'(N_{pr}') \rightarrow V_t(N_{pr}',NP_4')))$.

k. the N was V_t[PAS] by N_{pr} CONJ if N_{pr} V_i then N_{pr} V_t the N — $6G_1$
$\Rightarrow (V_t'(N_{pr}',\text{the-N}') \text{ CONJ}' (V_i'(N_{pr}') \rightarrow V_t(N_{pr}',\text{the-N}')))$.

l. The cake was eaten by Chester and if Ethel laughed, then Ethel poisoned the dog — Lex
$\Rightarrow$ (eat'(chester',the-cake') & (laugh'(ethel') $\rightarrow$ poison'(ethel',the-dog'))).

As before, derivations may also be represented by analysis trees, i.e. phrase structure trees annotated with their translations. (10), below, shows the tree associated with the sentence *If it didn't rain, it snowed*.

Exercise 3.1:
Translate the sentences in (1.a), (1.c), (5.a) and (5.c), using either the derivational or the analysis tree method.

In the grammar of the Chapter 2, the only source of ambiguity was homonymy, but logically more interesting forms of ambiguity arise when sentential co-ordination and negation are introduced into the grammar. For example, both (11.a) and (11.b), which are generated by G_1, are **structurally ambiguous**. That is, they each have two translations depending on the two syntactic structures that analyse them.

(10)

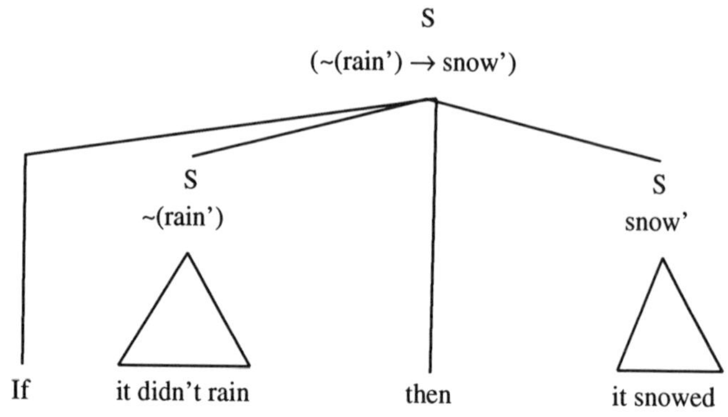

(11) a. It is not the case that the dog howled and Bertie screamed.
b. The cat ate the cake or the dog ate the cake and Fiona laughed.

The ambiguity in (11.a) depends on the relative **scopes** of the conjunction *and* and the negation *it is not the case that*. On one interpretation, the latter has scope over the conjunction of *the dog howled* and *Bertie screamed* whereas on the second interpretation the reverse is the case: the conjunction has scope over the negation which only has scope over *the dog howled*. In the grammar fragment, G_1, the two translations that correspond to these two interpretations are derived by applying the rules $13G_1$ and $15G_1$ in different orders. If the latter is applied first, then the reading of the sentence is that the dog did not howl and Bertie did not scream as in (12). The interpretation in which the dog did not howl but Bertie did scream is the one given to the translation derived by applying rule $13G_1$ before $15G_1$ as in (13).

As we will see in Section 3.3, the two L_P expressions in (12.h) and (13.h) have different truth-conditions and so give rise to the two interpretations described above. The difference between the two expressions is shown by the bracketing of the component formulae which indicate the relative scopes of the two logical operators, ~ and &. In the first expression, (12.h), *~(howl'(the-dog') & scream'(bertie'))* the connective, &, comes inside the brackets that are introduced by rule $15G_1$ in (12.b). These brackets define the domain over which the negation has effect. This is called the **scope of the negation** and the conjunction operator comes inside this. In the second expression, (13.h), *(~(howl'(the-dog')) & scream'(bertie'))* the reverse is the case. The negation operator now comes within the scope of the conjunction, because it appears within the brackets introduced by $13G_1$ in (13.b). The scope of a connective is crucial to the interpretation of any formula containing it. Where formulae contain different operators and connectives, different readings result from the relative scopes of the latter. A second example appears in (14) where the two translations of (11.b) are given. The first formula has the disjunction operator within the scope of the conjunction, giving the reading where Fiona is laughing and either the dog or the cat ate the cake. The second reading reverses the scopes of the connectives to give the reading where the cat ate the cake and either the dog ate the cake or Fiona laughed. It is, therefore, very important to include the brackets introduced by rules $13G_1$, $14G_1$ and $15G_1$, whenever there is more than one conjunction or negation in the sentence. Without them, the L_P expressions translating the sentences remain ambiguous, contrary to the requirement that L_P be an unambiguous language. Certain pairs of brackets, e.g. the very outermost ones in a formula, do not really serve a useful purpose and will often be omitted and, later on in the book, when the reader has more familiarity with the logical system, other sets of brackets will occasionally be omitted where there is no risk of ambiguity.

(12) a. S
⇒ S'.
b. it is not the case that S — $15G_1$
⇒ ~(S').
c. it is not the case that S CONJ S — $13G_1$
⇒ ~((S' CONJ' S')).
d. it is not the case that NP V_i CONJ S — $1G_1$
⇒ ~((V_i'(NP') CONJ' S')).
e. it is not the case that N_{pr} V_i CONJ S — $6G_1$
⇒ ~((V_i'(the-N') CONJ' S')).
f. it is not the case that N_{pr} V_i CONJ NP V_i — $1G_1$
⇒ ~((V_i'(the-N') CONJ' V_i'(NP'))).
g. it is not the case that N_{pr} V_i CONJ N_{pr} V_i — $6G_1$
⇒ ~((V_i'(the-N') CONJ' V_i'(N_{pr}'))).
h. it is not the case that the dog howled and Bertie screamed — Lex
⇒ ~((howl'(the-dog') & scream'(bertie'))).

(13) a. S
⇒ S'.
b. S CONJ S — $13G_1$
⇒ (S' CONJ' S').
c. it is not the case that S CONJ S — $15G_1$
⇒ (~(S') CONJ' S').
d. it is not the case that NP V_i CONJ S — $1G_1$
⇒ (~(V_i'(NP')) CONJ' S').
e. it is not the case that N_{pr} V_i CONJ S — $6G_1$
⇒ (~(V_i'(the-N')) CONJ' S').
f. it is not the case that N_{pr} V_i CONJ NP V_i — $1G_1$
⇒ (~(V_i'(the-N')) CONJ' V_i'(NP')).
g. it is not the case that N_{pr} V_i CONJ N_{pr} V_i — $6G_1$
⇒ (~(V_i'(the-N')) CONJ' V_i'(N_{pr}')).
h. it is not the case that the dog howled and Bertie screamed — Lex
⇒ (~(howl'(the-dog')) & scream'(bertie')).

(14) a. ((eat'(the-cat',the-cake') ∨ eat'(the-dog',the-cake')) & laugh'(fiona')).
b. (eat'(the-cat',the-cake') ∨ (eat'(the-dog',the-cake') & laugh'(fiona'))).

Exercise 3.2:
Letting the translation of *Fiona laughed* be represented by the symbol p and that of *Bertie screamed* be represented by the symbol q, how many different translations into L_P do each of the following have?

i. It is not the case that it is not the case that Fiona laughed or Bertie screamed.
ii. Fiona laughed or it was not the case that Fiona laughed and Bertie screamed.

3.3 Interpretation

We must now turn our attention to the interpretation of formulae that contain the logical connectives or the negation operator. In defining the truth-conditions of complex formulae that contain these expressions, the internal structure of the component formulae is irrelevant as it does not affect the way the truth or falsity of the formula is computed. All that is significant is whether the component formulae of a complex formula are true or false, not what the predicates and arguments that make up these formulae denote in the model. For this reason, ~, &, ∨, and → are known as **truth-conditional connectives**. This section shows how the connectives in L_P contribute to the truth-conditional meaning of the formulae in which they appear, taking each in turn and beginning with the negation operator ~.

3.3.1 Negation

The simplest of the five connectives is the negation operator, ~, used in the translations of the negated sentence rules in G_1. This operator takes only a single formula in its scope and reverses the truth value of that formula. In other words, if a formula ϕ is false ~(ϕ) is true and if ϕ is true then ~(ϕ) is false. This provides the truth-conditions for negative formulae, which can be stated as in (15).

(15) **Truth-conditions for negation**: A formula ~(S') is true if, and only if, S' is false. ~(S') is false otherwise.

Using (15) it is possible to work out the truth value of negative formulae with respect to particular models. For example, the truth value of the formula *~(run'(chester'))* with respect to M_1 can be worked out as follows:

(16) a. run'(chester') is true in M_1 iff the extension of chester', i.e. **DOG**, is a member of the set of entities denoted by run', i.e. {**DOG,CAT**}.
b. Since **DOG** ∈ {**DOG,CAT**} is true, run'(chester') is true in M_1 and so ~(run'(chester')) is false in M_1.

Logicians have devised another way of representing the truth-conditions for operators like ~, and connectives like &, etc., which is, perhaps, clearer than a verbal statement. This method sets out a **truth table** giving all the possible combinations of truth and falsity for all the component formulae and showing the truth value of the resultant complex formula containing the appropriate connective. To show the truth conditions of the connectives using the **truth table** method, the component formulae are represented by **propositional variables**. Variables do not have a fixed interpretation in some model, like constants, but range over extensions of the appropriate sort. Given that formulae denote truth values, propositional variables range over the values true and false. Such variables are usually represented by lower case letters from the middle of the alphabet: *p* (mnemonic for proposition) is used where only one variable is required, *p* and *q* are used when two are needed and *r* is added if a third is required.

To draw a truth table for a connective, you take an appropriate number of propositional variables, one in the case of negation and two for the other connectives. Underneath the variables you write the letter **t** or the letter **f** standing for truth and falsity, respectively, and put all possible combinations of the letters on different lines. If there is one component formula in the complex formula, then there are only two lines, one for **t** and one for **f**, while if there are two formulae there are four lines, for cases where both formulae are true, where both are false and where they differ in truth value. Each combination of truth and falsity is associated with the appropriate truth value for the complex proposition involving the operator or connective. Hence, for negation, there are two lines in the truth table and the resulting complex formula has the opposite truth value to the component formula. This is shown in (17) where the variable p stands for the component formula.

(17) **Truth table for negation**

p	~p
t	f
f	t

The use of variables in truth tables means that we can replace them by actual formulae to get the particular truth value of a compound formula very easily. All that needs to be done is to take a component formula, e.g. *(ethel' = the-golfer')* that translates *Ethel was the golfer* and replace all occurrences of a variable in a table with this formula. Once the truth value of the component formula (or formulae) with respect to some model has been determined, it is possible just to go to the line in the truth table with that truth value and read off the truth value for the complex formula. Thus, to find out the truth value of *~(ethel' = the-golfer')*, we need first to determine the truth or falsity of *(ethel' = the-golfer')* with respect to M_1 by checking whether the expression *ethel'* denotes an entity identical to that denoted by the expression *the-golfer'* in that model. Since this is the case, *(ethel' = the-golfer')* is true with respect to M_1. Looking at the line in the truth table for negation where the propositional variable has the value **t**, we find the truth value of the negated formula shown to the right, i.e. **f**. Hence, *~(ethel' = the-golfer')* is false with respect to the model M_1.

Negation in L_P is recursive and the truth-conditions given in (15) allow the truth value of formulae that contain more than one or two embedded formulae to be computed in a mechanical fashion. For example, the translation of the sentence *It is not the case that the lecturer didn't scream* contains two instances of the negation operator, i.e. *~(~(scream'(the-lecturer')))*. To find out the truth value of this formula with respect to some model, we need to find out the truth of the most deeply embedded formula, *scream'(the-lecturer')*. The truth-conditions for ~ then provide the truth value of *~(scream'(the-lecturer'))* and a re-application of these truth-conditions yields the value of the formula *~(~(scream'(the-lecturer')))*. Thus, the truth value of this particular formula with respect to M_1 can be worked out as in (18).

(18) a. scream'(the-lecturer') is false in M_1 because **$WOMAN_2$**, the extension of the-lecturer', is not a member of Ø, the extension of scream' in M_1.

b. Hence, ~(scream'(the-lecturer')) is true in M_1 by the truth-conditions for negation.

c. Hence, ~(~(scream'(the-lecturer'))) is false in M_1 again by the truth-conditions for negation.

A more succinct way of showing these steps is again to use a truth table. There are a number of ways of showing this, but we shall adopt the clearest. Here you write a propositional variable *p* on the left with its two possible truth values, then you write the next embedded formula to its right with the corresponding truth values, and so on, until you reach the largest formula. At every stage you use the truth table for negation to give you the truth values for the current column by treating the previous column as the base formula. All you have to do then is find out the actual truth value of the formula that you are substituting for *p*, and look along that line to get the truth value of the whole compound formula. The truth-conditions for a doubly negated formula can thus be represented by the truth table in (19) which combines two instances of the truth table for negation.

(19)

p	~p	~(~p)
t	f	t
f	t	f

The truth table for ~(~*p*) is identical to that for *p* itself. This means that in logical form double negatives give rise to the same interpretation as the corresponding positive. In other words, ~(~*p*) has exactly the same truth value as *p*, whatever *p* happens to be. Thus, something that may not have been completely obvious from just looking at the truth-conditions for negation becomes obvious when we use truth tables. In translating sentences with double negatives in them, however, it is often the case that only single negation is intended. For example, translating *Chester never did nothing* with two negatives, the formula expressed is semantically equivalent to *Chester always did something*. It is often the case, however, that sentences containing multiple negatives in many languages serve only to express a single negation, the extra negatives merely serving as reinforcements of this and not as independent negations. For example, the expression *Chester never did nothing* in many dialects of English is interpreted as *Chester never did anything*; the second negative expression *nothing* does not independently negate but emphasises the negation of the expression *never*. In the logical language L_P, on the other hand, multiple negatives are always interpreted as independent negations. Thus, *~(~(p))* is always equivalent to *p*, never to *~(p)*. Hence, if a sentence in some natural language is analysed as containing multiple negative expressions with only a single negation intended, that sentence must be translated into L_P with only one negation operator.

3.3.2 Conjunction

Specifying the truth-conditions for formulae containing &, the logical translation of *and*, involves reference to the truth values of the two formulae that the expression conjoins: such a formula is true only when both component formulae are true and is false in every other situation. This is guaranteed by the truth-conditions stated in (20) which can also be represented by the truth table in (21).

(20) **Truth-conditions for conjunction**: A formula (S_1' & S_2') is true iff S_1' is true and S_2' is also true. (S_1' & S_2') is false otherwise.

(21) **Truth Table for &**

p	q	p & q
t	t	t
t	f	f
f	t	f
f	f	f

To interpret a formula containing & thus involves finding out the truth values of the formulae it conjoins and then checking the truth table to ascertain the truth or falsity of the complex expression. For example, the translation of *The dog howled and the cat ate the dog* with respect to M_1 is *(howl'(the- dog') & eat'(the-cat',the-dog'))*. The steps in interpretation of this formula with respect to M_1 are set out in (22), a situation that corresponds to the third line of the truth table in (21).

(22) a. howl'(the-dog') is true in M_1 because the entity denoted by the-dog' in M_1 is a member of the extension of howl' in M_1, i.e. **DOG** $\in$ {**DOG**}.

b. eat'(the-cat',the-dog') is false in M_1 because the ordered pair formed from the entities denoted by the-cat' and the-dog', respectively, are not in the set of ordered pairs denoted by eat' in M_1, i.e. **<CAT,DOG>** $\notin$ {**<DOG,CAKE>**}.

c. Hence, (howl'(the-dog') & eat'(the-cat', the-dog')) is false in M_1 by the truth-conditions for &.

More complex examples can be constructed using negation and conjunction. Let us work through an example in detail, interpreting the sentence *It is not the case that Ethel loathed Chester and Ethel wasn't happy*. The structure of one of the formulae this ambiguous sentence can be translated into is set out in tree form in (23) which is parallel, of course, to the structure of the translated sentence.

(23)

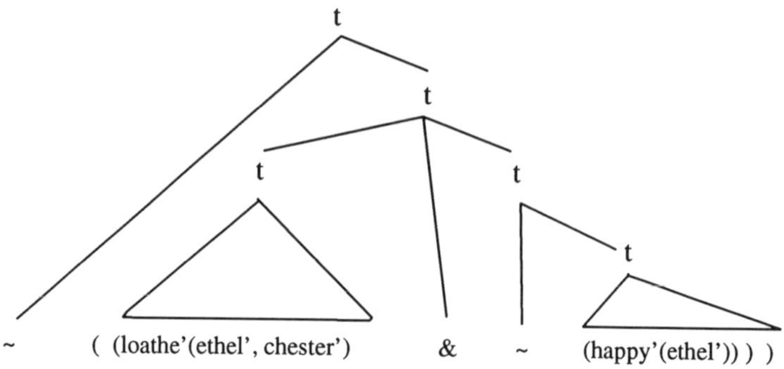

The interpretation of this formula begins with the specification of the truth-conditions of the whole complex formula and works downwards to those of the simplex component formulae. Once we have reached this level, the truth of the whole expression can be ascertained by finding the extensions of the constants in the expression in some model. Thus, the interpretation procedure of (22) with respect to the model M_1 follows the steps laid out in (24) which begins by specifying the truth-conditions of the outermost operator, i.e. negation, and then moves on to those for the conjunction connective, &. Since one of the conjuncts is negative, the truth-conditions for negation are repeated. Finally, the truth of the simplex propositions is checked with respect to the model by applying the truth-conditions for two-place and one-place predicates, as set out in the last chapter. Having ascertained these truth values, those of the more complex formulae are worked out until we finally get to the operator with the widest scope, where the truth of the whole formula can be computed.

(24) a. ~((loathe'(ethel',chester') & ~(happy'(ethel')))). is true in M_1 iff (loathe'(ethel',chester') & ~(happy'(ethel'))) is false (by (15)).

b. (loathe'(ethel',chester') & ~(happy'(ethel'))) is true iff loathe'(ethel',chester') is true and ~(happy'(ethel')) is also true (by (20)).

c. loathe'(ethel',chester') is true iff the ordered pair consisting of the entities denoted by ethel' and chester', respectively, is in the set denoted by loathe'.

d. Since, ethel' denotes **WOMAN**$_1$ and chester' denotes **DOG** and loathe' denotes {**<MAN**$_1$**,DOG>**,**<MAN**$_2$**,DOG>**,**<WOMAN**$_1$**,DOG>**, **<WOMAN**$_2$**,DOG>**,**<WOMAN**$_2$**,MAN**$_1$**>**}, loathe'(ethel',chester') is true in M_1.

e. ~(happy'(ethel')) is true iff happy'(ethel') is false (by (15)).

f. happy'(ethel') is true iff the entity denoted by ethel' is in the set denoted by happy'.

g. Since the entity denoted by ethel' is $\mathbf{WOMAN_1}$ and the extension of happy' is {$\mathbf{WOMAN_1}$,$\mathbf{WOMAN_2}$,$\mathbf{MAN_1}$}, happy'(ethel') is true in M_1.
h. Hence, ~(happy'(ethel')) is false in M_1.
i. hence, (loathe'(ethel',chester') & ~(happy'(ethel'))) is false in M_1.
j. hence, ~((loathe'(ethel',chester') & ~(happy'(ethel')))) is true in M_1.

As before, the truth table method can be used to get the same result. Firstly, the structure of the formula is made more transparent by replacing the simplex formulae by the variables *p* and *q* to get the formula *~(p &~(q))*. Then, a truth table is set up showing all the combinations of the truth values of the basic formulae and columns are constructed showing the truth values of each of the more complex formulae within the expression. The final column gives the truth value of the whole expression determined from the combination of truth values of the basic formulae. Once the truth values of the simplex formulae have been ascertained with respect to a particular model, the final value of the expression can be read off the appropriate line. Thus, line 1 in (25) gives the truth value of the expression in M_1 where *p* is associated with the formula *loathe'(ethel',chester')* and *q* is associated with the formula *happy'(ethel')*.

(25)

p	q	~q	p & ~q	~(p & ~q)
t	t	f	f	t
t	f	t	t	f
f	t	f	f	t
f	f	t	f	t

Exercise 3.3:
Work through the interpretation of the other formula of L_P that translates *It was not the case that Ethel loathed Chester and Ethel wasn't happy*, using both the method illustrated in (24) and the truth table method illustrated in (25).

According to G_1, a sentence containing two or more instances of the conjunction *and* has two or more derivations. Hence, they have more than two translations, because of the parallelism between syntactic derivation and translation. Thus, *Bertie laughed and Fiona laughed and the dog howled* has the two translations in (26) where the difference resides in the comparative scopes of the two instances of &, shown by the bracketing.

(26) a. (laugh'(bertie') & (laugh'(fiona') & howl'(the-dog'))).
b. ((laugh'(bertie') & laugh'(fiona')) & howl'(the-dog')).

This ambiguity does not, however, give rise to any difference in interpretation. The truth-conditions for (26.a) and (26.b) are identical: three formulae conjoined by & give rise to a true formula if, and only if, all three component formulae are true. This can be proved by constructing truth tables for the two readings, representing the basic formulae as *p*, *q* and *r*. Because the pattern of truth and falsity is identical in the first and final columns, the different formulae must have the same truth-conditions: they are true or false in the same situations. This is shown in the truth tables in (27) and (28).

(27)

p	q	r	(q & r)	(p & (q & r))
t	t	t	t	t
t	t	f	f	f
t	f	t	f	f
f	t	t	t	f
t	f	f	f	f
f	t	f	f	f
f	f	t	f	f
f	f	f	f	f

(28)

p	q	r	(p & q)	((p & q) & r)
t	t	t	t	t
t	t	f	t	f
t	f	t	f	f
f	t	t	f	f
t	f	f	f	f
f	t	f	f	f
f	f	t	f	f
f	f	f	f	f

In fact, no matter how many formulae are strung together using the conjunction connective, the actual bracketing of the conjoined formulae does not matter to the final truth value (provided that no other connective appears in the expression). Thus, for any formulae *p*, *q* and *r*, *(p & (q & r))* has the same truth value as *((p & q) & r)*. This property is called **associativity** and & is known as an **associative operator**. Associativity is a property also found with certain arithmetical functions like addition and multiplication (but not subtraction and division). Thus, for example, $(3 + 2) + 4 = 3 + (2 + 4) = 9$ and $(2 \times 3) \times 4 = 2 \times (3 \times 4) = 24$ or, in general, $(x + y) + z = x + (y + z)$ and $(x \times y) \times z = x \times (y \times z)$. This is an important property which, as we shall see in Chapter 7, enables us to make some useful inferences from formulae with this structure. Nothing more will be said about this here, but remember that in working out the truth value of a formula containing a string of formulae all connected by & (or sentences conjoined by *and*) the different derivations do not affect the truth-conditions; the ambiguity is only apparent, not real. In other words, our translation procedure overdisambiguates, as it were. But this is not a problem, because the interpretation procedure ensures that no semantic ambiguity is produced.

3.3.3 *Disjunction*

The next connective is ∨ which we have used to translate English *or*. This is known as the **logical disjunction operator** and a formula containing this connective is true when at least one of the component formulae is true:

(29) **Truth-conditions for disjunction**: A formula of the form (S_1' ∨ S_2') is true, iff S_1' is true or S_2' is true. (S_1' ∨ S_2') is false otherwise.

(30) **Truth table for disjunction**

p	q	p ∨ q
t	t	t
t	f	t
f	t	t
f	f	f

It follows from (29) that the sentence *The lecturer poisoned the cat or Chester howled* is translated into a formula that is true in M_1, as can be seen from the detailed interpretation in (31).

(31) a. (poison'(the-lecturer',the-cat') ∨ howl'(chester')) is true with respect to M_1 iff poison'(the-lecturer',the-cat') is true or howl'(chester') is true.

b. poison'(the-lecturer',the-cat') is true iff the ordered pair consisting of the entity denoted by the-lecturer' and that denoted by the-cat' is a member of the set denoted by poison' in M_1.

c. Since the entity denoted by the-lecturer' is **WOMAN₂**, that denoted by the-cat' is **CAT** and the extension of poison' is {<**CAKE**,**DOG**>}, poison'(the-lecturer',the-cat') is false in M_1.

d. howl'(chester') is true iff the entity denoted by chester' is a member of the set denoted by howl'.

e. Since the entity denoted by chester' is **DOG** and that of howl' is {**DOG**}, howl'(chester') is true in M_1.

f. Since howl'(chester') is true in M_1, (poison'(the-lecturer',the-cat') ∨ howl'(chester')) is true with respect to M_1.

You may have already noticed that there are some odd things about this treatment of disjunction, particularly in the fact that a disjunctive formula is true if both of its disjuncts are true. For example, under this interpretation the formula translating the sentence *The student was crazy or the student was happy* is true in a model in which both disjuncts are true. Yet we often tend, when using disjunctions, to assume that one of the disjuncts must be false if the other is true. Such disjunctions are said to have an **exclusive** interpretation, one which disallows situations where both disjuncts are true. For example, on hearing the sentence in (32), a speaker of English would normally assume that the jacket being referred to was not simultaneously red and blue, a situation that is not excluded by the truth of the formula in (32.b), according to the truth-conditions for the **inclusive disjunction** operator ∨.

(32) a. The jacket was blue or red.
b. (blue'(the-jacket') $\vee$ red'(the-jacket')).

The fact that sentences like (32) receive an interpretation that excludes the situation in which both disjuncts are true can be captured directly in the semantics by interpreting *or*, not as $\vee$ in (30) above, but as a different operator $\vee_e$ which has the truth-conditions specified in (33) which gives rise to the truth table in (34).

(33) **Truth-conditions for Exclusive Disjunction**: A formula of the form (S_1' $\vee_e$ S_2') is true, iff S_1' is true and S_2' is false or S_2' is true and S_1' is false. (S_1' $\vee_e$ S_2') is false otherwise.

(34) **Truth table for exclusive disjunction**

p	q	p $\vee_e$ q
t	t	f
t	f	t
f	t	t
f	f	f

There is, however, a compelling reason for not translating the English conjunction *or* as $\vee_e$ and thus interpreting all disjunctive sentences exclusively. While many uses of disjunction do imply that only one of the disjuncts holds, there are many occasions where we do not want to preclude a situation in which both disjoined formulae are true. For example, the propositions expressed by the sentences in (35) are not obviously false of situations where both of the disjuncts are true, i.e. where there are students who have a private income and rich parents, or where a job applicant has two Higher and five 'O' grade passes, or where the lecturer does not want to rule out the possibility of a zealous student reading both articles.

(35) a. Students who have a private income or rich parents are better off at University than those who do not.
b. Applicants for the job must have two Higher, or five Ordinary, grade passes.
c. You must read the article on presupposition or the article on implicature by next Wednesday.

The sentences in (35) (and many others like them) show that exclusive disjunction on its own makes too strong a claim about the truth-conditions of English *or*, since inclusive, as well as exclusive, readings of disjunctive sentences must be allowed for. For this reason, *or* is translated as $\vee$ and interpreted as inclusive disjunction. The problem of accounting for the exclusive readings of *or* as illustrated in (32) will be addressed in Chapter 7 where different sorts of inference are discussed.

As can be seen from checking truth tables, disjunction, both inclusive and exclusive, like conjunction, is associative. Thus, $(p \vee (q \vee r))$ has the same truth-conditions as $((p \vee q) \vee r)$: they are both true if any one of the component formulae is true. (The reader is invited to show that this is indeed so by drawing the appropriate truth tables.) However, when *or* is used to combine clauses which are negative or contain *and*, genuine ambiguities may result. For example, the expression *It is not the case that it rained or it snowed and the dog howled* has no fewer than five different interpretations, depending on the scopes of the negation, the disjunction and the conjunction. Letting *p* stand for the formula *rain'*, *q* stand for *snow'* and *r* stand for *howl'(the-dog')*, we get the schematic formulae in (36). The two truth tables in (37) and (38) show that at least the readings in (36.a) and (36.b) have different truth-conditions. A formula of the form of (36.a) is true only when p and q are both false and r is true, while one with the form in (36.b) is true in all situations except where r is true and either p or q or both are also true.

(36) a. (~((p ∨ q)) & r).
b. ~(((p ∨ q) & r)).
c. ~((p ∨ (q & r))).
d. ((~(p) ∨ q) & r).
e. (~(p) ∨ (q & r)).

(37)

p	q	r	(p ∨ q)	((p ∨ q) & r)	~(((p ∨ q)) & r))
t	t	t	t	t	f
t	t	f	t	f	t
t	f	t	t	t	f
f	t	t	t	t	f
t	f	f	t	f	t
f	t	f	t	f	t
f	f	t	f	f	t
f	f	f	f	f	t

(38)

p	q	r	(p ∨ q)	~((p ∨ q))	(~((p ∨ q)) & r))
t	t	t	t	f	f
t	t	f	t	f	f
t	f	t	t	f	f
f	t	t	t	f	f
t	f	f	t	f	f
f	t	f	t	f	f
f	f	t	f	t	t
f	f	f	f	t	f

Exercise 3.4:
Write out the truth tables for the other formulae in (36). Which, if any, of these interpretations do you think would be the most likely ones to be given to an utterance of the expression *It is not the case that it rained or it snowed and the dog howled* by a speaker of English and why do you think this might be the case? Does the expression *It didn't rain or snow and the dog howled* have the possible translations into L_P shown in (36)? If not, why not?

There is another property that should be mentioned with respect to disjunction and that is that the relative order of the **disjuncts** is not truth-conditionally significant. Thus, the sentence *It rained or it snowed* has the same truth-conditions as *It snowed or it rained.* This is reflected in the truth-conditions for disjunction given above, which do not mention the order of the formulae, thus ensuring that $(p \vee q)$ is truth-conditionally equivalent to $(q \vee p)$.This property is technically known as **commutativity** and disjunction is a **commutative operator**. Commutativity does indeed seem to be a property of English disjunctive sentences, as shown by the fact that *Bertie laughed or Fiona sang* may be used to describe the same situations as *Fiona sang or Bertie laughed.* On the other hand, most speakers of English consider there to be a semantic difference between *Bertie laughed and Fiona sang* and *Fiona sang and Bertie laughed.* However, the conjunction operator also turns out to be commutative in L_P, since $(p \;\&\; q)$ is truth-conditionally equivalent to $(q \;\&\; p)$, as readers can check for themselves. This potential problem will be put to one side for the moment and taken up again in Chapter 7.

3.3.4 Implication

The final connective used in the grammar fragment of Section 3.1 is the one that we have used to translate English *if...then* sentences. This is $\rightarrow$, the logicians' **material implication**. A formula consisting of two formulae, p and q, conjoined by $\rightarrow$ is interpreted as true, provided that the second formula, q, called the **consequent**, is true whenever the first formula, p, called the **antecedent**, is also true. A formula of the form $p \rightarrow q$ is thus false only when p is true and q is false. The truth-conditions for formulae containing $\rightarrow$ are given in (39) and its associated truth table is given in (40).

(39) **Truth-conditions for material implication**: A formula $(S_1' \rightarrow S_2')$ is true iff S_1' is false or S_2' is true. $(S_1' \rightarrow S_2')$ is false, otherwise.

(40) **Truth table for material implication**:

p	q	$p \rightarrow q$
t	t	t
t	f	f
f	t	t
f	f	t

A good way to help you remember the truth table is to remember the sentence in (41).

(41) If Jo is over six feet tall, then Jo is over four feet tall.

There are only three possible ways that someone's height may relate to being over (i.e. greater than) four feet or over six feet: either they are over six foot and hence over four foot, or they are under six foot but over four or they are under four foot. No-one, however, can be under four foot but over six. These possibilities are illustrated in the diagram in (42) where the variable *p* stands for the formula translating *Jo is over six foot tall* and *q* stands for *Jo is over four foot tall.* Notice that the fourth situation cannot be represented diagrammatically and this gives you the situation in which the conditional would have to be false.

(42) If Jo is over six feet tall, then Jo is over four feet tall

Material implication is neither associative nor commutative. *If it rained, then Bertie was happy* does not mean the same as *If Bertie was happy, then it rained.* This is guaranteed by the truth-conditions in (39), as in the former case the formula *rain' → happy'(bertie')* is true provided that it is not raining, but Bertie is happy, while *happy'(bertie') → rain'* is true with respect to the latter situation. The non-associativity of → can be shown by looking at the truth tables associated with the two schematic formulae $((p \rightarrow q) \rightarrow r)$ and $(p \rightarrow (q \rightarrow r))$. As can be seen by comparing (43) and (44), the formula $((p \rightarrow q) \rightarrow r)$ is false in three situations, i.e. where r is false and either p and q are both true or where p is false. The latter formula *(p → (q → r))* is, however, only false where *p* and *q* are both true, but *r* is false. The definition of the truth-conditional meaning of *if ... then* thus ensures that the indirect interpretation of *If if it rained then the dog howled then Bertie screamed* (a sentence that is better expressed in English by *If, when it rained, then the dog howled, then Bertie screamed*) is truth-conditionally distinct from *If it rained then if the dog howled then Bertie screamed*.

(43)

p	q	r	(p → q)	((p → q) → r)
t	t	t	t	t
t	t	f	t	f
t	f	t	f	t
f	t	t	t	t
t	f	f	f	t
f	t	f	t	f
f	f	t	t	t
f	f	f	t	f

(44)

p	q	r	(q → r)	(p → (q → r))
t	t	t	t	t
t	t	f	f	f
t	f	t	t	t
f	t	t	t	t
t	f	f	t	t
f	t	f	f	t
f	f	t	t	t
f	f	f	t	t

There are, however, strange things about this interpretation of *if...then*. One of the peculiar aspects has to do with the situations in which it is possible to assert a true conditional formula. The only situation in which it is possible for a conditional to be false according to the truth table in (40) seems intuitively plausible. Consider the sentence *If it rained, then it didn't snow*. A situation in which it was raining and it was also snowing would be a counterexample to the conditional statement and sufficient to falsify it. This is, of course, exactly what the truth-conditions for → tell us, because the antecedent would be true but the consequent false. Hence, the conditional formula must be false. The assertion of this sentence in other situations involving rain and snow would give rise, however, to the expression of a true statement which appears much less intuitively satisfying. In a situation in which it was raining and it wasn't snowing, the sentence would express a true proposition. The situation could be said to be a confirming instance of the conditional, but it would be most peculiar to utter such a sentence unless the speaker were committed to there being a causal connection between rain and a lack of snow.

Knowing simply that two formulae happen to be true does not justify a belief in any sort of a connection between them, something that would be conveyed by the assertion of a conditional containing them. Even more peculiar would be the assertion of *If it rained, then it didn't snow* with respect to a situation in which it was not raining but was also not snowing. The truth table for material implication, however, ensures that the conditional formula is true because the formula expressed by the antecedent is false.

These peculiarities may be explained, not by the truth-conditions of *if..then*, but from what we consider to be an appropriate utterance of a conditional sentence. In other words, associating material implication with natural language conditionals merely gives the central core of the meaning of *if...then*, its truth-conditions. It has nothing to say about the appropriateness or otherwise of the assertion of a conditional statement. Hence, irrespective of the connectivity of antecedent and consequent, someone who utters *if it rained then it didn't snow* with respect to a situation in which it did indeed rain and did not snow, makes a true assertion, the situation being a confirming instance of the conditional. With respect to situations in which it didn't snow and also did not rain, the sentence may also be truthfully asserted, because there are many situations in which it didn't snow (e.g. if the sun was shining). The sentence could also be truthfully asserted with respect to the last possible situation, one in which it is not raining but it is snowing. If the sentence is asserted as a general rule about the weather, a day on which rain didn't fall, but snow did does not disconfirm the rule. Thus, it would be possible for someone to say *See, it's true. If it rained, then it didn't snow.* Isn't this a true statement? It is certainly not a false one, and given that the theory of truth put forward in this book is **bivalent**, and so only allows formulae to have one of two possible truth values, the sentence must express a true proposition with respect to this situation. The truth table in (40) does, therefore, provide some of the meaning of simple conditionals in English, and for the moment let us accept it as a reasonable interpretation of the *if..then* sentences generated by G_1. We will, however, return to a discussion of the adequacy of material implication as the interpretation of natural language conditionals in Chapter 7.

3.3.5 Equivalence

Logicians usually operate with another logical connective which is not in G_1, but which we have been using in the definitions of truth-conditions. This is the **equivalence operator** which is represented in L_P as $\leftrightarrow$ and in English by the phrase *if, and only if.* We could introduce this into the grammar by putting the English phrase into the lexicon as a CONJ so that it could be introduced via the same syntactic rule, Rule 13, that introduces *and* and *or*. Although the phrase is little used in everyday English, adopting it into the grammar fragment allows us at least to see what contribution it makes to the truth-conditions of the definitions that are given. The truth-conditions of the equivalence connective, $\leftrightarrow$, are captured by requiring a formula $p \leftrightarrow q$ to be true just in case p and q have the same truth value. The truth-conditions for this connective are spelled out in (45) and its corresponding truth table is given in (46).

(45) **Truth-conditions for equivalence**: A formula $(S_1' \leftrightarrow S_2')$ is true iff either S_1' is true and S_2' is true or S_1' is false and S_2' is false. $(S_1' \leftrightarrow S_2')$ is false, otherwise.

(46) **Truth Table for equivalence**

p	q	p ↔ q
t	t	t
t	f	f
f	t	f
f	f	t

Notice that equivalence has the same truth-conditions as a double material implication conjoined by &, as you can see by comparing the truth table in (47) with that in (46). The final columns in these two tables show the same patterns of truth and falsity for the same combinations of truth and falsity of the component formulae, thus proving their semantic equivalence.

(47)

p	q	(p → q)	(q → p)	((p → q) & (q → p))
t	t	t	t	t
t	f	f	t	f
f	t	t	f	f
f	f	t	t	t

Exercise 3.5:
(46) and (47) show that a formula of the form $(p \leftrightarrow q)$ is truth-conditionally equivalent to one of the form $((p \rightarrow q) \ \& \ (q \rightarrow p))$. Write out the truth table for the formula $((p \leftrightarrow q) \leftrightarrow ((p \rightarrow q) \ \& \ (q \rightarrow p)))$. What, if anything, is odd about this truth table?

3.4 Formal interpretation

The specification of the truth-conditions for formulae containing the connectives completes the interpretation of the logical language L_P used to translate the set of English sentences generated by G_1. This informal definition of the interpretation of L_P provides (indirectly) the truth-conditional semantics of a small fragment of English. We end this chapter by providing a more rigorous definition of the theory set up so far. This is primarily concerned with the replacement of informal English as the **metalanguage** and the definition of models and the theory of interpretation by a more formal language. The metalanguage that is defined in this section is still partly based on English, but is much less open to misinterpretation and provides a properly rigorous and unambiguous specification of the whole of the interpretation procedure. Formalisation of this sort is, as in any discipline, an aid to understanding and shows precisely what the theory being formalised predicts. It is to this task that we now address ourselves. The notation and the points made in this section are of necessity somewhat technical, but no concepts are introduced that have not already been informally presented. Those unused to formal theories should try not to overreact to the symbolic nature of the formalism. A symbol is not something mystical or arcane, but a tool to aid analysis and understanding. When presented with a string of symbols, readers should take care to recall what each symbol is intended to represent and to assign the symbol the intended interpretation. Unlike words or phrases in natural languages, each symbol in a formalism is unambiguous and the pedantry of the metalanguage is designed so that there can be no possibility of ambiguity. The formalism thus provides an unambiguous and rigorous specification of what has been said about truth-conditional meaning in this chapter and in Chapter 2 which allows the predictions of the theory to be checked.

3.4.1 Formal models

As we have already seen, there are two parts to the theory of interpretation that we are developing: the construction of **models** which are the representations of situations or states of affairs, and the theory of interpretation, called the **model theory**, which provides the means of relating all the expressions in some object language to denotations in these models. As discussed in Chapter 2, a model consists of an ontology and a function that assigns extensions to basic expressions in the object language. The ontology is defined as a set of entities, usually symbolised as the set **A**, which contains the entities that exist in the state of affairs being modelled. Extensions are assigned to basic, or constant, expressions of the object language by a function **F** which associates each constant expression with some entity in **A** or some subset of **A** or some set of ordered n-tuples in **A**, depending on the logical category of the constant expression. Crucially, **F** is a **function**, something that assigns a unique denotation to each constant in the object language. More is said about functions in Chapter 4, but their importance lies in the fact that they always provide a unique **value** (here an extension in the model) for a particular **argument** (here a basic expression in the object language, L_P). This ensures that the interpretation of some L_P expression is properly unambiguous. Thus, **F** always applies to some constant *a* in the object language to yield a unique extension, Δ (*delta*). If **F** were not a function, it would be possible for a constant to be assigned two different extensions. In such a case, we could not necessarily decide whether a formula involving the expression was true or not and, therefore, could get no information from it.

For example, if a predicate like *scream'* denoted two different sets, say ∅ and {$\mathbf{MAN_1}$,$\mathbf{WOMAN_2}$}, then a formula like *scream'(jo')* could be either true or false depending on which extension is chosen. On a particular occasion of utterance, however, the sentence *Jo screamed* expresses a proposition that is either true or false, but not both, assuming that Jo has a unique extension in the context. Furthermore, although we may come across homonymous or polysemous expressions in speech, these are interpreted with the aid of the context as if they were properly unambiguous.

In other words, they are treated as denoting a unique extension in the given context. The fact that **F** is a function does not, of course, prevent two lexemes from having the same extension, like two synonyms e.g. *mercury* and *quicksilver*. Items that are not synonymous may also have the same extensions. In the real world, this is true of the words *unicorn* and *gryphon* on the assumption that they denote nothing (i.e. nothing that exists in our world is either a unicorn or a gryphon). The significance of this will be examined further in Chapters 9 and 10.

As discussed in Chapter 2, the denotation assignment function must also specify a denotation of every constant in the object language, even if there is nothing in its extension. This is because, even if nothing in a model has a certain property or stands in a certain relation to anything else, we can use expressions with null extensions to describe some state of affairs and to make true statements using the negation operator. An expression like *Jo threw the cat to Fiona*, however, is strictly both ungrammatical and meaningless in the fragment generated by G_1, because *threw* is not a word in the lexicon of the grammar. Such an expression would be grammatical, of course, if the ditransitive verb *threw* were introduced into the lexicon. If this is done, however, its translation into L_P, *throw'*, must be included in the specification of the denotation function assignment in any model used to interpret L_P. Otherwise formulae containing this constant would remain meaningless.

Any model for interpreting expressions in L_P can be defined as an ordered pair consisting of the ontology and the denotation assignment function, i.e. **M = «A,F»**. The model M_1 may thus be formally defined as in (48). This specifies everything that exists in the model, i.e. the ontology **A**, and the extensions of all the constants in L_P that are associated with lexemes in G_1. The situation thus represented involves two men, two women, a dog, a cat, a book and a cake, with the properties and relations assigned informally in Chapter 2. $\mathbf{F_1}$ is specified as a set of statements of the form $\mathbf{F_1(a)} = \alpha$ where **a** is the **argument** of the function, a constant in L_P and α is the **value** of the function applied to this argument, i.e. its extension in the model M_1. It is important to remember that the upper case words in (48) and elsewhere represent real world entities and are not words of English or L_P.

(48) M_1 = «A,F_1», where

a. A = {$\mathbf{MAN_1}$,$\mathbf{WOMAN_2}$,$\mathbf{MAN_2}$,$\mathbf{WOMAN_1}$,**DOG**,**CAT**,**BOOK**,**CAKE**}

b. F_1 =

{F_1(jo') = $\mathbf{MAN_1}$,
F_1(the-student') = $\mathbf{MAN_1}$,
F_1(bertie') = $\mathbf{MAN_2}$,
F_1(ethel') = $\mathbf{WOMAN_1}$,
F_1(the-golfer') = $\mathbf{WOMAN_1}$,
F_1(fiona') = $\mathbf{WOMAN_2}$,
F_1(the-singer') = $\mathbf{WOMAN_2}$,
F_1(the-lecturer') = $\mathbf{WOMAN_2}$,
F_1(the-cat') = **CAT**,
F_1(prudence') = **CAT**,
F_1(chester') = **DOG**,
F_1(the-dog') = **DOG**,
F_1(the-book') = **BOOK**,

F_1(the-cake') = **CAKE**,
F_1(run') = {**DOG**,**CAT**},
F_1(laugh') = {**MAN$_1$**, **WOMAN$_1$**},
F_1(howl') = {**DOG**},
F_1(crazy') = ∅ ,
F_1(happy') = {**WOMAN$_1$**,**WOMAN$_2$**,**MAN$_1$**} ,
F_1(disgusting') = {**CAKE**},
F_1(scream') = ∅ ,
F_1(messy') = ∅ ,
F_1(sing') = {**WOMAN$_2$**},
F_1(like') = {**<MAN$_1$,WOMAN$_1$>**, **<MAN$_1$,WOMAN$_2$>**,
<WOMAN$_1$,WOMAN$_2$>, **<WOMAN$_2$,CAT>**, **<MAN$_1$,MAN$_1$>**,
<WOMAN$_2$,WOMAN$_1$>, **<MAN$_1$,MAN$_2$>**}
F_1(loathe') = {**<MAN$_1$,DOG>**, **<MAN$_2$,DOG>**, **<WOMAN$_1$,DOG>**,
<WOMAN$_2$,DOG>, **<WOMAN$_2$,MAN$_1$>**, **<CAT,DOG>**},
F_1(poison') = {**<CAKE,DOG>**},
F_1(eat') = {**<DOG,CAKE>**},
F_1(kick') = ∅ ,
F_1(read') = {**<WOMAN$_1$,BOOK>**, **<MAN$_1$,BOOK>**},
F_1(give') = {**<WOMAN$_2$,CAKE,MAN$_2$>**, **<MAN$_1$,CAKE,DOG>**,
<MAN$_1$,BOOK,MAN$_2$>, **<MAN$_2$,BOOK,WOMAN$_2$>**,
<MAN$_1$,CAT,WOMAN$_2$>},
F_1(rain') = **1**,
F_1(snow') = **0**}.

The last two entries in the specification of F_1 may seem a bit strange. The symbols **1** and **0** are not in **A** and in Chapter 2 the expressions *rain'* and *snow'* were directly associated with a truth value, their extensions in the model M_1 being true and false, respectively. It is not just these two constants that are defined as having truth values as their extensions, but all formulae are ultimately assigned a value, **true** or **false**, by the interpretation procedure. What is meant by the terms *true* and *false* in semantics is not, however, quite the same as what is meant by the same words in English. In order to emphasise this the English words, *true* and *false* are replaced in model-theoretic semantics by two neutral symbols which are traditionally shown as **0** and **1**, for falsity and truth, respectively. It does not really matter what these symbols actually are - they could be a cup of coffee and a biscuit - as long as they have a specific interpretation in the theory. This interpretation is defined by the theory of interpretation itself (ie. by the set of truth-conditions): a formula denotes **1** just in case it corresponds to the structure of some model according to the rules of interpretation, in which case we say it is true, or it denotes **0** if it doesn't correspond, in which case we say it is false. This statement may seem somewhat peculiar and perhaps even circular, but it is not. *True* and *false* are informal (English) terms which help us remember what we are getting at in our semantic analysis, whereas **0** and **1** are precise (logical) terms, whose interpretation is defined by the theory. For this latter reason, the symbols **1** and **0** are not included in the ontology of the model, but are part of the theory of interpretation. If they were members of **A**, some models might not contain them and so have no means of representing truth and falsity.

However, it is part of the theory that all formulae have determinate truth values and so it is in the theoretical part of the interpretation procedure that they are defined.

3.4.2 Model theory

We have now given a formal definition of the structure that models have and given a specification of one such model, M_1. The next thing to be done is to provide a formalisation of the theory of interpretation which defines how formulae are interpreted with respect to some model, the **model theory**. The model theory provides a means of determining the extensions of all expressions in L_P, whether simple or complex. Formally, the denotation of an expression is represented by putting it within square brackets, [.]. Thus, for example, [*the-cat'*] represents the denotation of *the-cat'* and [*scream'(jo')* ∨ *laugh'(fiona')*] represents the denotation of the formula that translates *Jo screamed or Fiona laughed.* As we have seen, however, expressions do not have denotations *tout court*, but only with respect to a particular model. For this reason, the name of the model being used to interpret the expression is written as a superscript to the right of the square brackets. For example, the denotation of *laugh'(fiona')* with respect to the model, M_1, is written as $[laugh'(fiona')]^{M_1}$ and that of *the-cat'* is $[the\text{-}cat']^{M_1}$.

Formally, the model theory is stated as a **recursive definition** of the notion of denotation in a model, i.e. of $[\alpha]^M$ where α is any expression in the object language. The **base** of the recursive definition is given by the equation of the model-theoretic denotation of constants with the extension assigned to that constant by **F** in the relevant model (see (49.1)). This means that while the denotation function, **F**, can vary from model to model, it always provides the basis of the interpretation of complex expressions. In other words, the truth value of a sentence is determined by the denotations of the words it contains. For example, because the expression *the-cat'* is a constant in L_P, its extension with respect to M_1, $[the\text{-}cat']^{M_1}$, is the result of applying $\mathbf{F}_1$, the denotation assignment function in M_1, to the expression *the-cat'*. By (48), F_1(*the-cat'*) is **CAT**, so $[the\text{-}cat']^{M_1}$ is also **CAT**. From the denotations of the constants supplied by **F** in a particular model, the denotations of all other expressions in the language are built up by a series of **recursive clauses** which define how to build up the denotations of complex expressions from the denotations of their parts, in accordance with the principle of compositionality. Anything not specified by the base and recursive clauses does not count as a possible denotation in the model.

The recursive clauses state formally the truth-conditions of formulae in L_P by defining what must be the case for a formula with a particular structure to be true in any model. Thus, the truth-conditions for formulae constructed from an n-place predicate and n arguments is formally set out in general form in (49.2) and requires that the n-tuple formed by taking the extensions of each of the arguments in order to be in the extension of the predicate for the formula to be true. (49.3) states that an equative formula is true only when the entities denoted by the two individual constants being equated are one and the same entity. The next four clauses in the model theory in (49) deal with the interpretations of complex formulae given the extensions of their component parts: a negative formula is true if the component formula is false; two formulae must be true for their conjunction by & to be true; at least one of two formulae must be true for their disjunction by ∨ to be true; for conditionals to be true, either the antecedent must be false or the consequent true; and two formulae are equivalent only if they have the same truth value. This completes the formal definition of the model theory used to interpret L_P. (49) does nothing more than formally state the model theory that has been informally presented in Chapter 2 and the earlier part of this chapter. No new information about interpretation is introduced.

(49) Given a model, **M = «A,F»**, then
1. For any constant α , $[\alpha]^M$ is $F(\alpha)$.
2. If f is an n-place predicate, and $a_1,...,a_n$ are individual constants, then $[f(a_1,...,a_n)]^M$ is **1**, iff $<[a_1]^M,...,[a_n]^M> \in [f]^M$. Otherwise, $[f(a_1,...,a_n)]^M$ is **0**.
3. If a and b are individual constants, then $[a = b]^M$ is **1** iff $[a]^M$ is extensionally identical to $[b]^M$. Otherwise, $[a = b]^M$ is **0**.
4. If ϕ is a formula, then $[\sim(\phi)]^M$ is **1**, iff $[\phi]^M$ is **0**. Otherwise, $[\sim(\phi)]^M$ is **0**.
5. If ϕ and ψ are formulae, then $[\phi \mathbin{\&} \psi]^M$ is **1**, iff $[\phi]^M$ is **1** and $[\psi]^M$ is **1**. Otherwise, $[\phi \mathbin{\&} \psi]^M$ is **0**.
6. If ϕ and ψ are formulae, then $[(\phi \vee \psi)]^M$ is **1**, iff $[\phi]^M$ is **1** or $[\psi]^M$ is **1**. Otherwise, $[(\phi \vee \psi)]^M$ is **0**.
7. If ϕ and ψ are formulae, then $[(\phi \rightarrow \psi)]^M$ is **1**, iff $[\phi]^M$ is **0** or $[\psi]^M$ is **1**. Otherwise, $[(\phi \rightarrow \psi)]^M$ is **0**.
8. If ϕ and ψ are formulae, then $[\phi \leftrightarrow \psi]^M$ is **1**, iff $[\phi]^M$ is $[\psi]^M$. Otherwise, $[\phi \leftrightarrow \psi]^M$ is **0.**

To show how the model theory works, we shall look at the interpretation of the formula that translates the sentence *If Jo was the student, then the lecturer loathed Jo*, *(jo'= the-student' → loathe'(the-lecturer', jo'))*. To specify the interpretation of this L_P formula, we begin by defining the truth-conditions of the complex formula according to the model theory and then find out whether these are met in the model under consideration. If they are, the formula is true. If not, then it is false. Since the formula is a conditional, the first step in interpreting it is given by the truth-conditions for material implication set out in (49.7). In other words, we replace ϕ and ψ in this clause with the component formulae to get (50).

(50) [(jo' = the-student' → loathe'(the-lecturer',jo'))]^{M_1} is **1**, iff [jo' = the-student']^{M_1} is **0** or [loathe'(the-lecturer',jo')]^{M_1} is **1**.

It is then necessary to interpret the component formulae to see whether these truth-conditions are met. The antecedent formula is equative, the truth-conditions of which are provided by the clause in (49.3). We now come to constants of the language L_P whose extensions are provided by the model. So, the base clause (49.1) is applied twice to get the extension of *jo'* and *the-student'* in M_1, allowing us to determine the truth value of the antecedent formula with respect to the model, as shown in (51).

(51) a. [jo' = the-student']^{M_1} is **1** iff [jo']^{M_1} is extensionally identical to [the-student']^{M_1} (by (49.3)).
b. [jo']^{M_1} = F_1(jo') = $\mathbf{MAN_1}$ (by (49.1) and definition of F_1 in (48.b)).
c. [the-student']^{M_1} = F_1(the-student') = $\mathbf{MAN_1}$ (by (49.1) and definition of F_1).
d. Therefore, as $\mathbf{MAN_1}$ is identical to $\mathbf{MAN_1}$, [jo = the-student']^{M_1} is **1**.

Because the antecedent is true with respect to the model, we cannot yet tell whether the conditional is true and must find out the truth value of the consequent. This contains a two-place predicate, *loathe'* and two arguments, *the-lecturer'* and *jo'*.By the clause in (49.2) the truth-conditions of this formula are met if entities denoted by *the-lecturer'* and *jo'* form an ordered pair which is in the extension of *loathe'* in M_1, as set out in (52). Since this is the case, it follows from (50) that the whole conditional is true with respect to M_1. Hence, we have indirectly interpreted the English sentence *If Jo was the student, then the lecturer loathed Jo* as being true of the situation modelled by M_1, as required.

(52) a. $[\text{loathe'(the-lecturer',jo')}]^{M_1}$ is **1** iff $\langle[\text{the-lecturer'}]^{M_1},[\text{jo'}]^{M_1}\rangle \in [\text{loathe'}]^{M_1}$ (by (49.2)).

b. $[\text{loathe'}]^{M_1} = F_1(\text{loathe'}) = \{\langle\mathbf{MAN}_1,\mathbf{DOG}\rangle, \langle\mathbf{MAN}_2,\mathbf{DOG}\rangle, \langle\mathbf{WOMAN}_1,\mathbf{DOG}\rangle, \langle\mathbf{WOMAN}_2,\mathbf{DOG}\rangle, \langle\mathbf{WOMAN}_2,\mathbf{MAN}_1\rangle, \langle\mathbf{CAT},\mathbf{DOG}\rangle\}$ (by (49.1) and the definition of F_1 in (48.b)).

c. $[\text{the-lecturer'}]^{M_1} = F_1(\text{the-lecturer'}) = \mathbf{WOMAN}_2$ (by (49.1) and F_1 in (48.b)).

d. $[\text{jo'}]^{M_1} = F_1(\text{jo'}) = \mathbf{MAN}_1$ (by (49.1) and F_1 in (48.b)).

e. Because $\langle\mathbf{WOMAN}_2,\mathbf{MAN}_1\rangle \in \{\langle\mathbf{MAN}_1,\mathbf{DOG}\rangle, \langle\mathbf{MAN}_2,\mathbf{DOG}\rangle, \langle\mathbf{WOMAN}_1,\mathbf{DOG}\rangle, \langle\mathbf{WOMAN}_2,\mathbf{DOG}\rangle, \langle\mathbf{WOMAN}_2,\mathbf{MAN}_1\rangle, \langle\mathbf{CAT},\mathbf{DOG}\rangle\}$, $[\text{loathe'(the-lecturer',jo')}]^{M_1}$ is **1**.

This process, which may seem rather tedious (as indeed it is!), is a rigorous specification of the truth-conditional meaning of the formula that translates the sentence *If Jo was the student, then the lecturer loathed Jo.* Each step is automatic and the final conclusion is reached just by following the rules set out in (49). Thus, the model theory makes absolutely explicit how the interpretation of formulae that translate sentences generated by G_1 is to be carried out. Note that the theory is not intended to represent the steps that we, as speakers of English, carry out in our heads when interpreting expressions generated by this small grammar. It does, however, provide an automatic procedure for determining the truth or falsity of any formula associated with a sentence in G_1 with respect to the model M_1 and thus constitutes a theory of the truth-conditional meaning of the grammar fragment. (49) thus provides an explicit theory of semantic interpretation whose precision enables us to check its predictions and see if they do indeed match up with our intuitions about what English sentences mean. In the following chapters, it will be shown that the theory in (49) is not sufficient in itself to provide a full theory of interpretation for English (or any other natural language), but it does provide a firm foundation for the more adequate theories to be discussed later.

Exercise 3.6:

Translate the following sentences into L_P and determine their truth or falsity with respect to M_1 using the formal method shown in (50) to (52):

i. Jo didn't give the cat to the lecturer.
ii. The dog ate the cat or the dog ate the cake.
iii. If Chester was messy, then the cat didn't loathe the dog.

3.5 Further reading

The logical operators ~, &, ∨ , → and ↔ and their truth-conditional interpretations form the basis of **propositional logic** and there are many introductions to this system: see, in particular, Guttenplan (1986: 42-88) (which also discusses translation on pp. 105-124), Allwood, Andersen and Dahl (1977: ch. 4), Lyons (1977: 138-150), Partee, ter Meulen and Wall (1990: 99-107), Martin (1987: 8-30) and McCawley (1981: chs. 2 & 3) which gives a discussion of the syntax and semantics of propositional logic and inference, but uses a different notation that is potentially confusing to the novice. (Barwise and Etchemendy (1987) offers an introductory text and a computer program for learning predicate logic on a Macintosh computer.) The formal approach to interpretation discussed in Section 3.4 is discussed in Dowty, Wall and Peters (1981: ch. 2) which also touches on matters that will become important in later chapters.

4 Type Theory

4.1 Verb phrases and other constituents

One of the conditions of adequacy for a semantic theory set up in Chapter 1 is that it conform to the Principle of Compositionality. This principle requires the meaning of a sentence to be derived from the meaning of its parts and the way they are put together. The interpretation procedure for the grammar fragment set up in the last two chapters adheres to this principle insofar as the translations of sentences, and thereby their interpretations, are derived from the translations of their parts and the syntactic rules used to combine them. Thus, for example, the translation of the sentence *Ethel kicked the student* is derived from the translations of the two noun phrases *Ethel* and *the student* and the verb *kicked*. These are combined using the translation rule for transitive sentences to give *kick'(ethel',the-student')*. The truth or falsity of the resulting formula can then be directly ascertained by checking whether the ordered pair of entities denoted by the subject and object in that order is in the set of ordered pairs denoted by the predicate, *kick'*.

Unfortunately, in the theory of Chapters 2 and 3, compositionality is maintained only at the expense of the syntax. The 'flat' structure of the predicate-argument syntax of L_P and its interpretation requires a flat sentence structure in the English syntax in order to maintain a direct correspondence between syntax and translation, and thus a transparent relation between elements in the interpretation and constituents of the English sentence. There is, however, strong syntactic evidence that many languages, including English, do not have a flat sentence structure, but one that contains a number of hierarchically defined constituents. In particular, English sentences are usually analysed as containing verb phrases consisting of the verb and its complements and modifiers. According to the principle of compositionality, all constituents within a sentence must have a well-formed translation and thus be assigned a denotation by the model. Hence, if the sentence *Ethel kicked the student* were analysed as containing a verb phrase, a properly compositional semantics would need to assign a logical representation and denotation to the phrase *kicked the student*. It is not too difficult to see what sort of thing such a phrase denotes: verb phrases denote the same things as intransitive verbs, i.e. sets of entities, because the simplest verb phrases consist only of a single intransitive verb. Hence, in the same way that the verb *ran* may be associated with a predicate *run'* denoting the set of things that have the property of running, so the verb phrase *kicked the student* ought to be associated with some predicate denoting the set of all entities that kicked the student. In formal terms, the extension of this verb phrase should be derived from the extension of predicate representing the verb *kick'* by taking the first element of each of the ordered pairs in this set where the second element of the pair is the entity denoted by the direct object, $[$*the-student'*$]^M$ in this case. There is, however, no expression in L_P that could be assigned such an interpretation. It is not possible, for example, to represent verb phrases by leaving out the subject expression from a formula. Expressions like *kick'(the-student')* or *kick'(_,the-student')* are not well-formed expressions of L_P because they do not conform to the construction rule for formulae given in Chapter

2, repeated in (1), below, which requires n-place predicates to have n arguments to make a formula. The expression *kick'* is a two-place predicate, and so must combine with two individual expressions to make a well-formed formula.

(1) $t = Pred_n(e^1,...,e^n)$.

There are also, of course, many other constituents that the logical language L_P cannot represent. For example, adverbs like *slowly* or prepositional phrases like *in the garden* have no obvious representation or interpretation within the theory of the previous chapters. The word *slowly* in the sentence *Chester ran slowly* cannot be treated as a simple predicate because such expressions do not define properties of individuals. It makes no sense to translate *Chester ran slowly* as *run'(chester') & slowly'(chester')* because the idea of Chester 'being slowly' is not coherent. Even if the adverb were translated as if it were equivalent to its adjectival base form to give *run'(chester') & slow'(chester')*, this would not provide an adequate interpretation for *Chester ran slowly*. This is because it is Chester's running that is described as slow, not Chester himself. It is possible that Chester's slow running is still fast and thus to predicate slow of Chester would not capture the meaning intended to be conveyed by the use of the adverb. Adverbs and prepositional phrases (in some of their uses) predicate properties, not of individuals, but of predicates themselves. Since L_P only contains expressions that are predicates, individuals or connectives, it is not capable of representing **higher order** concepts like predicates of predicates.

4.2 A typed logical language

There is no way to represent verb phrases or verb phrase modifiers in L_P in such a way as to give their intuitively correct denotations. A new logical language is therefore needed to represent more adequately the semantic structure of natural languages like English. This logical language must have more flexibility than L_P and, in particular, it should have a more complex system of semantic categories, to allow formulae to be given more structure in order to better represent the rich constituent structure of natural languages. From now on, we will distinguish logical semantic categories, like e and t, from syntactic ones, like NP, S, etc., by referring to the former as **semantic types** (or just **types**). The theory behind them is referred to as **Type Theory** and the new logical language is called $\mathbf{L_{type}}$. Although L_{type} is a very different language from L_P in many ways, it contains many of its features. In particular, it contains the propositional operators and the notion of predicate/argument structure, albeit in a slightly modified form. The interpretation of the language is also similar in that it is based on set theory, although again this is somewhat modified. We now turn to the definition of the syntax of the language L_{type} and see how translation into this language maintains the constituent structure of a sentence.

4.2.1 Semantic types

In L_P, there are only five logical types: individual constant (e), formula (t), one-place connective (i.e. ~), two-place connective (i.e. &, $\vee$, $\rightarrow$, $\leftrightarrow$) and n-place predicate ($Pred_n$). These types are all primitive in L_P, i.e. they have no internal structure and cannot be further decomposed. It is possible, however, to define them in such a way that only two of the types are primitive and the other three are defined in terms of these. In order to do this, we must consider a different way of viewing the construction of logical formulae.

The main formula construction rule in (1) is a rule schema that collapses all the rules in (2) and (infinitely) many more.

(2) a. $t \rightarrow Pred_0$.
b. $t \rightarrow Pred_1(e)$.
c. $t \rightarrow Pred_2(e^1,e^2)$.
d. $t \rightarrow Pred_3(e^1,e^2,e^3)$.

In most phrase structure grammars, the combinatorial properties of expressions of particular categories, like e and $Pred_n$ in (2) (or NP and S in the grammar fragment G_1), have to be inferred from the set of rules that govern their distribution. For example, from the grammar fragment G_1, we can extract the information that transitive verbs combine with two noun phrases to make a sentence or that a conjunction combines with two sentences to make another sentence. In the same way, we can think of a two-place predicate as an expression that combines with two individual constants to give a formula, or a connective like & as an expression that combines with two formulae to make a complex formula. Such information, however, instead of being encoded within a set of rules, could as well be directly encoded in syntactic categories or semantic types. For example, instead of treating a two-place predicate like *kick'* as having a primitive type, $Pred_2$, we may give it a complex type which itself contains the information that the expression combines with two individuals to make a formula. Such complex types thus provide information about the number and types of the arguments with which particular expressions combine and the type of the expression that results after the combination. Hence, the type of an expression directly encodes what other types of expression it can combine with and we only need to know exactly how the combination is effected to perform the required operation. It is as if we have an equation like that in (3) where we need to replace the *e*'s with particular individual expressions (like *ethel'* and *the-student'*) and to know what the combination operation × means to get to the resulting expression which is a formula of type t.

(3) $\text{kick'} \times e \times e = t$.

Generalising this idea and making it more formal, we can define non-primitive types as **ordered pairs** of types. The first element of the pair indicates the required type of the expression which expressions of the complex type combine with, the **input type** and the second element gives the type of the resulting expression, the **output type**. Thus, a one-place predicate, like *scream'*, which combines with an individual expression (an expression of type e) to give a formula (an expression of type t), has the complex type <e,t>. Similarly, the negation operator, ~, which combines with a formula to make a formula that has the complex type <t,t>.

(4) **Complex types**: <input type,output type>.

What, however, of expressions that combine with more than one argument, like n-place predicates and two-place connectives? It would be possible to allow types to have an ordered list of types as their first element, instead of just a single type. This list would give the types of all the expressions with which another expression combines and the order in which they are combined. On this definition, a two-place predicate would have two instances of type e as its input list and t as the type of the output, i.e. have a type <[e,e],t>. A two-place connective, like &, would have two instances of t as its input and t again as its output, i.e. <[t,t],t> and so on. It would then be a simple matter to state a rule that combines an expression with a complex type with expressions of all of its input types at the same time: a two-place predicate would combine with two expressions of type e to give a formula (as in the equation in (3)), and a two-place connective would combine with two formulae to give a formula and so on. This approach would, however, maintain the basic syntax of L_P, since it combines a predicate expression with its argument expressions all in one go. As such it is subject to the same problems in defining representations for constituents like VP as L_P itself.

Instead of defining complex types as having an ordered list as the first element, however, it is possible to restrict the number of input types to one, allowing only **binary types** and so only binary combination of logical expressions into more complex expressions. This may seem far too strict. If complex types only have one possible input type, how can n-place predicates be defined? The answer is quite simple. The types for one-place predicates, <e,t>, and the negation operator, ~, <t,t> have a primitive type, t, as its output type. The output type could, however, be complex, not primitive. For example, an expression could combine with an individual constant to give an expression that itself requires an individual constant in order to make a formula. The type of such an expression would therefore be <e,<e,t>> and, since an expression of this type ultimately requires two individual expressions to make a formula, we may associate this type with two-place predicates. The combination of such expressions with their arguments would not be a one stage process as shown in (3) but a two stage process as shown in (5). First, the predicate is combined with one expression of type e to make an expression of type <e,t> as in (5.a) and then this expression is combined with another expression of type e to yield an expression of type t, i.e. a formula.

(5) a. <e,<e,t>> × e = <e,t>.
b. <e,t> × e = t.

It is not only the result types that can be complex but argument ones as well. For example, an expression may combine with a one-place predicate to give an expression of the same type. As we have seen, one-place predicates have the type <e,t> because they combine with an individual to make a formula. A **predicate modifier** would, therefore, have the type <<e,t>,<e,t>>, giving the type of a VP adverb, like *slowly*. In fact, the theory imposes no constraints on the complexity of semantic types, beyond the fact that types must be binary: there must be only one input type and one output type. Given this lack of constraint, there is an infinite number of types which must, therefore, be defined **recursively**. The base of the recursion is given by the statement of what constitutes a primitive type, i.e. individuals and formulae, and the recursive clause defines complex types based on these, as fully specified in (6).

(6) **Types for L_{type}:**

a. e is a type,
b. t is a type,
c. If a is a type and b is a type, then <a,b> is a type.

From (6), we can construct types like <e,t>, and <t,t>. From the latter we can construct types like <<e,t>,<e,t>>, <<e,t>,t>, <t,<t,t>>. From these we can construct more complex types like <<e,t>,<<e,t>,t>>, <<<e,t>,t>,<<e,t>,<e,t>>> and so on. All the types in (7.a) are thus well-formed according to the definition in (6) but those in (7.b) are not.

(7) a. <e,<e,<e,t>>>, <<t,t>,t>, <t,e>, <<<e,t>,t>,<e,t>>, <<<e,t>,<e,t>>,<e,t>>.
b. <e,e,t>, <e,<α,t>>, <<e,e,e>,t>, <$Pred_n$>.

Now that the system of types has been given, the syntactic rules that combine expressions with different types must be specified in order to complete the definition of the language L_{type}. One of the advantages of encoding combinatorial properties directly in the types themselves is that it is not necessary to state individual rules for combining expressions of different types. Instead, only one syntactic rule needs to be stated. Because types are binary, the rule combines at most (and at least) two expressions. The **rule of functional application** (or **RFA** for short), defined in (8), combines an expression with type, <a,b>, with an expression of type a to yield an expression of type b. The expression with the type <a,b> is called the **functor** and the expression with which it combines is called the **argument**. The result of applying the functor to its argument is obtained by writing the functor to the left of the argument, which is enclosed in parentheses. So, in general, if *f* is the functor expression and *a* is the argument, then the **functional application** of *f* to *a* is *f(a)* (which is often read as *f applied to a* or just *f of a*).

(8) **Rule of functional application (RFA)**: If *f* is an expression of type <a,b>, and *a* an expression of type a, then *f(a)* is an expression of type b.

The rule of functional application can be thought of as performing some sort of logical cancellation analogous to the sort of cancelling that goes on in arithmetical multiplication. If the cancelling yields a single result at the end, then the combination of expressions is well-formed. If no cancelling takes place, however, or if it is anomalous, then the resulting expression is ungrammatical in L_{type}. As an arithmetical illustration, consider the simple multiplication in (9.a). The result of this multiplication is determined by cancelling out the identical multiplier and divisor to leave the unique uncancelled dividend as the result. In (9.b), on the other hand, because multiplier and divisor do not cancel each other out, the result is not equal to the dividend but must be computed.

(9) a. $2/4 \times 4 = 2$.
b. $2/4 \times 3 \neq 2$.

Similarly, to get the type of two expressions when they are combined by RFA, the type of the argument is cancelled with the identical first element of the type of the functor, as illustrated schematically in (10.a). The type of the resulting expression is given by the (uncancelled) output type of the functor category. If no cancellation can take place, because the argument type and the first element of the functor's type are not identical, then the result of the combination has no type in L_{type} and so is not a well-formed expression in the language, e.g. (10.b). To see whether a combination of expressions is well-formed, the types of the functor and the argument need to be checked: if the input type of the functor can be cancelled with the type of the argument expression then the functor can be applied to the argument. If not, then there is no well-formed expression in L_{type} that combines just those two expressions.

(10) a. f + a = f(a).
<e,t> × e = t
b. g + a ≠ g(a).
<t,t> × e

As a more concrete example, consider how the three expressions ~, *scream'* and *bertie'* may be combined. In (11.a), the functor expression, *scream'* of type <e,t>, is applied to the argument, *bertie'*, of type e, to get an expression of type t (a formula). The negation operator (type <t,t>) can now be applied to this expression to get the resulting formula in (11.b). No other combination of these expressions yields a well-formed expression of L_{type}, as illustrated in (11.c) and (11.d).

(11) a. scream' + bertie' = scream'(bertie').
<e,t> × e = t
b. ~ + scream'(bertie') = ~(scream'(bertie')).
<t,t> × t = t
c. ~ + scream'.
<t,t> × <e,t>
d. ~ + bertie'.
<t,t> + e

The formula in (11.b) looks the same as an equivalent combination of these three expressions in L_P. However, this is only true of a very restricted number of formulae in L_{type}. As we will see in Section 4.2.2, formulae containing two-place predicates look rather different from their L_P counterparts and contain in particular a subexpression that corresponds to a verb phrase in the syntax of the English sentence being translated. It is to the matter of translating English into L_{type} that we now turn.

Exercise 4.1:
Given the following abstract expressions with their types, state whether the complex expressions that follow are well-formed according to RFA. If they are, what are the types of the resulting expressions?

f is an expression of type <e,t>. a is an expression of type <e>.
h is an expression of type <t,t>. j is an expression of type <<e,t>,t>.
g is an expression of type <<e,t>,<e,t>>.

i. f(a) ii. g(f) iii. g(a)
iv. h(f) v. j(f) vi. (g(f))(a)

4.2.2 *Translating verb phrases*

To see how the language defined in Section 4.2.1 is able to represent the translations of verb phrases, consider how the sentence *Ethel kicked the student* might be translated into L_{type}. In a grammar of English descriptively more adequate than G_1, there will be a rule that combines a transitive verb, e.g. *kicked,* with a noun phrase, e.g. *the student*, to give a verb phrase, *kicked the student*. L_{type} contains a parallel means of combining two-place predicates, like *kick'* with its arguments. In L_{type} a two-place predicate is analysed as having a type that requires an individual expression to yield an expression that needs an individual expression to make a formula, i.e. <e,<e,t>>, as has already been seen above. An expression of such a type, like *kick'*, will combine, according to the RFA, with an individual expression like *the-student'* to give an expression of type <e,t>, i.e. *kick'(the-student')*. The parallelism between the syntactic construction of a verb phrase in English and the combination of a two-place functor with an argument in L_{type} is shown in (12). (12.a) gives the English expressions that are combined according to the (backwards) phrase structure rule in (12.b), while in (12.c), the L_{type} counterparts are combined according to the RFA shown by the valid 'cancellation' in (12.d).

(12) a. kicked + the student = kicked the student.
b. V_t NP ← VP.
c. kick' + the-student' ⇒ kick'(the-student').
d. <e,<e,t>> × e = <e,t>.

Similarly, the construction of the sentence *Ethel kicked the student* from the verb phrase in (12.a) and the noun phrase *Ethel* is paralleled by the functional application of the one-place predicate in (12.c) with an individual constant, *ethel'*, as shown in (13).

(13) a. Ethel + kicked the student = Ethel kicked the student.
b. NP VP ← S.
c. ethel' + kick'(the-student') ⇒ (kick'(the-student'))(ethel').
d. e × <e,t> = t.

Notice that the translation of the sentence into the formula in L_{type} given in (13.c) is not equivalent to the translation of the same sentence into L_P. Translation into the latter would result in the expression *kick'(ethel',the-student')*. Here the translation of the syntactic subject appears as the first argument of the predicate and that of the (direct) object as the second. In the L_{type} expression, on the other hand, this order is reversed. The translation of the object is combined with the predicate before the subject and so appears to the left of the translation of the latter. This better accords with traditional grammar and with traditional semantic notions of subject and predicate which both include the direct object as part of the predicate. It is possible, following Dowty (1982), to identify the positions of the translations of noun phrases in a formula in L_{type} that translates some English sentence with the grammatical functions those noun phrases perform in that sentence. In general, the more oblique the grammatical function of the noun phrase the closer its translation appears to the translation of the verb. Thus, the translation of an **indirect object** (if present) appears next to the predicate, being combined first. The translation of the **direct object** comes next, while the translations of syntactic **subjects** are always combined last of all. (14) gives a schematic representation of the relative order of the translations of noun phrases performing the three functions within some sentence. Obviously, if not all three functions are represented in a sentence, the relative ordering remains the same: the translation of the object always precedes that of the subject in the **functor-argument structure** of the predicate. If this is borne in mind while translating sentences of English into L_{type}, the trap of mimicking the order of arguments in L_P translations can be avoided.

(14) (((verb'(indirect-object'))(object'))(subject')).

Let us now put the procedure for translating from English into L_{type} on a firmer footing by specifying the new grammar fragment and stating its translation rules. As in the previous chapters, the new grammar, G_2, is defined in terms of phrase structure rules with the translation rules operating in parallel to the syntactic ones, in accordance with the **rule-to-rule hypothesis**. The grammar G_2 has much the same coverage as G_1 of Chapters 2 and 3, but with a more adequate constituent analysis. Discussion and specification of rules for accounting for passive, copular and co-ordination constructions will, however, be left until Chapter 5.

Since it is now possible to have verb phrase constituents, the basic finite sentence of English can be constructed by the familiar rule in (15.a), the first rule of the new grammar G_2. Verb phrase rules can also be stated in their more usual form and intransitive, transitive and ditransitive VPs are analysed by the rules in (15.b) to (15.e). The variable α in these rules ranges over the values + and - so that these rules generate finite ([+FIN]) and non-finite ([-FIN]) verb phrases. The NP, PP and impersonal sentence rules are the same in G_2 as in G_1 and are repeated in (16).

(15) a. Rule $1G_2$: S $\rightarrow$ NP VP[+FIN].
b. Rule $2G_2$: VP[αFIN] $\rightarrow$ V_i[αFIN].
c. Rule $3G_2$: VP[αFIN] $\rightarrow$ V_t[αFIN] NP.
d. Rule $4G_2$: VP[αFIN] $\rightarrow$ V_{dt}[αFIN] NP_1 NP_2.
e. Rule $5G_2$: VP[αFIN] $\rightarrow$ V_{dt}[αFIN] NP PP_{to}.

(16) a. Rule $6G_2$: NP $\rightarrow$ N_{pr}.
b. Rule $7G_2$: NP $\rightarrow$ the N.
c. Rule $8G_2$: PP_{to} $\rightarrow$ to NP.
g. Rule $9G_2$: S $\rightarrow$ it V_0[+FIN].

As mentioned above, conjunction rules will be omitted for the time being, but, at the cost of compositionality, we can continue to include one of the negation rules of G_1 in G_2 as (17.a). The category *Neg* which is rewritten as *it is not the case that*, cf. (17.b), is treated as a single unanalysed constituent. The other negation rules of G_1 can be collapsed into the single rule in (17.c). This introduces the negated auxiliary *didn't* followed by a non-finite VP. Because the VP rules given above can be expanded as finite or non-finite, nothing else is required to generate negative sentences.

(17) a. Rule $10G_2$: S $\rightarrow$ Neg S.
b. Neg $\rightarrow$ {it is not the case that}.
c. Rule $11G_2$: S $\rightarrow$ NP didn't VP[-FIN].

In order to begin translating English expressions generated by G_2 into L_{type}, the syntactic categories of G_2 must first be linked up with corresponding logical types. This is done by a **type assignment function** (often also called a **type mapping**) that associates each syntactic category with a unique type. The reason that each syntactic category must be assigned only a single type is to ensure that no ambiguity is present in the logical translation and that each syntactic rule is paired with a unique translation rule. Although each syntactic category must be associated with a unique type, it is not the case that that type is necessarily unique to that category, as can be seen from (18), below. The type assignment function is called **TYPE;** its **domain** is the set of syntactic categories and its **range** is the set of types. (See Section 4.3 for a definition of these terms.) The part of this function that assigns types to phrasal categories is given in (18). Notice that although there are six categories they only map into four types, since both NP and PP_{to} translate into expressions with the type of an individual, i.e. e, as in G_1.

(18) a. TYPE(S) = t.
b. TYPE(VP) = <e,t>.
c. TYPE(NP) = e.
d. TYPE(PP_{to}) = e.

Types for lexical categories are slightly more interesting. V_i has the same type as VP, i.e. that of a one-place predicate, <e,t>. The type for a proper name remains that of an individual constant and that for an impersonal verb is t, but the types of the other three categories, Neg, V_{dt} and V_t, are more complex. Transitive verbs, as we have seen, translate into expressions with a type whose argument type is an individual constant and whose resultant type is that of a one-place predicate (19.b). Ditransitive verbs have a type that takes an individual constant to yield something of the type of a transitive verb (19.c). The negation operator, ~, has the type <t,t> because it combines with a formula to give another formula. These lexical types are summarised in (19). (The type of a common noun, N, will be ignored until Chapter 6.)

(19) a. TYPE(V_i) = <e,t>.
b. TYPE(V_t) = <e,<e,t>>.
c. TYPE(V_{dt}) = <e,<e,<e,t>>>.
d. TYPE(V_0) = t.
e. TYPE(N_{pr}) = e.
f. TYPE(Neg) = <t,t>.

The translation rules for G_2 are of two sorts. In the first place, there are rules where there is only a single category (as in Rules $2G_2$ and $6G_2$) or where there is a meaningless element plus one other category (as with the preposition *to* in Rule $8G_2$ and dummy *it* in rule $9G_2$) on the righthand side of the rule. In all of these cases, the translation of the phrase is identical to that of the meaningful category, cf. (20.a), (20.b) and (20.c). The rule introducing definite NPs, $7G_2$, is given the non-compositional translation in (20.d) which is identical to its counterpart in G_1. This is for expedience only and will be rectified in Chapter 6 when we look in more detail at the semantics of noun phrases.

(20) a. $T2G_2$: V_i'.
b. $T6G_2$: N_{pr}'.
c. $T9G_2$: V_0'.
d. $T7G_2$: the-N'.

In the other cases, the translation is given by the functional application of the translation of a category with a functor type over the translation of one (or more) expressions of the argument types. Thus, the translation of the transitive VP rule in (15.c) is provided by applying the translation of the verb, of type <e,<e,t>> to that of the NP of type e, to give an expression of the correct type for a VP, i.e. <e,t>. One thing that becomes apparent with the translation of the ditransitive VP rules is that L_{type}, instead of being too flat like L_P, appears, from a syntactic point of view, to be too structured. This is because the logical language constructs complex expressions only through binary combination while VPs, in the analysis of English at any rate, are usually given a flatter structure. This is not, however, a major problem and too much structure is preferable to too little (provided that it is the correct structure, of course). For our own purposes, it is a simple matter to state for both of the ditransitive VPs the order of combination of the objects. This, of course, follows the pattern set out in (14) above, but in the **double object** construction in (21.c) the NP immediately following the verb is interpreted as its indirect object. This allows the paraphrase relationship between sentences like *Bertie gave Fiona the book* and *Bertie gave the book to Fiona* to be captured directly within the translation rules. The lexicon of G_1 may be carried over to G_2 and lexical items are translated in the same way as outlined in Chapter 2.

(21) a. $T1G_2$: VP'(NP').
b. $T3G_2$: V_t'(NP').
c. $T4G_2$: V_{dt}'(NP_1')(NP_2').
d. $T5G_2$: V_{dt}'(PP_{to}')(NP').
e. $T10G_2$: NEG'(S').
f. $T11G_2$: ~(VP'(NP')).

As before, the translation of a sentence proceeds via a syntactic derivation using the rule-to-rule translation algorithm of Chapter 2. Thus, every time a syntactic rule is applied expanding a syntactic category, the parallel translation rule also applies to give the corresponding translation. An example derivation of the sentence *Fiona didn't give Chester the cake* appears in (22) where the numbers on the righthand side of the derivation indicate the syntactic and translation rule used in each step. The derivation in (22) has a corresponding phrase structure analysis which appears in (23). In this analysis tree, each node is labelled with a syntactic category, its type and a translation constructed from the translations of the nodes it dominates.

(22) a. S
$\Rightarrow$ S'.

b. NP_1 didn't VP[-FIN] $11G_2$
$\Rightarrow$ ~(VP'(NP')).

c. N_{pr} didn't VP[-FIN] $6G_2$
$\Rightarrow$ ~(VP'(N_{pr}')).

d. N_{pr} didn't V_{dt}[-FIN] NP_2 NP_3 $4G_2$
$\Rightarrow$ ~((V_{dt}'(NP_2')(NP_3'))(N_{pr}')).

e. N_{pr} didn't V_{dt}[-FIN] N_{pr} NP_3 $6G_2$
$\Rightarrow$ ~((V_{dt}'(N_{pr}')(NP_3'))(N_{pr}')).

f. N_{pr} didn't V_{dt}[-FIN] N_{pr} the N $7G_2$
$\Rightarrow$ ~((V_{dt}'(N_{pr}')(the-N'))(N_{pr}')).

g. Fiona didn't give Chester the cake Lex
$\Rightarrow$ ~((give(chester')(the-cake'))(fiona')).

(23)

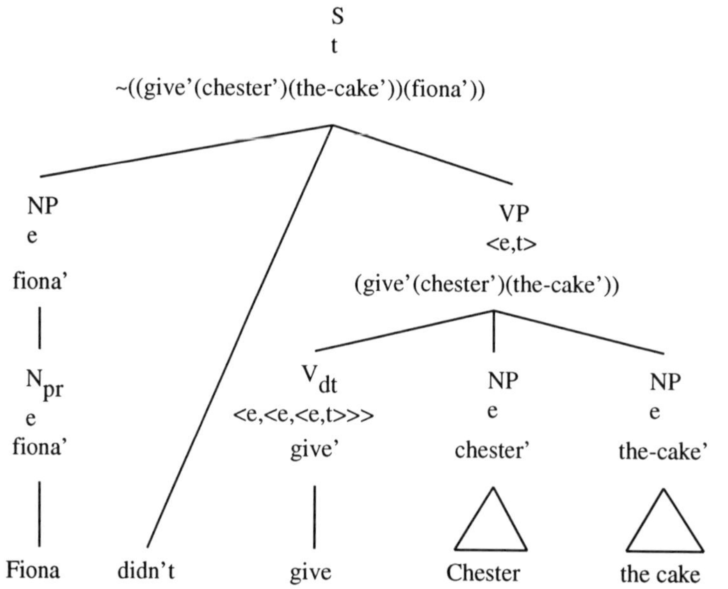

Exercise 4.2:
Draw analysis trees, i.e. phrase structures trees annotated with the translations and types of each node as illustrated in (23), for the following sentences:

i. It is not the case that Chester liked Jo.
ii. The cat ate the cake.
iii. Ethel didn't scream.

4.3 More set theory

As (23) shows, the adoption of L_{type} as the translation language allows us to provide a much better syntactic analysis of (a subset of) English sentences. In particular, of course, our syntax now contains a verb phrase constituent that has a well-formed translation, one that is of the same type as an intransitive verb, i.e. <e,t>. As these are desirable properties according to the discussion in Section 4.1, it seems that our original problem is solved, since we now have a means of representing VPs in the translation language. This is not sufficient, however, as we still need to provide an interpretation of these constituents that conforms to our intuitions about the meaning of the sentences in which they appear. Before this can be done, however, we need to take another look at sets and relations and to discuss further the notion of **function** introduced in Chapter 3.

4.3.1 Relations and functions

As we saw in Chapter 2, sets consist of collections of elements called its **members** which may be single items (entities), ordered n-tuples or even sets themselves. Sets that contain ordered pairs of elements are said to specify **relations** which have so far been represented by sets of ordered pairs consisting of **<(extension of) subject,(extension of) object>**. Thus, the relation denoted by *loathe'* in the model M_1 is represented by the set in (24).

(24) {**<MAN$_1$,DOG>**, **<WOMAN$_1$,DOG>**, **<WOMAN$_2$,DOG>**, **<WOMAN$_2$,MAN$_1$>**, **<CAT,DOG>**}.

This relation could, however, also be represented diagrammatically by drawing arrows between individual elements showing that the first element bears a particular relation (e.g. of loathing) to the second. This is shown in the diagram in (25) where X represents the set of loathers and Y the set of the loathed. The arrows show who loathed whom.

(25)

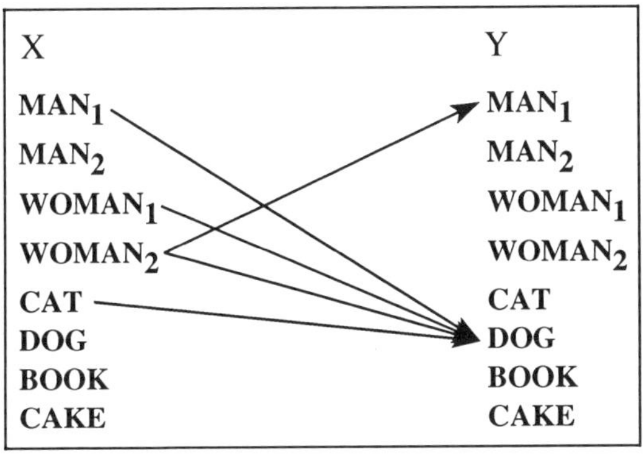

In (25), both the first and second elements of the relation are taken from the same set, i.e. the set, **A**, of entities in the model, M_1, but this is, of course, not necessary. A relation can be stated between the elements of any two sets, even sets that have complex members like ordered n-tuples or other sets. For example, we could represent the relation *being loathed by* in M_1 as a relation between entities and the sets of entities that loathe them, as in (26). In talking about relations, we refer to the set of first elements of the ordered pairs in the relation (X in (25) and (26)) as the **domain** of the relation and the set of the second elements (Y in (25) and (26)) as its **range**. In (25), the set **A** forms both the domain and the range while in (26) it forms the domain only and the range is a set of subsets of **A**.

(26)

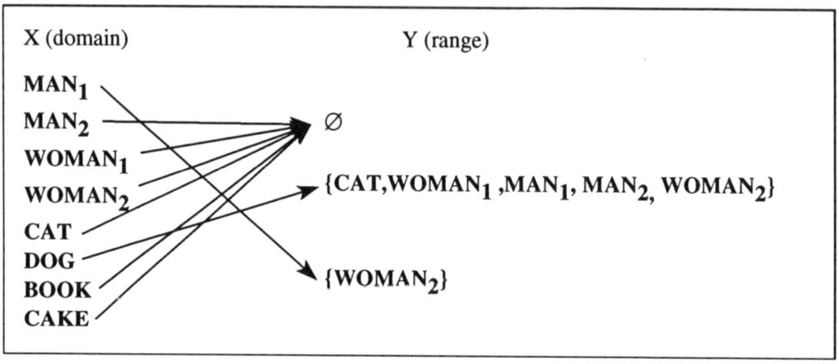

Certain relations have a special property: they assign every element in the domain to a single element in the range. Relations of this sort are called **functions** and are very important in logic and mathematics. Their importance has to do with the fact that they are complete (every element in the domain is assigned some value by the relation) and unambiguous (each element in the domain is assigned one and only one element in the range). Thus, functions, unlike relations in general, admit of no gaps in the domain and provide one and only one **value** for each such element. In (27), four relations between two sets are represented. The domain contains four letters of the alphabet and the range contains the first five positive whole numbers. Of these relations, those in (27.a) and (27.b) both represent functions, but those in (27.c) and (27.d) do not. (27.c) does not assign a value in the range to every element in the domain, while (27.d) assigns some members of the domain two values in the range.

(27)

a.

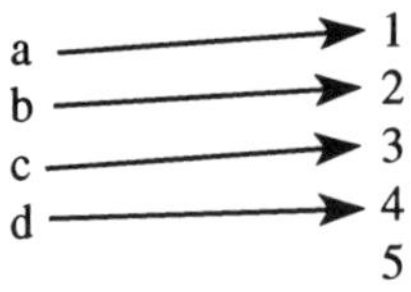

b.

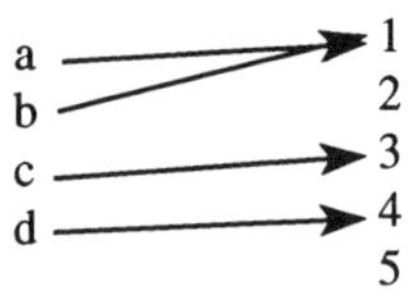

c.

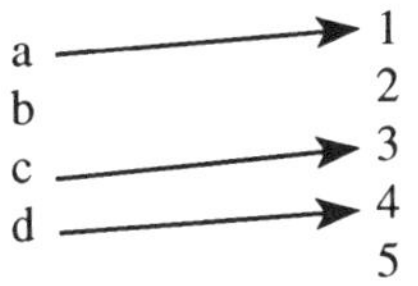

d.

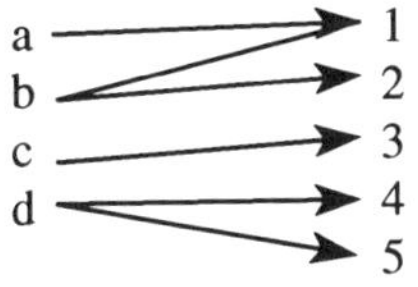

There is some terminology that is associated with mathematical functions that should be learnt at this point. In the first place, assuming that **F** is a function with domain **D** and range **R**, **F** is said to **map D** to **R**. Secondly, if **a** is an element in the domain **D**, then **F** applied to **a** is written as **F(a)** and read as '**F** of **a**'. **a** is then said to be the **argument** of **F**. Thirdly, if **a** is an element in the domain **D** and **b** is an element in the range **R**, and **F** assigns **b** to **a** then **b** is called the **value** of **F** applied to **a** (written **F(a) = b**). Fourthly, if **a** is an element in the domain **D** and **b** is an element in the range **R**, and **F** assigns **b** to **a** then we say that **F maps a onto b**. Finally, if the domain and range are the same, i.e. **D,** then **F** is said to be an **operation on D.**

The two characteristic properties of functions, that of providing a value for every element in the domain and ensuring that that value is unique, make them very useful in linguistics, and especially in semantics. We have already come across things that can be modelled by a function. For example, in the truth-conditional semantics we have been developing, every formula is either true or false and cannot be both. Hence, we could represent our model theory as a function from formulae (the domain) to truth values (the range) with respect to some model. A very small part of this function is given in (28) for the formulae that translate sentences in G_1 with respect to M_1.

(28)

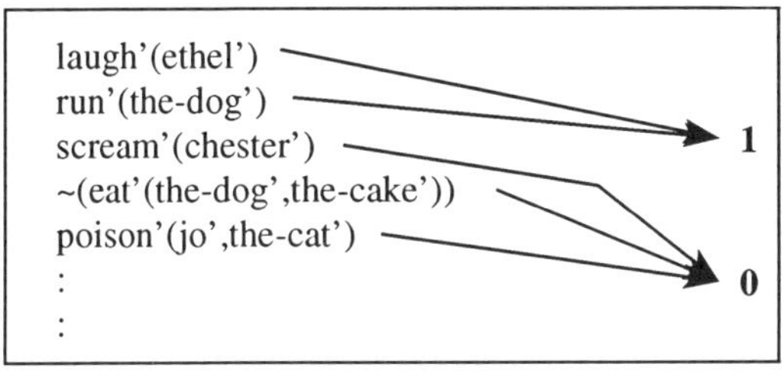

Another example of a function that has already been introduced is the denotation assignment function, **F**, used in the specification of models. As we have seen, this is a function from basic expressions to some element or set of n-tuples of elements in **A**, the set of entities in the model. As discussed in Chapter 3, **F** assigns every constant in the object language a unique denotation in the model, since otherwise sentences containing words whose translations have no denotation would be meaningless. Furthermore, **F** is required not to assign more than one denotation to some lexeme, as this would make the translation language semantically ambiguous. Since both of these properties are properties of functions, denotation assignment is best treated as a function of the appropriate sort. In fact, most aspects of the interpretation procedure of Chapter 3 can be reformulated in terms of functions over some appropriate domain and from now on functions start to play an increasingly important part in the theory. In particular, the interpretation of L_{type} is defined in terms of functions and it is to a discussion of the model theory required to interpret this language that we now turn.

4.3.2 Sets again

The last piece of groundwork that needs to be done before we can re-examine the model theory involves a re-characterisation of sets. Until now we have been describing sets by listing their members. It is possible, however, to describe them using a function that picks out just those entities that are members of the set and rejects anything else. In other words, given each element of some domain, a function that defines a set gives *yes* or *no* as a value according to whether the element is in the set or not. As an example, consider the set assigned as the extension of the expression *run'* in M_1, i.e. **{DOG,CAT}**. This can be represented as the function given in (29), which maps **DOG** and **CAT** onto *yes* and everything else in the domain (i.e. **A - {DOG,CAT}**) onto ***no***.

(29) $[\text{run'}]^{M1}$

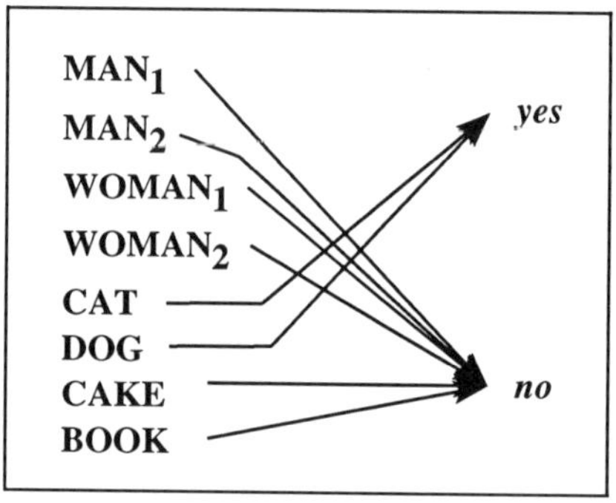

Functions that map all the elements in a domain onto one of two values, e.g. *yes* and *no*, are called **characteristic functions** of sets of elements of the domain, because they characterise the sets they are associated with. Formally, the characteristic function of a set, Σ, can be defined as a function from a domain, **A**, into the set **{0,1}** (the truth values) so that every element in Σ is mapped onto **1** (i.e. *yes*) and everything else is mapped onto **0** (i.e. *no*). Thus, every subset, Σ, of a set of individuals, **A**, can be associated with a characteristic function, f_Σ, which has the following formal definition:

(30) **Characteristic function of a set**: For all $a \in A$, $f_\Sigma(a) = \mathbf{1}$, if $a \in \Sigma$, and $f_\Sigma(a) = 0$, if $a \notin \Sigma$.

The characteristic function, f_Σ, of a set, therefore, divides the domain **A** into two subsets of **A**: the set Σ and every element that is in **A** but not in Σ. The latter set is called the **complement** of Σ relative to **A**. This is often written as $\overline{\Sigma}$ and is equivalent to **A** - Σ, as shown in the diagram in (31).

(31) **A set and its complement**

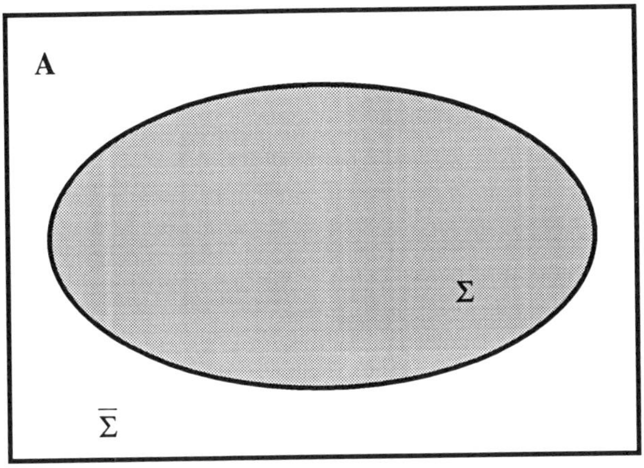

The diagram in (29) above represents the characteristic function of the set **{DOG,CAT}** with respect to M_1 and (32) provides two more illustrations of the concept. (32.a) represents the characteristic function, f_N, of the set N, where N is the set of even numbers with respect to the set consisting of the first nine positive whole numbers, i.e. N = {2,4,6,8}. (32.b) represents the characteristic function of the set, B, of bilabial consonants in the set {b, d, g, t, k, p, v, β, θ }.

(32)

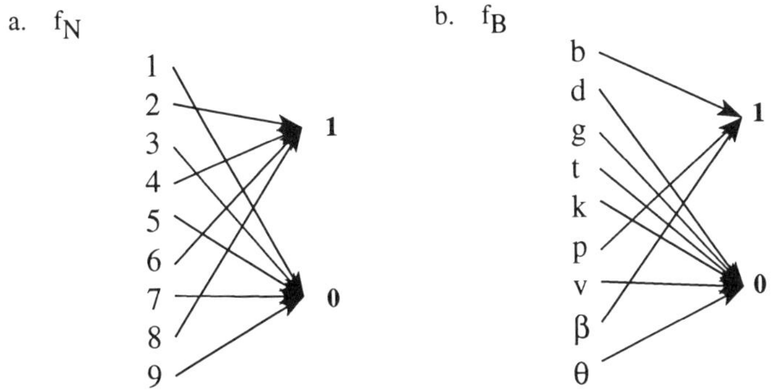

Exercise 4.3:
Draw diagrams representing the characteristic functions of the following sets in the manner of (30) and (32) above:

i. the set of all square numbers in the positive integers between 1 and 20.
ii. the set {a,e,i,o,u} with respect to the Roman alphabet.
iii. the extension of *happy'* and *scream'* in the model M_1 with respect to A.

Instead of talking about a single function with a particular domain and range, we often need to refer to all the functions that have the same domain and the same range. For example, it is often necessary to refer to all possible subsets of the set of entities, **A**, in some model, but we do not want to have to laboriously write out all the actual subsets of A, (e.g. in M_1, ∅ , **{DOG}, {CAT,DOG}**, {**DOG**,**MAN**$_1$}, etc.), or to draw diagrams representing all the characteristic functions of these sets. There is a way of referring to a set of functions which all have the same domain and range: the name of the set defining the domain is written as a righthand **superscript** to that of the set defining the range. Hence, the set of all functions with domain A and range B is written as $\mathbf{B}^{\mathbf{A}}$. For example, the characteristic functions of all subsets of **A** have **A** as their domain and **{0,1}** as their range and so we can refer to all such functions as $\mathbf{\{0,1\}}^{\mathbf{A}}$. This is an important piece of notation that will be used to a considerable extent in the following chapters, so it is necessary to learn its significance.

(33) $\mathbf{RANGE}^{\mathrm{DOMAIN}} =_{\mathrm{def}}$ the set of all functions from DOMAIN to RANGE.

4.4 Interpreting $\mathbf{L}_{\mathrm{type}}$

We are now in a position to provide an interpretation for L_{type} and begin by looking at the sorts of denotations that expressions of particular types have in a model. The model theory of Chapter 3 will then be revised to take the revisions in denotation and the syntax of expressions into account.

4.4.1 Denotation

As discussed in Chapter 2, the extension of an expression is the entity, property or relation that the expression is associated with in some model. Although it is not useful to specify the actual denotation of some expression in every possible model, it is useful to define the sort of denotation it should have in any possible model. The specification of the sorts of denotations associated with expressions of different types was done in L_P by directly assigning possible denotations to the types. For example, one-place predicates were defined as denoting subsets of **A**, two-place predicates as denoting sets of ordered pairs of **A**, and so on. Because L_{type} contains an infinite number of different types, however, we cannot list the types and the sorts of denotation expressions of that type should have in some model, but must provide a recursive definition of such denotations. To refer to the set of possible denotations that expressions of some type, τ, can have, we use the symbol $\mathbf{D}_\tau$ which is defined in a way that is parallel to the definitions given to the types themselves. Firstly, the sort of denotations assigned to expressions of the primitive types, e and t, is given and then a general rule is specified for determining the sorts of denotations expressions of complex types have.

The basis for the interpretation of L_{type} is the same as for the L_P: i.e. a set **A** of entities given by a model and the set of truth values, **{0,1}**. As before, individual constants, i.e. expressions of type e, denote members of **A** and formulae, i.e. expressions of type t, denote truth values. In other words, the set of possible denotations for expressions of type e, D_e, is the set **A** and the set of possible denotations for expressions of type t, D_t, is **{0,1}**. This provides the base of the recursive definition of D_{type}, the sets of possible denotations of expressions in L_{Type}. The denotations of expressions of complex types are defined in terms of the possible denotations of their input types and those of their output types. Because L_{type} is an unambiguous language, the denotation of an expression must be properly and uniquely determined within a model. Furthermore, the Principle of Compositionality requires the denotation of a composite expression to be determined by the denotations of its parts. Hence, because L_{type} allows only binary combination of expressions, consisting of a functor and a single argument, the functor must denote a function that when applied to its argument yields a unique value, the denotation of the complex expression. Since functors must, by definition, combine with an expression of a particular type to yield an expression of another type, they must denote functions from the denotations of the type of their arguments to denotations of the types of expression that result after combination. For example, one-place predicates in L_{type} have the type <e,t>, as we have already seen. Thus, they combine with expressions of type e to yield expressions of type t. Hence, by the above reasoning, expressions of type <e,t> must denote functions from domain D_e to range D_t. As we saw at the end of Section 4.3, the set of all functions from a domain **A** to a range **B** is written $\mathbf{B}^{\mathbf{A}}$, so that we can define $D_{<e,t>}$ as $D_t^{D_e}$, the set of all functions from D_e to D_t, as shown schematically in (34).

(34) $D_{<e,t>}$

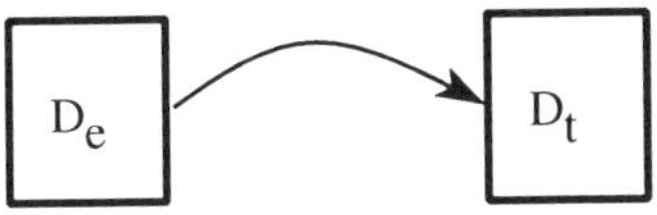

The set of possible denotations of expressions of type e, D_e, is the set **A** and the set of possible denotations of expressions of type t, D_t, is the set of truth values, **{0,1}**. Hence, $D_{<e,t>}$ is the set of all functions from the set of entities **A** to the set of truth values **{0,1}**, i.e. $\mathbf{\{0,1\}}^{\mathbf{A}}$. As we saw in Section 4.3.2, functions from **A** to **{0,1}** are characteristic functions of subsets of **A** and so we maintain the intuitively appealing idea from L_P that one-place predicates denote such sets, although they are now being defined in terms of functions.

Generalising this approach, we may interpret the denotations of expressions with a complex type, <a,b>, as functions from the set of possible denotations of the input (first) type, a, to the set of possible denotations of the output (second) type, b. In other words, $D_{<a,b>}$ is the set of all functions from D_a to D_b, written $D_a^{D_b}$ and shown schematically in (35). The full recursive definition of the possible denotations of expressions of some type is given in (36) which directly parallels the recursive definition of types given in (6), above.

(35) $D_{<a,b>}$

(36) **The denotations of types**:

a. D_e is **A**.

b. D_t is **{0,1}**.

c. If a and b are types then $D_{<a,b>}$ is $D_b^{D_a}$.

This definition thus provides a transparent relationship between the types of L_{type} and the sort of denotations they are associated with in the model. However complicated the type is, the sort of denotation it can have can be worked out by checking the possible denotations of its argument and result types. For example, the denotation of an expression of type <<e,t>,t> is a function from $D_{<e,t>}$ to D_t, i.e. $D_t^{D_{<e,t>}}$. But $D_{<e,t>}$ is also a function, from D_e to D_t so $D_{<<e,t>,t>}$ is $\{0,1\}^{\{0,1\}^A}$, the set of all functions from functions from entities to truth values to truth values. This is shown more perspicuously by the schematic diagram in (37).

(37) $D_{<<e,t>,t>}$

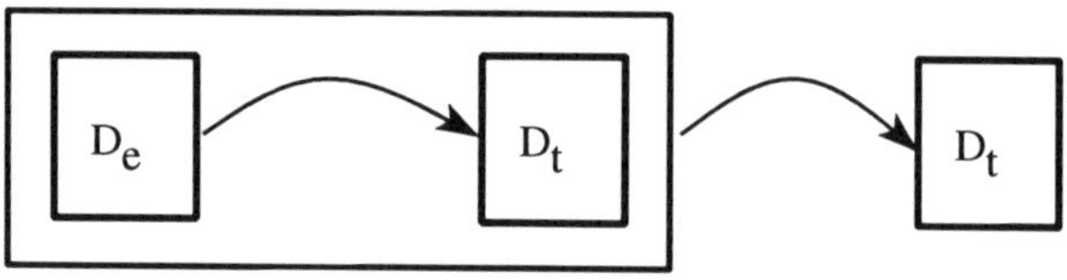

Exercise 4.4:

Given the definition in (36), what are the sets of possible denotations associated with the following types?

i. <t,t>. ii. <<e,t>,<e,t>>. iii. <e,<e,t>>. iv. <<e,t>,t>.

Let us now take a more concrete example and look at the sort of denotation that is assigned to a two-place predicate, i.e. an expression of type <e,<e,t>>. According to (37), an expression of type <e,<e,t>> denotes a function from domain, D_e, of entities to a range, $D_{<e,t>}$, itself a set of functions from D_e to D_t. Thus, $D_{<e,<e,t>>}$ is worked out according to the steps in (38), with (38.e) giving the set of possible denotations of expressions of this type as functions from entities to functions from entities to truth values. The reference on each line is to the line of the recursive definition in (36) that provides the justification for each step.

(38) a. $D_{<e,<e,t>>} = D_{<e,t>}{}^{De}$. (36.c)
b. $D_{<e,t>} = D_t{}^{De}$. (36.c)
c. $D_t = \{\mathbf{0,1}\}$. (36.b)
d. $D_e = \mathbf{A}$. (36.a)
e. $D_{<e,<e,t>>} = (\{\mathbf{0,1}\}^{\mathbf{A}})^{\mathbf{A}}$.

A two-place predicate therefore denotes a function that, when applied to an entity, yields a function that picks out the set of entities that bear a particular relation to the first. As an example, consider a simple situation where Jo and Ethel (from M_1) are both kicking the dog, Chester, and the dog is kicking Jo. No-one else in **A** (of M_1) is doing any kicking at all. This relation, which provides the extension of the two-place predicate *kick'* with respect to a model (let us call it M_2), can be represented by a function that associates each element in **A** with the set of elements in **A** that kick it. Thus, assuming the association of entities and names of M_1, **DOG** is associated with the set {$\mathbf{MAN_1}$,$\mathbf{WOMAN_1}$}, $\mathbf{MAN_1}$ is associated with the set {**DOG**} and all the other entities in **A** are associated with the empty set ∅ , as shown in (39).

(39)

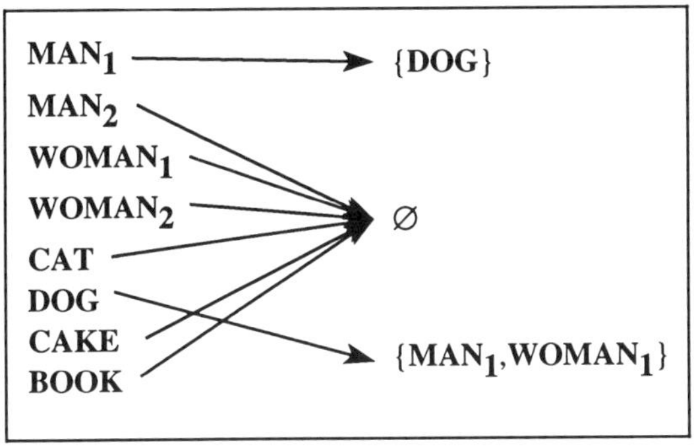

As we have seen, sets of entities in **A** can be defined as characteristic functions, functions from **A** to {**0,1**}. Hence, the extension of *kick'* with respect to M_2 should more properly be represented as a function from elements in **A** to the characteristic functions that pick out the sets of entities that kick them. This is shown in (40), where f_1 represents the characteristic function of the set {**DOG**}, f_2 represents that of ∅ and f_3 that of {$\mathbf{MAN_1}$,$\mathbf{WOMAN_1}$}.

The complex function in (40) defines a relation between entities in the set **A**, something that can also be represented as a set of ordered pairs, as we have seen. To recover this set, each entity in the characteristic functions, f_1, f_2 and f_3, in (40) is made the first element of an ordered pair if it is mapped onto **1**. The second element of each pair is provided by the entity that is associated with the relevant characteristic function. Thus, in f_1 **DOG** is mapped onto **1** and so forms the first element of an

(40) [kick']^{M2}

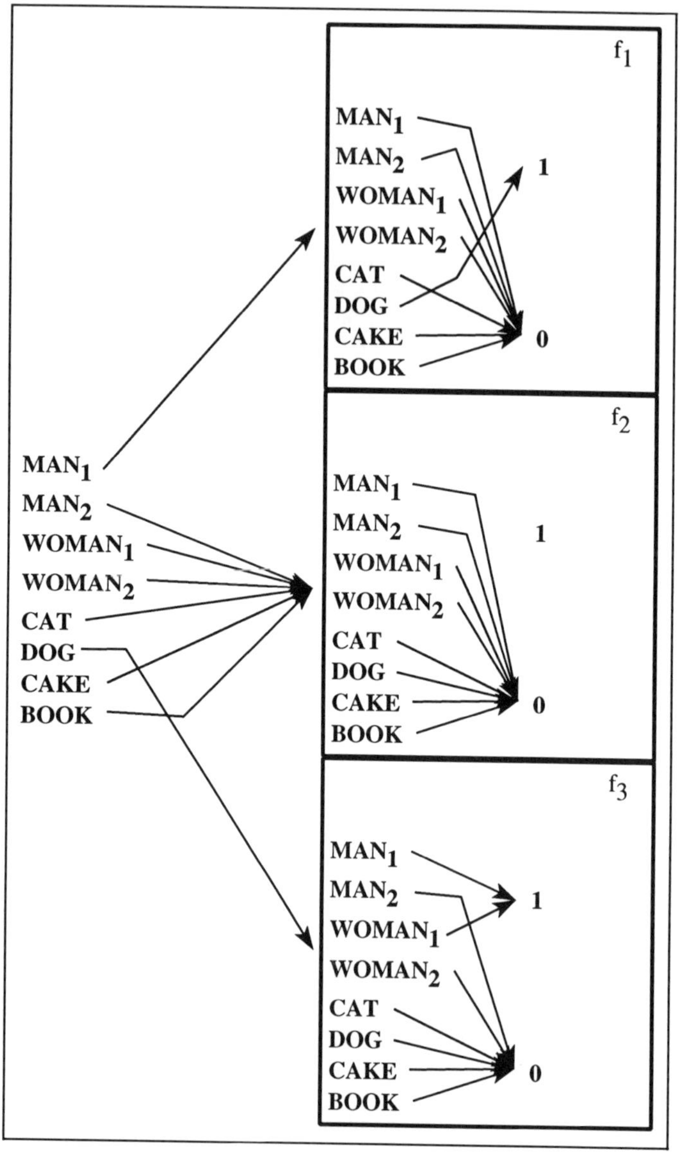

ordered pair with **MAN**$_1$, the entity mapped onto f_1, to give the pair **<DOG,MAN$_1$>**. Nothing in f_2 is mapped onto **1** and so we turn straight to f_3 where both **MAN**$_1$ and **WOMAN**$_1$ are mapped onto **1**. These thus form the first elements of two ordered pairs whose second element is **DOG**, since (40) maps the latter onto f_3. This yields the set

$\{\langle\textbf{MAN}_1,\textbf{DOG}\rangle,\langle\textbf{WOMAN}_1,\textbf{DOG}\rangle,\langle\textbf{DOG},\textbf{MAN}_1\rangle\}$ which is the extension assigned to *kick'* in M_1 by the denotation assignment function of Chapter 3. In other words, functions from entities to characteristic functions are semantically equivalent to sets of ordered pairs. Hence, the sort of denotation assigned to two-place predicates has not been significantly changed but just reformulated to allow for the interpretation of VPs.

The extensions of three-place predicates have the same pattern as the extensions of two-place ones, except that they are functions from entities to functions from entities to characteristic functions. In other words, they denote functions from entities to the sorts of thing denoted by two-place predicates. To illustrate, let's take a quite complex example using the ditransitive verb, *gave*, that translates into an expression in L_{type} of type <e,<e,<e,t>>>. In M_1, Fiona gave the cake to Bertie who gave it to the dog. Jo also gave the book to Bertie who gave it to Fiona who was also given the cat by Jo. This situation can be represented by the function in (41) which looks somewhat complicated but it just defines in terms of functions the set of ordered triples, $\{\langle\textbf{WOMAN}_2,\textbf{CAKE},\textbf{MAN}_2\rangle, \langle\textbf{MAN}_2,\textbf{CAKE},\textbf{DOG}\rangle, \langle\textbf{MAN}_1,\textbf{BOOK},\textbf{MAN}_2\rangle, \langle\textbf{MAN}_2,\textbf{BOOK},\textbf{WOMAN}_2\rangle, \langle\textbf{MAN}_1,\textbf{CAT},\textbf{WOMAN}_2\rangle\}$, the extension assigned to *give'* in M_1. This can be checked by taking those entities that are mapped onto **1** by the characteristic functions, f_4 to f_7 and letting them form the first elements of ordered triples. The second elements are provided by the entities mapped onto these functions and the third elements are given by the leftmost entities that are mapped onto the latter. The order of the mapping from entities to functions in these diagrammatic representations of functions follows the order of the arguments in L_{type} expressions containing the appropriate functors. In other words, in (41) the leftmost entities are those denoted by the indirect object, the second set of entities gives those denoted by the direct object and the third set those denoted by the subject. Such diagrams thus go from most oblique object on the left to least oblique on the right.

4.4.2 Revising the theory

It is not difficult to redefine the model structure so that it can be used to interpret expressions in the language, L_{type}. First of all, the denotations in a model of all predicates must be redefined as functions of some sort rather than as sets. For expressions of types e (e.g. *ethel'*) and t (e.g. *rain'*), there is no change from previous models. These are assigned entities and truth values, respectively, as before. The denotation assignment function, **F**, however, assigns appropriate functions to all expressions with complex types, instead of sets of n-tuples of entities. Thus, one-place predicates, of type <e,t>, are assigned characteristic functions over **A** (as in (43), below); two-place predicates, of type <e,<e,t>>, are assigned functions from entities to characteristic functions (as in (40)) and three-place predicates, of type <e,<e,<e,t>>>, are assigned functions from entities to functions from entities to characteristic functions (as in (41)). As we have seen, this is equivalent to assigning sets of entities, sets of ordered pairs and sets of ordered triples, respectively, but allows the interpretation of expressions other than basic expressions and formulae, as we will see directly.

(41) [give']^{M2}

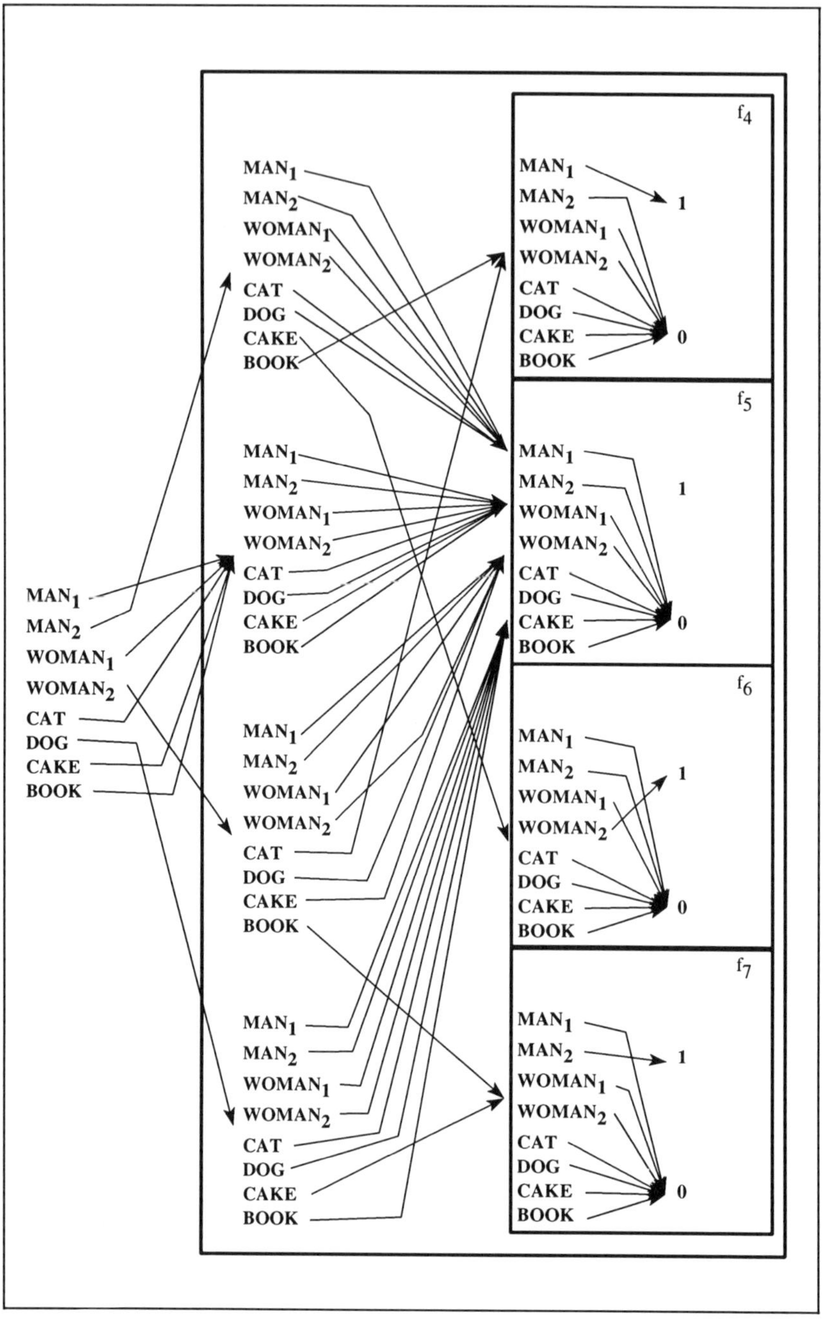

Given a model containing a set of entities **A**, as before, and a denotation assignment function, **F**, revised to assign functions rather than sets, the interpretation of all expressions in L_{type} (excluding formulae containing the connectives) can be specified by two clauses. The first clause equates the interpretation of any basic expression with the denotation assigned to it in the model (i.e. by **F**). This gives the basis of the interpretation which is built on by the recursive application of the second clause which provides the means of interpreting all complex expressions formed from these. This clause derives the denotation of a well-formed expression in L_{type} consisting of a functor expression, *f*, and an argument expression, *a*, from the application of the denotation of *f* in some model to that of *a* in the same model. In other words, the denotation in a model of an expression *f(a)* is as the value of a function denoted by *f* applied to the denotation of an argument *a*. The two clauses of the model theory needed to interpret L_{type} are formally specified in (42).

(42) Given a model, M = «A,F», then

1. For any constant *a*, $[a]^M = F(a)$.
2. If *f* is of type <a,b> and the type of *a* is a, then $[f(a)]^M = [f]^M([a]^M)$.

The simplicity of the model theory results directly from the adoption of mathematical functions as the denotations of complex types. If the output type of the functor (the second member of the ordered pair of types defining the complex type) is basic then the value obtained when the function is applied to some argument is either a truth value or an entity (usually the former). If, on the other hand, it is a complex type, then the denotation resulting from the application of the function to some argument is itself a function.

To make this more concrete, let us take over the extension of the predicate *laugh'* in the model, M_1, into M_2 (assuming that M_2 has the same ontology, i.e. **A,** and the same assignment of entities to individual constants as M_1). The situation modelled is thus one where only Jo and Ethel are laughing, which is represented by the characteristic function in (43).

(43) $[\text{laugh'}]^{M2}$

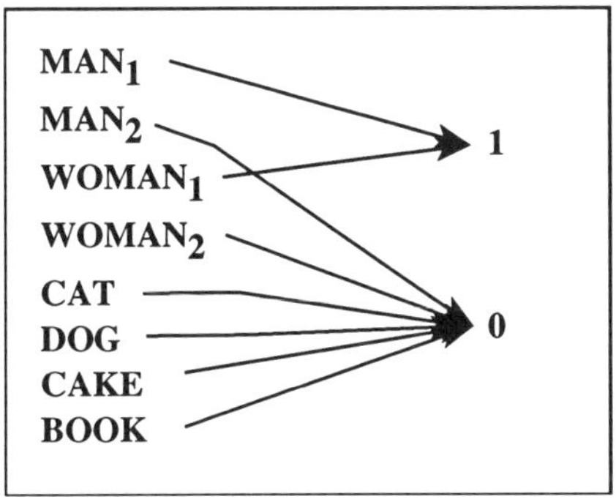

Given this function, it is simple to work out the extension (i.e. truth value) of a formula containing *laugh'*. Once the extension of the subject expression has been ascertained, the function is applied to it and the automatic result is a truth value, the value of the function denoted by the predicate applied to the argument. So, for example, to find out the truth value of a formula *laugh'(jo')* (translating the sentence *Jo laughed*) we go through the steps in (45), where the number on the righthand side refers to the clause in the model theory or the representation of the extension that justifies the step taken. We see from the last line that the formula is true in M_1, since the function denoted by *laugh'* in M_2 returns the value **1** when applied to $\mathbf{MAN_1}$ which is the extension of *jo'* in the same model.

(44) a. $[\text{laugh'(jo')}]^{M2}$ is $[\text{laugh'}]^{M2}([\text{jo'}]^{M2})$. (42.2)
b. $[\text{laugh'}]^{M2}$ is F_2(laugh') is the function in (43) (call it f_{43}). (42.1)
c. $[\text{jo'}]^{M2}$ is F_2(jo') = $\mathbf{MAN_1}$. (42.1)
d. $f_{43}(\mathbf{MAN_1})$ is **1**. (43)
e. Hence, $[\text{laugh'(jo')}]^{M2}$ is **1**.

More complex formulae are interpreted in the same way, except that more applications of the rule in (42.2) are involved. The interpretation of a formula containing a two-place predicate like *kick'* or a three-place predicate like *give'* proceeds by reducing the complexity of the function until a truth value is arrived at. In the former case, the function denoted by the predicate is applied to the entity denoted by the direct object, the first argument combined with the predicate, to give a characteristic function. Applying this function to the entity denoted by the subject yields a truth value, the truth value of the whole formula. With the translations of ditransitive verbs, the function denoted by the predicate is first applied to the extension of the indirect object and then to that of the direct object to get the characteristic function that yields the truth value of the formula when applied to the extension of the subject.

As an example, consider the interpretation of the formula, *(kick'(the-dog'))(the-singer')* translating the sentence *The singer kicked the dog*. First of all, the rule in (42.2) is applied to the formula to unpack the function/argument structure, starting with the rightmost argument and working inwards until the constant expressions are reached, as shown in (45).

(45) a. $[\text{(kick'(the-dog'))(the-singer')}]^{M2}$.
b. $[\text{kick'(the-dog')}]^{M2}([\text{the-singer'}]^{M2})$. (42.2)
c. $([\text{kick'}]^{M2}([\text{the-dog'}]^{M2}))([\text{the-singer'}]^{M2})$. (42.2)

The constants in (45.c) can then be then 'cashed out' in terms of their extensions in the model M_2 as specified by F. The value of each function is computed at every step, starting from the functor and working outwards. Thus, we first retrieve the extension of *kick'* in M_2, i.e. the function in (40) (which we may call $\mathbf{f_{40}}$, for convenience). Then, this is applied to the extension of *the-dog'*, i.e. **DOG**, to get the extension of the expression *kick'(the-dog')* which is the characteristic function $\mathbf{f_3}$ in (40). Applying the latter to the extension of *the-singer'*, i.e. $\mathbf{WOMAN_2}$, gives a truth value, in this case **0**. Hence, the formula *(kick'(the-dog'))(the-singer')* is false with respect to M_2. These automatic steps are spelled out in (46) which should be compared to the function denoted by *kick'* given in (40) to see how the final result is obtained.

(46) a. $[\text{kick'}]^{M2} = F_2(\text{kick'}) = f_{40}$.
b. $[\text{the-dog'}]^{M2} = F_2(\text{the-dog'}) = \mathbf{DOG}$.
c. $[\text{kick'}]^{M2}([\text{the-dog'}]^{M2}) = f_{40}(\mathbf{DOG}) = f_3$.
d. $[\text{the-singer'}]^{M2} = F_2(\text{the-singer'}) = \mathbf{WOMAN_2}$.
e. $([\text{kick'}]^{M2}([\text{the-dog'}]^{M2}))([\text{the-singer'}]^{M2}) = f_3(\mathbf{WOMAN_2}) = \mathbf{0}$.

We have now properly solved the problem posed in Section 4.1: how to incorporate verb phrases into the grammar. In our example sentence, the VP, *kicked the dog*, has the translation *kick'(the-dog')* whose extension is given in (46.c) as $\mathbf{f_3}$ in (41). This results from the application of the function denoted by the two-place predicate to the extension of the direct object. Since this is a characteristic function over **A**, and such characteristic functions define sets of entities, we have neatly captured the intuition that verb phrases should pick out sets, the sets of entities that bear the appropriate relation to their subjects. Indeed, the adoption of L_{type} gives us a powerful logical language into which to translate natural language sentences, one that can reflect the syntactic structure of the object language. By taking the denotations of L_{type} expressions to be either truth values, entities or more or less complex functions based on these two sets, we can ensure that the syntactic structure of an expression is maintained in the interpretation, as shown in the earlier examples. Thus, in addition to having a L_{type} representation, a VP also has a model-theoretic interpretation, i.e. as some function from entities to truth values. Hence, each independently meaningful expression generated by the grammar is associated with an extensional meaning and so compositionality is maintained.

Exercise 4.5:

1. Assuming that the negation operator, ~, is of type <t,t> what is the actual function that it denotes?
2. Using the step-by-step interpretation method outlined above, work out the truth value of the translation of the sentence *The student didn't give the book to Ethel* with respect to M_2 (i.e. using the function drawn in (41)), assuming the interpretation of negation given in Chapter 3.

4.5 Adverbs

The grammar fragment G_2 as yet covers only the same ground as the earlier G_1 (although without the recursion allowed by conjunction) but our new theory of translation and interpretation allows us to extend the grammar in a number of new and interesting directions. In particular, we are now in a position to tackle certain sorts of adverbial modification, including simple English adverbs of manner like *slowly, happily, pathetically*, etc. Such adverbs modify verbs, or more correctly, verb phrases and so may be syntactically analysed as combining with a VP to give another VP, as in the rule in (47).

(47) a. Rule $12G_2$: VP[αFIN] → VP[αFIN] Adv.
b. Adv → {slowly, happily, stupidly, crazily}.

Since VPs have the type of one-place predicates, i.e. $<e,t>$, adverbs introduced by this rule must be associated with L_{type} expressions that combine with one-place predicates as arguments to yield one-place predicates. In other words, the type of an adverb is $<<e,t>,<e,t>>$. This type assignment entails that the translation rule associated with Rule $12G_2$ is given by the functional application of the translation of the adverb to that of the VP, as in (48). A verb phrase like *walked slowly* is thus translated into L_{type} as *slowly'(walk')*.

(48) TRule $12G_2$: Adv'(VP').

The question that must be asked whenever we augment the grammar with a new category and an associated type is *Does the type assignment make sense semantically?*. In the case of manner adverbs, the suggestion made above does accord with intuition. VPs with simple *-ly* adverbials in English pick out a subset of the set of entities denoted by the VP without the adverbial. So, for example, the set of things that walk slowly in any situation is a subset of the set of things that walk in that situation. The semantic effect of *slowly* can thus be analysed as a function that maps a set, the extension of the translation of a VP, onto a subset of that set. This parallels the semantic relation between adjectives like *slow* or *happy* to their common nouns in phrases like *a happy student*. Such adjectives pick out a subset of the set of entities denoted by the common nouns, so that, for example, the phrase *happy student* denotes a subset of the set of all students, i.e. the happy ones. The relation between such adjectives and common nouns will be discussed in Chapter 6, but the functions that are denoted by both manner adverbials and their adjectives have characteristic functions as both their domain and range. In other words, such expressions have denotations in $D_{<e,t>}^{D_{<e,t>}}$ which is the set of denotations associated with the type $<<e,t>,<e,t>>$, as shown in (49).

(49) $D_{<<e,t>,<e,t>>}$

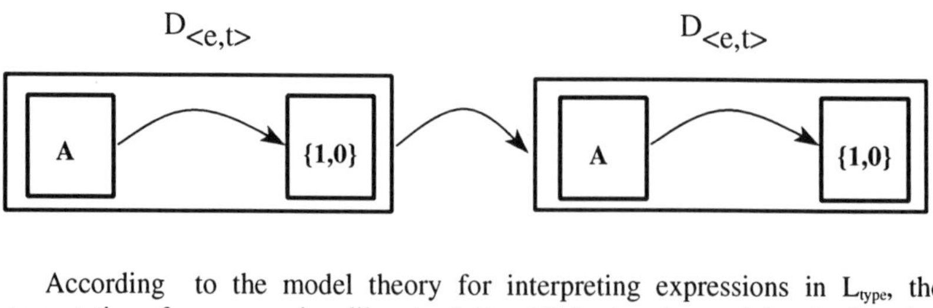

According to the model theory for interpreting expressions in L_{type}, the interpretation of an expression like *slowly'(walk')* is given by applying the function denoted by *slowly'* to that denoted by *walk'*, i.e. $[slowly'(walk')]^M$ is $[slowly']^M([walk']^M)$ or more generally as in (50).

(50) $[Adv'(VP')]^M = [Adv']^M([VP']^M)$.

As an example, let us assume that in M_2 Bertie, Ethel and the cat are the only entities that are walking, a situation that can be represented as the function in (51), supplying the extension of *walk'* in M_2. The things that are slowly walking in M_2 are Bertie and the cat, giving us the extension of *slowly'(walk')* in (52). The effect of applying $[slowly']^{M2}$ to $[walk']^{M2}$, then, is to pick out a subset of the set of things that walk, i.e. the set of things that walk slowly. This means that part of the function denoted by *slowly'* is that given in (53). Note that this is only a part because the function applies to other characteristic functions of sets (i.e. VP extensions) to yield other results.

(51) $[walk']^{M2}$

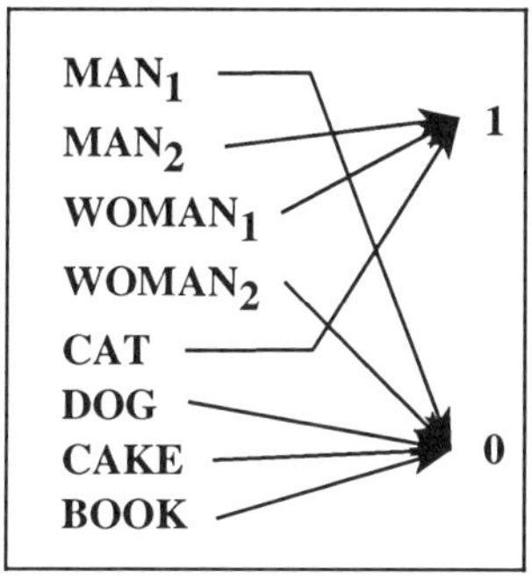

(52) $[slowly'(walk')]^{M2}$

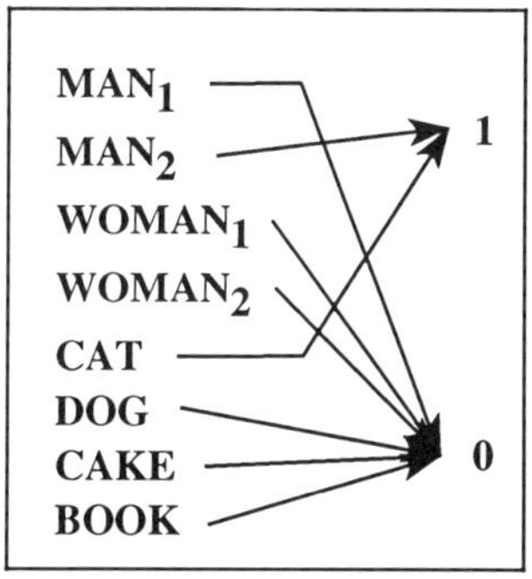

(53) [slowly']^{M2}

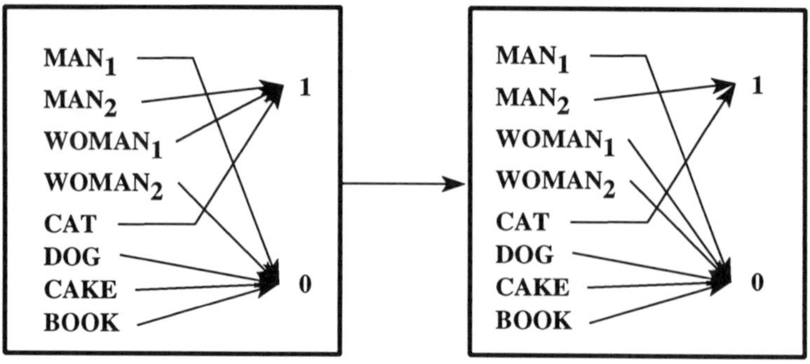

Exercise 4.6:

Assume that in M_2, the man, Ethel, the cat, the dog and the bike are all moving, and that the man, the cat and the bike are all moving slowly.

i. Draw the characteristic function denoted by [*move'*]^{M2}.

ii. Draw the characteristic function denoted by [*slowly'(move')*]^{M2}.

iii. Draw the function now associated with *slowly'* in M_2, assuming that nothing else is happening slowly and representing all characteristic functions apart from those associated with *move'* and *walk'* as ϕ.

There is much more that could be said about the extensions of adverbs. In particular, we need to constrain the functions denoted by adverbs like *slowly* so that they do pick out subsets of the sets denoted by their associated VPs in every model (cf. subsequent chapters, particularly Chapter 7, for details of how to do this). Furthermore, in a more extensive fragment, we would need to provide the means for interpreting other VP modifiers like prepositional phrases, other classes of adverbials and sentential modifiers (like *necessarily*, *unfortunately*, etc.). Such constructions present their own problems in semantics (which may or may not necessitate the extension or revision of certain aspects of the theory presented so far), but the introduction of a typed logical language and its transparent relation to possible denotations at least allows for the expressions to be representable in the logical translation language. Hence, for the rest of this book, L_{type} will form the basis for all revisions to the translation language required by the development of the grammar fragment and the basis of the model theory will remain the binary application of functions to their arguments in the way that we have seen.

4.6 Further reading

The idea that the combinatory properties of expressions can be encoded directly in their categorial definition is central to **categorial grammar** which evolved out of the work of certain logicians, most particularly Ajdukiewicz (1937) and Bar-Hillel (1953). A simple introduction can be found in Allwood, Andersen and Dahl (1977: 132-135) and more detailed discussions can be found in the articles in Oehrle, Bach and Wheeler (1988). Montague himself used categorial grammar for his syntactic analysis in Montague (1973) which is therefore also used in Dowty, Wall and Peters (1981). The definition of logical types can be found in Dowty, Wall and Peters (1981: 83-97) and Partee, ter Meulen and Wall (1990: 338-341). Discussions of type theory, translation and the syntax of natural languages can be found in Dowty (1982) and Gazdar, Klein, Pullum and Sag (1985: ch. 9). The notion of a function is introduced in Partee, ter Meulen and Wall (1990: 30-33), Allwood, Andersen and Dahl (1977: 9-13) and Chierchia and McConnell-Ginet (1990: 438-440). An early discussion of the semantic representation of adverbs can be found in Thomason and Stalnaker (1973). Cresswell (1985a) contains a collection of papers on adverbial and prepositional phrases, primarily with respect to temporal and spatial modification; and see also Parsons (1980). The discussion in the latter two references is somewhat technical and uses concepts that have not yet been presented or discussed in the present work and readers are advised to consult this book only after they have tackled subsequent chapters (particularly Chapters 8 and 9). The application of type theory to natural languages is discussed in Parsons (1979). There is a current debate about whether higher order types are necessary for the analysis of the semantics of natural languages. Representative articles on this subject are Thomason (1989), Turner (1989), and Chierchia and Turner (1989), but these are very technical and should not be tackled until the reader has read most of this book.

5 The Lambda Operator

5.1 The passive

In discussing the translation from English into L_{type} in Chapter 4, rules for generating and interpreting simple passives were omitted. Although it is possible to define the extension of a passive verb phrase like *kicked by Jo* as the characteristic function of the set of things that Jo kicks, it is not possible with the apparatus we currently have to link this function directly with the extension of the active verb *kick, kicks, kicked.* The appropriate relationship between the two voices is that, in the relation denoted by the passive, the entity denoted by the object of the preposition *by* corresponds to the entity denoted by the subject of the active and the entity denoted by the passive subject corresponds to that denoted by the object in the active. This correspondence was handled in Chapter 2 directly in the translation for the passive rule by switching around the individual constants translating the two noun phrases in the passive rule to yield an identical translation to that of the active. So, for example, *Jo kicked Chester* and *Chester was kicked by Jo* are both translated into L_P as *kick'(jo',chester')*. Unfortunately, this simple expedient is no longer open to us because of the existence in G_2 of a verb phrase constituent. This prevents subject and complement NPs from being ordered with respect to each other in a translation rule because they are no longer introduced by the same syntactic rule.

To see the problem that passives pose, together with other constructions that involve a change in grammatical functions, let us devise an extension of G_2 that not only generates passive sentences but also ensures that active and passive pairs of sentences are semantic paraphrases. The appropriate syntactic rules to generate passives are easy to define and appear in (1). In accordance with the general policy of this book, no attempt is made to draw out the syntactic regularities shown by different constructions. The rules in (1) clearly lose the obvious syntactic relations with their active counterparts and this problem may be resolved in a number of ways according to the system of syntax with which the theory of semantics is associated. Readers who are familiar with one of the many other systems of generative grammar currently used by linguists are invited to adapt the following grammar and its interpretation to suit the requirements of the theory they know. The important thing from the point of view of the semantics, however, is that, no matter what the appropriate syntactic relationship between active and passive happens to be and however it is formalised, active and passive pairs are truth-conditionally synonymous and this, at least, must be shown by an adequate semantic theory.

(1) a. $13G_2$: VP $\rightarrow$ was VP[PAS].
  b. $14G_2$: VP[PAS] $\rightarrow$ V_t[PAS] PP_{by}.
  c. $15G_2$: VP[PAS] $\rightarrow$ V_{dt}[PAS] PP_{to} PP_{by}.
  d. $16G_2$: VP[PAS] $\rightarrow$ V_{dt}[PAS] NP PP_{by}.
  e. $17G_2$: PP_{by} $\rightarrow$ by NP.
  f. V_t[PAS] = {kicked, loathed, poisoned, read, eaten, liked}.
  g. V_{dt}[PAS] = {given}.

For ease of exposition, it is assumed that the prepositions in passive *by* phrases function simply as syntactic case markers, like indirect objects marked by the preposition *to,* and the syntactic problems posed by this assumption will be ignored. The syntactic category, PP_{by}, thus has the same type and translation as the noun phrase it contains. Given this, it is possible to assign to the translations of passive verbs the same type as that assigned to their active counterparts, as shown in (2). These give rise to the set of translation rules in (3) for the syntactic rules in (1).

(2) a. TYPE(V_t[PAS]) = <e,<e,t>>. (= TYPE(V_t))
b. TYPE(V_{dt}[PAS]) = <e,<e,<e,t>>>. (= TYPE(V_{dt}))

(3) a. T13G_2: VP[PAS]'.
b. T14G_2: V_t[PAS]'(PP_{by}').
c. T15G_2: V_{dt}[PAS]'(PP_{to}')(PP_{by}').
d. T16G_2: V_{dt}[PAS]'(NP')(PP_{by}').
e. T17G_2: NP'.

The question that must now be addressed is: how to translate/interpret passive verbs to ensure that the rules in (3) yield the appropriate truth-conditions? If we stick to the rules for translating lexical items that we have been using until now, we should translate passive verbs exactly like their active counterparts, because translation is based on the lexeme underlying the word form. Given the usual assumption that passive morphology in English is inflectional, the lexeme associated with the form *kicked*, passive and active past tense, is KICK, so both ought to translate as *kick'* (as in Chapter 2). However, if we do this we will end up with the incorrect interpretations for passive sentences: they will come out with different truth-conditions from the corresponding active sentences. To see why this is so, consider the diagram in (4) which represents part of the extension for *kick'* in the model, M_2.

The translation of a sentence like *Ethel kicked the dog* comes out as true here with the translation of the VP, *kick'(the-dog')*, having the extension shown by the function f_3 which picks out the set of entities kicking the dog, i.e. {**MAN_1**, **$WOMAN_1$**}. If the passive participle is translated by the expression *kick'*, however, the translation of the corresponding passive *The dog was kicked by Ethel* comes out as false, because the VP translation, by T17G_2, is *kick'(ethel')* which denotes the function represented by f_2, i.e. the characteristic function of the null set. This, of course, picks out the set of things that kick Ethel, not that kick the dog, but, intuitively, the phrase *be kicked by Ethel* does not denote this set but the set of things that Ethel kicked. There is unfortunately no way of representing this set in L_{type} directly without assigning an extension to the passive participle *kicked* that is unconnected with that of the active verb *kicked*. The required function is that shown in (5).

Although the two diagrams in (4) and (5) represent different functions, there is an obvious relation between them. The function in (5) switches around the entities denoted by the first and second arguments of the function in (4). Unfortunately, this generalisation is not actually expressed in the grammar. If we give *kick'* and *kicked'* separate extensions as specified by the denotation assignment function, **F**, we lose the semantic generalisation about the passive-active relation and cannot guarantee that the extensions of passive participles do not depart radically from the extensions of their active counterparts. This would mean that the grammar was descriptively inadequate, because it failed to capture an intuition about the relation between active and passive. To maintain the adequacy of our theory, therefore, some way must be found of relating the extensions of active and passive verbs.

(4)

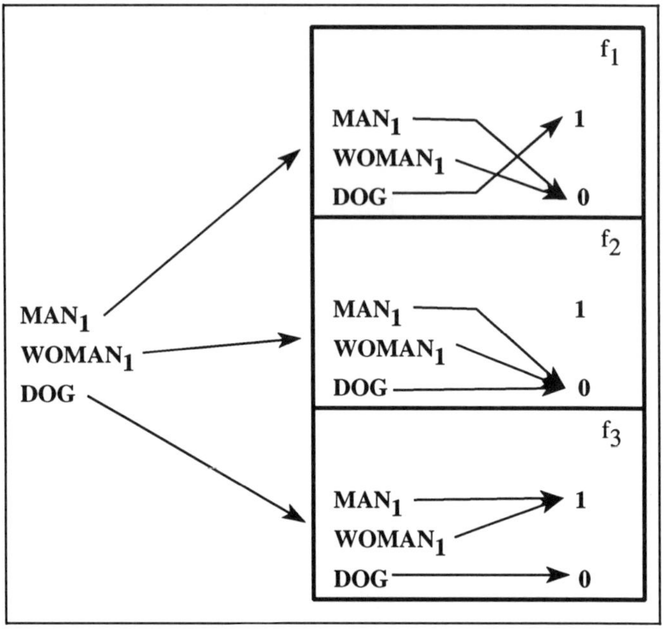

(5)

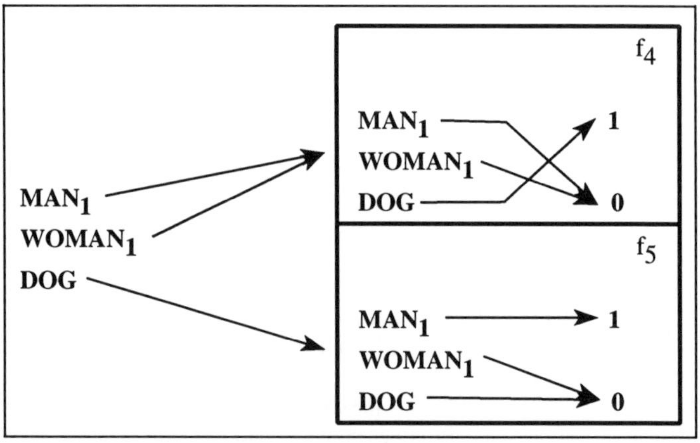

5.2 Introducing the lambda operator

To solve this problem, we need to take another look at sets. As we have seen, a set can be specified by listing of all its members or by defining a characteristic function for that set. These two methods of defining a set are easy to do if the set being defined is **finite**, but if the set is not finite but **infinite** a simple listing is not sufficient because, by definition, the list or the function will never be complete. It is possible, however, to define infinite sets by describing in general terms the property that picks out all the members of the set. Thus, instead of giving the definition of a set by listing its members, we can give a definition that describes the general property that determines which entities are members of that set. For example, the set of all natural numbers is an infinite set for which we can give a partial listing, e.g. {1,2,3,4,5,6,7,8,9,10,...} (the three dots before the right hand curly bracket conventionally indicates that the set is open and not fully listed), but we could also describe this set as the set consisting of all the natural numbers. Slightly more formally, we can define it as *the set of all things that are natural numbers*, or more formally still, as *the set of all x such that x is a natural number*. This latter definition selects a **variable** and specifies a property that any entity substituting for the variable must have in order to be a member of the set in question. Traditionally, individual variables (i.e. variables ranging over individual entities) are written as lower case members of the end of the alphabet, i.e. x, y, z, which sometimes appear with subscripts, e.g. x_1, y_{243}, z_{15}, etc., if a large number of such variables are required. The intensional description of a set may be symbolised by writing some individual variable before a vertical stroke, |, which both precede a quasi-English expression where the variable takes the place of some noun phrase in the expression, e.g. *x is a natural number.* The resulting expression is enclosed in curly brackets, {·} to indicate that what is being defined is a set. So, the set of natural numbers may be defined as *{x | x is a natural number}*. Although this is the most convenient way of specifying an infinite set, we can, of course, use it to specify a finite one. For example, we might specify the sets in (6), which are all presumably finite, and which could be used to describe the extensions of the English phrases *kicked Chester*, *was kicked by Jo* and *was a drunken lecturer*, respectively.

(6) a. {x | x kicked Chester}.
b. {y | Jo kicked y}.
c. {z | z was drunk and z was a lecturer}.

The semi-English set descriptions in (6) may easily be translated into formulae in L_{type}, but with the formulae containing a variable in place of one of the argument individuals. Hence, *x kicked Chester* can be represented in L_{type} as *(kick'(chester'))(x)*, (6.b) can be represented as *(kick'(y))(jo')* and (6.c) as *drunk'(z) & lecturer'(z)*.

Formulae containing variables are semantically incomplete, since variables do not have a fixed interpretation like constants but take their meaning from being associated with specific entities in specific situations, rather like pronouns in natural languages. Thus, a formula like *(kick'(chester'))(x)* does not denote a truth value until the variable, *x*, is associated with some entity in the model. Thus, to interpret such a formula, some entity, say $\mathbf{MAN_2}$, must be assigned to the variable *x* and the formula *(kick'(chester'))(x)* thus gets assigned the same truth value in the model as *(kick'(chester'))(bertie')*, since *bertie'* denotes $\mathbf{MAN_2}$. Interpreting formulae containing variables of this sort is thus like trying to ascertain the meaning of a sentence containing a pronoun, like *Chester was kicked by him.* The pronoun must be associated with a referent through the context before interpretation can proceed. Formulae in L_{type} (and other logical languages) which contain a **free variable**, i.e. a variable not associated with some operator (see below), are referred to as **propositional functions** or **open formulae**.

5.2.1 Extending L_{type}

Each of the descriptions in (6) provides the intensional property that determines the membership of some set of entities. The semantic theory developed so far has little to say about intensional things such as properties, but we may instead interpret them extensionally as equivalent to the sets they pick out. In other words, we may equate the set descriptions in (6) with one-place predicates in L_{type} which denote characteristic functions of sets of entities, as we saw in Chapter 4. Thus, given any entity, **a**, in some domain, if **a** substitutes for the variable in a set description to give a true statement, then **a** is in the set denoted by that description. If the resulting statement is false, however, then **a** is not in the set.

The propositional functions used at the end of the last section to translate the descriptions in (6) do not, however, denote sets. They are expressions of type t and not of type <e,t>. Such expressions can be turned into one-place predicates by the use of a special logical symbol, written λ (lambda), called the **lambda operator**. This operator picks up, or, more technically, **abstracts on**, a variable contained in a propositional function and turns the expression into something that denotes a characteristic function. The lambda operator is paired with the variable it abstracts upon which it is said to **bind**. For example, λx abstracts on the x variable and binds all instances of x in some propositional function while λy abstracts on and binds the y variable, and so on. The operator together with the variable it selects is written to the left of a propositional function which is itself enclosed in square brackets. For example, given the propositional function *(kick'(chester'))(x)* we can form the **lambda expression** *λx [(kick'(chester'))(x)]* which is a well-formed L_{type} expression of type <e,t>. The fact that all instances of the variable abstracted upon by the lambda operator which are contained in the propositional function are **bound** by the operator is an important point that will be returned to below. Generally, given a propositional function ϕ, containing an instance of the variable x, of type e, $\lambda x\,[\phi]$ is a well-formed expression of type <e,t>. This requires the addition to the syntax of L_{type} of the rule in (7) which allows expressions like those in (8), but not those in (9):

(7) If ϕ is an expression of type t containing an unbound instance of a variable x of type e, then $\lambda x[\phi]$ is a well-formed expression of type <e,t>.

(8) a. λy [(kick'(y))(jo')].
b. λz [drunk'(z) & lecturer'(z)].
c. λx [~(crazy'(x))].
d. λx [(kick'(y))(x)].
e. λz [(kick'(z))(z)].

(9) a. λx [(kick'(y))(jo)].
b. λy [(kick'(chester'))(jo)].
c. λz λz [[kick'(z)]].

In effect, the lambda operator turns a propositional function containing a free individual variable into a one-place predicate which denotes the characteristic function of the set of entities that **satisfy** the propositional function. An entity is said to satisfy a propositional function, ϕ, containing a variable, *x*, if the association of x with that entity gives rise to a true formula. A lambda expression λx [ϕ] is thus interpreted as if it were a set-theoretic expression {x | ϕ}, extensionally denoting the set of all x such that ϕ . For example, the one-place predicate λ*x [(kick'(chester'))(x)]* denotes the set of all x such that x kicked Chester, while the predicate λ*y [(kick'(y))(jo')]* is interpreted as the set of all y such that Jo kicked y and λ*z [drunk'(z) & lecturer'(z)]* denotes the set of all z such that z was drunk and z was a lecturer. Indeed, because propositional functions are formulae with at least one free variable, λ-expressions can be set-denoting expressions of indefinitely complex internal structure. An expression like λ*x [(((loathe'(x))(jo') ∨ (like'(x))(jo')) & ((x = the-cake') → (eat'(x))(jo')))]* is perfectly well-formed in L_{type} and denotes the set of all x such that either Jo loathed x or he liked x and if x was the cake then Jo ate x. Thus, λ-expressions provide a representation in L_{type} of the sorts of set descriptions introduced above.

Exercise 5.1:
Give an informal description of the sets denoted by the following lambda expressions:

i. λy [(like'(y))(jo') & ~((like'(y))(ethel'))].
ii. λz [(give'(z)(the-cake'))(z)].
iii. λx [x = jo'].
iv. λz [student'(z) & (like'(jo'))(z)].

Because lambda expressions of the sort given above are of type <e,t>, they can combine with expressions of type e by the rule of functional application to yield an expression of type t. Applying the predicate λ*x [(kick'(chester'))(x)]* to the individual constant *jo'* we get the expression λ*x [(kick'(chester'))(x)](jo')*. This formula, which may be read as *Jo is an x such that x kicks Chester*, has identical truth-conditions to the one obtained by replacing the bound variable x in the propositional function following the lambda operator by the argument expression, *jo'* and removing the lambda operator. Thus, λ*x [(kick'(chester'))(x)](jo')* is equivalent to *(kick'(chester'))(jo')*. The process of replacing variables by constants and removing the lambda operator is known as **lambda conversion** because it converts a complex lambda expression into a simple one.

(10) **Lambda Conversion**: If λx [ϕ] is a lambda expression of type <e,t> and a is an expression of type e, then λx [ϕ](a) is an expression of type t and is truth-conditionally equivalent to the expression ϕ* where ϕ* is derived from ϕ by replacing every occurrence of x in ϕ bound by λ by the expression a.

The rule for lambda conversion in (10) requires all instances of the variable bound by lambda to be replaced by an instance of the argument expression. If this were not done, the expression after conversion would still contain a variable and so would not be a formula but a propositional function that does not directly denote a truth value. The equivalence would, therefore, not hold. For example, *λz[drunk'(z) & lecturer'(z)](ethel')* is equivalent to *drunk'(ethel') & lecturer'(ethel')*, but not to *drunk'(ethel') & lecturer'(z)* nor *drunk'(z) & lecturer'(ethel')*, which are both propositional functions and not full formulae.

A second very important point about the use of the lambda operator is that, in the definition of lambda abstraction given in (7) above, mention was made of the fact that the variable abstracted on by the lambda operator must itself not be bound, i.e. not abstracted on by any other lambda operator. As an illustration, consider the lambda expression *λx [(like'(x))(fiona')]* where the x variable is bound by the lambda operator. This can be applied to an individual constant to yield a formula, *λx[(like'(x))(fiona')](ethel')* which in turn could be coordinated with a propositional function like *laugh(x)* to give the expression *λx [(like'(x))(fiona')](ethel') & laugh'(x)*. The second instance of the variable x in this expression is not bound by the lambda operator, as can be seen from the application of lambda conversion to the expression. The rule of lambda conversion in (10) allows the variable bound by λ to be replaced by the argument expression of the λ-expression to yield a truth-conditionally equivalent formula. In the case of the expression *λx[(like'(x))(fiona')](ethel') & laugh'(x)*, *ethel'* is the argument of the functor *λx[(like'(x))(fiona')]* so that the result of lambda conversion is *(like'(ethel'))(fiona') & laugh'(x)*, a propositional function. Thus, if we now take the original expression before lambda conversion *λx [(like'(x))(fiona')](ethel') & laugh'(x)*, we can abstract on the variable x again to get the one-place predicate *λx [λx [(like'(x))(fiona')](ethel') & laugh'(x)]*. The variable x in *(like'(x))(fiona')* in the latter expression is not bound by the outermost lambda operator, but only by the inner one. This means that the extension of the expression *λx [λx [(like'(x))(fiona')](ethel') & laugh'(x)]* is *the set of all x such that Ethel is in the set of things such that Fiona liked x and x laughed*, but not *the set of all x such that Fiona liked x (who is Ethel) and x laughed*. If this expression is applied to an individual constant like *jo'* to yield *λx[λx[(like'(x))(fiona')](ethel') & laugh'(x)](jo')* and is then lambda converted, the resulting expression is *[λx [(like'(x))(fiona')](ethel') & laugh'(jo')]* and not *[λx[(like'(jo'))(fiona')](ethel') & laugh'(jo')]*. The latter would have a very strange extension something like *Ethel is an x such that Fiona liked Jo and Jo laughed*, i.e. no properties are predicated of Ethel at all. It is necessary, therefore, to be careful when using variables. Even if two variables look the same in an expression, they may not behave in the same way in the expression concerned, as they may be bound by different operators and so behave differently semantically. For your own lambda expressions, try to differentiate variables as much as possible, writing the same symbol for different instances of variables only when they are bound by the same operator. This helps in keeping track of what conversions to make and ensuring that constants are not accidentally put where they shouldn't go. Using the symbol » to stand for λ-*converts into* the statements in (11) are all true and valid instances of lambda conversion, according to (10), while those in (12) are not.

(11) a. λy [(kick'(y))(jo')](chester')
» (kick'(chester'))(jo').
b. λx [(kick'(x))(x)](jo')
» (kick'(jo'))(jo').
c. λx [λ y [(kick'(y))(x)](jo')](bertie')
» λy [(kick'(y))(bertie')](jo')
» (kick'(jo'))(bertie').

(12) a. λx [(kick'(x))(x)](jo')
» (kick'(x))(jo').
b. λx [λx [howl'(x)](the-cat')](the-dog')
» λx [howl'(the-dog')](the-cat').
c. λy [(like'(jo'))(x)](bertie')
» (like'(jo'))(bertie').
d. λz [crazy'(z)](ethel') ∨ drunk'(z)
» crazy'(ethel') ∨ drunk'(ethel').

Exercise 5.2:

1. Explain why are the λ-conversions in (12) wrong.
2. Convert the following lambda expressions plus arguments into their equivalent formulae:
   i. λy [(like'(y))(jo') & ~((like'(y))(ethel'))](the-dog').
   ii. λz [(give'(z)(the-cat'))(z)](bertie').
   iii. λx [~(x = jo')](bertie').
   iv. λy [(like'(the-cat'))(y) ∨ ~(like'(the-dog'))(y)](bertie').
   v. λx [λy [crazy'(x) & (like'(x))(y)](jo') ∨ ~(crazy'(x))](bertie').

5.2.2 *Interpreting lambda expressions*

What lambda expressions denote has already been briefly discussed above. Essentially the idea is that by abstracting on a variable using the lambda operator, an expression is formed that denotes a set, the set of things that have the property specified by the propositional function in the scope of the operator. So, an expression like λ*x [(like'(x))(ethel')]* denotes the set of things that Ethel liked. It is now time to put this on a more formal footing and specify precisely how the denotation of a lambda expression can be determined from the denotation of the propositional function it is made from. Although the fundamental idea behind lambda abstraction is a simple one, i.e. that it is a set-forming operator, the formal definition is unfortunately quite complicated, but, as with all formal definitions given in this book, it does no more than restate explicitly the informal definition given earlier.

To see how the formal semantics of lambda abstraction works, let us look at what happens in lambda conversion. The equivalence between ϕ* and λx [ϕ] in (10) provides the interpretation of the lambda expression when applied to an appropriate argument. As we have seen, an expression like *λx[(kick'(x))(jo')](chester')* is, by the rule of lambda conversion, equivalent to *(kick'(chester'))(jo')*, i.e. the formula that is obtained when (all occurrences of) the abstracted variable are replaced by the argument expression. In yet other words, the truth-conditions of a lambda expression λx [ϕ] (where ϕ is a propositional function containing x) applied to an individual argument a are identical to those of the expression ϕ* derived by substituting a for all free occurrences of x in ϕ . From the semantic point of view what this equivalence expresses is that the value of the function denoted by λx[ϕ] applied to the denotation of a in a model is identical to that denoted by ϕ* in the same model. This can be more formally represented as (13), but at the moment we have no way of formally expressing what ϕ* is, or, more exactly, what its semantics is. To do this, the model theory needs to be extended to cope properly with the existence of variables in L_{type} expressions.

(13) $[\lambda x\ [\phi](a)]^{M}$ if, and only if, $[\phi^{*}]^{M}$.

In a number of places in this book, it has been said that variables are like pronouns: if the referent of a pronoun is unknown, there is no way that an expression containing it can be interpreted (assigned a truth value). For example, to know whether *She didn't like him* expresses a true proposition, one has to know who *she* and *him* refer to. In a similar way, the truth value of a formula containing a variable cannot be ascertained until the variable is associated with some entity in the model. In an expression λx [ϕ](a), the lambda operator binding a variable x gives the information that x is to be associated with the entity denoted by a, the argument that the lambda expression applies to. For example, *λx [(kick'(x))(jo')](chester')* is a formula that associates x in the model with $[chester']^{M2}$, i.e. **DOG**. On the other hand, the equation of x with **DOG** is not appropriate for every occurrence of x in any formula, since variables are not uniquely associated with particular entities in any particular model. The point of a variable is that it can be associated with different things in different circumstances, unlike constants, whose denotations are fixed by the denotation assignment function of a model. The association of variables with entities in a model is something in addition to, and separate from, the model itself.

Because variables do not have a fixed denotation, they are associated with entities in a model not by the denotation assignment function **F**, but by a **variable assignment function**, usually represented by the symbol **g**. This function assigns to each variable an entity in the model as its **value**. It is usually assumed that the number of variables available is infinite, but of course we are only ever interested in a small number of variables and in particular only the ones appearing in the L_{type} expressions we are interpreting. Because of this, and because infinite functions pose no real problem in interpretation, we shall ignore all but a very few of the infinite number of variables mentioned in any variable assignment function. Formally, then, **g** is an infinite function but in practice we will deal with only a very small part of it. Because the number of variables is infinite, the number of variable assignment functions for any set of entities in a model is infinite and varies quite considerably. For instance, there is a function that maps every variable onto only a single entity in the model, one that maps every seventeenth variable onto the same entity or one that maps variables onto entities in strict rotation. These are all perfectly valid functions but not really very useful for our purposes. The sorts of function we will be dealing with are very restricted, and the only important thing to bear in mind is that because **g** is a function, every variable is assigned one and only one entity as its value. From now on, therefore, expressions in L_{type} are interpreted with respect not just to a model, **M**, but also to a variable assignment **g**. Denotations of expressions are written between square brackets with the names of the model and the variable assignment function as superscripts outside the right bracket:

(14) If α is an expression in L_{type}, then $[\alpha]^{M,g}$ is its denotation with respect to a model, M, and a variable assignment g.

We need to look at the interpretations of expressions with respect to the same model, but different assignments of values to variables and, in particular, with respect to similar variable assignments. For example, we might have a (partial) variable assignment like that in (15) and we could also have one that is almost identical except that x is assigned **DOG** as value as in (16)

(15) g

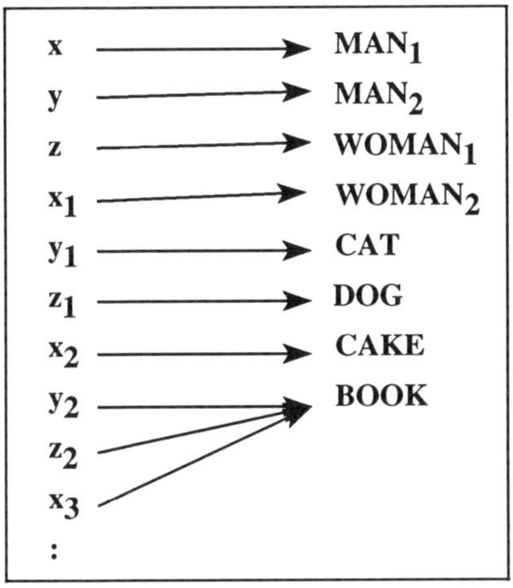

In the case of the variable assignments in (15) and (16), we say that **g'** is exactly like **g** except for the fact that x is assigned **DOG** as value. The relation between **g** and **g'** can be symbolised as: **g'** = $\mathbf{g}^{DOG/x}$, where the notation **a/x** indicates that **a** is assigned as the value of x in the appropriate function. Hence, $\mathbf{g}^{DOG/x}$ is that function exactly like **g** but with the value **DOG** assigned to x, i.e. **g'**. This notation is useful in discussing the interpretations of expressions with respect to the same model but slightly different variable assignments; in particular, variable assignments that may differ only in the value of one variable.

(16) **g'**

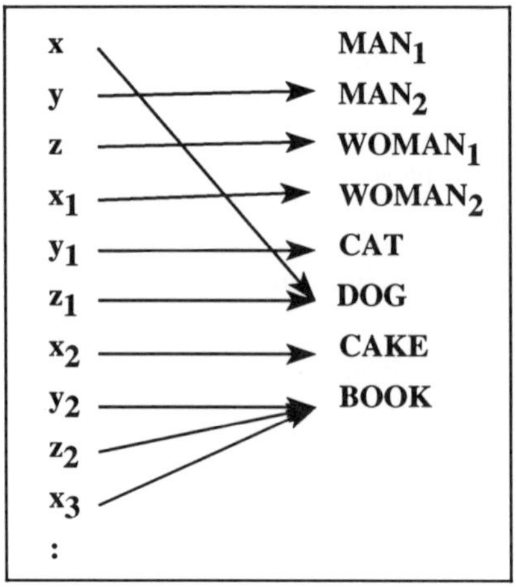

For expressions that contain no variables, the choice of variable assignment function is irrelevant. If there are no variables, it obviously makes no difference to the interpretation what variables are assigned to what entities. Hence, the interpretation of $[laugh'(ethel')]^{M,g}$ is identical to $[laugh'(ethel')]^{M,g'}$, where **g'** is not identical to **g**. Such expressions are still assumed to be interpreted with respect to an assignment of values to variables in order to make the theory more general, i.e. without having to refer to whether or not an expression contains a variable or not. Just bear in mind that the assignment is significant only when the interpreted expression does contain a variable.

The introduction of the variable assignment function provides a way of formally characterising ϕ^* in (13) in terms of the semantics rather than by the syntactic method of substituting the argument expression of a λ-expression for every occurrence of the abstracted variable. Given the use of variable assignment functions, the interpretation of an expression like *λx [(kick'(x))(jo')](chester')* with respect to a model, $\mathbf{M_2}$, and a variable assignment, **g**, can be defined as being identical to the interpretation of the expression *(kick'(x))(jo')* with respect to the same model $\mathbf{M_2}$ but a different variable assignment function **g'**. The assignment function required is that one exactly like **g** except that the variable bound by λ, x in this instance, is assigned as value the extension of the argument *chester'* in M_2. In the example given, $[chester']^{M2}$ is the entity **DOG**, so that **g'** maps the variable x onto this entity (i.e. **g'** is $\mathbf{g}^{DOG/x}$). Because x is associated with an entity, **DOG**, the truth value of $[(kick'(x))(jo')]^{M2,g'}$ is determined by first applying the function denoted by *kick'* in M_2 (with respect to **g'**) to the entity **DOG** and then applying the resulting function to $[jo']^{M2,g'}$. This is, of course, equivalent to the truth value that is assigned to the expression *(kick'(chester'))(jo')* in M_2, as required. More generally, then, we can restate the equivalence in (13) more accurately as in (17), where ϕ is a propositional function, and a is an individual constant.

(17) **Lambda conversion**: $[\lambda x\ [\phi](a)]^{M,g} \leftrightarrow [\phi]^{M,g[a]M/x}$.

The equivalence in (17) needs, however, to be shown to be true. In order to do this, it is necessary to define how the denotation of a lambda expression is determined and how the application of this denotation to that of its argument guarantees the truth of (17). It has already been established that the type of a lambda expression, $\lambda x[\phi]$, is <e,t> and so it must denote a characteristic function (i.e. a function from entities to truth values), but what function? To find this out, let us consider a concrete example. The function denoted by the (active) verb **liked** in M_2 (more strictly the extension of its translation, *like'*) is shown in (19), overleaf. This is equivalent to . the set of ordered pairs {**<MAN_1,$WOMAN_1$>**, **<MAN_1,$WOMAN_2$>**, **<MAN_1,MAN_1>**, **<MAN_1,MAN_2>**, **<$WOMAN_1$,MAN_1>**, **<$WOMAN_1$,$WOMAN_2$>**, **<$WOMAN_2$,CAT>**, **<$WOMAN_2$,$WOMAN_1$>**}.

It is now our task to work out the denotation of the lambda expression *λx[(like'(x))(jo')]* based on this function. Clearly, the characteristic function denoted by this expression must pick out the set of entities that Jo liked in the model, i.e. **$WOMAN_1$**, **$WOMAN_2$**, **MAN_2** and himself, **MAN_1**. This function can be defined formally by using different variable assignment functions and checking the truth value of the expression *(like'(x))(jo')* with respect to the model and the appropriate variable assignment function. To get the function denoted by the lambda expression, therefore, we ascertain the truth value of $[(like'(x))(jo')]^{M2,g}$ for every assignment function **g'** exactly like **g** except that x is assigned to a different member of **A**, the set of entities in the model. If the truth value of the expression for some assignment of a value to x is **1** (i.e. true), then in the function denoted by the lambda expression, the entity assigned to x is mapped onto **1**. Otherwise, it is mapped onto **0**. To see how this works, let us go through the construction of the characteristic function denoted by *λx [(like'(x))(jo')]* with respect to M_2, step by step.

In the first place, let **g** be the assignment function in (15). Here x is mapped onto **MAN_1** and the value of $[(like'(x))(jo')]^{M2,g}$ is **1** because Jo did like himself. This result can be checked by comparing the function in (19), where **MAN_1** is mapped onto a function that maps **MAN_1** onto **1**. Hence, the information in (18) must be part of the function denoted by $[\lambda x\,[(like'(x))(jo')]]^{M2,g}$.

(18)

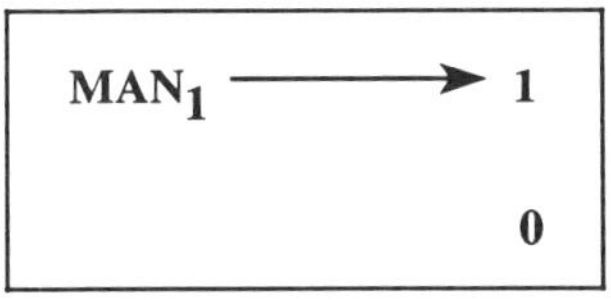

Next, we look at the truth value of *(like'(x))(jo')* with respect to a variable assignment function exactly like **g** except that x is mapped on to some other member of **A**, say **MAN_2**. This function is $g^{MAN2/x}$ and, as shown by (19), $[(like'(x))(jo')]^{M2,g^{MAN2/x}}$ is **1** and so the function $[\lambda x\,[(like'(x))(jo')]]^{M2,g}$ maps **MAN_2** onto **1** as well, giving (20).

(19)

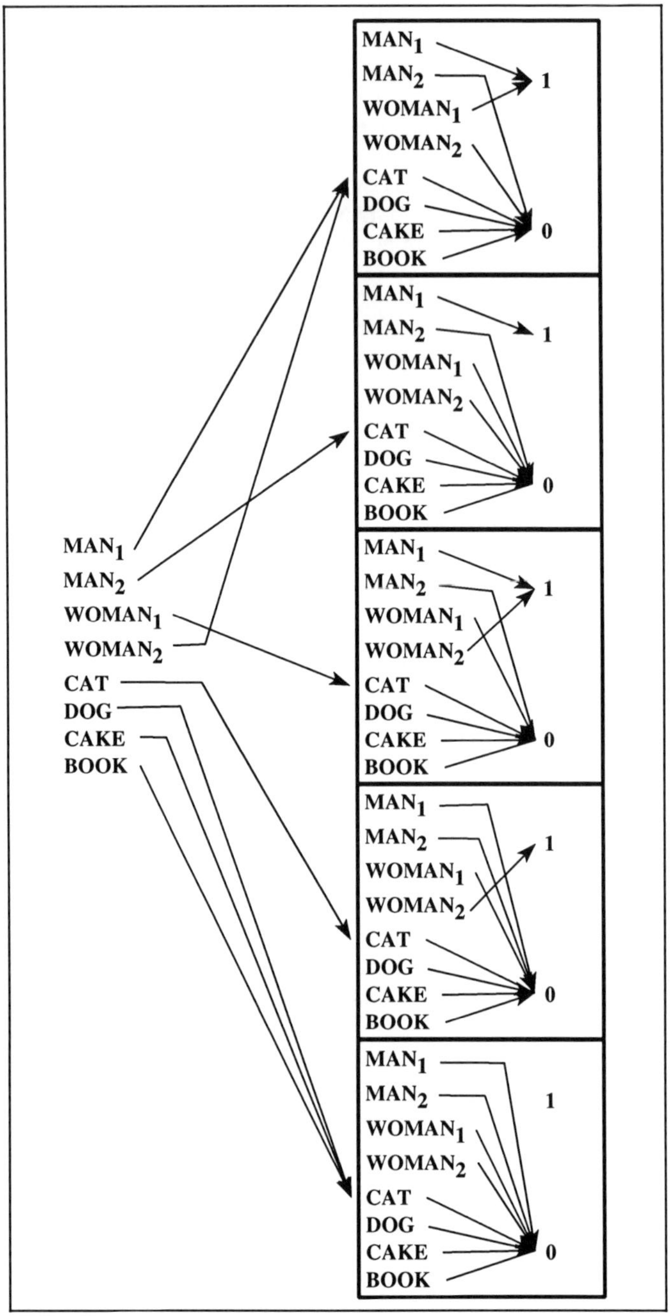

(20)

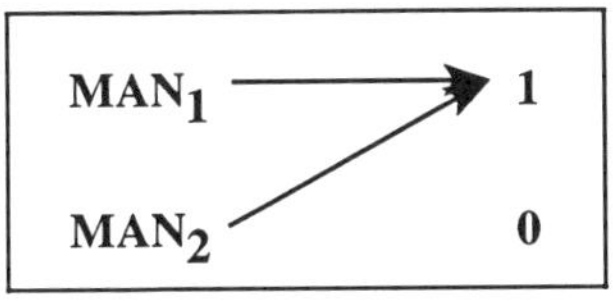

This process is repeated with a new variable assignment function like **g** but where x is mapped onto **WOMAN**$_1$ to get the value of $[(like'(x))(jo')]^{M2,g_{WOMAN1/x}}$ which again is **1**. This is repeated again and again until the value of $[(like'(x))(jo')]^{M2,g_{\alpha}/x}$ has been ascertained for every member of **A**. This yields the complete characteristic function in (21) which provides the extension of the expression λx *[(like'(x))(jo')]* with respect to the model M_2 and the variable assignment function, **g**.

(21)

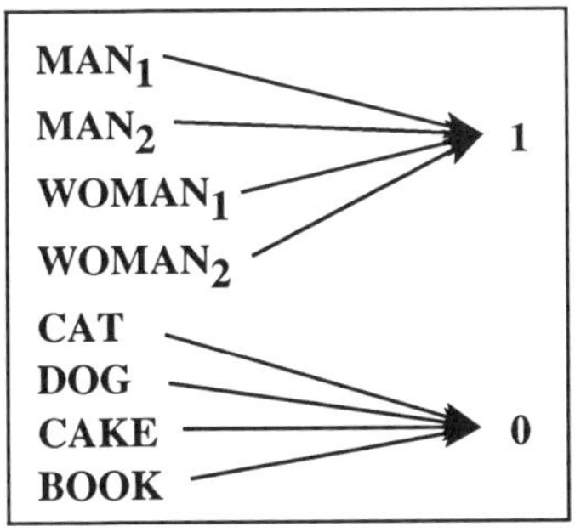

This description of the way in which the denotations of lambda expressions containing abstracted individual variables are constructed provides the basis for the formal definition for ascertaining the denotations of such λ-expressions. The definition is added to the model theory used to interpret L_{type} as the new clause which appears in (22). This restates in a more general and precise fashion how the function in (21) was determined and introduces no new concepts.

(22) For any model M = «A,F», if ϕ is an expression of type t containing an unbound instance of the individual variable x (of type e), then $[\lambda x\ [\phi]]^{M,g}$ is that characteristic function κ such that for all individuals, **a** , in A, κ(**a**) = 1 if, and only if, $[\phi]^{M,g_{a}/x}$ = **1** and κ(**a**) = 0, otherwise.

(22) guarantees that the equivalence in (13) holds for any model. The reason is that, according to (13), the truth value of an expression $\lambda x[\phi\ ](a)$ with respect to **M** and **g** is given by assigning the value of $[a]^{M,g}$, say **a**, to x and ascertaining the truth value of $[\phi]^{M,g_{a}/x}$. Since the denotation of $\lambda x\ [\phi]$, according to (22), includes a mapping from $[a]^{M,g}$ to $[\phi]^{M,g_{a}/x}$, the equivalence always holds. Hence, the informal syntactic process of λ-conversion can be carried out validly, because the semantics of λ -expressions in (22) entails that $\lambda x\ [\phi](a)$ is always truth-conditionally equivalent to $\phi^{a/x}$, no matter what model is being used for the purposes of interpretation.

Exercise 5.3:
Using the definition in (22) and assuming that the model M_2 is the same as M_1, except for parts already specified, work out the extensions of the following L_{type} lambda expressions:

i. λy [happy'(y) & laugh'(y)].
ii. λz [(give'(bertie')(z))(jo')].
iii. λx [laugh'(x)].
iv. λy [~((y = the-lecturer') ∨ (y = the-student'))].

5.2.3 *The passive again*

The lambda operator, as should be clear from the above discussion, provides an elegant way of capturing the semantic relation between active and passive verbs, or, more precisely, verb phrases. As we have already noted, the syntactic subject of a passive sentence corresponds semantically to the direct object of the active. In order to capture this relation, all that needs to be done is to translate passive VPs by a lambda expression that abstracts on a variable in the appropriate position. So, for example, we can translate the passive VP *kicked by Jo* as *λx [(kick'(x))(jo')]* which denotes the set of things that Jo kicked. Assuming that copular *be* adds nothing to the truth-conditions of the passive sentence (beyond tense), this is the expression that is functionally applied to the translation of the subject. Hence, *Chester was kicked by Jo* translates into L_{type} as *λx [(kick'(x))(jo')](chester')*. By lambda conversion, this is equivalent to *(kick'(chester'))(jo')* which is, of course, the translation of the active sentence *Jo kicked Chester*, exactly as required.

To complete the analysis of the simple passive in G_2, here are the translation rules for the syntactic rules $13G_2$ to $17G_2$. The rule in (23.b) is for the passive of transitive verbs, and so the abstracted variable *x* appears in the object position nearest the verb. The two rules for ditransitive passives in (23.c) and (23.d) differ in the place where the variable appears. In the former rule, the λ-operator binds the second, direct object, position while in the latter it binds the indirect object position, nearest the verb, capturing the difference between ordinary ditransitive passives like *the book was given to Ethel by Bertie* and the ones associated with double object ditransitive sentences like *Ethel was given the book by Bertie*.

(23) a. $T13G_2$: VP[PAS]'.
b. $T14G_2$: λx [V_t[PAS]'(x)(PP_{by}')].
c. $T15G_2$: λx [V_{dt}[PAS]'(PP_{to}')(x)(PP_{by}')].
d. $T16G_2$: λx [V_{dt}[PAS]'(x)(NP')(PP_{by}')].
e. $T17G_2$: NP'.

(24) presents a sample derivation and translation of the ditransitive passive sentence, *Ethel was given the book by Bertie*. That this translation is equivalent to that of the active sentence *Bertie gave the book to Ethel* can be seen by deriving the translation of the latter. This is left as an exercise to the reader.

(24) a. S
$\Rightarrow$ S'.
b. NP VP[+FIN] $1G_2$
$\Rightarrow$ VP'(NP').
c. N_{pr} VP[+FIN] $6G_2$
$\Rightarrow$ VP'(N_{pr}').
d. N_{pr} was VP[PAS] $13G_2$
$\Rightarrow$ VP[PAS]'(N_{pr}').
e. N_{pr} was $V_{dt\text{-}pas}$ NP PP_{by} $16G_2$
$\Rightarrow \lambda x$ [$V_{dt\text{-}pas}$'(x)(NP')(PP_{by}')](N_{pr}').
f. N_{pr} was $V_{dt\text{-}pas}$ the N PP_{by} $7G_2$
$\Rightarrow \lambda x$ [$V_{dt\text{-}pas}$'(x)(the-N')(PP_{by}')](N_{pr}').
g. N_{pr} was $V_{dt\text{-}pas}$ the N by NP $17G_2$
$\Rightarrow \lambda x$ [$V_{dt\text{-}pas}$'(x)(the-N')(NP')](N_{pr}').
h. N_{pr} was $V_{dt\text{-}pas}$ the N by N_{pr2} $6G_2$
$\Rightarrow \lambda x$ [$V_{dt\text{-}pas}$'(x)(the-N')(N_{pr2}')](N_{pr}').
i. Ethel was given the book by Bertie Lex
$\Rightarrow \lambda x$ [give'(x)(the-book')(bertie')](ethel')
» give'(ethel')(the-book')(bertie').

Exercise 5.4:
Translate the following passive sentences into L_{type} and compare their translations with their active counterparts:

i. The cake was eaten by Chester.
ii. The book was given to Fiona by Ethel.

5.3 Generalising lambda expressions

Because propositional functions may contain more than one free variable, it is possible to construct expressions that have more than one instance of the lambda operator in them. According to the formulation we gave above, however, this is not possible because we have restricted lambda abstraction to binding individual variables in propositional functions. There is, however, no sound reason to adhere to this restriction and the theory benefits from generalising the definition of lambda abstraction to allow the lambda operator to bind a variable of any type contained within an expression of any type.

For example, instead of introducing the lambda operator in the translation rules for the passive VPs, it is possible to state the semantics of the passive participle directly by manipulating the argument structure of the verb using multiple lambda abstraction. For the passive of a transitive verb, this allows the first and second arguments to be permuted in the translation. For example, it is possible to derive the semantics of the passive participle *kicked* from that of its active counterpart *kicked, kicks, kick* by creating an open formula from the translation of the active verb using two variables. This would give the propositional function *(kick'(y))(x)*. Because the direct object argument (the second to last argument to be combined with by a predicate) appears last in the passive, surfacing as the syntactic subject, we abstract on the y variable first to give the expression *λy [(kick'(y))(x)]* of type <e,t>. This expression contains the free variable x associated with the subject, or final, argument of the verb which appears in the passive as the object of the preposition *by.* Abstracting on this variable gives an expression of type <e,<e,t>>, *λx[λy[(kick'(y))(x)]]*. Using this approach, the translation of a passive VP like *kicked by Ethel* comes out as *λx [*λy [(kick'(y))(x)]](ethel'), which by lambda conversion is equivalent to *λy [(kick'(y))(ethel')]*, which has the form of the output of the translation rule T14G_2 in (23.b). The translation of the sentence *Prudence was kicked by Ethel* is thus equivalent to the application of this latter expression to the translation of the subject, i.e. *λy [(kick'(y))(ethel')](prudence')* which, of course, is equivalent to *(kick'(prudence'))(ethel')* by lambda conversion, as shown in (25).

(25) a. *kicked*
⇒ λx [λy [(kick'(y))(x)]].
b. *kicked by Ethel*
⇒ λ x [λy [(kick'(y))(x)]](ethel').
c. *Prudence was kicked by Ethel*
⇒ (λx [λy [(kick'(y))(x)]](ethel'))(prudence').
d. » λy [(kick'(y))(ethel')](prudence').
e. » (kick'(prudence'))(ethel').

If lambda abstraction is allowed to operate over expressions of any type in this way, then the rule of lambda conversion must be relaxed to allow this. All that needs to be done is to say that a lambda expression, λx [φ], applied to an individual argument is semantically equivalent to φ with the denotation of the argument as value of the free variable x, as in (26).

(26) **Lambda conversion**: If φ is an expression of type a containing a free instance of x, a variable of type e, and a is an expression of type e, then $[\lambda x\,[\phi](a)]^{M,g} \leftrightarrow [\phi]^{M,g\mathbf{a}/x}$ where **a** is $[a]^{M,g}$.

When converting lambda expressions with multiple abstractions, it is very important to make sure that the correct variable is replaced by the correct argument. (26) requires that lambda conversion be **successive**. Conversion starts from the leftmost lambda operator and the first argument after the square brackets demarcating the scope of the operator, then moves on to the next lambda and the argument it combines with and so on until there are no more lambdas left. Thus in (25.c), the leftmost lambda abstracts on the variable *x* and the first argument after the square brackets is *ethel'*. Hence, it is this argument that must replace instances of *x*. The second argument *prudence'* becomes the first argument after this lambda conversion and because the leftmost λ is now associated with the variable *y*, *prudence'* replaces the instance of *y* to give the correct expression after λ-conversion, i.e. *(kick'(prudence'))(ethel')*. A further example is given in (27) which shows the necessary steps in the conversion of the triple abstraction in the lambda expression *((λx[λy[λz[(give'(x)(z))(y)]]](fiona'))(bertie'))(the-book')*, the translation of the sentence *The book was given to Fiona by Bertie.* In this example, each variable is given a different subscript which also appears with the arguments that are to replace them. Although strictly speaking unnecessary, this co-indexing of variable and argument shows the dependencies between them very clearly and allows the order of λ-conversion to be more easily traced.

(27) a. » $((\lambda x_1\ [\lambda y_2\ [\lambda z_3\ [give'(x_1)(z_3)(y_2)]]](fiona'_1))(bertie'_2))(the\text{-}book'_3)$
b. » $(\lambda y_2\ [\lambda z_3\ [give'(fiona'_1)(z_3)(y_2)]](bertie'_2))(the\text{-}book'_3)$
c. » $\lambda z_3\ [give'(fiona'_1)(z_3)(bertie'_2)](the\text{-}book'_3)$
d. » $[give'(fiona'_1)(the\text{-}book'_3)(bertie'_2)]$.

Exercise 5.5:
Which of the following lambda conversions are well-formed?

i. λx [λz [(like'(x))(z)](jo')](bertie')
» (like'(jo'))(bertie').
ii. (λx [λz [(like'(x))(z)]](jo'))(bertie')
» (like'(jo'))(bertie').
iii. (λx [λy [(like'(x))(y) & laugh'(y)]](the-cat'))(ethel')
» (like'(the-cat'))(ethel') & laugh'(ethel').
iv. λx [scream'(x)] ∨ λx [~(laugh'(x))](jo')
» scream'(jo') ∨ ~(laugh'(jo')).
v. λx [scream'(x) ∨ ~(laugh'(x))](jo')
» scream'(jo') ∨ ~(laugh'(jo')).

---

*Exercise 5.6:
Construct a lexical rule for passivisation in English along the lines suggested in the text above.

---

*Exercise 5.7
Another process by which grammatical functions are altered in English is the one often referred to as **dative shift** whereby a prepositional indirect object becomes the direct object and the direct object appears in second place, as shown in the relation between a and b below. Using the λ-operator, construct a rule that relates the semantic structure of the non-dative-shifted verb in i to that in ii, making sure that the paraphrase relation that holds between these sentences is maintained.

i. Ethel gave the cake to the dog.
ii. Ethel gave the dog the cake.

Not only is it possible to abstract over expressions of any type, it is also possible to abstract on variables of any type. Thus, we can generalise the definition of lambda abstraction given in (7) to derive lambda expressions of all types. For example, variables of type t, usually written using the letters p, q and r, may be abstracted upon in an expression like *snow'* ↔ *p* to create an expression λ*p [snow' ↔ p]* of type <t,t>. This denotes the set of all truth values that are identical to that assigned to *snow'* in a model. Alternatively, a one-place predicate variable, P, may apply to an individual constant like *the-cat'* to give the expression *P(the-cat')*. The free predicate variable can then be abstracted upon to yield the expression, λ*P[P(the-cat')]*, of type <<e,t>,t> which denotes the set of all sets of which the cat is a member. Indeed, L_{type} contains variables of every type and allows any of these to be bound by the lambda operator in any expression of whatever type. Hence, the rules for constructing well-formed expressions in L_{type} include the general syntactic rule for lambda expressions in (28).

(28) **Lambda Abstraction**: If ϕ is an expression of type b, and u is an unbound variable of type a contained in ϕ, then $\lambda u\ [\phi]$ is a well-formed expression of type <a,b>.

The type of a lambda expression is derived from taking the type of the abstracted variable as the argument type and the type of the expression abstracted over as the result type. Thus, taking *p* and *q* to be variables of type t, an expression like $\lambda p[p \rightarrow q]$ is of type <t,t>, because *p* and $p \rightarrow q$ are both of type t. The expression $\lambda q[\lambda p[p \rightarrow q]]$, on the other hand, is of type <t,<t,t>>, because q is of type t and $\lambda p[p \rightarrow q]$ is of type <t,t>, and so on.

Exercise 5.8:
Given the variables below, what are the types of the lambda expressions that follow? (Where a is a type, the set of variables of type a can be symbolised as $\mathbf{Var_a}$.)

$P,Q \in Var_{<e,t>}$	$p,q \in Var_t$	$R \in Var_{<e,<e,t>>}$
$x,y,z \in Var_e$	$A \in Var_{<<e,t>,<e,t>>}$	

i. λR [(R(jo'))(bertie')].
ii. λx [λy [λz [(give'(x)(y))(z)]]].
iii. λP [λA [A(P)]].
iv. λp [p ↔ rain'].
v. λQ [Q(ethel')].
vi. λp [λq [p ↔ q]].

The interpretation of these generalised lambda expressions is similar to that for expressions where the abstracted variable is an entity contained in a propositional function. The denotations, however, have different domains and ranges. For example, the expression *λP [P(chester')]* is of type <<e,t>,t> and so denotes a function from sets (denotations of type <e,t>) to truth values. This function maps every set of entities onto **1** if the extension of *chester'* is in the set, i.e. if $[P(chester')]^{M,g^{s/P}}$ is **1** where **s** is some subset of **A**. Otherwise $[\lambda P\ [P(chester')]]^{M,g}$ maps **s** onto **0**. In other words, the expression *λP [P(chester')]* denotes the set of all subsets of **A** of which Chester is a member. A more complex example is given by the denotation of an expression that has more than one instance of lambda operator, e.g. *λx[λy[(like'(y))(x)]]*. This expression denotes a set of ordered pairs: the set of all pairs of entities <β,α> such that β is liked by α, or, more formally, $\{<\beta,\alpha> \mid <\alpha,\beta> \in [like']^{M,g}\}$. More examples of informally described denotations of complex lambda expressions appear in (29) where the variables have the types given in exercise 5.8.

(29) a. λx [(hate'(x))(jo') & (hate'(x))(ethel')] denotes the set of all x such that Jo and Ethel hate x.

b. λP [P(bertie') → P(chester')] denotes the set of all sets P such that if Jo is in P then Chester is also in P.

c. λR [(R(chester'))(bertie')] denotes the set of all relations R that hold between Chester and Bertie.

d. λy [λx [give'(y)(the-book')(x)]] denotes the set of all ordered pairs <x,y> such that x gives the book to y.

e. λP [λx [P(x)]] denotes the set of ordered pairs of entities and sets <x,P> such that x is in the set P.

f. λR [λx [(R(x))(chester')]] denotes the set of ordered pairs of entities and sets of ordered pairs <x,R> such that Chester stands in the relation R to x.

g. λP [λQ [Q(ethel') & P(ethel')]] denotes the set of ordered pairs of sets of entities <Q,P> such that Ethel is a member of both sets.

Exercise 5.9:
Give informal descriptions of the denotations of the lambda expressions given in exercise 5.8 along the lines of those in (29).

The formal definition for the denotations of generalised lambda expressions is very similar to that given in (22) for simple lambda expressions involving only individual variables and propositional functions. Any lambda expression λu [ϕ] denotes a function from the denotations of the type of the abstracted variable, u, to denotations of the type of the expression that is abstracted over, i.e. ϕ. The actual function denoted by λu [ϕ] is one that when applied to any object in the domain of the function (i.e. of the type of the abstracted variable) yields a semantic object that is identical to the interpretation of the expression abstracted upon, ϕ, with respect to a variable assignment where the abstracted variable, u, is associated with the object denoted by the argument. The formal definition is given in (30), which forms part of the model theory interpreting L_{type}.

(30) If u is a variable of type a and ϕ an expression of type b containing a free instance of u, then $[\lambda u\ [\phi]]^{M,g}$ is that function **h** from D^a into D^b such that for all elements **a** in D^a, **h**(**a**) is $[\phi]^{M,g^{a/u}}$.

To make this definition clearer, consider the interpretation of the expression *λx[λy[(like'(y))(x)]]*. Informally, as we have seen, this denotes the set of ordered pairs of entities such that the first is liked by the second. Formally, it denotes a function from entities to characteristic functions where each member of the set of entities, **A**, is mapped onto the characteristic function obtained from the extension of *λy [(like'(y))(x)]* where *x* is associated with the relevant element in **A**. For example, if the function $[\lambda x\ [\lambda y\ [(like'(y))(x)]]]^{M2,g}$ is applied to the entity **DOG**, then the result is $[\lambda y\ [(like'(y))(x)]]^{M2,g^{DOG/x}}$, which denotes the set of entities that the dog likes. Since the latter is truth-conditionally equivalent to the expression *λy[(like'(y))(chester')]*, we get the effects of lambda conversion. Hence, it again follows from the definition of the interpretation of lambda expressions in (30) that lambda conversion holds and $\lambda x\ [\lambda y\ [(like'(y))(x)]](chester')$ is equivalent to $\lambda y[(like'(y))(chester')]$. Thus, the generalised version of the definition of lambda conversion in (17) given below is valid for all lambda expressions whatever the type of the variable abstracted upon and whatever the type of the expression abstracted over. (But see Chapter 10 for some environments in which it is not valid.)

(31) $[\lambda u\ [\phi](a)]^{M,g} = [\phi]^{M,g[a]M/u}$.

To complete the example of generalised lambda abstraction, let us work through the construction of the function denoted by $\lambda x\ [\lambda y\ [(like'(y))(x)]]$ in M_2. To do this, it is necessary to construct the denotation of the lambda expression $\lambda y\ [(like'(y))(x)]$ for all values of x. In M_2, the extension of *like'* is the function in (19) above. We begin constructing the function $[\lambda x\ [\lambda y[(like'(y))(x)]]]^{M2,g}$ by taking an arbitrary member of the set of entities, **A**, say $\mathbf{MAN_1}$, and working out the value of $[\lambda y[(like'(y))(x)]]^{M2,gMAN1/x}$. The latter is, of course, the characteristic function that picks out the set of things Jo liked, i.e. himself, Bertie, Fiona and Ethel. This function can be laboriously constructed by working out the value of $[(like'(y))(x)]^{M2,g'a/y}$ for all members α of **A** where **g'** is $\mathbf{g}^{MAN1/x}$. Working out the values of *(like'(y))(x)* with respect to M_2 and the variable assignment function noted above (which may also be written as $\mathbf{g}^{[MAN1/x],\alpha/y}$) yields the function in (32).

(32) $[\lambda y\ [(like'(y))(x)]]^{M2,gMAN1/x}$

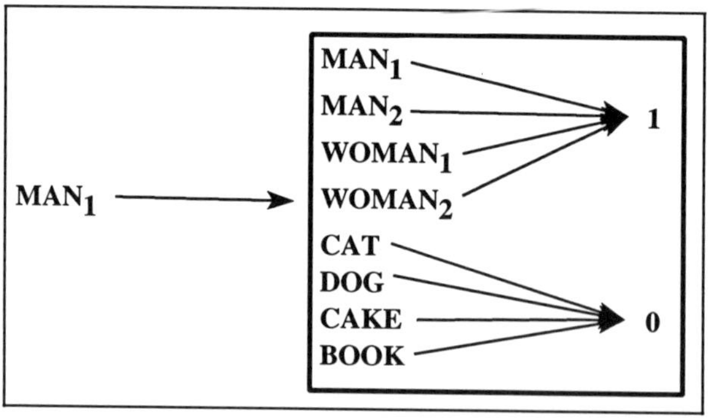

Next we take another member of **A**, say **DOG**, and compute the value of $[\lambda y[(like'(y))(x)]]^{M,gDOG/x}$, the set of things that the dog liked. This gives another part of the extension of $\lambda x\ [\lambda y\ [(like'(y))(x)]]$. Stepping through this procedure for the remaining members of **A** we get the function in (33) which reverses the relations between the entities in the diagram in (19), as can be checked by interpreting the function in (33) in terms of sets of ordered pairs.

(33) $[\lambda x\ [\lambda y\ [(like'(y))(x)]]]^{M2,g}$

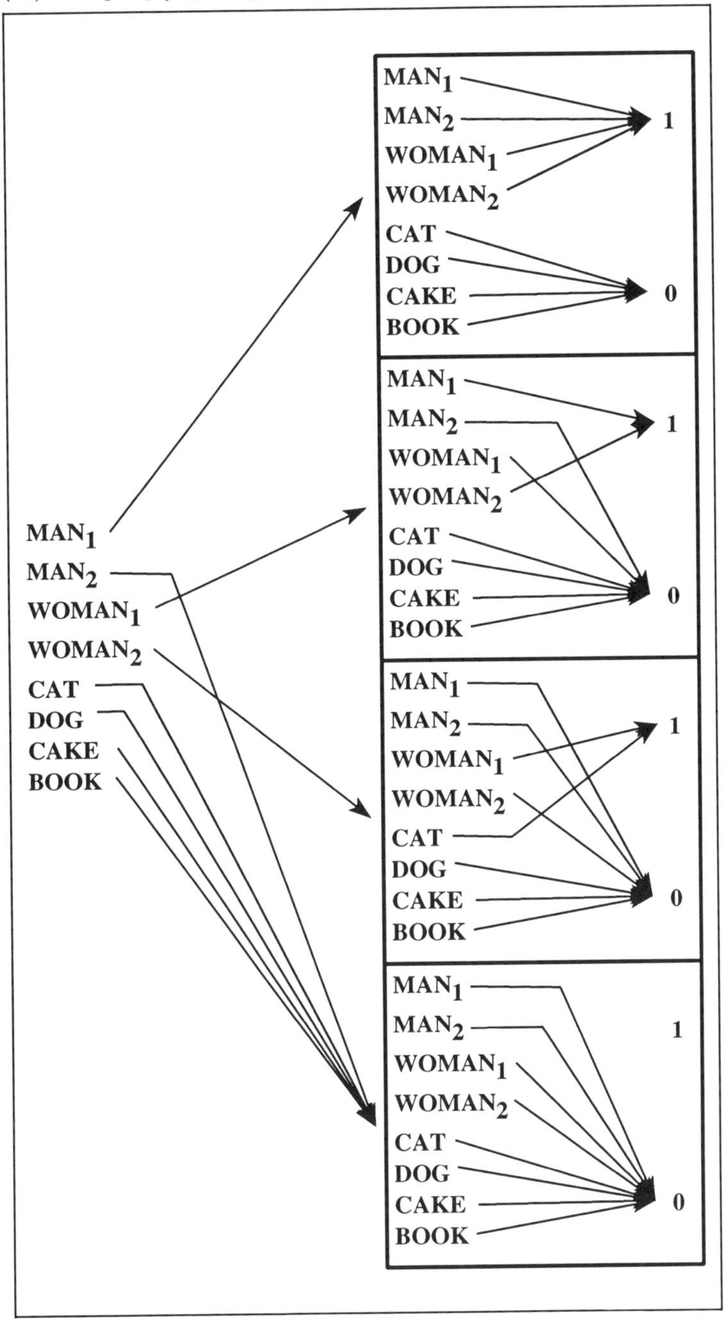

(34) $[\lambda y\ [(like'(y))(x)]]^{M2,gDOG/x}$

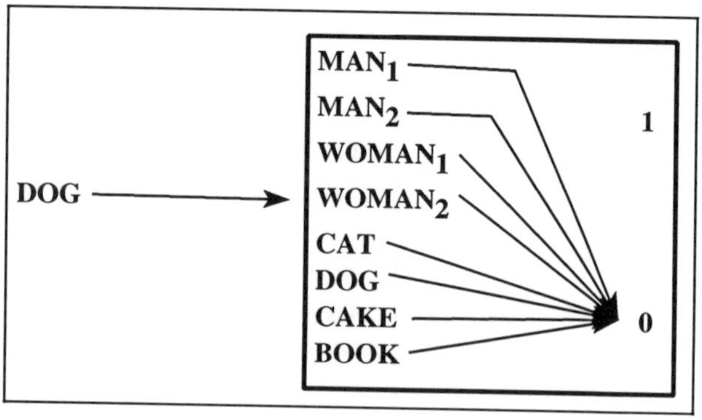

To further illustrate the formal interpretation of generalised lambda expressions, let us take a look at a second example expression, one that abstracts on a variable over one-place predicates, e.g. $\lambda P\ [P(ethel')]$. As mentioned above, this expression denotes the set of all sets of which Ethel is a member. In functional terms, this is construed as a function from characteristic functions to truth values, where each characteristic function, **k**, in the domain is mapped onto **1** if (and only if) $\mathbf{WOMAN_1}$ (the extension of $[ethel']^{M2,g}$) is mapped onto **1** in **k** itself, i.e. if $[P(ethel')]^{M2,gk/P}$ is true. For example, in M_2 (assuming the denotations in M_1 are carried over into M_2) the sets that contain Ethel include the sets denoted by the expressions *happy'* and *laugh'* but not the sets denoted by *run'* or $\lambda x\ [(like'(x))(bertie')]$. Hence, the function in (35) forms part of $[\lambda P\ [P(ethel')]]^{M2,g}$. The domain of the functions that expressions like $\lambda P\ [P(ethel')]$ denote include, not only the extensions of simple one-place predicates specified by the denotation function of a particular model, but all the characteristic functions denoted by some expression in the logical language. This includes the sets of entities liked by Jo, those given the book by the man, those that were loathed by the cake and more abstruse sets like the set of all entities that were eaten by the dog and did not poison it. (35) thus only represents a part of the function denoted by $\lambda P\ [P(ethel')]$ in M_2, but gives enough information to show what this function looks like.

Exercise 5.10:

Give the formal definitions of the denotations of the following lambda expressions in M_2 and represent these in the way shown in the examples in (33) and (35):

i. $\lambda p\ [p \leftrightarrow rain']$.
ii. $\lambda z\ [\lambda y\ [\lambda x\ [give'(x)(y)(z)]]]$.
iii. $\lambda P\ [slowly'(P)]$.

---

(35) $[\lambda P\ [P(ethel'))]]^{M2,g}$

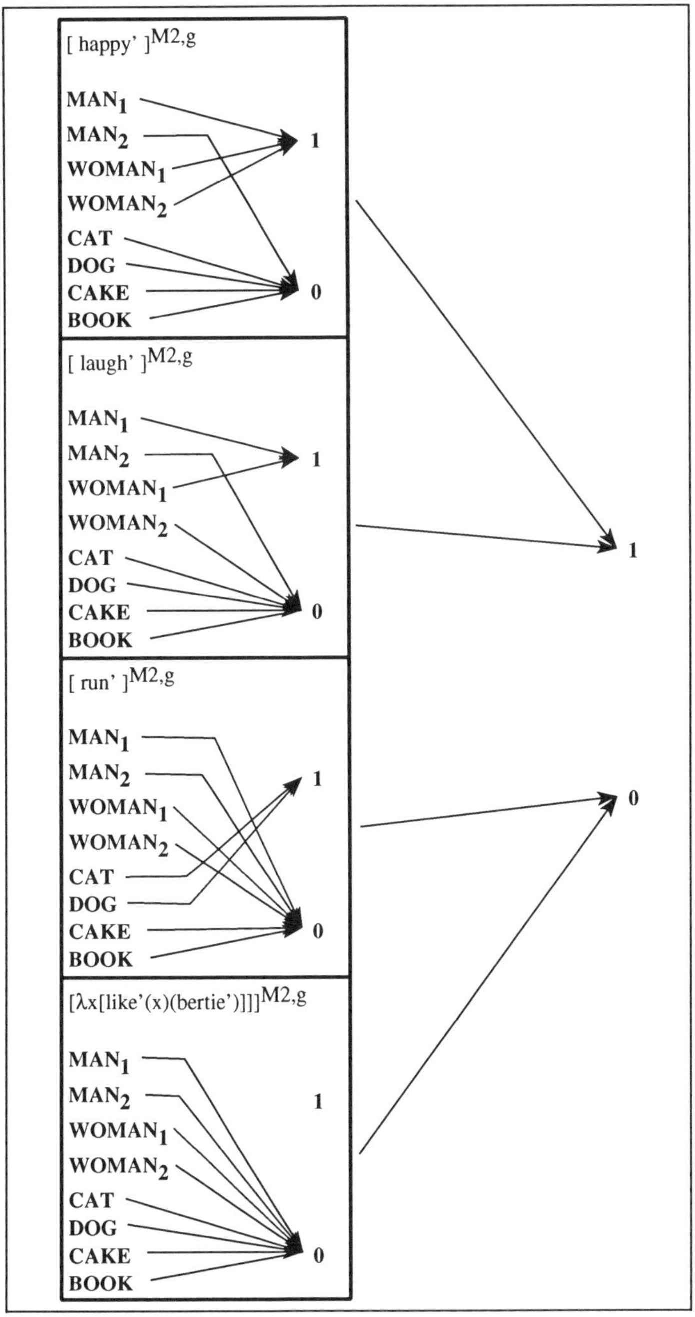

5.4 Reviewing co-ordination

So far, G_2 contains no means of generating compound sentences. This section will remedy the fault and show how lambda abstraction and an interpretation of propositional connectives in terms of functions can provide a more adequate account of English co-ordinate structures. The syntactic analysis of co-ordinate sentences in Chapter 3 is not the best that can be made. First of all, there is some evidence that a conjunction like *and* in English and the clause that follows it form a single binary constituent, rather than that they both combine with the preceding clause to give a flat ternary branching structure. Secondly, and more importantly, there are a number of constructions not handled in G_1, in particular conditional sentences where the **antecedent** follows the **consequent**, e.g. *Ethel sang, if Chester howled* and non-sentential co-ordination, e.g. *Bertie and Fiona loathed Chester*. It is not my intention to discuss the syntax of co-ordination in great detail, but a set of rules is presented below that remedy the above inadequacies. This analysis is a simplified version of the GPSG account presented in Weisler et al. (1986) and Gazdar et al. (1985), one of the better analyses of constituent co-ordination in the generative literature. In keeping with the spirit of the rest of the book, I will ignore the alternatives to this account that may be proposed.

5.4.1 Sentential co-ordination

We begin with a revision of sentential co-ordination. Syntactically the new analysis involves a rule that expands S as two sentential nodes one of which is marked with a syntactic feature of co-ordination. Another rule then realises this category, S[CONJ], as a conjunction plus an ordinary sentence. The new rules are given in (36) and a sample phrase structure tree generated by them appears in (37):

(36) a. $18G_2$: S → S S[CONJ].
b. $19G_2$: S[CONJ] → CONJ S.
c. CONJ → {*and, or, if and only if, if*}.

(37)

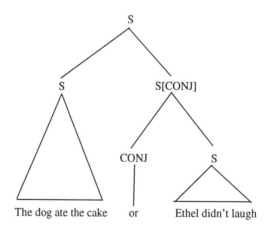

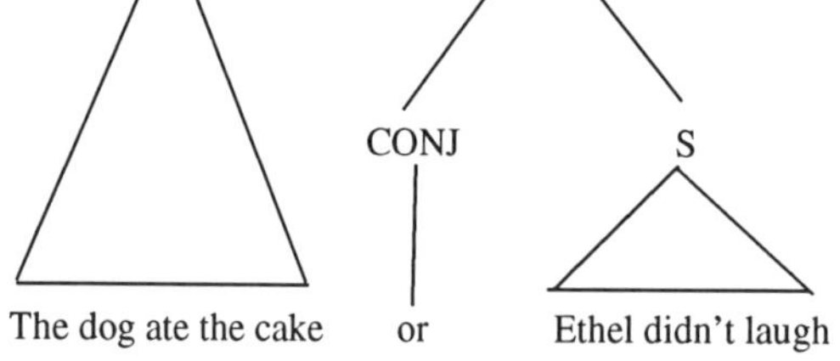

The interpretation of the logical connectives presented in Chapter 3 is, as we will see in Chapter 7, broadly adequate as an account of the semantics of the basic English conjunctions. In view of this, the truth-conditional interpretation of the connectives is maintained in the new grammar, as, for the sake of convenience, is the logical syntax of compound formulae familiar from L_P. Strictly speaking, in L_{type} the logical connectives which take two formulae to yield a formula have the type <t,<t,t>>, denoting functions from truth values to functions from truth values to truth values. If the connectives are treated as having this type, then by the usual rule of functional application we should get expressions like *(&(p))* of type <t,t> and *(&(p))(q)* of type t, where *p* and *q* are variables of type t. However, this notation is not as perspicuous as the infix notation used in L_P and, for the sake of clarity, we import into L_{type} the syntactic rule for generating complex formulae from L_P repeated in (38).

(38) a. $t \rightarrow t\ Op_2\ t$.
b. $OP_2 \in \{\&, \vee, \rightarrow, \leftrightarrow\}$.

This decision, however, poses a problem for the syntactic analysis proposed above, because the new co-ordination rules introduce the conjunctions as combining with only one of the two co-ordinated clauses. According to the construction rule in (38), however, these connectives require two formulae at a time to make a formula, not one. There is thus no simple translation of rule $19G_2$ in (36.b), since expressions like *(& S')* are not well-formed in L_P. It is possible, however, to use lambda abstraction to help out here, so that instead of translating *and* simply as &, *or* as $\vee$, *if* as $\rightarrow$ and *if, and only if* as $\leftrightarrow$, we can translate them as complex lambda expressions that combine with one formula at a time.

In order to obtain appropriate translations of the conjunctions, we first replace each of the formulae that they combine with by a different propositional variable, to get $p \,\&\, q$, $p \leftrightarrow q$, $p \vee q$, and $p \rightarrow q$. These propositional functions are turned into expressions of the correct type (i.e. <t,<t,t>>) by using the lambda operator to bind the variables. This provides the revised translations of the connectives shown in (39).

(39) a. and $\Rightarrow \lambda p\ [\lambda q\ [q \,\&\, p]]$.
b. or $\Rightarrow \lambda p\ [\lambda q\ [q \vee p]]$.
c. if $\Rightarrow \lambda p\ [\lambda q\ [p \rightarrow q]]$.
d. if, and only if $\Rightarrow \lambda p\ [\lambda q\ [p \leftrightarrow q]]$.

Adopting these translations allows the translation of rule $19G_2$ to combine the translations of the conjunction and the clause it combines with simply by functional application. The translation rule in (40.a) thus induces translations like *λp [λq [q ∨ p]](laugh'(ethel'))* for the phrase *or Ethel laughed*, and *λp [λq [p → q]](rain')* for *If it rained*, expressions which can be reduced by λ-conversion to *λq [q ∨ laugh'(ethel')]* and *λ q[rain' → q]*, respectively. It follows from this that the type of S[CONJ] must be <t,t> and so the translation of rule $18G_2$ results directly from the application of the translation of the sentence containing the co-ordinating morpheme to that of the higher sentence, yielding a full formula. The translation rules and appropriate type assignment appear in (40) and give rise to the translation tree in (41) which parallels the syntactic analysis in (37). The translation of the topmost sentence node in (41) can be simplified by lambda conversion to the expression in (42.c), the

(42.c), the latter being identical to the L_P translation of the same sentence. The fact that the order of the formulae is permuted in these examples from the order found in previous chapters is semantically insignificant because of the commutativity of ∨ and &, as discussed in Chapter 3.

(40) a. $T19G_2$: CONJ'(S').
 b. TYPE(S[CONJ]) = <t,t>.
 c. $T18G_2$: S[CONJ]'(S').

(41)

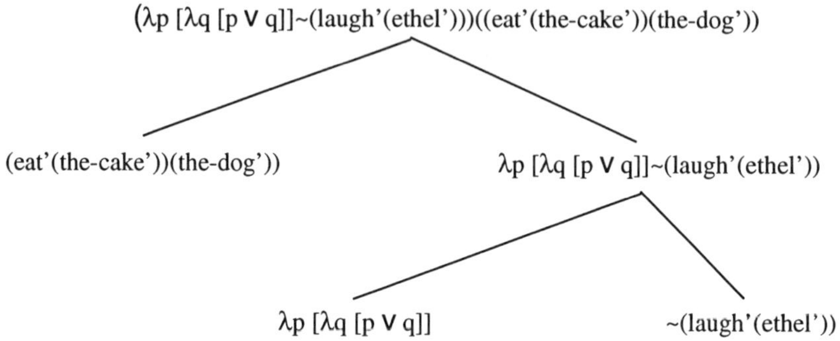

$$(\lambda p \; [\lambda q \; [p \; \vee \; q]] {\sim} (laugh'(ethel')))((eat'(the\text{-}cake'))(the\text{-}dog'))$$

(eat'(the-cake'))(the-dog') $\lambda p \; [\lambda q \; [p \; \vee \; q]] {\sim} (laugh'(ethel'))$

$\lambda p \; [\lambda q \; [p \; \vee \; q]]$ ${\sim}(laugh'(ethel'))$

(42) a. $(\lambda p \; [\lambda q \; [p \vee q]] {\sim} (laugh'(ethel')))((eat'(the\text{-}cake'))(the\text{-}dog'))$.
 b. » $\lambda q \; [{\sim}(laugh'(ethel')) \vee q]((eat'(the\text{-}cake'))(the\text{-}dog'))$.
 c. » $[{\sim}(laugh'(ethel')) \vee (eat'(the\text{-}cake'))(the\text{-}dog')]$.

A further example of this approach is shown in the analysis tree of the sentence *It rained if it didn't snow* in (45). This tree assumes a negative counterpart of the rule introducing impersonal verbs, i.e. S → it didn't V_0[-FIN] which translates as ${\sim}(V_0)$ (call this rule $9'G_2$). Again although the translation of the topmost sentence node looks complicated, it reduces to the more familiar logical expression in (43.c).

(43) a. $(\lambda p \; [\lambda q \; [p \rightarrow q]]({\sim}snow'))(rain')$.
 b. » $\lambda q \; [{\sim}snow' \rightarrow q](rain')$.
 c. » ${\sim}snow' \rightarrow rain'$.

The grammar does not yet contain a rule for generating sentences containing *if...then*. For the sake of completeness, this is remedied by the rules in (44), which specifically mention the appropriate morphemes. A more elegant solution could be proposed but this is sufficient for our purposes.

(44) a. $20G_2$: S → S[if] S[then].
 b. $21G_2$: S[if] → if S.
 c. $22G_2$: S[then] → then S.

(45)

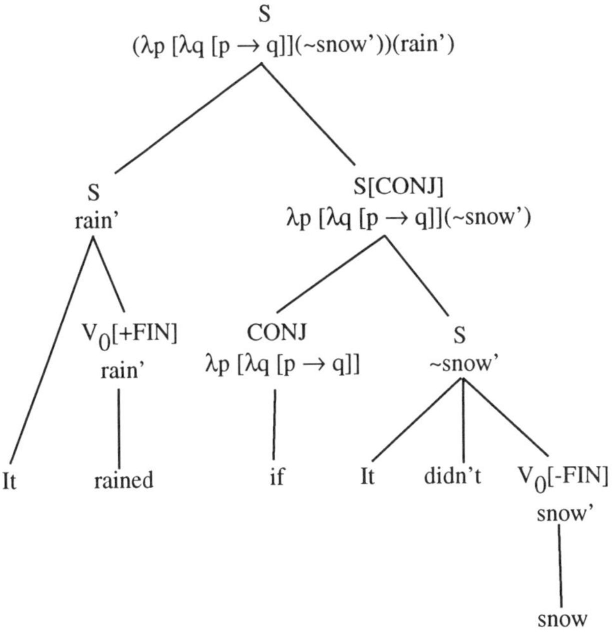

Assuming that the sentences generated by these rules are truth-conditionally equivalent to those generated by rules $17G_2$ and $18G_2$, where CONJ rewrites as *if*, we get the translation rules in (46).

(46) a. $T20G_2$: S[if]'(S[then]').
  b. $T21G_2$: if'(S').
  c. $T22G_2$: then'(S').

The translation rule for $22G_2$ assumes that the expression *then* is also translated and so interpreted, just as if it were an ordinary conjunction morpheme. Unlike the others, however, the word *then* does not add any semantic information to the sentence. It should, therefore, be given a translation (and interpretation) that reflects this. According to the translation rules in (46), *then'* combines with a formula to yield an expression that forms an argument to *if'(S')*. The latter, as we have already seen, is an expression of type <t,t> and so S[then] must be a formula and *then'* must therefore be an expression of type <t,t>, as well. Expressions of this type denote functions from truth values to truth values. One of the four possible functions of this sort is the one that maps falsity onto falsity and truth onto truth as shown in (47). This function, which is called the **identity function** over truth values because it maps a truth value onto itself, is denoted by a lambda expression of type <t,t> that applies to a formula to give an expression that is truth-conditionally equivalent to the argument formula. This expression is *λp [p]* which applies to a formula like *crazy'(ethel')* to give *λp[p](crazy'(ethel'))*, an expression that λ-converts into *crazy'(ethel')*. This truth-conditionally empty expression, which denotes the function represented in (47), thus provides an appropriate translation of the meaningless element *then*.

(47) $[\lambda p\ [p]]^{M,g}$

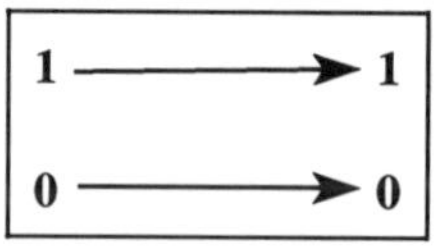

As an example of the way the rules and translations in (44) and (46) work, the derivation of the sentence *If it didn't snow, then it rained* is given in (48). The translation, as can be seen from the lambda conversion equivalents, turns out to be truth-conditionally synonymous with *It rained, if it didn't snow*, as desired.

(48) a. S
⇒ S'.
b. S[if] S[then] — $20G_2$
⇒ S[if]'(S[then]').
c. if S S[then] — $21G_2$
⇒ (λp [λq [p → q]](S'))(S[then]').
d. if S then S — $22G_2$
⇒ (λp [λq [p → q]](S'))(λr [r](S')).
e. if it didn't V_0[-FIN] then S — $9'G_2$
⇒ (λp [λq [p → q]](~V_0'))(λr [r](S')).
f. if it didn't V_0[-FIN] then it V_0[+FIN] — $9'G_2$
⇒ (λp [λq [p → q]](~V_0'))(λr [r](V_0')).
g. if it didn't snow then it rained — Lex
⇒ (λp [λq [p → q]](~snow'))(λr [r](rain'))
h. » λq [(~snow') → q](λr [r](rain'))
i. » [(~snow') → (λr [r](rain'))]
j. » [(~snow') → (rain')].

Exercise 5.11:
Translate the following formulae into L_{type} using grammar G_2, giving the full translations and their converted equivalents:

i. The dog ate the cake and the cake poisoned the dog.
ii. Ethel was crazy or the student didn't like Ethel and Chester didn't like Ethel.
iii. Jo laughed, if Chester howled or the cat yowled.

The truth-conditional connectives are interpreted in the same way as in Chapter 3 and, as in the model theory of that chapter, the truth-conditions of compound formulae are specified directly in the model theory used to interpret L_{type}. The full specification of this theory in (49) includes clauses for interpreting lambda abstraction and negation, as well as for functional application and the connectives. This will remain the basis of the interpretation procedure throughout the rest of the book, just as L_{type} will remain the basis of the translation language. There will, however, be additions to the theory in later chapters as more data are covered.

(49) Given a model, **M** = **«A,F»** and assignment of values to variables **g**, then:

1. For any item α in the lexicon, $[\alpha]^{M,g} = F(\alpha)$.
2. If a is of type a and f is of <a,b>, then $[f(a)]^{M,g} = [f]^{M,g}([a]^{M,g})$.
3. If u is a variable of type a and ϕ an expression of type b containing a free occurrence of u, then $[\lambda u/\phi]]^{M,g}$ is that function **h** from D_a into D_b such that for all objects, **a** in D_a, **h**(**a**) is $[\phi]^{M,g^{a/u}}$.
4. If ϕ is a formula, then $[\sim(\phi)]^{M,g}$ is **1**, iff $[\phi]^{M,g}$ is **0**. Otherwise, $[\sim(\phi)]^{M,g}$ is **0**.
5. If ϕ and ψ are formulae, then $[\phi \ \& \ \psi]^{M,g}$ is **1**, iff $[\phi]^{M,g}$ is **1** and $[\psi]^{M,g}$ is **1**. Otherwise, $[\phi \ \& \ \psi]^{M,g}$ is **0**.
6. If ϕ and ψ are formulae, then $[\phi \vee \psi]^{M,g}$ is **1**, iff $[\phi]^{M,g}$ is **1** or $[\psi]^{M,g}$ is **1**. Otherwise, $[\phi \vee \psi]^{M,g}$ is **0**.
7. If ϕ and ψ are formulae, then $[\phi \rightarrow \psi]^{M,g}$ is **1**, iff $[\phi]^{M,g}$ is **0** or $[\psi]^{M,g}$ is **1**. Otherwise, $[\phi \rightarrow \psi]^{M,g}$ is **0**.
8. If ϕ and ψ are formulae, then $[\phi \leftrightarrow \psi]^{M,g}$ is **1**, iff $[\phi]^{M,g}$ is $[\psi]^{M,g}$. Otherwise, $[\phi \leftrightarrow \psi]^{M,g}$ is **0**.

As discussed in Chapter 3, the meanings of the connectives are specified directly in the model theory above because their interpretation does not vary from model to model. Their interpretations can, however, be modelled as functions in the same way as other denotations in the grammar. For example, $\lambda p \, [\lambda q \, [p \ \& \ q]]$ is that function that when given a true formula yields a function which yields truth when given another true formula and yields falsity on all other occasions. The functions denoted by all the connectives, &, $\vee$, $\rightarrow$, $\leftrightarrow$ and ~, are set out diagrammatically in (50) to (54) and provide precisely the same information as the truth tables of Chapter 3.

(50) $\lambda p \, [\lambda q \, [p \ \& \ q]]$

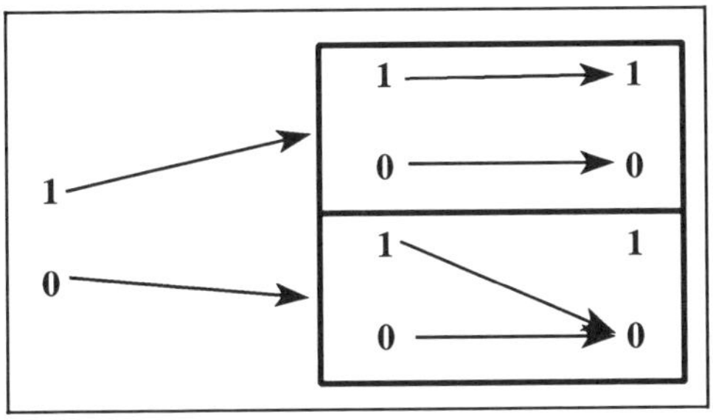

(51) λp [λq [p v q]]

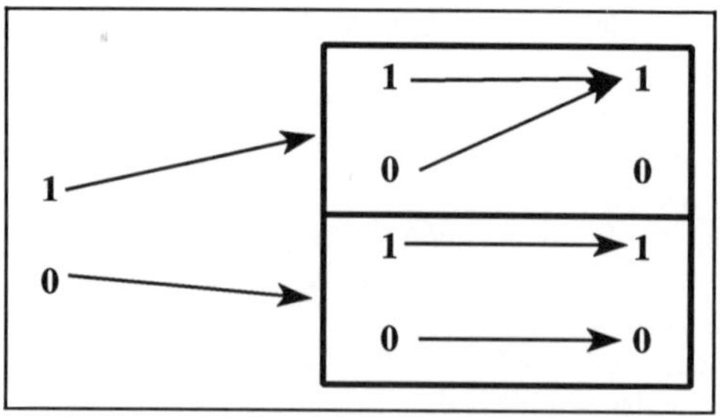

(52) λp [λq [p → q]]

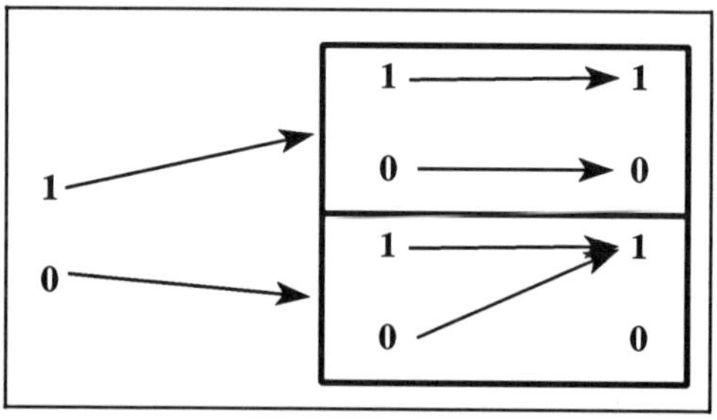

(53) λp [λq [p ↔ q]]

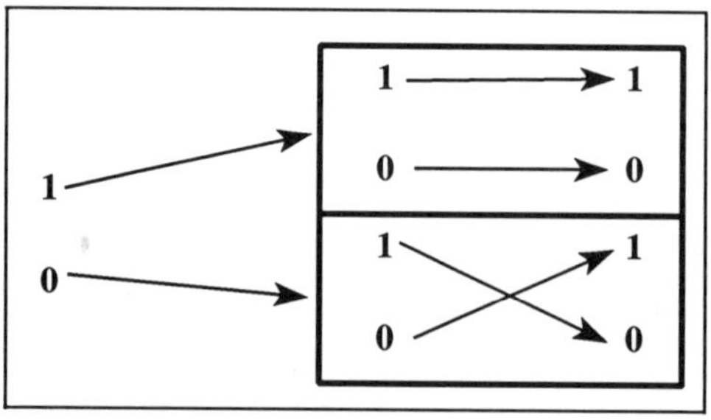

(54) ~p

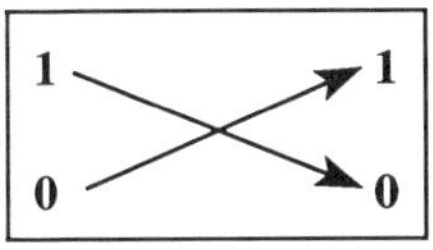

5.4.2 Co-ordinating other categories

In the last section, sentential co-ordination was (re-)introduced into the grammar, but the lambda operator allows an extension of the grammar to include some types of NP and VP co-ordination, while still maintaining a propositional interpretation of the conjunctions themselves. The sorts of VP and NP co-ordination that we can now handle are those like (55.a & b) which are truth-conditionally identical to the sentences in (55.c & d), respectively.

(55) a. Jo loathed the dog and liked the cat.
b. The student and the lecturer loathed Chester.
c. Jo loathed the dog and Jo liked the cat.
d. The student loathed Chester and the lecturer loathed Chester.

The phrase structure rules to generate VPs and NPs conjoined by *and* and *or* are relatively straightforward and the appropriate rules are given in (56). In these rules, φ stands for any features associated with the VP (e.g. [+/-FIN]) which are passed down onto both conjuncts and the PL marking on the mother NP node is for agreement purposes. In the latter case, conjunction is restricted to subject NPs (again to avoid unnecessary confusion) and so some slight revision needs to be made to rule $1G_2$ to allow for singular and plural verbs. The revised Rule $1G_2$ appears in (56.e), but the other revisions to make sure that the right forms of verbs appear in the right places are again left as an exercise for the reader. Because the conjunctions *if* and *if, and only if,* do not appear in VP and NP co-ordination the rules must be restricted to the conjunctions *and* and *or* which can be done by specifying the value of the conjunction.

(56) a. $23G_2$: VP[φ] $\rightarrow$ VP[φ] VP[φ,CONJ:α] $\alpha \in$ {*and, or*}.
b. $24G_2$: NP[+PL] $\rightarrow$ NP NP[CONJ:α] $\alpha \in$ {*and, or*}.
c. $25G_2$: VP[φ,CONJ:α] $\rightarrow$ α VP[φ].
d. $26G_2$: NP[CONJ:α] $\rightarrow$ α NP.
e. $1'G_2$: S $\rightarrow$ NP[αPL] VP[+FIN,αPL].

Since the truth-conditions of sentences like (55.a & b) are identical to those of (55.c & d), respectively, the conjunctions *and* and *or* should have the same interpretation in sentences containing NP and VP co-ordination as in sentential co-ordination. But this gives rise to a problem in the translation of rule $23G_2$ and $24G_2$: the conjunctions are of type <t,<t,t>> and so cannot directly combine with expressions of type <e,t> (the type of a VP) or of type e (the type of a NP). To see how the lambda operator can solve this apparent problem, let us work through the analysis of (55.a) backwards, as it were, undoing lambda conversions as we go along. First of all here is the syntactic analysis of the sentence according to G_2. (The numerical subscripts on the VP nodes are for ease of reference.)

(57)

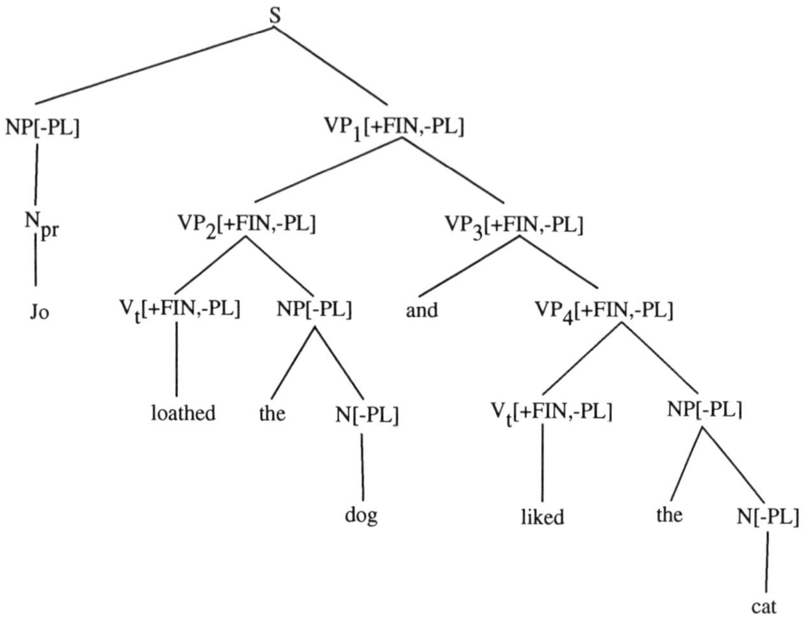

As mentioned above *Jo loathed the dog and liked the cat* is truth-conditionally equivalent to *Jo loathed the dog and Jo liked the cat.* The translation of the latter sentence is shown in (58.a) and, because of the equivalence noted above, this translation can be analysed as the λ-converted equivalent of that of the S node in (57). According to the translation rule $T1G_2$, (58.a) must result from λ-converting an expression derived from the application of the translation of VP_1 to that of the subject NP as in (58.b). To find the first stage of the λ-conversion the result of which is shown in (58.b), the rule is applied backwards to (58.a) in order to arrive at an expression that is truth-conditionally equivalent to VP_1. Since the argument of VP_1' is *jo'*, each instance of the individual expression *jo'* in (58.a) is replaced by an individual variable *x* which is then abstracted on to give the expression in (59). This expression when applied to the argument *jo'* gives an expression equivalent to (58.a).

(58) a. (loathe'(the-dog'))(jo') & (like'(the-cat'))(jo').
b. VP_1'(NP') = VP_1'(jo')
» (loathe'(the-dog'))(jo') & (like'(the-cat'))(jo').

(59) VP_1'
» λx [(loathe'(the-dog'))(x) & (like'(the-cat'))(x)].

The syntax of the co-ordinate VP consists of two VPs, one of which contains a conjunction morpheme. In order to obtain the correct type for *VP_1'*, the latter should translate into a functor over VP expressions, i.e. of type <<e,t>,<e,t>> so that the translation rule T23G_2 must be derived from the application of *VP[CONJ]'* to *VP'* as shown in (60.b). Thus, the expression in (59), translating VP_1, must be derived from the application of VP_3' to VP_2 (cf. (60.c)). Since VP_2 translates directly into the expression *loathe'(the-dog')*, we can apply backwards λ-conversion to (59) by replacing the latter with a variable P, of type <e,t>, and abstracting on this to give the expression in (60.f), of type <<e,t>,<e,t>> as required.

(60) a. TYPE(VP[CONJ:α]') = <<e,t>,<e,t>>.
b. T23G_2: VP[CONJ:α]'(VP').
c. VP_3[CONJ:and]'(VP_2')
» λx [(loathe'(the-dog'))(x) & (like'(the-cat'))(x)].
d. VP_2' = loathe'(the-dog').
e. VP_1'
» λP [λx [P(x) & (like'(the-cat'))(x)]](loathe'(the-dog')).
f. VP_3[CONJ:and]'
» λP [λx [P(x) & (like'(the-cat'))(x)]].

The translation in (60.f) is derived in turn from the combination of the translations of the conjunction *and* and the VP *liked the cat*. The translation of the former is *λp [λ q [p & q]]*, as we have already seen, and that of VP_4 is *like'(the-cat')*. However, because the type of the translation of the conjunction is <t,<t,t>> and that of the VP is <e,t>, the combination of these expressions cannot result directly from the functional application of one expression to the other. Hence, the translation of the rule expanding VP[CONJ:α], rule 25G_2, must directly specify the way these translations are combined. As can be seen from (60.f), the rule must introduce and abstract upon the predicate variable P and the individual variable x, since these do not appear in the translations of *and* or *liked the cat.* Furthermore, the expressions P(x) and *like'(the-cat')* must be associated with the p and the q variables in the translation of the conjunction (the order is immaterial because of the commutativity of & as mentioned in Chapter 3). Hence, (60.f) must be derived by λ-conversion from the expression in (61.a) and the appropriate translation rule for VP[CONJ:α] must be that in (61.b).

(61) a. VP_3' = λP [λx [(λp [λq [p & q]](P(x)))((like'(the-cat'))(x))]]
» λP [λx [P(x) & (like'(the-cat'))(x)]].
b. T25G_2: λP [λx [(α'(P(y)))(VP'(y))]].

(62) shows that the rules that we have come up with for VP co-ordination by applying backwards λ-conversion work in the way intended by giving the derivation and translation of the example sentence *Jo loathed the dog and liked the cat*. The λ-conversion of the resulting complex expression is carried out in (63) to show its equivalence to (58.a) as required.

(62) a. S
$\Rightarrow S'$.

b. NP VP_1[+FIN,-PL] 1'G_2
$\Rightarrow VP_1'(NP')$.

c. N_{pr} VP_1[+FIN,-PL] 6G_2
$\Rightarrow VP_1'(N_{pr}')$.

d. N_{pr} VP_2[+FIN,-PL] VP_3[CONJ:and,+FIN,-PL] 23G_2
$\Rightarrow (VP_3[CONJ{:}and]'(VP_2'))(N_{pr}')$.

e. N_{pr} V_t[+FIN,-PL] NP VP_3[CONJ:and,+FIN,-PL] 3G_2
$\Rightarrow (VP_3[CONJ{:}and]'(V_t'(NP')))(N_{pr}')$.

f. N_{pr} V_t[+FIN,-PL] NP and VP_4[+FIN,-PL] 25G_2
$\Rightarrow (\lambda P\ [\lambda x\ [(\lambda p\ [\lambda q\ [p\ \&\ q]](P(x)))(VP_4'(x))]](V_t'(NP')))(N_{pr}')$.

g. N_{pr} V_t[+FIN,-PL] NP and V_t NP 3G_2
$\Rightarrow (\lambda P\ [\lambda x\ [(\lambda p\ [\lambda q\ [p\ \&\ q]](P(x)))((V_t'(NP'))(x))]](V_t'(NP')))(N_{pr}')$.

h. N_{pr} V_t[+FIN,-PL] the N and V_t NP 7G_2
$\Rightarrow (\lambda P\ [\lambda x\ [(\lambda p\ [\lambda q\ [p\ \&\ q]](P(x)))((V_t'(NP'))(x))]](V_t'(the\text{-}N')))(N_{pr}')$.

i. N_{pr} V_t[+FIN,-PL] the N and V_t the N 7G_2
$\Rightarrow (\lambda P\ [\lambda x\ [(\lambda p\ [\lambda q\ [p\ \&\ q]](P(x)))((V_t'(the\text{-}N'))(x))]](V_t'(the\text{-}N')))(N_{pr}')$.

j. Jo loathed the dog and liked the cat Lex
$\Rightarrow (\lambda P\ [\lambda x\ [(\lambda p\ [\lambda q\ [p\ \&\ q]](P(x)))((like'(the\text{-}cat'))(x))]]$
$(loathe'(the\text{-}dog')))(jo')$.

(63) a. $(\lambda P\ [\lambda x\ [(\lambda p\ [\lambda q\ [p\ \&\ q]](P(x)))((like'(the\text{-}cat'))(x))]]$
$(loathe'(the\text{-}dog')))(jo')$.

b. » $(\lambda P\ [\lambda x\ [\lambda q\ [P(x)\ \&\ q]((like'(the\text{-}cat'))(x))]](loathe'(the\text{-}dog')))(jo')$.

c. » $(\lambda P\ [\lambda x\ [P(x)\ \&\ (like'(the\text{-}cat'))(x)]](loathe'(the\text{-}dog')))(jo')$.

d. » $\lambda x\ [(loathe'(the\text{-}dog'))(x)\ \&\ (like'(the\text{-}cat'))(x)](jo')$.

e. » $[(loathe'(the\text{-}dog'))(jo')\ \&\ (like'(the\text{-}cat'))(jo')]$.

This method of arriving at translation rules, while perhaps not strictly interesting from a purely semantic viewpoint, does illustrate one of the advantages of the semantic theory being advanced here. It is possible, using this formal theory, to work out the meanings of expressions in a language from the interpretation of expressions with which they are synonymous and from the interpretations of the entailments of the phrase. So from the equivalence of (58.a) and (58.c) we were able to work out that the translation of the VP *and liked the cat* is $\lambda P\ [\lambda x\ [P(x)\ \&\ (like'(the\text{-}cat'))(x)]]$, something that was not previously obvious. By working backwards like this, we can be sure that entailment and paraphrase relations are maintained in the semantics and that constituents of complex sentences are assigned appropriate denotations.

Exercise 5.12:
It is also possible to co-ordinate transitive verbs as in the following sentences:

i. Ethel loathed and detested Jo.
ii. The farmer shot and killed the dog.
iii. The student loved or loathed the lecturer.

State a syntactic rule and an appropriate translation rule like that for VP co-ordination above to generate co-ordinate transitive verbs, making sure that the translations given to the above sentences are truth-conditionally equivalent to the respective co-ordinate sentences that follow:

iv. Ethel loathed Jo and Ethel detested Jo.
v. The farmer shot the dog and the farmer killed the dog.
vi. The student loved the lecturer or the student loathed the lecturer.

A similar process can be gone through to obtain the translations of the NP co-ordination rules which are given in (56.b) and (56.d). We begin by noticing the truth-conditional equivalence between the sentences in (64.a) and (64.b), the latter of which has the simple translation in (64.c).

(64) a. Ethel or Bertie was the golfer.
b. Ethel was the golfer or Bertie is the golfer.
c. (ethel' = the-golfer') ∨ (bertie' = the-golfer').

The formula in (64.c) is truth-conditionally equivalent to some expression constructed from the translations of the VP *was the golfer* and the NP *Ethel or Bertie*. The former is given by the L_{type} expression in (65.a) (denoting the set of entities that are identical to the golfer). An L_{type} expression that combines with this to give an expression that λ-converts to (64.c) is given in (65.b) which may be taken to be the translation of the subject NP.

(65) a. was the golfer ⇒ λx [x = the-golfer'].
b. Ethel or Bertie ⇒ λP [P(ethel') ∨ P(bertie')].

(65.b) must be derived from the translations of *or Bertie* and *Ethel*, i.e. *ethel'*, while the former is derived from the translations of *or*, i.e. λp [λq [p ∨ q]], and *Bertie*, i.e. *bertie'*. Without going into further details, the appropriate translation rules and type assignments are given in (66) and the derivation of the NP *Ethel or Bertie* according to these is given in (67). (68) provides the appropriate λ-conversion showing the equivalence of the translation to (65.b).

(66) a. TYPE(NP[CONJ:α]') = $<e,<<e,t>,t>>$.
b. TR 24G_2: NP[CONJ:α]'(NP').
c. TR 26G_2: λx [λP [(α'(P(x)))(P'(NP'))]].

(67) a. NP
$\Rightarrow$ NP'.
b. NP NP[CONJ:or] $24G_2$
$\Rightarrow$ NP[CONJ]'(NP').
c. N_{pr} NP[CONJ:or] $7G_2$
$\Rightarrow$ NP[CONJ]'(N_{pr}').
d. N_{pr} or NP $26G_2$
$\Rightarrow \lambda x\ [\lambda P\ [(\lambda p\ [\lambda q\ [p \vee q]](P(x)))(P(NP'))]](N_{pr}')$.
e. N_{pr} or N_{pr} $7G_2$
$\Rightarrow \lambda\ x\ [\lambda P\ [(\lambda p\ [\lambda q\ [p \vee q]](P(x)))(P(N_{pr}'))]](N_{pr}')$.
f. Ethel or Bertie Lex
$\Rightarrow \lambda\ x\ [\lambda P\ [\lambda p\ [\lambda q\ [p \vee q]](P(x)))(P(bertie'))]](ethel')$.

(68) a. $\lambda x\ [\lambda P\ [(\lambda p\ [\lambda q\ [p \vee q]](P(x)))(P(bertie'))]](ethel')$.
b. » $\lambda x\ [\lambda p\ [\lambda q\ [P(x) \vee q](P(bertie'))]](ethel')$.
c. » $\lambda x\ [\lambda P\ [P(x) \vee P(bertie')]](ethel')$.
d. » $\lambda P\ [P(ethel') \vee P(bertie')]$.

There is an important thing to notice about the expressions that result from the application of the rules in (66) (and the equivalent expressions in (68)) and that is their type. In (68.d), we have a formula containing two instances of a predicate variable, P, bound by the λ operator. Since the type of the variable is <e,t> and that of the expression in its scope is t, the type of the whole expression is <<e,t>,t>, denoting a function from sets to truth values. This is not, however, the type previously assigned to noun phrases, i.e. e, which we have been assuming is appropriate up until now. This leads us into our next topic, the interpretation of noun phrases generally, which is taken up in Chapter 6.

---

*Exercise 5.13:
It is often argued nowadays that auxiliary verbs in English like *does/didn't* form a constituent with its dependent content VP (e.g. like the cat) (cf. Pullum and Wilson (1977), Gazdar, Klein and Sag (1981)). However, G_2 assigns a flat structure to sentences negated by *didn't*. Revise the grammar to capture the fact that *didn't VP* is a constituent, giving *didn't* a translation that ensures that a sentence like *Ethel didn't like the cat* is a paraphrase of *It is not the case that Ethel likes the cat.*

---

*Exercise 5.14:
G_2 has three rules for VP that introduce the positive copula *was* and an additional two sentential rules introducing the negative copula *wasn't*. Furthermore, the grammar gives no translation to the copula, encoding the appropriate translations directly into the rules themselves. Revise the grammar so that negative and positive copulas are introduced by the same rules (hint: use a feature NEG in the syntax) giving the positive and negative copulas appropriate translations. In your answer, you should have noticed that you have to give the copula appearing with an NP complement a different translation to that appearing with A or VP[PAS]. Propose a way to modify the grammar so that the interpretation of the copula remains constant but

the translation of a NP in predicate position has a different translation to its non-predicative counterpart, one that is of the same type as a predicative adjective (hint: you may find the identity operator useful here).

5.5 Further reading

A logical account of the lambda operator can be found in Church (1956), and linguistic introductions to the operator are found in Partee, ter Meulen and Wall (1990: 338-351), Dowty, Wall and Peters (1981: 98-104), Allwood, Andersen and Dahl (1977: 155-157), Chierchia and McConnell-Ginet (1990: 318-330) and McCawley (1981: 395-401). Applications of the λ-operator are not hard to find. Dowty (1982) uses it to discuss cross-linguistic analyses of passive formation and other grammatical-function-changing operations. The approach to co-ordination discussed in Section 5.4 owes a lot to the discussion in Montague (1973) and the specific analyses of Sag, Wasow, Gazdar and Weisler (1985) and Gazdar, Klein, Pullum and Sag (1985: ch. 8). (A more sophisticated approach to the co-ordination of all syntactic categories within a slightly different framework can be found in Keenan and Faltz (1985) and Partee and Rooth (1983).) Partee, ter Meulen and Wall (1990: 351-367) has a discussion of linguistic applications of the λ-operator including passive, phrasal co-ordination, VP-deletion, and relative clauses. These constructions are also discussed in Chierchia and McConnell-Ginet (1990: 330-348) which also discusses VP anaphora. The interpretation of unbounded dependencies in Gazdar, Klein, Pullum and Sag (1985: ch. 7; 229-236) relies heavily on the use of this device. (See also Cresswell (1973).)

6 Quantification

6.1 The variety of noun phrases

We have so far in this book been looking at the meaning of sentences primarily in terms of the properties that entities have and the relations that hold between them. This has meant a concentration on the interpretations of verbs and verb phrases, with the meanings of the phrases that serve as their arguments, noun phrases, taking second place. Indeed, only two sorts of English noun phrase have been analysed in the grammar fragments so far: proper names and simple definite noun phrases. But there are, of course, many other types of noun phrase in English, including indefinite noun phrases like those in (1.a & b), quantified noun phrases as in (1.c & d), noun phrases containing adjectives or relative clauses (1.e & f), noun phrases with possessive modifiers (1.g), and many more.

(1) a. a book.
  b. some cat.
  c. every dog.
  d. each person.
  e. the happy student.
  f. any student who gives a good report.
  g. Ethel's friend's dog.

The noun phrases in (1) all require a more sophisticated interpretation than the one supplied for proper names and definite descriptions in earlier chapters. Both of these expressions have been translated as expressions of type e, denoting entities in the model. Such an analysis is, however, not ultimately tenable for proper nouns, is suspect for definite noun phrases and cannot be sustained at all for the other types of noun phrase in (1). For example, that noun phrases like (1.a) and (1.c) cannot denote a specific entity in the model can be seen from a consideration of the meaning of a sentence like *Every student read a book*. If the phrase *a book* denoted a single entity unique in any model, say *Jane Eyre*, then the proposition expressed by this sentence is true only if all students read the same book. But this is not necessarily what the sentence means. It may well be true that all the students did read *Jane Eyre*, but the proposition expressed is also true if one student read *Agnes Grey*, one read *Villette*, one read *Wuthering Heights*, and so on. Hence, the phrase *a book* can pick out different entities on different occasions, provided only that they are all books. Thus, an indefinite noun phrase cannot be directly associated with a unique entity in the model and so cannot be translated into an expression of type e. For similar reasons the subject NP *every student* also cannot denote a single individual in the model. The example sentence is not verified by the fact that one entity, say Jo, was a student and read *Jane Eyre*, but is true only if all those entities in the model that are students read the book.

The appearance of nominal modifiers in noun phrases (as in (1.e) and (1.f)) also provides evidence against letting NPs denote individuals. In earlier chapters, each definite description is associated with a unique entity in the model by the denotation assignment function. Thus, *the dog* is specified as extensionally denoting **DOG** and *the student* **MAN**$_1$, etc. If this is maintained for a larger fragment of English including modifiers, the denotation assignment function of each model must be extended to provide a unique extension for every modified and non-modified definite NP in the object language. Hence, not only will an extension be assigned to *the student*, but also to *the happy student*, *the tall, happy student*, *the happy student with a cold*, and so on. One argument against this approach is that, if attributive modification is recursive, as usually assumed in the generative literature, then the denotation assignment function will be required to assign an extension to an infinite number of phrases, and will thus itself be infinite. A more cogent argument against treating modified definite NPs as entity-denoting expressions concerns the fact that there are clear semantic relations between all these noun phrases. The extension of the phrase *happy student* is related to those of *happy* and *student* and the extension of *tall happy student* is related to those of *tall* and *happy student* and so on. The information provided by nominal modifiers in definite noun phrases narrows down the domain in which the referent of the definite description is sought. In a roomful of students, the entity being referred to by the phrase *the student with green hair* can be identified by looking at the entities in the room that are students and seeing which one also has green hair. If the only entity in the room with these two properties happens to be Fiona, we can identify her as the referent of the NP without having previously known that the student with green hair is actually Fiona. In other words, the semantics of definite noun phrases, like those of other NPs, is compositional, the meaning of the whole being derived from the meaning of the parts. Hence, even definite NPs must have more semantic structure than that provided by an individual constant. The approach to NP denotation of Chapters 2 to 5 is thus inadequate and must be revised to account for the points just raised. It is the purpose of this chapter to provide the basis for such a theory which is compositional and assigns meanings to full noun phrases according to the meanings of the adjectives, nouns and determiners that they contain.

6.2 Introducing the logical quantifiers

We begin our analysis of noun phrases by looking at a now traditional semantic treatment of NPs like those in (1.a) to (1.d). This analysis comes directly from the logical tradition and has been adopted by many linguists as a basis for the interpretation of **universal** NPs like *everyone, all gardeners, every dog*, etc. and **existential** ones like *someone, some gardener, a dog*, etc. This analysis goes back to the work of Gottlob Frege, a German philosopher of the nineteenth century, who first provided the now standard technical means of analysing sentences containing quantified noun phrases (QNPs), which have been the object of philosophical study in the Western tradition since Aristotle. Since this book is about the semantics of natural languages, many of the logical aspects of this analysis are ignored and this chapter is concerned only with the contribution it makes to the understanding of quantified noun phrases in English and other human languages that have been seriously investigated. As with the analyses of other constructions in this book, interpretation is not carried out on English sentences directly but on logical representations of these. Hence to provide a semantic analysis of quantified sentences, we must first provide a logical language which can represent them and then define the interpretation of that language. The language that is used to translate English with noun phrases like those in (1) is based on L_{type}, but contains two new logical operators and is called L_Q. In this section, we define this language and discuss its interpretation.

6.2.1 The quantifiers

To begin the analysis of quantified sentences, consider the sentence *Someone liked Jo.* This provides the information that some entity liked (at some time in the past) some, possibly different, entity called Jo and it may thus be paraphrased by the formal English sentence in (2).

(2) For some entity, that entity liked Jo.

Replacing the word *entity* in (2) by a variable gives the quasi-logical sentence in (3) which brings out the fact that the something being talked about is the thing that liked Jo.

(3) For some z, z liked Jo.

The second part of this expression is easily represented in L_{type} as *(like'(jo'))(z)*, a propositional function containing a free variable, *z*. Such an expression is not suitable as the translation of (3), however, as, although it is of the right type to translate a sentence, i.e. t, it does not denote a truth value because it contains an unbound variable. To make the propositional function into a formula the free variable must be bound by some operator which, unlike the lambda operator, must not alter the type of the logical expression; which must be a formula, since the expression translates a sentence and not a predicate. The relevant operator is $\exists$ (or V, in some notations) and is known as the **existential operator**. Like the lambda operator, $\exists$ is written before the variable it binds and comes to the left of square brackets which enclose the propositional function over which the operator ranges. Ignoring for the moment the fact that the English expression *someone* is used only of people (or, less commonly, of other animate entities), the sentence in (2) can be translated into the formula in (4).

(4) $\exists$z [(like'(jo'))(z)].

Care is needed in specifying the right scope for the existential operator, as it is for lambda. Thus, neither (5.b) nor (5.c) are correct representations of the sentence in (5.a). In the former, *(like'(jo'))(x)* is not in the scope of the operator while in (5.c) it is in its scope, but the variable x is not bound by the operator. The correct representation is given in (5.d).

(5) a. Someone liked Ethel and Jo.
b. $\exists$x [(like'(ethel'))(x)] & (like'(jo'))(x).
c. $\exists$y [(like'(ethel'))(y) & (like'(jo'))(x)].
d. $\exists$z [(like'(ethel'))(z) & (like'(jo'))(z)].

Associated with the existential operator is the **universal operator**. This is used in the translations of sentences that contain noun phrases with *all* and *every* and is written as $\forall$ (or Λ). This is again prefixed to a propositional function containing the variable it is associated with and has all the usual properties in terms of variable binding and scope. The representation of (6.a) can be given the quasi-logical translation in (6.b) which translates into the fully logical expression in (6.c).

(6) a. Everyone liked Fiona.
b. For all x, x liked Fiona.
c. $\forall$x [(like'(fiona'))(x)].

The operators, $\exists$ and $\forall$, are more generally known as **quantifiers** and their use has now become standard in logic, forming the backbone of the predicate calculus and more complex logical languages. If we add the quantifiers to the typed language with the λ-operator of Chapter 5, we get the language L_Q, which is defined by the same rules as L_{type} with the additional rule introducing quantified formulae given in (7).

(7) **Quantifier rule**: If ϕ is an expression of type t containing a free instance of a variable u of type e, then $\exists$u [ϕ] and $\forall$u [ϕ] are expressions of type t.

In writing a syntactic rule for generating quantified formulae, logicians do not specify that ϕ should contain an unbound instance of the variable to be bound by the quantifier, as this does not affect the semantics. As we will see below, an expression like $\forall$*x [(like'(fiona'))(jo')]* is truth-conditionally equivalent to *(like'(fiona'))(jo')*. However, the string most nearly equivalent to the former expression in English *Everyone Jo liked Fiona* is ungrammatical (as are the equivalent expressions in many other languages). As the semantic theory being developed in this book is intended for the interpretation of natural languages, the rule in (7) has been written specifically to disallow quantifiers from combining with formulae that are not propositional functions. In L_Q, therefore, expressions like $\forall$*x [sing'(jo')]* are not well-formed, even though they are perfectly acceptable in ordinary predicate logic.

The definition in (7) allows quantifiers to bind more than one instance of a variable in its scope (as in (5.d)), and more than one quantifier to bind distinct free variables in propositional functions. For example, (8) shows four well-formed formulae that can be constructed from the propositional function *(like'(x))(y)* using the two quantifiers, $\forall$ and $\exists$, with an English sentence that it can be used to translate following each logical expression.

(8) a. $\exists$x [$\exists$y [(like'(y))(x)]].
(Someone liked someone.)
b. $\forall$x [$\forall$y [(like'(y))(x)]].
(Everyone liked everyone.)
c. $\forall$x [$\exists$y [(like'(y))(x)]].
(Everyone liked someone.)
d. $\exists$x [$\forall$y [(like'(y))(x)]].
(Someone liked everyone.)

Just as with the lambda operator, different formulae can be constructed by binding variables in different orders. Thus, there are four other well-formed formulae based on the propositional function *(like'(y))(x)* which parallel the expressions given in (8). These are given in (9) which again has examples of English sentences that the logical expressions can be used to translate.

(9) a. $\exists$y [$\exists$x [(like'(y))(x)]].
(Someone liked someone.)
b. $\forall$y [$\forall$x [(like'(y))(x)]].
(Everyone liked everyone.)
c. $\exists$y [$\forall$x [(like'(y))(x)]].
(There was someone that everyone liked.)
d. $\forall$y [$\exists$x [(like'(y))(x)]].
(Everyone was liked by someone.)

Where two formulae differ in the relative orders of quantifiers binding the same variables, they show a difference in the scope of the quantifiers. Thus, the formulae in (9.a to d) reverse the quantifier scopes of the corresponding formulae in (8). As there are situations in which different orders of quantifiers change the truth-conditions of a formula, it is necessary to be careful to put them in the right order. This topic will be taken up in Section 6.4.2, but for the moment look at the logical expressions in (8) and (9) carefully and compare them with their English counterparts. Where the latter are the same for more than one of the expressions, the relative order of the quantifiers is not truth-conditionally significant. With the others, the differences in the order in which multiple quantifiers appear in expressions is significant.

Exercise 6.1:
Pair the English sentences in i to iv with one of the L_Q expressions in a to h which represents a possible translation into L_Q.

i. Someone liked herself.
ii. Someone liked Jo and hated Fiona.
iii. Someone was liked by everyone.
iv. Everyone gave something to someone.

a. $\exists$x [(like'(jo'))(x)] & (hate'(fiona'))(x).
b. $\exists$x [$\exists$y [(like'(y))(x)]].
c. $\exists$x [$\forall$y [(like'(y))(x)]].
d. $\exists$x [(like'(jo'))(x) & (hate'(fiona'))(x)].
e. $\exists$x [$\forall$y [(like'(x))(y)]].
f. $\forall$x [$\exists$y [(give'(y)(y))(x)]].
g. $\exists$x [(like'(x))(x)].
h. $\forall$x [$\exists$y [$\exists$z [(give'(z)(y))(x)]]].

6.2.2 *Interpreting L_Q*

To understand the interpretation of expressions containing quantifiers, we must consider the conditions under which the formulae translating quantified sentences are true. We have already seen that a sentence like *Fiona liked Jo* (or more properly the formula it translates into) is true if (and only if) the entity conventionally referred to by the word *Fiona* is a member of the set of entities denoted by the verb phrase *liked Jo*. Once the entity denoted by *Fiona* has been identified, therefore, and providing the extension of *liked Jo* is also determined, the truth or falsity of the proposition expressed by the sentence can be assessed. On the other hand, the utterance of a sentence like *Someone liked Jo* (in the interpretation with which we are concerned) does not assert that a specific entity is in the extension of the verb phrase, but just states that some entity in the universe of discourse is in that extension. In other words, if the set denoted by an expression like *like'(jo')* contains at least one element, then the formula is true, otherwise it is not. Similarly, the proposition expressed by the sentence *Jo liked someone* is true if, and only if, there is some entity in the universe of discourse such that Jo liked it (or, equivalently for our purposes, if the extension of *was liked by Jo* contains at least one element).

On a simple level, one can think about the truth of the propositions expressed by sentences containing *someone* as being guaranteed if there is a sentence in the object language that contains a name or a definite description in place of the quantified pronoun that can be uttered to make a true statement. Thus, the truth of the proposition expressed by the sentence *Someone liked Jo* is guaranteed by that of *Fiona liked Jo* or *Ethel liked Jo* or any of the other sentences formed in this way. This is rather how the formal definition of the semantics of these sentences is given, except that it does not involve the substitution of names or definite descriptions in place of the quantified pronoun (which can give rise to problems in intensional contexts; see Chapters 9 and 10). The formal interpretation of a quantified formula involves the assignment of different values to the variable bound by the quantifier in the formula and checking the truth or falsity of the propositional function in its scope with respect to the value assignment.

In Chapter 5, the operation of lambda-conversion was discussed in terms of looking at different ways of associating variables with constants in a model. The truth value of any formula formed by applying a lambda expression of type <e,t> to a constant of type e in L_{type} is the same as that of the propositional function in the lambda expression when the abstracted variable is assigned the same value as the constant. In other words, $[\lambda u\,[\phi](a)]^{M,g}$ is equivalent to $[\phi]^{M,g[a]M/u}$ (see Chapter 5). The interpretation of a formula containing the quantifier $\exists$ also requires us to look at different assignments of values to variables, except that we may need to look at more than one. Essentially an existentially quantified formula, $\exists x\,[\phi]$, is true if there is some assignment of values to variables which makes the propositional function, ϕ, true. (10) expresses this formally.

(10) **Truth-conditions for existential formulae**: If ϕ is an expression of type t containing a free occurrence of a variable, u, of type e, then $[\exists u\,[\phi]]^{M,g}$ is **1**, iff there is some value assignment **g'**, exactly like **g** except perhaps for the individual assigned to u, such that $[\phi]^{M,g'}$ is **1**.

As an example of how this works, consider the interpretation of the L_Q formula representing the sentence *Someone liked Jo*, i.e. $\exists$*z[(like'(jo'))(z)]*. According to (10), this is true if there is some value that can be assigned to *z* that makes *(like'(jo'))(z)* true. Assume that the model against which we want to assess the truth of the proposition is M_2 of Chapter 5 and in particular that the extension of *like'* is that shown in the diagram in (19) of that chapter. The interpretation of $\exists$*z [(like'(jo'))(z)]* with respect to M_2 and the value assignment **g** in (11) requires us to look at value assignments like $\mathbf{g}_1$ to $\mathbf{g}_4$ in (12), which are all exactly like **g** except for the value assigned to *z*. From the extension of *like'* in M_2 shown by the diagram (19) in Chapter 5, we can see that the value assignment $\mathbf{g_3}$ is the one that shows that $\exists z$ *[(like'(jo'))(z)]* is true. This is because $\mathbf{g_3}$ assigns the value $\mathbf{MAN_1}$ to *z* and the function denoted by *like'(jo')* in M_2 maps this entity onto **1**, showing that Jo liked himself. Hence, since the variable assignment, $\mathbf{g_3}$, is exactly like **g** except for the value assigned to *z*, $[\exists z\, [(like'(jo'))(z)]]^{M2,g}$ is **1** and we say that $\mathbf{g_3}$ **satisfies** the formula *(like'(jo'))(z)*, because this value assignment makes the formula true.

(11)

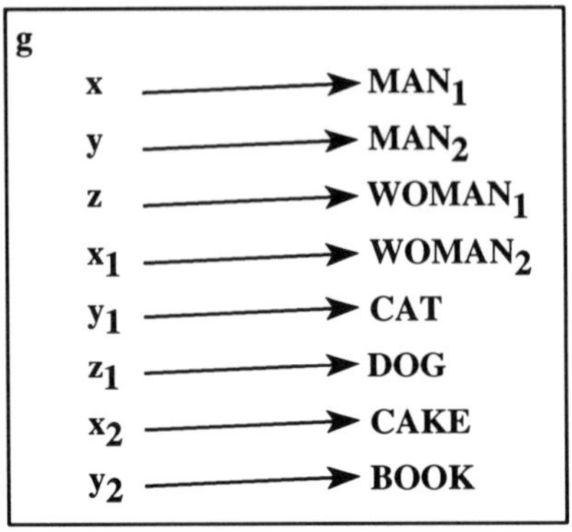

(12)

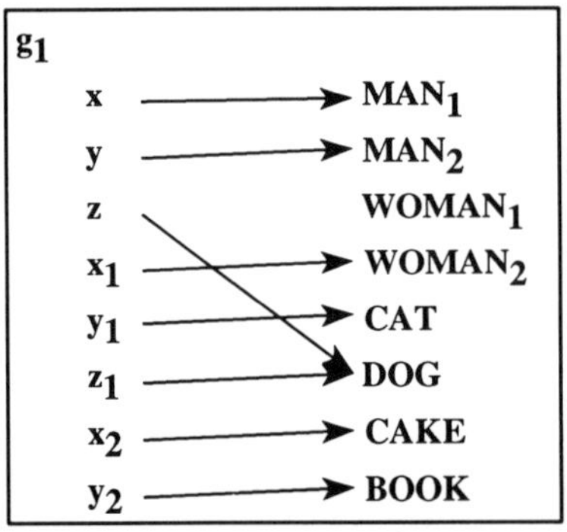

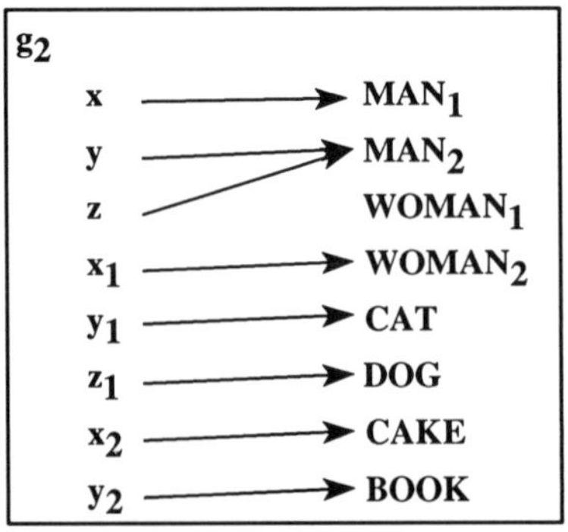

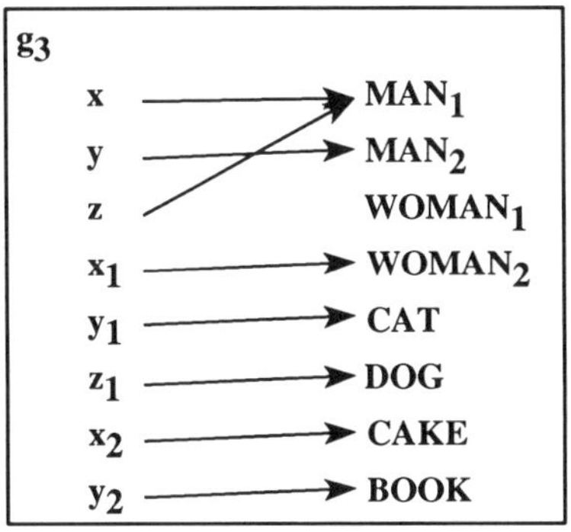

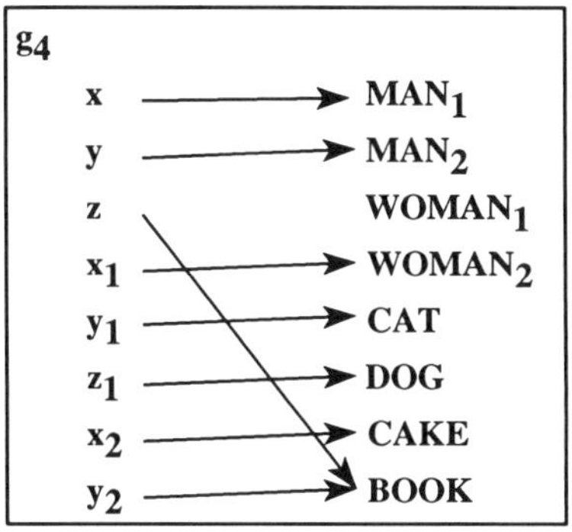

The interpretation of the universal quantifier follows the same lines, except that here we require that every value assigned to *z* make the propositional function true. In other words, the truth of the proposition expressed by the sentence *Jo liked everyone* on some occasion of utterance is guaranteed, if the propositions expressed by the sentences *Jo liked himself* and *Jo liked Fiona* and *Jo liked Ethel*, and so on, are all true on the same occasion. The formal interpretation of universally quantified formulae is given in (13).

(13) **Truth-conditions for universal formulae**: If ϕ is an expression of type t containing a free occurrence of a variable, u, of type e, then $[\forall u[\phi]]^{M,g}$ is **1**, iff there for every value assignment **g'**, exactly like **g** except perhaps for the individual assigned to u, $[\phi]^{M,g'}$ is **1**.

Clearly, the formula $\forall z$ *[(like'(z))(jo')]* is false with respect to M_2 because there at least one value assignment that makes *(like'(z))(jo')* false; e.g. $\mathbf{g}_1$ which assigns the value **DOG** to *z* and **<MAN$_1$,DOG>** is not in the denotation of $[like']^{M_2}$. Thus, while an existentially quantified formula is verified by a single value assignment that satisfies the propositional function containing the bound variable, a universally quantified one is falsified by a single value assignment that does not satisfy its propositional function.

Exercise 6.2:
Work out the truth values of the following formulae with respect to model M_3, where this model is exactly like M_2 with the addition of the denotation assignments shown below. For each formula, also give an English sentence that might be translated into it.

> F_3(exist') = {**MAN$_1$,MAN$_2$,WOMAN$_1$,WOMAN$_2$,CAT,DOG,CAKE,BOOK**}.
> F_3(touch') = {**<WOMAN$_1$,MAN$_1$>**, **<WOMAN$_1$,WOMAN$_1$>**,
> **<WOMAN$_1$,CAT>**, **<WOMAN$_1$,WOMAN$_2$>**, **<WOMAN$_1$,DOG>**,
> **<WOMAN$_1$,CAKE>**, **<WOMAN$_1$,CAKE>**, **<WOMAN1,BOOK>**}.
> F_3(like') = F_2(like') (= (18) of Chapter 5).

i. ∀x [(like'(x))(x)].
ii. ∃x [like'(fiona')(x) & (like'(x))(fiona')].
iii. ∀x [exist'(x)].
iv. ∀x [(touch'(x))(ethel')].
v. ∀x [∃y [(like'(x))(y)]].

6.2.3 *Quantification and negation*

Before tackling the question of how the logical quantifiers can be incorporated into a theory of natural language semantics (the topic of Section 6.3), let us look briefly at the way the negation operator, ~, interacts with the quantifiers, ∃ and ∀. Given a propositional function like *(like'(jo'))(z)*, there are four possible formulae that can be constructed using ~, ∃ and ∀, depending on their relative scopes. (14) gives the relevant L_Q expressions and (15) gives sentences in English that can be translated by the respective formulae in (14).

(14) a. ∃z [~((like'(jo'))(z))].
b. ∀z [~((like'(jo'))(z))].
c. ~(∃z [(like'(jo'))(z)]).
d. ~(∀z [(like'(jo'))(z)]).

(15) a. Someone doesn't like Jo.
b. No-one liked Jo.
c. No-one liked Jo.
d. Not everyone liked Jo.

Notice that two of the formulae in (14) are taken as translating the same English sentence. Since the sentence *No-one liked Jo* is not ambiguous, if the two translations accurately represent its truth-conditional meaning, they must be equivalent, i.e. have the same truth-conditions. For (14.b) to be true, the interpretation rule in (13) requires that the formula *~((like'(jo'))(z))* be true for all values assigned to *z*. But the semantics of negation, of course, means that it can be true only if there is no assignment of a value to *z* that satisfies the propositional function *(like'(jo'))(z)*, i.e. if no-one liked Jo. The formula *~(∃z [(like'(jo'))(z)])*, is true, however, if, and only if, *∃z [(like'(jo'))(z)]* is false. Since the latter is only false where there is no value assignment that satisfies *(like'(jo'))(z)*, the formula in (14.c) is true if, and only if no-one actually liked Jo. (14.b) and (14.c) are, therefore, truth-conditionally equivalent, giving us two ways of representing sentences containing the pronoun *no-one*: either with the universal quantifier having scope over a negated propositional function (i.e. $\forall x\ [\sim\phi]$) or with the negation operator having scope over an existentially quantified formula (i.e. $\sim(\exists x\ [\phi])$).

It is important to ensure that the relative scopes of the quantifiers and negation in the representation for *no-one* that is being used are correct: universal before negation or negation before existential. This is because formulae that have the scopes of the operators reversed have very different interpretations. Where the existential quantifier has scope over the negation operator, as in (14.a), the formula is true if there is some assignment of a value to *x* which satisfies *~((like'(jo'))(z))*, i.e. there is some element in the universe of discourse that does not like Jo. Where the negation scopes over a universally quantified formula, as in (14.d), on the other hand, the whole formula is true if, and only if, the formula $\forall z$ *[(like'(jo'))(z)]* is false, i.e. if there is some value assignment to x that does not satisfy *(like'(jo'))(z)*. These two sets of truth-conditions are the same and so, like (14.b) and (14.c), (14.a) and (14.d) are truth-conditionally equivalent. However, these truth-conditions are not the same as those for the former. A single variable assignment that fails to satisfy *(like'(jo'))(z)* which is sufficient to guarantee the truth of $\exists z$ *[~((like'(jo'))(z))]* and *~(*$\forall z$ *[(like'(jo'))(z)])* is not sufficient to guarantee the truth of $\forall z$ *[~((like'(jo'))(z))]* and *~(*$\exists z$ *[(like'(jo'))(z)])* which require every value assignment to fail to satisfy the propositional function. Hence, (14.a) (and (14.d)) may be true in models in which (14.b) and (14.c) are not and so the formulae in (14.a) and (14.d) are not truth-conditionally equivalent to those in (14.b) and (14.c). Intuitively this is the correct result, since the formula that translates *No-one liked Jo* may be false even though the formula that translates *Someone doesn't like Jo* is true. Relative scope is thus semantically significant and care must be exercised when translating sentences that contain negatively quantified noun phrases.

6.3 A compositional approach

The previous section gives an introduction to the logical quantifiers, but does not do so as part of a compositional theory of natural language semantics. No translation rules from English to L_Q have been given and there has been no attempt to analyse more complex noun phrases involving the quantifiers. This is remedied in this section where a type-theoretic analysis of NPs is given that follows Richard Montague's approach. As we shall see, this analysis is general enough to allow the translation and interpretation of most universally and existentially quantified noun phrases in English.

6.3.1 Translating quantifier pronouns

In order to simplify matters, let us first work out a way of translating sentences containing quantifier pronouns in subject position like those in (16) in line with their syntactic structure. Obviously, the first thing we need to do is add a new syntactic rule to the grammar fragment G_2 that allows a noun phrase to be rewritten as a pronoun.

This is given in (17.a) and with the addition of the pronouns in (17.b) to the lexicon, we can now analyse the sentence in (16.a) as having the structure in (18).

(16) a. Everyone liked Jo.
b. Someone sang.
c. No-one laughed.

(17) a. $27G_2$: NP $\rightarrow$ Pro.
b. Pro = {everyone, someone, no-one, everything, something, nothing, nobody}.

(18)

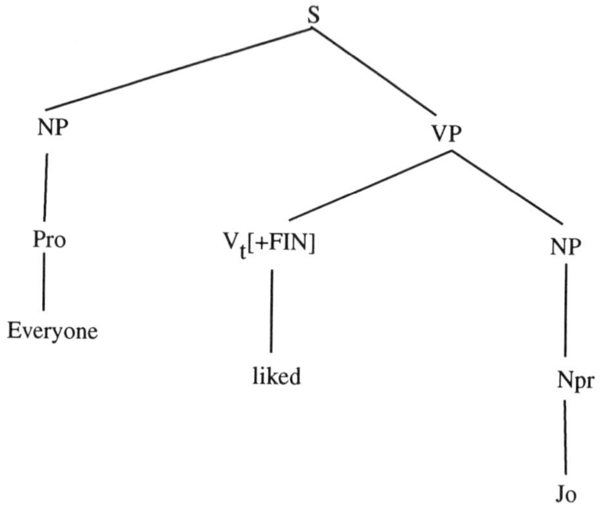

According to the previous section, the translation of sentence (16.a) into L_Q is equivalent to the formula in (19):

(19) $\forall$x [(like'(jo'))(x)].

Assuming that proper names are still translated as individual constants (an assumption that will be revised in Section 6.3), the translation of the VP in (18) is (20).

(20) VP $\Rightarrow$ like'(jo').

The rule of functional application requires the translation of the pronoun *everyone* to combine with the translation in (20) to give an expression that is equivalent to (19). There are two ways in which VP' and Pro' may be combined: either Pro' is an argument of VP' or VP' is an argument of Pro'. As we saw in Section 6.1 above, the pronoun cannot be translated into an expression with the type of an entity and so cannot serve as the argument of VP. Hence, it must denote a function from VP denotations to sentence denotations, and so have the type assignment in (21). (Notice that this type was proposed for conjoined subject NPs at the end of Chapter 5.)

(21) TYPE(Pro) = <<e,t>,t>.

The type assignment in (21) requires the translation rule for basic sentences to be revised to allow the subject to act as a functor over the VP translation. The appropriate revision appears in (22).

(22) $T1G_2$: S $\Rightarrow$ NP'(VP').

As we have seen, the translation that is assigned to the sentence *Everyone likes Jo* is truth-conditionally equivalent to the formula in (19). Assuming that this equivalence follows from λ-conversion, we may apply this rule backwards to arrive at the translation of the unconverted formula and hence recover the translation of the pronoun *everyone*. Thus, from (22) we can infer the schematic conversion in (23.a), since the expression *like'(jo')* is the translation of the VP. To get the translation of the pronoun we can replace this expression in the formula in (19) by a predicate variable to get the propositional function in (23.b). As this expression is of type t and contains a variable, P, of type <e,t>, we can abstract on this to obtain the expression in (23.c) which is of type <<e,t>,t>, the type required for subject NPs. The resulting expression provides an appropriate translation of the pronoun *everyone* and the application of this expression to the VP translation *like'(jo')* gives (23.d) which can be λ-converted into (19), as required.

(23) a. Pro'(like'(jo'))
» ∀x [(like'(jo'))(x)].
b. ∀x [P(x)]. (type t)
c. λP [∀x [P(x)]]. (type <<e,t>,t>)
d. λP [∀x [P(x)]](like'(jo'))
» ∀x [(like'(jo'))(x)].

Exercise 6.3:
Using the sentences in (16.b) and (16.c), provide translations for the pronouns *someone* and *no-one* along the lines of that given for *everyone* above.

The domain of denotations for expressions with the type assigned to quantifier pronouns in (21) (and other quantified noun phrases) is the set of functions from sets of entities (VP extensions) to truth values (S extensions), as shown in (24). We may thus think of a QNP as denoting a function that maps the extension of a VP (a characteristic function) onto the value **1** if it satisfies the property expressed by the quantifier, and **0** otherwise. Since a function from some denotation type onto the truth values is a characteristic function, another way of defining a set, QNPs are analysed as denoting sets of sets of entities in the model.

(24) a. $D_{<<e,t>,t>} = D_t^{D<e,t>} = \mathbf{\{0,1\}}^{(\{0,1\}A)}$.

b.

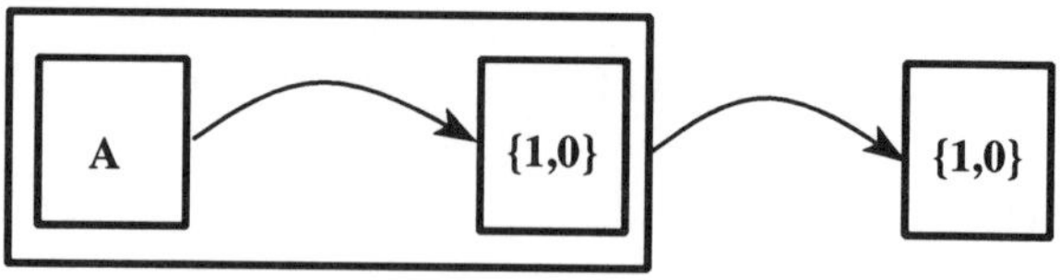

As an illustration, consider the denotation of the pronoun *someone*. As shown in the answer to Exercise 6.3, this translates into an expression λP [∃x [P(x)]], again of type <<e,t>,t>. According to the interpretation given to the existential quantifier in (10), the translation of the pronoun combines with a VP translation to give a true formula, if the extension of VP' contains at least one element. Hence, $[\lambda P\ [\exists x\ [P(x)]]]^{M,g}$ is that function that maps $[VP']^{M,g}$ onto **1** if $[VP']^{M,g}$ does not denote the empty set and onto **0** if it does. Hence, we may say that $[\lambda P\ [\exists x\ [P(x)]]]^{M,g}$ is the set of all subsets of **A** (the universe of discourse) that are non-null. In set-theoretic terms, this can be represented as (25.a).

(25) $[\lambda P\ [\exists x\ [P(x)]]]^{M,g} = \{X \subseteq A \mid X \neq \emptyset\}$.

Exercise 6.4:
What are the extensions of the translations of *everyone* and *no-one* in set-theoretic terms?

6.3.2 Complex NPs

The translation and interpretation of quantifier pronouns presented above provides the basis of an approach to the treatment of quantified noun phrases of all sorts. It needs, however, to be extended to cover more complex QNPs like those in (26.a) to (26.c) and to bring out the fact that the quantifier pronouns ending in *-one* are applicable only to human entities and those ending in *-thing* (primarily) to non-human ones, as in (26.d) and (26.e).

(26) a. Every student liked Jo.
b. A lecturer screamed.
c. No woman laughed.
d. No-one moved.
e. Nothing moved.

Information is conveyed in these sentences by the common noun in the subject NP and so this must be represented in their translations. To incorporate the noun translations, we first need to know their type. Common nouns, like verb phrases, extensionally denote sets of entities: sets that consist of just those entities of which it is true to say *That is a N*, for any common noun N. Thus, the extension of a noun like *chair* is the set of all chairs, that of *student* is the set of all students, and so on. The type of a common noun must, therefore, be that of a set-denoting expression, i.e. <e,t>. Given this type assignment, the translations of sentences like those in (26) is based on two open formulae which contain instances of the same variable: one formula derived by applying the translation of the VP to a variable and the other derived by applying the translation of the common noun to an instance of the same variable. For example, the translation of the sentence *Every student liked Jo* in (26.a) is derived from some combination of the open formulae *student'(x)* and *(like'(jo'))(x)*. The free variable in the open formulae must be bound by a quantifier appropriate to the determiner and the two open formulae must be combined by some propositional connective, &, $\vee$, $\rightarrow$ or $\leftrightarrow$, to form a well-formed formula with no free variables.

The question of how the two open formulae are connected can be answered by considering the truth-conditions associated with particular sentences. For example, the formula associated with the sentence in (26.a) is true if everything in the model that is a student also liked Jo. This interpretation can be made more explicit by paraphrasing (26.a) as the semi-formal English sentence in (27.a) which can be translated directly into L_Q as the formula in (27.b).

(27) a. For every x, if x was a student, then x liked Jo.
b. $\forall$x [student'(x) $\rightarrow$ (like'(jo'))(x)].

Given the interpretation rule for the universal quantifier, the formula in (27.b) is true as long as every value assignment to *x* makes the formula *student'(x)* $\rightarrow$ *(like'(jo'))(x)* true. By the semantics of material implication, this is the case if every constant instantiating the variable in a value assignment is in the extension of *like'(jo')*, if it is also in the extension of *student'*. In other words, the formula in (27.b) is true provided [*student'*]^{M,g} is a subset of [*like'(jo')*]^{M,g}. This situation can be represented by the diagram in (28) where the main box represents the set of entities in the model.

(28) Every student liked Jo

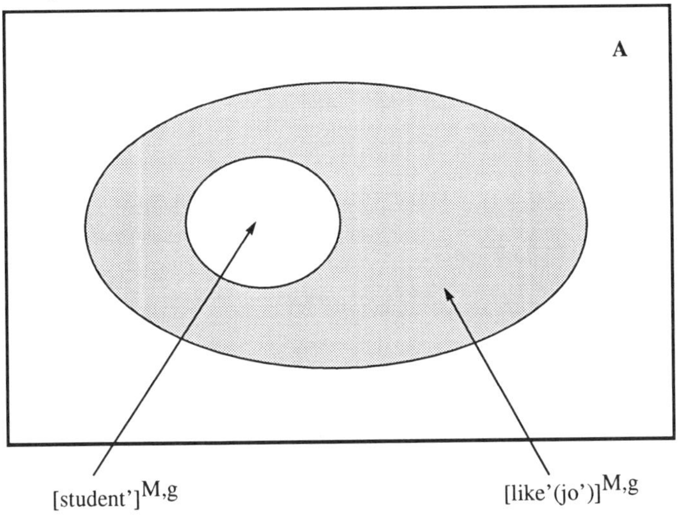

To get the translation of a noun phrase like *every student* we can apply backwards lambda-conversion to (27.b). The revised translation rule for basic sentences in (22.a) requires this formula to be derived by the application of the noun phrase translation to that of the verb phrase. Since the VP translation is *like'(jo')* (of type <e,t>), we can replace this expression in (27.b) with a predicate variable to get an open formula and then abstract on this to get an expression of type <<e,t>,t>, as is done in (29). This yields (29.d) as the translation of the NP *every student*.

(29) a. NP'(VP')
» $\forall$x [student'(x) $\rightarrow$ (like'(jo'))(x)].
b. NP'(like'(jo'))
» $\forall$x [student'(x) $\rightarrow$ (like'(jo'))(x)].
c. λP [$\forall$x [student'(x) $\rightarrow$ P(x)]](like'(jo'))
» $\forall$x [student'(x) $\rightarrow$ (like'(jo'))(x)].
d. NP $\Rightarrow$ λP [$\forall$x [student'(x) $\rightarrow$ P(x)]].

We have not, of course, completed the analysis of the example sentence, as we still need to show how the NP translation in (29.d) is obtained. Syntactically the phrase *every student* is made up of a determiner (*every*) followed by a noun (*student*) so the rule in (30.a) needs to be added to the grammar G_2, as well as a list of determiners to the lexicon (30.b).

(30) a. 28G_2: NP $\rightarrow$ Det N.
b. Det $\rightarrow$ {every, a, some, no, ...}.

As we have seen, quantified NPs have the type <<e,t>,t> and nouns have the type <e,t>. This means that determiners must have a type that takes a noun expression into a noun phrase expression, i.e. <<e,t>,<<e,t>,t>>, yielding the translation rule in (31) for the rule in (30.a).

(31) T28G_2: NP $\Rightarrow$ Det'(N').

Since we are treating Det' as a functor over N', we can apply backwards λ-conversion to (29.d). To get the translation of the determiner *every*, the translation of the common noun in (29.d) is replaced by another predicate variable, Q, which again is bound by the lambda operator, as in (32.c). This gives (32.d) as the appropriate translation for the determiner *every*.

(32) a. Det'(N')
» λP [$\forall$x [student'(x) $\rightarrow$ P(x)]].
b. Det'(student')
» λP [$\forall$x [student'(x) $\rightarrow$ P(x)]].
c. λQ [λP [$\forall$x [Q(x) $\rightarrow$ P(x)]]](student')
» λP [$\forall$x [student'(x) $\rightarrow$ P(x)]].
d. *every* $\Rightarrow$ λQ [λP [$\forall$x [Q(x) $\rightarrow$ P(x)]]].

The analysis tree for (26.a) is shown in (33) with the translations of the constituent phrases shown as usual on the nodes. Applying lambda-conversion to the translation of the S node gives the equivalent formula in (27.b), as readers can check for themselves.

(33)

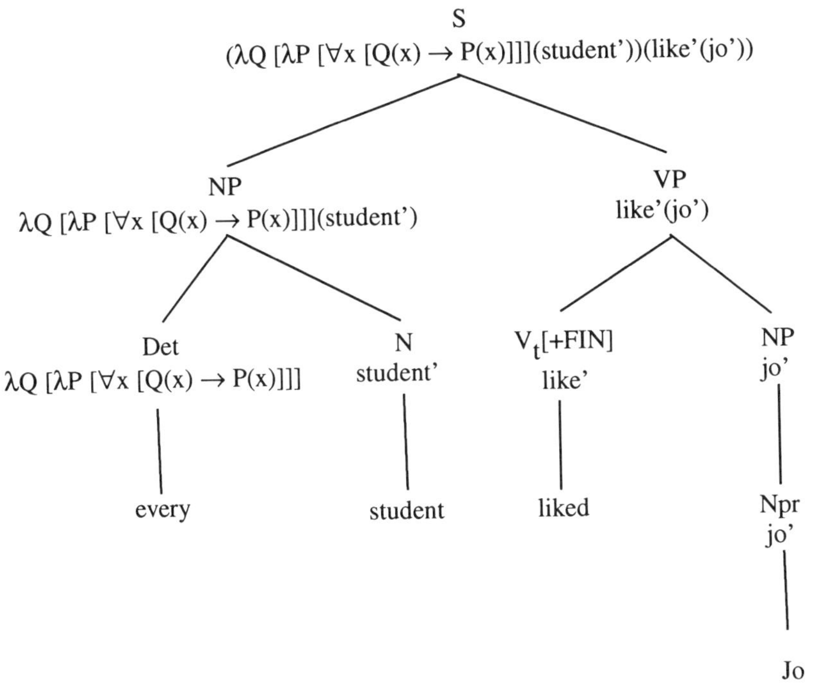

The translations of *some* (or *a*) and *no* are determined in the same fashion, but there is a difference in the way the open formulae formed from the noun and VP translations are connected. The existential sentence in (26.b) translates into a formula that is true if, and only if, there is something that was a lecturer *and* that something screamed. Hence, a conjunction is used in place of the material implication of the universally quantified formula. The force of this may be brought out by the semi-formal English sentence in (34.a) and its translation into L_Q in (34.b).

(34) a. For some x, x was a lecturer and x screamed.
b. ∃x [lecturer'(x) & scream'(x)].

According to the truth-conditions for formulae containing ∃, given in (10), above, (34.b) is true if (and only if) there is at least one entity in **A** that satisfies both *lecturer'(x)* and *scream'(x)*. Set-theoretically, this requires that the intersection of the extension of the common noun in the subject NP and that of the verb phrase is not empty, a situation that can be represented by the diagram in (35).

(35)

A lecturer screamed

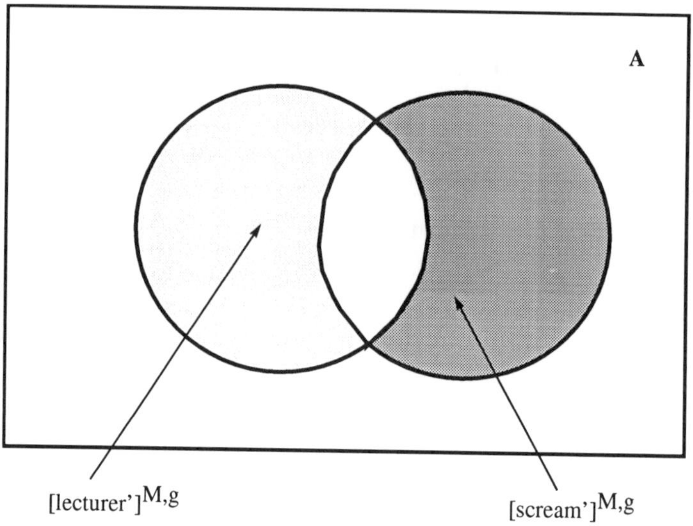

As before, it is possible to get to the translation of the NP *a lecturer* and that of the determiner by applying lambda-conversion backwards. The steps are shown in (36). (36.c) shows the translation of the NP *a lecturer* applied to the VP translation and (36.f) that of the determiner *a* applied to its head noun and then to the VP translation. This leaves (36.g) as the translation of the determiner *a*.

(36) a. $\text{NP'}(\text{VP'})$
$\gg \exists x\, [\text{lecturer'}(x)\ \&\ \text{scream'}(x)]$.

b. $\text{NP'}(\text{scream'})$
$\gg \exists x\, [\text{lecturer'}(x)\ \&\ \text{scream'}(x)]$.

c. $\lambda P\, [\exists x\, [\text{lecturer'}(x)\ \&\ P(x)]](\text{scream'})$
$\gg \exists x\, [\text{lecturer'}(x)\ \&\ \text{scream'}(x)]$.

d. $(\text{Det'}(\text{N'}))(\text{scream'})$
$\gg \lambda P\, [\exists x\, [\text{lecturer'}(x)\ \&\ P(x)]](\text{scream'})$.

e. $(\text{Det'}(\text{lecturer'}))(\text{scream'})$
$\gg \lambda P\, [\exists x\, [\text{lecturer'}(x)\ \&\ P(x)]](\text{scream'})$.

f. $(\lambda Q\, [\lambda P\, [\exists x\, [Q(x)\ \&\ P(x)]]](\text{lecturer'}))(\text{scream'})$
$\gg \lambda P\, [\exists x\, [\text{lecturer'}(x)\ \&\ P(x)]](\text{scream'})$.

g. $\text{a} \Rightarrow \lambda Q\, [\lambda P\, [\exists x\, [Q(x)\ \&\ P(x)]]]$.

In translating NPs, one must be careful to associate the correct connective with the correct quantifier, as a mistake gives rise to a formula with very different truth-conditions. Replacing & by $\rightarrow$ in (34.b), for example, yields (37.a) which, by the truth-conditions of material implication, is true even if there is nothing in the extension of *lecturer'*, i.e. *a lecturer screamed* expresses a true proposition even if there are no lecturers. Replacing $\rightarrow$ by & in (27.b), on the other hand, yields the formula in (37.b) which states that everything in the model was a student that liked Jo, which is not what the sentence *Every student liked Jo* means.

(37) a. $\exists$x [lecturer'(x) $\rightarrow$ scream'(x)].
b. $\forall$x [student'(x) & (like'(jo'))(x)].

Exercise 6.5:
Give a translation of the NP *no dog* and of the determiner *no*, following the steps used above. NB: There are two possible translations for *no*. Make sure that the connective used is the right one for the translation.

Exercise 6.6:
Translate the following sentences into L_Q, giving for each one both the logical expression as it is generated by the translation rules and its equivalent lambda converted form.

i. Every lecturer sang and laughed.
ii. Some student didn't sing.
iii. If no student sang, then no lecturer screamed.

In this way, sentences containing quantified noun phrases in subject position can be translated compositionally, but what sort of thing does a quantified noun phrase denote in a model? As with the quantifier pronouns, quantified NPs have the type <<e,t>,t> and so denote functions from sets to truth values or, equivalently, sets of sets of entities. Because of the interaction between the extension of the common noun in the NP and that of the VP, these functions are more complex than those associated with the quantifier pronouns.

The diagrams in (28) and (35) give a clue as to the denotations of universally and existentially quantified noun phrases. In (28), the diagram representing the truth-conditions for the sentence *Every student liked Jo* shows that the extension of the common noun, *student'*, must be contained in that of the VP, *like'(jo')*. We can, therefore, think of the noun phrase *every student* as (indirectly) denoting a function that maps every set of entities that contains the set of students onto **1** and every other set onto **0**. In other words, the phrase denotes the set of all supersets of $[student']^{M,g}$, as shown in (38.a), which generalises to (38.b) for all noun phrases containing the determiner *every*.

(38) a. $\{X \subseteq A \mid [student']^{M,g} \subseteq X\}$.
b. *every N* denotes $\{X \subseteq A \mid [N']^{M,g} \subseteq X\}$.

The extension of *every student* is called the **universal sublimation** of the property of being a student. This identifies the set of all sets of which every student is a member, as represented by the diagram in (39) where the central circle represents the extension of *student'* (or the relevant common noun), each P_n represents the extension of some other property and the whole thing represents the extension of $\lambda P\ [\forall x\ [student'(x) \rightarrow P(x)]]$.

(39) **Universal sublimation of [student']^{M}**

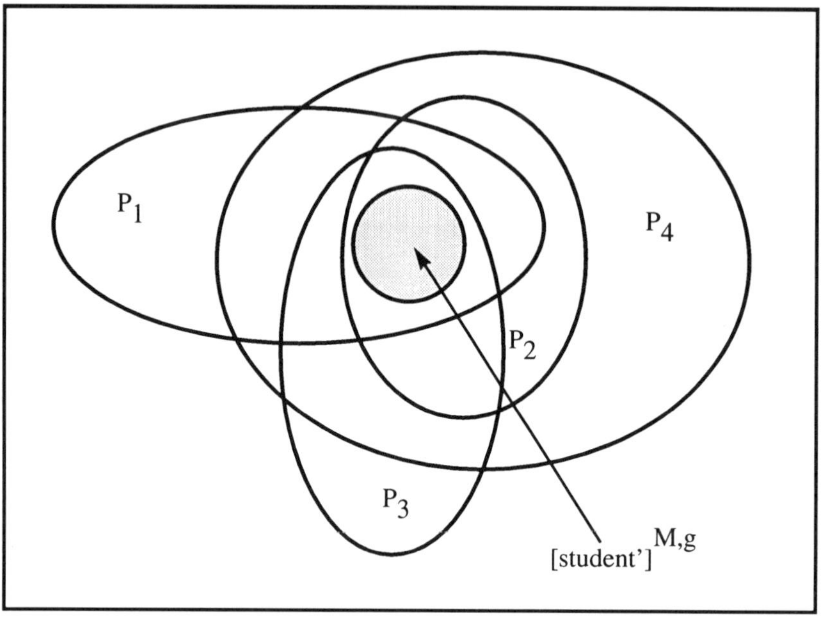

As can be seen from (35), a formula translating a sentence with an existential subject NP is true if the extension of the common noun in the subject NP has a non-null intersection with the extension of the VP. Thus, the extension of $\lambda P\ [\exists x\ [lecturer'(x)\ \&\ P(x)]]$, is a function that maps every set in the model onto **1** if its intersection with $[lecturer']^{M,g}$ contains at least one element. The extension of the NP *a lecturer* is therefore given the set-theoretic definition in (40) which is read as 'the set of all subsets of **A** that have a non-null intersection with the set denoted by *lecturer*''.

(40) $\{X \subseteq A \mid X \cap [lecturer']^{M,g} \neq \emptyset\}$.

(40) is called the **existential sublimation** of the property of being a lecturer, since it picks out the set of all properties that some lecturer has. This can be represented by the diagram in (41) where again the central circle represents the extension of *lecturer'* in the model, each P_n represents the extension of some other property and the whole thing represents the extension of *a lecturer*. We will return to this sort of representation for NP denotations in Section 6.6.

(41) **Existential sublimation of [lecturer']^M**

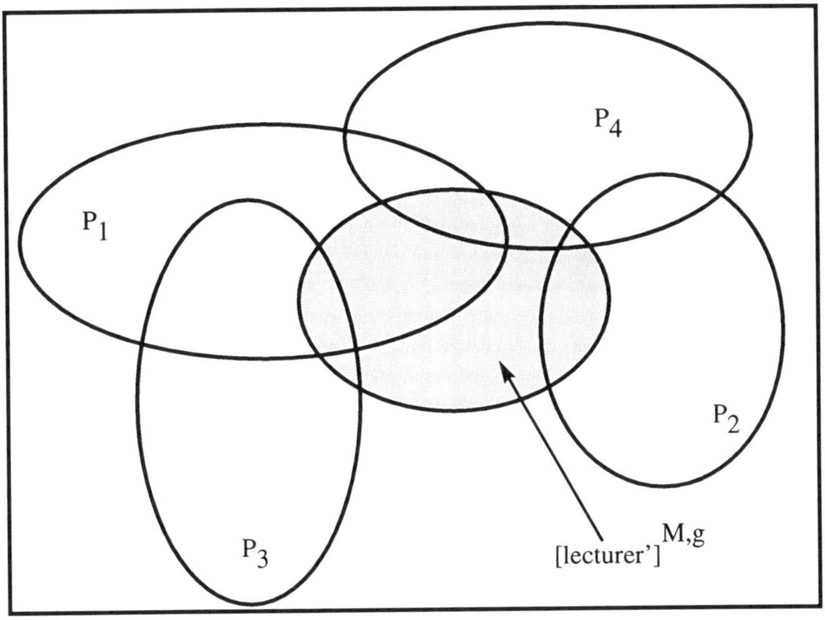

Exercise 6.7:
What is the set-theoretic definition of the extension of *no dog*? How could the negative sublimation of *dog* be represented diagrammatically?

6.3.3 Nominal modifiers

The approach to NP translation and interpretation discussed above is general enough to allow for the introduction of attributive modifiers into noun phrases. In English, nouns may be modified by adjectives, prepositional phrases or relative clauses. The proper analysis of PP modification requires an analysis of the meaning of prepositions, something that is not discussed in this book and so, in this section, we look only at how certain simple attributive adjectives can be introduced into our grammar fragment, leaving the analysis of relative clauses as an exercise for the reader.

Syntactically, attributive adjectives like *happy* and *fat* combine with a common noun to give a common noun phrase (CNP) (equivalent to N^1 in X-bar theory). Since more than one adjective (or other nominal modifier) can appear with a single noun, it is customary to adopt the recursive rule in (42.a) which distinguishes attributive adjectives from predicative ones by the use of a feature [PRD], the former being negatively marked for this property. This requires a slight alteration of the grammar to realise CNPs as simple nouns and allow determiners to combine with CNPs rather than with nouns directly. (42.d) gives a list of some attributive adjectives.

(42) a. $29G_2$: CNP → A[-PRD] CNP.
b. $30G_2$: CNP → N.
c. $28'G_2$: NP → Det CNP.
d. A[-PRD] = {happy, sad, silly, fat}.

Since determiners, of type <<e,t>,<<e,t>,t>>, combine with CNPs to give NPs, CNPs must have the same type as a common noun, i.e. <e,t>, so that the translation of the rule in (42.b) must be identical to the translation of the noun. This means that the type of an attributive adjective must be <<e,t>,<e,t>> as it takes a one-place predicate into a one-place predicate. But how should adjectives like *happy* be translated? We could, of course, simply write it as *happy'* and let the denotation assignment function in each model specify for each property the set of happy entities with that property. However, this would miss two things. In the first place, it would lose the relationship between the predicative use of the adjective as in *Every student is happy* and its attributive use as in *Every happy student*. Secondly, we want to capture the fact that every happy student is a student (and indeed that every happy student is happy). This does not necessarily follow if each model specifies for each property what set results from applying the function denoted by an attributive adjective to that property. Thus, if we take the set of students in a model to be {$\mathbf{MAN_1}$, $\mathbf{WOMAN_2}$}, for example, it is possible to define $[happy']^{M,g}$ as a function that maps this set into {$\mathbf{WOMAN_1}$,**DOG**}. In other words, it might be possible for some model to pick out a set of happy students that are not actually students! Hence, we need to ensure in the interpretation that the set of happy students is a subset of the set of students.

To do this, we take as a starting point the interpretation of the predicative use of such adjectives from Chapter 3. There, sentences like *Fiona was happy* were assigned the same logical structure as sentences containing intransitive verbs like *Fiona sang*, i.e. they are translated as one-place predicates combined with an individual constant. In L_{type} (and L_Q, of course), this gives predicative adjectives the type of a one-place predicate, <e,t>, with sets of entities as their extension. Using this type assignment (and assuming that the copula is pleonastic), the sentence *Every student was happy* is translated into L_Q as (43), a formula that is true provided that the set of students is a subset of the set of happy entities.

(43) $\forall x$ [student'(x) → happy'(x)].

A sentence like *Every happy student sang*, on the other hand, must translate into a formula that is true if, and only if, the set of happy students is a subset of the set of singers, or, more explicitly, if the set of entities that were both happy and students is a subset of the set of entities that sang. A formula that has precisely these truth-conditions appears in (44.a). If we assume that the equivalence between the formula in (44.a) and the one translating *every happy student sang* derives from λ-conversion, the rule can be applied backwards to work out the translations of the constituents of the sentence. (44.b) shows a λ-expression applied to the VP translation *sing'* which is equivalent to the formula in (44.a).

(44) a. $\forall x$ [(happy'(x) & student'(x)) $\rightarrow$ sing'(x)].
b. λP [$\forall x$ [(happy'(x) & student'(x)) $\rightarrow$ P(x)]](sing').

As we have seen, the translation of *every* is the expression in (32.d) so that (44.b) must be equivalent to the expression derived by applying *λQ [λP [∀x [Q(x) → P(x)]]]* to the translation of the CNP *happy student* as shown in (45.a) and (45.b). Because CNPs translate into one-place predicates, the expression translating *happy student* must be of type <e,t>. It must also contain the propositional function *happy'(y) & student'(y)* that is factored out of (44.b) when the translation of the determiner is removed. This propositional function can, of course, be turned into an expression of the appropriate type by abstracting on the free variable *y*, as in (45.c). This is, therefore, the translation of the common noun phrase *happy student*.

(45) a. every CNP
$\Rightarrow \lambda Q$ [λP [$\forall x$ [Q(x) $\rightarrow$ P(x)]]](CNP').
b. » λP [$\forall x$ [(happy'(x) & student'(x)) $\rightarrow$ P(x)]].
c. happy student
$\Rightarrow \lambda y$ [happy'(y) & student'(y)].

We can assume that the expression in (45.b) results from the functional application of the translation of the adjective to that of the noun. The former can thus be restored by replacing the translation of the noun, *student'*, by another predicate variable, P_1, and abstracting on this to give the expression in (46). This expression is of type <<e,t>,<e,t>> and denotes a function that maps the set of entities denoted by the common noun to the set of entities which appear in the intersection of this set with the set of entities denoted by the predicative adjective *happy'*. This interpretation guarantees that every happy student is happy and every happy student is a student.

(46) happy $\Rightarrow \lambda P_1$ [λy [happy'(y) & P_1(y)]].

Attributive adjectives like *happy'* with the same general translation and interpretation as shown in (46) are often referred to as **intersective adjectives** and a general rule may be written that takes the predicative adjective translation and outputs its attributive counterpart. This is given in (47) and, as with *happy*, the translation yields an expression that combines with that of a common noun to yield an expression that picks out the set of entities that appear in the extensions of the common noun and the related predicative adjective.

(47) If *a* is a predicative adjective with translation *a'*, then its attributive counterpart has a translation λP [λx [*a'*(x) & P(x)]].

Not all adjectives are intersective, however, and even adjectives like *happy* do not always have the interpretation captured by the rule in (47). The interpretation of *happy student* discussed above entails that any entity in its extension is happy in some absolute sense. However, there are situations where this is not the appropriate interpretation. A sentence like *The happy student was not a happy cook* is not (necessarily) contradictory, as is predicted from the translation of *happy* defined by (47). Furthermore, the translation of a sentence like *Jo was a happy student, but an unhappy lecturer* given by the above rule makes incorrect predictions about the entailments of this sentence. The appropriate translation is something like *(happy'(jo') & student'(jo')) & ~(happy'(jo') & lecturer'(jo'))*. Such a formula can only be true if Jo was a student and was happy (in some absolute sense), but was not a lecturer. The English sentence, however, conveys the information that Jo is a lecturer, but unhappy in that role, whereas he is happy in the role of a student. This interpretation requires the extension of *happy* to depend on that of the common noun with which it combines and is thus not simply intersective. Thus, while all happy students are students, there is an interpretation in which they are not happy in any absolute sense, but only happy as students. Many adjectives like *small, good, skilful* and so on, have the same properties as this use of *happy*, but others like *alleged* and *fake* are even more restricted in their entailments. For example, a fake gun is not a gun and an alleged murderer is not necessarily a murderer. The interpretation of all these adjectives goes beyond the extensional semantics that has so far been developed and requires a definition of intensionality. Although the apparatus for dealing with intensional expressions is introduced in Chapter 10, the proper treatment of intensional adjectives remains controversial and so will not be further discussed. The interested reader is encouraged to pursue the references cited at the end of this chapter for an idea of how complex adjective interpretation may be. The analysis of intersective adjectives given here is just a beginning, but it gives a basis from which to start.

---

*Exercise 6.8:
Devise a way of translating simple relative clauses like that in the following sentence that guarantees that a student that liked Jo, liked Jo and a student that liked Jo, was a student.

i. A student that liked Jo kicked the cat.

6.4 Proper names and definite descriptions

We have now seen how quantified NPs can be treated as having the type <<e,t>,t>, but what about proper names and definite descriptions? Proper names clearly pick out individual entities in the universe of discourse and so their assignment to type e seems the most reasonable assumption to make, since they thereby directly denote unique entities in the model. However, if this analysis is maintained, an imbalance in the treatment of noun phrases is created that is not represented in syntax. In English, quantified noun phrases and proper names have the same syntactic distribution, which is, of course, why they are assigned to the same syntactic category, NP. But the difference in the apparent denotations of proper names and QNPs implies a difference in syntactic category, since no syntactic category may be assigned more than one type without giving rise to unacceptable ambiguity in the translation language. If this is done, however, then clearly different syntactic rules have to be written for expressions of the same category according to whether they contain QNPs or proper names, thus missing the obvious syntactic generalisation that they have the same distribution. Richard Montague's solution to this dilemma is to give both proper names and quantified NPs the same type, thus allowing them to be treated the same syntactically. Since, as we have seen, QNPs cannot have the type of an entity, the type of N_{pr} must be raised to the type of a QNP. At the same time, however, we must make sure that the distinctive property of proper nouns, that, in a given context, they name a specific entity, is not lost.

As we have seen before, the translation into L_{type} of the sentence *Fiona sang* is *sing'(fiona')*, which is true only in those situations in which the set of singers includes some specific entity called Fiona. Simply changing the type of proper names to <<e,t>,t> and translating the sentence as *fiona'(sing')* obscures this simple interpretation and requires a complex interpretation of the constant *fiona'* to get the truth-conditions right. However, we can get a more transparent translation for *Fiona* by applying backwards lambda-conversion to the formula that best provides the semantics for the sentence. Thus, assuming that proper names have the same type as QNPs, i.e. <<e,t>,t>, the formula *sing'(fiona')* must be equivalent to an expression where the NP translation is functionally applied to *sing'*, the translation of the VP. Replacing the latter by a predicate variable we get the propositional function *P(fiona')* which may be turned into an expression of type <<e,t>,t> by abstraction to give the translation of *Fiona* in (48.a) which denotes the set in (48.b), i.e. the set of all sets of entities of which Fiona is a member.

(48) a. $[\lambda P\ [P(\text{fiona'})]]^{M,g}$.
b. $\{X \subseteq A \mid [\text{fiona'}]^{M,g} \in X\}$.

As (48.b) shows, the proper name *Fiona* denotes a set of sets like the other noun phrases dealt with so far in this chapter. In this case, the NP denotes the set of all sets that contain the entity denoted by the constant *fiona'*. That is, instead of picking out an entity directly, a proper name picks out the properties that the entity has. This is shown in the diagram in (49) which represents the **individual sublimation** of Fiona where there is just one thing in the intersection of all the sets P_n, i.e. Fiona herself.

At this point, it may be objected that just looking at the properties individuals have may not be sufficient to identify a single individual uniquely. For example, the model may contain two distinct entities which both have the same name, are both female, both with red hair and both students studying artificial intelligence at the same university. If they both have the same likes and dislikes as well, then how can just looking at the properties they have tell them apart? The answer is that every distinct entity has one property not shared by any other individual in the model and this is the property of being identical to itself. This property, which may be represented in L_Q by the expression $\lambda x\ [x = c]$ where *c* is some individual constant, always denotes the unit set consisting only of the individual denoted by *c* (for example, $\lambda x\ [x = \textit{fiona'}]$ denotes the set {$\mathbf{WOMAN_2}$} in M_3). Hence, any individual sublimation may be reduced to a unique individual in the model and so may be taken as equivalent semantically to an individual constant. NPs, whether quantified or proper, may therefore be treated in exactly the same way both syntactically and semantically, while still maintaining the differences between them.

(49) **Individual sublimation of $[\text{fiona}']^M$**

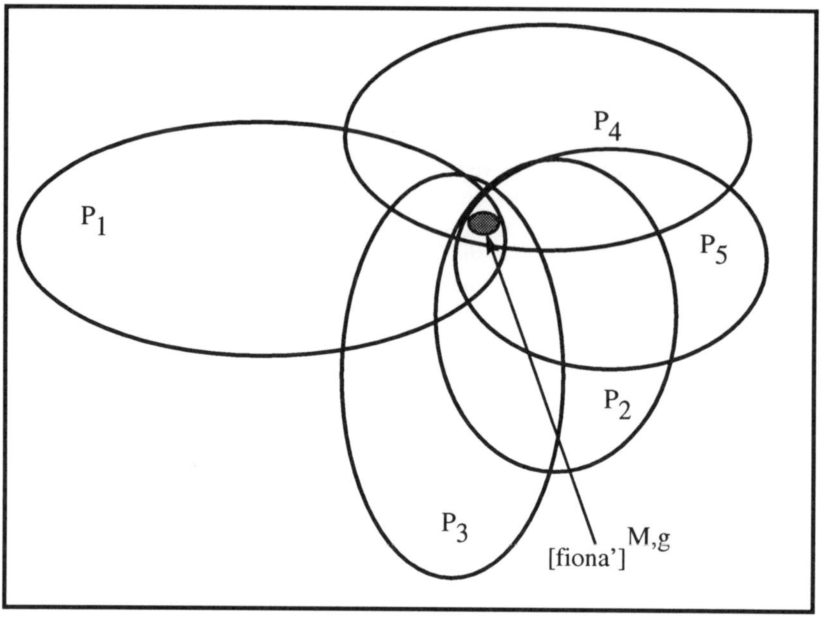

While an expression like $\lambda P\ [P(c)]$, where c is an individual constant, translates an expression in English, the individual constant, c, is itself the translation of no English expression. No expression in English (or, by hypothesis, any other human language) directly denotes an entity. All reference is done via reference to the set of properties that a particular entity has. Amongst other things, this means that definite descriptions also cannot translate into expressions of type e. This is perhaps not such a difficult concept to grasp as that of proper names no longer directly denoting individuals, partly because definite noun phrases in English contain a determiner *the* and a common noun of type <e,t>. The definite article in English and other languages is used in a number of different ways, none of which have an uncontroversial semantic interpretation, as can be seen by a glance at the articles and books referred to at the end of the chapter. Here, we look only at one treatment of one aspect of definiteness which for a long time held a dominant place in the logical analysis of definiteness. Although there are other treatments and obvious faults with the one to be discussed, it is an interesting proposal and deserves mention here.

The philosopher Bertrand Russell proposed in (1905) that a noun phrase like *the king of France* is logically complex and combines with a predicate to make a true formula only if there is at least and at most one entity that is the king of France and satisfies the predicate. Montague followed Russell's lead and gave the definite article an analysis that translates the sentence in (50.a) by the formula in (50.b). According to the truth-conditions of $\forall$, $\exists$, and the connectives, this formula is true if, and only if, there is at least one entity that kicked Prudence (the cat) and every entity that is fat and a philosopher is identical to it. This guarantees that the formula is true if, and only if, there is one, and only one, entity in the universe of discourse that fits the description of being a fat philosopher.

(50) a. The fat philosopher kicked Prudence.
b. $\exists x\ [\forall y\ [(\text{fat'}(y)\ \&\ \text{philosopher'}(y)) \leftrightarrow (x = y)]\ \&\ (\text{kick'}(\text{prudence'}))(x)]$.

Adopting this analysis, the definite NP in the sentence in (50.a) has the translation in (51.a) and the definite article itself that in (51.b), which can again be derived through backwards λ-conversion. (The reader is invited to work through the derivation of the sentence in (50.a) to show how the translations of the individual words combine to give a translation that is equivalent to the formula in (50.b).)

(51) a. the fat philosopher
$\Rightarrow \lambda P\ [\exists x\ [\forall y\ [(\text{fat'}(y)\ \&\ \text{philosopher'}(y)) \leftrightarrow (x = y)]\ \&\ P(x)]]$.
b. the $\Rightarrow \lambda Q\ [\lambda P\ [\exists x\ [\forall y\ [Q(y) \leftrightarrow (x = y)]\ \&\ P(x)]]]$.

As mentioned above, there are numerous problems with Russell's analysis of definite descriptions. The most obvious fault is that the sentence in (50.a) does not usually imply that there is only one fat philosopher in the whole of the world. There may well be many such, but the use of the definite article indicates that only one is relevant to the current discourse situation. Thus, some means of relating the uniqueness aspect to the immediate context is necessary to give a more accurate representation of the way definite descriptions are used. One way in which this may be done is to restrict the domain of the universal quantifier in the representation of a definite description to some pragmatically specified set containing only those entities of the model that are currently in the context of discourse. The translation of *the fat philosopher* might then be interpreted with respect not just to a model and a variable assignment, but also to such a pragmatically determined set. The semantics of the quantifiers must then be restricted to quantifying over this set (call it **D**) by, for example, checking the truth values of quantified formulae only with respect to the entities in **D**. Such a revision of the semantics for the universal and existential quantifiers is given in (52) where only those value assignments that associate variables with members of **D** are relevant for ascertaining the truth of quantified formulae.

(52) a. If ϕ is an expression of type t containing a free occurrence of a variable, u, of type e, then $[\exists u\ [\phi]]^{M,g,D}$ is **1**, iff there is some value assignment **g'**, exactly like **g** except perhaps for the individual assigned to u, such that $[\phi]^{M,g',D}$ is **1** and **g'**(u) is a member of **D**.
b. If ϕ is an expression of type t containing a free occurrence of a variable, u, of type e, then $[\forall u\ [\phi]]^{M,g,D}$ is **1**, iff for every value assignment **g'**, exactly like **g** except perhaps for the individual assigned to u, $[\phi]^{M,g',D}$ is **1** and **g'**(u) is a member of **D**.

In terms of the Russellian analysis of *the fat philosopher*, the revisions in (52) have the effect of requiring there to be a unique fat philosopher in **D**, the current context, but says nothing about the existence of other fat philosophers in the model. Furthermore, this revision has desired effects in the interpretation of universal sentences like *Everyone was drunk* which is not usually interpreted as describing a situation where everyone in the whole world was drunk, but just some contextually salient set of people was drunk. As an example of how this interpretation works, consider a situation in which Jo, the cat and Fiona are fat, Jo and Fiona are philosophers and Jo kicked the cat. When the sentence in (50.a) is uttered there are three entities in the discourse context, Jo, Ethel and Prudence the cat. At this point, therefore, we interpret the formula in (50.b) with respect to the model of this situation (M_3), an assignment of values to variables, **g**, and the set **{MAN$_1$, WOMAN$_1$,CAT}**. The first two steps in ascertaining the truth of this expression with respect to the relevant context are given in (53), which follow the definitions in (52).

(53) a. ∃x [∀y [(fat'(y) & philosopher'(y)) ↔ (x = y)] & (kick'(prudence'))(x)] is **1** with respect to M_3, **g** and {**MAN$_1$,CAT,WOMAN$_1$**} iff there is a value assignment **g'** like **g** where **g'**(x) ∈ {**MAN$_1$,CAT,WOMAN$_1$**} such that ∀y [(fat'(y) & philosopher'(y)) ↔ (x = y)] & (kick'(prudence'))(x)] is also **1**.

b. ∀y [(fat'(y) & philosopher'(y)) ↔ (x = y)] & (kick'(prudence'))(x)] is **1** with respect to M_3, **g** and {**MAN$_1$,CAT,WOMAN$_1$**} iff for every value assignment **g"** exactly like **g'** where **g"**(y) ∈ {**MAN$_1$,CAT,WOMAN$_1$**} [[(fat'(y) & philosopher'(y)) ↔ (x = y)] & (kick'(prudence'))(x)] is **1**.

Because interpretation is restricted to the set of entities that are salient in the discourse (i.e. to Jo, Ethel and Prudence), it is easy to show that (50.b) is true. First of all, we let **g'** be a function that assigns **MAN$_1$** to x and **WOMAN$_1$** to y. This satisfies the expression *[(fat'(y) & philosopher'(y)) ↔(x = y)] & (kick'(prudence'))(x)* with respect to M_3, because Jo (**MAN$_1$**) kicked Prudence (**CAT**), and [*(fat'(y) & philosopher'(y))*]$^{M3,g',\{MAN1,CAT,WOMAN1\}}$ has the same truth value as [x = y]$^{M3,g',\{MAN1,CAT,WOMAN1\}}$ (since **MAN$_1$**, the value of **g'** applied to x, is not identical to **WOMAN$_1$**, the value of **g'** applied to y, and the latter is neither a philosopher nor fat). There are then only two other relevant value assignments that we need to look at to verify (53.b), **g'**$^{MAN1/y}$ and **g'**$^{CAT/y}$. Both of these do satisfy *[(fat'(y) & philosopher'(y)) ↔ (x = y)] & (kick'(prudence'))(x)* with respect to M_3. The first satisfies the expression because x and y are assigned to the same entity, **MAN$_1$**, which makes [*x = y*]$^{M3,g',\{MAN1,CAT,WOMAN1\}}$ true and satisfies *philosopher'(x) & fat'(x)* because **MAN$_1$** is both a philosopher and is fat. Since both sides of the equivalence *(fat'(y) & philosopher'(y)) ↔ x = y* are true, the whole formula is true, and so the conjunction with *(kick'(prudence'))(x)* is also true. The final value assignment with y assigned to **CAT** satisfies the expression for the same reason that **g'** itself does, i.e. because the cat is not Jo nor is it a fat philosopher. Hence, where the domain of quantification is restricted to Jo, Ethel and Prudence (50.b) is true. Notice, however, that if the domain is unrestricted the formula is false of the situation being described. This is because a value assignment that assigns **WOMAN$_2$** to y (and **MAN$_1$** to x, as before) fails to satisfy the formula *[(fat'(y) & philosopher'(y)) ↔ (x = y)] & (kick'(prudence'))(x)*, since **WOMAN$_2$** is both a philosopher and fat, but, crucially, is not identical to **MAN$_1$**, the value of **g'**(x), and so the two formulae in the equivalence do not have the same truth value, making the equivalence (and the whole conjunction) false. There is thus more than one fat philosopher in the domain and so, according to Russell, the proposition expressed by the sentence *The fat philosopher kicked the cat* is false, since the phrase *the fat philosopher* fails to pick out a unique entity. Hence, the introduction of a context set, **D**, as part of the interpretation enables one to capture more accurately some of the meaning of the definite article *the* (and indeed the uses of the other quantifiers and proper names). The truth values of quantified formulae differ depending on the set of salient entities in the discourse.

There is much more that can be said about Russell's analysis and Strawson's criticisms. There is also much more to be said about the meaning of the word *the* in its anaphoric use (e.g. *Bill is my boss and the bastard really keeps me at it*) or in its generic use (e.g. *The tiger is a fierce animal*) where it appears to have the force of the universal quantifier. Indeed, much controversy surrounds the proper treatment of the definite article and definiteness in general. For the purposes of this book, however, despite its problems, the Russellian interpretation of *the* is the one that will be assumed whenever definite descriptions are used.

Exercise 6.9:
Translate the following sentences into L_Q, giving both the full translation as generated by the translation rules and the simplified equivalent form that results from lambda-conversion.

i. Jo laughed and cried.
ii. The linguist was not happy.
iii. If Ethel sang, then the dog howled.

6.5 Two problems

There are two problems facing the approach to noun phrase interpretation discussed above. One is more of a technical problem to do with translation and concerns the way non-subject noun phrases combine with their verbs to form verb phrases. The second concerns the ambiguity of sentences that contain more than one quantified noun phrase. We will look at these in turn.

6.5.1 Type raising

If we give NPs the type <<e,t>,t>, it is no longer possible to combine the translations of object NPs directly with those of their verbs, because the latter translate into expressions of type <e,<e,t>> that cannot functionally apply with expressions of type <<e,t>,t>. To combine NP' and V_t', therefore, the type of the latter must be changed so that its arguments have the correct type; so that transitive verbs must be assigned the complex type <<<e,t>,t>,<e,t>> and ditransitive verbs the type <<<e,t>,t>,<<<e,t>,t>,<e,t>>>. This would, of course, be a simple matter if all we were interested in was getting verb translations to combine with NP ones. But the point of translation into a logical language is the interpretation it receives. Just asserting that verb types are now all changed is not sufficient. We need to make sure that the verbs retain their fundamental interpretation as denoting relations between entities. To do this, the translations of verbs like *like* and *give* must be made more complex so that their type is the appropriate one to combine with non-subject NPs, but they still end up identifying relations between entities.

The solution to the problem, as before, can be found in the use of the lambda operator and, as in previous sections, the easiest way to get to the translation of a constituent is to start with a formula that expresses the truth-conditions of a particular sentence that contains that constituent. Consider the sentence in (54.a) whose truth-conditions require that for every entity that is a student in some model, there is a lecturer that that student liked. The force of this can be brought out by the semi-formal English sentence in (54.b) which has the transparent representation in L_Q shown in (54.c).

(54) a. Every student liked a lecturer.
b. For every x, if x is a student then there is a y such that y is a lecturer and x liked y.
c. $\forall x$ [student'(x) $\rightarrow \exists y$ [lecturer'(y) & (like'(y))(x)]].

As we have seen, the translation into L_Q of the subject NP *every student* is the λ-expression in (55.a) which combines with the translation of the VP to give a formula truth-conditionally equivalent to (54.c). The VP itself translates as an expression of type <e,t> that contains the remnants of the formula in (54.c) once the subject NP translation in (55.a) has been removed. This remnant is an open formula *$\exists y$ [lecturer'(y) & (like'(y))(x)]* and abstracting on the free variable, x, yields the one-place predicate in (55.b) which is equivalent to the translation of the VP. (The variable in (55.b) has been changed to z to bring out the fact that it is a different variable from the x in (54.c) which is supplied by the NP translation in (55.a).)

(55) a. λP [$\forall x$ [student'(x) $\rightarrow$ P(x)]](VP')
» $\forall x$ [student'(x) $\rightarrow \exists y$ [lecturer'(y) & (like'(y))(x)]].
b. VP $\Rightarrow \lambda z$ [$\exists y$ [lecturer'(y) & like'(y)(z)]].

The predicate in (55.b) is equivalent to the expression that results from combination of the translation of the transitive verb *like* with that of the NP *a lecturer*. Assuming that the verb is the functor (in order to keep the types of subject and object NPs uniform), V_t' must apply to the translation of the object NP in (56.a) to give an expression equivalent to (55.b), as shown in (56.b). In performing this λ-conversion, there must be a step where the NP translation in (56.a) applies to a one-place predicate which is bound to the variable *Q* and becomes *like'(y)(z)* after lambda-conversion. Since *z* is bound by the outermost lambda operator and *y* is supplied by the NP translation, the latter can be replaced by a new variable *x* which is abstracted upon to give the one-place predicate in (56.c) which yields (56.d) as the intermediate expression equivalent to the VP translation in (55.b).

(56) a. λQ [$\exists y$ [lecturer'(y) & Q(y)]].
b. V_t'(λQ [$\exists y$ [lecturer'(y) & Q(y)]])
» λz [$\exists y$ [lecturer'(y) & like'(y)(z)]].
c. λx [(like'(x))(z)].
d. λz [λQ [$\exists y$ [lecturer'(y) & Q(y)]](λx [(like'(x))(z)])].

One final step remains to be done to get to the translation of the verb. (56.c) is, as we have seen, equivalent to the translation of a verb phrase formed by applying the translation of the verb *like* to that of the NP *a lecturer*. To transform (56.c) into an L_Q

expression with such a structure, the NP translation can be replaced with a variable of the appropriate sort and placed as an argument after the λ-expression formed by abstraction on this variable. Taking $\boldsymbol{P}$ to be a variable of type <<e,t>,t>, backwards λ-abstraction yields (57.a) as the full (unconverted) form of the VP translation of *liked a lecturer* which is truth-conditionally equivalent to (56.c) and (55.b). The expression in (57.b) is thus the translation of the verb *like*, an expression that has the correct type, <<<e,t>,t>,<e,t>>, denoting a function from NP extensions to VP extensions. The derivation of the example sentence in (54.a) is given in (58) showing the way the translation is built up and then reduced to the equivalent expression in (54.c).

(57) a. $\lambda \boldsymbol{P}\, [\lambda z\, [\boldsymbol{P}(\lambda x\, [(\text{like}'(x))(z)])]](\lambda Q\, [\exists y\, [\text{lecturer}'(y) \,\&\, Q(y)]])$.
b. *like* $\Rightarrow \lambda \boldsymbol{P}\, [\lambda z\, [\boldsymbol{P}(\lambda x\, [(\text{like}'(x))(z)])]]$.

(58) a. S
$\Rightarrow$ S'.
b. NP VP[+FIN] — $1G_2$
$\Rightarrow$ NP'(VP').
c. Det CNP VP[+FIN] — $28'G_2$
$\Rightarrow$ (Det'(CNP'))(VP').
d. Det N VP[+FIN] — $30G_2$
$\Rightarrow$ (Det'(N'))(VP').
e. Det N V[+FIN] NP — $2G_2$
$\Rightarrow$ (Det'(N'))(V'(NP')).
f. Det N V[+FIN] Det CNP — $28'G_2$
$\Rightarrow$ (Det'(N'))(V'(Det'(CNP'))).
g. Det N V[+FIN] Det N — $30G_2$
$\Rightarrow$ (Det'(N'))(V'(Det'(N'))).
h. every student liked a lecturer. — Lex
$\Rightarrow (\lambda Q\, [\lambda P\, [\forall x\, [Q(x) \rightarrow P(x)]]](\text{student}'))$
$(\lambda \boldsymbol{P}\, [\lambda z\, [\boldsymbol{P}(\lambda x\, [(\text{like}'(x))(z)])]](\lambda Q\, [\lambda P\, [\exists y\, [Q(y) \,\&\, P(y)]]](\text{lecturer}')))$.
i. » $(\lambda P\, [\forall x\, [\text{student}'(x) \rightarrow P(x)]])$
$(\lambda \boldsymbol{P}\, [\lambda z\, [\boldsymbol{P}(\lambda x\, [(\text{like}'(x))(z)])]](\lambda Q\, [\lambda P\, [\exists y\, [Q(y) \,\&\, P(y)]]](\text{lecturer}')))$.
j. » $(\lambda P\, [\forall x\, [\text{student}'(x) \rightarrow P(x)]])$
$(\lambda \boldsymbol{P}\, [\lambda z\, [\boldsymbol{P}(\lambda x\, [(\text{like}'(x))(z)])]](\lambda P\, [\exists y\, [\text{lecturer}'(y) \,\&\, P(y)]]))$.
k. » $(\lambda P\, [\forall x\, [\text{student}'(x) \rightarrow P(x)]])$
$(\lambda z\, [\lambda P\, [\exists y\, [\text{lecturer}'(y) \,\&\, P(y)]](\lambda x\, [(\text{like}'(x))(z)])])$.
l. » $(\lambda P\, [\forall x\, [\text{student}'(x) \rightarrow P(x)]])(\lambda z\, [\exists y\, [\text{lecturer}'(y) \,\&\, \text{like}'(y)(z)]])$.
m. » $\forall x\, [\text{student}'(x) \rightarrow \lambda z\, [\exists y\, [\text{lecturer}'(y) \,\&\, (\text{like}'(y))(z)]](x)]$.
n. » $\forall x\, [\text{student}'(x) \rightarrow \exists y\, [\text{lecturer}'(y) \,\&\, (\text{like}'(y))(x)]]$.

This translation for *like*, which is generalised to cover all other transitive verbs, may seem unnecessarily complex, but it does allow noun phrases to be given a uniform treatment whatever position they happen to occupy in a sentence, whilst maintaining the insight that such verbs denote two-place relations between entities. Although the gain may seem slight as compared to the increased complexity in translating verbs, in Chapter 10 we will see that there are verbs which must be analysed as denoting functions from NP extensions to VP extensions directly, without there being any direct relation between two entities. Thus, to give a uniform syntactic treatment to such verbs and verbs that denote simple relations between entities, the increased complexity in translating the latter is a small price to pay.

Exercise 6.10:
Using translations of the transitive verbs of the sort given to *like*, translate the following sentences into L_Q, giving the formulae as they are generated by the translation rules and the equivalent formulae that result from lambda-conversion.

i. Ethel shot a philosopher.
ii. No student liked the lecturer.
iii. A linguist slapped Jo.

---

*Exercise 6.11:
Owing to the type changes introduced above, the translation rules for passive verb phrases given in Chapter 5 no longer give the right results. Show why this should be so and devise new rules that ensure that the correct interpretation is given to each passive sentence.

6.5.2 *Scope ambiguities*

Sentences containing more than one quantified NP are often ambiguous, depending on how wide the relative scopes of the quantifiers contained in the NPs are taken. Consider the sentence in (59.a) which could be followed by either of the sentences in (59.b) or (59.c), without contradiction.

(59) a. Every critic enjoyed a play.
b. Charles enjoyed Macbeth, Philippa enjoyed Bedroom Farce, Wendy enjoyed Happy Days and Kevin enjoyed all the plays.
c. The play that everyone enjoyed was Salome.

The reading of (59.a) that (59.b) picks up on is the one where each critic indeed enjoyed some play, but the one enjoyed is not necessarily the same for them all. (59.c), on the other hand, forces the stronger reading, where it is the same play that is enjoyed by everyone. The difference between these two interpretations is brought out by the semi-formal English sentences in (60) which may be represented in L_Q by the formulae in (61).

(60) a. For every x, if x was a critic then there was a y such that y was a play and x enjoyed y.
b. There was a y such that y was a play and for every x, if x was a critic then x enjoyed y.

(61) a. $\forall x\ [\text{critic'}(x) \rightarrow \exists y\ [\text{play'}(y)\ \&\ \text{enjoy'}(y)(x)]]$. (= (59.b)/(60.a))
b. $\exists y\ [\text{play'}(y)\ \&\ \forall x\ [\text{critic'}(x) \rightarrow \text{enjoy'}(y)(x)]]$. (= (59.c)/(60.b))

The difference between the two formulae in (61) resides in the relative scopes of the NP translations and the quantifiers and propositional connectives they contain. In

(61.a), the universal quantifier has scope over the existential one, whilst in (61.b) the reverse is the case and, because of the way we have translated universal and existential NPs, the material implication in (61.a) has wider scope than the conjunction, a situation reversed in (61.b). This difference is semantically significant, since it is possible for (61.a) to be true in a situation in which (61.b) is false (although the reverse is not the case; see below). This is the case in the situation shown in (62) which represents the relation between the set of critics and the plays that they enjoy in some model (call it M_6), as illustrated by (59.b). (NB: the diagram shows the relation, not the function, denoted by *enjoy'*.)

(62)

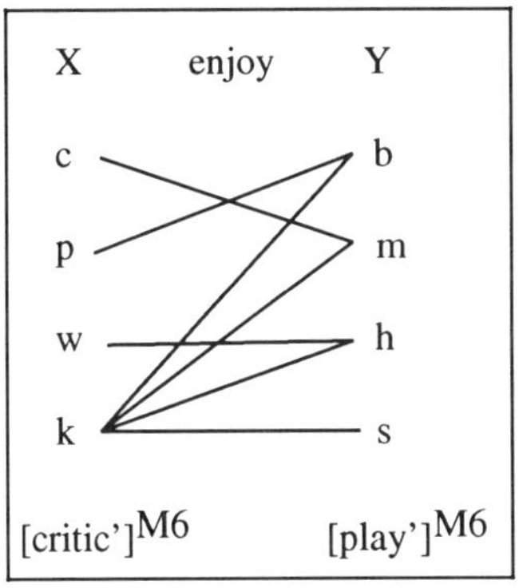

To prove that the interpretation we have given to the quantifiers does give the formulae in (61) different truth values with respect to M (and thus assign them different truth-conditions), let us work through the formal interpretation of the formulae in turn. The procedure for doing so, however, is somewhat involved, because of the fact that the truth-conditions of quantified sentences are defined in terms of value assignments to variables. All that is required to understand the method is a bit of patience to keep track of the different value assignments, but the effort helps in the understanding of the way the interpretation rules in Section 6.2.2 work.

According to the truth-conditions for ∃ and ∀ in (10) and (13), above, the formula in (61.a) is true with respect to the model M if, and only if, for every entity that can be assigned to x there is an entity that can be assigned to y that makes *critic'(x) → (play'(y) & (enjoy'(y))(x))* true. To show that this is so, we need to look at all possible assignments for x where x is a member of $[critic']^{M,g}$ and see if there is a value assignment that keeps the entity assigned to x constant, but assigns an entity to y which is in the set of plays and the set of things that x enjoyed. We do not need to look any further than those value assignments that associate x with a critic, because, by the semantics of material implication, *critic'(x) → (play'(y) & (enjoy'(y))(x))* is always true if x is not a critic, because *critic'(x)* is false on such a value assignment. Nor do we need to look at assignments of values to y that are not plays, because these make *play'(y) & enjoy(y)(x)* false for any value of x and thus are irrelevant for ascertaining the truth of the existential formula. We begin by looking at the value assignment **g** with respect to which (61.a) is to be interpreted. The relevant part of this is shown in (63), which specifies only the values assigned to x, y (the only variables in (61)) and to z, for good measure. There is no need to specify the rest of the function, as this remains constant throughout the interpretation procedure.

(63) **g**

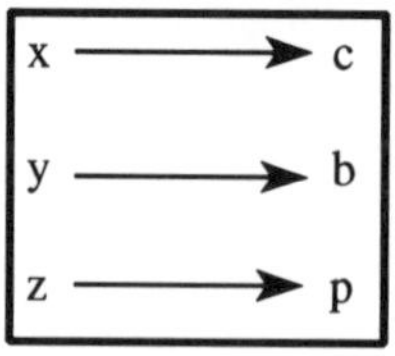

With respect to **g** (and M_6), the formula $critic'(x) \rightarrow (play'(y) \& (enjoy'(y))(x))$ is false because **c** is a critic but the pair **<c,b>** is not in the extension of $[enjoy']^{M6}$, where **c** is the value assigned to x and **b** is that assigned to y. However, the existential formula $\exists y\ [play'(y) \& (enjoy'(y))(x)]$ is not thus falsified, because it is still true if there is some value assignment exactly like **g** except for the value assigned to y that satisfies $play'(y) \& (enjoy'(y))(x)$. Hence, we must look at the value assignment just like **g** except that y is assigned another value, say **m**. This function is symbolised $\mathbf{g}^{m/y}$, as we saw in Chapter 5, and the part of this function that we are interested in is shown in (64). This assignment of values to variables satisfies $play'(y) \& (enjoy'(y))(x)$, because **<c,m>** is a member of $[enjoy']^{M6,g}$. Hence, the existential formula $[\exists y\ [play'(y) \& (enjoy'(y))(x)]]^{M6,g}$ is true, thus making $[critic'(x) \rightarrow \exists y\ [play'(y) \& (enjoy'(y))(x)]]^{M6,g}$ also true by the truth-conditions of material implication.

(64) $\mathbf{g}^{m/y}$

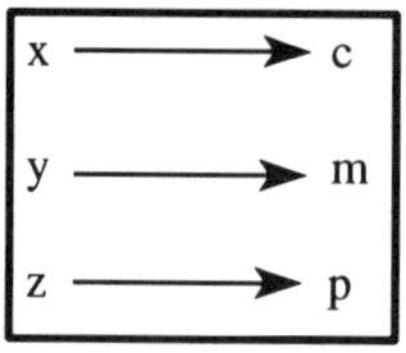

While we have shown that the formula $critic'(x) \rightarrow \exists y\ [play'(y) \& (enjoy'(y))(x)]$ is true with respect to M_6 and **g**, we have not, of course, yet completed the interpretation of (61.a), as we need to see what happens with all other assignments of values to x. Thus, we next look at the value assignment $\mathbf{g}^{p/x}$ shown in (65). Since the pair **<p,b>** is in the extension of $enjoy'$ in M_6 (and **p** is in $[critic']^{M6,g}$ and **b** is in $[play']^{M6,g}$), $\mathbf{g}^{p/x}$ again satisfies $critic'(x) \rightarrow (play'(y) \& (enjoy'(y))(x))$.

(65) $\mathbf{g}^{p/x}$

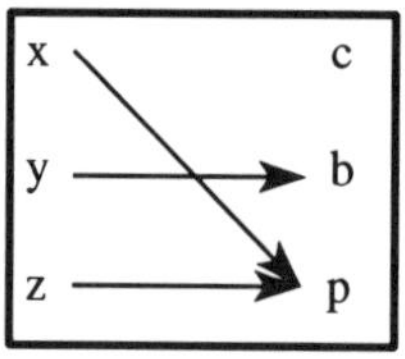

The next assignment of a value to x, $\mathbf{g}^{w/x}$ in (66.a), however, fails to satisfy the target formula, since Wendy did not enjoy Bedroom Farce, so we need to look at the value assignments just like this except for the values assigned to y. Assigning the value of **m** to y yields the assignment $\mathbf{g}^{[w/x]m/y}$ shown in (66.b). This does not help, as **<w,m>** is not in the extension of *enjoy'*. The next assignment $\mathbf{g}^{[w/x]h/y}$, however, which is shown in (66.c) does verify the formula *critic'(x)* → ∃*y [play'(y) & (enjoy'(y))(x)]*, because **<w,h>** is in $[enjoy']^{M6,g}$.

(66)

a. $\mathbf{g}^{w/x}$ b. $\mathbf{g}^{[w/x]m/y}$ c. $\mathbf{g}^{[w/x]h/y}$

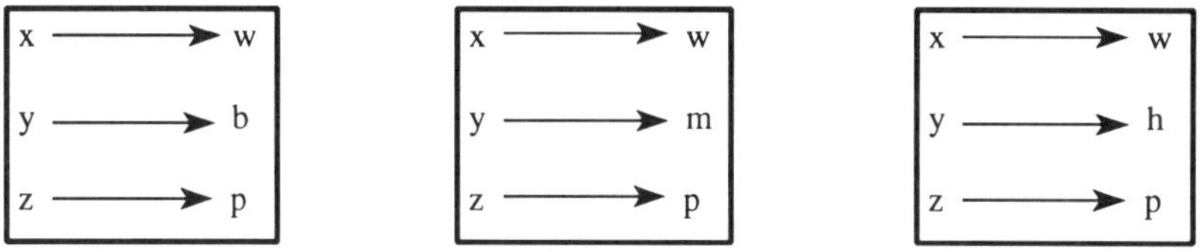

As there is one more critic in the model, there is one more assignment to x that must be looked at, i.e. $\mathbf{g}^{k/x}$. Since Kevin enjoyed all the plays in $\mathbf{M}_6$, this value assignment (shown in (67)) satisfies *critic'(x)* → *(play'(y) & (enjoy'(y))(x))*. Thus, we have now shown that for every value assignment like **g** but for the value of x which makes *critic'(x)* true, there is a value assignment exactly alike except possibly for the value of y that satisfies *critic'(x)* → *play'(y) & (enjoy'(y))(x)*. Hence, the formula in (61.a) is true with respect to M_6 and **g**. Furthermore, because the value assignment, **g**, was chosen arbitrarily, we can say that the formula is also true just with respect to the model $\mathbf{M}_6$. In other words, the formula is true irrespective of which value assignment is chosen.

(67) $\mathbf{g}^{k/x}$

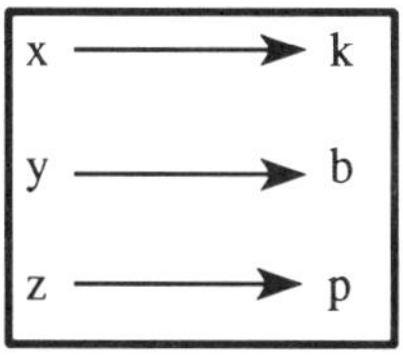

In ascertaining the truth of the formula in (61.a), the value of y may be varied for each value of x in order to satisfy the relevant propositional function. To show that the formula in (61.b) is true, on the other hand, it is necessary to find some value for y that makes the formula *play'(y) & (critic(x)* → *(enjoy'(y))(x))* true for all values of x. In other words, every value for x must satisfy the formula for some constant value of y. Since any value for y not in the extension of *play'* necessarily makes the formula false, we may restrict our attention only to those values for y which are plays. Furthermore, we need only look at values of x which are critics since all other assignments make the implication true. First, therefore, we may take the value assignment, **g**, and then look at all the assignments that vary from this in their value for *x*. If there is one variant that makes the target formula false then we move on to look at the next assignment like **g** except for the value assigned to *y* and go through all the values that may be assigned to *x*.

With respect to **g**, *play'(y) & (critic(x) → (enjoy'(y))(x))* is false in the model M_6, because **<c,b>** is not in the extension of *enjoy'* while **c** is in that of *critic'* in the model. As there is thus at least one critic in the model that fails to enjoy Bedroom Farce, we may go directly to an examination of another variable assignment, e.g. $\mathbf{g}^{m/y}$ in (64). This satisfies the formula and so another for *x* is tested. $\mathbf{g}^{[m/y]b/x}$ in (68.a), however, does not satisfy the target formula, so that $\mathbf{g}^{m/y}$ itself fails to satisfy the formula. A new assignment to *y* must therefore be investigated. This is $\mathbf{g}^{h/y}$ in (68.b) which fails to satisfy the target formula, as indeed does the last possible assignment to *y* that makes *play'(y)* true, i.e. $\mathbf{g}^{s/y}$ in (68.c), since neither **<c,h>** nor **<c,s>** are in $[enjoy']^{M6,g}$. As no value assigned to *y* makes *critic'(x) & (enjoy'(y))(x)* true for all values of *x*, the formula in (61.b) is false with respect to M_6. Hence, we have shown that there are situations like that modelled by M_6 in which the formula in (61.a) is true, but in which that in (61.b) is not. Thus, the truth-conditions of the two formulae must differ and so the sentence *Every critic enjoyed a play* in (59.a) is shown to be truly ambiguous.

(68)

a. $\mathbf{g}^{[m/y]h/x}$ b. $\mathbf{g}^{h/y}$ c. $\mathbf{g}^{s/y}$

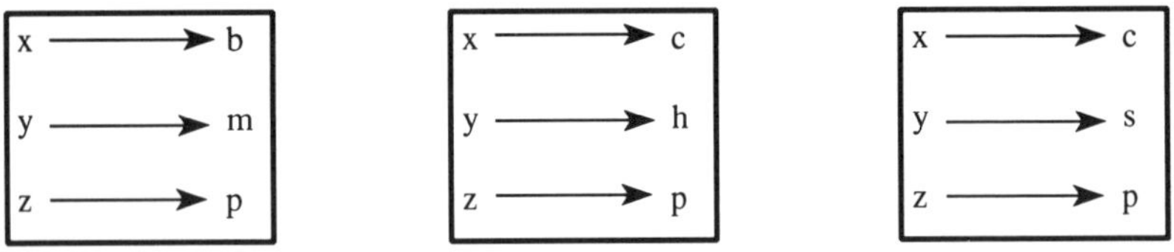

There are situations, of course, in which (61.b) is true. One such is shown in (69) which shows the criticizing relation between critics and plays in a model, $\mathbf{M_6}$**'**. The formula in (61.b) can be shown to be true with respect to M_6' and **g** by the value assignments in (70) which show all possible values for *x* when the value of *y* is held constant as **s** (i.e. the value assignments are all variants of $\mathbf{g}^{s/y}$). Since all these assignments satisfy *(play'(y) & critic'(x)) → (enjoy'(y))(x)*, (61.b) is also true.

The formula in (61.a) is also true with respect to M_6' because, for each critic, there is a play that they enjoy. It just happens to be the same play in each case. Any true formula where an existential quantifier has wider scope than a universal entails the truth of the corresponding formula with the scopes of the quantifiers reversed. Thus, where ϕ is any formula, the formula in (71) is a **tautology**, allowing $\forall x\ [\exists y \phi]$ to be inferred from $\exists y\ [\forall x \phi]$ in all cases. The reading of (59.a) in (61.b) thus **entails** that in (61.a). (See Chapter 7 for further details.)

(69)

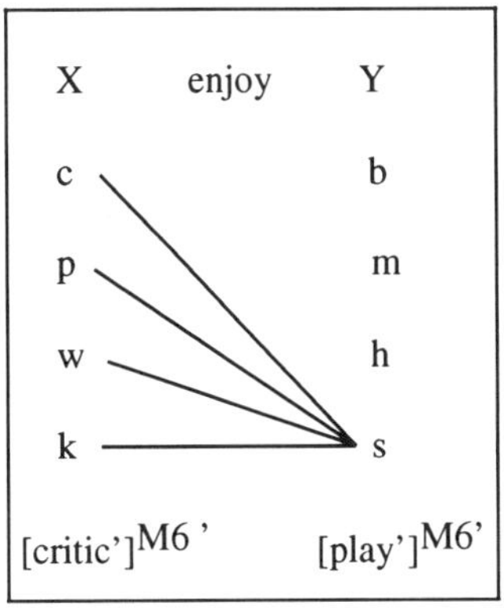

(70)

a. $g^{s/y}$ b. $g^{[s/y]p/x}$ c. $g^{[s/y]w/x}$ d. $g^{[s/y]k/x}$

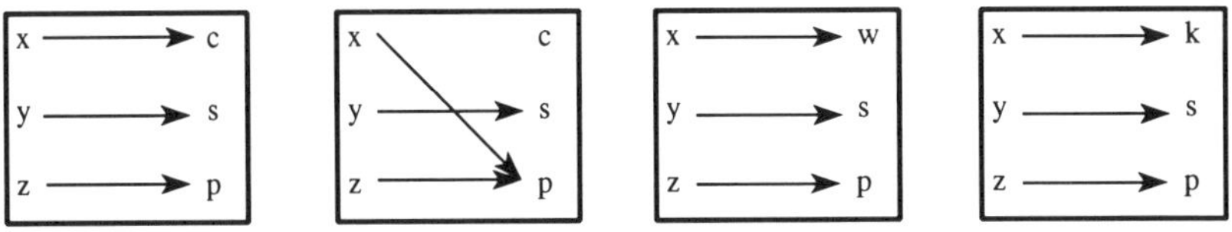

(71) $\exists x\ [\forall y\ [\phi]] \rightarrow \forall y\ [\exists x\ [\phi]]$.

Exercise 6.12:
Ascertain the truth values of the following two formulae with respect to the model, M_6, and the value assignment **g**, by examining different value assignments as was done above. Do the differences in scope of the quantifiers between i and iii and ii and iv affect the truth-conditions of the formulae?

i. $\exists x$ [critic'(x) & $\exists y$ [play'(y) & (enjoy'(y))(x)]].
ii. $\forall x$ [play'(x) $\rightarrow$ $\forall y$ [critic'(y) $\rightarrow$ (enjoy'(y))(x)]].
iii. $\exists y$ [play'(y) & $\exists x$ [critic'(x) & (enjoy'(y))(x)]].
iv. $\forall y$ [critic'(y) $\rightarrow$ $\forall x$ [play'(x) $\rightarrow$ (enjoy'(y))(x)]].

The existence of ambiguous sentences like that in (59.a) poses a problem for the grammar fragment set up so far in that the grammar rules given in Section 6.2 only generate one translation for the sentence in (59.a), the one where the quantifier in the subject NP has widest scope. The derivation of the L_Q formula that shows this reading parallels that for the sentence *Every student liked a lecturer* in (58). The second reading of (59.a) cannot, however, be generated by the grammar as it stands, because it requires the quantifier in the object NP to appear to the left of that of the subject. In other words, the object is semantically combined with the verb after the subject in some way, although, of course, in the syntax the object combines with the verb before the subject. This is a problem for the rule-to-rule hypothesis, because this is a semantic process that has no syntactic reflex. In the other cases of ambiguity that we have come across in this book, any semantic ambiguity can be seen in the syntactic derivation. A number of ways have been suggested to obtain different scope readings. In transformational grammar, noun phrases are moved to sentence initial position after the surface structure has been derived, but before semantic interpretation is carried out (i.e. at **LF**). In monostratal grammars, it has been suggested that the interpretation of a noun phrase may be stored during the derivation of a sentence and then utilised later to give the different readings.

No attempt will be made here to formally extend the grammar and derivation procedures developed so far to cope with scope ambiguities. However, a means of accounting for wide scope quantification in the semantics can be given using a process that Montague refers to as **quantifying in**. This process has the effect of replacing an argument of a verb by a variable of the appropriate sort and then combining a noun phrase translation with the λ-expression of type t formed by abstracting on this variable once all other arguments have been combined. Because object noun phrases have the type <<e,t>,t>, as we have seen, a predicate must combine with the individual sublimation of an individual variable, rather than an individual variable itself, i.e. $\lambda P\ [P(x)]$ rather than x. The rule is stated in (72) as an operation on well-formed formulae and has the effect of associating sentences with more than one translation (e.g. with wide scope readings for object NPs) and may, therefore, be thought of an an **ambiguating relation.**

(72) **Quantifying in**: If a sentence S is translated by a formula ϕ containing an expression α of type <<e,t>,t>, then S may also be translated as $\alpha(\lambda x\ [\phi'])$ where ϕ' is exactly like ϕ except that α is replaced by the expression $\lambda P[P(x)]$ where x is a variable of type e not bound in ϕ' .

As an example, the derivation of the second reading of the sentence in (59.a) can be shown by the semantic analysis tree in (73). Here, the translation of the direct object is replaced by the individual sublimation of the variable x_1 which combines with the translation of the transitive verb to give the translation of the VP. The latter is then combined with the translation of the subject NP to give a formula containing a free instance of the variable x_1. Finally, the translation of the direct object noun phrase *a play* is combined with the predicate formed by lambda abstraction on this variable. (74) shows the successive lambda-conversions that guarantee that this derivation is equivalent to the formula in (61.b). Other scope effects will be seen in Chapters 8 and 10 involving tense and intensionality, but they can all be derived in the semantics using the rule of quantifying in (72).

(73)

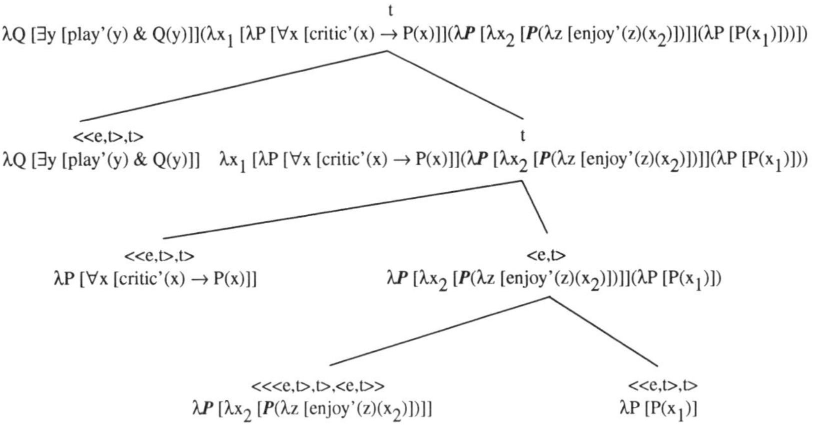

(74) a. $\lambda Q\, [\exists y\, [play'(y)\, \&\, Q(y)]](\lambda x_1\, [\lambda P\, [\forall x\, [critic'(x) \rightarrow P(x)]]$
$(\lambda \boldsymbol{P}\, [\lambda x_2[\boldsymbol{P}(\lambda z\, [(enjoy'(z))(x_2)])]](\lambda P\, [P(x_1)]))])$.

b. » $\lambda Q\, [\exists y\, [play'(y)\, \&\, Q(y)]](\lambda x_1\, [\lambda P\, [\forall x\, [critic'(x) \rightarrow P(x)]]$
$(\lambda x_2[\lambda P\, [P(x_1)](\lambda z\, [(enjoy'(z))(x_2)])])])$.

c. » $\lambda Q\, [\exists y\, [play'(y)\, \&\, Q(y)]](\lambda x_1\, [\lambda P\, [\forall x\, [critic'(x) \rightarrow P(x)]]$
$(\lambda x_2\, [\lambda z\, [(enjoy'(z))(x_2)](x_1)])])$.

d. » $\lambda Q\, [\exists y\, [play'(y)\, \&\, Q(y)]](\lambda x_1[\lambda P\, [\forall x\, [critic'(x) \rightarrow P(x)]]$
$(\lambda x_2\, [enjoy'(x_1)(x_2)])])$.

e. » $\lambda Q\, [\exists y\, [play'(y)\, \&\, Q(y)]]\, (\lambda x_1[\forall x\, [critic'(x) \rightarrow \lambda x_2[enjoy'(x_1)(x_2)](x)]])$.

f. » $\lambda Q\, [\exists y\, [play'(y)\, \&\, Q(y)]](\lambda x_1[\forall x\, [critic'(x) \rightarrow enjoy'(x_1)(x)]])$.

g. » $\exists y\, [play'(y)\, \&\, \lambda x_1[\forall x\, [critic'(x) \rightarrow enjoy'(x_1)(x)]](y)]$.

h. » $\exists y\, [play'(y)\, \&\, \forall x\, [critic'(x) \rightarrow (enjoy'(y))(x)]]$.

6.6 Generalised quantifiers

Certain English sentences containing quantifiers other than *every* (*all*), *no* and *a* (*some*) can be represented using the universal and existential quantifiers, as shown in (75).

(75) a. At least two students laughed
$\Rightarrow \quad \exists x\, [\exists y\, [student'(x)\, \&\, student'(y)\, \&\, {\sim}(x = y)\, \&\, laugh'(x)\, \&\, laugh'(y)]]$.

b. Both students laughed
$\Rightarrow \quad \exists x\, [\exists y\, [\forall z\, [(student'(x)\, \&\, student'(y)\, \&\, {\sim}(x = y)) \leftrightarrow (z = y \vee z = x)]\, \&\, laugh'(x)\, \&\, laugh'(y)]]$.

These representations, although truth-conditionally adequate, are very complex and counter-intuitive and illustrate a weak point in the translation procedure developed above for *every* and *some*: the translation of quantified English sentences introduces sentential connectives that are just not represented in the English syntax. Thus, although a compositional translation procedure for such sentences can be provided using the lambda operator, the interpretation requires a more complex structure for L_Q than is indicated in the object language. Furthermore, there are many quantified sentences that have no representation at all using the universal and existential quantifiers, examples of which appear in (76).

(76) a. More students than lecturers laughed.
b. Many linguists sneezed.
c. Few philosophers sang.
d. Most babies cried.
e. More than half the babies cried.

To end this chapter, we take a brief look at a recent development in the theory of quantification that has shown great promise in helping to solve these problems and which has led to the development of a series of constraints that can be imposed on the semantics of natural language quantifiers.

As mentioned in Sections 6.2.1 and 6.2.2, the semantics of universal and existential noun phrases can be defined in terms of set theory. A NP like *a student* denotes the set of sets of entities which have a non-null intersection with the set of students (cf. (40)) and *every student* denotes the set of sets of entities of which the set of students is a subset (cf. (38.b)). It is this analysis of NPs as denoting **generalised quantifiers** that has been so fruitful in linguistic semantics in recent years. Instead of NPs being translated into complex expressions of L_Q, their semantics is defined directly on a simple (lexical) translation. Thus instead of translating *every* into the complex expression $\lambda Q\ [\lambda P\ [\forall x\ [Q(x) \rightarrow P(x)]]]$ it is translated into *every'* like any other lexical item. This still has the type <<e,t>,<<e,t>,t>> and so gives rise to NP translations like *every'(student')* and sentential translations like *(every'(student'))(laugh')* which contains no extra sentential connectives. The semantics of *every'* (and *a*, *no*, etc.) is then directly defined by the model theory without the use of variables and value assignments. Each quantifier is associated with a function which assigns to each subset $[N]^{M,g}$ of **A** (i.e. the extension of each common noun), a set of subsets of **A** having a particular property. The definitions for *every* and *some* in these terms is given in (77). The truth value of a formula whose subject NP contains the quantifiers *every* or *some* can be ascertained by seeing whether the VP denotes a set that is in the set of sets denoted by the subject. Thus, the proposition expressed by a sentence like *Every student laughed* is true just in case $[laugh']^{M,g}$ is in $\{X \subseteq A \mid [student']^{M,g} \subseteq X\}$, i.e. if $[student']^{M,g} \subseteq [laugh']^{M,g}$.

(77) a. $[every']^{M,g}$ is that function which assigns to each $[N]^{M,g} \subseteq \mathbf{A}$, the set of sets $\{X \subseteq A \mid [N]^{M,g} \subseteq X\}$.
b. $[some']^{M,g}$ is that function which assigns to each $[N]^{M,g} \subseteq \mathbf{A}$, the set of sets $\{X \subseteq A \mid X \cap [N]^{M,g} \neq \emptyset\}$.

Using this set-theoretic method rather than the traditional quantifiers, it is possible to define the semantics of other quantifiers in terms of the set of sets that they assign to the extension of each common noun. The interpretation of many non-classical quantifiers (i.e. quantifiers other than $\exists$ and $\forall$) is based on the

cardinality of a set, i.e. the number of elements it contains. The cardinality of a set is symbolised by writing the set or its name within two single vertical lines, i.e. $|\cdot|$. Thus, the cardinality of the set {a,b,c}, written $|\{a,b,c\}|$, is 3, because the set has three members, while $|\mathbf{A}|$ is 8, because there are eight entities in the universe of discourse, and so on. Using this notation, we can also refer to the number of entities that have a certain property in a model. For example, the cardinality of the extension of *student'* with respect to some model, **M**, is written as $|[\textit{student}']^{M,g}|$. Quantifiers often involve the comparison of the cardinalities of two sets and the symbol is used to represent the relation *greater than*, while ≥ represents the *greater than or equal to* relation. Thus, the set-theoretic statement $|X| > |Y|$ means that the set X has more members than the set Y, while $|X| \geq |Y|$ means that X has more members or the same number of members as Y.

Exercise 6.13:
Given the sets A and B specified below, which of the statements that follow are true?

A = {a,b,c,d,e} B = {9,16,32,75,2,62} C = {q,3,s,t,1}

i. $|A| \geq |B|$. ii. $|B| > |C|$. iii. $|C| \geq |A|$. iv. $|A| > |C|$.

The treatment of the quantifiers *(at least) two* and *both* is much simpler using this method than the predicate logic translations in (75). Firstly, they are both translated directly according to the lexical translation rule in Chapter 2, as *two'* and *both'*. Both of these quantifiers put constraints on the cardinality of the intersection of two sets, that denoted by the common noun and that denoted by the VP, but the difference between them is that *two'* requires the intersection of these two sets to have two or more elements while *both'* requires the cardinality of the set to be exactly two. Under the analysis of the interpretation of the NP *two students* in (78.a), the formula translating *Two students laughed* is true just in case the intersection of the extension of *student'* with that of the VP, *laugh'*, has two or more members (i.e. if the set of students who laugh has a cardinality of greater than or equal to two). The translation of *Both students laughed*, on the other hand, is only true, according to the set-theoretic interpretation of the subject NP in (78.b), if (and only if) the intersection of the set of students and the set of laughing entities has exactly two members. These seem to prescribe the intuitively correct truth-conditions for these sentences in a considerably more simple fashion than is possible using the classical quantifiers, as can be seen from a comparison of the interpretations (78.c) and (78.d) with those of the formulae in (75.a) and (75.b), respectively.

(78) a. $[\text{two}'(\text{student}')]^{M,g} = \{X \subseteq A \mid |X \cap [\text{student}']^{M,g}| \geq 2\}$.
b. $[\text{both}'(\text{student}')]^{M,g} = \{X \subseteq A \mid |X \cap [\text{student}']^{M,g}| = 2\}$.
c. $[(\text{two}'(\text{student}'))(\text{laugh}')]^{M,g}$ is **1** iff $|[\text{laugh}']^{M,g} \cap [\text{student}']^{M,g}| \geq 2$.
d. $[(\text{both}'(\text{student}'))(\text{laugh}')]^{M,g}$ is **1** iff $|[\text{laugh}']^{M,g} \cap [\text{student}']^{M,g}| = 2$.

Using this method, it is also possible to give interpretations to the sentences in (76) that contain non-classical quantifiers. The first sentence, (76.a), *More students than lecturers laughed*, expresses a true proposition just in case the number of students who laughed is greater than the number of lecturers who laughed. *More...than* is a **discontinuous determiner** taking two common nouns and so has the type <<e,t>,<<e,t>,<<e,t>,t>>>. Noun phrases with this determiner and two common nouns, N_1 and N_2, can be interpreted as denoting the set of sets whose intersection with the extension of N_2 has more members than their intersection with the extension of N_1. Thus, the NP *more students than lecturers* receives the interpretation in (79.a), giving the formula translating the example sentence in (76.a) the truth-conditions in (79.b), which ensures that the formula is true if and only if there are more laughing students than laughing lecturers.

(79) a. $[\text{more\_than'(lecturer')(student')}]^{M,g} =$
$\{X \subseteq A \mid |X \cap [\text{student'}]^{M,g}| > |X \cap [\text{lecturer'}]^{M,g}|\}$.

b. $[(\text{more\_than'(lecturer')(student')})(\text{laugh'})]^{M,g}$ is **1** iff
$|[\text{laugh'}]^{M,g} \cap [\text{student'}]^{M,g}| > |[\text{laugh'}]^{M,g} \cap [\text{lecturer'}]^{M,g}|$.

On one interpretation, the sentence in (76.d), *Most babies cried,* can be interpreted as meaning that the number of babies who cried is greater than the number of babies who didn't cry. The denotation of the subject NP *most babies* can thus be defined as in (80).

(80) $[\text{most'(baby')}]^{M,g} = \{X \subseteq A \mid |X \cap [\text{baby'}]^{M,g}| > |[\text{baby'}]^{M,g} \cap (A - X)|\}$.

This interpretation, however, turns out to be truth-conditionally equivalent to the interpretation that might be given to the NP *more than half the babies* in the sentence in (76.e), *More than half the babies cried*. An appropriate interpretation for this noun phrase is given in (81) which guarantees that *more_than_half'(baby')(cry')*, the (simplified) translation of (76.e), is true if (and only if) the number of crying babies is greater than the number of non-crying ones.

(81) $[\text{more\_than\_half'(baby')}]^{M,g} = \{X \subseteq A \mid |X \cap [\text{baby'}]^{M,g}| > |[\text{baby'}]^{M,g} - X|\}$.

(81) is, however, equivalent to the interpretation given to *most babies* in (80), as the reader can check by showing that, where $B,X \subseteq A$, $B \cap (A - X) = B - X$. (76.e) and (76.d) thus turn out to be paraphrases. Many people, however, might feel that the sentence *most babies cried* implies that a significantly greater proportion of babies cried than didn't, and that (76.e) and (76.d) are not truly paraphrases. For example, in a situation where there are fifty babies and twenty-six were crying while twenty-four were not, the interpretation given to *most babies* in (80) and to *more than half the babies* in (81) verifies both sentences, but the sentence with the latter NP is more appropriate than the one with the former. It is possible that the implication here is a pragmatic one, determined by appropriate usage rather than truth-conditions so that, if speakers know that twenty-six out of fifty babies cried they are likely to utter the sentence *More than half the babies cried*, rather than *Most babies cried*. However, it is possible to incorporate the notion of context dependence more directly into the semantics by interpreting *most* with respect to some pragmatically determined numerical proportion of the number of entities in the extension of the common noun that is greater than 50 per cent. If we let *c* represent this proportion, we can give *most'(baby')* the interpretation in (82.a). Assuming that *most* in this context requires at least 85 per cent of the elements in the extension of the common noun to have the property denoted by the verb phrase and that there are fifty babies, the sentence in

(76.d) has the truth-conditions in (82.b). The truth-conditions of *More than half the babies cried* are also met in any situation in which (82.b) holds, so that *Most babies cried* entails that *More than half the babies cried* (cf. (82.c)). The converse, however, is no longer true, because there are situations (e.g. where only twenty-six out of fifty babies cried) in which the latter is true but the former is not. Thus, the two sentences turn out not to be paraphrases under this interpretation, since they do not have exactly the same truth-conditions.

(82) a. $[\text{most'(baby')}]^{M,g} =$
$\{X \subseteq A \mid |X \geq [\text{baby'}]^{M,g}| > c \cdot |[\text{baby'}]^{M,g}|\}$ where $c \geq \cdot 5$.
b. Let $c = \cdot 85$ and $|[\text{baby'}]^{M,g}| = 50$, then $[\text{most'(baby')(cry')}]^{M,g}$ is **1** iff $|[\text{cry'}]^{M,g} \cap [\text{baby'}]^{M,g}| \geq 43$.
c. $\text{most'(N')(VP')} \rightarrow \text{more\_than\_half'(N')(VP')}$.

Other quantifiers like *many* and *few* also need some reference to contextually determined proportions. For example, the sentence in (76.b), *Many linguists sneezed*, means that some number of linguists sneezed, the proportion being determined by the context. Although it seems to be the case that the relevant proportion for determining the truth of this should be greater than fifty per cent, this is not always the case. For example, a sentence like *Many civil servants have knighthoods* might describe a situation in which the number of civil servants in Britain who have knighthoods is proportionately greater than the number of people in other fields in Britain who also have knighthoods. It could thus be the case that on average a profession could expect three per cent of its most senior members to be knighted, but that the number of knighted civil servants is actually five per cent of the number of all civil servants. In such a situation, the proposition expressed by the sentence *Many civil servants have knighthoods* is true, despite the fact that nowhere near half of the number of such people are knighted. Thus, we may assign to a noun phrase like *Many civil servants* the interpretation in (83) where, as before, *c* is some pragmatically determined proportion.

(83) $[\text{many'(civil-servant')}]^{M,g} =$
$\{X \subseteq A \mid |X \cap [\text{civil-servant'}]^{M,g}| > c \cdot |[\text{civil-servant'}]^{M,g}|\}$.

The quantifier *few*, as in (76.c), *Few philosophers sang,* requires the number of singing philosophers to be less than fifty per cent, but again the exact proportion of singing to non-singing philosophers is determined by the context of utterance. It is not my intention to explore this issue further or to work out exactly how the proportion **c** relates to the context for the different quantifiers (references to works that do can be found at the end of the chapter). The generalised quantifier approach to NP interpretation does, however, offer greater hope for the interpretation of quantifiers other than the universal and existential quantifiers than the traditional treatment of quantification given in the earlier part of this chapter. Indeed, it can be argued, this approach has the advantage of providing an intuitively and empirically more satisfactory analysis of many of the examples which were analysed in terms of the classical universal and existential quantifiers in the earlier sections of this chapter. Without doubt the theory does provide a fairly simple and coherent account of quantifiers like *two*, *both* and those in the following exercise, which have an interpretation fixed independently of the context.

---

*Exercise 6.14:
Provide generalised quantifier interpretations for the determiners *the*, *at most five*, *all but three* and *exactly twelve*, using the truth-conditions of the following sentences as a guide.

i. The linguist screamed.
ii. At most five babies cried.
iii. All but three philosophers are insane.
iv. Exactly twelve students sang.

In addition to providing a framework within which more quantifiers than the traditional logical quantifiers can be defined, the theory of generalised quantifiers also allows the statement of constraints on the possible denotations of natural language quantifiers (a term which may cover just items like *every*, *all*, *most*, *few*, etc., or all determiners or the noun phrase itself, depending on the point of view being discussed). The study of **semantic universals** is a topic that has not been discussed so far, but those working within the framework of generalised quantifiers have begun to tackle this aspect of semantics with some success. The earliest proposals along these lines have, since the early part of the nineteen-eighties, been discussed and revised quite extensively, but one universal seems to be particularly robust and to be generally considered to be valid: the **conservativity universal**.

A quantifier phrase is called **conservative** if it has the conservativity property defined in (84). Here, Q represents the extension of a quantifier, N that of a common noun and X (which may be thought of as the extension of a VP) is any subset of **A**, the universe of discourse. The definition requires the intersection (i.e. the conjunction) of the extensions of the VP and the N to be a member of the set of sets denoted by a quantified NP containing the quantifier and the common noun, provided that the extension of the VP is also contained in this set of sets. The tautologous flavour of the examples in (85) shows that this property holds for some common quantified NPs in English. The conservativity universal requires every quantifier in any natural language to have the property in (84).

(84) A quantifier with extension Q is *conservative* iff, for $N, X \subseteq A$,
$X \in Q(N) \leftrightarrow (N \cap X) \in Q(N)$.

(85) a. Many students laughed iff Many students are students who laughed.
b. Every baby cried iff Every baby is a baby who cried.
c. Few lecturers screamed iff Few lecturers are lecturers who screamed.

(86) **Conservativity**: Every natural language quantifier is conservative.

This constraint may seem somewhat uninteresting, but it captures a fact about the denotations of natural language quantifiers that is not logically necessary. It is not, for example, logically necessary that if every man walks, then every man is a man who walks, but a fact about the meaning of *every* (and other natural language quantifiers). (86) rules out many logically possible quantifiers. For example, it rules out a quantifier that denotes a function that picks out every subset of **A** provided that it is not a subset of the extension of the common noun with which it is combined, i.e. one that denotes the set of sets $\{X \mid \sim(X \subseteq [N]^{M,g})\}$. Since the intersection of any two sets is a subset of both, such a quantifier does not include $X \cap [N]^{M,g}$ for any X and so it is not conservative, and thus by (86) not a natural language quantifier.

Conservativity ensures that the interpretation of a noun phrase containing a common noun N is not affected by those sets of entities that are not in the extension of N. If we are interpreting the sentence *Every dog barked*, we do not need to take account of cats, sheep, books or anything else in the domain of discourse that are not dogs. Furthermore, the conservativity property cuts down the number of possible extensions that quantifiers may have in any model. For example, in a model with just two elements in its universe of discourse there are 256 logically possible quantifier extensions (= $(2^4)^n$), where n = 2, the number of entities in the model). However, if only conservative extensions are permissible, natural language quantifiers may have only one of 64 possible extensions (= $(2^3)^n$). Thus, the space in which quantifiers may have their meanings located is considerably reduced in number.

As well as identifying other general properties for quantifiers (like their semantic independence from the identity, as opposed to the number, of entities in the extension of the common noun), there have also been attempts to characterise the properties of different subsets of quantifiers. In mathematics, a function, f^+, is said to be **monotone increasing** if for any two elements, *x* and *y*, in the domain where *x* is greater than *y* then $f^+(x)$ is also greater than $f^+(y)$. The converse of this is a **monotone decreasing** function, f where for any two elements, *x* and *y*, in the domain if *x* is greater than *y* then $f(x)$ is less than $f(y)$. In formal semantics, these definitions have been adapted to deal with the way an increase or a decrease in the number of entities in the extension of the common noun in a noun phrase or in the extension of the verb phrase affects truth values. For example, if we know that every philosopher sang in some model, then adding more singers to the model does not affect the truth value of the formula *every'(philosopher')(sing')*, but adding more philosophers to the model may affect its truth value because the newly introduced philosopher may not be a singer. On the other hand, taking away one of the philosophers (or picking out a subset of the philosophers) does not affect the truth value of the formula. If the addition of more entities to the extension of the common noun or the verb phrase does not affect the truth value of a formula with the structure *Qnt'(N')(VP')*, then we say that the quantifier is monotone increasing. If the subtraction of entities from the relevant extensions fails to affect the truth value, then we say that Qnt is monotone decreasing. We may make a further distinction between those quantifiers which are unaffected by increase or decrease in their common noun extensions (**subject monotone**) and those unaffected by increase or decrease of their associated VP extensions (**predicate monotone**) to give the four classes in (87). Examples of the different sorts of monotone quantifiers are given in (88) to (91). Each example contains four sentences illustrating the four properties in (87) in order. Those sentences that are not tautologous according to the interpretation of the quantifier are indicated by a percentage sign. The patterns show that *a* is both left and right monotone increasing; *every* is right monotone increasing, but left monotone decreasing; *no* is left and right monotone decreasing and *most* is just right monotone increasing.

(87) a. A quantifier Qnt is *subject monotone increasing* iff Qnt N_1 VP entails Qnt N_2 VP, where $[N_1]^{M,g} \subseteq [N_2]^{M,g}$.
b. A quantifier Qnt is *predicate monotone increasing* iff Qnt N VP_1 entails Qnt N VP_2, where $[VP_1]^{M,g} \subseteq [VP_2]^{M,g}$.
c. A quantifier Qnt is *subject monotone decreasing* iff Qnt N_1 VP entails Qnt N_2 VP, where $[N_2]^{M,g} \subseteq [N_1]^{M,g}$.
d. A quantifier Qnt is *predicate monotone decreasing* iff Qnt N VP_1 entails Qnt N VP_2, where $[VP_2]^{M,g} \subseteq [VP_1]^{M,g}$

(88) a. If a philosopher with red hair sang, then a philosopher sang.
b. If a philosopher sang well, then a philosopher sang.
c. %If a philosopher sang, then a philosopher with red hair sang.
d. %If a philosopher sang, then a philosopher sang well.

(89) a. %If every philosopher with red hair sang, then every philosopher sang.
b. If every philosopher sang well, then every philosopher sang.
c. If every philosopher sang, then every philosopher with red hair sang.
d. %If every philosopher sang, then every philosopher sang well.

(90) a. %If no philosopher with red hair sang, then no philosopher sang.
b. %If no philosopher sang well, then no philosopher sang.
c. If no philosopher sang, then no philosopher with red hair sang.
d. If no philosopher sang, then no philosopher sang well.

(91) a. %If most philosophers with red hair sang, then most philosophers sang.
b. If most philosophers sang well, then most philosophers sang.
c. %If most philosophers sang, then most philosophers with red hair sang.
d. %If most philosophers sang, then most philosophers sang well.

Not all quantifiers or other determiners are either monotone increasing or decreasing, however. For example, the pre-modifying quantifier phrase *exactly half* in English is not monotone in either subject or predicate position, as illustrated by the sentences in (92). (This result holds for all English phrases *exactly n* where n is some number.)

(92) a. %If exactly half the philosophers with red hair sang, then exactly half the philosophers sang.
b. %If exactly half the philosophers sang well, then exactly half the philosophers sang.
c. %If exactly half the philosophers sang, then exactly half the philosophers with red hair sang.
d. %If exactly half the philosophers sang, then exactly half the philosophers sang well.

A number of interesting linguistic universals can be stated about noun phrases according to the different sorts of monotone quantifiers that they contain. One of these is that noun phrases can be conjoined by *and* or *or* only if they have quantifiers with the same monotone direction. Thus, according to (93) we may conjoin noun phrases containing *no* and *every* (as in (94.a)) or *most* and *every* (cf. (94.b)), but not *most* and *no* (94.c) or *no* and *a* (94.d).

(93) **Co-ordination constraint**: Two NPs can be co-ordinated by conjunction (*and*) and disjunction (*or*) iff they are both monotone increasing or both monotone decreasing.

(94) a. No student and every lecturer liked the book.
b. Most students and every lecturer liked the book.
c. *No student and most lecturers liked the book.
d. *No student and a lecturer liked the book.

The classification of the quantifiers into the classes in (87) have other benefits in enabling us to identify and explain other linguistic phenomena (for example, **negative polarity items** cannot appear in the scope of monotone increasing functors). Other entailment patterns have also been identified and these, together with further general properties of quantifiers, allow more universals to be stated. These universals and constraint are somewhat technical in nature, and no more will be presented here, but I hope that the short discussion in this section gives some idea of the fascinating and fruitful ideas resulting from the study of generalised quantifiers.

6.7 Further Reading

There is a good deal written about quantification and the interpretation of noun phrases and this section can do no more than indicate the more important texts on particular topics. The classical quantifiers are given extensive treatment in many introductory logic and linguistic textbooks of which the most accessible introduction (which includes a discussion on translation) can be found in Guttenplan (1986: 166-246). The linguistic introductions to logic also discuss the classical quantifiers in detail: see Allwood, Andersen and Dahl (1977: ch. 4), Partee, ter Meulen and Wall (1990: 137-154), McCawley (1981: ch. 4), Chierchia and McConnell-Ginet (1990: ch. 3) and, for a more formal discussion, Dowty, Wall and Peters (1981: ch. 3). The decomposition of quantified NPs using the λ-operator can be found in Montague (1973) and Dowty, Wall and Peters (1981: 104-111). Partee (1986) discusses the type change from e to <<e,t>,t>. There are a number of discussions about adjectives, of which Klein (1980) and Siegel (1979) are the most accessible, while Kamp (1975), Chierchia and McConnell-Ginet (1990: 370-377) and Keenan and Faltz (1985: 118-150; 308-333) require an acquaintance with intensional semantics. The literature about definiteness and the interpretation of definite noun phrases is already vast and still growing. The analysis of *the* in this chapter owes its origins to Russell (1905) and Montague (1973) with Strawson (1950) providing the antithesis. See also Allwood, Andersen and Dahl (1977: 148-155), McCawley (1981: 176-182) and the more extended discussions in Hawkins (1978), Heim (1989), Kamp (1981), Ludlow and Neale (1991) and the papers in Reuland and ter Meulen (1987). (Carlson (1989) and Ojeda (1991) discuss the generic use of the definite article in English.) The issue of quantifier scope ambiguities is addressed, inter alia, in Cooper (1983) and May (1985). The literature on generalised quantifiers has grown steadily since the publication of Barwise and Cooper (1984). Partee, ter Meulen and Wall (1990: ch. 14) and Chierchia and McConnell-Ginet (1990: ch. 9) both provide introductions to the topic, and more detailed discussions can be found in Keenan and Stavi (1986), Zwarts (1983) and van Benthem (1986: chs. 1 & 3). McCawley (1981: ch. 14) discusses other types of quantifier and touches on mass terms and generics. Mass terms and plurals are not discussed in this book, but the reader will find interesting, if difficult, discussions of these topics in Link (1983), Hoeksema (1983) and Lønning (1987).

7 Inference

7.1 Making inferences

The semantic theory developed up to Chapter 6 has concentrated mainly on the interpretation of sentences and phrases in isolation from each other, but one of the criteria for assessing the adequacy of a semantic theory set out in Chapter 1 is that it should account for the meaning relations that hold between different expressions in a language. This means, amongst other things, that the semantic theory proposed here ought to guarantee that, where reference and context are kept constant, the sentences in (1.b) and (1.c) are **paraphrases** of (1.a) while (1.d) and (1.e) are **entailments** of it and (1.f) and (1.g) are **contradictions** of it.

(1) a. Jo stroked the cat and kicked the dog.
  b. Jo kicked the dog and stroked the cat.
  c. The cat was stroked by Jo and the dog was kicked by Jo.
  d. Jo stroked the cat.
  e. Someone kicked the dog.
  f. The dog wasn't kicked.
  g. No-one stroked anything.

The intuitively identified relations between the sentences in (1) derive from the interpretations of the conjunction *and*, the negative *not* and the quantifier pronouns *no-one* and *someone*. Such relations are generally referred to as **logical** entailments, paraphrases or contradictions. (Note that these terms are used ambiguously between the relation that holds amongst sentences, as here, and the product sentences themselves, as in the first paragraph above.) Because of their logical nature, these relations should be directly explained by the interpretation given to the logical elements associated with the relevant grammatical expressions (&, ~ and ∃) by the model theory. Meaning relations of this sort are used to make **inferences**. An inference is the recovery of information from a discourse which is implicitly or explicitly presented as true by the speaker, but which is not stated directly. For example, an interlocutor, say Bertie, may infer the sentence in (2.b) from the utterance of (2.a) in a situation where Bertie knows that Chester did eat the cake.

(2) a. If Chester ate the cake, then he will probably die.
  b. Chester will probably die.

More interesting chains of inference result from combining different bits of information, expressed in sentences or formulae, to arrive at some conclusion. For example, from the sentence in (3.a) it is possible to arrive at the inference in (3.f) using the information expressed in the sentences in (3.b) to (3.e). In logical terms, (3) has the structure of a **valid inference pattern**, since the truth of the **conclusion** in (3.f) is guaranteed by the truth of all of the **premisses** in (3.a) to (3.e). We may indeed think of an inference pattern of this sort as an extended entailment relation where the set of premisses are treated as a compound sentence conjoined by *and* which directly entails the conclusion. Such a pattern is called an **argument** by logicians, but the term will not be used here in order to avoid a potentially confusing ambiguity with the argument of a functor. In order to show the extent to which the semantic theory set up so far is adequate, it is necessary to show the extent to which it can capture the meaning relations that hold between sentences and account for intuitively valid inference patterns like that in (3).

(3) a. The dog has eaten the cake.
b. The cake is poisonous.
c. If something poisonous is eaten, the entity that ate the poisonous substance will become ill.
d. A dog is an animal.
e. If an animal is ill, a vet should be called.
f. Someone should call a vet.

Inference of the sort shown in (2) and (3) is called **deductive inference** because the truth of the conclusion results from the logical interpretation of the premisses. There are, however, inference processes that rely on **non-logical** relations between expressions in a particular language. One such relation results from **lexical meaning** and the lexical relations that hold in the vocabulary of some language. The term lexical meaning is to be interpreted as concerning that part of the meaning of a sentence that results, not from its logical structure (in terms of conjunctions and quantifiers), but from the idiosyncratic meanings of its component words. A distinction is thus being made between the meanings of grammatical or functional words like *a*, *every*, *and*, *if* and so on, and content lexemes that translate into constants in the logical translation language. Expressions of the former sort are interpreted in the same way with respect to all models, whilst the denotations of the latter expressions may change from model to model. There are, however, relations that are expected to hold between content expressions within particular models. For example, in (4), (4.b) and (4.c) may be inferred from (4.a), the first due to the meaning of the word *kill* and its relation to the word *dead* and the latter due to that of the words *owl* and *mouse* and their relations to the words *bird* and *mammal*, respectively.

(4) a. An owl killed a mouse.
b. A mouse is dead.
c. A bird killed a mammal.

The inferences recovered from the meanings of words, however, are weaker than those that derive from the interpretation of logical expressions in that they can more readily be cancelled. This is most obvious in figurative or metaphorical speech where properties usually associated with certain words are influenced by those associated with other words in the sentence. The sentence in (5.a), for example, is not contradictory in the same way that (5.b) is, and conveys more obvious information, despite the fact that the semi-formal sentences in (5.c), (5.d) and (5.e) describe apparent entailments associated with the words *idea* and *swallow* that ought to license the contradictory inference in (5.b). The position is taken here that lexical meaning relations are not therefore absolute constraints on models, so not purely logical and thus able to be overridden in certain circumstances.

(5) a. Jo swallowed the idea.
b. An idea is and is not abstract.
c. If x swallows y, then y is concrete.
d. If x is concrete, x is not abstract.
e. An idea is abstract.

Other types of inference exist, weaker than those derived through the meaning relations of words and sentences which derive from **presupposition** and **implicature**. The former has already been mentioned briefly with respect to definiteness and uniqueness in Chapter 6 and Chapter 1. The difference between presupposition and entailment is that presuppositions persist for both positive and negative sentences and that the falsity of the presupposition does not so obviously falsify the original sentence as does the falsity of an entailment. This is illustrated in (6) where the truth of (6.a) presupposes that of (6.b) and where the falsity of (6.b) does not falsify (6.a) as does the falsity of (6.c) (an entailment of (6.a)). This topic is a controversial and interesting one, but does not directly concern us here and no more will be said about it.

(6) a. The King of France is not bald.
b. There exists an entity that is King of France.
c. There exists an entity that is not bald.

Another form of pragmatic inference is briefly discussed in Section 7.4 to account for some of the apparent anomalies between the interpretations of certain natural language constructions and their logical counterparts. This type of inference results from the implicatures of an utterance. Implicature is probably the weakest form of inference that can be made, since it holds only where there is no information to the contrary and can be contradicted without contradicting the original sentence. For example, the truth of (7.a) implicates the truth of (7.b), but this implicature can be cancelled without contradiction as shown by the sentence in (7.c) which is not obviously contradictory despite the fact that it denies the truth of (7.b) (although most speakers of English might judge the former to be odd or paradoxical).

(7) a. Every boy in the room kissed Fiona.
b. Someone kissed Fiona.
c. Yes, that's true. Every boy in the room did kiss Fiona, but there were no boys in the room!

The different sorts of inference mentioned above seem to form a hierarchy in terms of how they relate to the sentence (or sentences) from which the inference is made. Inference deriving from entailment (or paraphrase or contradiction) must always hold, while that made through implicature need not hold. The inferences determined by lexical meaning (and presupposition) fill intermediate slots in the **inference hierarchy** shown in (8).

(8) **Inference hierarchy**: entailment > lexical meaning > implicature.

In this chapter, we will concentrate on deductive inference that can be made using the logical operators and connectives that have been introduced in previous chapters, showing how the interpretation given to them explains common inference strategies. We will then take an all too brief look at a way of incorporating lexical meaning into the theory and end with a short discussion of the way implicature can account for some non-truth-functional aspects of the English counterparts of the logical connectives &, $\vee$ and $\rightarrow$.

7.2 Logical deduction

Deductive inference derives from the primary meaning relations between sentences, entailment, paraphrase and contradiction. By formally defining the latter, therefore, we can show how adequately the model theory defined in Chapter 6 accounts for valid inferences. Within truth-conditional semantics, the primary logical meaning relations can be given general definitions in terms of the relation between the truth or falsity of the proposition expressed by one sentence and that expressed by another.

One sentence is an entailment of another only if the truth of the former is guaranteed by that of the latter. In other words, whenever (the proposition expressed by) a sentence is true, (the propositions expressed by) its entailments are also true, although the reverse need not be the case. These are, of course, just the truth-conditions of material implication and so we can characterise entailment between two sentences in terms of their combination using $\rightarrow$. Since entailment, like the other logical meaning relations, holds in all situations, the material implication must be true in all situations. This allows us to define entailment as holding between two sentences when the formulae associated with each of the sentences conjoined by the material implication sign, $\rightarrow$, make a **tautology**, a formula that is always true no matter what the denotations of its component parts happen to be. Adopting the symbol $\vdash$ to signify the relation **entails** (so that $S_1 \vdash S_2$ means sentence S_1 entails sentence S_2) provides the definition of entailment in (9).

(9) **Entailment**: $S_1 \vdash S_2$ iff $S_1' \rightarrow S_2'$ is a tautology.

To see how this definition works, we can take as an example the simplest entailment in our fragment which results from an **inference rule** that logicians call **conjunction elimination**. This rule allows the inference that each conjunct of a true formula is also true. For example, in (10), the truth of both (10.b) and (10.c) may be inferred from that of (10.a) according to this rule.

(10) a. $\exists x\ [\forall y[\text{cake}'(y) \leftrightarrow x = y]\ \&\ (\text{eat}'(x))(\text{chester}')]\ \&\ \text{sick}'(\text{chester}')$.
b. $\exists x\ [\forall y[\text{cake}'(y) \leftrightarrow x = y]\ \&\ (\text{eat}'(x))(\text{chester}')]$.
c. $\text{sick}'(\text{chester}')$.

According to (9), if conjunction elimination is a valid rule, a sentence that translates into a formula conjoined by & (e.g. (10.a)) entails the sentences that translate into the conjuncts (e.g. (10.b) and (10.c)), provided that the material implication formed from the conjoined formula and each of its conjuncts is always true no matter what truth values are associated with the antecedent or the consequent. In other words, the sentence in (11.a) entails both (11.b) and (11.c) if (and only if) (12.a) and (12.b) are tautologies.

(11) a. Chester ate the cake and was sick.
b. Chester ate the cake.
c. Chester was sick.

(12) a. $(\exists x\ [\forall y[\text{cake'}(y) \leftrightarrow x = y]\ \&\ \text{eat'}(x)(\text{chester'})]\ \&\ \text{sick'}(\text{chester'}))$
$\rightarrow \exists x\ [\forall y[\text{cake'}(y) \leftrightarrow x = y]\ \&\ \text{eat'}(x)(\text{chester'})]$.

b. $(\exists x\ [\forall y[\text{cake'}(y) \leftrightarrow x = y]\ \&\ \text{eat'}(x)(\text{chester'})]\ \&\ \text{sick'}(\text{chester'}))$
$\rightarrow \text{sick'}(\text{chester'})$.

It is easy to show that both formulae in (12) are indeed tautologies by using the truth table method introduced in Chapter 3. If we represent the formula denoted by *Chester ate the cake* as p and that expressed by *Chester was sick* as q, we can see that the formula (p & q) → p is a tautology because the final implication always has the value *t* (or **1**) no matter what truth values are assigned to p and q as shown in (13). Hence, according to (9), the entailments in (11) are valid and our theory successfully guarantees that a sentence of the form S_1 *and* S_2 entails both S_1 and S_2 (and hence that both these sentences may be inferred from the former).

(13)

p	q	p & q	(p & q) → p
t	t	t	t
t	f	f	t
f	t	f	t
f	f	f	t

The two other sentential meaning relations of paraphrase and contradiction can also be defined in terms of tautologies that result from combining appropriate formulae with particular connectives. Two sentences paraphrase each other if they both have precisely the same truth-conditions. In other words, sentences that are paraphrases of each other express propositions that are both true or both false (i.e. logically equivalent) in all the same situations. Hence, we may show that two sentences are paraphrases by showing that the formulae they express, when conjoined by the equivalence connective, ↔, make a tautology. This is expressed by the definition in (14) where the symbol ⊣⊢ is used to signify the relation **paraphrases**.

(14) **Paraphrase**: $S_1 \dashv\vdash S_2$ iff $S_1' \leftrightarrow S_2'$ is a tautology.

We have already seen the equivalence that holds between λ-expressions applied to an argument and their λ-converted equivalents in Chapter 5. By (14), this is sufficient to make passive and active pairs paraphrases as, intuitively, they should be. For example, the semantics of the lambda operator ensures that the formulae in (15.c) and (15.d) are truth-conditionally equivalent (so that their conjunction by ↔ is always true) and, thus, by (14), the English sentences that they translate, (15.a) and (15.b), respectively, are paraphrases as required.

(15) a. Chester was kicked by Jo.

b. Jo kicked Chester.

c. $\lambda x\ [(\text{kick'}(x))(\text{jo'})](\text{chester'})$.

d. $(\text{kick'}(\text{chester'}))(\text{jo'})$.

There is another simple logical paraphrase between sentences which was mentioned in Chapter 3 and involves the truth-conditional equivalence between positive formulae and their doubly negated counterparts. As we saw in Chapter 3, two negatives in logical expressions are equivalent to a positive, so that ~(~p) is truth-conditionally equivalent to p, where p is any formula. This is shown in the truth table in (16) and so, according to (14), (17.a) and (17.b) are paraphrases because (17.c) is a tautology.

(16)

p	~p	~(~p)	p ↔ ~(~p)
t	f	t	t
f	t	f	t

(17) a. It rained.
b. It is not the case that it didn't rain.
c. rain' ↔ ~(~rain').

Because the definition of paraphrase in (15) utilises truth-conditional equivalence, it also predicts that two paraphrases entail each other. This results from the fact that a formula of the form p ↔ q is truth-conditionally equivalent to one of the form ((p → q) & (q → p)) (as shown in the truth table in (43) of Chapter 3). By conjunction elimination, therefore, we can infer that both p → q and q → p hold and so by the definition of entailment in (9), paraphrases that translate into p and q are also entailments of each other. Thus, the definition of paraphrase in (14) treats the relation as equivalent to mutual entailment, as suggested in Chapter 1.

The final relation between sentences that we need to look at is contradiction. Here, the truth of the proposition expressed by one sentence guarantees the falsity of that expressed by another. There are a number of ways this can be defined using the connectives, one of which is to use material implication and negation to bring out the relation between contradiction and entailment. Essentially, the definition of contradiction in (18), which uses the symbol ⊨ to denote the relation **contradicts**, defines one sentence as contradicting another if the latter entails the negation of the former.

(18) **Contradiction**: $S_1 \vDash S_2$ iff $S_1' \rightarrow \sim S_2'$ is a tautology.

From (18) it is easy to see that the negation of any entailment is a contradiction. Thus, the sentence in (19.a) is contradicted by that in (19.b) which is the negation of an entailment derived from conjunction elimination. This is guaranteed by the fact that (19.c) is a tautology, which is shown by the truth table in (20) where p represents the translation of *Chester ate the cake* and q that of *Chester was sick.*

(19) a. Chester ate the cake and was sick.
b. Chester wasn't sick.
c. (∃x [∀y[cake'(y) ↔ x = y] & eat'(x)(chester')] & sick'(chester'))
→ ~(~(sick'(chester'))).

(20)

p	q	p & q	~q	~(~q)	((p & q) → ~(~q))
t	t	t	f	t	t
t	f	f	t	f	t
f	t	f	f	t	t
f	f	f	t	f	t

Having given a formal definition of the primary meaning relations between sentences, we can proceed to an examination of some of the valid deductive inferences that are captured by the semantic theory proposed in Chapters 2 to 6. Clearly, any entailment or paraphrase of a sentence is a valid inference that can be made from that sentence. But, as we have seen, inferences often operate over sets of sentences rather than single ones. In other words, deductive inference normally takes the shape of an inference pattern that contains a set of **premisses** and a **conclusion**. An inference pattern is valid if, and only if, the truth of all its premisses guarantees the truth of the conclusion. This is like entailment in an extended sense where the entailing sentence is a conjunction of all the premisses and the conclusion is entailed by this conjunction. An inference pattern may therefore be defined as valid, if the material implication formed with the conjunction of the translations of its premisses and that of its conclusion as the consequent is a tautology, as in (21).

(21) An inference pattern $S_1,...,S_{n-1} \vdash S_n$ is valid iff $(S_1' \; \& \; .... \; \& \; S_{n-1}') \rightarrow S_n'$ is a tautology.

A simple inference pattern that is intuitively valid is shown in (22) where (22.a) and (22.b) are the premisses and (22.c) is the conclusion.

(22) a. Fiona is either at home or in the library.
b. She isn't in the library.
c. Then she is at home.

According to (21), we can show that this is valid according to the model theory by proving that a formula with the structure $\phi \rightarrow \psi$ is a tautology, where ψ is the translation of (22.c) and ϕ is the conjunction of the translations of (22.a) and (22.b). If we let p stand for the formula translating *Fiona was at home* and q stand for that translating *Fiona was in the library*, then the logical structure of the inference pattern is $((p \vee q) \; \& \; {\sim}q) \rightarrow p$. The truth table in (23) shows that this expression is tautologous, thus proving that the inference pattern in (22) is actually valid according to the semantic interpretation provided for *or* and *not*.

(23)

p	q	p ∨ q	~q	(p ∨ q) & ~q	((p ∨ q) & ~q) → p
t	t	t	f	f	t
t	f	t	t	t	t
f	t	t	f	f	t
f	f	f	t	f	t

7.2.1 Using the connectives

In this section, we look at some of the many valid inference patterns that can be constructed using the propositional connectives. Only a few of these are discussed here and the reader is referred to a good introduction to propositional logic for a fuller discussion. Only the most commonly used patterns involving the expressions *and*, *or*, *not* and *if* are discussed below.

We have already seen one valid inference pattern involving disjunction and negation in (22) above. Another one, called **disjunction elimination** by logicians, exploits the relation between disjunction and implication to arrive at a particular conclusion. An inference pattern with the appropriate structure is shown in (24), where (24.a), (24.b) and (24.c) are the premisses and (24.d) is the conclusion. The logical structure of the premisses and conclusion in terms of propositional variables and connectives is shown on the right hand side of the example where p stands for *Jo kicked Bertie*, q for *Jo kicked Ethel* and r for *Ethel hit Jo*. The validity of this inference pattern is shown by the truth table in (25) which is constructed from (24) along the lines set out in (21). Since the complex formula on the right is always true no matter what values are assigned to the basic formulae, the inference pattern is valid and the conclusion in (24.d) may be inferred from the premisses, as required. (Note that the formula ((p ∨ q) & (p → r) & (q → r)) → r is false if, and only if, all of the conjuncts in the antecedent are true and the consequent is false. To show that it is true, therefore, it is sufficient to show that one of the conjuncts is false or that the consequent is true. Hence, the intermediate step of showing the truth value of the antecedent (p ∨ q) & (p → r) & (q → r) is omitted from (25).)

(24) a. Jo kicked Bertie or Ethel. p ∨ q
b. If Jo kicked Bertie, then Ethel hit Jo. p → r
c. If Jo kicked Ethel, then Ethel hit Jo. q → r
d. Ethel hit Jo. r

Other important inference rules involve material implication. Given the truth of an *if ... then* sentence and its antecedent, we can confidently infer the truth of the consequent, as illustrated in (26). This inference pattern is called **modus ponens** by logicians and its validity is shown by the truth table in (27).

(25)

p	q	r	(p ∨ q)	p → r	q → r	((p ∨ q) & (p → r) & (q → r)) → r
t	t	t	t	t	t	t
t	t	f	t	f	f	t
t	f	t	t	t	t	t
f	t	t	t	t	t	t
t	f	f	t	f	t	t
f	t	f	t	t	f	t
f	f	t	f	t	t	t
f	f	f	f	t	t	t

(26) a. If Ethel was not at home, then she was in the pub. $p \rightarrow q$
b. Ethel was not at home. p
c. Ethel was in the pub. q

(27)

p	q	(p → q)	(p → q) & p	((p → q) & p) → q)
t	t	t	t	t
t	f	f	f	t
f	t	t	f	t
f	f	t	f	t

Another inference rule involving material implication is called **modus tollens** and is in effect the reverse of modus ponens. Given a conditional and the negation of its consequent, it is possible to infer that the antecedent is also false. In other words, given two sentences *If S1 then* S_2 and *It is not the case that* S_2, we infer *It is not the case that* S_1. An example of this type of inference pattern is given in (28) where the final conclusion in (28.d) relies on the equivalence between p and ~~p discussed above.

(28) a. If Ethel was not at home, then she was in the pub. $\sim p \rightarrow q$
b. Ethel was not in the pub. $\sim q$
c. It is not the case that Ethel was not at home. $\sim\sim p$
d. Ethel was at home. p

Exercise 7.1:
Prove that modus tollens is valid by constructing the appropriate truth table.

These inference pattern types can be put together to construct quite complex chains of inference with new premisses being deduced from old ones to arrive at an ultimate conclusion. In texts, however, the premisses and intermediate conclusions of a chain of inference are often not expressed. This is illustrated in the short dialogue between Bertie and Fiona in (29).

(29) a. Fiona: That's Ethel now.
b. Bertie: What is she doing?
c. Fiona: Well, she didn't kick the cat.
d. Bertie: OK, I'll slice the lemon.

The interesting thing about this exchange from our point of view is how Bertie's response in (29.d) relates to Fiona's statement in (29.c). We can show how Bertie gets to his conclusion by making explicit the unexpressed premisses that he uses with Fiona's statement in (29.c) to come to intermediate conclusions that ultimately lead to his assertion of (29.d). The full inference pattern in English is set out in (30). (30.a) is the initial premiss asserted by Fiona. Bertie uses the (implicit) premiss in (30.b) to arrive at the intermediate conclusion in (30.c) via modus tollens. The latter sentence is, as we have seen, a paraphrase of (30.d) which can then be used to derive (30.f) from the premiss in (30.e) via modus ponens. This conclusion can then be combined with another conditional premiss in (30.g) to give the conjunction in (30.h). Applying conjunction elimination to this (cf. (12) above) yields (30.i) which combines with the final premiss in (30.j) to give the final conclusion in (30.k) again via modus ponens.

(30) a. Ethel didn't kick the cat.
b. If Ethel doesn't win a golf match, she kicks the cat.
c. It is not the case that Ethel didn't win the golf match.
d. Ethel won the golf match.
e. If Ethel won the golf match, she wants a drink.
f. Ethel wants a drink.
g. If Ethel wants a drink, we need gin and sliced lemon.
h. We need gin and sliced lemon.
i. We need sliced lemon.
j. If we need sliced lemon, I'll slice it.
k. I'll slice the lemon.

The logical structure of this inference pattern is set out in (31) where q stands for *Ethel kicked the cat*, p for *Ethel won the golf match*, r for *Ethel wants a drink*, s for *We need gin*, u for *We need sliced lemon* and v for *I'll slice the lemon*. The inference rule that licenses the steps taken at each point in the inference pattern is indicated on the right hand side and inasmuch as each of these small steps is valid, so the whole inference pattern is validated by the semantic interpretation given to the connectives in the model theory.

(31) a.	$\sim q$.	premiss
b.	$\sim p \rightarrow q$.	premiss
c.	$\sim\sim p$.	deduction from a & b via modus tollens
d.	p.	deduction from c via negation elimination
e.	$p \rightarrow r$.	premiss

f. r. deduction from d & e via modus ponens
g. r → (s & u). premiss
h. s & u. deduction from f & g via modus ponens
i. u. deduction from h via conjunction elimination
j. u → v. premiss
k. v. deduction from i & j via modus ponens

So far we have looked at the way inference patterns are constructed from information gleaned from entailments and paraphrases, but conclusions can also be drawn from the use of contradictions. The most obvious way that contradictions are used in discourse is to challenge or disprove the truth of other assertions, as exemplified in the simple exchange in (32).

(32) a. Jo: Fiona said she's working hard on her thesis today.
b. Bertie: But I've just seen her in the pub.
c. Jo: Oh dear! She lied to me.

The reasoning that lies behind this exchange is fairly simple. Suppose that Fiona has said to Jo that she is working hard on her thesis and so he asserts (32.a) to Bertie. On standard assumptions that people generally speak the truth, both Jo and Bertie can infer from this that *Fiona is working hard on her thesis* is true (let p represent the formula that translates this sentence). Bertie, however, has seen Fiona in the pub and asserts (32.b) (call the formula that translates *Fiona is in the pub* q). At this point an unexpressed premiss comes into play to the effect that if someone is in the pub then they are not working hard, from which we can get the formula q → ~p. However, from this and Bertie's assertion, we can infer ~p, via modus ponens. This, of course, contradicts the earlier inference p. Although this does not contradict (32.a), since Fiona did say that she was working hard, Jo can infer that she did not assert p truthfully and his knowledge of lexical meaning allows him to infer that she lied. Hence, while Bertie does not directly contradict Fiona's assertion, he provides information that can be used to show that Fiona has been economical with the truth with respect to her working hard on her thesis.

There is another use of contradictory information that involves a form of indirect reasoning called a **reductio ad absurdum** argument (or **negation introduction**) by logicians. In this form of reasoning, an assumption is made in the course of an inference pattern which is not itself validated by the current premisses. This assumption is then used to deduce logically that some other sentence is both true and false. From this logically false conclusion, it follows that the assumption must be false, since one cannot deduce a false conclusion from a true premiss. This form of reasoning thus allows one to eliminate different possible explanations; any assumption that leads to a contradiction must be false and so can be discarded. This may sound a bit peculiar, but is exemplified in the dialogue in (33) which takes place between Jo and Ethel after Jo has discovered that the poisoned cake has been eaten.

(33) a. Jo: The dog ate the poisoned cake.
b. Ethel: I've just seen him playing with a ball.
c. Jo: Then who did eat the cake?

This exchange might seem peculiar because Jo asserts in (33.a) that a certain entity ate the poisoned cake, but in (33.c) asks Ethel who that entity is. Ethel's response to Jo's initial statement does not directly contradict Jo's statement in (33.a) but she supplies information that when combined with certain unexpressed premisses show that it must be false. Suppose that Jo finds the plate holding the poisoned cake empty and so concludes that it has been eaten. In order to show that this is the case, he must, by the interpretation given to such a sentence, find some entity that ate the cake. In logical terms, he must find something that can be associated with the variable *z* that satisfies the open formula $\exists x\ [\forall y[cake'(y)\ \&\ poisoned'(y) \leftrightarrow x = y]\ \&\ eat'(x)(z)]$. He makes a first assumption that Chester is the culprit, but when Fiona makes her assertion in (33.b), he brings to bear three background premisses that show that his assumption must be false. The first is that if someone has eaten the poisoned cake then they are dead; the second is that if someone is playing with a ball then they are alive; and the third one derives from the meaning of the word *alive* to the effect that if something is alive then it is not dead. From the second of the implicational premisses and Ethel's assertion, we infer, via modus ponens, that Chester is alive. From this conclusion and the third implicational premiss, modus ponens again allows us to infer that Chester is not dead. However, from Jo's assumption and the first of the additional premisses, we conclude that Chester is dead. There is another deduction rule whose validity is intuitively obvious (and provable) that allows us to construct a conjunction from two true formulae (this is often called **conjunction introduction**). Since we have proved that *Chester is dead* is true and that *Chester is not dead* is also true, we can infer that *Chester is dead and not dead* is also true, but a formula of the form p & ~p can never be true. Hence, we are forced to conclude that the original assumption, that Chester ate the cake, must be false, since it was this that led to the contradiction. Hence, Jo can infer from Ethel's statement that Chester didn't eat the cake so he is none the wiser as to who did and responds with a question.

This somewhat convoluted chain of argument is spelled out in English in (34) and the logical form of the inference pattern is shown in (35). Again, in the latter, the rule that licenses each step is given on the right hand side. The sentence *Chester ate the poisoned cake* is represented by p, *Chester is dead* is represented by q, *Chester is playing with a ball* is represented by r and *Chester is alive* is represented by s.

(34) (Someone ate the poisoned cake.)
- a. Chester ate the poisoned cake.
- b. If Chester ate the poisoned cake, then he is dead.
- c. Chester is dead.
- d. If Chester is playing with a ball, then he is alive.
- e. Chester is playing with a ball.
- f. Chester is alive.
- g. If Chester is alive, then he is not dead.
- h. Chester is not dead.
- i. Chester is dead and he isn't dead.
- j. Chester didn't eat the poisoned cake.

(35) a. p. assumption
b. $p \rightarrow q$. premiss
c. q. deduction from a & b via modus ponens
d. $r \rightarrow s$. premiss
e. r. premiss
f. s. deduction from d & e via modus ponens
g. $s \rightarrow \sim q$. premiss
h. $\sim q$. deduction from f & g via modus ponens
i. $q \& \sim q$. deduction from c & f via conjunction introduction.
j. $\sim p$. reductio ad absurdum

The reason that reductio ad absurdum arguments work can be seen by considering the logical structure of the inference pattern in (35). From the assumption of p, i.e. that Chester ate the poisoned cake, we come step by step to the contradictory conclusion in (35.i), i.e. that Chester is and is not dead. As we have seen above, a conclusion is truth-conditionally related to its premisses by material implication. Hence, we can link the assumption p with the conclusion $q \& \sim q$ in a conditional expression as in (36.a). The creation of an implication combining an assumption with a conclusion reached from that assumption by standard deductive rules is a valid rule of logic, called **conditional introduction**. Because the consequent is a logical contradiction, i.e. it can never be true, the conditional, by the semantics of $\rightarrow$, can only be true if p is false. Hence, the generation of a contradiction from an assumption must lead to the conclusion that the original assumption was false (a version of modus tollens). This is clearly brought out in the conditional English sentence in (36.b) from which it is intuitively necessary to conclude that Chester did not eat the poisoned cake. Logically valid reductio ad absurdum arguments thus mirror certain human deductive processes and our theory thus provides an explanation of these in formal terms.

(36) a. $p \rightarrow (q \& \sim q)$.
b. If Chester ate the poisoned cake, then Chester is and is not dead.

There are many other logical deductions utilising the connectives that follow validly from the interpretation that has been given to them in earlier chapters. However, the examples given here should be sufficient for the reader to see how they work. Most inference patterns can be reduced to repeated steps involving the seven rules introduced above, repeated as (37.a) to (37.g). (37.h) introduces another valid inference pattern involving disjunction and negation which the reader can check is indeed valid by showing that $((p \vee q) \& \sim p) \rightarrow q$ is a tautology.

(37) a. **Conjunction elimination (CE)**: $p \& q \vdash p$.
b. **Conjunction introduction (CI)**: $p, q \vdash p \& q$.
c. **Disjunction elimination (DE1)**: $p \vee q, p \rightarrow r, q \rightarrow r \vdash r$.
d. **Disjunction elimination 2 (DE2)**: $p \vee q, \sim p \vdash q$.
e. **Modus ponens (MP)**: $p \rightarrow q, p \vdash q$.
f. **Modus tollens (MT)**: $p \rightarrow q, \sim q \vdash \sim p$.
g. **Conditional introduction (CndI)**: $(p \vdash q) \vdash p \rightarrow q$.
h. **Reductio ad absurdum (RA)**: $(p \vdash (q \& \sim q)) \vdash \sim p$
i. **Negation Elimination (NE)**: $\sim\sim p \vdash p$.

Exercise 7.2:
Using the rules of deduction in (37), show why the following deductions are valid. Some ancillary premisses derived from the meanings of some of the words may need to be invoked. Make sure that these are included in the structure of the inference pattern.

i. Either Fiona or Bertie poisoned the cake. If Fiona poisoned the cake, then she will have a bottle of poison in her bedroom and a book about unsolved murders on her bedside table. Therefore, if Bertie didn't poison the cake, then Fiona will have a book about unsolved murders on her bedside table.
ii. If Ethel lost the golf match, then she will be tired and unhappy and if she is unhappy, there will be no gin left. But there is some gin left, so Ethel won the golf match.
iii. If Jo likes Ethel, then he will give her a copy of *Jane Eyre* or a new bottle of gin. If he gives her *Jane Eyre*, she will not be pleased and think he's a creep, but if he gives her a new bottle of gin, she will be pleased but still think he's a creep. So if Ethel doesn't think Jo is a creep, then he doesn't like her!

7.2.2 *Reasoning with quantifiers*

At the end of Chapter 6, a number of entailments were mentioned that are associated with different types of quantifier in terms of (left or right) monotonicity and also a very general entailment, that of conservativity, which is believed by many formal semanticists to be applicable to all quantifiers in every natural language. There are, however, many other entailments from sentences containing noun phrases with different quantifiers. In this section, however, we consider only deduction rules that are associated with the classical quantifiers, $\forall$ and $\exists$.

Consider the inference pattern in (38) which is valid, according to (21), if, and only if, the formula in (39) is a tautology.

(38) a. Every student is intelligent.
b. Fiona is a student.
c. Therefore, Fiona is intelligent.

(39) $(\forall x\ [\text{student'}(x) \rightarrow \text{intelligent'}(x)]\ \&\ \text{student'}(\text{fiona'})) \rightarrow \text{intelligent'}(\text{fiona'})$.

Because the formula in (39) is in the form of a material implication, it is false only if the antecedent is true and the consequent is false. To prove that (39) is always true, therefore, it suffices to show that this cannot ever be the case, i.e. that it is impossible for every student to be intelligent and for Fiona to be a student but for Fiona not to be intelligent. It is relatively easy to show that this is the case by using a reductio ad absurdum argument, i.e. by showing that the assumption that (39) is false leads to a contradiction. Assuming, then, that (39) is false, the antecedent formula $\forall x$ *[student'(x)* $\rightarrow$ *intelligent'(x)] & student'(fiona')* must be true. Since this is a conjunction, both *student'(fiona')* and $\forall x$ *[student'(x)* $\rightarrow$ *intelligent'(x)]* must also be true by conjunction elimination. For the latter formula to be true according to the truth-conditions for universally quantified formulae discussed in the last chapter, the open formula *student'(x)* $\rightarrow$ *intelligent'(x)* must be satisfied by every possible assignment of a value to x. One of these assignments associates x with the entity denoted by *fiona'*, i.e. **WOMAN**$_2$, and satisfies *student'(x)* $\rightarrow$ *intelligent'(x)* only if it satisfies *intelligent'(x)* or fails to satisfy *student'(x)*. Since we have assumed that *student'(fiona')* is true, $g^{\text{WOMAN2/x}}$ does satisfy *student'(x)* and so must also satisfy *intelligent'(x)*. However, our original assumption that (39) is false requires *intelligent'(fiona')* also to be false, but this leads to the contradiction that Fiona is both intelligent and not intelligent. By the reductio ad absurdum argument, therefore, we are forced to conclude that the assumption that (39) is false must itself be false. In other words, (39) must always be true and so we have proved that (38.c) is validly derived from (38.a) and (38.b). This type of inference, shown schematically in (40), is called **universal instantiation**, because the premiss allows a variable bound by the universal quantifier to be instantiated as any constant, *a*.

(40) **Universal instantiation**: $\forall$x [P(x)] $\vdash$ P(a).

There is a parallel inference rule for existential formulae which is in a sense the inverse of (40). Instead of instantiating a variable as a constant, the rule of **existential generalisation** replaces a constant by a variable which is then bound by the existential quantifier. This rule is stated in (41) and exemplified in (42). The premiss in (42.a) licenses the conclusion in (42.b) because the formula in (42.c) is a tautology. Again, this can be shown by assuming that it is false and showing that this assumption leads to a contradiction. If (41.c) is false, then *intelligent'(fiona')* is true, and so the assignment of the entity denoted by *Fiona* to *x* satisfies *intelligent'(x)*. However, the falsity of (41.c) requires $\exists x$ *[intelligent'(x)]* to be false so that there must be no value assignment satisfying this open formula. We are therefore forced to conclude that there is and is not a value assignment that satisfies *intelligent'(x)* which in turn entails that (42.c) can never be false, thus proving that (41) is a valid deduction.

(41) **Existential generalisation**: P(a) $\vdash$ $\exists$x [P(x)].

(42) a. Fiona is intelligent.
b. Therefore, someone is intelligent.
c. intelligent'(fiona') $\rightarrow$ $\exists$x [intelligent'(x)].

As an example of how the two deduction rules in (40) and (41) interact with each other and with other rules of deduction, consider the inference pattern in (43). The steps taken to get to the conclusion (43.d) from the premisses in (43.a) to (43.c) are shown in (44). As before, the deduction rule used for each step appears on the right hand side together with the number of the line on which relevant formulae appear. In order to simplify matters, we assume that *gin* translates into an individual constant and that *alcoholic beverage* is translated as the predicate *a-b'*.

(43) a. Ethel likes gin.
b. Gin is an alcoholic beverage.
c. All alcoholic beverages are bad.
d. Therefore, Ethel likes something that is bad.

(44) a. $(like'(gin'))(ethel')$. premiss
b. $a\text{-}b'(gin')$. premiss
c. $\forall x\ [a\text{-}b'(x) \rightarrow bad'(x)]$. premiss
d. $a\text{-}b'(gin') \rightarrow bad'(gin')$. from c via universal instantiation
e. $bad'(gin')$. from b & d via modus ponens
f. $(like'(gin'))(ethel')\ \&\ bad'(gin')$.from a & e via conjunction introduction
g. $\exists x\ [(like'(x))(ethel')\ \&\ bad'(x)]$. from f via existential generalisation.

Further entailments and paraphrases involving the interaction of the existential and universal quantifiers with the negation operator were mentioned in Chapter 6. There it was noted that a sentence like (45.a) is a paraphrase of (45.b) and a sentence like (45.c) is a paraphrase of both (45.d) and (45.e). In addition, each of the sentences in (45.c), (45.d) and (45.e) all entail both (45.a) and (45.b).

(45) a. Someone didn't like Jo
b. Not everyone liked Jo.
c. Everyone didn't like Jo.
d. It is not the case that someone liked Jo.
e. No-one liked Jo.

According to the formal definitions of entailment and paraphrase in (9) and (14), we can show that these entailment and paraphrase relations in (45) hold by showing that their translations can be combined to form tautologies, using $\leftrightarrow$ and $\rightarrow$ respectively. The relevant formula to show the paraphrase relation between (45.a) and (45.b) is shown in (46.a), that between (45.c), (45.d) and (45.e) appears in (46.b) and the entailment relation is shown in (46.c).

(46) a. $\exists x\ [\sim(like'(jo'))(x)] \leftrightarrow \sim(\forall x\ [(like'(jo'))(x)])$.
b. $\forall x\ [\sim(like'(jo'))(x)] \leftrightarrow \sim(\exists x\ [(like'(jo'))(x)])$.
c. $\forall x\ [\sim(like'(jo'))(x)] \rightarrow \sim(\forall x\ [(like'(jo'))(x)])$.

Again the proof that the formulae in (46) are tautologies can be made by showing that they can never be false. As an example of the reasoning, let us take the formula in (46.a) and assume it is false. For this to be so, either $\exists x\ [\sim(like'(jo'))(x)]$ is true and $\sim(\forall x\ [(like'(jo'))(x)])$ is false, or vice versa. Let us take the first possibility. For $\exists x\ [\sim(like'(jo'))(x)]$ to be true, there must be some value assignment **g'** that satisfies $[\sim(like'(jo'))(x)]$. By the semantics of negation, such a value assignment fails to satisfy $[(like'(jo'))(x)]$. Hence, $\exists x\ [\sim(like'(jo'))(x)]$ is true only if there is some value assigned to x that makes $[(like'(jo'))(x)]$ false. For $\sim(\forall x\ [(like'(jo'))(x)])$ to be false, on the other hand, $\forall x\ [(like'(jo'))(x)]$ must be true, which is so only if every value assigned to x satisfies the propositional function $[(like'(jo'))(x)]$. However, we have already seen that for the left hand side of the equivalence to be true there must be at least one value of x that fails to satisfy this open formula, so that we arrive at a contradiction: that there is and is not some value assignment that falsifies $[(like'(jo'))(x)]$, which shows that our first assumption is false.

Because there are two possibilities that guarantee the falsity of the equivalence in (46.a), we have not yet shown that it can never be false. To complete the proof, we must show that the reverse situation, where $\exists x$ *[~(like'(jo'))(x)]* is false and ~($\forall x$ *[(like'(jo'))(x)])* is true, also cannot occur. For the latter formula to be true, it must not be the case that every value assigned to x satisfies *(like'(jo'))(x)*, i.e. that there is some value assignment that makes this propositional function false. For $\exists x$ *[~(like'(jo'))(x)]* to be false, however, it must be the case that no value assigned to x satisfies *(like'(jo'))(x)*. Again we arrive at the same contradiction as before: that there is some value for x that does and does not satisfy the propositional function. Hence, we have shown that neither of the component formulae in (46.a) can be true while the other is false and so have confirmed the validity of the paraphrase.

Exercise 7.3:
Show that the formulae in (46.b) and (46.c) are tautologies by showing that the assumption that they are false leads to a contradiction.

There is one final important point that needs to be made here with respect to the entailments of quantified formulae. This concerns the difference between the universal and existential quantifiers in terms of the existence in a model of entities that satisfy the propositional functions that they combine with. As required by the truth-conditions for $\exists$ given in Chapter 6, existentially quantified formulae that are true entail the existence in a model of at least one entity that has the property described, and thus that something actually exists in the model. For example, if the formula translating *A lecturer screamed* is true with respect to some model, then so are those translating *Some entity screamed*, *There was a lecturer* and *Some entity existed*; i.e. given the truth of (47.a) the formulae in (47.b) to (47.d) are also true.

(47) a. $\exists$x [lecturer'(x) & scream'(x)].
b. $\exists$x [scream'(x)].
c. $\exists$x [lecturer'(x)].
d. $\exists$x [exist'(x)].

The truth of (47.d) follows under the assumption that the extension of the predicate *exist'* is always the set of all entities that exist in the model, i.e. **A**. If there is some entity that satisfies any of (47.a) to (47.c), then this must be a member of **A** and so must exist. The truth of (47.b) and (47.c), on the other hand, follows from the truth of (47.a) by a generalised version of the rule of conjunction elimination given above. That this inference is valid is shown in (48) which uses a form of inference sometimes called **existential elimination**. Because (48.a) is true (by assumption), there must be some value assignment, **g**, that satisfies *lecturer'(x) & scream'(x)* This allows us to infer the truth of a formula where x is replaced by an individual constant that denotes whatever entity is assigned to x by **g**. We do not necessarily know the identity of this individual, but just that there is some individual that screamed. Thus, in (48.b) x is replaced by an arbitrary individual constant, symbolised as *c*, but not by an actual individual constant like *jo'* or *bertie'*. From this step, the rest of the deduction follows straightforwardly. Note that care must be taken in using this type of deduction that inferences are not made about specific individuals. The extension of the arbitrary constant *c* is not known, and so inferences with respect to particular individuals are not licensed. Hence, we are not permitted to infer the truth of, say, *Fiona screamed* from *A lecturer screamed*, only that someone or other screamed.

(48) a. ∃x [lecturer'(x) & scream'(x)].
b. lecturer'(c) & scream'(c). existential elimination
c. lecturer'(c). conjunction elimination from b
d. ∃x [lecturer'(x)]. existential generalisation from c

No existential commitment follows from the truth of a universally quantified formula, however. It is not possible to infer from the truth of the formula translating a sentence like *Every lecturer screams* either that something screams or that something is a lecturer or indeed that anything exists at all. Thus, the truth of (49.a) does not guarantee those of (49.b) to (49.d).

(49) a. ∀x [lecturer'(x) → scream'(x)].
b. ∃x [lecturer'(x)].
c. ∃x [scream'(x)].
d. ∃x [exist'(x)].

The reason that these inferences cannot be made has to do with the implicational nature of (49.a). Since an implication is true whenever its antecedent is false, the formula in (49.a) is true if no value for x satisfies *lecturer'(x)*, i.e. if there is nothing in the extension of *lecturer'* in some model. Hence, we cannot infer (49.b), as it cannot be guaranteed that there are any entities in the extension of *lecturer'*. Nor can we infer (49.c), as (49.a) is true if both (49.c) and (49.b) are false, i.e. if there are no lecturers and no screamers in the model. Furthermore, since there may be no entity that satisfies *lecturer'(x)* or *scream'(x)*, we cannot even infer that any entities exist at all and so (49.d) also does not follow from the truth of (49.a). This has the consequence that all the sentences in (50) express true propositions in our world (in 1991).

(50) a. Every blue sheep lives in the Highlands.
b. All pink elephants have green trunks.
c. Every Green Party member of the British parliament supports nuclear power.

Although this may seem peculiar, it presents no very serious problems for a theory that allows pragmatics to explain why sentences like (50.a) and (50.b) are unlikely to be uttered as serious assertions outside of stories and jokes. More importantly, we can use the lack of existential commitment in universally quantified formulae to make intuitively valid inferences. Consider, for example, a situation in which the sentence in (50.c) is uttered to someone in 1992 who has the background knowledge that Green Party politicians do not support nuclear power. Assuming the rough translations of (50.c) and the background knowledge as in (51.a) and (51.b), where *gp'* stands for the translation of *is a member of the Green Party*, *mp'* that of *is a member of the British parliament* and *s'* of *supports nuclear power*, the hearer can make the inference in (51.c), that Green Party members of the British parliament do and do not support nuclear power. Since the latter formula is contradictory (always false whatever value is assigned to x), the hearer applies modus tollens to the implication in (51.a) to derive (51.d), the conclusion that there are currently no Green members of parliament. Hence, even the apparently bizarre lack of existential commitment of universally quantified formulae helps to explain certain intuitively valid inferences.

(51) a. $\forall x\ [(gp'(x)\ \&\ mp'(x)) \rightarrow s'(x)]$. premiss
b. $\forall x\ [gp'(x) \rightarrow \sim(s'(x))]$. premiss
c. $\forall x\ [(gp'(x)\ \&\ mp'(x)) \rightarrow (s'(x)\ \&\ \sim s'(x))]$. conjunction introduction
d. $\forall x\ [\sim(gp'(x)\ \&\ mp'(x))]$. modus tollens

7.3 Lexical meaning

The inferences discussed in Section 7.2 are explained with reference to the interpretations given to logical operators, but there are valid inferences that are not licensed by the model theory. For example, from the truth of (52.a) one can infer the truth of the propositions expressed by each of the sentences in (52.b) to (52.d). Yet there is nothing in the translations (and interpretations) of these sentences (shown in (53)) that directly guarantees that these inferences hold in any model.

(52) a. Chester was killed by the poisoned cake.
b. Chester is dead.
c. Chester is not alive.
d. The poisoned cake caused Chester's death.

(53) a. $\exists x\ [\forall y[(cake'(y)\ \&\ poisoned'(y)) \leftrightarrow x = y]\ \&\ (kill'(chester'))(x)]$.
b. $dead'(chester')$.
c. $\sim(alive'(chester'))$.
d. $\exists x\ [\forall y\ [(cake'(y)\ \&\ poisoned'(y)) \leftrightarrow x = y]\ \&\ (cause'(die'(chester')))(x)]$.

The inferences in (52) all depend, of course, on words in the sentences, not on the logical structure of the sentences themselves. It is thus a property of the particular English word *kill* that its extension relates to the extension of the English phrase *cause to die* or that *dead* is the complementary of *alive*. Such relationships are not purely logical in the way that, for example, *no* is logically related to *not all*. There is nothing in the interpretation of the predicate *kill'* itself that requires all those things that are killed to be in the extension of the predicate *dead'* in the same model, or that requires nothing that is dead to be in the extension of the predicate *alive'*. Moreover, as we saw in (5) above, inferences derived from lexical meaning are weaker than those derived from the interpretations of logical operators, since the former can be suppressed to give rise to non-literal interpretations, while the latter cannot without incoherence.

Content words are much more likely to undergo semantic change over time than grammatical words. For example, the word *sely* in Middle English which gives us *silly* in Modern English did not mean *foolish* or *feeble minded*, but rather *pitiable* or *deserving of compassion*, a meaning still retained in parts of Scotland. The ancestor of the Modern English word *girl* used to denote any human youth, but now, of course, this has been restricted to female humans. Examples such as these are commonplace in all languages whose earlier history is known.

Moreover, it is a commonplace observation that the vocabularies of different natural languages divide the world in different ways. This means that the inferences that can be derived from particular words in one language may be different from those derived from a near equivalent in another. For example, the Modern German word *fahren* implies motion by conveyance other than by foot, which is not the case for the nearest equivalent in Modern English, i.e. the verb *go*. On the other hand, the nearest equivalent to the English word *granddaughter* in Lakhota, an American Indian language, is *thakóža* which has no implication of female gender and whose translation into English would be *grandchild*. Thus, the German sentence in (54.a) implies that in (54.b) while their English translations are not so related. On the other hand, the English sentence in (54.c) implies that in (54.d) while the Lakhota sentence in (54.e) has no such implication.

(54) a. Gestern ist Jo zum Kino gefahren.
yesterday is Jo to-the cinema gone
'Jo went to the cinema yesterday.'
b. Jo ist zum Kino zu Fuss nicht gegangen.
Jo is to-the cinema on foot not gone
'Jo did not go to the cinema on foot.'
c. My granddaughter is ill.
d. A female is ill.
e. mithakóža khuže.
my-grandchild is-sick
'My grandchild is sick.'

Inferences derived from lexical meaning are thus here interpreted as language particular and subject to semantic change (although there are those who would not adopt this position). The model-theoretic interpretation of logical expressions, however, captures general aspects of the meaning of grammatical/logical expressions which are, by hypothesis, unchanging and constant across all natural languages all of which have words, morphemes or other ways of indicating these fundamental semantic concepts. There appears thus to be a considerable difference between the meaning relations that result from the meaning of content words and those that result from the interpretation of the logical operators. The latter have an invariant interpretation that guides the interpretation of the whole system and thus have their meaning encoded within the model theory itself. Lexical meaning, on the other hand, being language particular, subject to change and weaker than logical meaning, must be specified in some other way, outside the model theory.

Lexical implications of the sort noted above result from the **sense** of a lexeme rather than its **denotation**. The denotation of a lexeme is its relation to things external to the linguistic system. In the theory presented in earlier chapters, it is this aspect of lexical meaning that is paramount and captured by associating each lexeme with the entity, set of entities, etc., of which it is correct to predicate the lexeme. This is the **extension** of the lexeme, which has already been contrasted with its **intension** and which will be discussed further in Chapters 9 and 10. The sense of a lexeme, on the other hand, has a number of different interpretations within the philosophical and linguistic literature on linguistic meaning. Some philosophers, like Montague following Frege and Carnap, interpret sense in the way that intension will be interpreted in later chapters, as a logical function that determines the extension of an expression (basic or derived) in different situations (see Chapters 9 and 10). Many linguists, on the other hand, interpret sense in a relational way as concerned only with the set of meaning relations lexemes bear to other lexemes (or expressions) within a particular language. There seems some benefit in maintaining a distinction between these two notions (see Chapter 10) and so it is the latter interpretation of sense that is used here. In other words, the notion of sense is to be defined in terms of the different sorts of **sense relations** that hold between lexemes in a language.

Many different types of sense relations have been recognised between the words and expressions in a language, some of which are central to the linguist's notion of sense. One important sense relation is that of **hyponymy** where the sense of one lexeme, the **hyponym,** is included in that of another, the **superordinate**, and the extension of the latter includes that of the former (e.g. *rose* and *flower*). The relation of **synonymy** is defined where two lexemes have the same sense and extension, and so may be defined as **mutually hyponymous**. Total synonymy is rare (an example may be *quicksilver* and *mercury*, although the former term is now archaic), but partial synonymy occurs relatively frequently where two lexemes have almost the same sense and almost the same extension (e.g. *pullover* and *jumper* or *sweater* in British English). On the other hand, two lexemes are described as **opposites** if their extensions are required to be distinct and their senses are contradictory with respect to each other. There are a number of specific types of opposites. **Antonymy** (in the restricted sense of this term) covers **gradable opposites** like *hot/cold*. Gradable antonyms form instances of **contraries** (see below) and implicitly or explicitly invoke a field over which the grading takes place, i.e. a standard of comparison. So, for example, the adjective *tall* changes its extension according to the properties of the entities of which it is predicated (e.g. *tall gerbil* vs. *tall giraffe*). **Complementaries** (or **binary antonyms**) are all **non-gradable** opposites which, from the extensional point of view, divide the universe of discourse into two disjoint sets (e.g. *dead* vs. *alive* and *abstract* vs. *concrete*). The last opposite relation is that of the **contraries** which involve the general opposition sense relation but without the negation of one of the lexemes implying the truth of the other (thus excluding contradictories). We can use this term to refer to non-binary contrasts found among **co-hyponyms** like *peony, rose, tulip*, etc or **ranks** (e.g. *Monday, Tuesday, Wednesday*, etc.).

Finally, there are three more general sense relations that involve more complex properties of the arguments of predicates. The first is that of the **selectional restrictions** that predicates impose on their arguments. For example, the verb *kick* requires an animate (and legged) subject and a concrete direct object while the verb *solve* requires an animate and usually human subject and an abstract object (e.g. *The child solved the problem* versus ?*The rock solved the problem* versus ?*The student solved the chair*). Next, we have **converses** which are **relational terms** where the relation denoted by one lexeme is reversed to give the relation denoted by another (and vice versa). These often get called antonyms but they do not conform to the general definition given above, since there need not be an oppositeness relation involved. For example, *sell* is the converse of *buy*, but *Bertie bought some gin from Ethel* does not imply that *Bertie didn't sell some gin to Ethel*, though it does imply that *Ethel sold some gin to Bertie*. Finally for our purposes, the meaning of lexemes may be related by **decomposition** to the meanings of expressions involving fundamental notions like causality (e.g. if *x kills y* then *x causes y to die*) or change of state (e.g. *soften* and *cause to become soft*).

To define the sense of a word, it is sufficient to define the sense relations that it bears to other expressions in the language, i.e. identifying its homonyms, hyponyms, superordinates and opposites as well as any other selectional or decompositional properties it may have. The important question is thus how to capture the sense relations within truth-conditional semantics. The theory of semantics that has been adopted here gives primacy to sentence meaning over lexical meaning, or, more precisely, to the interpretation of the formulae that translate sentences rather than to the interpretation of constants. Until now, the semantic contribution of words has been restricted to the contribution they make to the truth-conditions of every sentence in which they can appear. Since content lexemes are translated (and interpreted) as constants in the logical representation of a sentence, this makes their extension their primary contribution to the meaning of a formula. Given that, in truth-conditional semantics, the central aspect of the meaning of an expression is taken to be its denotation, one may think of sense relations as specifying relations between the extensions of different lexemes and expressions. For example, *tulip* and *rose* are both hyponyms of *flower* which means that every tulip and every rose is a flower or, more formally, that the extensions of the predicates *tulip'* and *rose'* are subsets of the extension of *flower'*. Furthermore, *rose* and *tulip* are opposites (incompatible co-hyponyms) and so their extensions are disjoint. Thus, the sense of a lexeme may be defined as the constraints it imposes on the extensions of other expressions with respect to its own extension. The meaning of a lexeme in truth-conditional semantics can thus be defined in terms of both its extension and its sense relations, as in (55).

(55) **Lexical meaning**: The meaning of a lexeme is the contribution it makes to the truth or falsity of the proposition expressed by any sentence in which it can appear together with the constraints it imposes on the extensions of other expressions in those sentences.

Defining sense relations in terms of constraints on the denotations of expressions allows them to be given a representation in L_Q and thus a transparent interpretation within the theory. It is common within lexical semantics to identify the sense relations of particular lexemes by inserting a lexeme into a particular sentence frame and seeing whether the sentence so formed appears to be tautologous. For example, to test for hyponymy, the hyponymous lexeme is substituted for X and its superordinate for Y in the sentence frame *Every X is a Y*. Thus, the tautologous feel of *Every tulip is a flower* indicates the hyponymy between *tulip* and *flower* whereas the sentence *No tulip is a rose* indicates the incompatibility between *tulip* and *rose* and so on. Such sentences have a simple and direct translation into formulae in L_Q as in (56) where (56.a) requires the set of all tulips to be a subset of the set of all flowers and (56.b) requires the set of tulips to have a null intersection with the set of roses.

(56) a. $\forall x\ [\text{tulip}'(x) \rightarrow \text{flower}'(x)]$.
b. $\forall x\ [\text{tulip}'(x) \rightarrow \sim\text{rose}'(x)]$.

Formulae like those in (56) are called **meaning postulates** and have the form of statements in the logical metalanguage that specifically relate formulae containing different logical constants which translate particular lexemes and other expressions. Meaning postulates all have the form of an implication where the antecedent consists of a formula constructed from a single constant whose argument places are bound by universal quantifiers. The consequent of the implicational statement is a more or less complex formula consisting of related constants at least one of whose argument places contains a bound variable shared with the antecedent and whose other argument places are either existentially or universally bound. For example, the meaning postulates in (57) capture the relations between the sentences in (52). (57.a) relates the extension of *kill'* to that of *cause to die*; (57.b) allows the inference from *Someone caused something to occur* to the fact that something did occur; (57.c) relates dying and becoming dead and (57.d) relates the extensions of *dead* and *alive*. The steps used to make the inferences in (52) using these meaning postulates are shown in (58). The latter inference pattern assumes appropriate interpretations for tense, aspect and the (actually problematic) expressions *become'* and *cause'*. Indeed, many decompositional meaning postulates like those in (57.a) to (57.c) need to make reference to tense, aspect and modality, matters that are the topics of the final chapters of the book.

(57) a. $\forall x\, [\forall y\, [\text{kill'}(y)(x) \rightarrow (\text{cause'}(\text{die'}(y)))(x)]]$.
b. $\forall P\, [\forall x\, [\forall y\, [(\text{cause'}(P(x)))(y) \rightarrow P(x)]]]$.
c. $\forall x\, [\text{die'}(x) \rightarrow \text{become'}(\text{dead'}(x))]$.
d. $\forall x\, [\text{dead'}(x) \rightarrow {\sim}\text{alive'}(x)]$.

(58) a. $\exists x\, [\forall y\, [(\text{cake'}(y)\ \&\ \text{poisoned'}(y)) \leftrightarrow x = y]\ \&\ (\text{kill'}(\text{chester'}))(x)]$.
b. $\exists x\, [(\text{kill'}(\text{chester'}))(x)]$. conjunction elimination
c. $\exists x\, [(\text{cause'}(\text{die'}(\text{chester'})))(x)]$. modus ponens from b & (57.a)
d. $\text{die'}(\text{chester'})$. modus ponens from c & (57.b)
e. $\text{become'}(\text{dead'}(\text{chester'}))$. modus ponens from d & (57.c)
f. $\text{become'}({\sim}\text{alive'}(\text{chester'}))$. modus ponens from e & (57.d)

Using meaning postulates, we can define the sense relations in terms of how they relate the extensional denotations of lexemes and other expressions in the language. Hyponymy, for example, is defined between two lexemes if there is a meaning postulate connecting the constants that they translate into which has the structure specified in (59.a), i.e. as an implicational statement with the argument place universally quantified, as the examples in (59.b) to (59.d) show.

(59) a. **Hyponymy**: X is a hyponym of Y iff there is a meaning postulate relating X' and Y' of the form: $\forall x\, [X'(x) \rightarrow Y'(x)]$ (the extension of X is a subset of that of Y).
b. $\forall x\, [\text{dog'}(x) \rightarrow \text{mammal'}(x)]$.
c. $\forall x\, [\text{mammal'}(x) \rightarrow \text{animal'}(x)]$.
d. $\forall x\, [\text{terrier'}(x) \rightarrow \text{dog'}(x)]$.

Because of the fact that two formulae $p \rightarrow q$ and $q \rightarrow r$ logically entail $p \rightarrow r$ (as readers can check for themselves), it follows that any sense relations defined for the consequent are also defined for the antecedent. We can, therefore, construct further meaning postulates for hyponyms from meaning postulates associated with their superordinates like those in (60) which are derived from those in (59). If we then define the sense of a lexeme to be the set of meaning postulates that have the constant translating the lexeme in the antecedent of the implicational formula, the sense of a superordinate is contained in the sense of the hyponym. Notice also that by this definition, it turns out that a hyponym, X, with superordinate, Y, is also a hyponym of all superordinates of Y.

(60) a. $\forall x$ [dog'(x) $\rightarrow$ animal'(x)].
b. $\forall x$ [terrier'(x) $\rightarrow$ mammal'(x)].
c. $\forall x$ [terrier'(x) $\rightarrow$ animal'(x)].

Synonymy, as we have seen, is defined where two lexemes are mutually hyponymous, in other words where their extensions (and senses) are required to be identical, as shown in (61).

(61) a. **Synonymy**: X is a synonym of Y iff there is a meaning postulate relating X' and Y' of the form: $\forall x$ [X'(x) $\leftrightarrow$ Y'(x)] (X and Y have identical extensions).
b. $\forall x$ [pullover'(x) $\leftrightarrow$ sweater'(x)].

Unfortunately this definition does not allow for partial synonymy, since extensions in the theory are discrete, i.e. there are no fuzzy edges where, for example, there may be things that are almost pullovers but that are not sweaters. Since, as we have noted, full synonymy is rarely, if ever, attested, this makes the definition in (61) less useful than it might be. It is possible that a pragmatic explanation may be found for the interpretation of synonymy as partial rather than full, but in the meantime, the effect of partial synonymy may be incorporated by replacing the universal quantifier in (61) by the quantifier *most*, so that we interpret synonymy as *Most X are Y* and *Most Y are X*.

The definition of the general property of oppositeness has the form of the meaning postulate in (56.b). Because p $\rightarrow$ ~q has the same truth-conditions as q $\rightarrow$ ~p through modus tollens, we can infer from meaning postulates like that in (62.b) that if the positive counterpart of the consequent is true then the antecedent cannot be. Hence, from (62.b) we can infer a meaning postulate to the effect that no dogs are cats, i.e. $\forall x$ *[dog'(x) $\rightarrow$ ~cat'(x)].*

(62) a. **Opposites**: X is an opposite of Y iff there is a meaning postulate relating X' and Y' of the form: $\forall x$ [X'(x) $\rightarrow$ ~Y'(x)] (the extension of X is distinct from that of Y).
b. $\forall x$ [cat'(x) $\rightarrow$ ~dog'(x)].

All opposites must conform to the general definition in (62.a) but the different types may distinguished by imposing further restrictions. For example, complementaries are opposites where the negation of one also implies the positive of the other, as defined and exemplified in (63).

(63) a. **Complementaries**: X is the complementary of Y iff there is a meaning postulate relating X' and Y' of the form:
$\forall x$ [(X'(x) $\rightarrow$ ~Y'(x)) & (~X'(x) $\rightarrow$ Y'(x))] (the extensions of X and Y are distinct and the complement of the extension of X is equal to the extension of Y).
b. $\forall x$ [~concrete'(x) $\rightarrow$ abstract'(x)].
c. $\forall x$ [~alive'(x) $\rightarrow$ dead'(x)].

Again, we can infer that if X is the complementary of Y then Y is the complementary of X. This follows from (63.a) by modus tollens, since $\sim Y'(x)$ implies $\sim\sim X'(x)$, i.e. $X'(x)$. This gives rise to the postulates in (64) paralleling those in (63.b) and (63.c).

(64) a. $\forall x\, [\sim abstract'(x) \rightarrow concrete'(x)]$.
b. $\forall x\, [\sim dead'(x) \rightarrow alive'(x)]$.

Antonyms are opposites restricted to some particular domain. For example, a big mouse is not small for a mouse although it may be small for an elephant. Letting *P* stand for some property, like being a mouse or an elephant, we can define antonymy as in (65). Strictly speaking such meaning postulates go beyond the extensional semantics so far developed, but they can be modelled in the semantic theory put forward in Chapter 10 and they are included here for the sake of completeness. The intended interpretation of *(big'(P))(x)* is that *x is big for a P* or *x is a big P*, whatever constant P may be. (The meaning postulate in (65.c) results from (65.b) by modus tollens.)

(65) a. **Antonyms**: X and Y are antonyms iff there is a meaning postulate relating X' and Y' of the form: $\forall x\, [\forall P\, [(X'(P))(x) \rightarrow \sim(Y'(P))(x)]]$ (the extensions of X and Y are distinct for some given domain).
b. $\forall x\, [\forall P\, [(big'(P))(x) \rightarrow \sim(small'(P))(x)]]$.
c. $\forall x\, [\forall P\, [(small'(P))(x) \rightarrow \sim(big'(P))(x)]]$.

The definition of converses in (66.a) requires a schematic meaning postulate that allows for predicates with different valencies. Many converses are also opposites as illustrated in (67).

(66) a. **Converses**: X is the converse of Y iff there is a meaning postulate relating X' and Y' of the form: $\forall x ... \forall y\, [X'(y)...(x) \rightarrow Y'(x)...(y)]$ (wherever $<e_1,e_2,...,e_n>$ is in the extension of X, $<e_n,e_{n-1},...,e_1>$ is in the extension of Y).
b. $\forall x\, [\forall y\, [\forall z\, [(buy'(x)(y))(z) \rightarrow (sell'(z)(y))(x)]]]$.
c. $\forall x\, [\forall y\, [\forall z\, [(sell'(x)(y))(z) \rightarrow (buy'(z)(y))(x)]]]$.

(67) a. $\forall x\, [\forall y\, [(left\_of'(x))(y) \rightarrow (right\_of'(y))(x)]]$
b. $\forall x\, [\forall y\, [(left\_of'(x))(y) \rightarrow \sim(right\_of'(x))(y)]]$
c. $\forall x\, [\forall y\, [(daughter'(x))(y) \rightarrow (parent'(y))(x)]]$
d. $\forall x\, [\forall y\, [(daughter'(x))(y) \rightarrow \sim(parent'(x))(y)]]$

Selectional restrictions and decomposition have similar definitions involving the specification of further required properties of arguments. The latter differs in containing information about causation, change of state and possibly other cognitively important properties. An example of a simple selectional restrictions appears in (68.b) and (68.c) and (68.d) show the decompositional properties of the verb *melt*, where *melt"* is the translation of the transitive verb and *melt'* is that of the intransitive .

(68) a. **Selectional restrictions/decomposition**: A lexeme X imposes some condition on the extension of one of its arguments.
b. $\forall x\, [sing'(x) \rightarrow \sim abstract'(x)]$.
c. $\forall x\, [\forall y\, [(melt''(y))(x) \rightarrow [(cause'(melt'(y)))(x)]]$.
d. $\forall x\, [melt'(x) \rightarrow become'(\sim solid'(x))]$.

Exercise 7.4:
Write a set of meaning postulates that specify the sense relations that hold between the sets of words that follow. Are there other sense relations that involve these words and are all the sense relations noted as strong (or necessary) as each other?

i. run, move, walk, saunter, stroll.
ii. abstract, concrete, human, animate, inanimate, liquid, solid, think, flow, interpret, crumble.
iii. horse, mare, filly, foal, offspring, child, mature, adult, human, animal, mammal.

Meaning postulates are intended to impose constraints on the extensions of certain expressions, and the sense relations defined above hold only where there is such a constraint. It is not sufficient to define one lexeme α as the opposite of another, β, merely because within some model $\forall x\, [\alpha'(x) \rightarrow \sim\beta'(x)]$ happens to be true. For example, it is not the case that *student* is the opposite of *dog*, merely because in our formal models no student is a dog (and vice versa). Nor is it the case that *genius* and *lecturer* are synonyms merely because $\forall x\, [genius'(x) \leftrightarrow lecturer'(x)]$ happens to be true in M_2. Rather, these lexemes are unrelated in terms of sense, because there are no meaning postulates connecting them. The sense of a lexeme is defined exclusively by the set of meaning postulates that specify the relationship of its extension with those of other expressions within the language. This remains the case whatever the truth of particular postulates within a particular model, but this brings up the problem of the status of the meaning postulates with respect to different models or states of affairs and to the theory as a whole.

There has been a tendency within the logical tradition, including Montague, to interpret meaning postulates as constraints on admissible models. In other words, meaning postulates restrict the set of all possible models (the denotation assignment functions) which can be used to interpret a language with respect to the situation being represented. Only those models are admissible in which the meaning postulates associated with the set of constants are true. Under this interpretation, meaning postulates are raised to the status of logical (or **analytic**) truths, since they are true of all situations that can be described in some language. This means that inferences derived from these have the same status as deductive inferences derived from the interpretation of logical operators. As we have already seen, however, it is not always the case that inferences derived from lexical meaning behave in the same way. It is possible to suppress inferences derived from lexical meaning in a way that is not possible with deductive inferences. When this happens, it gives rise either to a figurative interpretation or to a generalisation of the applicability of a term. An example of the latter appears in (69). The sentence in (69.a) is generally supposed to capture the meaning of the noun *bachelor*, but the term may be applied to a woman, as in (69.b), without causing the reader any difficulty in interpretation. This is so, despite the fact that it seems to be equivalent to the less acceptable sentence in (69.c), which states directly that the entity denoted by the subject noun phrase is both a woman and a man (cf. the formula in (69.e)). The sentence in (69.b) would, in normal circumstances, be interpreted as stating that the relevant woman is unmarried, i.e. the maleness of bachelorhood is suppressed given the stated information that the subject is a woman (and the complementary relation between *man* and *woman* with respect to humans). The interpretation of (69.c), however, is less clear than this and could be interpreted in a number of ways: that the person referred to behaves socially like an unmarried man, that the person is a transvestite (i.e. looks like a woman) or that the person is a transsexual (i.e. is genetically male). The interpretation of the logically contradictory sentence in (69.d), on the other hand, which is derived from (69.c) through the sense of *man*, is even less informative than the latter. It requires much more contextual information for its interpretation and sounds much more bizarre in isolation than (69.c) and has a very different status from (69.b). This is not explicable if meaning postulates have the status of analytic truths, since all three example sentences would be true in all the same circumstances and so convey the same information.

(69) a. All bachelors are unmarried men.
b. That woman is a bachelor.
c. ?That woman is an unmarried man.
d. *That woman is not a woman and is unmarried.
e. $\exists y$ [woman'(y) & $\sim\exists x$ [(marry'(x))(y) & man'(y)]].

Instead of taking meaning postulates to be necessary conditions on models, we can interpret them as independent statements (perhaps located in the lexicon) that provide information about normal circumstances. Inferences made from them then are assumed to hold where there is no information to the contrary. So, for example, the statement in (69.a) about *bachelor* is assumed to be generally, rather than universally, true. It holds unless there is a stronger reason to believe that part of the information that can be deduced from the postulate cannot be true, because if it did it would lead to a logical contradiction. In such a situation, only part of the information encoded in the meaning postulate is inferred. It is as if the implicational connective in formal meaning postulates were not interpreted exactly as $\rightarrow$ but as a similar connective, call it $\downarrow$, for which the inference pattern structure in (70) is valid. Applying this inference pattern to (69), we infer that Fiona is unmarried and the information derived from (69.a) as to her being a man is dropped, because it is explicitly stated that she is a woman.

(70) a.	p $\downarrow$ (q & r).	MP
b.	p.	premiss
c.	~r.	premiss
d.	q.	conclusion

The formal interpretation of a connective like $\downarrow$ will not be further pursued as there is much more to the retrieval of lexical inferences than just setting up meaning postulates containing such an implicational connective. In particular, pragmatics (mainly in the guise of **cognitive relevance**) must come into play in examples like (69) to explain why, for example, it is a bachelor's maleness that is suppressed rather than a woman's non-maleness (i.e. it is the inference derived from *bachelor* that is altered, not that derived from *woman*). Furthermore, the notion of sense put forward here allows a distinction to be made between sentences and situations in terms of how few or how many lexical inferences need to be suppressed to avoid contradiction, but this requires more semantic machinery than is yet available. (But see Chapters 9 and 10 for some further discussion of the matter.) For these reasons, a proper formalisation of the way meaning postulates work will not be spelled out here. It is unfortunate that while lexical semantics has, at least until very recently, been the primary focus of linguistic semantics, a great deal of work remains to be done on this topic within logical semantics. It does, however, seem a reasonable hypothesis that central aspects of lexical meaning can be analysed in terms of the definition of sense relations as constraints on the denotations of expressions within a particular language. It also seems reasonable that such constraints cannot be stated as part of the model theory (as conditions on admissible models), if their comparative weakness with respect to the logical operators is to be captured. Thus, however the formal procedure for making inferences from meaning postulates is to be set up, these two points must be incorporated.

7.4 Non-truth-conditional aspects of the connectives

In this last section, we take a look at some aspects of the meaning of sentences containing the conjunctions *and*, *or* and *if...then* that are not explained by the truth-conditional interpretation of their logical counterparts, &, $\vee$ and $\rightarrow$. This discussion is by no means exhaustive and there are aspects of the meanings of the connectives that are not discussed. The point of this section, however, is to indicate how inference patterns can be constructed to account for certain aspects of meaning not determined by truth-conditional interpretation by considering language use. The success of this enterprise provides support for the hypothesis that truth-conditional semantics can provide a sufficient basis for a general theory of meaning, as long as it is supplemented by a rich enough theory of pragmatics.

7.4.1 And

First, let us look at the semantics of sentences containing *and*. As discussed in Chapter 3, the truth-conditions of a formula containing the connective & are met if, and only if, both conjunct formulae are true. This holds irrespective of the order in which the conjunct formulae appear, because & is a commutative operator, as we have already seen. The sentence in (71.a) is thus truth-conditionally equivalent to that in (71.b).

(71) a. The skier fell over and broke her ankle.
     b. The skier broke her ankle and fell over.

Most speakers of English, however, would interpret an utterance of (71.a) as meaning something different from an utterance of (71.b). This is because there is a tendency to assume that conjuncts are causally or temporally related, if the events described are such that they can be so related under normal assumptions. In (71.a), for example, the sentence *The skier fell over* comes before *(she) broke her ankle* and so the most likely interpretation is that the falling preceded, and possibly caused, the breaking of the ankle. This temporal/causal relation is reversed in (71.b) where the order of the constituent clauses are reversed: the skier's breaking her leg precedes, and possibly causes, her falling over. This difference between (71.a) and (71.b) could be taken as an indication of the incorrectness of the semantic interpretation provided for the conjunction *and* by the truth table for &. To establish whether or not this is so, we have to ask ourselves a few questions: is the temporal/causal relation between two conjoined clauses found between clauses in other contexts? If it is, can a unified treatment of the two constructions be proposed without invoking the semantics of the conjunction? We must also ask whether the causal/temporal implication always holds of conjoined clauses and finally whether it is possible for two conjoined clauses to translate into a true formula if the truth-conditions provided for *and* are not met.

The answer to the first question is quite straightforward: exactly the same temporal/causal effect is found when two or more sentences are strung together in a text without any overt co-ordinating morpheme. Thus, the simple text in (72.a) appears to be more coherent than that in (72.b) where the order of the sentences is changed, despite the fact that they could both be said to describe the same situation.

(72) a. Fiona gave the cake to Bertie. Bertie gave the cake to the dog. The dog ate the cake. The dog died. Bertie laughed.

b. Bertie laughed. The dog died. Fiona gave the cake to Bertie. The dog ate the cake. Bertie gave the cake to the dog.

The peculiarity of the text in (72.b) may be, at least in part, ascribed to the fact that texts of this sort are taken to describe a series of events occurring in the order in which the sentences appear. Imposing such a temporal order on (72.b), however, makes it difficult to construct a sensible causal chain out of the events and so it appears incoherent. Temporal and causal order is thus imposed on a series of non-conjoined sentences forming a text as well as on conjoined sentences. This strongly suggests that this aspect of the meaning of conjunctions has nothing to do with the meaning of the word *and* but with the way texts are constructed. This hypothesis is confirmed by the fact that situations can be presented (and often are, in practice) with later events being described before earlier ones.

Furthermore, the causal/temporal implications of *and* are not always in evidence. For example, sentences like *The skier broke her ankle and the instructor cracked his ribs* and *Jo's aunt is insane and his grandfather was in jail for many years* do not imply that the situations described by each of the conjuncts is connected causally or temporally. On the other hand, it is never possible for a conjoined sentence to describe a true state of affairs when one of its component sentences describes something actually false. So for example, it is perfectly possible for (71.a) and (71.b) to describe the same temporal state of affairs, but it is not possible for such a statement to be true, if, in fact, the skier did not break her ankle. Thus, the temporal/causal effects associated with conjunction can be cancelled or weakened and appear in other textual situations which do not contain *and*, whereas the truth of each conjunct cannot be denied without denying the truth of the whole sentence. This is evidence, therefore, that the truth-conditions for & provide the central core of the meaning of *and* while temporal and causal effects are secondary and can be explained by a theory of language use.

7.4.2 Or

A similar argument may be applied to one of the apparent oddities in the truth-conditions associated with *or* via its translation as logical disjunction, as discussed in Chapter 1. Because of the truth-conditions of $\vee$, a disjunctive formula may be true if both of the disjuncts are true. However, in English, the use of a disjunctive sentence often implies that only one of the disjuncts is true. It would, for example, be extremely odd for someone to utter the sentences in (73) knowing that both disjuncts are true.

(73) a. Fiona was a Professor of Linguistics or Dean of the Arts Faculty.
b. Bertie's jacket was in the bedroom or in the cloakroom.

Although the truth-conditional interpretation of *or* allows both sentences in (73) to be true of situations in which Fiona was a professorial Dean of the Arts Faculty and Bertie's jacket was both in the bedroom and in the cloak-room, these statements would not usually be given such an interpretation. Very often disjunctive sentences have an **exclusive** meaning, i.e. one which disallows situations where both disjuncts are true. Hence, the sentence in (73.a) would normally be interpreted so that Fiona was either a Professor of Linguistics or Dean of the Arts Faculty, but not both. To capture this intuition, *or* could be interpreted, not as **inclusive disjunction**, but as exclusive disjunction, $\vee_e$, which has the truth-conditions in (74) and truth table in (75), repeated from Chapter 3.

(74) **Truth-conditions for exclusive disjunction**: If ϕ and ψ are formulae then $[\phi \vee_e \psi]^{M,g}$ is **1** iff $[\phi \ \& \ \psi]^{M,g}$ is **0** or $[\sim\phi \ \& \sim\psi]^{M,g}$ is **0**.

(75)

p	q	p $\vee_e$ q
t	t	f
t	f	t
f	t	t
f	f	f

The problem with adopting exclusive disjunction as the truth-conditional meaning of *or* is that while many uses of disjunction do imply that only one of the disjuncts holds, there are some occasions where we do not want to preclude a situation in which both component formulae are true. Consider, for example, the sentences in (77) which we do not want to be falsified by situations where both disjuncts are true, i.e. where there are students who have a private income and rich parents, or where a job applicant has two Higher and five 'O' grade passes, or where the lecturer does not want to rule out the possibility of a zealous student reading both articles.

(76) a. Students who have a private income or rich parents are better off at University than those who do not.
b. Applicants for the job must have two Higher, or five Ordinary, grade passes.
c. You must read the article on presupposition or the article on implicature by next Wednesday.

The sentences in (76) (and many others like them) show that exclusive disjunction on its own makes too strong a claim about the truth-conditions of English *or*, since inclusive readings of disjunctive sentences must be allowed for. This could be taken as an indication that *or* is ambiguous between $\vee$ and $\vee_e$. While this is not an unreasonable suggestion, it is probably incorrect. Gazdar (1979) presents logical arguments against the ambiguity theory by showing that the use of exclusive disjunction leads to bizarre logical consequences in negative sentences. For example, under the ambiguity hypothesis the sentence in (77.a) has a propositional structure that may be represented as either (77.b) or (77.c).

(77) a. Edinburgh isn't boring or provincial.
b. $\sim(p \vee q)$.
c. $\sim(p \vee_e q)$.

The problem with (77.c) is that it can be shown to be truth-conditionally equivalent to the formula in (78.a) which, by the definition of paraphrase in (14), entails that (77.a) is a paraphrase of (78.b). Intuitively, however, these two sentences are not paraphrases, thus indicating that the exclusive reading of (77.a) is not acceptable. Since there appears to be no reason why the ambiguity should fail in this example, the implication is that *or* is never ambiguous.

(78) a. $((\sim p \;\&\; \sim q) \vee (p \;\&\; q))$.
b. Either Edinburgh isn't boring and isn't provincial, or it's both.

A less technical way of showing that the ambiguity theory is not the best account of the semantics of English *or* is to show, as we did with *and*, that the apparent differences can be traced to other factors. Because of sentences like those in (76), we cannot take exclusive disjunction as basic because otherwise the formulae that translate such examples would be false where both disjuncts are true; an undesirable consequence, as we have seen. If we assume that inclusive disjunction is basic, however, we can show that the exclusivity effects result from non-truth-conditional aspects of meaning. There are two major sources for exclusive readings of disjunctions. In one type of disjunction, exemplified in (73.b), the disjunction is interpreted exclusively because of our knowledge of the way the (real) world is. Knowing that a jacket is an entity and rooms are locations, we are forced to give the sentence an exclusive reading, otherwise it could be the case that the jacket in question was in two different locations at once, something that our knowledge of the world tells us is impossible. A sentence like *Bertie's jacket is in the bedroom or on the floor*, however, can be given an inclusive reading, because the properties of being on the floor and being in a bedroom are not mutually exclusive. Hence, there are no real world constraints on interpreting the disjunction inclusively and the exclusive reading is not forced.

The exclusive reading of the sentence in (73.a), however, cannot be accounted for in precisely the same way, since it is perfectly possible for someone to be a Professor of Linguistics and a Dean of a Faculty at the same time. To account for the preferred reading here, we must turn, as we did with *and*, to a theory of language use. As discussed in the introduction, Grice (1975) suggests that there are a number of rules that speakers adhere to when engaging in conversation. In conversations, participants are assumed to be being co-operative and are sticking to certain principles governing conversational behaviour. One of the maxims can be used to account for the oddity of someone uttering a sentence like (73.a), when, in fact, they know perfectly well that Fiona is both Professor of Linguistics and Dean of the Faculty. The relevant maxim is repeated in (79):

(79) **Maxim of quantity**: Make your exchange as informative as is required.

Amongst other things, the maxim of quantity requires speakers to use a conjunction if they believe that two sentences express true propositions or to state that two disjoined sentences may both be true. In a situation in which speakers conceive that it may be possible that both component formulae expressed in (73.a) may be true, they ought to say something like *Fiona is Professor of Linguistics or Dean of the Faculty or both.* By using disjunction, rather than conjunction, therefore, a co-operative speaker implies that they do not think that Fiona is both Professor and Dean. Hence, from the use of the *or*, there is an **implicature** that the speaker believes that it is not the case that both disjuncts are true. This gives rise to the effect of exclusive disjunction, without resorting to an interpretation of *or* as $\vee_e$. Furthermore, the implication of exclusivity can be cancelled, allowing (73.a) to be true even if both disjuncts are true. After all, someone who uttered this sentence would be somewhat aggrieved at being accused of lying if it so happened that Fiona was, in fact, both Professor and Dean. This would not be explained if the exclusive reading of this sentence was part of the truth-conditions of *or* and not an implicature derived from conversational use. The English disjunction morpheme *or* should not, therefore, be treated as a homonym, but non-ambiguously as inclusive disjunction. Its interpretation in particular contexts may give rise to exclusive interpretations by the meanings of its component formulae and knowledge of the world or through the operation of pragmatic principles like the maxim of quantity. A theory of language use again can be shown to interact with basic principles of semantic interpretation to give the desired results.

Before going on to look at conditionals, there is one entailment relation involving disjunction that is problematic and that should be mentioned here. The truth-conditions for $\vee$ guarantee that a complex formula $p \vee q$ is true if p is true, irrespective of the truth value of the other component formula. This has the effect of making the formula $p \rightarrow (p \vee q)$ a tautology. According to the definition of entailment in (9), this means that we predict that a true sentence S_1 entails S_1 *or* S_2 where S_2 is any other sentence at all. In other words, any sentence that expresses a true proposition entails a disjunctive sentence containing it. But this is bizarre, as the examples in (80) show.

(80) a. Grass is green. Therefore, grass is green or violets are blue.

b. Chester ate the cake. Therefore, Chester ate the cake or Ethel was crazy.

The oddity of these examples, however, can again be explained with reference to pragmatic factors. Indeed, we may again appeal to the maxim of quantity. Clearly, if it is the truth of a single proposition that needs to be conveyed, then the maxim of quantity requires the utterance only of the sentence that expresses that proposition. Any addition, like an extra disjunction, is extra unnecessary information and so a flouting of the conversational maxim.

7.4.3 If

There are a number of peculiar things about the interpretation of conditional sentences as logical material implication. One of these is the peculiarity of asserting conditional sentences when there appears to be no apparent causal relation between the antecedent and the consequent. Compare, for example, the sentences in (81).

(81) a. If the cake was poisoned, then the dog will die.
b. If the cake was poisoned, then the dog will eat it.
c. If the cake was poisoned, then the dog won't be hungry.
d. If the cake was poisoned, then the dog was called Chester.
e. If the cake was poisoned, then the dog is a space alien from Alpha Centauri.

The acceptability of the sentences in (81) declines from (81.a) to (81.e) as it becomes more difficult to connect the situation described by the antecedent with that described by the consequent. This feeling of connectivity between the two sentences is much stronger with conditionals than with conjunctions and is not so easily accounted for (particularly as material implication is not commutative, i.e. $p \rightarrow q$ is not truth-conditionally equivalent to $q \rightarrow p$). However, we can again provide a pragmatic explanation for this phenomenon using Gricean principles of conversation. The explanation utilises the maxim of quantity in (79) and the **maxim of quality**, repeated in (82).

(82) **Maxim of quality**: Do not say what you believe to be false and do not say that for which you lack adequate evidence.

To see how these maxims help explain the gradation of acceptability in (81), consider what one is trying to convey in asserting a conditional sentence. In general, the utterance of a conditional sentence asserts that, as far as the speaker is aware, it is not true that the antecedent is true and the consequent is false simultaneously, i.e. the maxim of quality is adhered to by avoiding the assertion of something known to be false. For listeners to believe such a conditional, they should be able to pick out a connection between the two clauses that enables them to be certain that their truth-conditions are met. If there is no such connection then they could believe the formula expressed by the conditional only by having reasonable grounds for believing that the antecedent is false or the consequent true. By the maxim of quantity, however, the speaker is then revealed as being un-co-operative because he or she should either have simply stated the consequent or denied the truth of the antecedent. The conditional says too much, as it were. Thus, the assertion of a conditional is only felicitous if there is some connection between the antecedent and the consequent and if the speaker believes the conditional to be true.

The assertion of conditionals containing apparently unconnected component sentences, however, can sometimes be used felicitously. The utterance of the sentence in (81.e) may be felt to be more acceptable than that of the sentences in (81.c) and (81.d). The reason for this can be found in the interaction of typical beliefs held by interlocutors and modus tollens. From the truth-conditions of $\rightarrow$, this sentence is true if (and only if) the dog is a space alien from Alpha Centauri or the cake wasn't poisoned. Someone hearing an utterance of (81.e) is unlikely in ordinary circumstances to entertain the possibility that there are dogs which are space aliens from Alpha Centauri. If hearers have no other grounds for assuming that speakers are flouting the maxim of quantity by uttering something they know is untrue, the former must, by modus tollens, assume that the antecedent is false. Thus, anyone who utters the sentence in (81.e) is normally assumed to be conveying that they believe that the cake is not poisonous. In a similar fashion, it is possible to convey that a consequent really is true by having as an antecedent a sentence that expresses a well known truth, since, for the conditional to be true, the consequent must also be true. For example, the sentence *If two plus two equals four, then my client is innocent* strongly conveys that my client is innocent (example taken from McCawley (1981: 220)). Hence, Grice's conversational maxims, together with the truth-conditional interpretation we have provided, can be used to account for a number of peculiarities in the interpretation of conditionals.

That a pragmatic explanation of these facts is feasible is strengthened by the fact that the same connectivity is felt between paraphrases of conditionals that use a disjunction. A formula containing $\rightarrow$ is truth-conditionally equivalent to a disjunction where the antecedent formula is negated, as can be checked by showing that $(p \rightarrow q) \leftrightarrow (\sim(p) \vee q)$ is a tautology. Hence, our theory predicts that the sentences in (83) are paraphrases of those in (81).

(83) a. Either the cake wasn't poisoned or the dog will die.
b. Either the cake wasn't poisoned or the dog will eat it.
c. Either the cake wasn't poisoned or the dog won't be thirsty.
d. Either the cake wasn't poisoned or the dog is called Chester.
e. Either the cake wasn't poisoned or the dog is a space alien from Alpha Centauri.

The acceptability of the sentences in (83) declines in precisely the same way as their equivalents in (81). Hence, we can conclude that the relatedness between antecedent and consequent in a conditional does not result from the semantics of *if* and we are not in a position to reject the truth-conditional interpretation of natural language conditionals as material implication.

Unfortunately, while a theory of language use can be used to account for some of the vagaries of the use of material implication as the interpretation of English *if... then*, it is hard to see how it can account for all of them. Apart from the existence of **counterfactual conditionals** like *If Chester had not eaten the poisoned cake, he would have lived* and *If I were rich, I would spend every day gardening* which require something more than simple material implication for their interpretation, the very equivalence between material implication and disjunction noted above argues against the correctness of this analysis. Thus, while the sentences in (83) seem to be reasonable paraphrases of those in (81), there are many pairs of sentences with the same structure that are not paraphrases of each other. Consider, for example, the sentences in (84) (taken from Gazdar (1979:83)) and (85) (taken from McCawley (1981:222)). Neither of these pairs of sentences are paraphrases, despite the fact that the use of $\rightarrow$ to translate *if* predicts that they are.

(84) a. If you have your ankle removed your foot will drop off.
b. Either your foot will drop off or you will not have your ankle removed.

(85) a. If you come a step closer, I'll scream.
b. Either you won't come a step closer or I'll scream.

It is considerations like these, rather than the problem of conditionals with false antecedents, that militate against the use of material implication to translate conditional sentences in natural languages. Many suggestions have been put forward for the analysis of such sentences and all go well beyond ascertaining the truth of conditionals over a single state of affairs. That is to say, the truth of a conditional like *If it doesn't rain, then there is drought* depends not just on whether it is not raining and there is drought here and now, but on whether in all or the majority of cases in which it doesn't rain, there is drought. Such approaches take us beyond the extensional semantics that has been developed in Chapters 2 to 6 into the realm of intensionality, the topic of the final chapters of this book. Conditionals, however, will not be further discussed, as the topic is extremely controversial and requires more space than can be given here. The reader is referred to the books and articles mentioned in the next section for more information, but these should not be tackled until the reader has discovered more about intensionality.

7.5 Further Reading

For a general discussion of inference, see Sperber and Wilson (1986: ch. 2). Logical deduction figures largely in textbooks on logic and the rules mentioned in this chapter (and many others) can be found by looking at any reasonable introductory book on predicate and propositional logic. As before, the most accessible account is given in Guttenplan (1986: 124-165), which deals with the inferences that are generated by the propositional operators, and pp. 245-276, which deals with the quantifiers. Allwood, Andersen and Dahl (1977: ch. 6) provides a concise summary, as does Partee, ter Meulen and Wall (1990: 115-136; 154-180), while Martin (1987: ch. 5) gives a rather more formal account of logical deduction. For a detailed discussion of lexical meaning in general linguistic semantics, see Cruse (1986) and also the discussions in Lyons (1977: 250-335) and Lyons (1981: chs. 2 to 4). Pulman (1983) gives an interesting discussion of the possibility of constructing a theory of lexical meaning, taking up the challenge of the philosophers W. V. O. Quine (see Quine (1960)) and H. Putnam (see Putnam (1975)). There is not a great deal of literature specifically about lexical meaning within formal semantics: there is a slightly dated discussion in Kempson (1977: ch. 6) and a more sophisticated one in Chierchia and McConnell-Ginet (1990: ch. 8). Dowty (1979: 193-321) provides a lengthy discussion of the topic with particular reference to grammatical aspect. Thematic (participant) roles are given an analysis in terms of lexical entailments defined by meaning postulates in Dowty (1989) and Dowty and Ladusaw (1988). See also the articles in Eikmeyer (1981) and Ballmer and Pinkal (1983). The non-truth-functional aspects of the propositional connectives have received a considerable amount of attention since Grice (1975; 1978): Levinson (1983: ch.3) discusses the topic, as do McCawley (1981: 215- 233) and Chierchia and McConnell-Ginet (1990: 187-203). Gazdar (1979: chs. 3 & 4) provides a formalisation of the notion of implicature and a discussion of the truth-functional connectives. These problems have been re-addressed within the literature on Relevance Theory: see, especially, Blakemore (1987; 1989) and, for a critique of some aspects of the Gricean approach, Carston (1988). The literature on conditionals is predictably large. Gazdar (1979: 83-87) provides semantic reasons for rejecting material implication as a reasonable interpretation of the meaning of *if.* McCawley (1981: 296-326) discusses modalised implication and counterfactual conditionals, the latter based on the seminal discussion in Lewis (1973). Van Benthem (1986: ch. 4) provides an account of conditionals as generalised quantifiers, while the papers in Traugott, ter Meulen, Reilly and Ferguson (1986) provide a good overview of the main issues for formal and general linguistic semantics and language typology.

8 Time, Tense and Aspect

8.1 Temporal contingency

The grammar fragment developed in previous chapters generates sentences only in the past tense form. This has been a matter of expediency to allow more natural English to be used for the examples. However, the temporal properties of the sentences implied by the use of this tense have, in fact, been completely absent from their interpretation. The models we have been working with only contain a set of basic entities, **A**, and a function **F** which assigns an extension to each lexeme in the language. The denotations assigned by the latter are, however, static and no notion of change or development is (or could be) incorporated. This means that really the model theory treats all formulas as **universal truths** or **universal falsehoods**, as if they were all of the same sort as sentences like $e = mc^2$, *All humans are mortal, No bachelors are unmarried, The square root of nine is seventeen*, and so on. The propositions expressed by such sentences have the same truth value at all times and so may be thought of as 'timeless'. Most of the sentences generated by the grammar fragment, however, translate into formulae that could vary in truth value according to time and place, and other contextual factors. For example, *A lecturer screamed* may be true if uttered today but false if uttered the day before yesterday. Such sentences do not denote universal truths or falsehoods but **contingent** ones, ones whose truth depends on what is happening or has happened at a particular time. Most, if not all, languages have ways to refer to situations that are happening now or that have happened in the past or that are going to happen in the future. Furthermore, many languages can present situations as ongoing or complete (e.g. *Fiona was singing a song* versus *Fiona sang a song*) and the duration or time of occurrence of events can be specified directly within sentences (e.g. *Fiona sang for five minutes yesterday afternoon*).

In this chapter, we are concerned with defining a theory that enables the difference between timeless and temporally bound sentences to be captured. To do this we will sketch a fairly simple theory of time and use this to provide an account of the way English may refer to present, past or future events (**tense**) and how such events are presented as ongoing or complete (**aspect**). The analysis concentrates on basic tense and aspect, and no attempt is made to incorporate temporal adjuncts like the adverbial phrases *yesterday, on Tuesday*, etc. or sentential adjuncts like *when* clauses.

8.2 Time

Before tense or aspect can be incorporated into the theory, the concept of **time** needs to be introduced. According to one view, time consists wholly of a series of **moments** which are all ordered with respect to each other so that each moment either precedes or follows all the others. This captures the intuition that time is directional, irreversible and uniform. This can be formally defined by a set, **T**, of moments of time and a relation *is earlier than* or *precedes* symbolised as < which has the properties in (1).

(1) For all $\mathbf{t_i}$ and $\mathbf{t_j} \in \mathbf{T}$:

a. $\sim(\mathbf{t_i} < \mathbf{t_i})$.

b. $((\mathbf{t_i} < \mathbf{t_j}) \ \& \ (\mathbf{t_j} < \mathbf{t_k})) \rightarrow (\mathbf{t_i} < \mathbf{t_k})$.

c. $(\mathbf{t_i} < \mathbf{t_j}) \rightarrow \sim(\mathbf{t_j} < \mathbf{t_i})$.

d. $(\mathbf{t_i} < \mathbf{t_j}) \vee (\mathbf{t_j} < \mathbf{t_i}) \vee (\mathbf{t_i} = \mathbf{t_j})$.

The condition in (1.a) disallows any moment of time from preceding itself, thus making **<** **irreflexive**; (1.b) imposes **transitivity** on the relation by requiring any moment of time that precedes another to precede all other moments that the latter precedes; and the third condition ensures that the relation < is **asymmetric** by disallowing moments of time from both preceding each other. The final condition in (1.d) makes the relation **dense** by ensuring that there are no moments of time outside the series **T** and that every moment precedes or follows every other moment except itself. Given these conditions, one may think of **T** as the set of natural numbers and **< as** the relation *is less than*. This concept of time may also be represented by the **time line** in (2) where the line represents moments of time ordered from the past into the future as indicated by the arrow and **t** is a particular moment on this series.

(2)

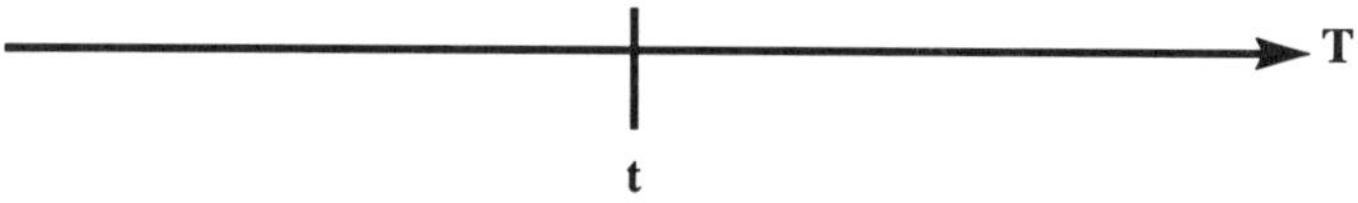

8.2.1 *Intervals of time*

Moments of time seem adequate for assessing the truth of formulae containing expressions referring to instantaneous events like *sneeze'*, but there are many activities like writing a book or painting a picture, which occur over a period of time during which it may not be true that for all moments in that period someone is actually in the process of writing or painting. Thus, while it is true that I am currently writing this textbook in August 1991, it is not true that I was actually writing three hours ago (since I was still in bed) and yet one of the interpretations of the sentence *Ronnie is writing a book on semantics* was as much true three hours ago as it is now. Furthermore, events may be presented as occurring during the period when some other event is occurring. For example, I may describe my current situation with the sentence *I am eating my breakfast while writing this sentence*, presenting two different events as occurring at the same time. To be able to account for situations such as book-writing and other non-instantaneous events and to allow for events to be contained in or overlap others, the truth of formulae may be assessed not at **moments** of time but at **intervals** of time. Thus, the proposition expressed by *Ronnie wrote a book* is assessed as being true if, over a period of time that has now finished, Ronnie was writing a (particular) book and that book is now complete. This sentence does not, however, require Ronnie to begin and complete the writing of a book at some particular moment in time, nor that it be true that Ronnie wrote at every moment of the time that he took to complete the book. In **interval semantics**, moments of time are primitive, and intervals of time are defined in terms of these, as a continuous set of moments of time ordered by the precedence relation, <. The set of all possible intervals of time is thus defined as in (3) as the set of all continuous subsets, **i**, of a set of moments of time, **T**, ordered by the precedence relation, <.

(3) $\mathbf{I} = \{i \subseteq T \mid ((\mathbf{t_i} \in i) \,\&\, (\mathbf{t_k} \in i) \,\&\, (\mathbf{t_i} < \mathbf{t_j} < \mathbf{t_k})) \rightarrow (\mathbf{t_j} \in i)\}$.

Intervals of time may **overlap with**, **be contained in**, or **precede**, other intervals. Two intervals **i** and **j** overlap (written $\mathbf{i} \circ \mathbf{j}$) if they share moments of time; one interval, **i**, is contained in another, **j**, (written $\mathbf{i} \subseteq \mathbf{j}$) if every moment in **i** is also in **j**; and one interval, **i**, precedes another, **j** (written $\mathbf{i} < \mathbf{j}$), if every moment in **i** precedes every moment in **j**. These definitions are summed up in (4) and a schematic example illustrating the concepts is given in (5). In the latter, the four lines under the time line marked **i**, **j**, **k** and **l** are all intervals of time such that **k** overlaps with **i** and **j**, **l** is a **subinterval** of (is contained in) **j**, and **i** and **j** are independent of each other, except that **i** precedes **j** (and **k** precedes **l**), as summarised in (6). (By the definition in (4.c) **i** does not precede **k** and **k** does not precede **j**, because they overlap.)

(4) For all temporal intervals **i** and **j** in **I**:

a. $\mathbf{i} \circ \mathbf{j}$ if, and only if, $\mathbf{i} \cap \mathbf{j} \neq \emptyset$.

b. $\mathbf{i} \subseteq \mathbf{j}$, if, and only if, $\mathbf{i} \cap \mathbf{j} = \mathbf{i}$ (or, equivalently, $\mathbf{i} \cup \mathbf{j} = \mathbf{j}$).

c. $\mathbf{i} < \mathbf{j}$, if, and only if, $\forall t \in \mathbf{i}\, [\forall \mathbf{t'} \in \mathbf{j}\, [\mathbf{t} < \mathbf{t'}]]$.

(5)

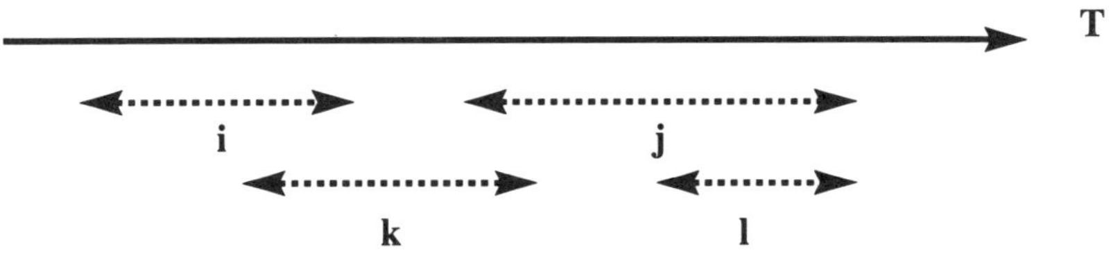

(6) a. $i < j$, $k < l$.

b. $i \circ k$, $j \circ l$, $j \circ k$.

c. $l \subseteq j$.

For notational convenience, an interval of time is represented, not by using set notation, but by enclosing the **endpoints** of the interval between square brackets. Thus, the interval symbolised as $[\mathbf{t_4},\mathbf{t_8}]$ is the set of all moments of time between $\mathbf{t_4}$ and $\mathbf{t_8}$, i.e. $\{\mathbf{t_4},\mathbf{t_5},\mathbf{t_6},\mathbf{t_7},\mathbf{t_8}\}$. An interval of time that is no more than a moment is represented within interval semantics as a **unit set** of times, i.e. as an interval consisting only of a single moment of time, $\{\mathbf{t}\}$, and is indicated by enclosing the moment of time between square brackets. For example, $[\mathbf{t_7}]$ is the interval of time consisting only of the moment $\mathbf{t_7}$, i.e. $\{\mathbf{t_7}\}$. These definitions are given in (7).

(7) a. **Interval of time**: $[\mathbf{t_1},\mathbf{t_2}] =_{def} \{\mathbf{t} \mid \mathbf{t_1} \leq \mathbf{t} \leq \mathbf{t_2}\}$.

b. **Moment of time**: $[\mathbf{t}] =_{def} \{\mathbf{t}\}$.

8.2.2 Temporal models

In order to incorporate time into our semantic theory, the models with respect to which the truth of a formula must be assessed must be extended to the ordered quadruple in (8).

(8) **Temporal model**: «A,F,T,<».

As before, **A** is a set of entities specifying the ontology of the model and **T** is a set of moments of time ordered by the dense linear ordering <, as defined in (1). Intervals of time as such are not part of the model directly as they are not primitive but derived from the set of moments of time, **T**, and the precedence relation, <, in the way specified in (4). As before, **F** is the function that assigns denotations to lexemes in the model, but now, of course, it must do so at particular temporal intervals. **F** may, therefore, be defined as a function from lexemes to sets of ordered pairs of times and extensions, $<\mathbf{i},\Delta>$, where **i** is a temporal interval and Δ (*Delta*) is the extensional denotation of a constant at the time **i**. The models defined in this book are all complete in the sense that it is always possible to determine the extension of any well-formed expression in the object language. It is therefore necessary to ensure that there are no times for which the extension of some expression is not specified. In other words, **F** assigns denotations to basic expressions in such a way that the extension of the latter can be ascertained for every interval defined on **T** so that there are no 'holes' in the model where the extension of a particular constant is unspecified at some particular time. This is done by requiring that the union of all temporal intervals in the range of **F**(α) for each constant α be equal to the largest possible interval, i.e. the set of times **T**. This strong condition on (complete) temporal models is formally written as the statement in (9) where the symbol $\bigcup_i$ indicates the union of all sets **i** where **i** is the interval of time that forms the first element in an ordered pair in **F**(α).

(9) $\bigcup_i <i,\Delta> \in F(\alpha) = T$, for all constants α in the object language.

As an example of a temporal model, let us consider a situation in which the four humans of our previous models, Jo, Fiona, Bertie and Ethel, previously unacquainted, meet for the first time. On first impressions, both Fiona and Ethel like Jo and Jo likes both of the others. Nobody likes Bertie at first and he likes no-one else. After a time, however, Fiona decides she doesn't like Jo, but likes Ethel instead. At the same time, Ethel decides she does like Bertie. After another period of time, Ethel too decides she doesn't like Jo but does like Fiona. Bertie also comes to like Ethel. This situation can be formally represented in a model, call it M_8, containing four entities $\mathbf{MAN_1}$ (Jo), $\mathbf{MAN_2}$ (Bertie), $\mathbf{WOMAN_1}$ (Ethel) and $\mathbf{WOMAN_2}$ (Fiona) and nine moments of time, $\mathbf{t_1}$ to $\mathbf{t_9}$ (a ludicrously small timescale in reality but sufficient to illustrate the idea). The denotation assignment function, $\mathbf{F_8}$, models the above situation by assigning the denotation to *like'* in (10), where there is no moment of time in which the lexeme does not have a specified extension (even if this is null for some moments). We assume here, and elsewhere, that individual constants denote the same entity at all times in a model so that $\mathbf{F_8}$ assigns to each individual constant, *jo', fiona', bertie'* and *ethel'*, a single member of **A** for the largest interval in **I**, i.e. **T** itself.

(10) a. $F_8(jo') = <[t_1,t_9], MAN_1>$.

b. $F_8(fiona') = <[t_1,t_9], WOMAN_2>$.

c. $F_8(bertie') = <[t_1,t_9], MAN_2>$.

d. $F_8(ethel') = <[t_1,t_9], WOMAN_1>$.

e. $F_8(like') = \{<[t_1], \emptyset>,$
$<[t_2,t_4], \{<MAN_1, WOMAN_1>, <MAN_1, WOMAN_2>,$
$<WOMAN_1, MAN_1>, <WOMAN_2, MAN_1>\}>,$
$<[t_4,t_6], \{<MAN_1, WOMAN_1>, <MAN_1, WOMAN_2>, <WOMAN_1, MAN_1>,$
$<WOMAN_2, WOMAN_1>, <WOMAN_1, MAN_2>\}>,$
$<[t_7,t_9], \{<MAN_1, WOMAN_1>, <MAN_1, WOMAN_2>,$
$<WOMAN_1, WOMAN_2>, <WOMAN_2, WOMAN_1>,$
$<WOMAN_1, MAN_2>, <MAN_2, WOMAN_1>\}>\}$.

The situation specified in (10) can be represented diagrammatically as (11), where each line bounded by square brackets under the time line indicates the interval during which one person likes another.

(11)

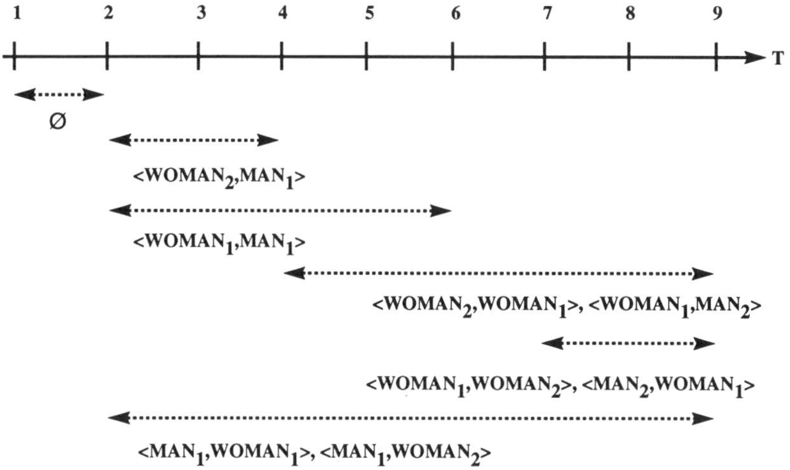

To ascertain the truth of temporal formulae, however, it is necessary to know not only the model, but also the time at which the formula is being assessed. For example, the formula *(like'(jo'))(fiona')* is true with respect to (10) at the interval $[t_3]$ (a moment of time), but false at $[t_7]$, while *(like'(fiona'))(jo')* is true at all intervals except $[t_1]$. Hence, all logical expressions must be interpreted with respect not only to a model, **M**, and an assignment of values to variables, **g**, but also an interval of time, **i**. The extension of an expression, α, with respect to **M**, **g** and **i** is symbolised as $[\alpha]^{M,g,i}$.

To interpret temporal formulae, the base clause of the model theory must be altered to identify the meaning of a constant at a particular time with its extension at that time as specified by the denotation assignment function of the model (12.a). Because the value of **F** applied to a constant α is a set of ordered pairs, $\mathbf{F}(\alpha)$ may be interpreted as a function from intervals to extensions. Thus, where $\langle\mathbf{i},\Delta\rangle$ is in $\mathbf{F}(\alpha)$, $\mathbf{F}(\alpha)(\mathbf{i})$ is the extension, Δ, of α at interval $\mathbf{i}$. For example, $\mathbf{F}_8$(*like'*)($[\mathbf{t}_2,\mathbf{t}_4]$) is the set $\{\langle\mathbf{MAN}_1,\mathbf{WOMAN}_1\rangle, \langle\mathbf{MAN}_1,\mathbf{WOMAN}_2\rangle, \langle\mathbf{WOMAN}_1,\mathbf{MAN}_1\rangle, \langle\mathbf{WOMAN}_2,\mathbf{MAN}_1\rangle\}$ (according to (8.e), above). The rule for interpreting functor/argument structures at a particular time is then given by the rule of functional application relativised to temporal intervals. Thus, the interpretation of an expression *f(a)* with respect to a model, a variable assignment and a particular interval of time, is determined by the application of the extension of the functor, *f*, at that time to that of the argument at the same time, cf. (12.b).

(12) Given a model M = «A,F,<,T»:
  a. If α is a constant, then $[\alpha]^{M,g,i} = F(\alpha)(i)$.
  b. If f(a) is an expression in L_Q, then $[f(a)]^{M,g,i} = [f]^{M,g,i}([a]^{M,g,i})$.

Given the revised model theory in (12), to obtain the interpretation of the expression *(like'(jo'))(fiona')* at the interval $[\mathbf{t}_2,\mathbf{t}_4]$, one must apply the function $[\textit{like'(jo')}]^{M8,g,[t2,t4]}$ to the argument $[\textit{fiona'}]^{M8,g,[t2,t4]}$. Since *fiona'* is a constant in the logic, $[\textit{fiona'}]^{M8,g,[t2,t4]}$ is given by $\mathbf{F}_8$(*fiona'*) applied to the interval, $[\mathbf{t}_2,\mathbf{t}_4]$. Under our assumption that individual constants like *fiona'* extensionally denote the same entity at all times, $\mathbf{F}_8$(*fiona'*)($[\mathbf{t}_2,\mathbf{t}_4]$) is the same as $\mathbf{F}_8$(*fiona'*)($[\mathbf{t}_1,\mathbf{t}_9]$), i.e. $\mathbf{WOMAN}_2$. The functor expression, on the other hand, *like'(jo')*, is not basic, and so its extension at the interval $[\mathbf{t}_2,\mathbf{t}_4]$ is computed by a second application of (12.b) from the extension of *like'* at this interval applied to that of *jo'* in M_8 at the same time. Since *Jo* translates as an individual constant, $[\textit{jo'}]^{M8,g,[t2,t4]}$ is $\mathbf{F}_8$(*jo'*)($[\mathbf{t}_1,\mathbf{t}_9]$), i.e. $\mathbf{MAN}_1$. The function denoted by $[\textit{like'}]^{M8,g,[t2,t4]}$ is given by $\mathbf{F}_8$(*like'*)($[\mathbf{t}_2,\mathbf{t}_4]$) which, as we saw above, is that function in $(\{\mathbf{0},\mathbf{1}\}^A)^A$ that defines the set $\{\langle\mathbf{MAN}_1,\mathbf{WOMAN}_1\rangle, \langle\mathbf{MAN}_1,\mathbf{WOMAN}_2\rangle, \langle\mathbf{WOMAN}_1,\mathbf{MAN}_1\rangle, \langle\mathbf{WOMAN}_2,\mathbf{MAN}_1\rangle\}$. Applying the appropriate function to the entity denoted by *jo'*, i.e. $\mathbf{MAN}_1$, gives the characteristic function of the set $\{\mathbf{WOMAN}_1,\mathbf{WOMAN}_2\}$, which is thus the value of $[\textit{like'(jo')}]^{M8,g,[t2,t4]}$. The application of this function to the extension of *fiona'* yields the value **1**, since $\mathbf{WOMAN}_2$ is in the set denoted by the predicate at that time. Hence, the formula *(like'(jo'))(fiona')* is true with respect to M_8 at the interval $[\mathbf{t}_2,\mathbf{t}_4]$. (13) summarises the steps taken to arrive at this interpretation.

(13) a. $[(\text{like'}(\text{jo'}))(\text{fiona'})]^{M8,g,[t2,t4]}$ is **1** iff $[\text{like'}(\text{jo'})]^{M8,g,[t2,t4]}([\text{fiona'}]^{M8,g,[t2,t4]})$ is **1**.
  b. $[\text{like'}(\text{jo'})]^{M8,g,[t2,t4]}([\text{fiona'}]^{M8,g,[t2,t4]})$ is **1** iff $([\text{like'}]^{M8,g,[t2,t4]}([\text{jo'}]^{M8,g,[t2,t4]}))([\text{fiona'}]^{M8,g,[t2,t4]})$ is **1**.
  c. $[\text{fiona'}]^{M8,g,[t2,t4]}$ is $F_8(\text{fiona'})([\mathbf{t}_2,\mathbf{t}_4])$ is $\mathbf{WOMAN}_2$.
  d. $[\text{jo'}]^{M8,g,[t2,t4]}$ is $F_8(\text{jo'})([\mathbf{t}_2,\mathbf{t}_4])$ is $\mathbf{MAN}_1$.
  e. $[\text{like'}]^{M8,g,[t2,t4]}$ is $F_8(\text{like'})([\mathbf{t}_2,\mathbf{t}_4])$, the function defining $\{\langle\mathbf{MAN}_1,\mathbf{WOMAN}_1\rangle, \langle\mathbf{MAN}_1,\mathbf{WOMAN}_2\rangle, \langle\mathbf{WOMAN}_1,\mathbf{MAN}_1\rangle, \langle\mathbf{WOMAN}_2,\mathbf{MAN}_1\rangle\}$ (call this κ).
  f. $\kappa(\mathbf{MAN}_1)(\mathbf{WOMAN}_2) = \mathbf{1}$.
  g. So $[(\text{like'}(\text{jo'}))(\text{fiona'})]^{M8,g,[t2,t4]}$ is **1**.

Exercise 8.1:
The verb *like* is a **stative** verb so that its extension at some interval of time remains the same for every subinterval of that interval. Assuming this to be so, work out the extensions of the following expressions at the intervals indicated with respect to the model in (10).

i. (like'(ethel'))(fiona') at $[\mathbf{t_7,t_8}]$.
ii. (like'(fiona'))(jo') at $[\mathbf{t_6}]$.

Ascertaining the truth or falsity of formulae with respect to temporal intervals that correspond to the times specified by the denotation assignment **F** is given directly by the theory of interpretation in (12), but problems arise in interpreting formulae with respect to intervals that are not specified by **F**. In the previous exercise, we assumed that, because *like* is stative, if *x* likes *y* at an interval **i**, then *x* likes *y* at all subintervals of **i**. Without any contextual information to the contrary, this seems intuitively correct and solves the problem of ascertaining the extension of certain types of constant (but not all; see section 8.3.2) at subintervals of the intervals specified by **F**.

A more intractable problem arises, however, when we consider the truth of a formula with respect to an interval of time which spans a change in the extension of a constant in the formula being interpreted. To illustrate the problem consider the interpretation of the formula *(like'(jo'))(fiona')* at the interval $[\mathbf{t_4,t_5}]$. According to (10), this formula is true at moment $[\mathbf{t_4}]$ but false at moment $[\mathbf{t_5}]$. What then is the truth value of $[(like'(jo'))(fiona')]^{M8,g,[t4,t5]}$? This question requires an answer to the more general question: what exactly is meant by the expression 'true at an interval of time'? Clearly if we mean 'true at some time during an interval', then the example formula is true with respect to the little model given above, since there is a subinterval ($[\mathbf{t_4}]$) at which *(like'(jo'))(fiona')* is true. On the other hand, if it means 'true throughout an interval of time', then, of course, $[(like'(jo'))(fiona')]^{M8,g,[t4,t5]}$ is false, because there is a subinterval ($[\mathbf{t_5}]$) at which the formula is false. Although this is not a problem that arises directly in this chapter, because of the way the truth of formulae is assessed with respect to arbitrary intervals of time, a grammar fragment that analyses temporal adverbials like *on Tuesday, last week, two years ago,* needs to have this problem solved in order that sentences like *Fiona sang last Tuesday* may be interpretable in a situation in which there are periods on the appropriate day in which Fiona did indeed sing, but other periods in which she didn't. Furthermore, a formula should in principle be interpretable with respect to any interval in the model, and so some solution must be provided whereby the extensions of expressions can be ascertained at all temporal intervals irrespective of whether or not those intervals are directly mentioned by the denotation assignment function of the model in question.

The solution that is adopted here takes the notion of *truth at an interval* to be equivalent to *truth at some time during an interval*. The reason for this decision can be seen from a consideration of the truth-conditions of sentences like the ones in (14).

(14) a. Jo kicked the dog yesterday.
b. Fiona sang the song last Tuesday.
c. Bertie will paint a picture next year.
d. Ethel knew how to play golf last year.

These sentences all express true propositions, if the event described by the verb and its arguments occurred at some time during the interval described by the adverbial expression. For example, the sentence in (14.b) translates into a formula that is true, if the person called Fiona sang the (contextually salient) song at some time on the Tuesday before the time of utterance. It does not, however, require that Fiona sang the song all throughout the day in question. The sentence in (14.d) appears to imply that Ethel knew how to play golf throughout the whole of the year preceding the one in which the sentence is uttered, but it would not be falsified if, for example, she knew how to play golf from January to September of that year and then was in an accident that made her forget that there exists a game called golf, let alone how to play it.

In general, therefore, we can take truth at an interval to be defined according to truth at some period in that interval. Formally, this can be defined by taking the denotation of a constant, α, at an interval **i** to be determined by the union of the extensions of α at all intervals that overlap with **i**, as specified by the denotation assignment function, **F**. For example, $[\mathit{like}']^{M8,g,[t4,t5]}$ is given by $\mathbf{F_8}$(*like'*)(**j**) for all intervals **j** that overlap with $[\mathbf{t_4},\mathbf{t_5}]$. According to the model, $\mathbf{M_8}$, there are two such intervals in the domain of **F**: $[\mathbf{t_2},\mathbf{t_4}]$ and $[\mathbf{t_5},\mathbf{t_6}]$ (see (10.c)). In the former interval *like'* denotes the set $\{\langle \mathbf{MAN_1},\mathbf{WOMAN_1}\rangle, \langle \mathbf{MAN_1},\mathbf{WOMAN_2}\rangle, \langle \mathbf{WOMAN_1},\mathbf{MAN_1}\rangle, \langle \mathbf{WOMAN_2},\mathbf{MAN_1}\rangle\}$, whilst in the latter it denotes the set $\{\langle \mathbf{MAN_1},\mathbf{WOMAN_1}\rangle, \langle \mathbf{MAN_1},\mathbf{WOMAN_2}\rangle, \langle \mathbf{WOMAN_1},\mathbf{MAN_1}\rangle, \langle \mathbf{WOMAN_2},\mathbf{WOMAN_1}\rangle, \langle \mathbf{WOMAN_1},\mathbf{MAN_2}\rangle\}$. The union of these two sets is $\{\langle \mathbf{MAN_1},\mathbf{WOMAN_1}\rangle, \langle \mathbf{MAN_1},\mathbf{WOMAN_2}\rangle, \langle \mathbf{WOMAN_1},\mathbf{MAN_1}\rangle, \langle \mathbf{WOMAN_2},\mathbf{MAN_1}\rangle, \langle \mathbf{WOMAN_1},\mathbf{MAN_2}\rangle, \langle \mathbf{WOMAN_2},\mathbf{WOMAN_1}\rangle\}$ which provides the extension of *like'* at the interval $[\mathbf{t_4},\mathbf{t_5}]$. The formula *(like'(jo'))(fiona')* is thus true with respect to model M_8 and interval of time $[\mathbf{t_4},\mathbf{t_5}]$.

The first clause in the model theory must now be revised as in (15) which also contains a restriction on the overlapping intervals that are relevant to the interpretation. According to the definitions in (4.a) and (4.b), above, proper subintervals also overlap with their containing intervals. Although the extensions of stative predicates at some particular time are maintained for all subintervals of that time, this property is not shared by all predicates. For example, a sentence like *Bertie painted a picture last week* should not be interpreted as expressing a true proposition with respect to a situation where Bertie painted a picture over a two week interval containing last week (see section 8.3.2 for more discussion of these sorts of predicate). Hence, (14) excludes from the definition of the extension of a constant at some time, **i**, the extensions of that constant at other times which properly contain **i**. However, if **i** is in the domain of **F** then the definition in (15) reduces to that in (12.a), under the assumption that **F** does not include overlapping intervals for individual constants.

(15) If α is a constant, then $[\alpha]^{M,g,i}$ is $\bigcup_{\Delta}$, where $F(\alpha)(j) = \Delta$ for all $\mathbf{i} \circ \mathbf{j}$ where **i** is not a proper subinterval of **j**.

The rest of the model theory, covering the interpretation of the propositional connectives, the lambda operator and the quantifiers, needs also to be revised in the light of the introduction of time. These are all straightforward revisions, and a fuller discussion of the model theory is postponed until Chapter 10.

8.3 Tense

Given the theory of time and temporal models presented in the last section, the interpretation of simple tensed formulae is fairly straightforward and is the topic of this section. In the following subsections, a general theory of tense will be presented, providing the basic interpretations of **Present tense**, **Past tense**, and **Future tense** and discussing certain combinations and entailments of these. Many languages do not have morphological tense systems and very few have a three-way tense system, but all languages seem to have ways of referring to times other than the time of utterance. The theory put forward in this chapter is a general one, in the sense that it does not claim to analyse specific tense systems, but provides the machinery to talk about present, past and future time reference. It should be emphasised that as we move away from a purely extensional semantics like that developed in Chapters 2 to 6, the amount of controversy and debate increases. Readers are asked to bear in mind, therefore, that what is presented here is no more than an outline of what is acknowledged to be an as yet incomplete theory in a fairly rudimentary state of development. Readers are invited to pursue their own ideas and are encouraged to compare the truth-conditions suggested for the interpretation of different tenses with their intuitions about their own language or their knowledge of languages other than English.

8.3.1 Past, present and future

Tense is a **deictic category** that locates in time the state of affairs described by a sentence. This location is not precise, but relative to some other time, a **temporal reference point**, the most important of which is the **time of utterance**, the interval (usually assumed to be a moment) in which a sentence is uttered by some speaker. It is with respect to this time that present, past and future for the speaker are computed. Thus, for those languages that have it, a declarative sentence in the present tense can be used to assert that the event described by the sentence occurs at the time the sentence is uttered, i.e. the time of the event is located at the time of utterance. A declarative sentence in the past tense, on the other hand, can be used to assert that the event occurred prior to the time of utterance and one in the future tense, that the event will occur after the time of utterance. Although in a discourse the time of utterance is always the main reference time, it is possible for other times to act as the principal reference time for the interpretation of a tensed sentence, particularly for multiply tensed sentences (see Section 8.2.2) or embedded clauses. Hence, the definitions given below refer only to principal reference times rather than the time of utterance, in order to maintain generality.

Since tense locates situations in time that are described by a sentence, the tenses can be represented in logic as operators over formulae. Thus, temporal logics contain a set of **tense operators** which, being expressions of type <t,t>, combine with formulae to yield tensed formulae. The introduction of these operators into the language L_Q gives the tensed logical language, $\mathbf{L_T}$. The present tense operator is symbolised as **Pres** and the representation of a sentence like *Fiona sings* in L_T is *Pres (sing'(fiona'))*, and that of *Every student sings* is *Pres* ($\forall x$ *[student'(x)* $\rightarrow$ *sing'(x)])*.

As mentioned above, the use of the present tense may indicate that the truth or falsity of a formula is to be assessed with respect to the primary reference time, usually the time of utterance. Thus, on one interpretation, the proposition expressed by the sentence *Fiona sings* is true if there is someone called Fiona who is singing at the time the sentence is uttered. In other words, the present tense locates the time of the event or situation described by a sentence at the time of utterance and so the interpretation of the L_T representation of *Fiona sings* is identical to $[sing'(fiona')]^{M8,g,i}$, where **i** is the time of utterance. Thus, the interpretation of formulae containing the present tense operator at some time **i** is equated with the interpretation of the formula without the operator at the same interval of time. The truth-conditions of such formulae are spelled out formally in (16) and represented diagrammatically in (17) where **i** is the reference time placed on the time line which clearly shows that the time at which the embedded formula ϕ is to be interpreted is the same as the principal reference time.

(16) **Present tense**: $[\text{Pres}\ (\phi)]^{M,g,i}$ is **1** iff $[\phi]^{M,g,i}$ is **1**.

(17)

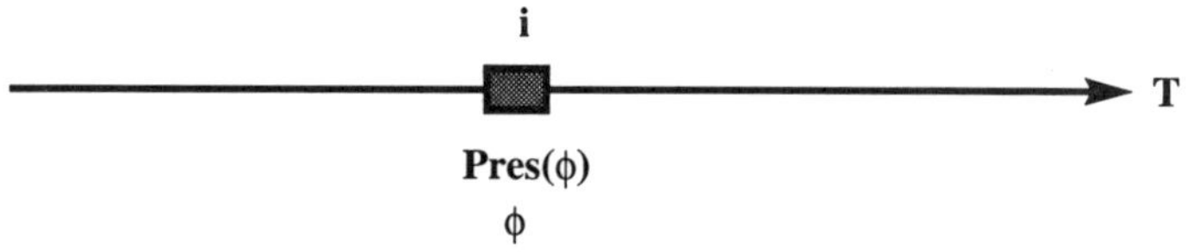

The fact that present tense formulae at a particular time are interpreted identically to the corresponding untensed formula at that time leads many logicians to omit the present tense operator altogether. However, many languages morphosyntactically mark the present tense and many distinguish tensed from untensed sentences. The linguistic evidence thus points to the need for a present tense operator, as well as past or future tense ones, even though this may be semantically unnecessary, according to the interpretation given in (16). In a discourse, however, it is possible that the use of tense introduces particular **reference times** that can be subsequently referred to by pronominal expressions (like *then*, *from that time on*, etc.). Untensed sentences, on the other hand, do not seem to have this property. A more sophisticated theory that considers the needs of discourses, rather than isolated sentences, would thus very likely make use of a present tense marker and so a present tense operator is adopted here, despite the fact that it is truth-conditionally otiose.

To capture the force of the past tense, an operator **Past** is used which gives rise to formulae like the ones in (18) which represent the formulae expressed by the English sentences in (19), respectively.

(18) a. Past (sing'(fiona')).
b. Past (∃x [student'(x) & (like'(jo'))(x)]).
c. ∀x [adult'(x) → Past (child'(x))].

(19) a. Fiona sang.
b. A student liked Fiona.
c. Everyone who is an adult was a child. (Every adult was a child.)

The interpretation of past tense formulae locates the time of the event described by the predicate at a time prior to the principal reference time, so that the truth or falsity of a formula like *Past (sing'(fiona'))* is determined by whether there is some interval of time before the moment of utterance at which the formula *sing'(fiona')* is true. If there is, then *Past (sing'(fiona'))* is true, if not, then it is false. (20) gives the formal definition of the interpretation of formulae in the scope of the past tense operator while (21) represents this diagrammatically and shows clearly the 'pastness' of the situation with respect to the principal reference time.

(20) **Past tense**: $[\text{Past}(\phi)]^{M,g,i}$ is **1** iff there is a time **j** such that **j** < **i** and $[\phi]^{M,g,j}$ is **1**.

(21)

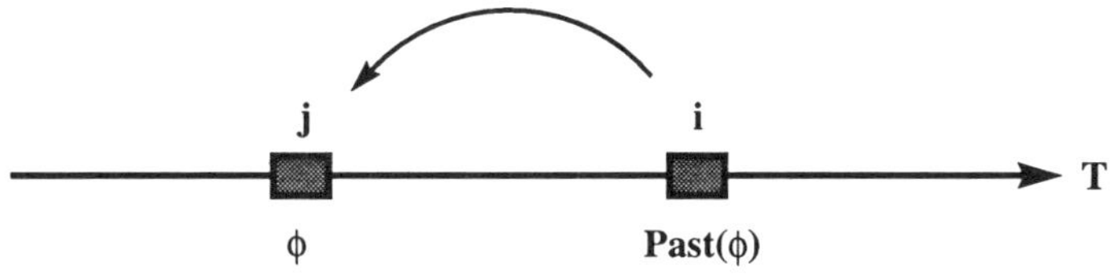

In order to see how past tense formulae are interpreted with respect to a particular model, let us adopt the simple model, M_8, presented in the last section augmented with the denotations of *sing'*, *student'* and *happy'* in (22).

(22) a. F_8(sing') = {<[t_1,t_2],{**WOMAN$_2$**}>,
<[t_3,t_8],{**MAN$_1$,WOMAN$_1$,WOMAN$_2$**}>,
<[t_9],{**MAN$_2$,MAN$_1$,WOMAN$_2$,WOMAN$_1$**}>}.
b. F_8(student') = {<[t_1],{**MAN$_1$**}>,
<[t_2,t_9],{**WOMAN$_2$,MAN$_1$**}>}.
c. F_8(happy') = {<[t_1,t_2],{**MAN$_1$,WOMAN$_1$**}>,
<[t_3,t_6],{**MAN$_1$**}>,
<[t_7],∅>,
<[t_8,t_9],{**MAN$_2$,WOMAN$_2$,WOMAN$_1$**}>}.

If the sentence *Fiona sang* was uttered at the moment **[t_8]**, the formula that represents it, i.e. *Past (sing'(fiona'))*, is true only if there is an interval of time **i** prior to **[t_8]** in which *sing'(fiona')* is true, i.e. if **WOMAN$_2$** (the entity denoted by *fiona'*) is in $[sing']^{M8,g,i}$. Clearly, there are a number of intervals at which this is so according to **F_8**, **[t_3,t_8]** being one of these (cf. (22.a)). Hence, *Past (sing'(fiona'))* is true with respect to M_8 and time **[t_8]**. On the other hand, the formula is not true at the interval **[t_1]**, since there is no prior interval in which Fiona sings.

(23) presents the formal procedure for verifying the more complex formula *Past (∀x [student'(x) → sing'(x)])* (the translation of the sentence *Every student sang*) with respect to $\mathbf{M_8}$ and time of utterance $\mathbf{[t_6]}$. The complexity of this example is due entirely to its rigour and nothing is introduced that was not in the discussion of the past given above. In (23) and the exercise that follows, it is assumed that the properties of singing, being a student, being a lecturer or being happy are all stative so that if someone has one of these properties at some interval of time, then they have it for all subintervals of that time.

(23) a. $[\text{Past}(\forall x\,[\text{student}'(x) \rightarrow \text{sing}'(x)])]^{M8,g,[t6]}$ is **1** iff there is an interval of time j such that $j < \mathbf{[t_6]}$ and $[\forall x\,[\text{student}'(x) \rightarrow \text{sing}'(x)]]^{M8,g,j}$ is **1**.

b. Let j be $\mathbf{[t_3,t_4]}$, then $[\forall x\,[\text{student}'(x) \rightarrow \text{sing}'(x)]]^{M8,g,[t3,t4]}$ is **1**, iff for every value assignment g' like g but for the value of x, $[\text{student}'(x) \rightarrow \text{sing}'(x)]^{M8,g',[t3,t4]}$ is **1**.

c. Let $g' = g^{MAN1/x}$, then $[\text{student}'(x) \rightarrow \text{sing}'(x)]^{M8,gMAN1/x,[t3,t4]}$ is **1** iff $[\text{student}']^{M8,gMAN1/x,[t3,t4]}$ is **0** or $[\text{sing}']^{M8,gMAN1/x,[t3,t4]}$ is **1**.

d. $[\text{student}'(x)]^{M8,gMAN1/x,[t3,t4]}$ is **1** since $\mathbf{MAN_1} \in F_8(\text{student}')(\mathbf{[t_2,t_9]})$, student' is stative and $\mathbf{[t_3,t_4]} \subseteq \mathbf{[t_2,t_9]}$.

e. $[\text{sing}'(x)]^{M8,gMAN1/x,[t3,t4]}$ is **1** since $\mathbf{MAN_1} \in F_8(\text{sing}')(\mathbf{[t_3,t_8]})$, sing' is stative and $\mathbf{[t_3,t_4]} \subseteq \mathbf{[t_3,t_8]}$.

f. Hence, $[\text{student}'(x) \rightarrow \text{sing}'(x)]^{M8,gMAN1/x,[t3,t4]}$ is **1**.

g. Let $g' = g^{MAN2/x}$, then $[\text{student}'(x) \rightarrow \text{sing}'(x)]^{M8,gMAN2/x,[t3,t4]}$ is **1** because $[\text{student}'(x)]^{M8,gMAN2/x,[t3,t4]}$ is **0** (as $\mathbf{MAN_2} \notin F_8(\text{student}')(\mathbf{[t_3,t_4]})$).

h. Let $g' = g^{WOMAN1/x}$, $[\text{student}'(x) \rightarrow \text{sing}'(x)]^{M8,gWOMAN1/x,[t3,t4]}$ is **1** because $[\text{student}'(x)]^{M8,gWOMAN1/x,[t3,t4]}$ is **0** (as $\mathbf{WOMAN_1} \notin F_8(\text{student}')(\mathbf{[t_3,t_4]})$).

i. Let $g' = g^{WOMAN2/x}$, $[\text{student}'(x) \rightarrow \text{sing}'(x)]^{M8,gWOMAN2/x,[t3,t4]}$ is **1**, because $[\text{student}'(x)]^{M8,gWOMAN2/x,[t3,t4]}$ is **1** ($\mathbf{WOMAN_2} \in F_8(\text{student}')(\mathbf{[t_3,t_4]})$ and $[\text{sing}'(x)]^{M8,gWOMAN2/x,[t3,t4]}$ is **1** ($\mathbf{WOMAN_2} \in F_8(\text{sing}')(\mathbf{[t_3,t_4]})$).

j. Hence, since there are no other g', $[\forall x\,[\text{student}'(x) \rightarrow \text{sing}'(x)]]^{M8,g,[t3,t4]}$ is **1**.

k. Hence, since $\mathbf{[t_3,t_4]} < \mathbf{[t_6]}$, $[\text{Past}(\forall x\,[\text{student}'(x) \rightarrow \text{sing}'(x)]]^{M8,g,[t6]}$ is **1**.

Exercise 8.2:
For each of the following formulae, give an English sentence which could express it and interpret it formally (as in (23)) with respect to the model M_8 and the time of utterance shown.

i. Past (~(∃x [student'(x) & happy'(x)])) at $\mathbf{[t_5]}$.
ii. Pres (∀x [student'(x) & Past (happy'(x))]) at $\mathbf{[t_2]}$.
iii. Past (sing'(jo') & (like'(jo'))(fiona')) at $\mathbf{[t_7]}$.

Very few languages have a morphological future tense and the interpretation of sentences that refer to future time is not straightforward because **modality** is usually involved. However, to represent simple future reference in L_T, there is another operator, **Fut**, which gives rise to formulae such as *Fut (sing'(fiona'))* which can be used to translate English sentences with the auxiliary *will* as in *Fiona will sing*. The interpretation of future tensed formulae proceeds in the same way as for past tense ones, except that we look for a time following the time of utterance at which the simple untensed formula is true. This gives the truth-conditions in (24) which again can be diagrammatically represented by the time line in (25).

(24) **Future tense**: $[\text{Fut}\ (\phi)]^{M,g,i}$ is **1** iff there is a time **j** such that **i** < **j** and $[\phi]^{M,g,j}$ is **1**.

(25)

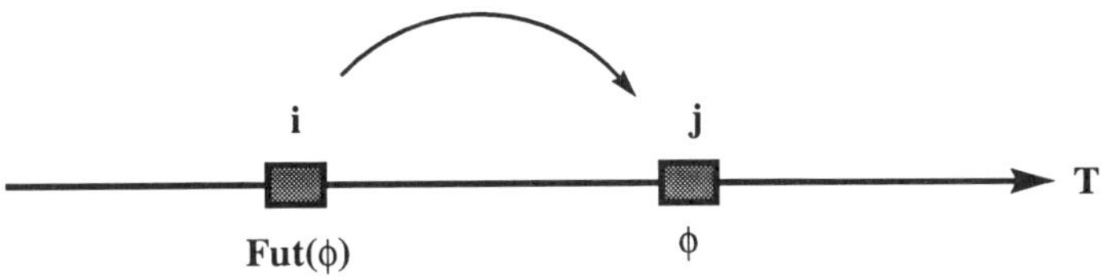

As an example, consider the interpretation of *Fut (sing'(fiona'))* with respect to $\mathbf{M_8}$ and the time of utterance $[\mathbf{t_3}]$. This is true if, and only if, there is an interval of time following $[\mathbf{t_3}]$ where Fiona actually sings. Since $[\textit{sing'}]^{M8,g,[t5,t7]}$ contains $\mathbf{WOMAN_2}$, the entity denoted by *fiona'*, and the time of utterance, $[\mathbf{t_3}]$, precedes the interval $[\mathbf{t_5,t_7}]$, the formula is true. (26) gives a further illustration of the semantics of *Fut*, and shows the formal interpretation of the formula *Fut (∃x [student'(x) & happy'(x)])*, one of the translations of *A student will be happy*, with respect to $\mathbf{M_8}$ and the time of utterance $[\mathbf{t_6}]$.

(26) a. $[\text{Fut}\ (\exists x\ [\text{student}'(x)\ \&\ \text{happy}'(x)])]^{M8,g,[t6]}$ is **1** iff there is a time j, where $[\mathbf{t_6}]$ < j, such that $[\exists x\ [\text{student}'(x)\ \&\ \text{happy}'(x)]]^{M8,g,j}$ is **1**.

b. Let j = $[\mathbf{t_8,t_9}]$. Then $[\exists x\ [\text{student}'(x)\ \&\ \text{happy}'(x)]]^{M8,g,[t8,t9]}$ is **1** iff there is a value assignment g' exactly like g except for the value assigned to x such that $[\text{student}'(x)\ \&\ \text{happy}'(x)]^{M8,g',[t8,t9]}$ is 1.

c. Let g' = $g^{WOMAN2/x}$. Then $[\text{student}'(x)\ \&\ \text{happy}'(x)]^{M8,gWOMAN2/x,[t8,t9]}$ is **1** iff $[\text{student}'(x)]^{M8,gWOMAN2/x,[t8,t9]}$ is **1** and $[\text{happy}'(x)]^{M8,gWOMAN2/x,[t8,t9]}$ is **1**.

d. Since $\mathbf{WOMAN_2} \in [\text{student}']^{M8,gWOMAN2/x,[t8,t9]}$, $[\text{student}'(x)]^{M8,gWOMAN2/x,[t8,t9]}$ is **1**.

e. Since $\mathbf{WOMAN_2} \in [\text{happy}']^{M8,gWOMAN2/x,[t8,t9]}$, $[\text{student}'(x)]^{M8,gWOMAN2/x,[t8,t9]}$ is **1**.

f. Hence, $[\text{student}'(x)\ \&\ \text{happy}'(x)]^{M8,g',[t8,t9]}$ is **1**.

g. Hence, $[\exists x\ [\text{student}'(x)\ \&\ \text{happy}'(x)]]^{M8,g,[t8,t9]}$ is **1**.

h. Hence, since $[\mathbf{t_6}] < [\mathbf{t_8,t_9}]$, $[\text{Fut}\ (\exists x\ [\text{student}'(x)\ \&\ \text{happy}'(x)])]^{M8,g,[t6]}$ is **1**.

Exercise 8.3:
What are the truth-conditions of the following future formulae? What English sentences might these translate and what do they reveal about the interaction of the operators Fut, ~ and ∃?

i. ~(Fut (∃x [student'(x) & happy'(x)])).
ii. ~(Fut (∃x [student'(x) & happy'(x)])).
iii. ∃x [Fut (~(student'(x) & happy'(x)))].
iv. ∃x [~(Fut (student'(x) & happy'(x)))].

8.3.2 Complex tenses

Because tenses are represented as operators over formulae in L_T, it is possible to iterate them, just as it is possible to have more than one quantifier in front of an open formula. Thus, according to the syntax of L_T all of the formulae in (27) are well-formed.

(27) a. Fut (Fut (sing'(fiona'))).
b. Past (Past (sing'(fiona'))).
c. Fut (Past (sing'(fiona'))).
d. Past (Fut (sing'(fiona'))).
e. Past (Fut (Past (Past (Fut (Fut (sing'(fiona'))))))).

The iteration of tenses in this way is a mixed blessing. Expressions like (27.e) are likely to translate no natural sentence in any human language, although they can be imitated using very formal language. For example, the expression in (27.e) can be represented in formal English by repeating the phrases *it was the case that* and *it will be the case that*, i.e. by the sentence *It was the case that it will be the case that it was the case that it was the case that it will be the case that Fiona will sing*. However, such expressions are unlikely ever to be uttered in any actual situation and, more importantly, finding a language that has a single tense in its inventory that would reflect this temporal contour is highly improbable. However, the fact that there is a sentence of English that can be translated into the formula in (27.e), no matter in how stilted a fashion, indicates that the explanation for its unnaturalness in terms of human language lies elsewhere than in semantics. We will not attempt to provide a pragmatic account of the improbability of a sentence expressing the formula in (27.e), but will assume that one can be constructed using Grice's maxims and so accept that tenses can be iterated.

Double combinations of tenses are, however, needed to provide an account of part of the tense/aspect systems of a number of languages, including English. The double past tense formula in (27.b), for example, reflects the temporal information contained in the English pluperfect. Consider the sentence in (28) which expresses a true formula if, on the day before the time of utterance, there is a time before that at which Fiona indeed sang the song.

(28) By yesterday, Fiona had sung the song.

Thus, two reference times, other than the time of utterance, are required to interpret such a sentence: *yesterday*, on which the formula *Past (sing'(fiona'))* is true, and some time before it when *sing'(fiona')* is true. These are the truth-conditions of the double past tense in (27.b), so that the pluperfect tense can be represented by the diagram in (29) where, as before, **i** is the time of utterance and **j** and **k** are two temporal intervals standing for the referent of *yesterday* and the time at which Fiona did the singing, respectively.

(29) **Pluperfect**:

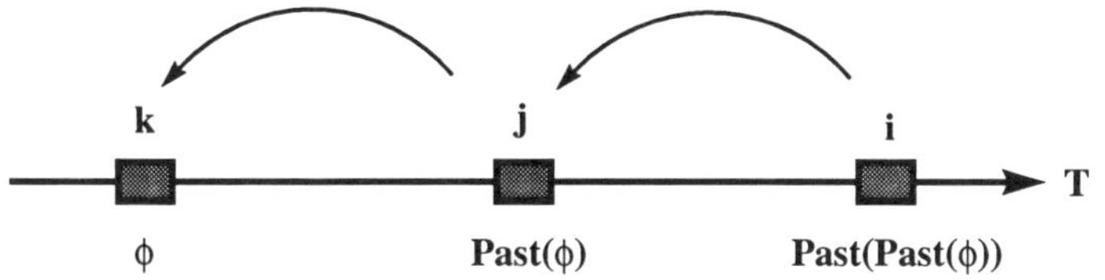

Double futures also underlie the temporal interpretation of certain constructions in human languages. Although English has no proper double future tense, the sense can be captured by using the construction *will be going to* as in (30).

(30) Fiona will be going to sing my favourite song (when she has learnt it).

Although the main clause of this sentence also conveys the intention of the entity denoted by the subject, the temporal information it conveys is that expressed by the formula in (27.a). Again there are two reference points in addition to the time of utterance: the time when she has learnt the song and the time after this when she actually sings it. Hence, the situation can be represented by the diagram in (31) where **j** represents the time Fiona learns the song and **k** when she sings it. The diagram of the truth-conditions associated with the formula in (27.a) shows only the temporal relation between the events described by the sentence in (30). It gives no indication of the modality or the aspect of the English sentence and thus does not provide a complete explication of the meaning of that sentence.

(31)

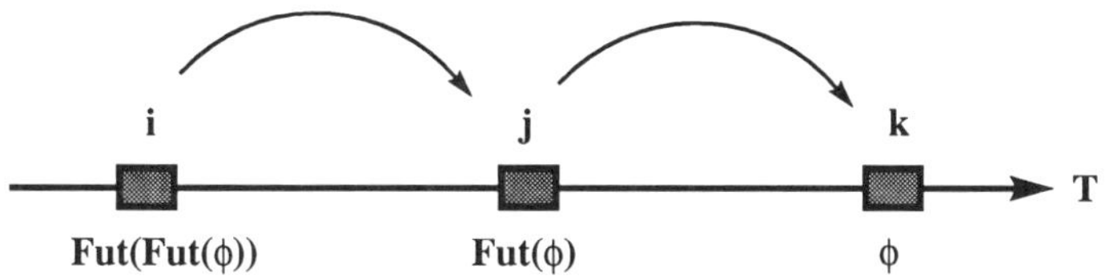

Exercise 8.4:
Show that the diagrams in (29) and (31) represent the truth-conditions for the pluperfect and the *be going to* construction in English, by working out formally the truth or falsity of the formulae in (27.a) and (27.b), with respect to M_8 and the moments of time **[t_3]** and **[t_9]**, respectively.

The two diagrams in (29) and (31) reveal an entailment that each of the formulae in (27.a) and (27.b) have. That is, if the proposition expressed by *Fiona had sung the song* is true at the time of utterance then so is that expressed by *Fiona sang the song* (32.b). Similarly if *Fiona will be going to sing the song* expresses a true proposition at a particular time, then so does *Fiona will sing the song* (32.a).

(32) a. Fut (Fut (ϕ)) → Fut (ϕ).
b. Past (Past (ϕ)) → Past (ϕ).

The mixed combinations of tenses in (27.c) and (27.d) also figure in English. The formula in (27.c) is expressed by the sentence in the future perfect given in (33) (ignoring the adverbial *by midnight* and the direct object for simplicity).

(33) Fiona will have sung my favourite song by midnight.

This expresses a true proposition only if there is a future time (before midnight) in which the proposition expressed by the sentence *Fiona sang my favourite song* is true. This situation can be shown schematically by the diagram in (34), which, as before, utilises three reference times including the time of utterance.

(34) **Future perfect**:

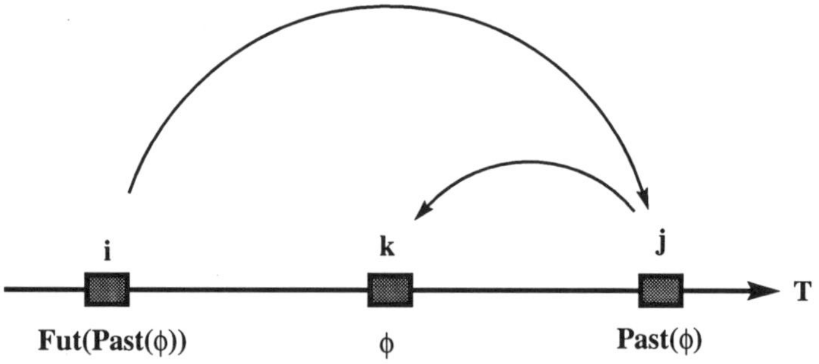

The semantics of the operators *Past* and *Fut* do not require the reference point **k** in (34) to be in the future with respect to **i**. The interval **j** must be in the future with respect to **i**, but the formula *Past (ϕ)* is true with respect to **j** if (and only if) **k** is before **j**, **i** being irrelevant to its interpretation. Hence, ϕ could be true in the future, past or present with respect to **i**. The implication in (35) is thus a tautology on this analysis.

(35) $Fut(Past(\phi)) \rightarrow (Past(\phi) \vee Pres(\phi) \vee Fut(\phi))$.

This interpretation of the future perfect is, therefore, rather weak because it does not determine when the event in question is likely to happen with respect to the time of utterance. On the other hand, the use of this tense apparently conveys the information that the simple formula, ϕ, is true with respect to **i**, so that one might want to extend the theory to make the time of utterance continue to be relevant at all subsequent evaluations of the truth of the embedded formulae at particular times. For example, one might evaluate *Fut (Past (*ϕ*))* as being true at **i** only if *Past (*ϕ*)* is true at an interval **j** following **i** and ϕ is true at an interval **k** also following **i** (and, of course, preceding **j**). This would make any future perfect formula true only in the situation diagrammed in (34). However, this seems an unnecessary move. In the first place, we can appeal to the Maxim of Quantity to account for the non-use of the future perfect where it is known whether *Past (*ϕ*)* or *Pres (*ϕ*)* is true. This is because in normal conversation we state what we believe to be true and no more or less. If we know that something has happened or is happening, then that is what we should say, by using the past or present. If we know that something has not happened in the past or is not happening in the present, then we must use a disjunction like *Fiona is singing the song now or will sing it soon* or *Fiona has already sung the song or will sing it soon*. Only if we know that something did not happen in the past and is not happening now, and that this something is to happen by a certain time, would we use the future perfect. Hence, we can account for the implicature of the futurity of ϕ in *Fut (Past (*ϕ*))*, using pragmatic principles.

Furthermore, it seems that the apparent futurity of **k** in (34) with respect to **i** is not contradicted by situations in which **k** is equal or prior to **i**. For example, (36) gives four possible responses to the sentence in (33). Only the response in (36.d) seems to deny the truth of (33), while the others merely specify the time at which Fiona sings the song. Hence, the apparent weakness of the future perfect on this interpretation appears to be borne out.

(36) a. She did, two hours ago! You must have missed it.
b. You'd better be quick; she's singing it now.
c. She's going to sing it in a quarter of an hour.
d. No, she won't. She's never sung that song and never will. She hates it!

Similar considerations apply as well to formulae with the structure in (27.d), where future formulae are evaluated in the past as shown in the diagram in (39). Again **k** may be before, after or identical to **i**, the implication in (37) again turning out to be a tautology. There is no recognised 'tense' in English that captures this temporal relationship, but the past tense of *be going to* as in (38) seems to come closest to it.

(37) $Past(Fut(\phi)) \rightarrow (Past(\phi) \vee \phi \vee Fut(\phi))$.

(38) Fiona was going to sing my favourite song by midnight.

This sentence can be used to imply that the speaker believes that Fiona has not sung, is not singing and will not sing my favourite song. However, such an assumption is cancellable as is shown by the fact that the replies in (36.a) to (36.c) contradict the assumption, while not contradicting what is said by the sentence in (38). Hence, we may take the speaker's belief as an implicature and not an entailment of the sentences and maintain the truth-conditional analysis captured in the (partial) translation in (27.d).

(39)

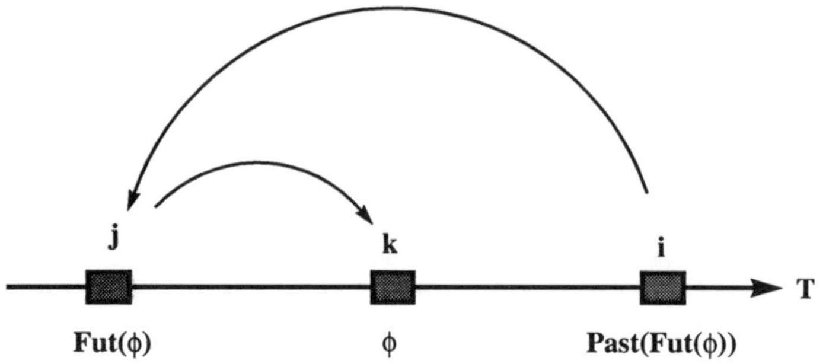

---

*Exercise 8.5:
Discuss the truth-conditions and provide an appropriate logical translation of sentences containing the adverbs *always* and *never* like those in (a) to (d), below. What problems arise with the interaction of the scope of the different operators in these translations?

i. Jo was always a fool.
ii. Jo will always be a fool.
iii. Jo was never clever.
iv. Jo will never be clever.

The theory of tense presented above is idealised with respect to actual linguistic data. The specifics of grammatical tense in particular languages often have different interpretations from those presented in Section 8.2.1. For example, in English, the grammatical tense that covers the present (the so-called present tense) also allows a future interpretation, although it does not allow a past tense reading (without pragmatic implicatures), as shown in (40).

(40) a. Jo goes home today.
b. Jo goes home tomorrow.
c. ?Jo goes home yesterday.

Furthermore, the semantic future tense is encoded using a periphrastic construction involving the auxiliary verb *will/shall* in English which emphasises the apparent **modality** of this tense. Thus, English may be said to distinguish semantic past and non-past and to lack a true future tense. The theory presented above, however, is not intended as a complete theory of the tense system of English (or any other language), but as the basis of such a theory. Clearly, in analysing the tense system of any human language, one needs a theory of time and some way of expressing past, present and future relative to some point of reference. This has been done and been shown to have certain interesting properties that hold, or appear to hold, of English. The theory provides a reasonable base for an analysis of the specifics of a particular system of tense.

8.4 Simple aspect

The previous section deals with the deictic category of tense, which locates an event in time with respect to other times, in particular the time of utterance. Temporal relations may, however, also be presented according to the perceived internal properties of the event or situation being described. For example, an activity can be presented as continuing at some interval of time without indicating how long the activity has lasted or will last in relation to that time, as illustrated by the sentences in (41). On the other hand, an event may be presented as complete or undifferentiated, as illustrated in (42).

(41) a. Fiona is singing the song.
b. Fiona was singing the song.
c. Fiona will be singing the song.

(42) a. Fiona sings the song.
b. Fiona sang the song.
c. Fiona will sing the song.

The examples in (41) are said to be in the **imperfective** aspect whilst those in (42) are in the **perfective** aspect. Other verbal aspects may be defined as subtypes of this basic distinction. For example, one can further subdivide the imperfective into **habitual** (43.a) and **continuous** (43.b).

(43) a. Jo used to kick the cat.
b. Jo was kicking the cat.

Finer grained distinctions may be made by dividing the continuous aspect into **progressive** and **non-progressive** types or recognising **punctual** versus **durative** events or a difference between events that involve the bringing into existence of some entity (e.g. *paint a picture*) and those that just involve an activity of some sort (e.g. *walk*), and so on. It is not the intention of this section, however, to discuss the category of aspect in all its manifestations (this would require a whole volume to itself). Instead, a basic definition of the perfective/imperfective distinction and some characterisation of some of the different types of event denoted by different verbs is given in terms of temporal intervals.

8.4.1 Perfective and imperfective

Despite the controversy that surrounds almost any formal definition of the semantics of the different aspects, the use of temporal intervals allows us to give at least a rudimentary definition of the semantics of the basic perfective/imperfective distinction. In this section, I present definitions of these that follow Bennett and Partee

(1978) and Dowty (1979). The analysis presented here is, however, far from complete and, for fuller treatments, the works cited at the end of this chapter should be consulted.

The perfective aspect, as mentioned above, presents a situation as temporally undifferentiated, but complete, and ignores any internal structure it may have. For example, the sentence *Jo kicked Chester* presents the event of Jo kicking Chester as a complete unit without indicating how long or how often it occurred. Hence, to know the truth value of the formula that translates this sentence, all we need to know is whether the event occurred or not (at some time in the past). Truth-conditionally, therefore, the perfective can be interpreted in the same way as we have been interpreting all formulae in this chapter, i.e. directly with respect to a model, a variable assignment and a time, the latter being the time of the event. The perfective, then, may be (and often is) treated as the semantically neutral aspect, without any need for an operator (like the tense operators, *Pres*, *Past* and *Fut*). Any sentence in the perfective aspect, therefore, translates directly into L_T and is interpreted using rules already given. Thus, the sentence *Jo kicked Chester* translates (after lambda conversion) into *Past ((kick'(chester'))(jo'))*, a formula that is true if, and only if, Jo actually kicks Chester at some time prior to the time of utterance.

It is possible, however, that, like the present tense, the perfective should also be signified by the use of an operator, particularly as there are languages that have morphosyntactically marked perfective aspects and others may combine perfective and imperfective aspects. Furthermore, it could be argued that the completeness property of the perfective should be represented in its semantics. This may be done by requiring the temporal interval at which the truth of a perfective formula is assessed to contain both **initial** and **final** moments of the event being described by the sentence. This would mean that the proposition expressed by a sentence like *Jo kicks Chester* would be true only if the event of Jo's kicking Chester is begun and finished at the time of utterance. Furthermore, by the semantics of the past tense given above, a sentence like *Ethel played a game of golf* would express a true proposition only if Ethel actually completed the game of golf at some point before the time of utterance. It would not be true, however, if, for example, she was still playing the last hole when the sentence was uttered. In the future tense, such an analysis would entail that the initial moment of the event being described must follow the time of utterance. So, for example, the sentence *Fiona will sing my favourite song* would express a true proposition only if Fiona had not already begun singing my favourite song at the time of utterance.

Given these informal descriptions of the truth-conditions of past, present and future perfective sentences, we may introduce a perfective aspect operator, **Perf**, whose formal interpretation is given in (44).

(44) **The perfective:** $[\text{Perf}\ (\phi)]^{M,g,i}$ is **1** iff $[\phi]^{M,g,i}$ is **1** and i contains initial and final points if ϕ inherently contains these.

Initial and final points are taken to be initial and final subintervals (as defined in (45)) which are no more than a moment (i.e. intervals consisting only of a single point in time). The requirement for initial and final points applies only to predicates that inherently contain them. This is to accommodate stative predicates like *be good* or *like* which do not necessarily have beginning or end points. For example, the sentence

Bertie is good expresses a true proposition, if Bertie is actually good at the moment of utterance. Its truth does not, however, depend on Bertie's ceasing to be good at this point. The proposition is true, even if Bertie continues to be good until the end of his life. Consequently, bounding points are only taken into account in situations (like playing a game of golf or singing a song) where these are inherently required by the meaning of the predicate. For those events, like being good, which do not necessarily have beginning or end points, the perfective reduces to the simple assessment of the truth of the formula at an interval. We will return to the inherent aspectual properties of predicates in the next section.

(45) a. **Initial subinterval**: **i** is a initial subinterval of **j**, iff **i** is a subinterval of **j** and there is no $\mathbf{t} \in \mathbf{j} - \mathbf{i}$ and $\mathbf{t'} \in \mathbf{i}$ such that $\mathbf{t} < \mathbf{t'}$.

b. **Final subinterval**: **i** is a final subinterval of **j** iff **i** is a subinterval of **j** and there is no $\mathbf{t} \in \mathbf{j} - \mathbf{i}$ and $\mathbf{t'} \in \mathbf{i}$ such that $\mathbf{t'} < \mathbf{t}$.

The definition of the perfective in (44) gives rise to the truth-conditional interpretation in (46) of the formula *Past (Perf(∃x [book'(x) & write'(x)(jo')]))* which translates the sentence *Jo wrote a book.* This formal description of the truth-conditions of the formula translating this sentence, given in (46), guarantees that it is true only in circumstances in which Jo completed a book some time prior to the time of utterance. It would not, however, be true if, for example, Jo had begun a book, but not actually finished it, i.e. if the end point of the action is not before the time of utterance.

(46) a. $[\text{Past (Perf } (\exists x\ [\exists x\ [\text{book'}(x)\ \&\ (\text{write'}(x))(\text{jo'})]]))]^{M8,g,i}$ is **1**, iff there is an interval **j** such that $\mathbf{j} < \mathbf{i}$ and $[\text{Perf } (\exists x\ [\text{book'}(x)\ \&\ (\text{write'}(x))(\text{jo'})])]^{M8,g,j}$ is **1**.

b. $[\text{Perf } (\exists x\ [\text{book'}(x)\ \&\ (\text{write'}(x))(\text{jo'})])]^{M8,g,j}$ is **1**, iff **j** includes beginning and final points and $[\exists x\ [\text{book'}(x)\ \&\ (\text{write'}(x))(\text{jo'})]]^{M8,g,j}$ is **1**.

c. $[\exists x\ [\text{book'}(x)\ \&\ (\text{write'}(x))(\text{jo'})]]^{M8,g,j}$ is **1** iff there is a value assignment **g'** exactly like **g** but perhaps for the value of x, such that $[\text{book'}(x)]^{M8,g',j}$ is **1** and $[(\text{write'}(x))(\text{jo'})]^{M8,g',j}$ is **1**.

While the perfective describes an event as complete, the imperfective aspect describes it as on-going or incomplete. To represent this aspect, we introduce the semantic operator, Impf, which is interpreted as requiring the event being described by the formula in its scope to be true of an interval of time properly containing the time at which the imperfective formula is being assessed. So, for example, the sentence *Jo is kicking Chester* is translated into the formula *Pres (Impf ((kick'(chester'))(jo')))* which is true with respect to an interval **i**, only if there is a larger interval, **j**, containing **i**, such that *(kick'(chester'))(jo')* is true at **j**. In plainer English, this means that the event described by an imperfective formula must go on around the time with respect to which it is to be interpreted. The formal definition of this appears in (47).

(47) **The Imperfective**: $[\text{Impf } (\phi)]^{M,g,i}$ is **1** iff there is an interval **j** such that **i** is a proper subinterval of **j** and $[\phi]^{M,g,j}$ is **1**.

To see the effects of this definition, consider the interpretation of the more complex sentence in (48). This expresses a true proposition if there is some time prior to the time of utterance at which someone called Jo enters and this event occurs in an interval, longer than that in which Jo enters, when someone called Fiona sings.

(48) Jo entered, while Fiona was singing.

If the model M_8 is extended to include denotations for the verb *enter* as in (49) and *while* is translated simply as a form of conjunction, then the truth of the formula translating (48) uttered at interval $[\mathbf{t_5}]$ with respect to M_8 is determined as in (50).

(49) a. F_8(enter')($[\mathbf{t_2,t_3}]$) = {**MAN**$_1$,**WOMAN**$_2$}.
b. F_8(enter')($[\mathbf{t_1}]$) = F_8(enter')($[\mathbf{t_3,t_9}]$) = ∅.

(50) a. [Past (Perf (enter'(jo')) & Impf (sing'(fiona')))]$^{M8,g,[t5]}$ is **1** iff there is an interval, **j**, such that **j** < $[\mathbf{t_5}]$ and [Perf (enter'(jo')) & Impf (sing'(fiona'))]^{M8,g,j} is **1**.
b. Let j = $[\mathbf{t_2,t_3}]$, then [Perf (enter'(jo')) & Impf (sing'(fiona'))]$^{M8,g,[t2,t3]}$ is **1** iff [Perf (enter'(jo'))]$^{M8,g,[t2,t3]}$ is **1** and [Impf (sing'(fiona'))]$^{M8,g,[t2,t3]}$ is **1**.
c. [Perf (enter'(jo'))]$^{M8,g,[t2,t3]}$ is **1** iff $[\mathbf{t_2,t_3}]$ contains initial and final points for [enter'(jo')]$^{M8,g,[t2,t3]}$ and [enter'(jo')]$^{M8,g,[t2,t3]}$ is **1**. Since $[\mathbf{t_2,t_3}]$ does contain beginning and end points for [enter'(jo')]$^{M8,g,[t2,t3]}$ and [enter'(jo')]$^{M8,g,[t2,t3]}$ is **1** (both from F_8(enter')($[\mathbf{t_2,t_3}]$) in (49.a)), [Perf (enter'(jo'))]$^{M8,g,[t2,t3]}$ is **1**.
d. [Impf (sing'(fiona'))]$^{M8,g,[t2,t3]}$ is **1** iff there is an interval of time, **k**, such that $[\mathbf{t_2,t_3}]$ is a proper subinterval of **k** and [sing'(fiona')]^{M8,g,k} is **1**.
e. Let k = $[\mathbf{t_1,t_5}]$.
f. F_8(sing')($[\mathbf{t_1,t_2}]$) and F_8(sing')($[\mathbf{t_3,t_8}]$) both contain **WOMAN**$_2$, the value of [fiona']$^{M8,g,[t1,t9]}$ and [sing']$^{M8,g,[t1,t8]}$ also contains **WOMAN**$_2$, since the interval $[\mathbf{t_1,t_8}]$ overlaps with both of these intervals. Because *sing* is an activity verb we can infer that [sing'(fiona')]^{M8,g,l} is the same for all subintervals l of $[\mathbf{t_1,t_8}]$ (see next section). Hence, [sing'(fiona')]$^{M8,g,[t1,t5]}$ is **1**.
g. Since $[\mathbf{t_2,t_3}]$ is a proper subinterval of $[\mathbf{t_1,t_5}]$ and [sing'(fiona')]$^{M8,g,[t1,t5]}$ is **1**, [Impf (sing'(fiona'))]$^{M8,g,[t2,t3]}$ is **1**.
h. Since [Perf (enter'(jo'))]$^{M8,g,[t2,t3]}$ is **1** and [Impf (sing'(fiona'))]$^{M8,g,[t2,t3]}$ is **1** and $[\mathbf{t_2,t_3}]$ < $[\mathbf{t_5}]$, [Past (Perf (enter'(jo')) & Impf (sing'(fiona')))]$^{M8,g,[t5]}$ is **1**.

We can represent this situation more succinctly using a timeline. The diagram in (51) shows the time of utterance, $[\mathbf{t_5}]$, as **i**, the time of Jo's entry, $[\mathbf{t_2,t_3}]$ as **j** and the period of Fiona's singing, $[\mathbf{t_1,t_8}]$, as **k**. It is not necessary that **k**, the period of Fiona's singing, be prior to the time of utterance, merely that **j** should be. This is generally true of all imperfective formulae: the tense requirements need only be met by the proper subinterval at which the truth of the formula is assessed, not by the wider interval at which the base formula is true. Intuitively this is the correct result, as we do not want to say that the proposition expressed by (48) is false if Fiona is still actually singing at the time of utterance.

(51)

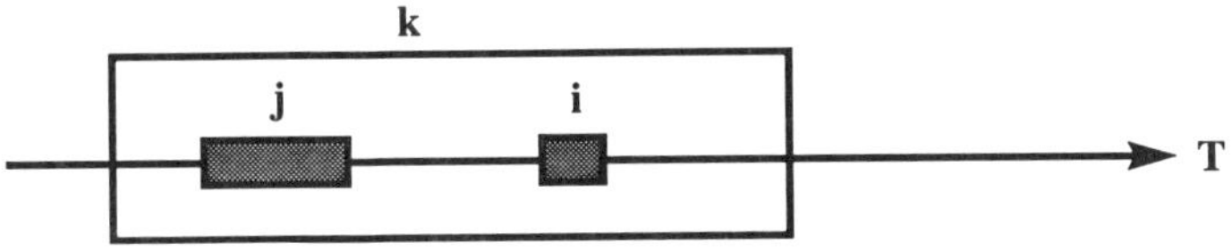

Although the truth-conditions given to the imperfective in (47) properly locate the principal reference time inside the time over which some event is occurring, it suffers from a serious deficiency. The problem is that if an imperfective sentence like *Fiona was singing my favourite song* expresses a true proposition, according to (47), then there must be some interval of time at which the perfective aspect of the sentence *Fiona sang my favourite song* is also true with respect to some reference time. The entailment relation in (52) is valid with respect to the model theory containing (47), as can be checked by showing that no situation can be constructed in which, for example, *Impf (Past (sing'(fiona')))* is true at some time **i**, but there is no other interval **j** in the model at which *Perf (Past (sing'(fiona')))* is true.

(52) If $[\mathrm{Impf}\ (\phi)]^{M,g,i}$ is **1**, then $[\mathrm{Perf}\ (\phi)]^{M,g,j}$ is **1** for some interval **j**.

However, although it may well be the case that the conditional in (52) holds for many situations, it does not always do so, as can be seen by considering the sentences in (53), where the truth of (53.b) does not necessarily follow from that of (53.a). It is possible, for example, that Fiona has never sung my favourite song before, but was singing it when she was electrocuted and thus never actually completed it. In such a situation, because Fiona did not complete the singing of the song, the formula *Perf* $((sing_t'(a))(fiona'))$ (where *a* stands for the translation of *the song* for convenience) is not true of any interval of time.

(53) a. Fiona was singing my favourite song, when she was electrocuted by a faulty microphone.

b. Fiona once sang my favourite song.

The reason (52) is valid in L_T is because the imperfective is defined as occurring if (and only if) the primary reference time is a proper subinterval of an interval of time over which some event took place. For *Impf* (ϕ) to be true at **i**, therefore, there must be an interval **j** properly containing **i**, at which ϕ is true. This problem is often referred to as the **imperfective paradox** and has led to a considerable debate about the proper meaning of the imperfective aspect and to suggestions for revising (47) to get around the problem. Discussion of alternative suggestions is not possible here, but I have drawn the reader's attention to the problem to show that analyses that appear to account for some part of the meaning of some grammatical construction may have unforeseen consequences. The advantage of formalisation is that such consequences can be made plain and steps taken to rectify the problem, while trying to maintain the original insight. Without formalisation, it is possible for undesirable consequences to remain hidden and to lead to further problems elsewhere in the theory.

Exercise 8.6:
Let us add the following to the model M_8, given above:

a. two entities $\mathbf{SONG}_1$ and $\mathbf{SONG}_2$ are added to A.
b. F is extended as follows:
$F_8(\text{song}') = \{<[t_1,t_9],\{\mathbf{SONG}_1,\mathbf{SONG}_2\}>\}$,
$F_8(\text{sing}_t') = \{<[t_1,t_2],\{<\mathbf{WOMAN}_2,\mathbf{SONG}_1>\}>$,
$<[t_3,t_5],\{<\mathbf{MAN}_1,\mathbf{SONG}_1>, <\mathbf{WOMAN}_2,\mathbf{SONG}_1>, <\mathbf{WOMAN}_1,\mathbf{SONG}_1>\}>$,
$<[t_6,t_8],\{<\mathbf{MAN}_1,\mathbf{SONG}_2>, <\mathbf{WOMAN}_2,\mathbf{SONG}_2>, <\mathbf{WOMAN}_1,\mathbf{SONG}_1>\}>$,
$<[t_9],\{<\mathbf{MAN}_1,\mathbf{SONG}_2>, <\mathbf{WOMAN}_2,\mathbf{SONG}_2>, <\mathbf{WOMAN}_1,\mathbf{SONG}_1>$,
$<\mathbf{MAN}_2,\mathbf{SONG}_1>\}>\}$

Assume that *sing$_t$'* (indicating the transitive use of the verb *sing*) inherently contains initial and final points and that these are provided by the intervals specified by $\mathbf{F_8}$, but that *sing'* (indicating intransitive use) does not. Work out the truth values of the following formulae with respect to this model and a moment of utterance $\mathbf{[t_5]}$.

i. Past (Perf ($\exists$x [(sing$_t$'(x))(jo')])).
ii. Fut (Perf ($\exists$x [(sing$_t$'(x))(ethel')])).
iii. Fut (Perf ($\exists$x [sing'(x)])).
iv. Past (Perf (~($\exists$x [sing'(x)]))).
v. Pres(Impf(sing'(jo'))).
vi. Fut(Impf($\exists$y [$\exists$x [(sing$_t$(x))(y)]])).

8.4.2 *States and actions*

One of the reasons why studies of aspect (both formal and informal) become so complex is that the semantics of individual words, or groups of words, within a sentence contributes almost as much to the aspectual interpretation of that sentence as any morphosyntactic marking of grammatical aspect. We have already come across this in our discussion of the perfective, where the notion of beginning and end points was required to account for the completeness property for predicates that have inherent boundaries, like *build a garage*, etc. We have also seen that the extensions of stative predicates (like *like, know, be good*) at some interval **i** are constant at all subintervals of **i**. The study of the different aspectual classes of predicates has a long history, going back at least to Aristotle in the fourth century BC. Aristotle's original classification has been the source of revision and debate by philosophers ever since and now the subject has been taken up, with somewhat different emphasis, by linguists. The literature on this complex topic is vast and we can do very little in this book but look briefly at one particular classification, that of Zeno Vendler, and some of the entailments associated with the classes he proposed. These properties are not strictly logical in the sense that the semantic theory can derive them as theorems. Rather they have to do with the lexical meanings of expressions and so must be stated separately from the model theory itself. As we saw in Chapter 7, this may be done by the use of meaning postulates which specify the idiosyncratic semantic properties of predicates as part of the lexicon of some language.

The basic distinction that can be made between predicates is that between **states** (or **stative predicates**) and **actions**. Syntactically these two classes can be distinguished (in English, at any rate; these syntactic properties do not necessarily carry over into other languages) by the facts that stative predicates do not easily go into the progressive (54.a) unlike actions (54.b); imperatives usually have an action reading, even where stative verbs are used (55); and the pseudo-cleft construction is more natural with action verbs than stative ones (56).

(54) a. ?Ethel is knowing the answer.
b. Ethel is playing golf.

(55) a. ?Know the answer!
b. Play golf!

(56) a. ?What Ethel did was know the answer.
b. What Ethel did was play golf.

We have already seen the primary semantic property of statives: the extensions of such predicates at one interval remain the same for all subintervals, including moments. We can capture this property by the meaning postulate in (57) which guarantees that sentences like that in (58) sound tautologous.

(57) If f is a stative predicate, then if $[f(a)]^{M,g,i}$ is true, then so is $[f(a)]^{M,g,j}$ for all subintervals **j** of **i**.

(58) If Jo was tall for his age between the ages of two and four years old, then Jo was tall for his age at the age of three.

Actions are subdivided by Vendler into three categories: **activities, accomplishments** and **achievements**. The first group includes predicates denoting general activities like running, walking, driving a car, singing, etc. These differ from achievements (e.g. *recognise*, *find*, *lose*, *die*, etc.) and accomplishments (e.g. *sing a song*, *paint a picture*, *write a book*, etc.) in having no inherent boundaries, i.e. no necessary initial and final points to the events they describe. There is nothing inherent in the meaning of the word *sing* that requires the action to have a beginning and an end. After all the sentence *The gods are singing* could express a proposition that is true at all times, past, present and future.

The main entailment of activity predicates involves a relation between their imperfective and perfective uses. Thus, if the imperfective use of an activity predicate is true, then its perfective (in the same tense) is also true. For example, if *the dog was howling* is true now, then *the dog howled* is also true. This is captured by the meaning postulate in (59). Because activities do not have inherent boundaries the perfective formula reduces truth-conditionally to the simple base formula, i.e. $[\text{Perf}\ (\phi)]^{M,g,i} = [\phi]^{M,g,i}$ for all formulae, ϕ, containing activity predicates.

(59) If f is an activity predicate, then if $[\text{Impf}\ (f(a))]^{M,g,i}$ is true, then so is $[\text{Perf}\ (f(a))]^{M,g,j}$.

A further entailment involves the truth of formulae containing activity predicates at subintervals. In general, it seems to be the case that if *Jo walked for an hour* then he walked for all periods in that hour, apart from individual moments of that hour (walking seems to have to be defined over periods greater than a moment, since a snapshot of someone walking shows no movement by the walker). We can symbolise the durational part of the activity as *for'(NP*$_{temp}$*)* (a predicate modifier) where NP_{temp} stands for some temporal NP (which we may allow directly to denote intervals of time, although this poses certain problems). Thus, we arrive at the meaning postulate in (60).

(60) If f is an activity predicate, then if $[for'(NP_{temp})(f(a))]^{M,g,i}$ is **1** where $[NP_{temp}]^{M,g,i} = \mathbf{j}$, then so is $[f(a)]^{M,g,k}$, for all subintervals **k** of **j** that are larger than a moment.

Finally, we must look at achievements and accomplishments. In the first place, the meaning postulates in (59) and (60) do not hold of these. One cannot infer from the truth of *Fiona was singing my favourite song*, that *Fiona sang my favourite song* is true: she may have been interrupted somehow and never finished the song. Nor can one assume that if Bertie wrote a book for an hour then he wrote a book at any time in that hour. Achievements differ from accomplishments in that they appear to be momentaneous events. Hence, durational phrases sound peculiar, if not totally ungrammatical, as witness the achievement predicates in (61) versus the accomplishments in (62).

(61) a. ?Jo recognised the dog for a few minutes.
b. ?The dog died for a few hours.

(62) a. Jo sketched the dog for a few minutes.
b. The dog barked for a few hours.

Furthermore, accomplishments which are complete in a particular period enable us to infer that the imperfective form of the accomplishment is true for all subintervals of that period, excluding final subintervals. Thus, if *in'(NP*$_{temp}$*)* is the logical representation of phrases such as *in an hour*, the meaning postulate in (63) guarantees the truth of (64) in all normal situations.

(63) If f is an accomplishment predicate, then if $[in'(NP_{temp})(Perf\ (f(a)))]^{M,g,i}$ is true, where $[NP_{temp}]^{M,g,i} = \mathbf{j}$, then $[Impf\ (f(a))]^{M,g,k}$ is also true for all subintervals **k** of **j** excluding final subintervals.

(64) If Jo painted a picture in an hour, then Jo was painting a picture during that hour.

There is a lot more that can be said on this subject and there are more subtle differences between the different classes of predicates that can be teased out, but this brief sketch should give some idea of the range of variation in entailments between them and how these may be captured formally in the semantic theory described in this book.

8.5 Scope ambiguities

So far we have been looking at tense and aspect from the purely semantic point of view. Translations of English sentences have been given without any attempt to specify the rules for deriving them in a compositional manner and reliance has been placed on the reader's ability to work out the relation between the sentences in the object language and the corresponding formulae in L_T. This relation should be clear enough, but specifying the translation rules from English into L_T depends so much on the syntactic theory that one adopts that it seems sensible at this point to dispense with our previous practice of constructing complete and precise grammar fragments. This should not give the impression that a translation procedure cannot be given, but different theoretical frameworks encounter different problems and have different advantages for providing a precise translation procedure. Hence, a procedure worked out for one syntactic theory is not necessarily going to provide insights into the procedure for another. Although no attempt will be made to give a comprehensive translation algorithm for all the constructions discussed above, this chapter ends with a discussion of one problem that arises with respect to the relative scopes of the tense (and aspect) operators and any quantifiers contained in subject phrases. This problem is analogous to that of quantifier scope ambiguities discussed in Chapter 6 and will have to be solved by the translation procedure for any theory.

To see the problem in more detail, let us update the grammar fragment of Chapter 6 to incorporate simple present and past tense verbs (i.e. ignoring entirely future tense and aspect). Using a binary feature **PAST**, the basic sentence rule is revised to become (65.a) and all the VP rules given in previous chapters are now assumed to allow a verb to be marked + or - PAST, according to whether the VP node that dominates it is + or -. There are two translations (65.a) depending on the value of the feature [PAST] which are given in (65.b) and (65.c). (Although this seems to be a violation of the rule-to-rule hypothesis, it is not, if different feature values in a syntactic rule are defined as giving rise to different rules.) The effect of the translation in (65.b) is to accommodate the present and future readings of the English present tense as illustrated in (40), above. Given these rules, a sentence like *Every student passed an examination* receives the partial analysis in (66). After applying lambda reduction to the translation in (66.c) we get the formula in (67) which has the truth-conditions in (68). These guarantee the truth of (67) only in situations where all students at some time prior to the time of utterance pass an examination at that same time.

(65) a. $S[\alpha PAST] \rightarrow NP\ VP[\alpha PAST]$.
b. $S[-PAST] \Rightarrow [Pres\ (NP'(VP)') \vee Fut\ (NP'(VP'))]$.
c. $S[+PAST] \Rightarrow [Past\ (NP'(VP'))]$.

(66) a. passed an examination
$\Rightarrow \lambda y\ [\exists z\ [examination'(z)\ \&\ (pass'(z))(y)]]$.
b. every student
$\Rightarrow \lambda Q\ [\forall x\ [student'(x) \rightarrow Q(x)]]$.
c. every student passed an examination
$\Rightarrow Past(\lambda Q\ [\forall x\ [student'(x) \rightarrow Q(x)]]$
$(\lambda y\ [\exists z\ [examination'(z)\ \&\ (pass'(z))(y)]]))$.

(67) $\text{Past}\ (\forall x\ [\text{student}'(x) \rightarrow \exists z\ [\text{examination}'(z)\ \&\ (\text{pass}'(z))(x)]])$.

(68) a. $[\text{Past}\ (\forall x\ [\text{student}'(x) \rightarrow \exists z\ [\text{examination}'(z)\ \&\ (\text{pass}'(z))(x)]])]^{M8,g,i}$ is **1** iff there is a time $\mathbf{j} < \mathbf{i}$ such that $[\forall x\ [\text{student}'(x) \rightarrow \exists z\ [\text{examination}'(z)\ \&\ (\text{pass}'(z))(x)]]]^{M8,g,j}$ is **1**.

b. $[\forall x\ [\text{student}'(x) \rightarrow \exists z\ [\text{examination}'(z)\ \&\ (\text{pass}'(z))(x)]]]^{M8,g,j}$ is **1** iff for every substitution $\mathbf{a} \in A$ for x $[\text{student}'(x) \rightarrow \exists z\ [\text{examination}'(z)\ \&\ (\text{pass}'(z))(x)]]^{M8,ga/x,j}$ is **1**.

c. $[\text{student}'(x) \rightarrow \exists z\ [\text{examination}'(z)\ \&\ (\text{pass}'(z))(x)]]^{M8,ga/x,j}$ is **1** iff either $[\text{student}'(x)]^{M8,ga/x,j}$ is **0** or $[\exists z\ [\text{examination}'(z)\ \&\ (\text{pass}'(z))(x)]]^{M8,ga/x,j}$ is **1**.

d. $[\exists z\ [\text{examination}'(z)\ \&\ (\text{pass}'(z))(x)]]^{M8,ga/x,j}$ is **1** iff there is a substitution **b** $\in$ A for z such that $[\text{examination}'(z)\ \&\ (\text{pass}'(z))(x)]^{M8,g[a/x]b/z,j}$ is **1**.

e. $[\text{examination}'(z)\ \&\ (\text{pass}'(z))(x)]^{M8,g[a/x]b/z,j}$ is **1** iff $[\text{examination}'(z)]^{M8,g[a/x]b/z,j}$ is **1** and $[(\text{pass}'(z))(x)]^{M8,g[a/x]b/z,j}$ is **1**.

The crucial point for our purposes is seen in (68.c) which shows that on this reading the entities passing the examination are also students at the time of passing. This is because *student'(x)* and $\exists z$ *[examination'(z) & (pass'(z))(x)]* are both assessed with respect to the interval **j**, in the past with respect to the time of utterance. However, there is another possible interpretation of this sentence where the entities passing the examination in question are not necessarily students at this past time, but are students at the time of utterance. For example, if the examination was an entrance exam to a university, the people passing it would in general not be students at the time of passing. To get this second reading, we can use the rule of quantifying in introduced to handle quantifier scope ambiguities in Chapter 6. Using this rule to postpone the combination of the translation of the subject phrase until after the tense operator has been introduced yields the translation for *Every student passed an examination* in (69.a) which reduces to (69.b). (69.a) is derived by supplying $\lambda P[P(y)]$ as the translation of the subject, then applying the tensed sentence rule, followed by quantifying in the translation of *every student*, as readers can check for themselves.

(69) a. $\lambda Q\ [\forall x\ [\text{student}'(x) \rightarrow Q(x)]]$
$(\lambda y\ [\text{Past}\ (\lambda P P(y)(\lambda x_1[\exists z\ [\text{examination}'(z)\ \&\ (\text{pass}'(z))(x_1)]]))])$.

b. $\forall x\ [\text{student}'(x) \rightarrow \text{Past}\ (\exists z\ [\text{examination}'(z)\ \&\ (\text{pass}'(z))(x)])]$.

The truth-conditions of (69.b) are computed as in (70) with the crucial information appearing in (70.a and b). These show that we are assessing the truth of *student'(x)* at the time of utterance, **i**, while the truth of $\exists z$ *[examination'(z) & (pass'(z))(x)]* is assessed at the past interval, **j**.

(70) a. $[\forall x\ [\text{student}'(x) \rightarrow \text{Past}\ (\exists z\ [\text{examination}'(z)\ \&\ (\text{pass}'(z))(x)])]]^{M8,g,i}$ is **1** for every substitution $\mathbf{a} \in A$ for x $[\text{student}'(x)]^{M8,ga/x,i}$ is **0** or $[\text{Past}\ (\exists z\ [\text{examination}'(z)\ \&\ (\text{pass}'(z))(x)])]^{M8]ga/x,i}$ is **1**.

b. $[\text{Past}\ (\exists z\ [\text{examination}'(z)\ \&\ (\text{pass}'(z))(x)])]^{M8,ga/x,i}$ is **1** iff there is a time **j** prior to **i** such that $[\exists z\ [\text{examination}'(z)\ \&\ (\text{pass}'(z))(x)]]^{M8,ga/x,j}$ is 1.

c. $[\exists z\ [\text{examination}'(z)\ \&\ (\text{pass}'(z))(x)]]^{M8,ga/x,j}$ is **1** iff there is a substitution **b** $\in$ A for z such that $[\text{examination}'(z)\ \&\ (\text{pass}'(z))(x)]^{M8,g[a/x]b/z,j}$ is **1**.

d. $[\text{examination}'(z)\ \&\ (\text{pass}'(z))(x)]^{M8,g[a/x]b/z,j}$ is **1** iff $[\text{examination}'(z)]^{M8,g[a/x]b/z,j}$ is **1** and $[(\text{pass}'(z))(x)]^{M8,g[a/x]b/z,j}$ is **1**.

Thus, we find further scope interactions between logical operators, quantifiers and tenses, which do appear to mirror certain genuine ambiguities in English sentences. Ignoring any aspectual operators, the sentence *every student passed an examination* turns out to be at least six ways ambiguous, according to the different scopes of the operators *Past*, ∃ and ∀. Two of these have already been discussed. The others are shown in (71).

(71) a. Past (∃z [examination'(z) & ∀x [student'(x) → (pass'(z))(x)]]).
b. ∃z [examination'(z) & Past (∀x [student'(x) → (pass'(z))(x)])].
c. ∃z [examination'(z) & ∀x [student'(x) → Past ((pass'(z))(x))]].
d. ∀x [student'(x) → ∃z [examination'(z) & Past ((pass'(z))(x))]].

Exercise 8.7:
Work through the truth-conditions of the formulae in (71) to show how they differ in meaning. Are all of these readings intuitively plausible as interpretations of the sentence *Every student passed an examination*?

The proliferation of scope ambiguities of this sort gives rise to a number of questions that need consideration. In particular, it is necessary to ask whether all the ambiguities predicted by the free application of the rule of quantifying in are plausible for some particular sentence. As scope ambiguities involve all the logical operators, readings involving scope differences between tenses and aspects also need to be considered. If certain readings do not seem to represent genuine readings of a particular sentence or set of sentences, then the limits to ambiguity need investigation and some motivated constraints need to be put on the operation of the rule of quantifying in to allow only those ambiguities that are felt to be valid and to reject all others. It is not my intention to pursue these weighty matters here, but the reader should be aware that much more research needs to be carried out into the domain of scope ambiguity, before we can be confident that the treatment of tenses and aspects as logical operators is the correct one.

Furthermore, one has to ask whether the rule-to-rule hypothesis can be maintained, given that any construction containing more than one logical operator has more than one output for any single input. Whether or not the rule-to-rule hypothesis should be abandoned depends on whether one's syntactic theory can provide alternative syntactic analyses, with the same output, mirroring the different semantic readings. Again, this topic will not be pursued here, bound up as it is with theory particular considerations. Scope ambiguities do, however, cast doubt on the validity of the rule-to-rule hypothesis (although not the principle of compositionality) as holding for the full range of semantic phenomena found in human languages.

8.6 Further reading

General linguistic discussions of tense and aspect can be found in Comrie (1985), Comrie (1976), Lyons (1977: 677-690; 703-718), and Dahl (1985) which all have good bibliographies. For discussions of tense logic with respect to moments of time rather than temporal intervals see, inter alia, Lyons (1977: 809-823), McCawley (1981: 340-359), Reichenbach (1947), Prior (1967), Rescher and Urquhart (1971), Günthner (1976), Dowty, Wall and Peters (1981: 112-121), and Chierchia and McConnell-Ginet (1990: 223-1234). The suggestion that temporal intervals are more useful for the analysis of natural languages is proposed in Bennett and Partee (1972) and developed subsequently in Bennett (1977), Dowty (1979: ch. 3), Åquist (1976), Baüerle (1979), Cresswell (1985a: ch. 3), and many others. The classification of verbs in terms of their aspectual properties is the subject of many books and articles, among which see especially Vendler (1967), Dowty (1979: ch. 2), Mourelatos (1978) and Verkuyl (1972; 1989). Discussions of tense and aspect can be found in many collections of papers, among which see, for example, Rohrer (1980) and Tedeschi and Zaenen (1981). A critique of interval semantics can be found in, for example, Tichý (1985) (but see also the reply in Cresswell (1985a: 85-95))). A considerable amount of discussion of aspect currently takes place with reference to the notion of **events** which are considered to be ontological primitives like the individual entities encountered in this book. **Event theory** owes its current popularity to Davidson (1967) (and see also the other articles in Davidson (1980)); some examples of this approach can be found in Dowty (1989), Bach (1986), ter Meulen (1983; 1984) and Parsons (1989) which gives a good discussion of the Imperfective Paradox and presents a solution.

9 Possible Worlds

9.1 Where entailments fail

In previous chapters (particularly Chapter 7), we looked at certain types of entailment relations that are guaranteed by the theory of interpretation set out in the earlier part of this book. Certain contexts exist, however, where expected entailments do not hold. Consider, for example, the inference pattern in (1).

(1) a. The Morning Star is the planet Venus.
    b. The Evening Star is the Morning Star.
    c. Therefore, the Evening Star is the planet Venus.

The validity of this inference pattern illustrates a general rule that holds in the extensional semantic theory developed in Chapters 2 to 6 of this book. This rule is called **Leibniz's Law** or the **Law of Substitution** and it allows the substitution of extensionally equivalent expressions for one another in a formula while maintaining the truth value of the original formula. Thus, in (1), since the Morning Star and the Evening Star denote the same entity, the latter expression may be substituted for the former in the first premiss to give the conclusion. Indeed, because all three terms in (1) have the same extension all of them may be substituted for each other *salva veritate* (the Latin phrase used by Leibniz meaning 'with truth unchanged'). The Law of Substitution can be formally defined as in (2) which, in words, says that if an expression a is extensionally equivalent to another expression b, then a formula ϕ is truth-conditionally equivalent to the formula formed from ϕ by substituting an instance of b for every instance of a.

(2) $(a = b) \rightarrow [\phi \leftrightarrow \phi^{b/a}]$.

That substitution of this sort does really hold in the semantic theory (without tense) developed up to Chapter 7 can be shown by trying to show that ϕ could be true while $\phi^{b/a}$ is false for any extensionally equivalent expressions a and b. No formal proof will be attempted here, but intuitively it should be fairly clear to the reader that the formula in (2) does indeed hold, because truth-conditions are defined in a model in terms of entities and functions over entities and not in terms of the *names* of entities or functions. Hence, the truth of a formula depends on the extension of an expression in a model and not on the expressions themselves. If two expressions, say *morning-star'* and *evening-star'*, denote the same thing, say the entity **VENUS**, then the truth of a formula containing either of these expressions depends only on whether the entity denoted, i.e. **VENUS**, is mapped onto **1** by the function denoted by some predicate, e.g. $[\lambda x\ [x = venus']]^{M,g}$ (the set of all entities identical with Venus).

The Law of Substitution in (2) does not, however, hold in all linguistic contexts. Consider the inference patterns in (3), (4) and (5).

(3) a. Necessarily, the Morning Star is the Morning Star.
    b. The Morning Star is the Evening Star.
    c. Therefore, necessarily, the Morning Star is the Evening Star.

(4) a. Bertie believes the Morning Star is the Planet Venus.
    b. The Morning Star is the Evening Star.
    c. Therefore, Bertie believes that the Evening Star is the planet Venus.

(5) a. Bertie wants to look at the Morning Star.
    b. The Morning Star is the Evening Star.
    c. Therefore, Bertie wants to look at the Evening Star.

None of these inference patterns is intuitively valid, despite the fact that they involve the substitution of extensionally equivalent expressions in a formula. The inference pattern in (3) fails because, while it is (logically) necessary that something is identical to itself, it is not necessary for two different names to have the same extension. We can imagine a possible state-of-affairs in which the Morning Star is the planet Venus, but the Evening Star is, for example, the planet Jupiter. The fact that the proposition expressed by the sentence *The Morning Star is the Evening Star* is **contingently true** is not sufficient grounds for asserting that it is **necessarily true**. Contingent formulae are those whose truth value could be otherwise than they are whilst non-contingent formulae are either always true or always false and whose truth or falsity is determined by their logical structure.

The invalidity of the inference patterns in (4) and (5) depends on the attitudes and beliefs of the referent of the subject of the main clause. The person called Bertie could well believe that the Morning Star is the planet Venus, but not believe that the Evening Star and the Morning Star are the same thing. Thus, while the second premiss in (4) is true, it is true outside Bertie's beliefs and so cannot be used to construct new statements about what Bertie believes from the original premise. In Bertie's system of beliefs, the Evening Star could be the planet Jupiter and not Venus at all. Similar reasoning argues against the validity of (5). Here, Bertie may easily want to see the Morning Star and so be intending to get up at dawn, but this is not the same as wanting to see the Evening Star at dusk. He may already have seen the Evening Star and merely wants to catch a sight of its manifestation as the Morning Star. Notice that here the failure in substitution in (5) may also persist even if Bertie knows that the Evening Star and the Morning Star are extensionally equivalent. What is important is a particular manifestation of some entity, the planet Venus.

Sentences containing verbs like *want* and *believe* exhibit another interesting property. Consider the sentences in (6).

(6) a. Jo believes that the Ladies' Scottish Golf Champion is rich.
    b. Jo believes that Ethel is poor.

In general, it is, of course, possible for these two sentences to express true propositions at the same time. If, however, it is true that Ethel is the Ladies' Scottish Golf Champion, it might seem that Jo has contradictory beliefs, believing of one and the same person that she is rich and that she is poor. However, the contingent fact that Ethel is a golf champion does not necessarily affect Jo's beliefs and we cannot substitute the name *Ethel* for the subject noun phrase in (6.a) (or vice versa) in order to infer the truth of the contradictory sentence (via conjunction introduction and the opposite relation between *rich* and *poor*) *Jo believes that Ethel is rich and Jo believes that Ethel is not rich.* If Jo does not know (or believe) that Ethel is the Ladies' Scottish Golf Champion, then (6.a) means that Jo has a belief about someone who carries the title of Ladies' Scottish Golf Champion without knowing (or perhaps caring) who that person is. In other words, (6.a) may be a reflection of Jo's pre-conceived ideas about those who win golfing tournaments and have nothing to do with the actual individuals concerned. Such belief is often said to be **de dicto**, a belief 'about what is said or mentioned'. In such contexts, the referents of noun phrases within the sentential complement of a verb like *believe* are, one might say, within the subject's 'belief worlds' and do not refer necessarily to entities outside those worlds.

There is a second way that (6.a) may be interpreted, however. The assertion of such a sentence, instead of being interpreted as a simple statement about Jo's beliefs, may be taken as asserting *of a certain individual* that Jo has a particular belief about them. In other words, the *speaker* may refer to the particular individual that is denoted by the expression *the Ladies' Scottish Golf Champion*, who may not be known to Jo, the subject of the belief. In these cases, the belief is said to be **de re**, belief 'about the thing' referred to. In such cases, the reference of a noun phrase in the sentential complement of *believe* is to an entity outside the subject's beliefs, something 'in the real world'. Furthermore, because *de re* reference is outside the subject's beliefs, substitution of extensional equivalents is valid, but, for the same reason, this does not lead to the conclusion that Jo has contradictory beliefs (see below).

This ambiguity between *de re* and *de dicto* reference is not confined to belief contexts, but may be found after verbs which denote mental states, acts and attitudes (a subclass of which, including *believe, doubt, consider,* are traditionally called by philosophers verbs of **propositional attitude**). For example, the sentences in (7) exhibit the same ambiguity as those in (6).

(7) a. Jo does not want to meet Ethel.
b. Jo wants to meet the Ladies' Scottish Golf Champion.

In the *de dicto* sense, if Ethel and the Ladies' Scottish Golf Champion are one and the same, these sentences are not contradictory. Jo may very well want to meet the Ladies' Scottish Golf Champion (perhaps under the illusion that she is a rich lady of leisure) but definitely not want to meet Ethel, his secretary, whose filing system he has ruined. On a *de re* reading, on the other hand, the sentences in (7) are contradictory, because the speaker is asserting of some individual (i.e. Ethel) that Jo does and does not want to meet her. People hearing a sentence like (7.b) meant in a *de dicto* sense might interpret it *de re*. So, for example, Fiona might utter (7.b) to Bertie and the latter might reply *Oh, he wants to meet Ethel*, i.e. he supplies the actual referent of the phrase *the Ladies' Scottish Golf Champion*, even though Jo may still not want to meet Ethel. We will return to this topic in Chapter 10.

There is one further problem with the verbs we have been discussing with respect to Leibniz' Law. The way this is defined in (3), above, allows for the substitution, not just of entity-denoting expressions, but of any two extensionally equivalent expressions of any type. By this law, therefore, if someone believes any true formula at all, then they should also believe every other true formula. Thus, if someone believes that grass is green then they must, by Leibniz' Law, also believe that the

Morning Star is the planet Venus, that 29 is the square root of 841 and that there is a pink water lily in flower in my garden pond! This patent absurdity follows from the fact every true formula denotes the value **1**, so that any sentence that translates into a formula with this value may be substituted for any other sentence with the same value. This is clearly not true and verbs like *believe* are not truth-functional in their complement position, because the truth of the whole proposition expressed by the sentence does not depend on the truth (or falsity) of the proposition expressed by the embedded sentence.

It is not only the law of substitution that is problematic in the above contexts. Scope effects involving the logical quantifiers may also fail to hold. Consider the inference pattern in (8).

(8) a. Jo met a secretary.
b. Therefore, there exists a secretary that Jo met.

As we saw in Chapter 6, the decomposition rule for transitive verbs ensures that any quantifier in an object noun phrase has scope over the verb. Thus, in L_Q, (9.a) provides the translation of the premiss in (8) which is, of course, also the translation of the conclusion of the inference pattern, hence ensuring that the truth of the premiss guarantees the truth of the conclusion. From conjunction elimination applied to (9.a), we can also conclude that a secretary exists (9.b) and that someone exists whom Jo met (9.c). In other words, the interpretation given to the translation of the premiss in (8) ensures that there exists someone specific whom Jo met, provided that the premiss is true.

(9) a. $\exists x\ [(\text{meet'}(x))(\text{jo'})\ \&\ \text{secretary'}(x)]$.
b. $\exists x\ [\text{secretary'}(x)]$.
c. $\exists x\ [(\text{meet'}(x))(\text{jo'})]$.

After verbs of needing, wanting, seeking, etc., however, this type of entailment does not necessarily follow. Thus, in (10), none of (10.b) to (10.d) necessarily follow from (10.a).

(10) a. Jo wanted to meet a secretary.
b. There exists a secretary that Jo met.
c. There exists a secretary.
d. There is someone whom Jo met.

If Jo met a secretary, then there is a specific secretary that Jo met, but if he wanted to meet a secretary, then it does not follow that there is a specific secretary that he wanted to meet. He may have in mind a particular individual secretary, but not necessarily. He may just want to meet someone who is a secretary, without caring which particular one. Indeed, (10.a) could be true even if no secretaries exist, a situation that is made more obvious in the sentence *Jo wants to meet a unicorn* which can clearly express a true proposition without there being any unicorns for someone to meet. Thus, certain verbs allow a **non-specific** reading for their objects (including objects of subordinate non-finite verbs), because there is no particular entity with the property defined in the noun phrase that is the object of the main predicate. In effect, then, these verbs may prevent an existential quantifier in an object phrase from having scope over the whole sentence. Again there is ambiguity, because a **specific** reading of the complement is possible. For example, Jo may have in mind a particular secretary who has been recommended to him as being particularly efficient, although he does not know exactly who this is. In this case, not every secretary will satisfy Jo's wanting to meet them, but only the specific one who has been recommended for their efficiency.

9.2 Intension and extension

The contexts in which straightforward entailments fail are often referred to as **referentially opaque** (or **oblique**) contexts, opposed to the **referentially transparent** contexts dealt with in Chapters 2 to 6. In order to make our semantics more adequate than it obviously is, we need to find some way of being able to distinguish between the objects of verbs like *want, look for* and those of verbs like *meet, find.* We also need to decide what complement clauses should denote, since, as we have seen, they cannot just denote truth values, but must still be associated with truth or falsity. The philosopher Gottlob Frege was the first to tackle this problem directly. He proposed that a distinction should be made between what he called the **reference** (German *Bedeutung*) of an expression and its **sense** (German *Sinn*). The reference of an expression is what we have been calling its extension, that is the entity or function that an expression refers to in any model. Its sense, on the other hand, is more abstract, more like the 'meaning' of the expression. We may think of the sense of an expression as being the thing that each of the elements in the reference of the expression have in common that cause them to be identified as such. As an illustration, the reference of the English word *red* is, according to Frege, the extension as defined in previous chapters, i.e. the set of all red entities. Its sense, however, is the property of being red, the 'redness' of all these entities abstracted away from the individuals themselves. In order to avoid confusion with the notion of reference as the *act* of picking out entities in the world and that of sense as the meaning relation between expressions in a particular language (see Chapter 7 and Lyons (1977:177ff)), it is better to follow the terminology of Carnap (1947) and use, as we have been doing, the term **extension** for Frege's *Bedeutung* and **intension** for *Sinn*.

Some may think of intensions as psychological concepts, but here the view is taken that they are external to human beings (in the world, so to speak) and so publicly accessible in some way. In either case, both **intension** and **extension** are intended to refer to things in the world and so constitute different aspects of the denotation of an expression, according to the definition of this concept in Chapter 1. This distinguishes both terms from **sense,** which is, from the linguistic point of view, language internal and defines the meaning relations between words and expressions of a particular language, as we saw in Chapter 7. We may thus picture the 'meaning' of an expression as minimally constructed from its sense and its denotation, as shown in the diagram in (11). (The role of sense in this system is briefly discussed in the next chapter.)

(11)

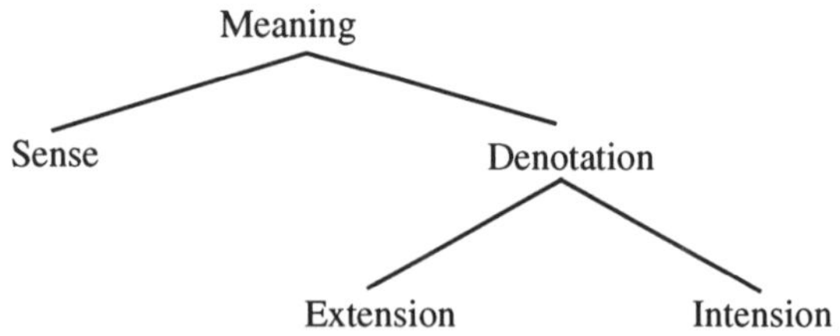

Making a distinction between extensional and intensional denotation allows a distinction to be made between referentially transparent and referentially opaque contexts. In the former case, a predicate is interpreted as a function over the extensional type of its argument, in the way familiar from previous chapters. Predicates that create opaque contexts, however, can be interpreted as denoting functions that take the intensional type of their arguments as their domain. Thus, while the verb *meet* denotes a relation between two entities, the verb *look for* denotes a relation between an entity, the searcher, and the intension (or concept) of another. In this way, we can distinguish the meanings of the sentences *Bertie is looking for an elf* and *Bertie is looking for a hobbit*. The expressions *elf* and *hobbit*, we assume, extensionally denote the null set in the actual world, and hence the noun phrases *an elf* and *a hobbit* also both denote the null set (since no set has a non-null intersection with ∅). Their intensions, on the other hand, differ, since the property that identifies an entity as an elf differs from that which identifies a hobbit, even though there are no actual elves or hobbits picked out in the real world and so if Bertie actually found one he would be able to identify it as such. Similarly, verbs like *believe* do not denote relations between entities and truth values, the extensions of sentences, but relations between entities and the intensions of sentences, which may be informally interpreted as the propositions they express. To believe that *the Morning Star is the planet Venus* is, therefore, not the same as believing that *the Evening Star is the planet Venus* because the propositions expressed by these two sentences differs. In the first case, the proposition expressed by the sentence is true if something called the Morning Star (which is visible at dawn) is the same as the planet Venus whilst the second is true if something called the Evening Star (which is visible at dusk) is the same entity as the planet Venus. Because the intensions of these sentences differ, Jo can 'stand in a belief relation' to one and not the other without contradiction, even if it is contingently true that the Evening Star and the Morning Star extensionally denote the same entity.

Furthermore, by appealing to the notion of intension, we can salvage the Principle of Compositionality. If the denotation of an expression can only be extensional, then the examples in Section 9.1 constitute a direct refutation of this principle, because the meaning of the whole does not rely on the extensions of the complements of the main verbs. However, for the purposes of compositionality, we can equate 'meaning' with intension and redefine the principle as in (12).

(12) **Principle of Intensional Compositionality**: The intension of a complex expression is a function of the intensions of its parts.

Frege attributed another important property to his concept of intension (*Sinn*) which is stated as the *Principle of Intensional Reference* in (13). This captures the traditional principle that intension (the defining property of some class) determines extension (the membership of a class).

(13) **Principle of Intensional Reference**: There is a relation between intensions and extensions such that each intension determines a unique extension.

The idea that an intension determines a unique extension for some expression allows the concept to be defined in terms of a function. The intension of an expression is the property that unifies all the members of its extension, and so it enables the identification of the extension to take place. Hence, an intension may be thought of as a function that picks out an extension for any possible state-of-affairs. For example, the intension of the word *red* can be considered to be the function that identifies the set of red entities in any situation, i.e. a function from situations to extensions.

Before we go on to look at intensionality in more detail in Chapter 10, however, we will first extend our semantic analysis to cover the simple **modal adverbs** *necessarily* and *possibly*. The introduction of modality leads to an introduction into the model of a set of **possible worlds** and lays the foundations for a discussion of Montague's formal approach to intensionality and intensional contexts.

9.3 Introducing other worlds

Human beings are capable of imagining situations that are not actual and all languages have the ability to refer to such states-of-affairs. Thus, while none of the sentences in (14) (presumably) express true propositions on 12 August 1990, we can interpret them well enough and imagine states-of-affairs of which they are true. Furthermore, as (15) shows, English has many ways of presenting non-actual situations for the purposes of conveying information. (15.a) contains a modal verb indicating the possibility of the truth of the situation described by the non-modal counterpart of the sentence, (15.b) illustrates a (slightly archaic) construction that presents the information of its modified sentence as untrue but desirable while (15.c) exemplifies conditionals whose component clauses are presumed to be untrue. Like the other constructions in (15), such **counterfactual** conditionals rely on our ability to entertain the idea that situations may be different from what they actually are (or are assumed to be).

(14) a. Richard Montague was the first person ever to win a Nobel Prize for Logic.
b. Hitler's postwar pact with Japan came unstuck when Hirohito invaded the USA, Germany's closest ally.
c. A team of robots from Mars began to clean up Earth's poisoned atmosphere.

(15) a. The depletion of the Ozone Layer might be caused by the excessive use of aerosol sprays.
b. Would that I had never agreed to write this book!
c. If Richard Montague had been a linguist, he would never have written PTQ.

It is in the notion of alternative situations that the formalisation of the concept of intension lies. This concept has already been used in this book in the representation of the meanings of the propositional connectives. As we saw in Chapter 3, the truth-conditional meanings of the connectives, &, ∨, ~, →, ↔, can be represented by truth tables, each line of which represents a different situation with regard to the truth or falsity of one or more formulae and provides the truth value in that situation of a complex formula formed from these using a connective. Logicians tend to talk, not of different situations, but of **possible worlds**, a term introduced by Leibniz. Just as we may think of our own world, the **actual world** (the 'best of all possible worlds' according to Leibniz) as a thing in its own right, so we may think of all possible worlds in the same way (although possibly not as existing). In constructing intensional models, therefore, we may introduce another set of ontological primitives, a set, **W**, of worlds alongside the set, **A**, of individual entities and the set, **T**, of times, in a temporal semantics. While Occam's Razor states that the postulation of different constructs should be avoided, it crucially states that entities should not be posited *beyond need* (*entia non sunt multiplicanda* ***praeter necessitatem***). Since we need to account for the existence of opaque contexts like those discussed in Section 9.1, and since a purely extensional semantics using only individuals (and times) cannot explain them, we clearly need something else to provide a semantic account of these expressions. Unlike the postulation of a set of primitive times in temporal semantics, however, the adoption of a set of primitive worlds is somewhat mysterious and less intuitively appealing. Indeed, the ontological status of possible worlds has been the subject of heated philosophical debate, but it is not my intention to go into this. If we assume that possible worlds are theoretical constructs (whose ontological status is similar to other mathematical constructs), then what we, as linguists, need to do is to assess their usefulness in achieving the general aims of semantic theory that were set out in Chapter 1. If the use of possible worlds enables an account of opaque contexts to be given in a clear and precise fashion and helps to capture the meaning relations that hold between different opaque sentences, then their adoption into the theory is justified. Of course, if another way of accounting for intensional phenomena is found that does not require the use of mysterious things like possible worlds, then, by Occam's Razor, we should dispense with their use. However, although alternative theories of intensionality have been suggested, none appear so far to have the scope and simplicity of the possible worlds approach and so this is the one that will be adopted here to provide an account of modality (and other intensional phenomena).

9.3.1 Simple modality

Some examples of modal sentences containing the **modal adverbs** *necessarily* and *possibly* and the **modal verbs** *may* and *must* are given in (16).

(16) a. Every proposition is necessarily either true or false, but not both.
b. Bertie possibly knows that the Morning Star is the Evening Star.
c. Every proposition must be either true or false, but not both.
d. Bertie may know the Morning Star is the Evening Star.

There are a number of different types of modality and so there are a number of different ways in which the necessity and possibility in the sentences in (16) may be taken. Some different types of modality will be discussed in the next section, but here we will concentrate only on logical necessity and possibility: that is to say, necessity and possibility that have to do with truth or falsity within a logical system. We may say that a formula is **necessarily true** (or false) in a logical sense (or **alethic** sense from the Greek *aletheia* meaning 'truth'), if the system of logic used ensures that a modal formula has to be true (or false), whatever model it is being interpreted with respect to. On the other hand, **possibly true** (or false) formulae are just those formulae that the logic does not define as necessarily false (or true). Thus, we may follow tradition and divide up the set of all formulae not only into true and false but also into **contingent** and **non-contingent** as represented in the diagram in (17) where the box

(17) **Contingent and non-contingent propositions**

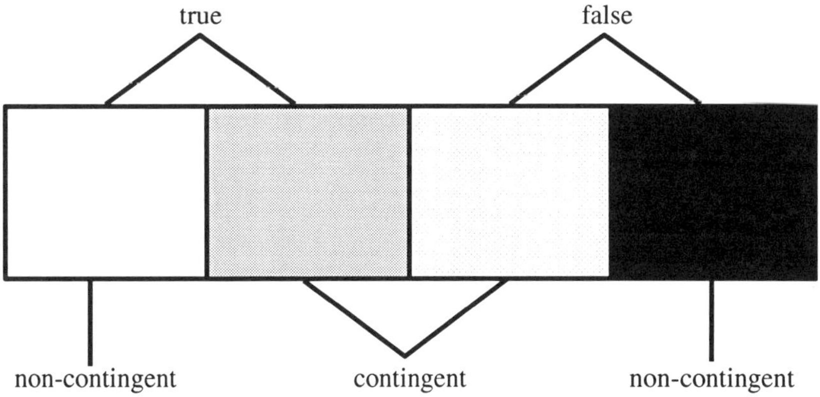

represents the set of all formulae.

The set of necessarily true formulae thus consists of all the non-contingent truths while the set of necessarily false formulae consists of the non-contingent falsehoods. Possibly true formulae are all those formulae that are not non-contingently false, i.e. all non-contingently true formulae plus all the contingently true and false ones. Formulae are possibly false if they are non-contingently false or contingently true or false. This is shown in the diagram in (18) on the following page. Under this interpretation of necessity and possibility, we may say that sentences like those in (16.a) and (16.c) express true propositions if (and only if) the formula translating the sentence *Every proposition is either true or false, but not both* is amongst the set of non-contingently true formulae. On the other hand sentences like (16.b) and (16.d) express true propositions if (and only if) the sentence *Bertie knows that the Morning Star is the Evening Star* translates into a formula that is not amongst those that are necessarily false.

(18) **Necessary and possible propositions**

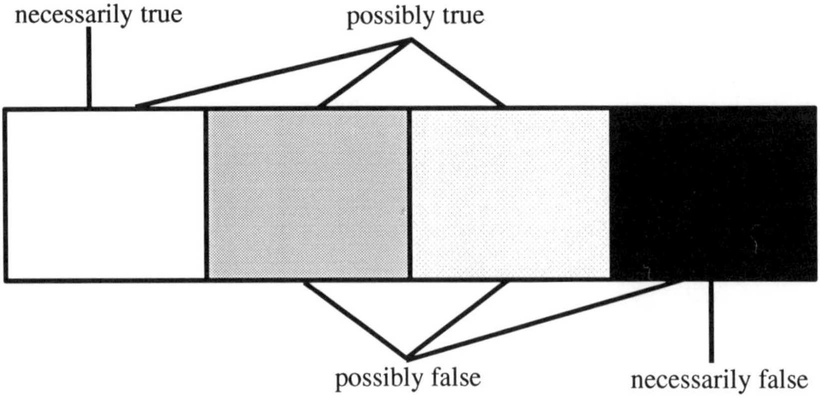

The fact that the interpretation of sentences expressing possibility and necessity may be defined in terms of their non-modal counterparts implies that these two concepts may be represented as operators like the tense and aspect operators of Chapter 8, an analysis that also reflects the fact that the adverbs *necessarily* and *possibly* are sentential modifiers. We may therefore introduce two logical operators: $\Box$ translating *necessarily* or *it is necessary that* and $\Diamond$ translating *possibly* or *it is possible that*. We may also associate English sentences containing the modal verb *may* with formulae containing $\Diamond$ and those containing the verb *must* with formulae containing $\Box$ (but see Chapter 10).

Possible worlds can be used to provide a formal definition of the semantics of these two operators. To do this, a set **W** of possible worlds is introduced into models, which (if tense is ignored for the moment) thus consist of an ordered triple «**A**,**F**,**W**». **A** is a set of entities, as before, **W** is a set of possible worlds and the denotation assignment function, **F**, assigns an extension to each constant in every world in **W**. An expression is thus interpreted with respect to a model, **M**, an assignment of values to variables, **g**, and a possible world, $\mathbf{w_n}$ (just as in a semantics with tense an interpretation refers to an interval of time). Thus, if ϕ is a formula, then its interpretation with respect to **M**, **g** and $\mathbf{w_n}$, i.e. $[\phi]^{M,g,wn}$, is the truth value of ϕ at $\mathbf{w_n}$. If ϕ is contingent, then the value of $[\phi]^{M,g,wn}$ may be different from $[\phi]^{M,g,wm}$ where $\mathbf{w_m}$ is some member of **W** other than $\mathbf{w_n}$.

We will not go into details of the translation and interpretation procedure for formulae in models with possible worlds at this point, but in order to illustrate how this is done let us consider the interpretation of the formula *laugh'(fiona')* with respect to a very simple model, M_9. In this model, there are five entities, two men, two women and a dog which are associated with the same logical name in each of the four worlds in the model, i.e. *jo'*, *bertie'*, *ethel'*, *fiona'* and *chester'*, respectively. The only predicate we are interested in is *laugh'* and both Jo and Fiona are laughing in one of the worlds ($\mathbf{w_1}$), only Chester is laughing in another ($\mathbf{w_2}$), no-one is laughing in a third ($\mathbf{w_3}$) and everyone is laughing in the last ($\mathbf{w_4}$). This model is formally set out in (19).

(19) M_9 = «{**MAN_1, MAN_2, $WOMAN_1$, $WOMAN_2$, DOG**},
F_9(jo') = {<w_1,**MAN_1**>, <w_2,**MAN_1**>, <w_3,**MAN_1**>, <w_4,**MAN_1**>},
F_9(bertie') = {<w_1,**MAN_2**>, <w_2,**MAN_2**>, <w_3,**MAN_2**>, <w_4,**MAN_2**>},
F_9(ethel') = {<w_1,**$WOMAN_1$**>, <w_2,**$WOMAN_1$**>, <w_3,**$WOMAN_1$**>, <w_4,**$WOMAN_1$**>},
F_9(fiona') = {<w_1,**$WOMAN_2$**>, <w_2,**$WOMAN_2$**>, <w_3,**$WOMAN_2$**>, <w_4,**$WOMAN_2$**>},
F_9(chester') = {<w_1,**DOG**>, <w_2,**DOG**>,< w_3,**DOG**>, <w_4,**DOG**>},
F_9(laugh') = {<w_1,{**MAN_1,$WOMAN_2$**}>, <w_2,{**DOG**}>, <w_3,∅>, <w_4,{**MAN_1,MAN_2,$WOMAN_1$,$WOMAN_2$,DOG**}>},
{w_1,w_2,w_3,w_4}»

As mentioned above, formulae are now interpreted with respect to a particular world, the **reference world**, just as they are to particular times in a temporal model. (We could also, if necessary, select a particular world, say w_1, to represent the *actual world* which may function as the base reference point in the same way as the moment of utterance in Chapter 8.) Constants have the extension they are assigned by **F** at the reference world and the values of function-argument structures are computed from the extension of the function and applied to that of the argument at the reference world. Thus, to compute the value of *laugh'(fiona')* at the world w_1, i.e. [*laugh'(fiona')*]^{M9,g,w1}, we take the value of *laugh'* with respect to M_9 and w_1 and apply it to the value of *fiona'* with respect to the same model and world, i.e. [*laugh'*]^{M9,g,w1}([*fiona'*]^{M9,g,w1}). Because *laugh'* is a constant, [*laugh'*]^{M9,g,w1} is determined by taking the value of F_9(*laugh'*) at w_1 which can be written as F_9(*laugh'*)(w_1), because the value of **F**(α) is a set of ordered pairs of worlds and extensions, i.e. a function from the former to the latter. The value of F_9(*laugh'*)(w_1) is, according to (19), the (characteristic function of the) set **{MAN_1,$WOMAN_2$}**. Since [*fiona'*]^{M9,g,w1}, F_9(*fiona'*)(w_1), is **$WOMAN_2$** and **$WOMAN_2$** is a member of the set **{MAN_1, $WOMAN_2$}**, the formula *laugh'(fiona')* is true with respect to **M_9** and w_1. On the other hand, this formula is not true in worlds w_2 and w_3, because **$WOMAN_2$** is not in the extension of *laugh'* in either of these worlds, as can be seen from the model in (19). Thus, a model containing possible worlds can provide characterisations of different situations, in some of which Fiona is laughing and in some of which she isn't.

Now we return to the interpretation of modal formulae. Because non-contingently true (i.e. necessarily true) formulae are true by virtue of the logical system used, they are true in every (logically) possible world, just as necessarily false formulae are false in every (logically) possible world. We can therefore define the truth-conditions of a formula containing the operator □by looking at the truth value of the formula without the operator in every world. Only if the latter is true in every world is the modal formula with □ be true. Hence, the truth-conditions of □ are defined as in (20).

(20) If ϕ is a formula then [□ϕ]^{M,g,wn} is **1** iff [ϕ]^{M,g,wm} is **1** for all w_m in **W**.

For example, given (20), the formula □(*laugh'(fiona')*) is true in world, w_1, if (and only if) *laugh'(fiona')* is true in all worlds in the model M_9. Since there is at least one world (in fact, there are two) in which Fiona is not laughing, [□(*laugh'(fiona')*)]^{M9,g,w1} is false. On the other hand, the disjunction of this formula with its negation, □(*laugh'(fiona') ∨ ~laugh'(fiona')*) is true with respect to M_9, **g** and w_1 because *laugh'(fiona')* ∨ *~laugh'(fiona')* is true in every world (as can be shown by looking at the truth table for $p \vee \sim p$ which yields the value **1** for all possible values of p).

Logically possibly true formulae, as we have seen, consist of all the necessarily true formulae plus all other contingent formulae, whether true or false. In fact, the possibly true formulae only exclude those that are necessarily false, i.e. those that can never be true. Translating this into a possible worlds context we can define a formula $\Diamond\phi$ as being true if, and only if, it is not false in every possible world, i.e. that it is true in some possible world. Therefore, we define the truth-conditions for possibility as in (21).

(21) If ϕ is a formula, then $[\Diamond\phi]^{M,g,w_n}$ is **1** iff $[\phi]^{M,g,w_m}$ is **1** for some $\mathbf{w}_m$ in **W**.

Given this definition, the formula ◇*(~laugh'(fiona'))* translating the sentence *It is possible that Fiona doesn't laugh* is true with respect to $\mathbf{M}_9$ and $\mathbf{w}_1$, because there is a world, $\mathbf{w}_2$, in which *~laugh'(fiona')* is true. On the other hand, the conjunction of this formula with its positive counterpart, ◇*(~laugh'(fiona') & laugh'(fiona'))*, is false because there is no world in which *(~laugh'(fiona') & laugh'(fiona'))* is (or could be) true.

Exercise 9.1:
Which of the following formulae are true in world $\mathbf{w}_1$ with respect to the model M_9?

- i. □~(laugh'(chester')).
- ii. ◇(~(laugh'(chester')) → laugh'(jo')).
- iii. ~(□laugh'(chester')).
- iv. ~(◇(laugh'(jo') → ~(laugh'(jo')))).
- v. ◇~(laugh'(fiona')).
- vi. ~(◇laugh'(fiona')).

Do the truth values of these expressions change depending on which world acts as the **reference world**? Explain your answer.

There are a number of important entailment rules that are valid in this semantics for modal formulae that also appear to be intuitively valid for the English sentences they are intended to translate. In the first place, the semantics for □ and ◇ involve quantification over possible worlds and so the entailment rules defined for the logical quantifiers have counterparts in this modal logic. Necessity is interpreted in terms of universal quantification over worlds, and a version of the rule of universal instantiation, given in Chapter 7, is valid for all worlds in all models. This rule is given in (22.a) and allows one to infer the truth of a formula ϕ from the truth of the formula $\Box\phi$. If we treat formulae as denoting functions from possible worlds to truth values, then the validity of (22.a) follows from that of the corresponding first order quantified formula in (22.b) for all worlds $\mathbf{w}_m$. It should, however, be clear without (22.b) that if some formula is necessarily true (true in every possible world), then it is true in any named world.

(22) a. $\Box\phi \rightarrow \phi$.

b. $\forall w\ [\phi(w)] \rightarrow \phi(w_m)$.

Logical possibility involves existential quantification over worlds and so the rule in (23.a) is valid for all models and worlds. Again this may be seen as a version of existential generalisation indicated in the formula in (23.b), where $\mathbf{w_m}$ is any named world. Intuitively, this too is valid, because if something is true at some named world, then it must be possibly true (nothing actually true can be necessarily false).

(23) a. $\phi \rightarrow \Diamond\phi$.

b. $\phi(w_m) \rightarrow \exists w\ [\phi(w)]$.

Other rules that are valid in the current logic are shown in (24) to (27) where each formula is followed by examples in English plus their schematic translations to illustrate their intuitive validity. (24) and (25) show the interdefinability of $\Diamond$ and $\Box$, while (26) shows that impossible formulae are those that are necessarily false and (27) shows that possibly false formulae are those that are not necessarily true.

(24) a. $\Box\phi \leftrightarrow \sim\Diamond\sim\phi$.

b. Fiona must be laughing or not laughing.
$\Box$(laugh'(fiona') $\vee$ ~laugh'(fiona')).

c. It is not possible that Fiona isn't laughing or not laughing.
~$\Diamond$~(laugh'(fiona') $\vee$ ~laugh'(fiona')).

(25) a. $\Diamond\phi \leftrightarrow \sim\Box\sim\phi$.

b. Fiona may be laughing.
$\Diamond$laugh'(fiona').

c. It is not the case that Fiona is necessarily not laughing.
~$\Box$~laugh'(fiona').

(26) a. $\sim\Diamond\phi \leftrightarrow \Box\sim\phi$.

b. It is not the case that Fiona may be laughing.
~$\Diamond$laugh'(fiona').

c. It must be the case that Fiona is not laughing.
$\Box$~laugh'(fiona').

(27) a. $\Diamond\sim\phi \leftrightarrow \sim\Box\phi$.

b. It may be the case that Fiona isn't laughing.
$\Diamond$~laugh'(fiona').

c. It is not the case that Fiona must be laughing.
~$\Box$laugh'(fiona').

Exercise 9.2:
Explain why the semantics given for $\Box$ and $\Diamond$ guarantees that the rules in (24) to (27) are valid.

The interpretation of necessity proposed above also has the desired property that it guarantees that the substitution of extensional equivalents is not valid in this context. Recall the invalid inference pattern in (3), repeated as (28). A schematic translation of this inference pattern appears in (29) where *ms'* is used for the translation of *the Morning Star* and *es'* for that of *the Evening Star*.

(28) a. Necessarily, the Morning Star is the Morning Star.
b. The Morning Star is the Evening Star.
c. Therefore, necessarily, the Morning Star is the Evening Star.

(29) a. $\Box(ms' = ms')$.
b. $ms' = es'$.
c. $\Box(ms' = es')$.

The inference pattern set out above is invalid in the terms of modal logic because the first premiss and the conclusion have different truth-conditions. (29.a) is true, as we have seen, relative to a model M and world $\mathbf{w_n}$ if, and only if, *ms' = ms'* is true in every possible world in M. Since every constant is, by the definition of identity, necessarily identical to itself, this formula is true of any set of possible worlds. (29.b), on the other hand, is true if and only if two different constants happen to extensionally denote the same entity. Although the premiss in (29.b) asserts that it is true that two different constants do denote the same entity, it is true non-modally, i.e. only with respect to some specified world (the actual one). Since it is not a logical impossibility that two different constants extensionally denote different things, there must be some logically possible world in which (29.b) is false. Hence, (29.c) must be false in a model that contains all logically possible worlds, i.e. in any model likely to provide an adequate interpretation for any natural language. The truth of (29.c) thus does not follow from the truth of the premises in (29.a) and (29.b).

The putative inference pattern in (28) is set out in (30) in terms of the truth-conditions of the expressions in (29). From this it is easy to see that (29.a) and (29.c) have different truth-conditions and that therefore (28.c) does not follow from (28.a) and (28.b). We have, therefore, provided a semantics that ensures that extensional substitution into one of the opaque contexts noted in Section 9.1 is not valid.

(30) a. $[\Box ms' = ms']^{M,g,wn}$ is **1** iff $[ms' = ms']^{M,g,wm}$ in all $\mathbf{w_m} \in \mathbf{W}$, i.e. if $[ms']^{M,g,wm}$ is identical to $[ms']^{M,g,wm}$ in every possible world.
b. $[ms' = es']^{M,g,wn}$ is **1** iff $[ms']^{M,g,wn}$ is identical to $[es']^{M,g,wn}$.
c. $[\Box es' = ms']^{M,g,wn}$ is **1** iff $[es' = ms']^{M,g,wm}$ in all $\mathbf{w_m} \in \mathbf{W}$, i.e. if $[ms']^{M,g,wm}$ is identical to $[es']^{M,g,wm}$ in every possible world.

9.3.2 Accessible worlds

In models more satisfactory than the simplistic M_9, the set of worlds would include all the logically possible worlds, i.e. a set of worlds in which each non-contradictory formula is true in at least one world. This has the consequence that every formula that is not a logical falsehood is possibly true and thus every sentence in (31) is associated with a true formula in some appropriate model.

(31) a. The Conservative Party might not win a fifth term of office in 1997.
b. Rabbits may be robots from Mars.
c. Snow may be a black sticky substance, hot to touch.
d. A tree may be an air-breathing quantifier that lives at the bottom of the sea on a diet of logic textbooks.

Although all the sentences in (31) describe situations that are *logically* possible, not all of them are as likely as the others. For example, (31.a) is much more likely than (31.b) and (31.d) is completely unlikely. Indeed, in the latter case the English word *tree* appears to have lost all of the properties generally associated with trees in the actual world and one could question whether a speaker asserting (31.d) as a true statement in some possible world was actually speaking English. Because of such differences in likelihood, the notion of possibility (and necessity) might be taken to be relative to a particular world and not absolute for all worlds. This notion of the relativity of modality can be defined in terms of a relation, **R**, of **accessibility** (or **alternativeness**) between possible worlds. A world $\mathbf{w_m}$ is thus **R-accessible** from another world $\mathbf{w_n}$, if, and only if, $\mathbf{w_nRw_m}$ is true (i.e. if $\mathbf{w_n}$ stands in relation **R** to $\mathbf{w_m}$) in which case $\mathbf{w_m}$ is a possible alternative to $\mathbf{w_n}$. The relation, **R**, thus imposes structure on the set of possible worlds, as the precedence relation, <, imposes structure on the set of possible times, **T**, in temporal models. The relations **R** and <, however, generally have different properties from <. For example, unlike <, **R** is not usually **transitive** so that if $\mathbf{w_nRw_m}$ and $\mathbf{w_mRw_o}$ it is not necessarily the case that $\mathbf{w_nRw_o}$. **R** is, however, often **reflexive**, so that $\mathbf{w_nRw_n}$ holds. The actual properties of **R** depend on the type of accessibility relation being modelled and thus no independent restrictions are put upon its definition.

The introduction of accessibility relations into the model allows possibility and necessity to be redefined in such a way as to refer only to worlds that are accessible to the reference world and not to every world in the model. This relativisation of modality to certain sets of worlds is reminiscent of the restriction of the domain of quantification to pragmatically determined context sets discussed in Chapter 6 with respect to definiteness, except that **R** is assumed to be given in the model itself, rather than by the pragmatics. The truth-conditions for $\diamond$ and $\Box$ relativised to accessible worlds are given in (32) where models contain a set of worlds plus an accessibility relation as well as a set of entities and a denotation assignment function, i.e. M = «A,F,W,R».

(32) a. If ϕ is a formula, then $[\Box\phi]^{M,g,wn}$ is **1** iff $[\phi]^{M,g,wm} = \mathbf{1}$ for all $\mathbf{w_m} \in \mathbf{W}$ where $\mathbf{w_nRw_m}$.
b. If ϕ is a formula, then $[\diamond\phi]^{M,g,wn}$ is **1** iff $[\phi]^{M,g,wm} = \mathbf{1}$ for some $\mathbf{w_m} \in \mathbf{W}$ where $\mathbf{w_nRw_m}$.

There are many different sorts of accessibility relation that may be defined over the set of possible worlds and these may yield different interpretations for modal formulae. Where logical necessity and possibility are involved, **R** relates all worlds that conform to the system of logic chosen. By (32), a formula that is logically necessarily true is one which is true in all logical worlds, but not in worlds where the logical structure breaks down. Whether the set of possible worlds should include worlds that do not conform to logical rules of inference like conjunction elimination is a matter of debate, but there are more interesting accessibility relations that do properly discriminate between logically possible worlds.

One such relation is that defined by the sense relations amongst words, such as those discussed in Chapter 7. We saw there that word meaning may be partly accounted for in terms of meaning postulates that relate the extensions of different expressions within a particular language. In a semantic theory that allows for the possibility of alternative states of affairs, the status of meaning postulates like those in (33) is unclear. Do they constrain the extensions of predicates in all permissible models or only in the actual world in particular models? We do not want to require all possible worlds to conform to all sense relations (thus elevating meaning postulates to the status of logical constraints) because we can, for example, happily accept talking trains and excitable cars within the space of a children's story or an adventure film. Nor do we want to restrict sense relations to holding only in the actual world, since we could not then explain why a sentence like *Colourless green ideas may sleep furiously* seems to describe an empirically impossible situation. If meaning postulates are interpreted as defining accessibility relations between worlds, however, then the anomaly associated with sentences like that just quoted or the peculiar sentence in (31.d) may be accounted for. For example, if a definition of the sense relations of English includes the statements in (33) and we interpret **R** to be $\mathbf{R}_s$, an accessibility relation that relates worlds that conforms to these sense relations, then (31.d) turns out to be false according to the definition of possibility in (32.b). Any world in which this sentence expresses a true proposition fails to conform to the constraints in (33), because it requires some entity to be both abstract and not abstract, a logical impossibility. Hence, such worlds are not accessible to the actual world and so *A tree may be an air-breathing quantifier that lives at the bottom of the sea on a diet of logic textbooks* is true in no world, $\mathbf{w}_m$, that is $\mathbf{R}_s$-accessible to the reference world, i.e. where $\mathbf{w}_n\mathbf{R}\mathbf{w}_m$ does not hold.

(33) a. $\forall x$ [tree'(x) $\rightarrow$ ~abstract'(x)].
b. $\forall x$ [quantifier'(x) $\rightarrow$ abstract'(x)].

We may conceive of **sense**, according to the definitions of Chapter 7, as defining a complex of accessibility relations that relate worlds according to how they conform to the different sets of meaning postulates associated with different lexical items. The sense of an expression, therefore, structures the set of worlds and makes it possible to differentiate those expressions that have the same intension. (This is discussed further in Chapter 10.) In this way, it is possible to give a more subtle account of the meaning of words and the sentences that contain them, one that may provide a semantic theory of figurative language in terms of possible worlds. Be that as it may, interpreting sense relations in terms of meaning postulates that define accessibility relations enables the differentiation of likely from unlikely possibilities.

*Exercise 9.3:

Consider a language with only two (one-place) predicate constants, P and Q, and two individual constants, a and b, and a model consisting of only two elements, e_1 and e_2, a denotation assignment function, F and a set of possible worlds W.

1. Define the set of all logically possible worlds, W, by listing the possible combinations of extensions of P and Q in this model (i.e. by defining F). How many worlds are there?
2. Which worlds are accessible to each other, if we add the accessibility relation R_1 to the model which is defined to hold between worlds that conform to the meaning postulate $\forall x\, [P(x) \rightarrow Q(x)]$? How many worlds are no longer accessible?
3. What are the truth values of the following expressions with respect to this model, assuming R_1 accessibility?

i. $\Box(\sim P(b) \vee Q(b))$.
ii. $\Diamond(P(a) \,\&\, \sim Q(a))$.
iii. $\sim\Diamond(\sim P(a) \vee \sim Q(a))$.
iv. $\sim\Box(P(a) \vee Q(a))$.

While the accessibility relation on worlds imposed by sense relations may be considered central to the meaning of non-figurative English expressions, other notions of accessibility can be used to account for other sorts of modal relations that are central to what one knows or what one's obligations are. In addition to the alethic modality discussed in the last section, philosophers also recognise **epistemic** and **deontic** modalities, amongst others. The former expression, derived from the Classical Greek word for 'knowledge', defines necessity and possibility in terms of states of knowledge while the second, a word derived from the Greek word meaning 'to be binding', has to do with permission and obligation.

The sentences in (34) would generally be construed epistemically, since it is likely that (34.a) is not logically true (we can conceive of worlds where room temperature is below the freezing point or above the boiling point of water) and (34.b) conveys little information from the logical point of view. Hence, the proposition expressed by (34.a) is true if (and only if) water is wet at room temperature in every world consistent with what is (objectively) known about the temperature of rooms and about the properties of water. Similarly, (34.b) expresses a true proposition if and only if in some world consistent with what is known about cold climates, precipitation and snow, precipitation does indeed fall as snow in cold climates. The truth of the propositions expressed by these sentences thus does not depend on worlds in which, for example, rooms generally have a temperature of -50°C or in which water is a solid at +20°C.

(34) a. At room temperature, water must be wet.
b. In cold climates, precipitation may fall as snow.

Epistemic modality may be interpreted as truth with respect, not to worlds consistent with what is generally known, but to worlds consistent with what an individual, speaker or hearer, knows. Consider the two sentences in (35).

(35) a. Fiona must be drunk.
b. Bertie may sing at the party.

In terms of what is objectively known, the proposition expressed by (35.a) is (probably) not true, since *Fiona is drunk* (at some particular time) is unlikely to be true in every world consistent with objective knowledge. However, it can be interpreted in such a way that it is true, provided that we take into consideration the knowledge of the person who utters the sentence. For example, according to what a speaker knows, it may indeed be necessarily true that Fiona is drunk, because she has drunk six glasses of wine and does not usually drink alcohol. In other words, *Fiona must be drunk* is true epistemically, if *Fiona is drunk* is true in every world consistent with what is known by the speaker. Similarly, a speaker-oriented epistemic interpretation of (35.b) requires there to be some world consistent with what is known by the speaker in which Bertie sings at the relevant party.

The two sentences in (35) are ambiguous not only according to the scope of knowledge assumed, but also according to the sort of modality intended. On a deontic interpretation, an utterance of (35.b) asserts that Bertie is being *allowed* to sing at the party while an utterance of (35.a) asserts that Fiona is *obliged* or required to be drunk (e.g. because she is acting in a play that requires this behaviour or is taking part in some initiation ceremony). More formally, (35.b) is true if (and only if) there is a world that is deontically accessible from the actual world where *Bertie sings at the party* is true and (35.a) is true if in every world deontically accessible from ours Fiona is indeed drunk. Exactly what deontic (or indeed epistemic) accessibility involves is a matter for the philosopher rather than the linguist, but the fact that different accessibility relations may alter the truth values of modal sentences allows us to begin to account for the different interpretations of sentences like those in (35).

Thus, the truth or falsity of modal statements depends on the different accessibility relations holding between different worlds. These accessibility relations have an effect, not only on the truth value of a formula translating a particular sentence, but also on the inferences that can be drawn within the modal system. For example, the entailment rule in (22.a), which allows the inference that ϕ is true whenever $\Box\phi$ is true, is valid only if **R** is **reflexive** (i.e. where for all worlds, $\mathbf{w_n}$, $\mathbf{w_n R w}$ is true). As pointed out in McCawley (1981:277), in certain interpretations of **moral necessity**, where **R** is interpreted something like *is morally better, or more desirable, than*, **R** is not reflexive. In such a modal system, we cannot infer from the truth of *All children must be good* that *All children are in fact good*, because the former sentence only requires the latter to be true in all morally more desirable worlds, of which the actual world is not necessarily one.

The definition of such relations is, therefore, very important for the interpretation of modal sentences and it is likely that an adequate semantic theory needs to contain many accessibility relations, providing a rich and complex structure to the worlds contained by any model. Context is then required for the hearer to identify the particular relation intended by the speaker. Despite the importance of the notion of accessibility, nothing further will be said about such relations. The reason for this is that, while particular interpretations and inferences are affected by the particular relation supposed, the general theory is not affected by which accessibility relation is assumed. Therefore, in the next chapter, it will be generally assumed that **R** defines logical accessibility, unless otherwise stated.

9.4 Further reading

Referentially opaque constructions are discussed in Lyons (1981: 157- 167), McCawley (1981: 326-340), Chierchia and McConnell-Ginet (1990: 204-208), Partee, ter Meulen and Wall (1990: 403-414) and Dowty, Wall and Peters (1981: 141-146). Frege's discussion on *Sinn* and *Bedeutung* can be found in Frege (1892) and Dummett (1981: chs. 5 & 6) gives a useful critical (philosophical) discussion of this. The notion of possible world is discussed at length in, for example, Lewis (1981), and, for a different point of view, Bradley & Swartz (1979). A full logical exposition of modal logic can be found in Hughes and Cresswell (1968), but the subject is given a simple introduction in Guttenplan (1986: ch. 16), McCawley (1981: 273-296) and Allwood, Andersen and Dahl (1977: 108-110). The logic is discussed in the terms used in this chapter in Dowty, Wall and Peters (1981: 121-131), and Chierchia and McConnell-Ginet (1990: 213-221). Different types of modality are discussed in Lyons (1977: ch. 7), Lyons (1981: ch. 10) and accessibility relations are discussed in McCawley (1981: 273 ff. & ch. 11), Partee, ter Meulen and Wall (1990: 414-423) and Martin (1987: 281-295).

10 Intensional Semantics

10.1 Modelling intensions

In Chapter 9, an interpretation of the modal adverbs *necessarily* and *possibly* was presented in terms of possible worlds, but the other contexts in which extensional entailments fail were not discussed. As proposed in Section 9.2, the general solution to the problem of referentially opaque contexts lies in the concept of intensionality, but the interpretation of modality given above was not stated in terms of this concept and it has not been made clear how possible worlds enable a formal definition of intension to be made. Let us now remedy the situation and provide a general semantic theory for opaque contexts, thus completing our survey of formal semantic theory.

The definitions for the interpretation of modal formulae given in Chapter 9 embody the idea that formulae may be true in some worlds but not in others, i.e. that the extensions of formulae (i.e. truth values) may vary from world to world. Furthermore, it was suggested at the end of Section 9.2 that an intension is something that picks out the extension of an expression in any state of affairs. The intension of a formula may thus be defined as something that specifies its truth value in every state of affairs. Equating states-of-affairs with possible worlds, we interpret the intensions of formulae as functions that map possible worlds onto truth values: functions that map a possible world onto **1** if the formula is true in that world and onto **0**, otherwise. For example, the truth values of the formula *laugh'(fiona')* with respect to the model $\mathbf{M_9}$ differ according to the reference world. As can be seen from the specification of this model in (19) of Chapter 9, this formula is true in worlds $\mathbf{w_1}$ and $\mathbf{w_4}$ but false in worlds $\mathbf{w_2}$ and $\mathbf{w_3}$. The intension of *laugh'(fiona')* in $\mathbf{M_9}$ is thus the function that maps $\mathbf{w_1}$ and $\mathbf{w_4}$ onto **1** and $\mathbf{w_2}$ and $\mathbf{w_3}$ onto **0**, as shown in (1).

(1) Intension of *laugh'(fiona')* in M_9

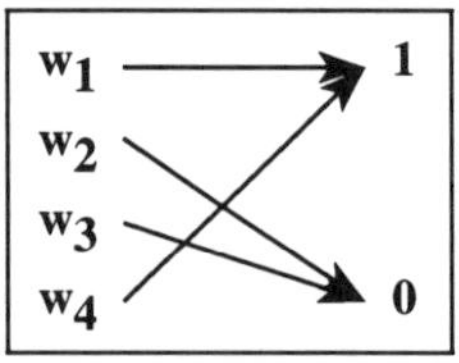

While the truth value of two formulae may be the same in some world, their intensions may differ. For example, both *laugh'(fiona')* and *~(laugh'(chester'))* are true in world $\mathbf{w_1}$ with respect to $\mathbf{M_9}$. However, the intension of the latter is the function that maps $\mathbf{w_1}$ and $\mathbf{w_3}$ onto **1** and $\mathbf{w_2}$ and $\mathbf{w_4}$ onto **0**, since in the latter worlds Chester does not laugh, as shown in (2.a). Furthermore, the formula *laugh'(jo')* $\vee$ *~laugh'(jo')* although again true in $\mathbf{w_1}$, differs in intension from both the previously considered formulae, since its intension is that function which maps every possible world onto **1**, cf. (2.b).

(2) a. Intension of *~(laugh'(chester'))* in M_9

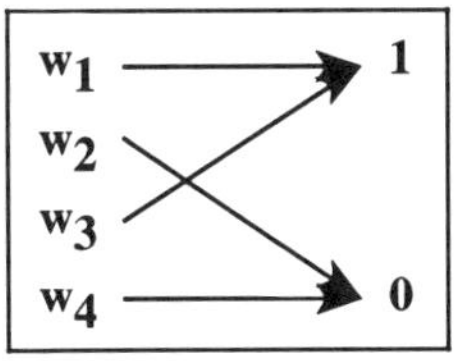

b. Intension of *laugh'(jo')* ∨ *~laugh'(jo')* in M_9

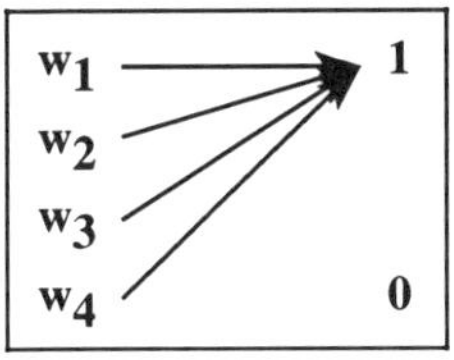

As the diagrams in (1) and (2) show, interpreting the intensions of formulae as functions from possible worlds to truth values allows semantic differentiation between formulae that happen to have the same extension in some world. Although there are some formulae that have the same intensions in M_9 (compare, for example, the intension of *laugh'(jo')* with (1)), but which are not true paraphrases, this is an artefact of the small scale of the model and not of the theory itself. In principle, if a full set of logically possible worlds is incorporated into the model, it is possible using this method to differentiate the intensions of all contingently true formulae.

Intensions cannot, however, be defined solely with respect to possible worlds. As we saw in the last chapter, the concept of time is necessary to account for tense and aspect distinctions. Since natural languages may combine tense and modality in particular sentences, as, for example, in *Jo possibly laughed yesterday* and *When she has finished her degree, Fiona may apply for a job as a gardener*, an adequate semantics for natural languages must also combine elements of modal and temporal interpretation. Models should, therefore, contain both times and possible worlds, as well as entities. Furthermore, because temporal models allow the extensions of expressions to change from interval to interval in the same way that modal models allow them to vary from world to world, our semantic models must allow extensions to vary along two dimensions: temporal interval and possible world. Thus, we may think of extensions as being defined for a particular world at a particular time. In other words, extensions are defined for a particular **co-ordinate** or **index** consisting of a possible world, $\mathbf{w_n}$, and an interval of time, **i**, i.e. with respect to an ordered pair $<\mathbf{w_n},\mathbf{i}>$. If one of the co-ordinates with respect to which an expression is interpreted changes then the extension of that expression may change. Hence, $[\alpha]^{M,g,wn,i}$, the extension of an expression α at the index $<\mathbf{w_n},\mathbf{i}>$ with respect to model **M** and variable assignment **g**, may differ from $[\alpha]^{M,g,wn,j}$ or $[\alpha]^{M,g,wm,i}$ where $\mathbf{w_n}$ differs from $\mathbf{w_m}$ and **i** differs from **j**.

As an illustration, consider the diagram in (3) which shows the changing extensions of the predicate *laugh'* in four worlds across four moments of time, to give part of the intensional model M_{10}. In (3), a line indicates an interval of time and the set below the line shows the extension of *laugh'* at that interval. The horizontal axis presents the different extensions for *laugh'* across the four moments of time within the same possible world while the vertical axis traces its extensions at the same time in different worlds.

(3)

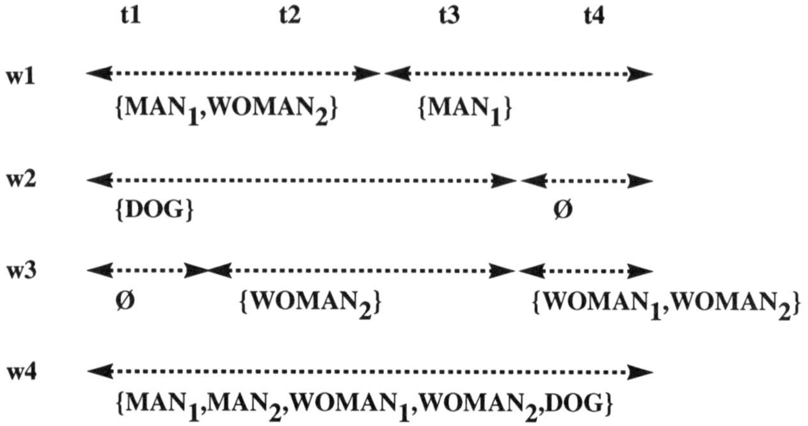

If intensions are defined as functions from states of affairs to extensions, then in models with times and worlds, they must have the set of all world-time co-ordinates (or indices) as their domain. Thus, the intension of the formula *laugh'(fiona')* with respect to $\mathbf{M_{10}}$ is a function from pairs consisting of a world and a time to the truth values, **0** and **1**. Because *laugh* is an activity verb, its extension holds for all subsets of an interval over which it is defined, as we saw in Chapter 8. Hence, we can define the intension of *laugh'(fiona')* in terms of its truth values at each ordered pair of world plus moment of time, as is done in (4), i.e. as a function from world/time pairs to truth values. The intension of an expression, α, with respect to a model, **M**, and an assignment of values to variables, **g**, is written as ${}_3[\alpha]^{M,g}$, so ${}_3[\text{laugh'(fiona')}]^{M10,g}$ represents the intension of the formula *laugh'(fiona')* with respect to M_{10} and **g**.

(4) $^3[\text{laugh'(fiona')}]^{M_{10},g}$

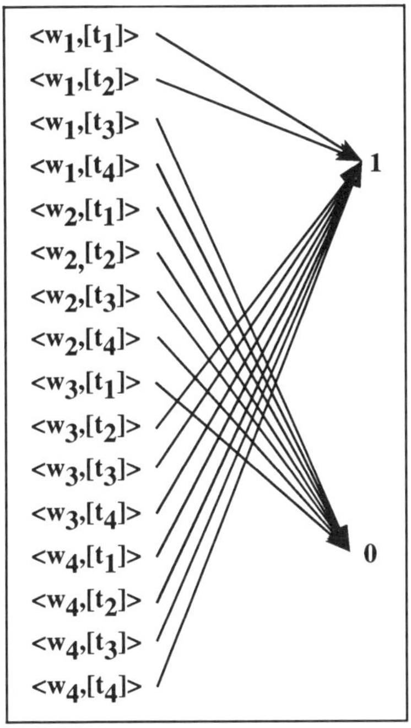

Exercise 10.1:
Diagram the intensions of the following formulae with respect to M_{10} (assuming that *jo', fiona'* and *chester'* have the same extensions in all worlds and times, i.e. **MAN**$_1$, **WOMAN**$_2$ and **DOG**, respectively):

i. laugh'(jo').
ii. laugh'(chester') ∨ laugh'(jo').
iii. laugh'(fiona') & ~laugh'(fiona').
iv. laugh'(fiona') → laugh'(jo').

It is possible to add more co-ordinates to the indices in terms of which intensions are defined. For example, it is often the case that locations are relevant to the interpretation of sentences. Thus, if the sentence *It is raining* is uttered, it is usually interpreted as an assertion that it is raining at the place in which the speaker is situated (at the present time in the actual world), not that it is raining everywhere. Hence, we might expand our semantic space to include locations and introduce into our models a set of places together with some relation of proximity. Furthermore, the fact that *I* and *you* are **indexical** (or **deictic**) expressions, like *here* and *there* or tense, indicates that co-ordinates for speaker and hearer should be added to the model. Indeed, as

Lewis (1972) points out, there are many other candidates for co-ordinates in defining an adequate semantics for any human language. Exactly what ones should be included is a matter for debate and empirical research, but at a minimum we would need worlds, times and places. In this book, however, we will utilise indices that consist only of worlds and times. The addition of a **topographical** co-ordinate will only complicate matters unduly without altering the basic properties of the semantic system. In principle, any (finite) number of co-ordinates may be added to the model theory presented below, allowing more and more contextual information to be included in the semantics, but without altering the fundamental structure of the theory.

The semantics of the modal operators can now be redefined in terms of the intensions of the formulae they have scope over, i.e. as functions from functions from co-ordinates to truth values to truth values. Since functions that map some set of entities into the truth values are characteristic functions of subsets of those entities, the intensions of formulae may be thought of as sets of indices. Hence, we can define the semantics of necessity and possibility in terms of functions from (the characteristic functions of) sets of world/time pairs to truth values. In the definitions in the previous chapter, $\Box\phi$ is true (with respect to a model and a reference world) if, and only if, ϕ is true in all accessible worlds in the model. $\Diamond\phi$, on the other hand, is true if, and only if, ϕ is true in some accessible world. The necessity operator can, therefore, be interpreted as that function that maps the set of all co-ordinates onto **1** and all other subsets of $\mathbf{W} \times \mathbf{I}$ onto **0** and the possibility operator is that function that maps the null set of co-ordinates onto **0** and all other subsets onto **1**. In order to differentiate this approach to necessity and possibility from the earlier approach, we will not use the modal operators, $\Box$ and $\Diamond$, but translate the words *necessarily* and *possibly* directly into *necessarily'* and *possibly'*. These expressions denote the functions over the intensions of formulae (over ʒ$[\phi]^{M,g}$) which are spelled out in (5) where **I** is the set of all temporal intervals defined on a set of moments **T**, $[\alpha]^{M,g,wn,i}$ is the extension of α with respect to **M**, **g** and index $<\mathbf{w_n},\mathbf{i}>$ (see Section 10.1.2) and ʒ$[\phi]^{M,g}(<\mathbf{w_m},\mathbf{i}>)$ is the value of the intension of ϕ at the index $<\mathbf{w_n},\mathbf{i}>$.

(5) a. $[\text{necessarily'}]^{M,g,wn,i}$ is that function which maps the intension of a formula ϕ onto **1** iff ʒ$[\phi]^{M,g}(<\mathbf{w_m},i'>)$ is **1** for all $\mathbf{w_m} \in \mathbf{W}$ such that $\mathbf{w_n R w_m}$ and $\mathbf{i} \in \mathbf{I}$ (i.e. where ʒ$[\phi]^{M,g}$ is the set of all possible world/time pairs).

b. $[\text{possibly'}]^{M,g,wn,i}$ is that function which maps the intension of a formula ϕ onto **1** iff ʒ$[\phi]^{M,g}(<\mathbf{w_m},i'>)$ is **1** for some $\mathbf{w_m} \in \mathbf{W}$ such that $\mathbf{w_n R w_m}$ and some $\mathbf{i'} \in \mathbf{I}$ (i.e. where ʒ$[\phi]^{M,g}$ is not null).

A question that arises with the interpretation of necessity within models which have times as well as possible worlds is whether to interpret it as necessity for all times and worlds, as in (5), or for particular times in all worlds. Should we analyse a sentence like *Necessarily, the Morning Star is the Morning Star* as expressing a true proposition if *The Morning Star is the Morning Star* is true always and in all situations or whether it is true *now* in all situations (and therefore perhaps false at some other time)? Although it would seem that with sentences like the above it is clear that the first interpretation is intended, with sentences containing modal verbs interpreted non-alethically, e.g. *Fiona must be singing*, it would seem preferable to have an interpretation in which the proposition expressed by the sentence comes out as true if *Fiona is singing* is true in every deontically or epistemically accessible world only at the time of utterance but not at *all* past and future times in those worlds. Montague adopts, without argument, the interpretation of necessity in (5.a). However, while this seems to work as an analysis of the adverb, *necessarily*, the modal verb *must* appears to require the less strict interpretation given in (6.a) which specifies that a formula *must'*(ϕ) is true as long as ϕ is true in all worlds at the appropriate reference time. Thus, according to (6.a) [*must'(Impf(sing'(fiona')))*]^{M,g,wn,i} is true provided that [*(Impf (sing'(fiona')))*]^{M,g,wm,i} is true in all worlds $\mathbf{w_m}$ at **i**. A parallel interpretation for the modal verb of possibility *may* is given in (6.b). This differs from that given for *possibly* in (5.b) in that a formula like *may'(Impf(sing'(fiona')))* (translating *Fiona may be singing*) is true as long as there is at least one world accessible to the reference world in which Fiona is singing at the time of utterance. Worlds in which she is singing at other times are irrelevant. Hence, while (6.a) gives a less restrictive form of necessity than (5.a), the definition of possibility in (6.b) is more restrictive than that in (5.b).

(6) a. [must']^{M,g,wn,i} is that function which maps the intension of a formula ϕ onto **1** iff $3[\phi]^{M,g}(<\mathbf{w_m},\mathbf{i}>)$ is **1** for all $\mathbf{w_m} \in \mathbf{W}$ such that $\mathbf{w_n R w_m}$.
b. [may']^{M,g,wn,i} is that function which maps the intension of a formula ϕ onto **1** iff $3[\phi]^{M,g}(<\mathbf{w_n},\mathbf{i}>)$ is **1** for some $\mathbf{w_m} \in \mathbf{W}$ such that $\mathbf{w_n R w_m}$.

Treating modal expressions as functors over intensional expressions in this way has the extremely desirable consequence that Leibniz' Law fails to be valid. The reason for this, of course, is that the intensions of formulae may differ even if their extensions happen to be the same at some index. Thus, the functions denoted by *necessarily', possibly', must'* and *may'* may map the intension of one formula, ϕ, onto true (or false) but that of another, ψ, onto the opposite truth value, where $3[\phi]^{M,g}$ is not identical to $3[\psi]^{M,g}$. As a concrete example, consider the interpretations of *Fiona must be laughing* and *Jo must be laughing* with respect to M_{10} and the index $<\mathbf{w_1},[\mathbf{t_2}]>$. Suppose that the accessibility relation of the model is one where $\mathbf{w_3}$ and $\mathbf{w_4}$ are both accessible to $\mathbf{w_1}$ which is accessible to itself, but $\mathbf{w_2}$ is not accessible to $\mathbf{w_1}$, i.e. where **R** is $\{<\mathbf{w_1},\mathbf{w_1}>,<\mathbf{w_1},\mathbf{w_3}>,<\mathbf{w_1},\mathbf{w_4}>\}$. The interpretation of *must'* in (6.a) entails that [*must'*]$^{M,g,w1,[t2]}$ is that function that maps a function from indices to truth values onto **1** if, and only if, that function maps the indices $<\mathbf{w_1},[\mathbf{t_2}]>$, $<\mathbf{w_3},[\mathbf{t_2}]>$, and $<\mathbf{w_4},[\mathbf{t_2}]>$ onto **1**, i.e. it picks out all those worlds accessible to $\mathbf{w_1}$ at time $[\mathbf{t_2}]$. Thus, [*must'*]$^{M,g,w1,[t2]}$(3[*laugh'(fiona')*]^{M,g}) is true if, and only if, 3[*laugh'(fiona')*]^{M,g} applied to each of these indices yields the value **1**. Looking at the diagram in (4) which represents the intension of *laugh'(fiona')*, we can see that this is the case. It is true that Fiona is laughing in all worlds accessible to $\mathbf{w_1}$ at the appropriate time $[\mathbf{t_2}]$. Hence, *Fiona must be laughing* is true. However, although it is true that *Jo is laughing* is true in world $\mathbf{w_1}$ at time $[\mathbf{t_2}]$, it is not the case that *Jo must be laughing* is true at that index. This is because the function 3[*laugh'(jo')*]^{M,g} maps the index $<\mathbf{w_3},[\mathbf{t_2}]>$ onto **0**, as can be checked by referring to the diagram in (3) showing the denotation of *laugh'* in M_{10}, and so *Jo is laughing* is not true in every accessible world at time $[\mathbf{t_2}]$. Hence, 3[*laugh'(jo')*]^{M,g} differs from 3[*laugh'(fiona')*]^{M,g} and so *must'(laugh'(jo'))* is false while *must'(laugh'(fiona'))* is true, despite the fact that Jo and Fiona are both laughing at the same **reference index**.

The fact that two expressions are extensionally equivalent at some index has no bearing at all on their intensional equivalence and so while substitution of the expressions preserves truth in extensional contexts, there is no guarantee that it does in intensional ones. As we saw at the end of Chapter 9, the inference pattern in (3) of that chapter fails because the extensional equivalence of the Morning Star with itself is necessary while that between the Morning Star and the Evening Star is contingent. The sentences *The Morning Star is the Morning Star* and *The Morning Star is the Evening Star* differ in intension and so are not intersubstitutable in intensional contexts. Leibniz' Law is thus valid only in extensional contexts and fails for all expressions that create intensional contexts. Thus, we must revise the definition of the Law of Substitution in (2) of Chapter 9 to exclude explicitly substitution into intensional contexts. These contexts also include the scopes of the past and future tense operators, because the extensions of expressions may vary over time and so those that are extensionally equivalent at one interval of time may not be at others. Thus, the truth of (8.c) does not follow from the truth of (8.a) and (8.b) because while Ethel may now be the Ladies' Scottish Golf Champion, someone else could have been when Jo met the then Ladies' Scottish Golf Champion. The revised version of the Law of Substitution is stated in (8), where the term **intensional functor** covers expressions like *necessarily'*, *may'* and the other opaque predicates discussed in later sections.

(7) a. Jo met the Ladies' Scottish Golf Champion.
    b. Ethel is the Ladies' Scottish Golf Champion.
    c. Jo met Ethel.

(8) $(a = b) \rightarrow [\phi \leftrightarrow \phi^{b/a}]$ where a is not in the scope of an intensional functor or the tense operators *Past* and *Fut*.

As we will see in Section 10.2, the analysis of modal expressions given above can be generalised to all opacity creating predicates. In this way, we can ensure that the Law of Substitution fails for the reasons shown above and we will see that this also has the effect of making the other false inference patterns noted in Section 9.1 truly invalid. Before this can be tackled properly, however, we need to construct a metalanguage that can represent intensional expressions and provide a proper and fully explicit semantics for this language. This will involve extending our definitions of possible types and revising the model theory of previous chapters to take account of intensions.

10.2 The intensional language L_{IL}

In this section, we look at Montague's definition of a co-ordinate semantics for a fully typed language, called L_{IL}, which is like L_Q but with tense and modal operators as well. First, we must revise the theory of types to take account of intensional expressions and look at how such expressions should be interpreted. No systematic attempt, however, is made to revise the grammar fragment so far constructed to take account of intensional contexts. From now on it is assumed that readers have the skill to see the relation between expressions in the intensional language and the English examples they are assumed to translate. While the construction of an adequate translation algorithm from syntax to L_{IL} is not without its problems or interest, to attempt the task here would unduly lengthen an already long book and would not particularly help the reader understand the most important matter, which is the semantic interpretation. Here more than ever the choice of the syntactic framework determines the precise nature of the translation algorithm and so setting out a particular algorithm would not necessarily be helpful or enlightening.

10.2.1 Intensional expressions ...

The intensional language L_{IL} has the language of Chapter 8, L_T, as its core, but also contains intensional expressions and intensional operators. To show that an expression is intensional, an **intension operator**, symbolised as ^, is used and, like all operators, it is written to the left of an extensional expression. For example, the intensional counterpart of *laugh'(fiona')* is *^laugh'(fiona')*, that of *laugh'* is *^laugh'*, that of *fiona'* is *^fiona'*. As might be expected, an intensional expression like *^laugh'(fiona')* denotes $\Im[\textit{laugh'(fiona')}]^{M,g}$, the intension of its extensional counterpart, *laugh'(fiona')*. This gives the general rule for intensional expressions in (9).

(9) If α is any extensional expression, $^\wedge\alpha$ is an intensional expression which denotes $\Im[\alpha]^{M,g}$.

Montague did not restrict the intensional operator to apply only to extensional expressions but allowed it to be recursive, thus allowing expressions like *^^laugh'(fiona')*, *^^^laugh'(fiona')* and so on. These expressions are not very interesting semantically, however, as they denote **constant functions** which pick out the same denotation for *^laugh'(fiona')* or *^^laugh'(fiona')* at every index. Furthermore, higher order intensions appear to be of little or no use in defining the semantics of any natural language and, as we are interested only in accounting for the interpretation of natural languages, ignoring the existence of higher order intensions is justified, at least as a temporary expedient.

Parallel to the intension operator is the **extension operator** written as ˇ which applies to an intensional expression α to yield an expression $^\vee\alpha$ which denotes the extension of α at some index. Thus, at any index the result of applying the extension operator to an intensional expression, $^\wedge\alpha$, is to cancel out the intensionality, making the expression so formed, $^{\vee\wedge}\alpha$ semantically equivalent to the original extensional expression α. For example, from *^laugh'(fiona')* the extensional expression *ˇ^laugh'(fiona')* can be formed which denotes at a particular index, say $\langle \mathbf{w}_3,[\mathbf{t}_2]\rangle$, the extension of *^laugh'(fiona')* at that index, i.e. $\Im[\textit{laugh'(fiona')}]^{M,g}(\langle \mathbf{w}_3,[\mathbf{t}_2]\rangle)$ which is, of course, equivalent to $[\textit{laugh'(fiona')}]^{M,g,w3,[t2]}$.The rule for using the extension operator is given more formally in (10) and the equivalence between $^{\vee\wedge}\alpha$ and α stated in (11) holds for all models, indices and variable assignments.

(10) If α is an intensional expression with denotation $\Im[\alpha]^{M,g}$, then $^\vee\alpha$ is an extensional expression whose denotation at any index $\langle \mathbf{w}_n,\mathbf{i}\rangle$, $[^\vee\alpha]^{M,g,wn,i}$, is the value of $\Im[\alpha]^{M,g}$ at $\langle \mathbf{w}_n,\mathbf{i}\rangle$ (i.e. $\Im[\alpha]^{M,g}(\langle \mathbf{w}_n,\mathbf{i}\rangle)$).

(11) $[^{\vee\wedge}\alpha]^{M,g,wn,i} = [\alpha]^{M,g,wn,i}$.

While the identity in (11) is valid, a parallel equivalence between $^{\wedge\vee}\alpha$ and α is not valid. As no expressions of this form are considered in this book, the explanation for this will not be given and readers are invited to try to work it out for themselves; or they may consult Dowty, Wall and Peters (1981: 175-176).

Because L_{IL} is a typed language, all intensional expressions must be assigned an appropriate intensional type. These are derived according to the rule in (12) which introduces a type that has the symbol **s** as its first element. Mnemonic for *sense* (after the Fregean *Sinn*), **s** is not itself a primitive type, like **e** and **t**, but is just used to indicate that a type is intensional. The fact that **s** is not treated as primitive means that no expressions directly denote indices, a reflection of the fact that natural languages have no way of referring directly to such things.

(12) **Intensional types**: If a is a type, then <s,a> is a type.

(12) is added to the rules defining types given in Chapter 4 and gives rise to types like those shown in (13). Recursive application of the intensional type rule will not be used in this book, as (10) already rules out the creation of 'higher order' intensional expressions so that types like that in (13.f) do not appear in the discussions below.

(13) a. <s,e>.
b. <s,t>.
c. <s,<e,t>>.
d. <s,<<s,<e,t>>,t>>.
e. <s,<<<s,<e,t>>,t>,<e,t>>>.
f. <<e,t>,<s,t>>.
g. <s,<s,<s,<e,t>>>>.

As in the language L_{type}, and the languages based on this, L_Q and L_T, complex expressions are derived by the rule of functional application, repeated in (14).

(14) If α is an expression of type <a,b> and β is an expression of type b, then $\alpha(\beta)$ is an expression of type a.

This rule must be strictly adhered to and caution must be taken when utilising it with expressions in intensional categories. Since there is no type s, there are no expressions of type s and so intensional types cannot directly combine with any expressions in L_{IL}. In order to combine an intensional functor with an argument, it is necessary first to 'de-intensionalise' the functor by applying the extension operator, $^\vee$, to it. Thus, one cannot directly apply an intensional functor $^\wedge\alpha$, of type <s,<a,b>>, to an argument β, of type a, but one can apply the extension of the functor $^\vee{}^\wedge\alpha$ to the same argument to get the well-formed expression $(^\vee{}^\wedge\alpha)(\beta)$ which, by the equivalence in (11), is semantically equivalent to $\alpha(\beta)$. By the general definition of types given in Chapter 4, intensional types may also appear as the argument or result types of other types. Examples of such types appear in (13.d,e & f) and care must be exercised in combining such functors with their arguments. Functors which have the general type <<s,a>,b> can be applied only to argument expressions that are themselves intensional, i.e. of type <s,a>. Thus, if α is of type <<s,a>,b> one cannot directly apply it to an expression β of type a. First, the latter must be made intensional using the intension operator to form the expression $^\wedge\beta$ of type <s,a> which can then be the argument of α to give $\alpha(^\wedge\beta)$. No problems arise in the application of functors with intensional result types of the form <a,<s,b>>, except that it must be borne in mind that the resulting expression is itself intensional and so may not directly combine with an argument and may only be an argument of a functor that takes an argument thathas an intensional type.

Exercise 10.2:
Assuming the type assignment that follows, which of the expressions below are well-formed expressions of L_{IL}? If they are well-formed say what types they have and if not, say why not.

Type:	Expression:
<s,e>	m
e	bertie', fiona'
<<s,e>,t>	change'
<e,t>	walk', student'
<<s,t>,t>	necessarily', possibly'
<t,t>	~
<<s,<e,t>>,<e,t>>	good'
<<e,t>,<e,t>>	happy'

i. change'(bertie').
ii. good'(^student').
iii. ~(˘^walk'(bertie')).
iv. necessarily'(^((good'(^student'))(fiona'))).
v. possibly'(change'(^m)).
vi. (happy'(student'))(˘m).
vii. good'(happy'(^student')).

The language L_{IL} also contains a full set of variables for each type, including the intensional types. Formally, the set of variables of any type a is formally symbolised as Var_a and particular variables of type a are formally indicated as $v_{n,a}$ where n is some natural number. This notation is somewhat cumbersome, however, and certain notational conventions are usually adopted. The conventions used in this chapter are set out in (15) and subscript numerals may be used with the various symbols where there are a number of variables of a particular type. The symbols used to indicate variables over extensional types (e.g. *x*, *P*, ***P*** and *R*) are the same as they have been in previous chapters, except for *p* and *q* which are here given an intensional type and so symbolise variables of type <s,t> and not of type t.

(15)

Type:	Variables:
e	x, y, z.
<s,e>	r.
<e,t>	P, Q.
<s,<e,t>>	A.
<s,t>	p, q.
<<e,t>,t>	***P***.
<s,<<e,t>,t>>	$\wp$.
<e,<e,t>>	R.
<s,<e,<e,t>>>	$\Re$.

Because L_{IL} contains both intensional and extensional variables, the lambda operator, λ, may bind intensional and extensional argument places. The definition of lambda abstraction remains as it was given in the final form in Chapter 5 (and as it is repeated in (16.d) below), but one must again be careful to use the correct type of variable. An extensional variable cannot be used where the position being bound is intensional, and vice versa. For example, given the type assignments in (15) and Exercise 10.2, λr *[change'(r)]* is well-formed, because *r* is of type <s,e> and *change'* is of type <<s,e>,t>, but neither λx *[change'(x)]* nor λx *[change'(r)]* is well-formed. The former is ill-formed because x is of type e and so not of a type appropriate to be the argument of *change'* while the latter is wrong because there is no instance of the variable bound by λ in the expression in its scope.

L_{IL} also contains the logical quantifiers $\forall$ and $\exists$ which like λ may bind variables of any type. So, for example, $\forall p$ *[necessarily'(p)]* is a well-formed formula which asserts that all expressions of type <s,t> are necessarily true while $\exists A$ *[(good'(A))(bertie')]* asserts that Bertie is a good something or, more accurately, there is some property with respect to which Bertie is good. The identity operator = in L_{IL} may also conjoin expressions of any type to yield a formula, as defined in (16.e). In the rules that construct quantified formulae in (16.k) and (16.l), the universal and existential operators are operators over *extensional* formulae (i.e. expressions of type t) and not over intensional ones (of type <s,t>) and their outputs are again extensional formulae. The same is true for the tense and aspect operators, *Past, Fut, Pres, Perf* and *Impf* and the propositional connectives, &, $\vee$, $\rightarrow$, $\leftrightarrow$ and ~.

The full definition of L_{IL} is given in (16) in the form of a recursive definition of what constitutes the set of **meaningful expressions** of a certain type. Anything that does not conform to one of these rules is not a meaningful expression of the logic and so does not have an interpretation in the model. (16) contains no rules for constructing modal expressions using the operators $\Box$ and $\Diamond$, as these these have now been supplanted by their counterparts *necessarily'* and *possibly'*, as discussed in Section 10.1.

(16) a. If α is an expression of type <b,a> and β is an expression of type b, then $\alpha(\beta)$ is an expression of type a.
b. If α is an extensional expression of type a, then $^\wedge\alpha$ is an expression of type <s,a>.
c. If α is an expression of type <s,a>, then $^\vee\alpha$ is an expression of type a.
d. If α is an expression of type a containing a free instance of a variable u of type b, then λu [α] is an expression of type <b,a>.
e. If α, β are expressions of type a, then $\alpha = \beta$ is an expression of type t.
f. If ϕ is an expression of type t, then $\sim\phi$ is an expression of type t.
g. If ϕ, ψ are expressions of type t, then (ϕ & ψ) is an expression of type t.
h. If ϕ, ψ are expressions of type t, then ($\phi \vee \psi$) is an expression of type t.
i. If ϕ, ψ are expressions of type t, then ($\phi \rightarrow \psi$) is an expression of type t.
j. If ϕ, ψ are expressions of type t, then ($\phi \leftrightarrow \psi$) is an expression of type t.
k. If ϕ is an expression of type t containing an instance of a free variable u of any type, then $\forall$u [ϕ] is an expression of type t.
l. If ϕ is an expression of type t containing an instance of a free variable u of any type, then $\exists$u [ϕ] is an expression of type t.

m. If ϕ is an expression of type t, then Past (ϕ) is an expression of type t.
n. If ϕ is an expression of type t, then Fut (ϕ) is an expression of type t.
o. If ϕ is an expression of type t, then Pres (ϕ) is an expression of type t.
p. If ϕ is an expression of type t, then Perf (ϕ) is an expression of type t.
q. If ϕ is an expression of type t, then Impf (ϕ) is an expression of type t.

10.2.2 ... And their interpretation

Having defined the language L_{IL}, into which expressions from English will now be translated, we must specify its interpretation, thus, as usual, providing an indirect interpretation of translated English expressions. First of all, we need a definition of the sorts of denotation that expressions of different intensional types may have and then we will move on to a consideration of intensional models and the formal definition of the model theory that will interpret all expressions in L_{IL} with respect to appropriate models.

Given the definition of an intension as a function from indices to extensions, from Section 10.1, the possible denotations of intensional types are easy to define. In all cases, an expression with an intensional type $<s,a>$ denotes a function from indices (i.e. world/time pairs) to denotations of type a. The set of all possible world/time pairs can be symbolised by the **Cartesian product** of the set **W** of possible worlds and the set **I** of temporal intervals defined by the set of times **T**. The Cartesian product of two sets **A** and **B** is written as **A** $\times$ **B** and is equivalent to the set of all *ordered pairs* where the first element is a member of set **A** and the second is a member of set **B**, as defined in (17).

(17) **Cartesian product**: $A \times B = \{<a,b> \mid a \in A \ \& \ b \in B\}$.

The Cartesian product of **W** and **I** is thus, by (17), the set of all pairs of possible worlds and temporal intervals, i.e. all indices defined by the model. The denotation of an expression of any intensional type is, therefore, taken from the set of functions from the Cartesian product of **W** and **I** to denotations associated with its associated extensional type as formally defined in (18.a) and exemplified in (18.b).

(18) a. $D_{<s,a>} = D_a^{W \times I}$

b.

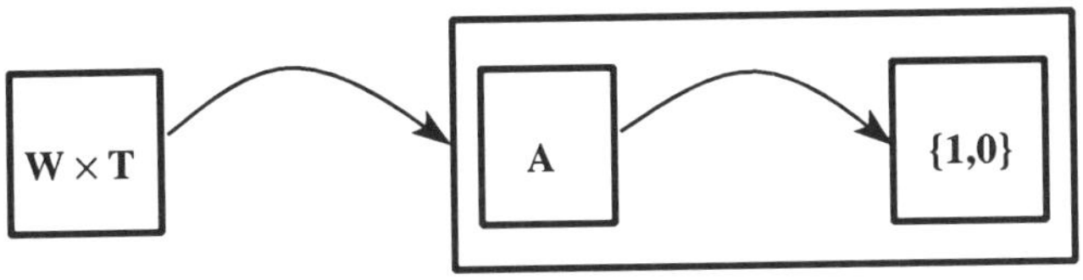

While all intensional expressions have the same sort of formal denotation as in (18.a), expressions of certain types have a special significance in translating expressions from a natural language like English and may be associated with particular philosophical concepts. For example, the intensions of formulae, which are expressions of type <s,t>, have as their denotations functions from world/time pairs to truth values, i.e. members of $\{0,1\}^{W \times I}$ (cf. e.g. (4) above which gives the denotation of the expression *^laugh'(fiona')* in M_{10}). Because such functions specify the truth value of a formula in any situation given by the model, they can be thought of as corresponding to **propositions**. This captures the intuition that the proposition expressed by a sentence is that part of its meaning that provides information about the situations that can be truly described by the sentence.

The intensions of individual constants of type <s,e> are called **individual concepts** and denote functions from indices to the set of entities in the model, i.e. $A^{W \times I}$, a function that picks out an individual entity at any index. In M_{10}, there are five such functions, one for each of the individual constants *ethel', jo', bertie', fiona'* and *chester'*. The denotation of the individual concepts of these names is, in each case, a **constant function**, i.e. a function that picks out the same entity at every index, i.e. $\mathbf{WOMAN_1}$, $\mathbf{MAN_1}$, $\mathbf{MAN_2}$, $\mathbf{WOMAN_2}$ and **DOG**, respectively. More interesting individual expressions are those that pick out different entities at different indices. The most obvious examples of such names are titles like *Queen of Scotland, President of the USSR, Mr Universe, Mayor of New York*, and so on. The extensions of these names differ from time to time and from world to world. So, for example, while the President of the Russian Republic in 1991 was Boris Yeltsin, in 1975 no-one bore this title and in 1995 it could refer to someone else. Furthermore, we can think of different situations in which other people bear these titles. So, it is possible to envisage a world in which the current Queen of Scotland is not also the current Queen of England, i.e. Elizabeth Windsor, but a descendant of Bonnie Prince Charlie called Morag Stuart; or one in which Britain had become a republic in the 1860s, and thus where there was no current Queen of England.

The intensions of one-place predicates are of type <s,<e,t>> and so denote functions from indices to sets of entities, i.e. functions in $(\{0,1\}^A)^{W \times I}$. Such functions pick out the set of all entities that are in the extension of a predicate at each index and so may be referred to as **properties**. Thus, formally, the extension of the predicate *red* is a set of entities that are red while the property of redness is a function that specifies the extension of the predicate in every situation, i.e. *^red'*. An example of such a property is specified for the model M_{10} in the diagram in (3) which represents the function that picks out the set of entities that are laughing at any index. We can follow Montague and generalise the term *property* to the denotations of expressions of any type with the structure <s,<a,t>> where a is any type. Such expressions denote functions in $(\{0,1\}^{D_a})^{W \times I}$ and, because such functions pick out sets of entities of the sort denoted by expressions of type a at every index, they may be said to be properties of such entities. Thus, expressions of type <s,<e,t>> denote properties of individual entities, those of type <s,<<e,t>,t>> denote properties of sets, those of type <s,<<s,t>,t>> denote properties of propositions, and so on.

Two-place predicates extensionally denote relations between entities, and the intensions of such expressions, of type <s,<e,<e,t>>>, are called **relations in intension** between entities, denoting functions in $((\{0,1\}^A)^A)^{W \times I}$. Like the term *property*, this term can also be generalised to cover all expressions that denote the intensions of two-place functions, i.e. those with the type structure <s,<a,<b,t>>> where a and b are any type. Thus, expressions of type <s,<<s,t>,<e,t>>> denote relations in intension between entities and propositions, expressions of type

<s,<<s,e>,<<s,e>,t>>> denote relations in intension between individual concepts, and so on. The different denotations of expressions are summarised in (19) according to whether they are intensional or extensional. There are, of course, many other intensional types and we will come across more in the sections that follow, but they all have the same sort of denotations, i.e. functions from indices (W × I) to extensional denotations.

(19)

Category Name	Extensional Type	Extensional Denotation	Intensional Type	Intensional Denotation
Individual constant	e	Entity A	<s,e>	Individual concept $A^{W \times I}$
Formula	t	Truth value $\{1,0\}$	<s,t>	Proposition $\{1,0\}^{W \times I}$
One-place predicate	<e,t>	Set of entities $\{1,0\}^{A}$	<s,<e,t>>	Property of entities $(\{1,0\}^{A})^{W \times I}$
Two-place predicate	<e,<e,t>>	Relations between entities $(\{0,1\}^{A})^{A}$	<s,<e,<e,t>>>	Relation in intension between entities $((\{0,1\}^{A})^{A})^{W \times I}$

Exercise 10.3:
What sorts of denotation do expressions of the following types have? Give the formal definition of the denotation, describe it in words and try and think of an English expression that might have such a denotation.

i. <s,<<e,t>,t>>.
ii. <<s,<e,t>>,t>.
iii. <<s,<e,t>>,<e,t>>.
iv. <s,<<<e,t>,t>,<e,t>>>.
v. <<s,t>,<e,t>>.
vi. <<s,e>,t>.

The models used to interpret expression of L_{IL} consist of the ordered sextuple in (20).

(20) **Intensional model**: M = «A,F,W,R,T,<».

As before, **A** is a set of entities defining the ontology of the model, containing all the entities that exist, have existed, will exist and might exist. **W** is a set of logically possible worlds and **R** is some relation of accessibility between them (or indeed a set of such relations; see Section 9.3.2). As in Chapter 8, **T** is a set of times ordered by the precedence relation, $<$. **F** is again a denotation assignment function, but now complicated to account for intensions. It assigns an intension to each lexeme in the object language, thus providing an extension for each basic expression at each world-time co-ordinate in the model. **F** can thus be defined as a function from lexemes to a function in $D_a^{W \times T}$, where a is an extensional type. As with temporal models, there must be no gaps in the intension assigned to a basic expression, either in worlds or in temporal intervals in those worlds. In other words, there must be no index for which the extension of any constant is not defined. Thus, the union of all worlds in the domain of **F** for some constant α must be equal to **W**, the set of all possible worlds, and the union of all time intervals mentioned by **F** must equal the set of times, **T**, for all worlds in **W**. Thus, **F** must conform to the two conditions in (21) for all basic expressions, α.

(21) a. $\bigcup_{wn} F(\alpha)(<\mathbf{w_n},i>) = \mathbf{W}$.

b. $\bigcup_{i} F(\alpha)(<\mathbf{w_n},i>) = \mathbf{T}$, for all $\mathbf{w_n} \in \mathbf{W}$.

The diagram in (4) that represents the intension of *laugh'* in M_{10} can thus more formally be specified as a set of extension plus co-ordinate pairs (or, equivalently, a function from indices to characteristic functions of entities), as in (22). The extension of $\mathbf{F_{10}}$(*laugh'*) need not be specified for every index, provided that there are meaning postulates that specify how to get to the extension of the constant at any index. Because *laugh* is an activity verb, there is a meaning postulate that specifies that the extensions of the predicate at any interval holds of all subintervals. Thus, in (22) the extension of *laugh'* at the index $<\mathbf{w_1},[\mathbf{t_2}]>$ is the same as $\mathbf{F_{10}}$(*laugh'*) at the index $(<\mathbf{w_1},[\mathbf{t_1},\mathbf{t_2}]>)$, i.e. $\{\mathbf{MAN_1},\mathbf{WOMAN_1}\}$, since $[\mathbf{t_2}]$ is a subinterval of $[\mathbf{t_1},\mathbf{t_2}]$. Furthermore, the rule for computing the extensions for intervals not specified by the denotation assignment function also holds (cf. Chapter 8). Strictly speaking, the meaning postulates defining the properties of predicates and the general rule determining extensions at other intervals hold of the denotations assigned by **F**, but do not determine them. Formally, therefore, the denotation assignment function should directly specify the extensions of a predicate at all indices. However, since such a specification is time consuming and tedious, in the example models in this chapter the denotation assignment functions give the denotations for only the minimum indices necessary to determine extensions at other indices, according to the rules given in Chapter 8.

(22) $F_{10}(\text{laugh'}) = \{<<\mathbf{w_1},[\mathbf{t_1},\mathbf{t_2}]>,\{\mathbf{MAN_1},\mathbf{WOMAN_2}\}>,$
$<<\mathbf{w_1},[\mathbf{t_3},\mathbf{t_4}]>,\{\mathbf{MAN_1}\}>,$
$<<\mathbf{w_2},[\mathbf{t_1},\mathbf{t_3}]>,\{\mathbf{DOG}\}>,$
$<<\mathbf{w_2},[\mathbf{t_4}]>,\varnothing>,$
$<<\mathbf{w_3},[\mathbf{t_1}]>,\varnothing>,$
$<<\mathbf{w_3},[\mathbf{t_2},\mathbf{t_3}]>,\{\mathbf{WOMAN_2}\}>,$
$<<\mathbf{w_3},[\mathbf{t_4}]>,\{\mathbf{WOMAN_1},\mathbf{WOMAN_2}\}>,$
$<<\mathbf{w_4},[\mathbf{t_1},\mathbf{t_4}]>,\{\mathbf{MAN_1},\mathbf{MAN_2},\mathbf{WOMAN_1},\mathbf{WOMAN_1},\mathbf{DOG}\}>\}$

The extension of a basic expression α at a particular index, $<\mathbf{w_n},\mathbf{i}>$, is thus the value of **F** at that index. Hence, the base of the model theory used to interpret L_{IL} is given by the statement in (23), where $F(\alpha)(<\mathbf{w_n},i>)$ is the function $F(\alpha)$ applied to the index $<w_n,i>$ which yields the extension of α at that index. This rule is generalised to obtain the extension of any intensional expression. Thus, where α has an intensional type, the denotation of $^\vee\alpha$ at an index $<w_n,i>$ is determined by the denotation of α (an intension) applied to the index $<w_n,i>$.

(23) a. If α is a basic expression, then $[\alpha]^{M,g,wn,i} = F(\alpha)(<w_n,i>)$.
b. $[^\vee\alpha]^{M,g,wn,i}$ is $[\alpha]^{M,g,wn,i}(<w_n,i>)$.

The intension of a basic expression, α, is **F** applied to α, i.e. $[^\wedge\alpha]^{M,g,wn,i} = F(\alpha)$. In general, the intension of an expression $^\wedge\alpha$ in L_{IL} is a function that picks out the denotation of α at each index, as formally defined in (24).

(24) If α is an extensional expression of type a, then $[^\wedge\alpha]^{M,g,wn,i}$ is that function, **h**, with domain $\mathbf{W} \times \mathbf{I}$ such that for all $<w_m,i'>$ in $\mathbf{W} \times \mathbf{I}$, $\mathbf{h}(<w_m,i'>) = [\alpha]^{M,g,wm,i'}$.

The intension of an expression is the same at every index, unlike the extension which may vary from index to index, because intensions are defined over all indices and make no special mention of the reference index. We may, therefore, equate $[^\wedge\alpha]^{M,g,wn,i}$ with $_{\Im}[\alpha]^{M,g}$, the intension of an expression with respect to a model and a variable assignment, irrespective of index.

To ascertain the denotations of complex expressions, whether intensional or extensional, we simply adopt a variant of the basic rule for interpreting expressions formed via functional application, relativised, not just to a temporal interval as in Chapter 8, but also to an index consisting of a world and a time. Thus, the value of $[\alpha(\beta)]^{M,g,wn,i}$ is ascertained by applying the value of the functor α at the reference index, $<w_n,i>$, to the value of β at the same index. Thus, for example, to ascertain the extension of the expression *laugh'(chester')* with respect to M_{10} and the index $<w_3,[t_2,t_3]>$, we apply the function denoted by *laugh'* at $<w_3,[t_2,t_3]>$ to the entity denoted by *chester'* at that index, i.e. $[laugh'(chester')]^{M,g,w3,[t2,t3]}$ is $[laugh']^{M,g,w3,[t2,t3]}([chester']^{M,g,w3,[t2,t3]})$. The value of $[laugh']^{M,g,w3,[t2,t3]}$ is the characteristic function of the set {$\mathbf{WOMAN_1}$} and the value of $[chester']^{M,g,w3,[t2,t3]}$ (as at every index) is **DOG**. Since the latter is not in the set denoted by the functor at the reference index $<w_3,[t_2,t_3]>$, *laugh'(chester')* is false at that index. Nothing has, therefore, changed in the interpretation of functor-argument expressions, except that care must now be taken to ensure that the denotations of the component parts of a complex expression are ascertained at the same index. Furthermore, caution must be exercised to ensure that the correct sort of denotation, intension or extension, is selected for each expression. This will be important in Section 10.3 and discussion of the details is postponed until then.

As for the rest of the model theory used for interpreting expressions in L_{IL}, very little differs from the rules we have already come across in previous chapters except again for the relativisation of denotations to indices. Note that the interpretation of a variable, *u*, is, as in Chapter 4 onwards, just the value assigned to *u* by the value assignment **g**, i.e. $[u]^{M,g,wn,i} = \mathbf{g}(u)$. In other words, assignments of values to variables are constant from index to index, as one might expect. Everything else remains much the same as before and the complete formal specification of the model theory is given in (25) which includes the interpretations of the expressions *necessarily'*, *possibly'*, *must'* and *may'*, since these are logical expressions whose interpretation does not vary from model to model. Students are advised to take some time to go through this before going on to the discussion of the important implications of this theory for an account of opaque contexts in the next section.

(25) a. If α is a basic expression, then $[\alpha]^{M,g,wn,i} = F(\alpha)(<\mathbf{w_n,i}>)$.
b. If α is a variable, then $[\alpha]^{M,g,wn,i} = g(\alpha)$.
c. If α is an expression of type <b,a> and β is an expression of type b, then $[\alpha(\beta)]^{M,g,wn,i}$ is $[\alpha]^{M,g,wn,i}([\beta]^{M,g,wn,i})$.
d. If α is an extensional expression of type a, then $[{}^\wedge\alpha]^{M,g,wn,i}$ is that function **h** with domain $\mathbf{W \times I}$ such that, for all $<\mathbf{w_m,i'}>$ in $\mathbf{W \times I}$, $\mathbf{h}(<\mathbf{w_m,i'}>) = [\alpha]^{M,g,wm,i'}$ (= $3[\alpha]^{M,g}$).
e. If α is an expression of type <s,a>, then $[{}^\vee\alpha]^{M,g,wn,i}$ is $[\alpha]^{M,g,wn,i}(<\mathbf{w_n,i}>)$.
f. If α is an expression of type a containing a free instance of a variable u of type b, then $[\lambda u\,[\alpha]]^{M,g,wn,i}$ is that function **h** with domain D_b such that for any object a in D_b, $\mathbf{h}(a) = [\alpha]^{M,g',wn,i}$ where **g'** is exactly the same as **g** except perhaps for the fact that $\mathbf{g'}(u) = a$.
g. If α and β are expressions of type a, then $[\alpha = \beta]^{M,g,wn,i}$ is **1** iff $[\alpha]^{M,g,wn,i}$ is identical to $[\beta]^{M,g,wn,i}$. Otherwise, $[\alpha = \beta]^{M,g,wn,i}$ is **0**.
h. If ϕ is an expression of type t, then $[\sim\phi]^{M,g,wn,i}$ is **1** iff $[\phi]^{M,g,wn,i}$ is **0**. Otherwise, $[\sim\phi]^{M,g,wn,i}$ is **0**.
i. If ϕ and ψ are expressions of type t, then $[(\phi\ \&\ \psi)]^{M,g,wn,i}$ is **1** iff $[\phi]^{M,g,wn,i}$ is **1** and $[\psi]^{M,g,wn,i}$ is also **1**. Otherwise, $[(\phi\ \&\ \psi)]^{M,g,wn,i}$ is **0**.
j. If ϕ and ψ are expressions of type t, then $[(\phi \vee \psi)]^{M,g,wn,i}$ is **1** iff $[\phi]^{M,g,wn,i}$ is **1** or $[\psi]^{M,g,wn,i}$ is **1**. Otherwise, $[(\phi \vee \psi)]^{M,g,wn,i}$ is **0**.
k. If ϕ and ψ are expressions of type t, then $[(\phi \rightarrow \psi)]^{M,g,wn,i}$ is **1** iff $[\phi]^{M,g,wn,i}$ is **0** or $[\psi]^{M,g,wn,i}$ is **1**. Otherwise, $[(\phi \rightarrow \psi)]^{M,g,wn,i}$ is **0**.
l. If ϕ and ψ are expressions of type t, then $[(\phi \leftrightarrow \psi)]^{M,g,wn,i}$ is **1** iff $[\phi]^{M,g,wn,i}$ and $[\psi]^{M,g,wn,i}$ both have the same truth value. Otherwise, $[(\phi \leftrightarrow \psi)]^{M,g,wn,i}$ is **0**.
m. If ϕ is an expression of type t containing an instance of a free variable u, then $[\forall u\,[\alpha]]^{M,g,wn,i}$ is **1** iff $[\phi]^{M,g',wn,i}$ is **1** for all value assignments **g'** exactly like **g** except perhaps for the value assigned to u.
n. If ϕ is an expression of type t containing an instance of a free variable u, then $[\exists u\,[\alpha]]^{M,g,wn,i}$ is **1** iff $[\phi]^{M,g',wn,i}$ is **1** for some value assignment **g'** exactly like **g** except perhaps for the value assigned to u.
o. If ϕ is an expression of type t, then $[\text{Pres}\ (\phi)]^{M,g,wn,i}$ is **1** iff $[\phi]^{M,g,wn,i}$ is **1**.
p. If ϕ is an expression of type t, then $[\text{Past}\ (\phi)]^{M,g,wn,i}$ is **1** iff $[\phi]^{M,g,wn,j}$ is **1** for some **j** in **I** where $\mathbf{j < i}$.
q. If ϕ is an expression of type t, then $[\text{Fut}\ (\phi)]^{M,g,wn,i}$ is **1** iff $[\phi]^{M,g,wn,j}$ is **1** for some **j** in **I** where $\mathbf{i < j}$.
r. If ϕ is an expression of type t, then $[\text{Perf}\ (\phi)]^{M,g,wn,i}$ is **1** iff $[\phi]^{M,g,wn,i}$ is **1** and **i** contains initial and final points if ϕ inherently contains these.
s. If ϕ is an expression of type t, then $[\text{Impf}\ (\phi)]^{M,g,wn,i}$ is **1** iff there is an interval **j** such that **i** is a proper subinterval of **j** and $[\phi]^{M,g,j}$ is **1**.
t. If ϕ is an expression of type t, then $[\mathit{necessarily}'({}^\wedge\phi)]^{M,g,wn,i}$ is **1** iff $[\phi]^{M,g,wm,j}$ is **1** for all $\mathbf{j} \in \mathbf{I}$ and all $\mathbf{w_m} \in \mathbf{W}$ such that $\mathbf{w_n R w_m}$.
u. If ϕ is an expression of type t, then $[\mathit{possibly}'({}^\wedge\phi)]^{M,g,wn,i}$ is **1** iff $[\phi]^{M,g,wm,j}$ is **1** for some $\mathbf{j} \in \mathbf{I}$ and some $\mathbf{w_m} \in \mathbf{W}$ such that $\mathbf{w_n R w_m}$.

v. If ϕ is an expression of type t, then $[must'(^\wedge\phi)]^{M,g,wn,i}$ is **1** iff $[\phi]^{M,g,wm,i}$ is **1** for all $\mathbf{w_m} \in \mathbf{W}$ such that $\mathbf{w_n R w_m}$.

w. If ϕ is an expression of type t, then $[may'(^\wedge\phi)]^{M,g,wn,i}$ is **1** iff $[\phi]^{M,g,wm,i}$ is **1** for some $\mathbf{w_m} \in \mathbf{W}$ such that $\mathbf{w_n R w_m}$.

10.3 Interpreting opaque contexts

We are now in a position to show to what extent the problems posed by the opaque constructions discussed in Section 9.1 are solved by the adoption of the intensional semantics defined above. We begin by considering the interpretation of verbs with opaque noun phrase or verb phrase object positions like *want, try* and *seem* and then move on to a consideration of verbs of propositional attitude like *believe, know*, etc.

10.3.1 Oblique transitive verbs

As we saw in Section 9.1, the fact that someone wants or is looking for something like a unicorn, a drink or a secretary does not entail that there is a specific unicorn, drink or secretary that they want or are looking for nor that any entity with the property specified actually exists. This differentiates such verbs from the ordinary transitive verbs like *like* and *stroke* with respect to which quantified object noun phrases always take wide scope, because the lexical decomposition of the latter guarantees that they denote relations between entities (cf. Chapter 6). For example, the sentence in (26.a) translates into L_Q as the complex expression in (26.b). After lambda conversion this reduces to (26.c) from which the entailments in (26.d) and (26.e) can be straightforwardly derived through conjunction elimination. These verbs also allow the substitution of referential equivalents in their object position, as shown by the valid inference pattern in (27).

(26) a. Jo liked a student.
b. λQ [Q(jo')](λ***P*** [λx [***P***(λy [(like'(y))(x)])]](λP [∃z [student'(z) & P(z)]])).
c. ∃z [student'(z) & (like'(z))(jo')].
d. ∃z [student'(z)].
e. ∃z [(like'(z))(jo')].

(27) a. Jo liked a student.
b. The student Jo liked is a wealthy Glaswegian.
c. Therefore, Jo liked a wealthy Glaswegian.

As we have seen, opaque transitive verbs do not have the same properties as transparent ones, as shown in (28): (28.b) cannot be inferred from (28.a) nor can (28.d) be inferred from (28.c) despite the fact *a unicorn* and *a gryphon* are referential equivalents in the actual world (i.e. they both extensionally denote the null set).

(28) a. Jo sought a student.
b. There is a student that Jo sought.
c. Bertie wanted a unicorn.
d. Bertie wanted a gryphon.

Because of the failure of Leibniz' Law in the object position of verbs like *want, seek, imagine* and *look for*, these are analysed as functors with an intensional argument position. It could be argued that, since ordinary transitive verbs ultimately denote relations between entities of type <e,<e,t>>, opaque verbs denote relations between *individual concepts* and entities, and so translate into expressions of type <<s,e>,<e,t>>. This would go some way towards a solution, since it allows one to distinguish between the particular *individuals* being sought or imagined. For example, the sentence in (29.a) translates into L_{IL} as the formula in (29.b), assuming the type of *imagine'* to be <<s,e>,<e,t>>. This translation ignores tense and treats the definite noun phrase *The Ladies' Scottish Golf Champion* as translating into the individual (sublimation of the) constant, *sgc'*, rather than as a proper Russellian definite description.

(29) a. Jo imagined the Ladies' Scottish Golf Champion.
b. (imagine'(^sgc))(jo').

According to the model theory specified in Section 10.2, the formula in (29.b) is true at an index **<w_n,i>**, if the entity denoted by *jo'* at **<w_n,i>** is 'in an imagining relation' not with the entity extensionally denoted by the Ladies' Scottish Golf Champion at that index, but with its associated individual concept, i.e. with [^*sgc'*]^{M,g} rather than [*sgc'*]^{M,g,w_n,i}. If Ethel and the Ladies' Scottish Golf Champion happen to be one and the same at some index, it does not therefore follow that because Jo is imagining the Ladies' Scottish Golf Champion, he is imagining Ethel. This is because the individual concept of *ethel'*, the function that picks out Ethel at every index, may differ from that of *sgc'*, the function that identifies the Ladies' Scottish Golf Champion at every index. In model M_{10}, the name *Ethel* refers to the same entity in every world at every time. Hence, 3[ethel']^{M10,g} is the constant function in (30.a). The Ladies' Scottish Golf Champion, however, is not the same person at every index but in world $\mathbf{w_1}$ *sgc'* extensionally denotes Ethel (**$WOMAN_1$**) at all times, but in $\mathbf{w_2}$ it denotes the dog at the interval **[t_1,t_2]** and Bertie at **[t_3,t_4]**. In world $\mathbf{w_3}$, Fiona is the Ladies' Scottish Golf Champion for the first three moments in the model, but Ethel in the last moment. In the final world $\mathbf{w_4}$, Fiona is the Ladies' Scottish Golf Champion at the interval **[t_1,t_4]**. The denotation of ^*sgc'* in M_{10} is, therefore, the function represented in (30.b).

(30) a. 3[ethel']^{M10,g}

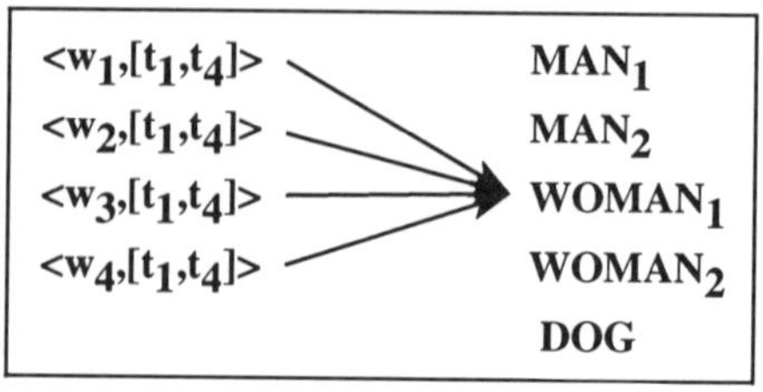

b. $[\![sgc]\!]^{M10,g}$

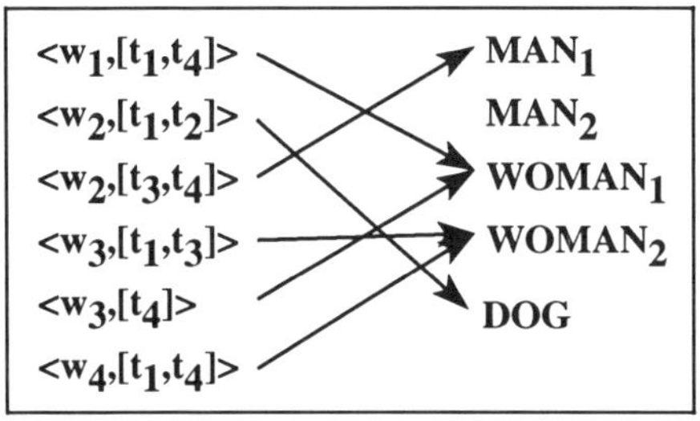

Because the intensions of *ethel'* and *sgc'* differ, it is possible for the denotation of *imagine'* at some index to map one of them onto the characteristic function of a set containing the entity denoted by *jo'*, but not the other. In other words, it is possible for Jo to imagine the concept of the Ladies' Scottish Golf Champion without imagining the concept of Ethel. Hence, Leibniz' Law fails in these contexts and so the inference pattern in (31) is correctly predicted to be invalid under the assumption that *imagine'* is of type <<s,e>,<e,t>>.

(31) a. Jo imagines the Ladies' Scottish Golf Champion.
b. Ethel is the Ladies' Scottish Golf Champion.
c. Therefore, Jo imagines Ethel.

Unfortunately, however, treating opaque verbs as relations between individual concepts and entities is not sufficient, because they may take quantified noun phrases as direct objects. If the argument type of predicates like *imagine'* is <s,e>, any quantifiers in the translation of an object noun phrase still have scope over the verb. The translation of a sentence like *Jo imagined a unicorn* is thus parallel to that of *Jo liked a student* in (26.c) except that the variable in the object position of *imagine'* is in an intensional position, i.e. $\exists x$ *[unicorn'(x) & (imagine'(^x))(jo')]*. This allows the application of standard entailment rules like conjunction elimination to get inferences like those shown in (26.d & e). The type of opaque verbs like these cannot, therefore, be as simple as <<s,e>,<e,t>>, but must be a functor over full noun phrase expressions. Indeed, this possibility is implicit in the type-raising of transitive verbs required by the higher type accorded to full noun phrases in Chapter 6. As we saw there, in order to maintain transitive verbs as functors over noun phrase denotations, it was necessary to raise their type from <e,<e,t>> to <<<e,t>,t>,<e,t>>. While transparent verbs like *like'* are lexically decomposed into a complex expression that maintains the intuition that they denote simple relations between entities, this is not the case for opaque verbs like *imagine* which must be interpreted as functors over the intensions of noun phrases.

To define the type and possible denotations of intensional transitive verbs, we need first to ascertain the types of noun phrases in L_{IL}. Montague analysed noun phrases as denoting, not sets of sets of entities, as we did in Chapter 6, but sets of properties of individual concepts. In other words, he translated noun phrases into expressions of type <<s,<<s,e>,t>>,t>, rather than as expressions of type <<e,t>,t>. His analysis, however, seems much more complex than is actually required for the interpretation of noun phrases. In the first place, there seems to be no reason to take VP denotations (the arguments of subject NPs) to be sets of individual concepts, i.e. to assign them the type <<s,e>,t>. The subject positions of most verbs are extensional and so require extensional arguments (of type e), not intensional ones (of type <s,e>). For those verbs that require intensional subjects (e.g. *appear*; see below), the argument position of the VP must be a full intensional NP denotation in order to include quantifiers, and not just an individual concept. Hence, we can maintain the translation of (most) VPs into one-place predicates. Furthermore, it seems unnecessary to require noun phrases to apply to properties (denoted by expressions of type <s,<e,t>>) rather than sets. If the translations of noun phrases were intensional in their argument position we would expect there to be noun phrases that do not allow substitution of extensional equivalents in this position. It seems likely, however, that there are no noun phrases of this sort and that wherever a noun phrase applies to a one-place predicate, truth is preserved if an extensionally equivalent predicate is substituted. For example, it seems intuitively correct to say that if *Every student sings well* is true and that all those things that sing well are also those things that are happy then *Every student is happy* is also true. Hence, we can maintain the assumption made in Chapter 6 that NPs denote extensional generalised quantifiers and so keep the same type in L_{IL} as they have in LQ.

Keeping the type of noun phrases as <<e,t>,t> means that the type of intensional transitive verbs must be <<s,<<e,t>,t>>,<e,t>>, denoting relations between the intensions of sets of sets of entities and sets of entities. A verb like *seek* thus translates into the constant *seek'*, denoting a function from noun phrase intensions to sets of entities. The translation of the syntactic rule generating VPs containing transitive verbs and their objects must thus combine the verb translation with the intension of the object NP, not its extension. A VP containing a transitive verb and its object is translated as V'(^NP') and the sentence in (32.a) is translated into the L_{IL} expression in (32.b) which is equivalent to (32.c) after lambda conversion.

(32) a. Bertie sought a unicorn.
b. Past (λQ [Q(bertie')](seek'(^λP [∃x [unicorn'(x) & P(x)]]))).
c. Past ((seek'(^λP [∃x [unicorn'(x) & P(x)]]))(bertie')).

Unlike ordinary transitive verbs, verbs like *seek* are not further semantically decomposed and so no further reduction of (32.c) can take place. Informally, (32.c) asserts of Bertie that he is seeking, not a specific unicorn, but the concept or idea of a unicorn. Hence, he need be seeking no specific unicorn and no unicorns need exist for him to be seeking them. Formally, (32.c) is true just in case at some time preceding the time of utterance in the actual world, the entity denoted by *bertie'* stood in a relation of seeking to the intension of *a unicorn*. The latter is a function that picks out the set of sets at each index that include some unicorn, i.e. one that picks out the existential sublimations of *unicorn'* at each index. Hence, [*seek'(^λP [∃x [unicorn'(x) & P(x)]])(bertie')*]^{M,g,w_n,i}. is true if, and only if, the function [*seek'*]^{M,g,w_n,i} maps the intension of the existential sublimation of *unicorn'*, i.e. ʒ[*λP [∃x [unicorn'(x) & P(x)]]*]^{M,g} onto a set that contains [*bertie'*]^{M,g,w_n,i} at <w_n,i>. Because ʒ[*λP [∃x [unicorn'(x) & P(x)]]*]^{M,g} is that function that picks out the existential sublimations of [*unicorn'*]^{M,g,w_n,i} at each index and not its particular existential sublimation at <w_n,i>, it follows that no specific entity need be being sought by Bertie at <w_n,i>.

Furthermore, since the intension of an existential sublimation may include indices like the actual world at the present time where there are no unicorns, i.e. where $[\lambda P\ [\exists x\ [unicorn'(x)\ \&\ P(x)]]]^{M,g,wn,i}$ is null, no unicorns need exist at the reference index for the expression in (32.c) to be true. Hence, this analysis properly accounts for the invalidity of the entailment between (28.a) and (28.b) in its non-specific reading. Because the object position of *seek* is an intensional one, Leibniz' Law is not valid and so we cannot infer from the truth of *Bertie sought a unicorn* that *Bertie sought a gryphon* is also true.

This analysis of verbs which have an opaque direct object position thus captures the semantic properties of non-specific readings. As we have seen, however, sentences like *Bertie sought a unicorn* and *Jo imagined the Ladies' Scottish Golf Champion* are ambiguous between the non-specific reading analysed above, and a reading where Bertie is seeking a specific unicorn and Jo is imagining a specific person who is the Ladies' Scottish Golf Champion. In these latter cases, one can infer the existence of an entity with the property specified by the object noun phrase and also that substitution of extensional equivalents is valid. Since these are semantic properties associated with transparent transitive constructions (ensured by giving any quantifier in the object noun phrase wide scope over the verb), the simplest way to analyse specific readings of intensional verbs is to analyse them in the same way as transparent verbs. Scope ambiguities between quantifiers in subject and object noun phrases and between the logical quantifiers and the tense operators were discussed in Chapters 6 and 8. Such ambiguities seem to be a general property of the semantics of natural language expressions: wherever sentences and the formulae into which they translate contain more than one operator the sentence has different readings according to the different scopes that the operators can have. If this is a general property of natural languages then we would expect ambiguity between the scopes of the intension operator ^ and quantifiers contained in noun phrases to parallel scope variations of the sort already seen. Since we have already identified an ambiguity in sentences containing opaque transitive verbs, it seems natural to treat them as deriving from differences in the scope of operators.

As discussed in Chapters 6 and 8, wide scope quantification can be derived in the semantics through the rule of quantifying in. In order to derive the specific reading of the sentence *Bertie sought a unicorn* using this rule, we first combine the predicate *seek'* with an expression containing a free variable of type e of the right type to combine with an intensional transitive verb. This expression is the intension of the individual sublimation of a free variable of type e, i.e. $^\wedge\lambda Q\ [Q(z)]$. The resulting expression, $seek'(^\wedge\lambda Q\ [Q(z)])$, is then combined with the subject translation $\lambda P\ [P(bertie')]$ to yield $\lambda P\ [P(bertie')](seek'(^\wedge\lambda Q\ [Q(z)]))$. Finally, the lambda operator is used to abstract on the free individual variable z and the resulting expression is combined with the translation of *a unicorn* to give a formula with no free variables, i.e. $\lambda P_1\ [\exists y\ [unicorn'(y)\ \&\ P_1(y)]](\lambda z\ [\lambda P\ [P(bertie')](seek'(^\wedge\lambda Q\ [Q(z)]))])$. This derivation is shown in (33) in the form of a semantic analysis tree, each line of which shows a functor to the left combining with an argument expression to its right. The types of the expressions being combined are written underneath to show that the combinations are valid according to the rule of functional application and the rule of quantifying in. (Tense is ignored for the sake of simplicity.)

(33)

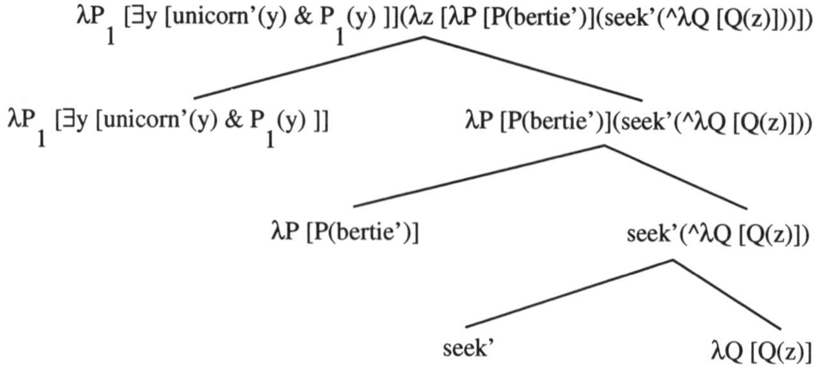

λP_1 [∃y [unicorn'(y) & P_1(y)]](λz [λP [P(bertie')](seek'(^λQ [Q(z)]))])
λP_1 [∃y [unicorn'(y) & P_1(y)]]
λP [P(bertie')](seek'(^λQ [Q(z)]))
λP [P(bertie')]
seek'(^λQ [Q(z)])
seek'
λQ [Q(z)]

The expression derived in (33) is equivalent to the formula in (34.a), as can be shown by applying lambda conversion to it. From the truth of this formula the truth of those in (34.b) and (34.c) can also be inferred by conjunction elimination.

(34) a. $\exists y\ [unicorn'(y)\ \&\ \lambda z\ [(seek'(\wedge\lambda Q\ [Q(z)]))(bertie')](y)]$.
b. $\exists y\ [unicorn'(y)]$.
c. $\exists y\ [\lambda z\ [(seek'(\wedge\lambda Q\ [Q(z)]))(bertie')](y)]$

Because the existential quantifier is outside the scope of ^ in (34.a), Leibniz' Law applies and so any extensionally equivalent expression may be substituted for *unicorn'* and maintain the truth value of the original formula. If this formula is true and all unicorns are one-horned horses, then we can infer from the specific reading of *Bertie sought a unicorn* that *Bertie sought a one-horned horse* is also true. The reason for this is that in the interpretation of (34.a) the extension of *unicorn'* is assessed at the reference index, i.e. at the world and time of utterance. Hence, any expression extensionally equivalent to *unicorn'* at the relevant index may be substituted *salva veritate*.

The interpretation of (34.a) may, however, seem a bit strange: what is it to be seeking the concept of the individual sublimation of a variable? Because there is one and only one individual sublimation for any individual at an index, being in a relation with an individual sublimation is tantamount to being in a relation with the individual that it is a sublimation of, as we saw in Chapter 6. Furthermore, the concepts of individual sublimations are also unique to that individual. The modal formula in (35) is thus valid in L_{IL} and it follows that predicating something of the concept of an individual sublimation is equivalent to predicating something of the individual itself. Thus, to be seeking the concept of an individual sublimation where that individual is a unicorn is to be seeking an actual individual with that property. Indeed, Montague provides a general formula to relate relations between entities and concepts of individual sublimations and the corresponding relations between entities. This is defined in (36.a) which relates an expression δ of type $\langle\langle s,\langle\langle e,t\rangle,t\rangle\rangle,\langle e,t\rangle\rangle$ to a corresponding expression δ_* of type $\langle e,\langle e,t\rangle\rangle$. How this applies to the example in (33) is shown in (36.b) to (36.f). This takes the formula in (33) after the translation of *Bertie* has combined with the predicate $seek'(^\wedge\lambda Q\, [Q(z)])$ but before the object noun phrase translation is quantified in, i.e. the expression in (36.b). Lambda conversion is applied to get (36.c) at which point the reduction in (36.a) can be applied to get the expression in (36.d). Quantifying in the translation of *a unicorn* yields the expression in (36.e) which is equivalent after lambda conversion to the formula in (36.f).

(35) $\forall x \forall y\, \Box[(x = y) \leftrightarrow ({}^\wedge\lambda P\, [P(x)] = {}^\wedge\lambda P\, [P(y)])]$

(36) a. $\delta_* =_{def} \lambda y\, [\lambda x\, [\delta({}^\wedge\lambda P\, [P(y)])(x)]]$.
b. $\lambda P\, [P(bertie')](seek'({}^\wedge\lambda Q\, [Q(z)]))$.
c. $(seek'({}^\wedge\lambda Q\, [Q(z)]))(bertie')$.
d. $(seek'_*(z))(bertie')$.
e. $\lambda P\, [\exists y\, [unicorn'(y)\ \&\ P(y)]](\lambda z\, [(seek'_*(z))(bertie')])$.
f. $\exists y\, [unicorn'(y)\ \&\ (seek'_*(y))(bertie')]$.

For reasons that will be discussed in Section 10.3.3, the λ-expression $\lambda z\, [(seek'({}^\wedge\lambda Q\ [Q(z)]))(bertie')](y)$ in (34.c) cannot be reduced to $(seek'({}^\wedge\lambda Q\, [Q(y)]))(bertie')$. However, the λ-conversion can take place if $seek'({}^\wedge\lambda Q\, [Q(z)])$ is reduced to $seek_*(z)$ using the definition in (36.a). The expression $(seek_*(y))(bertie')$ can be obtained from $\lambda z\, [(seek_*(z))(bertie')](y)$ by λ-conversion and so the full expression in (34.c) is equivalent to $\exists y\, [(seek_*(y))(bertie')]$. Hence, from the specific reading of *Bertie sought a unicorn*, it can be inferred that there was something that Bertie sought, as required.

Exercise 10.4:
In order to maintain a regular correspondence between syntactic rules and translation, it is necessary now to assume that the rule combining any verb with its direct object translates as the application of the translation of the verb to the intension of that of the object, i.e. VP' = V'(^NP'). This entails that the translations of transparent transitive verbs must be of type $\langle\langle s,\langle\langle e,t\rangle,t\rangle\rangle,\langle e,t\rangle\rangle$, the same as opaque transitive verbs. In order to maintain the fact that such verbs basically define a relation between two entities, they can continue to be semantically decomposed, but must contain a variable over the intensions of noun phrases. The translation for the verb *like* is the expression in i. below, an expression that takes the intension of a noun phrase, makes it extensional and applies this to the expression denoting the set of all things that are liked. The output is an expression denoting the set of all entities that like things with the properties given by the object NP. The two analyses described above for sentences containing intensional transitive verbs also applies to those containing transparent ones. Give both derivations for the sentence in ii. Is the ambiguity implied by the two derivations semantically significant?

i. $\lambda \wp\, [\lambda x\, [{}^\vee\wp(\lambda y\, [like'(y)(x)])]]$.
ii. Fiona liked a student.

10.3.2 Control verbs

The interpretation of sentences containing opaque transitive verbs given in Section 10.3.1 is one of the major achievements of Montague (1973). It captures in a very elegant way the primary semantic properties of the non-specific readings of such sentences and also provides a means of accounting for their specific counterparts. The general approach can be extended to account for verbs like *want* and *try* which take verb phrase objects which have an opaque reading (cf. the invalid inference patterns in Chapter 9). Such verbs, called **control verbs** in the linguistic literature, may thus be analysed as denoting relations between properties and entities. Hence, they translate into expressions of type $<<s,<e,t>>,<e,t>>$, as in the translation of the sentence in (37.a) given in (37.b).

(37) a. Jo wanted to find a secretary.
b. $\text{Past}\ (\text{want}'(\wedge\lambda y\ [\exists x\ [\text{secretary}'(x)\ \&\ (\text{find}'(x))(y)]])(\text{jo}'))$.

In sentences containing verbs like *want* and *try*, the matrix subject is interpreted also as the subject of the complement verb phrase. Thus, in (37.a), Jo is both the person doing the wanting and that doing the finding, and this needs to be brought out by the interpretation of the formula in (37.b). Since the identification of the subject of the matrix clause with the omitted subject of the subordinate infinitive is a lexical property of these verbs, we may use a meaning postulate to capture this relationship. This appears in (38.a) and ensures that a relation between properties and entities, like *want'*, of type $<<s,<e,t>>,<e,t>>$ is always associated with a relation between propositions and entities, like *want**, of type $<<s,t>,<e,t>>$, where the subject argument functions also as the subject of the embedded proposition to which it is related. According to this meaning postulate (which can also be represented as in (38.b)), the formula in (37.b) is truth-conditionally equivalent to that in (38.c), which is interpreted as asserting of Jo that he wants it to be the case that he finds a secretary.

(38) a. If δ is an expression of type $<<s,<e,t>>,<e,t>>$, P is an expression of type $<e,t>$, and x an expression of type e, then $\delta(\wedge P)(x)$ is truth-conditionally equivalent to $\delta^*(\wedge P(x))(x)$, where δ^* is an expression of type $<<s,t>,<e,t>>$.
b. $\forall P\ [\forall x\ [\delta(\wedge P)(x) \leftrightarrow \delta^*(\wedge P(x))(x)]]$.
c. $\text{Past}\ (\text{want}^*(\wedge\exists x\ [\text{secretary}'(x)\ \&\ (\text{find}'(x))(\text{jo}')])(\text{jo}'))$.

Because the existential quantifier in (37.b) and (38.c) is in the scope of the intension operator, we cannot infer from the latter that there is a specific secretary that Jo wants to find, nor, for the same reason, can we substitute any predicate in (37.b) which is extensionally equivalent to $\lambda y\ [\exists x\ [secretary'(x)\ \&\ (find'(x))(y)]]$ or any formula in (38.c) which has the same truth value as $\exists x\ [secretary'(x)\ \&\ (find'(x))(jo')]$. Hence, we can account for the fact that if Jo wants to find a unicorn it does not follow that he wants to find a gryphon.

The specific reading of (37.a) where there is a particular secretary that Jo wants to find can be achieved by quantifying in the translation of the object to yield the expression in (39.a) which, by (38.a), is equivalent to (39.b). (This equivalence does not result from λ-conversion, which is invalid in intensional contexts; see Section 10.3.3.)

(39) a. ∃x [secretary'(x) & want'(^λy [(find'(x))(y)])(jo')].
b. ∃x [secretary'(x) & want*(^(find'(x))(jo'))(jo')].

We can infer from the truth of the formulae in (39) that there is a (specific) secretary that Jo wants to find and that expressions extensionally equivalent to *secretary'* may be substituted for it. However, we are not in a position to substitute any other expression for the formula *(find'(x))(jo')* in (39.b) or the predicate λ*y [(find'(x))(y)]* in (39.a) because these are in the scope of the intension operator. Thus, we cannot infer from either reading of (37.a) that Jo wants to kiss a secretary, even if the set of things that Jo finds at some index is the same as the set of things that he kisses, i.e. if $[\lambda y\ [(find(y))(jo')]]^{M,g,wn,i}$ is the same as $[\lambda y\ [(kiss'(y))(jo')]]^{M,g,wn,i}$.

The analysis above provides a way of characterising the meaning of verbs like *want* in terms of relations between properties, propositions and entities. It is also possible to provide an analysis of verbs like *seem* or *appear* within the intensional semantics developed so far. The sentence in (40.a) has a non-specific reading in which it cannot be inferred from the truth of (40.a) that there exists a unicorn that is approaching nor indeed that anything at all is approaching. Thus, it is the *subject* position of such verbs that is intensional when they occur with a VP complement and it is necessary to make sure that all quantifiers in their subject NPs are in the scope of the intension operator. Hence, such verbs must denote relations between properties and the intensions of noun phrases, i.e. translate into expressions of the very complex type <<s,<e,t>>,<<s,<<e,t>,t>>,t>>. (40.b) thus provides the translation of (40.a).

(40) a. A unicorn appears to be approaching.
b. (appear'(^approach'))(^λP [∃x [unicorn'(x) & P(x)]]).

The sentence in (40.a) is a paraphrase of that in (41.a) where the verb *appear* takes a full complement clause and has as its subject the dummy element *it*. If we assume that the latter contributes nothing to the meaning of the sentence, we can interpret the verb *appear* as denoting a function from propositions to truth values, picking out just those propositions which appear to be true. Translating this category of the verb as the expression *appear** of type <<s,t>,t>, we thus get (41.b) as the translation of (41.a).

(41) a. It appears that a unicorn is approaching.
b. appear*(^∃x [unicorn'(x) & approach'(x)]).

The paraphrase relation between (40.a) and (41.a), which depends on the lexical interpretations of the verb *appear*, can be captured by the meaning postulate in (42.a) (with the formal representation in (42.b)) which relates an expression, δ, of type <<s,<e,t>>,<<<s,<e,t>>,t>,t>> to another one, δ*, of type <<s,t>,t>. The appropriate relation is stated as one of equivalence between formulae containing δ, predicated of a property, ^P, and the intension of a noun phrase, ℘, and those containing δ* which functionally applies to the intension of the formula derived from applying the translation of the subject to that of the complement, i.e. ^(ˇ℘(P)). In this way, we can guarantee that (40.a) and (41.a) are truth-conditionally equivalent. (43) shows the steps that are needed to derive (41.b) from the expression in (43.a) which is truth-conditionally equivalent to (40.b) according to (42). The formula in (43.b) is derived by 'down-up (ˇ^) cancellation' and that in (43.c) by λ-conversion.

(42) a. If δ is an expression of type <<s,<e,t>>,<<<s,<e,t>>,t>,t>>, P is an expression of type <e,t>, and $\wp$ an expression of type <<s,<e,t>>,t>, then $\delta(\wedge P)(\wp)$ is truth-conditionally equivalent to $\delta^{*}(\wedge(\vee\wp(P)))$, where δ^{*} is an expression of type <<s,t>,t>.

b. $\forall P\ [\forall\wp\ [\delta(\wedge P)(\wp) \leftrightarrow \delta^{*}(\wedge(\vee\wp(P)))]]$.

(43) a. appear*(^(ˇ^λP [∃x [unicorn'(x) & P(x)]](approach'))).

b. appear*(^(λP [∃x [unicorn'(x) & P(x)]](approach'))).

c. appear*(^(∃x [unicorn'(x) & approach'(x)])).

There is more to the semantics of these verbs than is touched on here and the implications of the intensionality of subjects of verbs like *appear* deserve more consideration, since this requires verb phrases to act as functors over their subjects, rather than vice versa. However, it should be clear that the analysis presented here does provide a reasonable basis for a satisfactory account of the opaque properties of these expressions and the way the properties denoted by complement VPs can be related to propositions involving subject noun phrases.

---

*Exercise 10.5:

The sentences in (40.a) and (41.a) appear to be three ways ambiguous. The sentence in i. below best corresponds to the reading in (40.b) and (41.b). Show how the reading in ii. may be derived using the quantifying in rule in Chapter 6. What problems arise in trying to derive the reading that best approximates to the reading in iii. and what implications does such a reading have for noun phrase interpretation in the analysis developed in this book?

i. It appears that there is a unicorn and that it is approaching.

ii. There is a unicorn and it appears to be approaching.

iii. There is something approaching and it appears to be a unicorn.

10.3.3 Propositional attitudes

Verbs of propositional attitude like *believe*, *know*, *doubt* and *consider* also create intensional contexts in their complement position, as we can see from the fact that the Law of Substitution fails and ambiguities arise between *de re* and *de dicto* readings of the same sentence (cf. Section 9.1). Because such verbs are opaque with respect to their complement clauses, they translate into L_{IL} expressions that denote functions over propositions, in fact relations between propositions and entities, and so translate into expressions of type <<s,t>,<e,t>>. To translate English sentences like those in (44) into the formulae in (45), the predicates translating the main verbs, *believe* or *know*, combine first with the intension of the formula translating their complement clause and then combine with the translation of the subject noun phrase to yield a formula.

(44) a. Fiona believes that the Ladies' Scottish Golf Champion is wealthy.
b. A Glaswegian knows that Ethel is not wealthy.
c. Ethel knows that a Glaswegian is wealthy.
d. Every student believes that every lecturer is wealthy.

(45) a. Pres (believe'(^Pres (wealthy'(sgc')))(fiona')).
b. Pres (∃x [glaswegian'(x) & know'(^(Pres (~wealthy'(ethel'))))(x)]).
c. Pres (know'(^(Pres (∃x [glaswegian'(x) & wealthy'(x)])))(ethel')).
d. Pres (∀x [student'(x) →
believe'(^(Pres (∀y [lecturer'(y) → wealthy'(y)])))(x)]).

Because the complements of the predicates *believe'* and *know'* in (45) are in the scope of the intension operator, Leibniz' Law does not hold in these positions, and so one cannot substitute extensionally equivalent expressions within the complement clause and preserve truth. As an demonstration that this is so, consider the sentences in (46).

(46) a. Jo believes that the Ladies' Scottish Golf Champion is wealthy.
b. Ethel is the Ladies' Scottish Golf Champion.
c. Jo believes that Ethel is wealthy.

The sentence in (46.c) is constructed from the other sentences in (46) by substitution into the complement of *believe*. As we have already seen, however, Jo's belief about the Ladies' Scottish Golf Champion in (46.a) is not the same as a belief about Ethel, despite the identity of these two entities at a particular index. This can be proved by showing that the propositions denoted by *The Ladies' Scottish Golf Champion is wealthy* and *Ethel is wealthy* formally define different functions from indices to truth values. If these functions differ, then the function denoted by *believe'* will not necessarily map them both onto the characteristic function of a set containing the entity denoted by the subject, Jo. In other words, the sentence in (46.c) may fail to be true even though both (46.a) and (46.b) are true.

The non-equivalence of (46.a) and (46.c) may be illustrated by working through the interpretations of the complement clauses in (46) with respect to the model M_{10}. (47) sets out the intension of the predicate *wealthy'* in this model.

(47)
$$\begin{aligned}F_{10}(\text{wealthy'}) = \{ & \langle\langle \mathbf{w_1,[t_1,t_4]}\rangle,\{\mathbf{MAN_2,WOMAN_2}\}\rangle, \\ & \langle\langle \mathbf{w_2,[t_1,t_2]}\rangle,\{\mathbf{DOG,WOMAN_2}\}\rangle, \\ & \langle\langle \mathbf{w_2,[t_3,t_4]}\rangle,\{\mathbf{WOMAN_2}\}\rangle, \\ & \langle\langle \mathbf{w_3,[t_1,t_3]}\rangle,\varnothing\rangle, \\ & \langle\langle \mathbf{w_3,[t_4]}\rangle,\{\mathbf{WOMAN_1}\}\rangle, \\ & \langle\langle \mathbf{w_4,[t_1]}\rangle,\{\mathbf{MAN_2}\}\rangle, \\ & \langle\langle \mathbf{w_4,[t_2,t_3]}\rangle,\{\mathbf{WOMAN_1,WOMAN_2,MAN_1}\}\rangle, \\ & \langle\langle \mathbf{w_4,[t_4]}\rangle,\{\mathbf{MAN_2}\}\rangle\}\end{aligned}$$

The denotation of the proposition *^(wealthy'(ethel'))* in M_{10} is that function that maps an index onto **1** if, and only if, the denotation of *ethel'* at that index is in the set of entities denoted by *wealthy'* at that index and maps the index onto **0**, otherwise. Since *^ethel'* denotes a constant function in M_{10} (cf. (30.a)), *^(wealthy'(ethel'))* picks out the set of indices at which $\mathbf{WOMAN_1}$ is in the extension of *wealthy'*. According to (47), Ethel is wealthy only in world $\mathbf{w_3}$ at moment $\mathbf{[t_4]}$ and world $\mathbf{w_4}$ at interval $\mathbf{[t_2,t_3]}$

and so the proposition denoted by *^(wealthy'(ethel'))* in M_{10} is the characteristic function represented in (48).

(48) $[\![wealthy'(ethel')]\!]^{M10,g}$

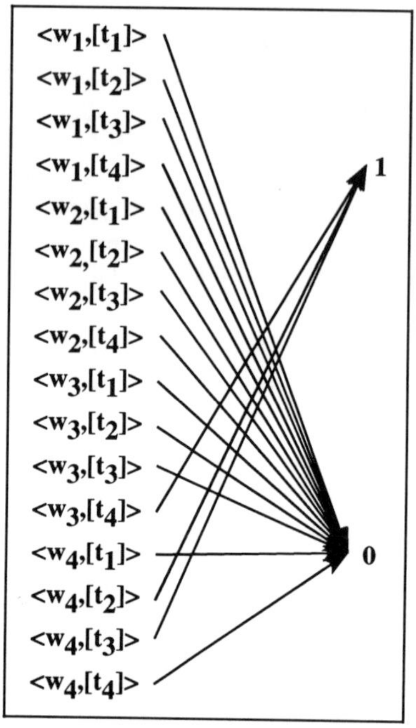

The proposition denoted by *^(wealthy'(sgc'))*, on the other hand, is the characteristic function defining the set of indices $\langle \mathbf{w_n},\mathbf{i}\rangle$ at which the denotation of *sgc'* at $\langle \mathbf{w_n},\mathbf{i}\rangle$ is in the set of entities denoted by *wealthy* at $\langle \mathbf{w_n},\mathbf{i}\rangle$. Since the extension of *sgc'* changes from index to index, one needs first to ascertain its denotation at a particular index and then check to see if this is in the set of wealthy entities at that index. Comparing the intension of *sgc'* in (30.b) with (47), we can construct the characteristic function in (49) defining the proposition denoted by *^(wealthy'(sgc'))*.

The function in (49) is the characteristic function of the set $\{\langle \mathbf{w_2},[\mathbf{t_1}]\rangle, \langle \mathbf{w_2},[\mathbf{t_2}]\rangle, \langle \mathbf{w_3},[\mathbf{t_4}]\rangle, \langle \mathbf{w_4},[\mathbf{t_2}]\rangle, \langle \mathbf{w_4},[\mathbf{t_3}]\rangle\}$ whilst that in (48) is the characteristic function of $\{\langle \mathbf{w_3},[\mathbf{t_4}]\rangle,\langle \mathbf{w_4},[\mathbf{t_2}]\rangle,\langle \mathbf{w_4},[\mathbf{t_3}]\rangle\}$. Since these two sets are different, the propositions denoted by *Ethel is wealthy* and *The Ladies' Scottish Golf Champion is wealthy* are different formal objects and so it is possible to believe (or know or doubt) one of them without believing (or knowing or doubting) the other. Although the function denoted by the predicate *believe'* may map the function in (49) onto the characteristic function of a set containing $\mathbf{MAN_1}$, the extension of *Jo*, it does not follow that it maps the function denoted by *^(wealthy'(ethel'))* onto a characteristic function of a set containing $\mathbf{MAN_1}$. The proposition expressed by the sentence *Jo believes that the*

Ladies' Scottish Golf Champion is wealthy may thus be true while that expressed by *Jo believes that Ethel is wealthy* may be false, despite Ethel's being the Ladies' Scottish Golf Champion at the reference index.

(49) $[\![\text{wealthy}'(\text{sgc}')]\!]^{M10,g}$

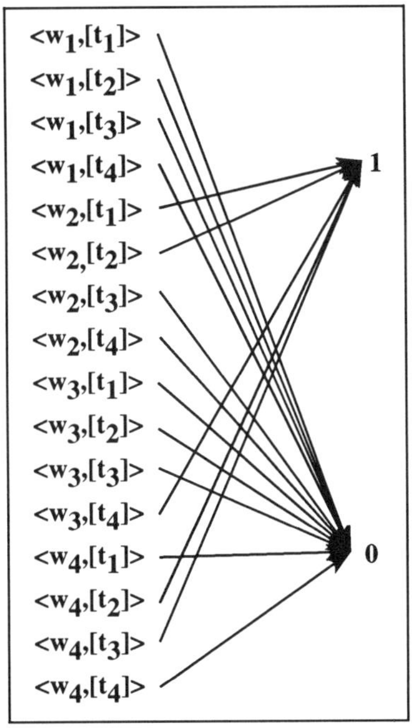

The fact that substitution is not valid in the complements of verbs like *believe* also accounts for why we cannot attribute a contradictory belief to Jo even if he happens to believe that Ethel is not wealthy, while also believing that the Ladies' Scottish Golf Champion is wealthy. If substitution were valid, (50.b) would be guaranteed to be true by the truth of (50.a) together with (46.a) and (46.b) by substitution and conjunction introduction. The full inference pattern is set out in L_{IL} formulae (ignoring the present tense operator for simplicity) in (51). (51.a) is the translation of (46.a), (51.b) that of (50.a), (51.c) is that of (46.b). Substituting *sgc'* for *ethel'* into (51.b) yields the formula in (51.d) which together with (51.a) leads to the formula in (51.e), the intended translation of (50.b), via conjunction introduction. Conjunction introduction, unlike substitution, is valid in intensional contexts provided that the contexts are kept constant. Thus, if someone believes that ϕ and also believes that ψ then they believe that ϕ and ψ.

(50) a. Jo believes that Ethel is not wealthy.

b. Jo believes that the Ladies' Scottish Golf Champion is wealthy and that the Ladies' Scottish Golf Champion is not wealthy.

(51) a. believe'(^[wealthy'(sgc')])(jo').
b. believe'(^[~wealthy'(ethel')])(jo').
c. ethel' = sgc'.
d. believe'(^[~wealthy'(sgc')])(jo').
e. believe'(^[wealthy'(sgc') & ~wealthy'(sgc')])(jo').

As we have seen, the inference pattern in (51) is invalid, because the formula in (51.d) cannot be inferred from (51.b) and (51.c) via substitution because of the intension operator. The truth of (51.e), which ascribes the contradictory belief to Jo that the Ladies' Scottish Golf Champion is both wealthy and unwealthy, thus does not follow from the truth of (51.a), (51.b) and (51.c).

There is, however, a reading of (50.b), that can be derived from the truth of the premises in (46.a), (46.b) and (50.a), which does not attribute a contradictory belief to Jo. In this reading, the first conjunct in (50.b) is interpreted *de dicto*, as in (51.a), but the second is interpreted *de re*. In other words, Jo's belief about the Ladies' Scottish Golf Champion being wealthy is taken as ascribing to Jo a belief about the wealth of whoever is named by the expression *the Ladies' Scottish Golf Champion*, whose identity he does not know but who exists within his 'belief worlds'. His second belief, on the other hand, is interpreted as a belief about the particular person referred to by this expression at a particular index, i.e. Ethel. Thus, while Jo believes *de dicto* that the Ladies' Scottish Golf Champion is wealthy, he also believes *de re*, i.e. from the speaker's perspective, that she is not wealthy.

This second reading of (50.b) can be derived in much the same way as the specific readings of opaque transitive verbs were derived in Section 10.2.2 through the use of the rule of quantifying in. The *de re* reading of the sentence in (46.a), *Jo believes that the Ladies' Scottish Golf Champion is wealthy*, can be constructed by combining the predicate *wealthy'* translating the verb phrase *is wealthy* with the individual sublimation of a variable, i.e. $\lambda Q\ [Q(x)]$. Once this is combined with the predicate *believe'* and the individual sublimation of *jo'*, we get the formula in (52.a), which λ-converts into the expression in (52.b). The rule of quantifying in allows us to abstract on the free variable x and combine the resulting predicate with the translation of *the Ladies' Scottish Golf Champion* to get (52.c), equivalent to the formula in (52.d).

(52) a. λP [P(jo')](believe'(^[~(λQ [Q(x)](wealthy'))])).
b. (believe'(^[~(wealthy'(x))]))(jo').
c. λQ [Q(sgc')](λx [(believe'(^[~(wealthy'(x))]))(jo')]).
d. λx [believe'(^[~(wealthy'(x))])(jo')](sgc').

It might seem that lambda conversion can be applied one more time to (52.d) to derive the formula in (51.d) which represents the *de dicto* reading of *Jo believes that the Ladies' Scottish Golf Champion is not wealthy*, from which we could derive the contradictory formula in (51.e) via conjunction introduction with (51.a). Like the Law of Substitution, however, the rule of Lambda Conversion is invalid in intensional contexts and must be revised to take account of this as in (53).

(53) $\lambda u\ [\phi](a) \leftrightarrow \phi^{a/u}$ provided that u is not in the scope of ^ or the tense operators *Past* and *Fut*.

To illustrate the fact that lambda conversion is not valid in intensional contexts and to show that (52.b) does indeed give the *de re* reading of (46.a), let us consider the interpretation of this formula with respect to M_{10} and the index **<w_1,[t_2]>**. The crucial point about this interpretation is that the denotation of *sgc'* is fixed by the reference index. This follows because the rule interpreting function/argument structures in L_{IL} given in (25.3) derives the interpretation of (54.a) from the application of the extension of the functor at <w_1,[t_2]> to that of the argument at the same index, as shown in (54.b). According to the function in (30.b), the denotation in M_{10} of *sgc'* at **<w_1,[t_2]>** is **$WOMAN_1$**. Hence, by the definition of lambda conversion in Chapter 5, the result of applying the extension of the λ-expression in (54.b) to that of its argument *sgc'* is equivalent to the interpretation of the former with respect to a variable assignment function where the variable *x* has the value **$WOMAN_1$**. Thus, (54.a) and (54.b) are equivalent to (54.c). In other words, the formula in (52.c) is true at some co-ordinate if, and only if, **$WOMAN_1$** is in the set of things that Jo believes are not wealthy. Since **$WOMAN_1$** is Ethel and Jo believes that Ethel is not a wealthy woman, we conclude the *de re* reading of *Jo believes the Ladies' Scottish Golf Champion is not wealthy* is true. Since the *de dicto* reading is false (given the truth of (46.a)), the *de re* and *de dicto* readings of this sentence represented by the formulae in (52.c) and (51.d) are thus truth-conditionally distinct.

(54) a. [λx [believe'(^[~wealthy'(x)])(jo')](sgc')]$^{M,g,w1,[t2]}$.

b. [λx [believe'(^[~wealthy'(x)])(jo')]]$^{M,g,w1,[t2]}$([(sgc')]$^{M,g,w1,[t2]}$).

c. [believe'(^[~wealthy'(x)])(jo')]$^{M,gWOMAN1/x,w1,[t2]}$.

The difference in interpretation between the *de re* and *de dicto* readings of (46.a) can be best appreciated by considering what propositions Jo is asserted to believe in each case. In the *de re* interpretation just discussed, the relevant proposition that Jo is said to believe is *^[wealthy'(x)]* where *x* is assigned **$WOMAN_1$** as a value. As we saw above, this proposition is given by the characteristic function of the set {**<w_3,[t_4]>,<w_4,[t_2]>,<w_4,[t_3]>**}. In the *de dicto* reading in (51.b), however, the proposition that Jo is said to believe is that denoted by *^[wealthy'(sgc')]*, the function in (49) that defines the set **{<w_2,[t_1]>, <w_2,[t_2]>, <w_3,[t_4]>, <w_4,[t_2]>, <w_4,[t_3]>}**. The functions denoted by *^[wealthy'(x)]* and *^[wealthy'(sgc')]* are thus different and so Jo may believe one proposition and not the other without inconsistency. We can thus see from this example that lambda conversion is indeed not valid in intensional contexts, because the non-converted formula has a different interpretation (and truth value in **M_{10}**) from the formula that would result after lambda conversion. Furthermore, because the referent of the embedded subject, *the Ladies' Scottish Golf Champion*, is determined by the reference index, the analysis adequately captures the fact that *de re* reference occurs outside the belief context and is therefore not dependent on the other beliefs of the referent of the subject of the main clause.

We are now in a position to provide the reading for the sentence in (50.b) which does not ascribe a contradictory belief to Jo. Recall that this sentence was constructed from a sentence ascribing to Jo a *de dicto* belief that the Ladies' Scottish Golf Champion is wealthy and another ascribing to him a belief that Ethel is not wealthy. Although direct substitution into an intensional context is not permitted, nevertheless if it is possible to ascribe a *de re* belief to someone, one can then substitute an extensionally equivalent expression for the directly referring expression. This obviously follows from the fact that the latter appears outside the intensional context created by *believe'* and so is subject to the Law of Substitution. In deriving the non-contradictory reading of (50.b), therefore, we construct from the *de dicto* belief about Ethel in (51.b), repeated in (55.b) below, the *de re* belief about Ethel in (55.c).

(55) a. believe'(^[wealthy'(sgc')])(jo').
b. believe'(^[~wealthy'(ethel')])(jo').
c. λx [believe'(^[~wealthy'(x)])(jo')](ethel').

It is not in general the case that the truth of the *de re* reading of a sentence is guaranteed by the truth of its *de dicto* counterpart. For example, the *de re* counterpart to (55.a), *λx [believe'(^[wealthy'(x)])(jo')](sgc')*, is not true in M_{10} and so not entailed by the former. However, where an expression, like *ethel'* and other proper names, denotes a constant function the *de re* and *de dicto* readings of the same belief sentence turn out to be equivalent. For example, *^[~wealthy'(ethel')]* denotes that proposition which picks out the set of indices at which it is true that the extension of *ethel'* is not in the set of wealthy entities in M_{10}, i.e. {$\langle w_1,[t_1,t_4]\rangle$, $\langle w_2,[t_1,t_4]\rangle$, $\langle w_3,[t_1,t_3]\rangle$, $\langle w_1,[t_1]\rangle$, $\langle w_4,[t_4]\rangle$}. Since *ethel'* picks out the same entity at each index, i.e. **WOMAN**$_1$, this proposition is equivalent to that denoted by *^[~wealthy'(x)]* where g(x) is **WOMAN**$_1$. Hence, where someone has a belief about a particular named individual, no semantic difference emerges between the *de re* and *de dicto* readings of the sentence. In fact, it is a general property of intensional expressions that denote constant functions from indices to extensions that lambda conversion continues to apply, even in intensional contexts. Hence, the rule of lambda conversion in (53) should be revised to allow the equivalence between λu [φ](*a*) and $[\phi]^{a/u}$ where the argument, a, has a constant intension.

Returning to the derivation of the non-contradictory reading of (50.b), we can validly infer the *de re* reading of *Jo believes that Ethel is not wealthy* in (55.c) from (55.b) via backwards λ-conversion. In (55.c), because *ethel'* is outside the scope of the intension operator, any extensionally equivalent expression may be substituted for it *salva veritate*. From (55.c) and the premiss in (56.a), therefore, we can construct (56.b), the *de re* interpretation of *Jo believes the Ladies' Scottish Golf Champion is not wealthy*. From this and the *de dicto* reading of *Jo believes that the Ladies' Scottish Golf Champion is wealthy* in (55.a), we get (56.c), the desired reading of *Jo believes that the Ladies' Scottish Golf Champion is wealthy and that the Ladies' Scottish Golf Champion is not wealthy*, which does not ascribe to Jo a contradictory belief about the Ladies' Scottish Golf Champion.

(56) a. ethel' = sgc'.
b. λx [believe'(^[~wealthy'(x)])(jo')](sgc').
c. λx [believe'(^[wealthy'(sgc') & ~wealthy'(x)])(jo')](sgc').

Individual constants with the semantic properties of *sgc'* are rare (and debatable) and phrases like *the Ladies' Scottish Golf Champion* and *the President of the USSR* ought more properly to be treated as definite noun phrases as in Chapter 6. However, the properties of belief contexts ensured by the analysis discussed above carry over to sentences containing verbs of propositional attitude and quantified noun phrases: i.e. that substitution fails in *de dicto* readings and that belief sentences are ambiguous between *de re* and *de dicto* readings. To illustrate this, let us work through both readings of the sentence in (57). Since no concepts are introduced here that have not already been met, it will suffice to go over the main points of the analysis and leave readers to work out the details for themselves.

(57) Fiona believes that a golf champion will be wealthy.

The derivation of the *de dicto* reading of (57) is straightforwardly derived without the application of the rule of quantifying in to get the translation in (58.a). The interpretation of this formula ascribes to Fiona a belief that a golf champion, whoever they may be, will in the future be wealthy. Because the existential quantifier is within the scope of the intension operator, no specific golf champion need be believed by Fiona to be going to be wealthy, nor need there be at the time of utterance any golf champions at all for the formula to be true. Furthermore, because the translation of the subordinate subject is within the scope of ^ no substitution of extensional equivalents may take place. The *de re* reading of (57) shown in (58.b) is derived from the application of the rule of quantifying in. Its interpretation states that there is some golf champion at the present time (and the actual world) of whom Fiona believes she will be wealthy. Hence, there must be a specific person who is a golf champion and of whom Fiona holds her belief. Furthermore, if all golf champions are currently secretaries then it follows from the truth of (58.b) that Fiona believes of a secretary that she will be wealthy. Hence, again, the analysis presented above enables one to distinguish *de re* from *de dicto* beliefs and to account for the failure of substitution within such contexts.

(58) a. (*de dicto*)
Pres(believe'(^[Fut(∃x [golf-champion'(x) & Pres(wealthy'(x))])])(fiona')).

b. (*de re*)
∃x [golf-champion'(x) & Pres (believe'(^[Fut(wealthy'(x))])(fiona'))].

Exercise 10.6:
Work out the semantic derivation of the formula in (58.b) using the rule of quantifying in. Interpreting the denotation of the predicate *golf-champion'* as the function in (30.b) with the entities replaced by unit sets of those entities (so that e.g. $[\text{golf-champion'}]^{M10,g,w1,[t1]}$ is {$\mathbf{WOMAN_1}$}), show that the complement propositions in (58.a) and (58.b) do denote different propositions with respect to M_{10} and the index $\langle \mathbf{w_1},[\mathbf{t_2}]\rangle$. Be careful to take full account of the tense operators in these formulae.

10.4 Two problems

The adoption of a co-ordinate semantics can thus solve the puzzles posed by the failure of expected entailments in certain contexts. By treating intensionality as an operator over formulae, we can also, as discussed above, account for ambiguities in intensional contexts in terms of scope differences between different sorts of operator (e.g. quantifiers and tense operators). There are, however, two major problems that arise from the analysis of intensional contexts given in Section 10.3. One has to do with the substitution of intensional equivalents and the other with referring to individuals at different indices.

10.4.1 Intensional equivalence

We have observed above that the substitution of extensional equivalents fails in intensional contexts. However, it was also observed in Section 9.2 that for Frege the intension (*Sinn*) of an expression is determined by the intensions of its component parts. Since the intensional semantics defined above preserves the version of the Principle of Compositionality in Chapter 9, the version of Leibniz' Law in (59) does hold in L_{IL}. This states that two expressions are intersubstitutable in intensional contexts if (and only if) their intensions are identical.

(59) $(\hat{}a = \hat{}b) \rightarrow [\phi \leftrightarrow \phi^{b/a}]$.

Exercise 10.7:
Explain informally why (59) is valid in L_{IL}. Illustrate your answer by showing that the two sentences below are truth-conditionally equivalent in M_{10} under the assumption that $\mathfrak{z}[\text{robert'}]^{M_{10},g}$ is the constant function that picks out $\mathbf{MAN_2}$ at every index.

i. Jo believes that Bertie is wealthy.
ii. Jo believes that Robert is wealthy.

The validity of (59) in L_{IL} presents a serious problem for the analysis of verbs of propositional attitude with respect to propositions that are necessarily true. In the technical sense of the term *proposition* given in this chapter, there is only one necessarily true proposition: the characteristic function that maps all possible indices (i.e. $\mathbf{W} \times \mathbf{I}$) onto **1**. Assuming that all logical and arithmetical truths are true at all indices, all the sentences in (60), therefore, denote the same proposition, i.e. the set $\mathbf{W} \times \mathbf{I}$.

(60) a. It is snowing or it is not snowing.
b. Four times four is sixteen.
c. All students are students.

Since there is only one necessarily true proposition, it follows that if someone believes or knows any necessarily true statement, then that person believes or knows all necessarily true statements. Thus, once someone has grasped the fact that four times four is sixteen, then they know every arithmetically and logically necessary truth. Not only do they then know the other sentences in (60) but also that the circumference of a circle is given by twice the radius of the circle times π and the law of *modus ponens*, and so on. There are no new necessarily true statements to be believed or known. This is patently absurd, of course. People may believe or know some necessary truths but not others but no-one would argue that since they know that it is either raining or not raining, then they know all necessarily true statements about the Universe!

The primary problem with logically necessary statements in belief contexts is that there are not enough worlds to differentiate the different statements from one another. As we have seen, contingent propositions are differentiated by the indices at which they are true which may differ from proposition to proposition. However, if the set of possible worlds is the set of all logically possible worlds, then obviously there is no possible world in which a logically true formula is false. Hence, the intensions of such formulae cannot be differentiated. To remedy this, it has been suggested that the set of worlds in a model should include not only the logically possible worlds but also logically impossible ones, i.e. worlds where the laws of classical logic fail to hold. These would include, for example, worlds where a sentence like *It is raining or it is not raining* is false or where it turns out not to be the case that four times four is sixteen. This certainly allows for differentiation in the intensions of the logically true (or logically false) statements, but only at the cost of introducing into the ontology worlds where the familiar rules of inference fail and which are thus so alien to our understanding that it is unlikely that we could ever comprehend them.

Other ways have been suggested to try and overcome the problem of intensional equivalence without undermining the whole basis of the possible worlds approach sketched in previous sections. There is no space here to deal with them all in any detail and the reader is referred to the suggested reading for fuller information. Most of them, however, involve the postulation of something more than an intension of the sort defined in this chapter. For example, Cresswell (1985) develops some ideas of Rudolf Carnap and David Lewis by defining a structural concept of meaning which interprets the objects of belief and knowledge as combinations of the intension of a formula plus all the intensions of its component parts. In other words, the meaning of a formula ϕ in this sense is something like a semantic derivation of the sort we have been using in deriving scope differences using the rule of quantifying in (cf. e.g. (33) above). Each node of the analysis tree, however, is labelled with the intension of some logical expression. rather than the expression itself. The meaning of the sentence *Jo is mad* in this system is thus something like (61.a). The difference in meaning between two logically true statements like *It is raining or it is not raining* and *It is snowing or it is not snowing* results from the differences in intension between the constants they contain, i.e. *rain'* and *snow'*. Hence, one may believe or know (61.b) without believing or knowing (61.c), since these are different formal objects.

(61) a. $<\mathfrak{I}[\text{Pres}\ (\text{mad'}(\text{jo'}))]^{M,g},<\mathfrak{I}[\lambda P P(\text{jo'})]^{M,g},\mathfrak{I}[\text{mad'}]^{M,g}>>.$
b. $<\mathfrak{I}[\text{rain'} \vee \sim\text{rain'}]^{M,g},<\mathfrak{I}[\text{rain'}]^{M,g},\mathfrak{I}[\sim\text{rain'}]^{M,g}>>.$
c. $<\mathfrak{I}[\text{snow'} \vee \sim\text{snow'}]^{M,g},<\mathfrak{I}[\text{snow'}]^{M,g},\mathfrak{I}[\sim\text{snow'}]^{M,g}>>.$

An alternative solution that does not involve complex intensional structures and which is somewhat closer to a linguist's intuitions about meaning was suggested in Section 9.2. This notion of the meaning of an expression defines it as the combination of the denotation of the expression, both its extension and its intension, and its sense, as defined in Chapter 7. As briefly discussed in Section 9.3.2, the set of meaning postulates that determine the sense of an expression can be interpreted as an accessibility relation $\mathbf{R}_\alpha$ on possible worlds. A world, $\mathbf{w}_m$, is $\mathbf{R}_\alpha$-accessible to another world, $\mathbf{w}_n$, if, and only if, all the meaning postulates associated with α hold in $\mathbf{w}_m$ and $\mathbf{w}_n$. Since different basic expressions are associated with different meaning postulates, they define different accessibility relations on the set of possible worlds. For example, given the three meaning postulates in (62), $\mathbf{R}_{\text{tree'}}$ selects all those worlds in which trees are plants and not flowers (but where flowers may not be plants or plants may be animals) while $\mathbf{R}_{plant'}$ selects those in which no plants are animals (but where trees may be flowers and flowers may not be plants) and so on.

(62) a. ∀x [tree'(x) → plant'(x)].
b. ∀x [tree'(x) → ~flower'(x)].
c. ∀x [plant'(x) → ~animal'(x)].
d. ∀x [flower'(x) → plant'(x)].

The sense of a constant α may, therefore, be defined as the set of all indices $<\mathbf{w}_m,\mathbf{i}>$ such that $\mathbf{wR}_\alpha\mathbf{w'}$ where $\mathbf{w}_n$ is the reference world. Generalising this to complex expressions, we can say that the sense of that expression is given by the set of indices where each world in each index is accessible to the reference world according to the sense relations of all the constants in the expression. Symbolising the sense of an expression α as $_\Sigma[\alpha]^{M,g,wn,i}$, we can formally define sense as in (63). Under this interpretation, the sense of a sentence like *Every tree is a plant* is that set of indices where trees are plants, are not flowers, and where plants are not animals, i.e. where each world is $\mathbf{R}_{tree'}$ and $\mathbf{R}_{plant'}$ accessible to this one.

(63) The sense of an expression α, $_\Sigma[\alpha]^{M,g,wn,i}$, is the set of indices, $<\mathbf{w}_m,\mathbf{i}>$, such that $\mathbf{wR}_{c1}\mathbf{w}_m$, $\mathbf{wR}_{c2}\mathbf{w}_m$ ... and $\mathbf{wR}_{ck}\mathbf{w}_m$ where $\mathbf{c}_1, \mathbf{c}_2, ..., \mathbf{c}_k$ are the constants in α.

A sentence like *Every tree is a plant*, that conforms to the structure of a meaning postulate associated with the subject, is thus true at every index in its sense. Hence, we can account for the apparent tautological (or **analytic**) properties of sentences like *Every bachelor is unmarried*, since it expresses a true proposition at every time in every **sensible world**, where the latter is defined as a world in which all meaning postulates are true for every basic expression in the language. Such sentences are not logical tautologies, however, because they are not true at every possible index and so can be distinguished from necessarily true sentences like *Every tree is a plant or not a plant*. On the other hand, the sense of the latter sentence is, of course, the same as that of *Every tree is a plant* because both sentences contain exactly the same content expressions, i.e. *tree'* and *plant'*. In order to distinguish the meanings of pairs of such sentences, we therefore need also to take into account their intensions as well as their senses. We may then call the combination of the sense and the intension of an expression the **meaning** of that expression and formally define the concept as in (64).

(64) The meaning of an expression α, $_M[\alpha]^{M,g,wn,i}$ is the ordered pair $<_\Sigma[\alpha]^{M,g,wn,i},_\Im[\alpha]^{M,g}>$.

This gives us sufficient structure to distinguish the meanings of logically true statements, since sentences containing different lexemes have different senses and those containing the same lexemes may have different intensions. For example, the meaning of *Every tree is a plant or not a plant* differs from that of *It is raining or it is not raining*, because, while their intensions are identical, their senses differ because there are worlds which conform to the patterns on extensions specified by the meaning postulates associated with *tree* and *plant* that do not conform to those of *rain* and vice versa. Furthermore, we can distinguish the meanings of two sentences which differ only in that they contain synonyms in the same position. Thus, while *Bertie has a red pullover* and *Bertie has a red jumper* both have the same sense, since *jumper* and *pullover* are synonyms (in British English), their intensions differ because there are indices that do not form part of the senses of these two words where Bertie's red jumper is not a pullover. Taking the objects of belief and knowledge to be meanings in the sense of (64), therefore, solves the problem of the substitution of intensional equivalents into such contexts. Whatever approach is adopted to solve this problem, however, it is clear that intensions in the technical sense are not sufficient to distinguish the meanings of all expressions. On the other hand, as illustrated in the approach to meaning that I have just sketched, this failure is not in itself sufficient to reject the possible worlds approach to intensionality (and meaning) entirely.

10.4.2 Cross-world reference

A second problem for the theory of intension defined in this chapter has to do with the interpretation of proper names. Indeed, this whole topic remains a thorny problem for linguists and philosophers which we can do no more than touch upon here. Essentially the problem revolves around whether named individuals in one world exist in others and, if they do, how they can be identified from one world to the next.

In the model M_{10}, the names *Bertie*, *Fiona*, *Ethel*, *Jo* and *Chester* are identified with (the individual sublimations of) individual constants that are assigned a constant intension by F_{10}. For example, *bertie'* denotes $\mathbf{MAN_2}$ and *fiona'* denotes $\mathbf{WOMAN_2}$ at every index in M_{10}. It has been cogently argued in the literature on this subject that this is the correct way to treat proper names, particularly as it allows one to refer to individuals with whom one has no direct acquaintance, like Queen Elizabeth II, or who may no longer be alive, like Socrates, or who may be fictional, like Jane Eyre. If proper names always pick out the same entity at whatever world or time, they always successfully refer and guarantee that when people talk about Jane Eyre, Socrates or Elizabeth Windsor they are talking about the same entity, even though that entity may not have corporeal existence in the actual world at the present time. Under this interpretation, names are **rigid designators** and the formula in (65) holds true of any model.

(65) $\exists x$ [necessarily'$(\alpha = x)$], where α translates a proper name.

Because the existential operator is outside the scope of the modal adverb, (65) asserts that there is some entity in **A** that is associated with the constant α at every index and that this entity is the same one at every index.

Unfortunately, once names are taken to be rigid designators, a familiar problem rears its ugly head. If two names denote the same entity at one index, then by (65) they must denote the same entity at every index. Thus, the Latin version of the Greek name for the Morning Star was *Hesperus* and that for the Evening Star was *Phosphorus*. We happen to know now that Hesperus and Phosphorus denote the same entity, the planet Venus. If names are rigid designators, then both Hesperus and Phosphorus must denote the planet Venus at every index and so have the same intension. Thus, by the revised version of Leibniz' Law in (59), the term *Hesperus* can be substituted for the term *Phosphorus* in all contexts and so, if the objects of belief are intensions, then we can infer from *The ancients believed that Hesperus is Hesperus* that *The ancients believed that Hesperus is Phosphorus* (in the *de dicto* reading), a conclusion that is not intuitively justified, as we have seen.

A further problem arises with sentences that assert the counterfactual identity of two elements. It is, for example, possible to imagine a person as being someone other than they are and making perfectly reasonable statements based on this assumption. All the sentences in (66) are well formed and easily interpretable, yet the interpretation of names as rigid designators means that we cannot take the assumption of the identity of two entities that are not in fact identical as being true in any possible world at any time.

(66) a. Clark Kent might not have been Superman.
b. I could have been Shakespeare, if I had lived in the sixteenth century.

Yet another problem concerns the properties that individuals may have at different worlds or times. For example, it is *logically* possible that at some index the entity denoted by *Bertie*, i.e. $\mathbf{MAN_2}$, could be a male human, at another a female frog, at another a dwarf tree, at another a Mozart sonata, and so on. Yet in what sense could a piece of music in one world be identified as the same entity as a man in another?

It is not clear that we can use the notion of meaning suggested in Section 10.4.1 to help out here, because it is not clear that proper names have sense in the same way that other expressions do. Indeed, it seems to be almost axiomatic in philosophy that names do not have sense. This is not a topic that I wish to get embroiled in here, but it may be the case that one should follow Aristotle in distinguishing the **essential properties** of an entity from its **accidental properties**. The essential properties of an individual may then be used to define an accessibility relation between worlds which excludes indices at which the individual in question does not have these properties. In that case, we could take the meaning of a proper name to be the set of indices in which the essential properties of the individual hold coupled with its (constant) intension. This could help in the cross-world identification of individuals, and, if identity is defined between essential properties, rather than referents, it might be possible to solve the problem of counterfactually equating distinct entities.

Other solutions to the problem of interpreting proper names can and have been put forward, but no one solution solves all the problems without posing more. It is clear that treating names as rigid designators intensionally is not sufficient, but it is possible that future research could produce a definition of meaning for proper names within a semantics based on possible worlds that is robust enough to account for the persistence of reference across worlds and times, but does not have the unfortunate consequences mentioned above.

10.5 Postscript

With this discussion of Montague's theory of intensionality, we come to the end of our excursion into formal semantics. It would seem appropriate, therefore, to end this chapter with a short review of the theory presented in the preceding chapters with respect to the criteria of adequacy discussed in Chapter 1.

With regard to the criteria for assessing the adequacy of semantic theories, the theory of interpretation defined in Section 10.2 comes out well. First and foremost, the Principle of Compositionality is adhered to throughout, since the denotations of all expressions are constructed from the intensional or extensional denotations of their component parts, depending on how these are put together. The information contained in an expression is not lost during its interpretation, and information not connected with the subparts of the expression does not arbitrarily contribute to the meaning of that expression. Apparent counterexamples to the Principle are treated in terms of intensions which allows a fully regular way of building up denotations in terms of functors and their arguments. The theory, therefore, provides an account of the way the meanings of expressions are built up from the meanings of their parts. The theory also provides an account of ambiguity. It predicts where this will occur: i.e. in expressions with homonyms and in those that contain more than one expression that translates into a logical operator. The interaction of the propositional connectives is determined by syntactic structure, while scope ambiguities involving the other operators are handled by the Rule of Quantifying In. The semantics proposed for the operators ensures that genuinely ambiguous expressions in the object language receive more than one set of truth-conditions. On the other hand, many genuinely non-ambiguous sentences (even those that are structurally ambiguous) are assigned only one set of truth-conditions, as required. The interaction of tense, aspect and modal operators, however, with each other and with the quantifiers may, as we have seen, provide too many readings for a single sentence, which is clearly a problem that needs to be resolved.

In Chapter 7 and subsequently, it has also been shown how truth-conditional semantics can account for relations of entailment, paraphrase and contradiction between sentences in English. The use of meaning postulates, interpreted as constraints on the extensions of related lexemes and phrases, provides the basis for a theory of sense, as the notion is generally used by linguists, rather than logicians. As discussed in this chapter and Chapter 9, it is possible to treat sense relations defined by meaning postulates as structuring the domain of possible worlds in terms of their accessibility to one another and, in so doing, to provide the basis of an account of anomaly and the likelihood of a sentence expressing a true proposition. This is achieved within an explicit and fully formulated theory of denotation, with both extensions and intensions determined formally in terms of the entities of a model and worlds (that may be thought of as possible alternative states-of-affairs) and times. Each basic expression in the object language is associated with a denotation in a model and the model theory determines how the denotations of all composite expressions are built up compositionally from these. Hence, the way linguistic expressions tie up with the world and convey information about possible or actual situations is made fully explicit within the theory.

Furthermore, in the course of this book, a theory has been provided of the core truth-conditional meanings of a number of constructions in English. These include: basic declarative sentences; negative sentences and sentences co-ordinated by *and* and *or*; simple passives; intersective adjectives; quantifiers, both classical and non-classical; grammatical tense and grammatical and lexical aspect; the modal adverbs *necessarily* and *possibly* and the modal verbs *must* and *may*; sentences of propositional attitude; control verbs and transitive verbs with a referentially opaque direct object position. There are, of course, many constructions that were omitted from the discussion (most notable **anaphora**) and there remain many problems with the theory of semantics presented in the text. However, formal semantics is now a thriving field of linguistics and is constantly being developed to analyse more constructions and to solve the problems that emerge. Indeed, there are now many variants of Montague's basic theory: some are primarily relatively compatible extensions to the theory and some are fairly radical revisions of it. Yet the theory presented in this introductory book remains the basis for much of the research that is carried out within formal semantics and there is no doubt that Montague's conviction that the syntax of natural languages is as amenable to formal interpretation as that of logical languages has introduced a valuable and robust strand of research into linguistic semantics.

10.6 Further reading

Lewis (1972) provides a general discussion of the programme adopted by Montague and discussed in this chapter. Montague discusses his intensional logic and its interpretation in Montague (1970a; 1970b; 1973), with the latter presenting the information in the form given in this chapter. Montague's general theory is discussed in Dowty (1979: ch. 1) and Dowty, Wall and Peters (1981: ch. 8) and the logic and its interpretation are sketched in McCawley (1981: 401-406), Allwood, Andersen and Dahl (1977: ch. 8) and Chierchia and McConnell-Ginet (1990: 208-219) and given a fuller discussion in Dowty, Wall and Peters (1981: ch. 6). The status of intensions as mathematical or psychological entities is discussed in Partee (1979) and Dowty (1979: ch. 8). Further discussion of the applications of the logic to intensional constructions in English presented in this chapter can be found in Chierchia and McConnell-Ginet (1990: 234-255) (modality, complement sentences and infinitives); McCawley (1981: 406-424) (intensional argument positions in e.g. *seek* and *change*); Dowty, Wall and Peters (1981: ch. 7) (which discusses the grammar of Montague (1973)); Bach (1979), Klein and Sag (1985) and Dowty (1985) (on control verbs). See also van Benthem (1988), the articles in Heny (1981), and, in a slightly different framework, Keenan and Faltz (1985), for discussions of different aspects of intensionality. The problem of intensional equivalence has generated a good deal of debate. Cresswell (1985b) provides the approach to the problems of propositional attitude verbs using structured meanings discussed in the text and this is taken up in Chierchia (1989). A radically different approach is taken in Barwise and Perry (1983) where the use of possible worlds is rejected entirely and subsequent developments in **situation semantics** have substantially revised the semantic programme that developed out of Montague's work (see, for example, Barwise (1986), the articles in Cooper, Mukai and Perry (1990) and, for some general discussion of the early form of the theory, the papers in *Linguistics and Philosophy* 8, no. 1). The analysis of proper names also remains controversial; see Kripke (1980). For representative examples of current developments in formal semantics, see the papers in Chierchia, Partee and Turner (1989a; 1989b), Cooper, Mukai and Perry (1990) and current issues of the journal *Linguistics and Philosophy*.

ANSWERS TO SELECTED EXERCISES

Chapter 2

Exercise 2.1:

i. poison'(ethel',the-cat')
ii. give'(the-student', the-cake', the-lecturer').
iii. crazy'(the-dog').

Exercise 2.3:

i. (ethel' = the-golfer'). True (both ethel' and the-golfer' denote $\mathbf{WOMAN_1}$).
ii. (the-student' = the-singer'). False (the-student' denotes $\mathbf{MAN_1}$ but the-singer' denotes $\mathbf{WOMAN_2}$).

Exercise 2.4:

1.	False.	2.	True.	3.	False.*
4.	True.	5.	False.	6.	False.
7.	True.	8.	False.	9.	False.
10.	True.	11.	False.	12.	True.
13.	False.	14.	True.	15.	True.
16.	False.				

* D represents *the set* consisting of the first four positive odd numbers.

Exercise 2.5:

i. laugh'(the-cat'). False ($\mathbf{CAT} \notin \{\mathbf{MAN_1}, \mathbf{WOMAN_1}\}$).
ii. happy'(jo'). True ($\mathbf{MAN_1} \in \{\mathbf{MAN_1}, \mathbf{WOMAN_1}, \mathbf{WOMAN_2}\}$).
iii. run'(fiona'). False ($\mathbf{WOMAN_2} \notin \{\mathbf{CAT}, \mathbf{DOG}\}$).

Exercise 2.6:

i. like'(the-lecturer', the-cat'). True ($\langle\mathbf{WOMAN_2},\mathbf{CAT}\rangle \in \{\langle\mathbf{MAN_1},\mathbf{WOMAN_1}\rangle, \langle\mathbf{MAN_1},\mathbf{MAN_2}\rangle, \langle\mathbf{MAN_1},\mathbf{WOMAN_2}\rangle, \langle\mathbf{MAN_1},\mathbf{MAN_1}\rangle, \langle\mathbf{WOMAN_1},\mathbf{WOMAN_2}\rangle, \langle\mathbf{WOMAN_1},\mathbf{MAN_1}\rangle, \langle\mathbf{WOMAN_2},\mathbf{CAT}\rangle, \langle\mathbf{WOMAN_2},\mathbf{WOMAN_1}\rangle\}$).
ii. kick'(ethel',the-student'). False. ($\langle\mathbf{WOMAN_1},\mathbf{MAN_1}\rangle \notin \varnothing$.)
iii. poison'(the-cake',the-cat'). False. ($\langle\mathbf{CAKE},\mathbf{CAT}\rangle \notin \{\langle\mathbf{CAKE},\mathbf{DOG}\rangle\}$.)

Exercise 2.7:

i. give'(the-golfer',the-book',the-golfer'). False.
ii. give'(the-student',the-book',the-lecturer'). False.
iii. give'(bertie', the-book', ethel'). True.

Exercise 2.8:

Truth conditions for n-place predicates: A formula $Pred_n(a_1,a_2,...,a_n)$ is true if and only if the ordered n-tuple $<E_1,E_2,...,E_n>$ is in the set of ordered n-tuples denoted by $Pred_n$, where E_1 is the entity denoted by a_1, E_2 is the entity denoted by a_2 and ... and E_n is the entity denoted by a_n. The formula is false otherwise.

Chapter 3

Exercise 3.2:

i. Three: $\sim(\sim(p \vee q))$, $\sim(\sim(p) \vee q)$, $(\sim(\sim(p)) \vee q)$.
ii. Three: $(p \vee \sim(p \,\&\, q))$, $((p \vee \sim(p)) \,\&\, q)$, $(p \vee (\sim(p) \vee q))$

Exercise 3.3:

p	q	~p	~q	(~p & ~q)
t	t	f	f	f
t	f	f	t	f
f	t	t	f	f
f	f	t	t	t

Exercise 3.5:

p	q	$(p \rightarrow q)$	$(q \rightarrow p)$	$(p \leftrightarrow q)$	$((p \leftrightarrow q) \leftrightarrow ((p \rightarrow q) \,\&\, (q \rightarrow p)))$
t	t	t	t	t	t
t	f	f	t	f	t
f	t	t	f	f	t
f	f	t	t	t	t

Exercise 3.6:

i. ~(give'(jo',the-cat',the-lecturer')). False. ($<$**MAN$_1$,CAT,WOMAN$_2$**$> \in [give']^{M1}$).
ii. (eat'(the-dog',the-cat') $\vee$ eat'(the-dog',the-cake')). True. ($<$**DOG,CAKE**$> \in [eat']^{M1}$).
iii. (messy'(chester') $\rightarrow$ ~(loathe'(the-cat',the-dog'))). True. (**DOG** $\notin [messy']^{M1}$).

Chapter 4

Exercise 4.1:

i. f(a): well-formed, type t.
ii. g(f): well-formed, type <e,t>.
iii. g(a): ill-formed.
iv. h(f): ill-formed.
v. j(f): well-formed, type t.
vi. (g(f))(a): well-formed, type t.

Exercise 4.3:

iii.

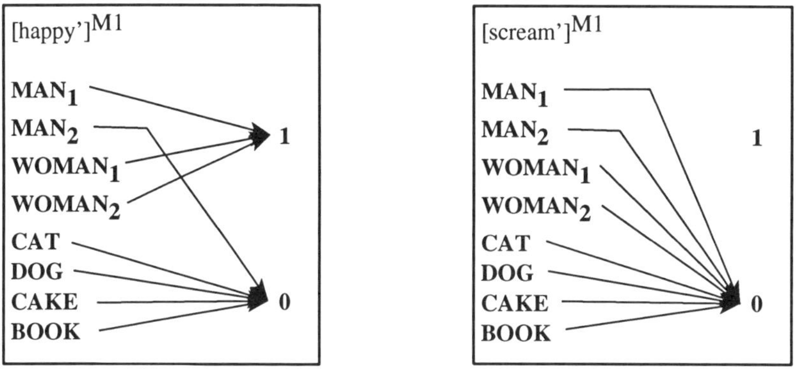

Exercise 4.4:

i. $D_t^{D_t} = \{0,1\}^{\{0,1\}}$. ii .$D_{<e,t>}^{D_{<e,t>}} = (\{0,1\}^A)^{(\{0,1\}^A)}$.

iii. $D_{<e,t>}^{D_e} = (\{0,1\}^A)^A$. iv. $D_t^{D_{<e,t>}} = \{0,1\}^{(\{0,1\}^A)}$.

Exercise 4.5:

1.

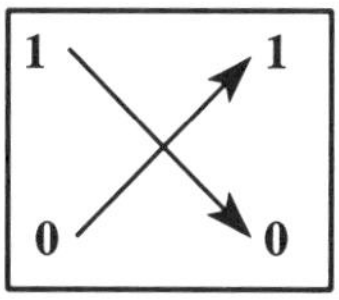

Chapter 5

Exercise 5.1:

i. The set of all entities y such that Jo liked y and Ethel didn't like y.

ii. The set of all entities z such that z gave the cake to themself.

iii. The set of all entities x that are identical to Jo.

iv. The set of all entities z such that z is a student and z liked Jo.

Exercise 5.2:

1. (12.a) should be (kick'(jo'))(jo').

(12.b) is ill-formed because λx [howl'(x)](the-cat') does not contain a free variable (x is bound by λx to the-cat').

(12.c) is ill-formed because λy does not bind the x variable in (like'(x))(jo') and so bertie' cannot be substituted for x.

(12.d) should be crazy'(ethel') ∨ drunk'(z).

2. i. (like'(the-dog'))(jo') & ~((like'(the-dog'))(ethel')).
   ii. (give'(bertie')(the-cat'))(bertie').
   iii. ~(bertie' = jo').
   iv. (like'(the-cat'))(bertie') ∨ ~((like'(the-dog'))(bertie')).
   v. (crazy'(bertie') & (like'(bertie'))(jo')) ∨ ~(crazy'(bertie')).

Exercise 5.3:

i. $[\lambda y\ [\text{happy'}(y)\ \&\ \text{laugh'}(y)]]^{M,g}$

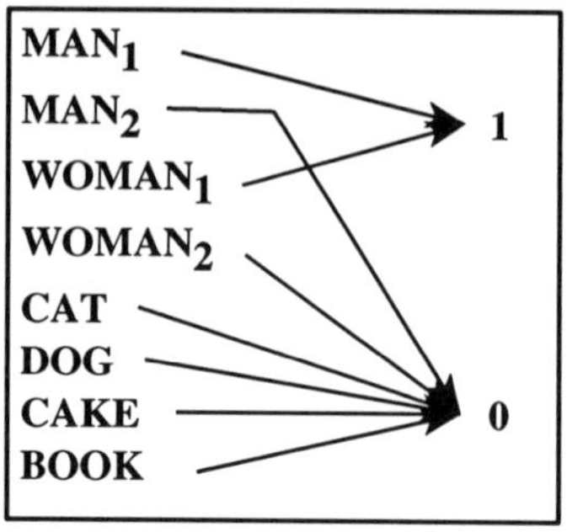

iv. $[\lambda y\ [\sim((y = \text{the-lecturer'}) \vee (y = \text{the-student'})]^{M,g}$

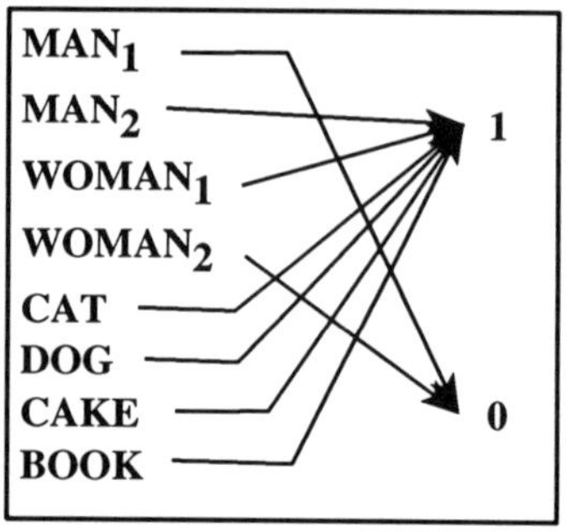

Exercise 5.4:

i. λx [(eat'(x))(chester')](the-cake').
ii. λy [(give'(fiona')(y))(ethel')](the-book').

Exercise 5.5:

i. Ill-formed. (The argument *jo'* is bound by λz not λx. The correct conversion is (like'(bertie'))(jo').)
ii. Well-formed.
iii. Well-formed.

iv. Ill-formed. (The argument *jo'* is not bound by the first λx. The correct conversion is λx [scream'(x)] ∨ ~(laugh'(jo')).)

v. Well-formed.

Exercise 5.8:

i. <<e,<e,t>>,t> ii. <e,<e,<e,t>>>

iii. <<e,t>,<<<e,t>,<e,t>>,<e,t>>> iv. <t,t>

v. <<e,t>,t>vi.<t,<t,t>>

Exercise 5.10:

i. [λp [p ↔ rain']]^{M2,g} is that function $\mathbf{h_1}$ from **{0,1}** to **{0,1}** such that for all elements α in **{0,1}** $\mathbf{h_1}$(α) is [p ↔ rain']$^{M2,g_{\alpha/p}}$.

iii. [λP [slowly'(P)]]^{M2,g} is that function $\mathbf{h_2}$ from **{0,1}**^{A} to **{0,1}**^{A} such that for all elements α in **{0,1}**^{A} $\mathbf{h_3}$(α) is [slowly'(P)]$^{M2,g_{\alpha/P}}$.

Exercise 5.11:

i. (λp [λq [p & q]]((poison'(the-dog'))(the-cake')))
((eat'(the-cake'))(the-dog'))
» (poison'(the-dog'))(the-cake') & (eat'(the-cake'))(the-dog').

Chapter 6

Exercise 6.1:

i. Someone liked herself:
∃x [(like'(x))(x)].

ii. Someone liked Jo and hated Fiona:
∃x [(like'(jo'))(x) & (hate'(fiona'))(x)].

iii. Someone was liked by everyone:
∃x [∀y [(like'(x))(y)]].

iv. Everyone gave something to someone:
∀x [∃y [∃z [(give'(z)(y))(x)]]].

Exercise 6.2:

i. False. (Not everyone likes themselves.)

ii. True. ($g^{WOMAN1/x}$ satisfies [(like'(fiona'))(x) & (like'(x))(fiona')].)

iii. True. (Every value assigned to x satisfies exist'(x).)

iv. True. (Every value assigned to x satisfies (touch'(x))(ethel').)

v. False. ($g^{MAN2/x}$ (and other value assignments) fails to satisfy (like'(x))(y) for any value assigned to y.)

Exercise 6.3:

someone ⇒ λP [∃x [P(x)]].
no-one ⇒ λP [~(∃x [P(x)])]. (or λP [∀x [~(P(x))]]).

Exercise 6.4:

everyone: {X ⊆ A | A = X}
no-one: {X ⊆ A | X = ∅}

Exercise 6.5:

no dog $\Rightarrow \lambda P\,[\sim(\exists x\,[dog'(x)\ \&\ P(x)])]$
(or $\lambda P\,[\forall x\,[dog'(x) \rightarrow \sim(P(x))]]$).
no $\Rightarrow \lambda Q\,[\lambda P\,[\sim(\exists x\,[Q(x)\ \&\ P(x)])]]$
(or $\lambda\,Q\,[\lambda P\,[\forall x\,[Q(x) \rightarrow \sim(P(x))]]]$).

Exercise 6.6:

ii. Some student didn't sing
$\Rightarrow (\lambda Q\,[\lambda P\,[\exists x\,[Q(x)\ \&\ P(x)]]](student'))(\lambda P_1\,[\lambda y\,[\sim(P_1(y))]](sing'))$
» $\exists x\,[student'(x)\ \&\ \sim(sing'(x))]$.

iii. If no student sang, then no lecturer screamed
$\Rightarrow (\lambda p\,[\lambda q\,[p \rightarrow q]]((\lambda Q\,[\lambda P\,[\sim(\exists x\,[Q(x)\ \&\ P(x)])]](student'))(sing'))$
$(\lambda Q_1\,[\lambda P_1\,[\sim(\exists y\,[Q_1(y)\ \&\ P_1(y)])]](lecturer'))(scream'))$
» $\sim(\exists x\,[\sim(student'(x)\ \&\ sing'(x))]) \rightarrow \sim(\exists y\,[lecturer'(y)\ \&\ scream'(y)])$.

Exercise 6.7:

$\{X \subseteq A \mid X \cap [dog']^{M,g} = \varnothing\}$

Negative sublimation of $[dog]^M$

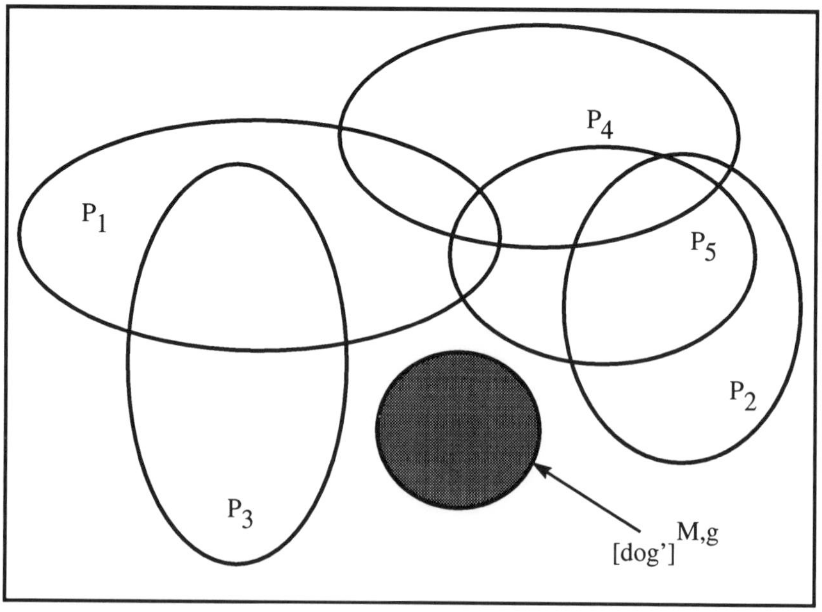

Exercise 6.9:

i. $\lambda P\ [P(jo')](\lambda x\ [(\lambda q\ [\lambda p\ [p\ \&\ q]](cry'(x)))(laugh'(x))])$
» $[laugh'(jo')\ \&\ cry'(jo')]$.

ii. $(\lambda Q\ [\lambda P\ [\exists x\ [\forall y\ [Q(y) \leftrightarrow x = y]\ \&\ P(x)]]](linguist'))(\lambda x\ [\sim(happy'(z))])$
» $\exists x\ [\forall y\ [linguist'(y) \leftrightarrow x = y]\ \&\ \sim(happy'(x))]$.

iii. $(\lambda p\ [\lambda q\ [p \rightarrow q]](\lambda P\ [P(ethel')](sing')))$
$((\lambda Q\ [\lambda P_1\ [\exists x\ [\forall y\ [Q(y) \leftrightarrow x = y]\ \&\ P_1(x)]]](dog'))(howl'))$
» $(sing'(ethel') \rightarrow \exists x\ [\forall y\ [dog'(y) \leftrightarrow x = y]\ \&\ howl'(x)])$

Exercise 6.10:

i. Ethel shot a philosopher
$\Rightarrow \lambda P\ [P(ethel')](\lambda \boldsymbol{P}\ [\lambda x\ [\boldsymbol{P}(\lambda y\ [(shoot'(y))(x)])]]$
$(\lambda Q\ [\lambda P_1\ [\exists z\ [Q(z)\ \&\ P_1(z)]]](philosopher')))$
» $\exists z\ [philosopher'(z)\ \&\ (shoot'(z))(ethel')]$.

Exercise 6.13:

i. False. ii. True. iii. True. iv. False.

Chapter 7

Exercise 7.1:

p	q	(p → q)	~q	((p → q) & ~q)	~p	((p → q) & ~q) → ~p)
t	t	t	f	f	f	t
t	f	f	t	f	f	t
f	t	t	f	f	t	t
f	f	t	t	t	t	t

Exercise 7.2:

i. Let p = *Fiona poisoned the cake.* Let q = *Bertie poisoned the cake.* Let r = *Fiona has a bottle of poison in her bedroom.* Let s = *Fiona has a book about unsolved murders on her bedside table*

a.	$p \vee q$	premiss
b.	$p \rightarrow (r\ \&\ s)$	premiss
c.	$\sim q$	assumption
d.	p	from a and c by DE2
e.	r & s	from b and d by MP
f.	s	from e by CI
g.	$\sim q \rightarrow s$	from c and f by CdI

Chapter 8

Exercise 8.1:

ii. a. $[(\text{like}'(\text{fiona}'))(\text{jo}')]^{M8,g,[t5]}$ is **1** iff $[\text{like}'(\text{fiona}')]^{M8,g,[t5]}([\text{jo}']^{M8,g,[t5]})$ is **1**.

b. $[\text{like}'(\text{fiona}')]^{M8,g,[t5]}([\text{jo}']^{M8,g,[t5]})$ is **1** iff $([\text{like}']^{M8,g,[t5]}([\text{fiona}']^{M8,g,[t5]}))([\text{jo}']^{M8,g,[t5]})$ is **1**.

c. Since $[t_5] \subseteq [t_1,t_9]$, $[\text{jo}']^{M8,g,[t5]}$ is $F_8(\text{jo}')([t_1,t_9])$ = $\mathbf{MAN_1}$.

d. Since $[t_5] \subseteq [t_1,t_9]$, $[\text{fiona}']^{M8,g,[t5]}$ is $F_8(\text{fiona}')([t_1,t_9])$ = $\mathbf{WOMAN_2}$.

e. Since $[t_5] \subseteq [t_7,t_9]$, $[\text{like}']^{M8,g,[t5]}$ is $F_8(\text{like}')([t_7,t_9])$ which is the function defining {<$\mathbf{MAN_1}$,$\mathbf{WOMAN_1}$>, <$\mathbf{MAN_1}$,$\mathbf{WOMAN_2}$>, <$\mathbf{WOMAN_1}$,$\mathbf{WOMAN_2}$>, <$\mathbf{WOMAN_2}$,$\mathbf{WOMAN_1}$>, <$\mathbf{WOMAN_1}$,$\mathbf{MAN_2}$>, <$\mathbf{MAN_2}$,$\mathbf{WOMAN_1}$>}, call this κ.

f. $\kappa(\mathbf{WOMAN_2})(\mathbf{MAN_1}) = \mathbf{1}$.

g. So $[(\text{like}'(\text{fiona}'))(\text{jo}')]^{M8,g,[t5]}$ is **1**.

Exercise 8.6:

i. $[\text{Past}\ (\text{Perf}\ (\exists x\ [(\text{sing}_t'(x))(\text{jo}')]))]^{M8,g,[t6]}$ is **1**. (Jo ($\mathbf{MAN_1}$) begins and ends singing $\mathbf{SONG_1}$ at interval $[t_3,t_5]$ which precedes $[t_6]$.)

ii. $[\text{Fut}\ (\text{Perf}\ (\exists x\ [(\text{sing}_t'(x))(\text{ethel}')]))]^{M8,g,[t6]}$ is **0**. (Although Ethel ($\mathbf{WOMAN_1}$) completes singing $\mathbf{SONG_2}$ at $[t_9]$, the interval in which she begins the singing includes $[t_6]$. Therefore, there is no future interval where she begins and completes the singing of a song.)

iii. $[\text{Fut}\ (\text{Perf}\ (\exists x\ [\text{sing}'(x)]))]^{M8,g,[t6]}$ is **1**. (There are intervals of time that follow $[t_6]$ in which someone sings (e.g. $\mathbf{WOMAN_2}$ at $[t_8]$.)

iv. $[\text{Past}\ (\text{Perf}\ ({\sim}(\exists x\ [\text{sing}'(x)])))]^{M8,g,[t6]}$ is **0**. (There is no interval of time preceding $[t_6]$ during which no-one is singing.)

v. $[\text{Pres}(\text{Impf}(\text{sing}'(\text{jo}')))]^{M,8,g,[t6]}$ is **1**. (There is an interval of time properly containing $\mathbf{[t_6]}$ (i.e. $\mathbf{[t_3,t_9]}$) at which $\mathbf{MAN_1}$ is singing.)

vi. $[\text{Fut}(\text{Impf}(\exists y\ [\exists x\ [(\text{sing}_t'(x))(y)]]))]^{M,g,t6}$ is 1. (There is an interval of time following $\mathbf{[t_6]}$ (e.g. $\mathbf{[t_8]}$) which is properly contained in an interval of time $\mathbf{[t_6,t_9]}$ during which $\mathbf{MAN_1}$ is singing $\mathbf{SONG_2}$.)

Chapter 9

Exercise 9.1:

i. $[\Box{\sim}\text{laugh}'(\text{chester}')]^{M9,g,w1}$ is **0**. (Chester (**DOG**) laughs in $\mathbf{w_2}$.)

ii. $[\Diamond({\sim}(\text{laugh}'(\text{chester}')) \rightarrow \text{laugh}'(\text{jo}'))]^{M9,g,w1}$ is **1**. (In world $\mathbf{w_2}$ in M_9, ${\sim}(\text{laugh}'(\text{chester}'))$ is **0**, so $({\sim}(\text{laugh}'(\text{chester}')) \rightarrow \text{laugh}'(\text{jo}'))$ is **1**.)

iii. $[{\sim}\Box\text{laugh}'(\text{chester}')]^{M9,g,w1}$ is **1**. (Chester does not laugh in $\mathbf{w_1}$, so $[\Box\text{laugh}'(\text{chester}')]^{M9,g,w1}$ is 0.)

iv. $[{\sim}(\Diamond(\text{laugh}'(\text{jo}')\ \&\ {\sim}\text{laugh}'(\text{jo}')))]^{M9,g,w1}$ is **1**. (There is no world, **w**, in which $[\text{laugh}'(\text{jo}')\ \&\ {\sim}\text{laugh}'(\text{jo}')]^{M9,g,w}$ is **1**, so $[\Diamond(\text{laugh}'(\text{jo}')\ \&\ {\sim}\text{laugh}'(\text{jo}'))]^{M9,g,w1}$ is **0**.)

v. $[\Diamond{\sim}\text{laugh}'(\text{fiona}')]^{M9,g,w1}$ is **1**. (Fiona does not laugh in $\mathbf{w_2}$, so $[{\sim}\text{laugh}'(\text{fiona}')]^{M9,g,w2}$ is **1**.)

vi. $[{\sim}\Diamond\text{laugh}'(\text{fiona}')]^{M9,g,w1}$ is **0**. (Fiona laughs in $\mathbf{w_1}$, so $[\Diamond\text{laugh}'(\text{fiona}')]^{M9,g,w1}$ is **1**.)

Chapter 10

Exercise 10.1:

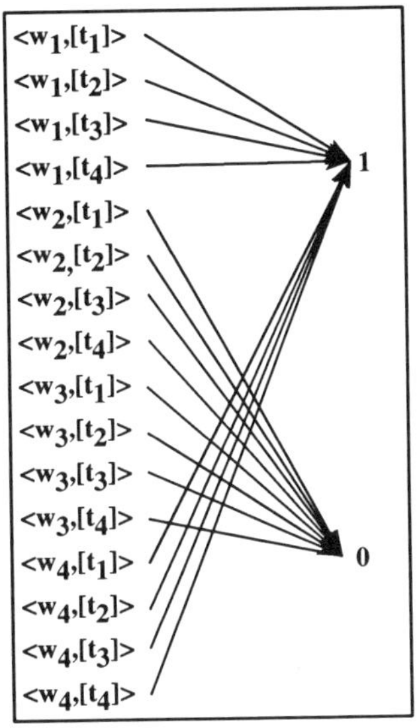

i. ɜ[laugh'(jo')]^{M10,g}

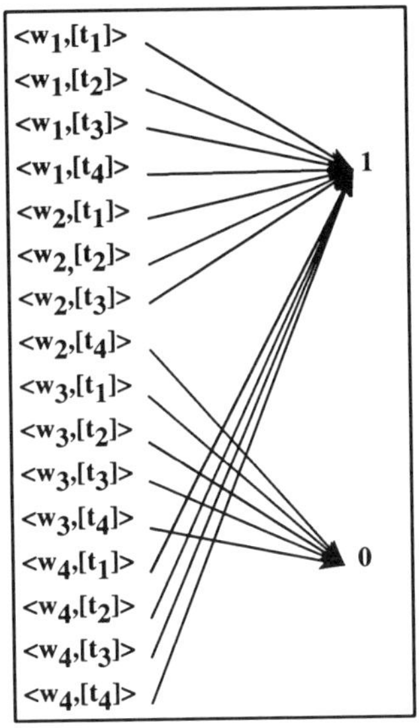

ii. ɜ[laugh'(chester') ∨ laugh'(jo')]^{M10,g}

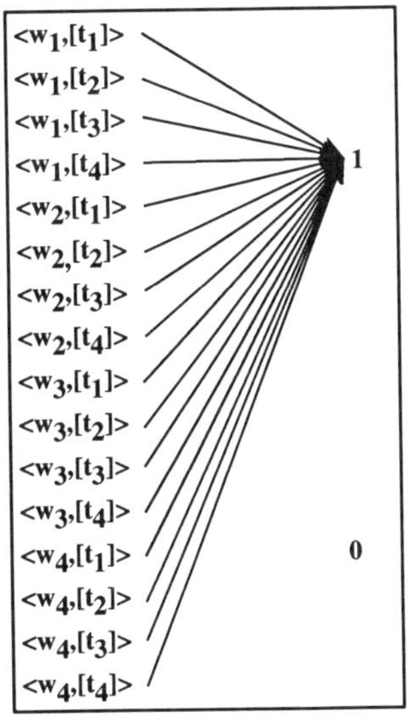

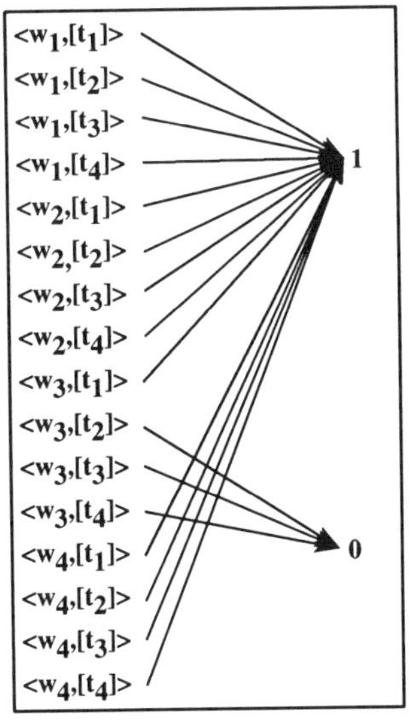

iii. $\Im[\text{laugh'(fiona')} \vee \sim\text{laugh'(fiona')}]^{M10,g}$ iv. $\Im[\text{laugh'(fiona')} \rightarrow \text{laugh'(jo')}]^{M10,g}$

Exercise 10.2:

i. Ill-formed.
ii. Well-formed (<e,t>).
iii. Well-formed (t).
iv. Well-formed (t).
v. Ill-formed.
vi. Well-formed (t).
vii. Ill-formed.

Exercise 10.3:

i. Functions from indices to functions from characteristic functions of entities to truth values: $(\{0,1\}^{(\{0,1\}^A)})^{W \times I}$.
ii. Functions from functions from indices to characteristic functions of entities to truth values: $\{0,1\}^{((\{0,1\}^A)^{W \times I})}$.
v. Functions from functions from indices to truth values to characteristic functions of entities: $(\{0,1\}^A)^{(\{0,1\}^{W \times I})}$.

REFERENCES

Ajdukiewicz, K. (1935) 'Die syntactische Konnexität'. *Studia Philosophica* 1: 1-27. (English translation in S. McCall ed. (1967) *Polish Logic*. Oxford, Oxford University Press.

Allwood, J., L. Andersen and O. Dahl (1977) *Logic in Linguistics*. Cambridge, Cambridge University Press.

Åquist, L (1976) 'A system of chronological tense logic'. In Günthner and S. Schmidt eds.: 223-254.

Bach, E. (1974) *Syntactic Theory*. New York, Holt, Rinehart and Wilson.

(1979) 'Control in Montague Grammar'. *Linguistic Inquiry* 10: 515-532.

(1986) 'The algebra of events'. *Linguistics and Philosophy* 9: 5-16.

Ballmer, T. and M. Pinkal eds. (1983) *Approaching Vagueness*. Amsterdam, North-Holland.

Bar-Hillel, Y. (1953) 'A quasi-arithmetical notation for syntactic description'. *Language* 29: 47-58.

Barwise, J. (1986) 'Conditionals and conditional information'. In Traugott, ter Meulen, Reilly and Ferguson eds.: 21-54.

Barwise, J. and R. Cooper (1984) 'Generalized quantifiers and natural language'. *Linguistics and Philosophy* 4: 159-219.

Barwise, J. and J. Etchemendy (1989) *Tarski's World*. Stanford, CSLI.

Barwise, J. and J. Perry (1983) *Situations and Attitudes*. Cambridge, Mass., MIT Press.

Baüerle, R. (1979) 'Tense logics and natural language'. *Synthèse* 40: 225-230.

Bennett, M. (1977) 'A guide to the logic of tense and aspect in English'. *Logique et Analyse* 20: 491-517.

(1978) 'Demonstratives and indexicals in Montague Grammar'. *Synthèse* 39: 1-80.

Bennett, M. and B. H. Partee (1972) 'Toward the logic of tense and aspect in English'. Mimeo, IULC.

van Benthem, J. (1986) *Essays in Logical Semantics*. Dordrecht, Reidel.

(1988) *A Manual of Intensional Logic*. Stanford, CSLI.

Blakemore, D. (1987) *Semantic Constraints on Relevance*. Oxford, Basil Blackwell.

(1989) 'Denial and contrast: a relevance theoretic analysis of *BUT*'. *Linguistics and Philosophy* 12: 15-38.

Borsley, R. (1990) *Syntactic Theory: a Unified Approach*. London, Edward Arnold.

Bradley, R. and N. Swartz (1979) *Possible Worlds: an Introduction to Logic and its Philosophy*. Oxford, Basil Blackwell.

Burton-Roberts, N. (1989) *The Limits to Debate: a Revised Theory of Semantic Presupposition*. Cambridge, Cambridge University Press.

Carlson, G. N. (1989) 'English generic sentences'. In Chierchia, Partee and Turner (1989b): 167-192.

Carnap, R. (1956) *Meaning and Necessity*. Chicago, Chicago University Press (Revised edn).

Carston, R. (1988) 'Implicature, explicature, and truth-theoretic semantics'. In R. Kempson ed.: 155-181.

Chierchia, G. (1989) 'Structured meanings'. In Chierchia, Partee and Turner eds. (1986b): 131-166.

Chierchia, G. and S. McConnel-Ginet (1990) *Meaning and Grammar: an Introduction to Semantics*. Cambridge, Mass., MIT Press.

Chierchia, G., B. H. Partee and R. Turner eds. (1989a) *Properties, Types and Meaning: Volume 1 Foundational Issues*. Dordrecht, Reidel.

(1989b) *Properties, Types and Meaning: Volume 2 Semantic Issues*. Dordrecht, Reidel.

Chierchia, G. and R. Turner (1988) 'Semantics and Property Theory'. In *Linguistics and Philosophy* 11: 261-302.

Church, A. (1956) *Introduction to Mathematical Logic*. Princeton, Princeton University Press.

Comrie, B. (1976) *Aspect*. Cambridge, Cambridge University Press.

(1985) *Tense*. Cambridge, Cambridge University Press.

Cooper, R. (1983) *Quantification and Syntactic Theory*. Dordrecht, Reidel.

Cooper, R., K. Mukai and J. Perry (1990) *Situation Theory and its Applications*. Stanford, CSLI.

Cresswell, M. J. (1973) *Logics and Languages*. London, Methuen.

(1985a) *Adverbial Modification*. Dordrecht, Reidel.

(1985b) *Structured Meanings*. Cambridge, Mass., MIT Press.

Cruse, D. (1986) *Lexical Semantics*. Cambridge, Cambridge University Press.

Dahl, O. (1985) *Tense and Aspect Systems*. Oxford, Basil Blackwell.

Davidson, D. (1967) 'The logical form of action sentences'. In N. Rescher ed. *The Logic of Decision and Action*. Pittsburgh, University of Pittsburgh Press: 81-95. (Reprinted in Davidson (1980).)

(1980) *Essays on Actions and Events*. Oxford, Clarendon.

(1984) *Inquiries into Truth and Interpretation*. Oxford, Oxford University Press.

Dowty, D. (1979) *Word Meaning and Montague Grammar*. Dordrecht, Reidel.

(1982) 'Grammatical relations and Montague Grammar'. In P. Jacobson and G. K. Pullum eds. *The Nature of Syntactic Representation*. Dordrecht, Reidel: 79-130.

(1985) 'On recent analyses of the semantics of control'. In *Linguistics and Philosophy* 8: 291-331.

(1989) 'On the semantic content of the notion of "thematic role"'. In Chierchia, Partee and Turner eds. (1989b): 69-129.

Dowty, D. and W. A. Ladusaw (1988) 'Toward a non-grammatical account of thematic roles'. In W. Wilkins ed. *Syntax and Semantics 21: Thematic Relations*. New York, Academic Press: 61-73.

Dowty, D., R. Wall and S. Peters (1981) *Introduction to Montague Semantics*. Dordrecht, Reidel.

Dummett, M. (1981) *Frege: Philosophy of Language*. London, Duckworth (2nd edn).

Eikmeyer, H-J. ed. (1981) *Words, Worlds and Contexts: New approaches to Word Semantics*. Berlin, de Gruyter.

Frege, G. (1892) 'Über Sinn und Bedeutung'. *Zeitschrift für Philosophie und philosophisches Kritik*: 22-50. (An English translation appears in P. Geach and M. Black eds. (1980) *Translations from the Philosophical Writings of Gottlob Frege*. Oxford, Basil Blackwell.)
Gazdar, G (1979) *Pragmatics: Implicature, Presupposition and Logical Form*. New York, Academic Press.
Gazdar, G., E. Klein, G. K. Pullum and I. A. Sag (1985) *Generalized Phrase Structure Grammar*. Oxford, Basil Blackwell.
Grice, P. (1975) 'Logic and conversation'. In P. Cole and J. Morgan eds. *Syntax and Semantics*, vol. 3. New York, Academic Press.
(1978) 'More on logic and conversation'. In P. Cole ed. *Syntax and Semantics*, vol. 9. New York, Academic Press.
Günthner, F. (1976) 'Time schemes, tense logic and the analysis of English tenses'. In Günthner, F. and S. Schmidt eds.: 201- 222.
Günthner, F. and S. Schmidt eds. (1976) *Formal Semantics and Pragmatics for Natural Languages*. Dordrecht, Reidel.
Guttenplan, S. (1986) *The Languages of Logic*. Oxford, Basil Blackwell.
Hawkins, J. A. (1978) *Definiteness and Indefiniteness*. London, Croom Helm.
Heim, I. (1989) *The Semantics of Definite and Indefinite NPs*. New York, Garland Press.
Heny, F. ed. (1981) *Ambiguities in Intensional Contexts*. Dordrecht, Reidel.
Hoeksema, J. (1983) 'Plurality and conjunction'. In ter Meulen ed.: 63-83.
Huddleston, R. (1984) *Introduction to the Grammar of English*. Cambridge, Cambridge University Press.
Hughes, G. E. and M. J. Cresswell (1968) *An Introduction to Modal Logic*. London, Methuen.
Hurford, J. R. and B. Heasley (1983) *Semantics: a Coursebook*. Cambridge, Cambridge University Press.
Kamp, J. A. W. (1975) 'Two theories about adjectives'. In E. L. Keenan ed. *Formal Semantics of Natural Language*. Cambridge, Cambridge University Press: 123-155.
Kamp, H. (1981) 'A theory of truth and discourse representation'. In J. Groenendijk, T. Janssen and M. Stokhof eds. *Formal Methods in the Study of Language*. Amsterdam: Mathematical Centre Tracts 135.
Keenan, E. and L. M. Faltz (1985) *Boolean Semantics for Natural Language*. Dordrecht, Reidel.
Keenan, E. and J. Stavi (1986) 'A semantic characterization of natural language determiners'. In *Linguistics and Philosophy* 9: 253-326.
Kempson, R. (1977) *Semantic Theory*. Cambridge, Cambridge University Press.
ed. (1988) *Mental Representations*. Cambridge, Cambridge University Press.
Klein, E. (1980) 'A semantics for positive and comparative adjectives'. In *Linguistics and Philosophy* 4: 1-45.
Klein, E. and I. A. Sag (1986) 'Type-driven translation'. *Linguistics and Philosophy* 8: 163-202.
Kripke, S. (1980) *Naming and Necessity*. Oxford, OUP.
Leech, G. N. (1974) *Semantics*. Harmondsworth, Penguin.
Levinson, S. C. (1983) *Pragmatics*. Cambridge, Cambridge University Press.

Lewis, D. (1972) 'General semantics'. In D. Davidson and G. Harman eds. *Semantics for Natural Language*. Dordrecht, Reidel.
(1973) *Counterfactuals*. Oxford, Basil Blackwell.
(1986) *The Plurality of Worlds*. Oxford, Basil Blackwell.
Link, G. (1983) 'The logical analysis of plural and mass terms: a lattice-theoretic approach'. In R. Baüerle, C. Schwarze and A. von Stechow eds. *Meaning, Use and Interpretation of Language*. Berlin, de Gruyter.
Lønning, J. T. (1987) 'Mass terms and quantification'. *Linguistics and Philosophy* 10: 1-52.
Ludlow, P. and S. Neale (1991) 'Indefinite descriptions: in defense of Russell'. *Linguistics and Philosophy* 14: 171-202.
Lycan, W. G. (1984) *Logical Form in Natural Language*. Cambridge, Mass., MIT Press.
Lyons, J. (1977) *Semantics*. Cambridge, Cambridge University Press.
(1981) *Language, Meaning and Context*. London, Fontana. (New edition to be published by Cambridge University Press.)
Martin, J. N. (1987) *Elements of Formal Semantics*. Orlando, Academic Press.
May, R. (1985) *Logical Form: its structure and derivation*. Cambridge, Mass., MIT Press.
McCawley, J. D. (1981) *Everything that Linguists have Always Wanted to Know about Logic**. Oxford, Basil Blackwell.
ter Meulen, A. G. B. (1983) 'The representation of time in natural language'. In ter Meulen ed.: 177-191.
ed. (1983) *Studies in Modeltheoretic Semantics*. Dordrecht, Foris.
(1984) 'Events, quantities and individuals'. In F. Landman and F. Veltman eds. *Varieties of Formal Semantics*. Dordrecht, Foris: 259-279.
Montague, R. (1970a) 'English as a formal language'. In B. Visentini et al. eds. *Linguaggi nella Società e nella Tecnica*. Milan, Editzione di Comunità: 189-224. (Reprinted in Montague (1974).)
(1970b) 'Universal grammar'. *Theoria* 36: 373-398. (Reprinted in Montague (1974).)
(1973) 'The proper treatment of quantification in ordinary English'. In J. Hintikka, J. Moravcsik and P. Suppes eds. *Approaches to Natural Language*. Dordrecht, Reidel. (Reprinted in Montague (1974).)
(1974) *Formal Philosophy: Selected Papers of Richard Montague*. Ed. by R. H. Thomason. New Haven, Yale University Press.
Mourelatos, A. P. D. (1978) 'Events, processes and states'. *Linguistics and Philosophy* 2: 425-434.
Oehrle, R. T., E. Bach and D. Wheeler eds. (1988) *Categorial Grammars and Natural Language Structures*. Dordrecht, Reidel.
Ojeda, A. E. (1991) 'Definite descriptions and definite generics'. *Linguistics and Philosophy* 14: 367-397.
Palmer, F. (1981) *Semantics: A New Outline*. Cambridge, Cambridge University Press.
Parsons, T. (1979) 'Type theory and ordinary language'. In S. Davis and M. Mithun eds. *Linguistics, Philosophy and Montague Grammar*. Austin, University of Texas Press: 127-152.

(1980) 'Modifiers and quantifiers in natural language'. *Canadian Journal of Philosophy* Supplementary Volume VI: 29-60.
(1989) 'The progressive in English: events, states and processes'. *Linguistics and Philosophy* 12: 213-241.
Partee, B. H. (1979) 'Semantics: mathematics or psychology?' In R. Baüerle, U. Egli and A. von Stechow eds. *Semantics From Different Points of View*. Berlin, Springer Verlag.
(1984) 'Compositionality'. In F. Landman and F. Veltman eds. *Varieties of Formal Semantics*. Dordrecht, Foris: 281-311.
(1986) 'Noun Phrase Interpretation and type-shifting principles'. In J. Groenendijk, D. de Jongh and M. Stokhof eds. *Studies in Discourse Representation Theory and the Theory of Generalized Quantifiers*. Dordrecht, Foris.
Partee, B. H. and M. Rooth (1983) 'Generalized conjunction and type ambiguity'. In R. Baüerle, C. Schwarze and A. von Stechow eds. *Meaning, Use and Interpretation of Language*. Berlin, de Gruyter.
Partee, B. H., A. ter Meulen and R. Wall (1990) *Mathematical Methods in Linguistics*. Dordrecht, Reidel.
Prior, A. N. (1967) *Past, Present and Future*. Oxford, Oxford University Press.
Pulman, S. G. (1983) *Word Meaning and Belief*. London, Croom Helm.
Putnam, H. (1975) 'The meaning of meaning'. In H. Putnam *Mind, Language and Reality: Philosophical Papers vol. 2*. Cambridge, Cambridge University Press.
Quine, W. V. O. (1960) *Word and Object*. Cambridge, Mass., MIT Press.
Reichenbach, H. (1947) *Elements of Symbolic Logic*. Berkeley, University of California Press.
Rescher, N. and A. Urquhart (1971) *Temporal Logic*. Berlin, Springer Verlag.
Reuland, E. J. and A. ter Meulen eds. (1987) *The Representation of (In)definiteness*. Cambridge, Mass., MIT Press.
Rohrer, C. ed. (1980) *Time, Tense and Quantifiers*. Tübingen, Niemeyer Verlag.
Russell, B. (1905) 'On denoting'. *Mind* 14: 479-493. (Reprinted in I. Copi and J. Gould eds. (1967) *Contemporary Readings in Logical Theory*. New York, MacMillan.)
Sag, I. A., T. Wasow, G. Gazdar and S. Weisler (1985) 'Co-ordination and how to distinguish categories'. In *Natural Language and Linguistic Theory* 3: 117-171.
Siegel, M. (1979) 'Measure adjectives in Montague Grammar'. In S. Davis and M. Mithun eds. *Linguistics, Philosophy and Montague Grammar*. Austin, University of Texas Press: 223-262.
Sperber, D. and D. Wilson (1986) *Relevance: Communication and Cognition*. Oxford, Basil Blackwell.
Strawson, P. F. (1950) 'On referring'. *Mind* 59: 320-344.
Tarski, A. (1944) 'The semantic conception of truth'. In *Philosophy and Phenomenological Research* 4: 341-375. (Reprinted in A. Martinich ed. (1985) *The Philosophy of Language*. Oxford, Oxford University Press.)
Tedeschi, P. J. and A. Zaenen eds. (1981) *Syntax and Semantics 14: Tense and Aspect*. New York, Academic Press.
Thomason, R. (1989) 'Motivating ramified type theory'. In Chierchia, Partee and Turner eds.: 47-62.

Thomason, R. and R. Stalnaker (1973) 'A semantic theory of adverbs'. *Linguistic Inquiry* 4: 195-220.

Tichý, P. (1985) 'Do we need interval semantics?' *Linguistics and Philosophy* 8: 263-282.

Traugott, E., A. ter Meulen, J. S. Reilly and C. A. Ferguson eds. (1986) *On Conditionals*. Cambridge, Cambridge University Press.

Turner, R. (1989) 'Foundations of semantic theory'. In Chierchia, Partee and Turner eds.: 63-84.

Vendler, Z. (1967) *Linguistics in Philosophy*. New York, Cornell University Press.

Verkuyl, H. J. (1972) *On the Compositional Nature of the Aspects*. Dordrecht, Reidel.

(1989) 'Aspectual classes and aspectual composition'. *Linguistics and Philosophy* 12: 39-94.

Wilson, D. and D. Sperber (1988) 'Representation and relevance'. In R. Kempson ed.: 133- 153.

Zwarts, F. (1983) 'Determiners: a relational perspective'. In ter Meulen ed.: 37-62.

INDEX

Pages where terms are discussed are indicated in **bold**

600